Vancouver Studies in Cognitive Science

General Editor

Steven Davis
  Professor of Philosophy, Simon Fraser University; Associate
  Member, CREA; Adjunct Professor, University of Montreal

Associate General Editors

Kathleen Akins
  Philosophy Department, Simon Fraser University

Nancy Hedberg
  Linguistics, Simon Fraser University

Fred Popowich
  Computing Science, Simon Fraser University

About Vancouver Studies in Cognitive Science

Vancouver Studies in Cognitive Science is a series of volumes in cognitive science. The volumes will appear annually and cover topics relevant to the nature of the higher cognitive faculties as they appear in cognitive systems, either human or machine. These will include such topics as natural language processing, modularity, the language faculty, perception, logical reasoning, scientific reasoning, and social interaction. The topics and authors are to be drawn from philosophy, linguistics, artificial intelligence, and psychology. Each volume will contain original articles by scholars from two or more of these disciplines. The core of the volumes will be articles and comments on these articles to be delivered at a conference held in Vancouver. The volumes will be supplemented by articles especially solicited for each volume, and will undergo peer review. The volumes should be of interest to those in philosophy working in philosophy of mind and philosophy of language; to those in linguistics in psycholinguistics, syntax, language acquisition and semantics; to those in psychology in psycholinguistics, cognition, perception, and learning; and to those in computer science in artificial intelligence, computer vision, robotics, natural language processing, and scientific reasoning.

Metarepresentations

A Multidisciplinary Perspective

edited by Dan Sperber

UNIVERSITY PRESS

2000

Oxford University Press

Oxford   New York

Athens   Auckland   Bangkok   Bogotá   Buenos Aires   Calcutta
Cape Town   Chennai   Dar es Salaam   Delhi   Florence   Hong Kong   Istanbul
Karachi   Kuala Lumpur   Madrid   Melbourne   Mexico City   Mumbai
Nairobi   Paris   São Paulo   Singapore   Taipei   Tokyo   Toronto   Warsaw

and associated companies in
Berlin   Ibadan

Published by Oxford University Press, Inc.
198 Madison Avenue, New York, New York 10016

Oxford is a registered trademark of Oxford University Press

Library of Congress Cataloging-in-Publication Data
Metarepresentations : a multidisciplinary perspective / [edited] by Dan Sperber.
p.   cm. — (Vancouver studies in cognitive science ; v. 10)
Includes bibliographical references and index.
ISBN 0-19-514114-8; ISBN 0-19-514115-6 (pbk.)
1. Mental representation—Congresses.
2. Thought and thinking —Congresses.
3. Cognitive science—Congresses.   I. Sperber, Dan.   II. Series.
BF316.6.M48   2000
121—dc21   00-035687

1 3 5 7 9 8 6 4 2

Printed in the United States of America
on acid-free paper

Acknowledgments

The conference and this collection would not have been possible without the support and assistance of a number of funding agencies, faculties, departments and people. Funding was received from the Social Sciences and Humanities Research Council of Canada and the Center for Systems Science, the Publications Committee, the Faculty of Arts, and the Cognitive Science Program of Simon Fraser University. There are a number of people who helped with the conference and collection. Steven Davis provided essential advice and aid with the preparation of the conference and of the volume. Merrily Allison and Dennis Bevington helped organize the conference. Eleanor O'Donnell did the copy editing and Arifin Graham, the cover design for the volume. The editor wants to express his deep gratitude for this ever efficient and gracious assistance.

Contents

Metarepresentations, Language and Meaning

Contributors

Susan Carey, Department of Psychology
   New York University

Leda Cosmides, Department of Psychology and Center for
   Evolutionary Psychology, University of California

Steven Davis, Department of Philosophy,
   Simon Fraser University and CREA

Daniel C. Dennett, Center for Cognitive Studies,
   Tufts University

Raymond W. Gibbs, Jr., Department of Psychology
   University of California, Santa Cruz

Alvin I. Goldman, Department of Philosophy and Program
   in Cognitive Science, University of Arizona

Susan C. Johnson, Department of Psychology
   University of Pittsburgh

Keith Lehrer, Department of Philosophy, University of Arizona
   and Karl-Franzens-Universität Graz

Alan M. Leslie, Department of Psychology and Center
   for Cognitive Science, Rutgers University

François Recanati, CREA and CNRS / École polytechnique,
   Paris, France

David M. Rosenthal, Graduate School, Philosophy and
   Cognitive Science, City University of New York

Dan Sperber, CNRS, Paris

John Tooby, Center for Evolutionary Psychology, Department
   of Anthropology, University of California

Andrew Whiten, School of Psychology
   University of St Andrews

Deirdre Wilson, Department of Linguistics
   University College London

Robert A. Wilson, Dep't of Philosophy and Cognitive Science Group,
   Beckman Institute, University of Illinois, Urbana-Champaign,
   and Deparmen.t of Philosophy, University of Alberta

Metarepresentations

Chapter 1

Introduction

Dan Sperber

Cognitive systems are characterized by their ability to construct and process mental representations. Cognitive systems capable of communicating also produce and interpret public representations. Representations, whether mental or public, are themselves objects in the world; they are found inside cognizers and in the vicinity of communicators; they are potential objects of second-order representations or "metarepresentations." While the term "metarepresentation" gained currency only in the late 1980s (early uses are found for instance in Pylyshyn, 1978; Sperber, 1985a; Leslie, 1987), the general idea is much older. Under a variety of other names, philosophers, psychologists, linguists, logicians, semioticians, literary theorists, theologians, and anthropologists have been interested in different types of metarepresentations. To give but one example, the seventeenth-century *Port-Royal Logic* devotes a chapter to the distinction between "ideas of things" and "ideas of signs," the latter being mental representations of public representations.

Mental representations of mental representations (e.g., the thought "John believes that it will rain"), mental representations of public representations (e.g., the thought "John said that it will rain"), public representations of mental representations (e.g., the utterance "John believes that it will rain"), and public representations of public representations (e.g., the utterance "John said that it will rain") are four main categories of metarepresentation. Most scholars have been predominantly interested in only one category: theory-of-mind psychologists, for instance, have studied mental representations of mental representations; reader-response theorists, mental representations of public representations; and semioticians, public representations of public representations.

Notwithstanding historical antecedents, much recent work on metarepresentations is truly novel as a result of being pursued within the framework of cognitive science and of philosophy of cognition. As such it gives great importance to mental representations of mental representations – drawing on relatively sophisticated notions of mental representation – whereas older work was mostly about the public representation of public representations – with elaborate taxonomies of public representations such as those found, for instance, in classical rhetoric or modern semiotics. Also, much current work is about the cognitive abilities that produce and exploit metarepresentations whereas older work was mostly about semi-formal properties of metarepresentations and about their role in communication. These earlier issues are still of great interest but their study is now approached from a cognitive rather than from a semiotic or hermeneutic point of view.

Reviewing past and present literature on metarepresentations would be a formidable task. Here, let me just briefly evoke four main areas where recent work on metarepresentations has been of particular importance: primate cognition, developmental psychology, philosophy of consciousness, and linguistic semantics and pragmatics.

While the ability to form representations is found in all animals with cognitive capacities, the ability to form metarepresentations is extremely rare. Most animal species, it is assumed, utterly lack metarepresentational abilities. In highly intelligent social animals such as primates, on the other hand, it has been argued that an ability to interpret and predict the behavior of others by recognizing their mental states may have evolved. In Dennett's terms (1987), some primates have been described as "second-order intentional systems," capable of having "beliefs and desires about beliefs and desires." Second-order intentional systems are, for instance, capable of deliberate deception. In a population of second-order intentional systems, a third-order intentional system would be at a real advantage, if only because it would be able to see through deception. Similarly, in a population of third-order intentional systems, a fourth-order intentional system would a greater advantage still, having greater abilities to deceive others and avoid being deceived itself, and so on. Hence, the hypothesis that an evolutionary arms race could have developed that resulted in a kind of "Machiavellian intelligence" consisting in higher-order metarepresentational abilities (Humphrey, 1976; Byrne & Whiten, 1988; Whiten & Byrne, 1997). Evolutionary and ethological arguments have sometimes converged with, sometimes diverged from, the experimental studies of primates' metarepresentational abilities that had started with Premack and Woodruff's pioneering article, "Does the chimpanzee have a theory of mind?" (1978).

Though the level of metarepresentational sophistication of other primates is still contentious, that of human beings is not. The human lineage may be the only one in which a true escalation of metarepresentational abilities has taken place.

Humans are all spontaneous psychologists. They attribute to one another many kinds of propositional attitudes: beliefs, regrets, opinions, desires, fears, intentions, and so on. Philosophers have described the basic tenets of this "folk psychology" and discussed its validity. Psychologists have focused on the individual development of this cognitive ability, often described as a "theory of mind." Philosophers and psychologists have been jointly involved in discussing the mechanism through which humans succeed in metarepresenting other people's thoughts and their own. This investigation has, in particular, taken the form of a debate between those who believe that attribution of mental states to others is done by means of simulation (e.g., Goldman, 1993; Gordon, 1986; Harris, 1989) and those who believe that it is done by deploying one kind or another of "theory" (e.g., Gopnik, 1993; Leslie, 1987; Perner, 1991, Wellman, 1990). In this debate between the simulation and the theory-theory views, much attention has been paid to different degrees of metarepresentational competence that may be involved in attributing mental states to others. In particular, the ability to attribute *false* beliefs has been seen as a sufficient, if not necessary, proof of basic metarepresentational competence. This metarepresentational competence can be impaired and this has been the basis of a new, cognitive approach to autism. Conversely, the study of autism has contributed to the development of a more fine-grained understanding of metarepresentations (see, Baron-Cohen, 1995; Frith, 1989; Happé 1994).

The ability to metarepresent one's own mental states plays an important role in consciousness and may even be seen as defining it. For David Rosenthal (1986, 1997), in particular, a mental state is conscious if it is represented in a higher-order thought. When a thought itself is conscious, then the higher-order thought that represents it is a straightforward metarepresentation. These higher-order thoughts may themselves be the object of thoughts of a yet higher order: the reflexive character of consciousness (i.e., the fact that one can be conscious of being conscious) is then explained in terms of a hierarchy of metarepresentations. (For other metarepresentational approaches to consciousness, see Carruthers 1996, Lycan 1996).

Cognitive approaches have stressed the metarepresentational complexity of human communication. It has been argued that the very act of communicating involves, on the part of the communicator and addressee, mutual metarepresentations of each other's mental states. In ordinary circumstances, the addressee of a speech act is interested in the linguistic meaning of the utterance only as a means to discover the speaker's meaning. Speaker's meaning has been analyzed by Paul Grice (1989) in terms of several layers of metarepresentational intentions, in particular the basic metarepresentational intention to cause in the addressee a certain mental state (e.g., a belief) and the higher-order metarepresentational intention to have that basic intention recognized by the addressee. Grice's analysis of metarepresentational intentions involved in communication has been discussed and developed by philosophers and linguists such as Bach & Harnish, 1979; Bennett, 1976;

Recanati, 1986; Schiffer, 1972; Searle, 1969; Sperber & Wilson, 1986. The metarepresentational complexity of human communication combines with that of language itself. It has long been observed that human languages have the semantic and syntactic resources to serve as their own metalanguage. In direct and indirect quotations, for instance, utterances and meanings are being metarepresented. The semantics of these metarepresentational uses has had a central issue in philosophy of language at least since Frege. Recent work in linguistics and pragmatics has suggested that there are several other, less obvious, metarepresentational dimensions of language use.

Under this name or another, a notion of metarepresentation has also been invoked in philosophical work on intentionality and on rationality (individual and collective), in the psychology of reasoning, and in epistemic logic, semantics, aesthetics, ethics, anthropology of religion, cognitive archeology, epistemology, philosophy of science, and artificial intelligence. This diversity of contributions is somewhat obscured by the extraordinary development of work in just one area: theory-of-mind (I am hyphenating the expression since it is often used without commitment to the view that the mind-reading ability in question is really theory-like; see, for instance, Alan Leslie, this volume). There have been, over the past 15 years, dozens of conferences, books, and special issues of journals devoted to the psychology of theory-of-mind (e.g. Baron-Cohen, Tager-Flusberg, & Cohen, 1993; Bogdan, 1997; Carruthers & Smith, 1996; Davies & Stone, 1995a; 1995b). In this literature, the link with autism, on the one hand, and with primate cognition, on the other, is often made. What is lacking is a much broader approach to metarepresentations, including theory-of-mind literature but not necessarily centered on it.

One could ask, though, whether there is a *general* story to be told about metarepresentations? Have works that make use of some notion of metarepresentation more in common than works that, in other domains, make use of, say, some notion of 'symmetry', or of 'reward'? Is there any good reason to have them confront one another? I have come to think that the answer to these questions is "yes."

In my own work, I have used a notion of metarepresentation in research on cultural symbolism (1975), on apparently irrational beliefs (1982/1985; 1997), on anthropological hermeneutics (1985b), on the evolution of language (1994), on the dynamics of culture (1985a; 1996) and, with Deirdre Wilson (Sperber & Wilson, 1986/1995), on communicative intentions, on irony and metaphor (Sperber & Wilson, 1981; 1990, Wilson & Sperber, 1992), on speech acts (Wilson & Sperber, 1988), and on higher-level explicatures (Wilson & Sperber, 1993). I have found it more and more illuminating to think of all these metarepresentational phenomena as based on a metarepresentational capacity no less fundamental than the faculty for language. Understanding the character and the role of this metarepresentational capacity might change our view of what it is to be human. This sentiment was reinforced by the interdisciplinary seminar on metarepresentations organized by Gloria Origgi at the CREA in Paris between 1994 and 1996, where many more metarepresentational issues were discussed, in particular with Daniel Andler, Pierre Jacob, and François Recanati. So, when Steven Davis invited me to organize the Tenth Vancouver Cognitive Science Conference, I had little hesitation: the conference would be on metarepresentations and would definitely bring together participants who had explored the notion in quite different ways.

The conference took place at Simon Fraser University in Vancouver, Canada, in February 1997. The present volume is a collection of essays based on the talks given at the conference and revised in the light of our debates. The chapters are organized in three parts: (1) The evolution of metarepresentation, (2) Metarepresentations in mind, and (3) Metarepresentations, language, and meaning. While this organization reflects three dominant themes of the conference, there is an unavoidable degree of arbitrariness in assigning individual chapters to parts. Several chapters are relevant to more than one major theme and other themes – the rudimentary forms of metarepresentation, the contrast between internalist and externalist views of representations, or the metarepresentational character of suppositional thinking – link chapters in yet other ways. Here is a brief guide to the contents of the volume.

The Evolution of Metarepresentation

In "Making tools for thinking," **Daniel Dennett** raises fundamental challenges. The notion of a metarepresentation cannot be clearer than that of a representation. The notion of a representation can be understood in a variety of senses, some shallower and wider, such that we would be willing to attribute representations to simpler animals and devices. Other senses are narrower and richer, such that we might be tempted to think of representation as specifically human. Do these richer senses of "representation" somehow presuppose that representations are being (or are capable of being) metarepresented? Can we conceive of the emergence in evolution and in cognitive development of metarepresentations – and of the type of representations that requires metarepresentation – in a way that is purely internal to the mind or should we see this emergence as linked to the availability in the environment of representational tools – linguistic symbols, for instance – that are there to be metarepresented? These issues are well worth keeping in mind when reading the rest of the book

In "The mind beyond itself," **Robert Wilson** speculates on issues similar to those raised by Dennett. He criticizes the individualistic approach to cognition and develops the idea that that many higher cognitive functions and, in particular, metarepresentational capacities are essentially world-involving. He discusses the cases of memory, theory-of-mind, and cultural evolution and argues that, in each case, external symbols and their metarepresentations play an essential role.

In "Consider the source: The evolution of adaptations for decoupling and metarepresentations," **Leda Cosmides and John Tooby** outline a novel and wide-ranging approach to the evolution of metarepresentational abilities. They start from the observation that human evolution is characterized by a dramatic increase in the use of contingent information for the regulation of improvised behavior tailored to local conditions. They argue that adaptations evolved to solve the problems posed by using local and contingent information include a specialized "scope syntax," decoupling systems, and a variety of metarepresentational devices. These adaptations are essential to planning, communication, mind-reading, pretence, deception, inference about past or hidden causal relations, mental simulation, and much else. Thus Cosmides and Tooby view mind-reading as only one of the functions that has driven the evolution of metarepresentational abilities and of human intelligence in general. One may note that the representational powers they see as having evolved in the human mind are interestingly similar to those François Recanati analyzes from a semantic point of view in his chapter.

In "Metarepresentations in an evolutionary perspective," **Dan Sperber** envisages the possibility that humans might be endowed, not with one, but with several evolved metarepresentational abilities. He argues that, beside the standard metapsychological mind-reading ability, humans might have a comprehension module aimed at the on-line interpretation of utterances, and a logico-argumentative module, aimed at persuading others and avoiding deception.

In "Chimpanzee cognition and the question of mental re-representation," **Andrew Whiten** examines the state of the evidence regarding the ability of chimpanzees to engage in imitation, mind-reading, and pretence. He argues that chimpanzees have a capacity for a most basic form of metarepresentation, which he calls "re-representation." These are mental representations whose content derives from other mental representations either in oneself or in others. He discusses how these abilities in apes relate to the different "grades" of metarepresentation envisaged in the theory-of-mind literature, in particular by A. M. Leslie and J. Perner. This chapter provides an appropriate transition to the second part.

Metarepresentations in Mind

In "The mentalizing folk," **Alvin Goldman** raises central questions regarding people's abilities to metarepresent mental representations. What concepts of mental states do people possess? How do they attribute specific instances of mental states to themselves and to others? How do these abilities develop? He reviews the main competing answers to these questions, criticizes various forms of the theory-theory approach, and defends a version of the simulation-theory approach where particular attention is paid to introspection.

In "How to acquire a representational theory of mind," **Alan Leslie** discusses several versions of the theory-theory of cognitive development in its application to the acquisition a representational theory-of-mind. Theory-theories associate the possession of a concept – in particular, the concept of belief – to some descriptive knowledge of the referents, in this case, of beliefs. Leslie argues against this view and for a "conceptual psycho-physical" approach where a concept such as that of belief might be causally correlated with, or "locked to," beliefs in the world and be that concept just because of this locking mechanism. The concept of belief, then, is not acquired as part of a proper "theory" of mind. Rather, the acquisition of a theory is made possible by the possession and deployment of the previously available concept. What makes this concept of belief available – as well as the basic metarepresentational abilities where it gets deployed – may well be an innate disposition rather than a learning process.

In "Metarepresentation and conceptual change: Evidence from Williams Syndrome," **Susan Carey and Susan Johnson** present a case study of abnormal cognitive development, specifically, the acquisition of a intuitive but non-core theory of biology by a population of retarded people with Williams Syndrome. They argue that the bootstrapping devices that underlie conceptual change require metarepresentational cognitive architecture. Metarepresentational capacities that are part of the theory-of-mind module support, for instance, noticing of contradictions and distinguishing appearance from reality, thus permitting conceptual change. However, in the case of retarded individuals, the lack of sufficient computational capacity serves as a bottleneck both in the construction of metaconceptual knowledge that goes beyond the core and in the construction of the first theories that likewise transcend the core. This study also throws light on the status of the four-year-old's theory-of-mind as core knowledge or constructed knowledge.

David Rosenthal's HOT (i.e., higher-order thought) theory of consciousness is a particularly clear and crisp case of metarepresentational thinking. In "Consciousness and metacognition," he defends this theory and discusses relevant evidence from current research on metacognition and, in particular, on feeling-of-knowing experiences. He argues that this evidence sheds light on what it is to be conscious of a mental state and on what it is, therefore, for a mental state to be conscious. He discusses important issues having to do with the development of metacognitive abilities and with their fallibility.

Metarepresentations, Language, and Meaning

In "Meaning, exemplarization and metarepresentation," **Keith Lehrer** argues that the human mind is essentially a "metamind" (see Lehrer, 1990), involving first-level representational states that are metarepresented and evaluated at a metalevel, thus becoming states of the metamind. This permits mental plasticity and the resolution of conflicts that, at the lower level, are unavoidable for a complex representational system. Such a metarepresentational view seems, however, threatened by a regress (as suggested by Wilfrid Sellars) or by circularity (as suggested by Jerry Fodor) in accounting for language learning. Drawing on Sellars theory of meaning, and on Nelson Goodman's notion of exemplarization, Lehrer argues that the problem of understanding meaning and of achieving representational transparency is resolved through a harmless referential loop of ascent to quotation and descent to disquotation.

In "The iconicity of metarepresentations," **François Recanati** develops an extensive and original formal treatment of the semantics of metarepresentations. He discusses the relevant philosophical literature on quotations and indirect reports of speech or thought and argues, against standard views, for a Principle of Iconicity according to which true metarepresentations essentially resemble the representations they are about. They are fundamentally "transparent," in that they represent what the metarepresented representation represents and not just, "opaquely," that representation itself. He contrast his approach to the simulation view of metarepresentations and speculates about the relationship between conditionals and metarepresentations.

In a series of influential papers, Tyler Burge has argued for the view that the intentional states of a subject are, in part, determined by the social practices of the members of his community. The disposition to defer to experts plays an important role in this externalist view. In "Social externalism and deference," **Steven Davis** discusses and refines Burge's account. He argues that a conditional disposition to defer is essential to the possession of concepts. He analyzes this disposition to defer as involving epistemic norms and a metarepresentational ability. This chapter thus relates the metarepresentational framework to some of the most interesting recent developments in the philosophy of language and mind.

In "Metarepresentations in staged communicative acts," **Raymond Gibbs** demonstrates, with linguistic and experimental evidence, how speakers' and listeners' recognition of specific metarepresentations affects their joint production and understanding of nonserious speech and, in particular, irony. The evidence tends to show that irony, because of its complex metarepresentational character, requires more processing effort to understand than tropes like metaphor. Gibbs concludes that the most general challenge that studying metarepresentations in language poses is to recognize how the coordination of mutual beliefs in ordinary speech reflects essential connections between the ways people think and the ways they produce and understand language.

In "Metarepresentation in linguistic communication," **Deirdre Wilson** examines the different types of metarepresentational ability involved in linguistic comprehension. She discusses Grice's metarepresentational view of speaker's meaning and of processes of comprehension. Focusing on the use of utterances to represent attributed utterances and thoughts, she surveys a range of linguistic metarepresentational devices and argues that their analysis can both benefit from, and provide useful evidence for, the study of more general metarepresentational abilities. From an historical point of view, current approaches to metarepresentations derive from semiotic and philosophical interest in metalinguistic devices. Deirdre Wilson's chapter, showing how this traditional interest is now being reframed in a cognitive perspective, provides a fitting conclusion for the whole volume.

References

Bach, Kent, & Harnish, Robert (1979). *Linguistic communication and speech acts.* Cambridge, MA.: Harvard University Press.

Baron-Cohen, Simon (1995). *Mindblindness: An essay on autism and theory of mind.* Cambridge, MA: MIT Press.

Baron-Cohen, Simon., Leslie, Alan, & Frith, Uta (1985). Does the autistic child have a "theory of mind"? *Cognition 21*, 37–46.

Baron-Cohen, S., Tager-Flusberg, H., & Cohen, D. J., Eds. (1993). *Understanding other minds: Perspectives from autism.* Oxford: Oxford University Press.

Bennett, J. (1976), *Linguistic behaviour.* Cambridge: Cambridge University Press.

Bogdan, R. J. (1997). *Interpreting minds: The evolution of a practice.* Cambridge, MA: MIT Press.

Byrne, R. W., & Whiten, A. (1988). *Machiavellian intelligence: Social expertise and the evolution of intellect in monkeys, apes and humans.* Oxford: Oxford University Press.

Carruthers, P. (1996). *Language, thought and consciousness.* Cambridge: Cambridge University Press.

Carruthers, P., & Smith, P., Eds. (1996). *Theories of theories of mind.* Cambridge: Cambridge University Press.

Davies, M., & Stone, T., Eds. (1995a). *Folk psychology: The theory of mind debate.* Oxford: Blackwell.

Davies, M., & Stone, T., Eds. (1995b). *Mental simulation: Evaluations and applications.* Oxford: Blackwell.

Dennett, D. (1987). *The intentional stance.* Cambridge: MIT Press.

Frith, U. (1989). *Autism: Explaining the enigma.* Oxford: Blackwell.

Gibbs, R. (1994). *The poetics of mind: Figurative thought, language and understanding.* Cambridge: Cambridge University Press.

Goldman, A. (1993). The psychology of folk psychology. *The Behavioral and Brain Sciences 16,* 15–28.

Gopnik, A. (1993). How we know our minds: The illusion of first-person knowledge of intentionality. *The Behavioral and Brain Sciences 16,* 1–14.

Gordon, R. M. (1986). Folk psychology as simulation. *Mind and Language 1,* 158–171.

Grice, H. P. (1989). *Studies in the way of words.* Cambridge, MA: Harvard University Press.

Happé, F. (1994). *Autism: An introduction to psychological theory.* London: UCL Press.

Harris, P. L. (1989). *Children and emotion: The development of psychological understanding.* Oxford: Blackwell.

Humphrey, Nicholas K. (1976). The social function of the intellect. In P. P. G. Bateson and R. A. Hinde (Eds.), *Growing points in ethology* (pp. 303–317). Cambridge: Cambridge University Press.

Lehrer, K. (1990). *Metamind.* Oxford: Oxford University Press.

Leslie, A. M. (1987). Pretence and representation: The origins of "theory of mind." *Psychological Review 94,* 412–426.

Lycan, William. (1996). *Consciousness and experience.* Cambridge, MA: MIT Press.

Perner, J. (1991). *Understanding the representational mind.* Cambridge, MA: MIT Press.

Premack, D., & Woodruff, G. (1978). Does the chimpanzee have a theory of mind? *Behavioral and Brain Science 1,* 515–526.

Pylyshyn, Zenon W. (1978). When is attribution of beliefs justified? *The Behavioral and Brain Sciences 1,* 592–526.

Recanati, F. (1986). On defining communicative intentions. *Mind and Language 1* (3), 213–242.

Rosenthal, D. M. (1986). Two concepts of consciousness. *Philosophical Studies 49* (3), 329–359.

Rosenthal, D.M. (1997). A theory of consciousness. In N. Block, O. Flanagan, & G. Güzeldere (Eds), *The nature of consciousness: Philosophical debates* (pp. 729–753). Cambridge, MA: MIT Press.

Schiffer, S. (1972). *Meaning.* Oxford: Clarendon Press,

Searle, J. (1969). *Speech acts.* Cambridge: Cambridge University Press.

Sperber, Dan (1975). *Rethinking symbolism.* Cambridge: Cambridge University Press.

Sperber, Dan (1982/1985). Apparently irrational beliefs. In S. Lukes & M. Hollis (Eds.), *Rationality and relativism* (pp. 149–180). Oxford: Blackwell. Revised edition in Dan Sperber (Ed.), *On anthropological knowledge.* Cambridge: Cambridge University Press.

Sperber, Dan (1985a). Anthropology and psychology: Towards an epidemiology of representations. (The Malinowski Memorial Lecture 1984).*Man (N.S.) 20*, 73–89.

Sperber, Dan (1985b). *On anthropological knowledge.* Cambridge: Cambridge University Press.

Sperber, Dan (1994). Understanding verbal understanding. In J. Khalfa (Ed.), *What is intelligence?* (pp. 179–198). Cambridge: Cambridge University Press.

Sperber, Dan (1996). *Explaining culture: A naturalistic approach.* Oxford: Blackwell.

Sperber, Dan (1997). Intuitive and reflective beliefs.*Mind and Language 12*, 67–83.

Sperber, Dan, & Wilson, Deirdre (1981). Irony and the use-mention distinction. In P. Cole (Ed.), *Radical pragmatics* (pp. 295–318). New York: Academic Press.

Sperber, Dan, & Wilson, Deirdre (1986/1995). *Relevance: Communication and cognition.* Oxford: Blackwell. Second Edition 1995.

Sperber, Dan, & Wilson, Deirdre (1990). Rhetoric and relevance. In John Bender & David Wellbery (Eds.), *The ends of rhetoric: History, theory, practice* (pp. 140–156). Stanford, CA: Stanford University Press.

Wellman, H. M. (1990). *The child's theory of mind.* Cambridge, MA: MIT Press.

Whiten, A. (1991). *Natural theories of mind: Evolution, development and simulation of everyday mind-reading.* Oxford: Basil Blackwell.

Whiten, A. & Byrne, R. W. (1997). *Machiavellian intelligence II: Evaluations and extensions.* Cambridge: Cambridge University Press.

Wilson, Deirdre, & Sperber, Dan (1988). Mood and the analysis of non-declarative sentences. In Jonathan Dancy, Julius Moravcsik, & Charles Taylor (Eds.), *Human agency: Language, duty and value* (pp. 77–101). Stanford, CA: Stanford University Press.

Wilson, Deirdre, & Sperber, Dan (1992). On verbal irony. *Lingua 87*, 53–76.

Wilson, Deirdre, & Sperber, Dan (1993). Linguistic form and relevance. *Lingua 90*, 1–25.

The Evolution of
Metarepresentation

Chapter 2

Making Tools for Thinking

Daniel C. Dennett

Representations are themselves objects in the world, and therefore potential objects of (second-order or meta-) representations. However, humans seem to be nearly unique in their ability to represent representations.

—Dan Sperber, 1996, in setting the topic for this conference

Just as you cannot do very much carpentry with your bare hands, there is not much thinking you can do with your bare brain.

—Bo Dahlbom and Lars-Erik Janlert (unpublished)

We use intelligence to structure our environment so that we can succeed with *less* intelligence. Our brains make the world smart so we can be dumb in peace!

—Andy Clark, 1997, p.180

If it be maintained that certain powers, such as self-consciousness, abstraction, etc. . . . are particular to man, it may well be that these are the incidental results of other highly advanced intellectual faculties; and these again are mainly the result of the continued use of a highly developed language.

—Charles Darwin, 1871, p. 101

Reflection on the issues raised by these observations has driven me to a tentative conclusion: in spite of what may well have been a surfeit of attention to definitional issues, we still do not know what we (all) mean when we talk about representation, and hence what we mean by metarepresentation. I am far from ready to offer a cure for this confusion, but I do have a few suggestions to offer about what the problems are and why they persist. My thinking has been much influenced recently by several new books that deal at least indirectly with these topics: Steven Mithen's *The Prehistory of the Mind* (1996), and Andy Clark's *Being There* (1997), but at this point I am still an asker, not answerer, of questions.

1. Florid and Pastel (Meta)representation

I must sneak up on the topic, not having figured out how to mount any frontal assault. The ethologists Robert Seyfarth and Dorothy Cheney once told me an unforgettable anecdote about some lions hunting in their neighborhood in Amboseli Park in Kenya. Robert and Dorothy had parked their Land Rover on high ground to show their guest, Don Griffin, the panorama, and below them nearby they spotted three lions crouching behind cover on some medium-high ground, overlooking a small herd of wildebeests. While the three ethologists watched in fascination, the lions put into execution a remarkable hunting ploy. One lion stepped forward into full view of the wildebeests, which all turned, with some nervousness, to eye her cautiously, ready to bolt the moment she made her move. While lion A held the herd's rapt attention in this fashion, lion B crept off to the left, circling around into position in a shallow ditch, unseen by the herd. Meanwhile lion C crept around to the right, more or less on the opposite side of the small herd from lion B. Once in place, lion C leapt out and gave chase. The herd bolted away, of course, and stampeded right over the ditch where lion B lay in wait. Lion B merely had to leap up to catch and bring down one animal, providing supper for all.

A delectable scenario; it leaves one wondering how much planning, how much coordination or even communication may have gone into the control and timing of that episode. It might be, of course, that appearances were deceptive – the lions' meal might have been more dumb luck than design. But probably not, and we can dimly imagine the sorts of cognitive mechanisms and practices that could account for their hunting success's not being an accident. Now let me add an embellishment that nobody would or should believe. Before the lions crept into their attack positions, lion A was observed to move a small bunch of twigs with her nose into a little group in the dust in front of the three lions; then she pushed three stones, one at a time, into another group, on a little bump in the dust. Then, checking for shared attention in lions B and C, she pushed two of the stones to left and right of the group of twigs, and then dashed the rightmost stone across the bunch of twigs, sending it over the stone on the left. And so forth.

Much too good to be true, of course. We have no grounds at all for believing that *that* sort of representing is within the talents or cognitive horizons of lions. Let us call this *florid representing*. What makes it florid, one sees dimly, is that it is deliberate representing, knowing representing, even self-conscious representing. It seems you cannot engage in florid representing without knowing and appreciating that you are engaging in florid representing. Or at least that will do for the moment as a mark of the florid. Now it is just a short and inviting step from this observation to the suggestion that such florid representing involves *metarepresentation*, since knowing that you are representing involves having a mental state that is itself *about* the representing you are doing and, moreover, about that representing qua representing. And this invites a further step, or slogan: No florid representation without metarepresentation.

This may be the right way to think about florid representation, but I want to move more cautiously. If that is florid representing, what is pastel representing? Is just seeing one's prey pastel representing? Is it representing at all? One has a mental or perceptual state that is surely *about* the prey (qua prey, one might add), and if that perceptual state plays an apposite role in guiding one to the prey, this state should count as a representation *in use*, or a representation that exists *for* the predator in question. That is enough, according to a familiar theme of mutual agreement, for us to speak of representation. Alan Leslie, according to his abstract for this volume, begins at this starting point. Rodney Brooks (e.g., 1991), however, uses the term "representation" in a way that would permit him to deny that such straightforward perceptual states count as representations. For Brooks, representations are the sorts of data structures GOFAI trafficked in – the manipulable items of "physical symbol systems" – and he thinks (with many others) we can get intelligent behavior without *them*.

Suppose, for the time being at least, we follow Brooks in denying the label of "representation" to such perceptual states. What, then, of the various sorts of phenomena that seem to be intermediate between such a perceptual state and a token playing its role in an instance of florid representation? What, for instance, of somebody – a young child, say – yelling "snake!" when a snake slithers into view? Is the child's utterance not a representation in a stronger sense than her visual state that provoked and guided her utterance?

Note that the child's utterance may very well not pass our makeshift test of floridity. It seems right to say that young children speak before they realize they are speaking, use language without noticing that they are doing so, respond appositely to all manner of linguistic moves, their own and those of others, without any self-conscious or deliberate metarepresentational machinery invoked at all. What young children do with language is, it seems, more like the leopard cries of vervet monkeys than the imaginary token-manipulations of our lions. And yet it clearly goes way beyond what the vervets do as well, being famously amenable to combinatorial authorship and elaboration, for one thing.

In any case, children soon enough come to be self-conscious about their use of words, and when that happens, if not before, they are capable of florid representation. What are the sure signs of this advance? I do not have a settled view on this yet, but I can offer an example. When my son was about five years old, he was captivated by what may have been the first joke he "got." "There's an old dead skunk lying in the middle of the road. I one it," I said. Now you say, "I two it." "I two it." "I three it" quoth I. "I four it!" he continued. "I five it." When it was his turn to say "I eight it," I looked at him with an expression of shock and disgust, and his eyes grew wide with delight. For several hours, we had to play this simple game, over and over, taking turns with the odd and even numbers. Such are the first faltering steps towards wit (and I have recently replicated this micro-experiment with my 5-year-old grandson). What shall we say about such moments? Then, if not before (and I am not at all sure about that), a child demonstrates a clear recognition of the existence of words as sounds, with roles to play, that might be combined in rule-bound ways – though of course the child would typically be incapable of putting it in such terms at the time.

But if this is an instance of unmistakable metarepresentational prowess, what are we to make, then, of a child's really quite adult and accomplished use of language preceding such an epiphany? (One is reminded, of course, of Molière's gentleman who was delighted to learn he'd been speaking prose all his life.) Was it somehow accompanied by, guided or informed by, metarepresentational states but just not *wittingly* so guided?[1]

2. Thinking about Thinking

I do not know how to answer that question yet, so I will turn to a related question which has recently been bothering me: Is there perhaps a big difference between *having beliefs about beliefs* and *thinking about thinking*?[2]

For some years now, I have been urging the importance of looking for evidence of "higher-order intentional states" – beliefs about beliefs, desires about beliefs, beliefs about desires about beliefs, and so forth – and all of this might very well be characterized as urging the importance of looking for evidence of metarepresentation. I do not at all mean to recant anything I have said on this score – not yet, at any rate – but I have begun to wonder whether it might not distract our attention from a neighboring source of insights, which might get us closer to an examination of the real powers of metarepresentation, properly so called.

Paying attention to *beliefs about beliefs* has certainly borne some good fruit. The theory-of-mind literature, the various paradigms of false-belief tests of children and animals, and all that surrounds this growth industry in investigation, has been more than routinely productive of insight in several fields, I think, but I have come to wonder if we are not missing some better questions in the immediate vicinity. A chimpanzee may be a natural psychologist, as Nicholas Humphrey has said, or may have a theory of mind, as David Premack (Premack & Woodruff 1978) and Alan Leslie (this volume) and Simon Baron-Cohen (1995) and many others have said, but – as I have recently been urging (e.g., in *Kinds of Minds*, 1996, pp. 130 ff.) – chimpanzees never have opportunities to compare notes with other psychologists, never get to *ask for the reasons* that ground the particular attributions of mentality to others, never get to communicate to others *or to themselves* about these mental states of others. I am tempted to say that even if they do have beliefs about beliefs, they may well be incapable of *thinking about thinking*. They may, indeed, not really be capable of *thinking* at all (in some florid but important sense of "thinking").

Our imaginary lions plotting their next moves were certainly thinking, using props as representations of the things in the world they were thinking about. But they were imaginary. When children playing touch football crouch down in the huddle and one says "Jimmy goes deep, Joey slants left, and I'll block for Tom who looks for the open man" (with or without a diagram traced with a finger on the ground or on an extended palm), this is an unmistakable instance of florid representation, and communal thinking. It is not necessarily thinking about thinking, but we can readily turn it into thinking about thinking, by letting their plans hinge on deception of some particular sort ("Jimmy will pretend to slip and fall, and then, as soon as they ignore him . . .")

What strikes me as clear enough is that there is *one* pathway to such florid thinking about thinking that moves from the outside in. It begins with the overt, public use of symbols and tokens of one sort or another (spoken words will do, perhaps, but only if they are used self-consciously), and creates practices that later can be internalized and rendered private. Since chimpanzees, for instance, lacking language, cannot play these external games any more than lions can, they cannot use *this* path as a route to private or covert thinking about thinking. This line of thought fits handsomely with the recent emphasis by Andy Clark, and indeed by me (in *Kinds of Minds*), on the claim that *minds are composed of tools for thinking* that we not only obtain from the wider (social) world, but largely leave in the world, instead of cluttering up our brains with them.

Might there, however, be other routes? Might there be pastel versions of metarepresentation that can arise by some process other than by the fading (or sophistication) of originally florid practices? It has commonly been supposed that there might indeed be such developments. The child's acquisition of a theory of mind, for instance, might seem to be a developmental story that does not at any point *depend on* the child's prior mastery of public, communal, florid practices of representation of the minds of others. After all, it has seemed quite clear that there is at least a strong genetic predisposition in our species – in normal, non-autistic children – to develop this way of "thinking about" other people, and indeed about animals and almost anything that moves.[3]

But if so, and if this penchant for *unwittingly* adopting the intentional stance is something we share with at least some of our cousin species, how do we, and we alone, come to metarepresent in the more florid, witting ways? How could such metarepresentational abilities arise in the first place? I do not think we philosophers have been sufficiently puzzled by these questions – indeed, we have hardly noticed them. We tend to take for granted the categories we find in folk psychology, which encourage us to impose a sorting in terms of these categories on all the intermediate cases. We ask: Is this one an instance of higher-order belief or not? Is this one an *echt* case of meta-representation, or should we put it in the "other" pigeonhole? These questions mask the developmental or evolutionary processes that must lead from the simple to the complex by a sequence of iffy or marginal candidates.

Sometimes I am struck by the weird complacency with which we are inclined to accept these categories at face value. How on earth *could* any agent, any organism, come to develop the *knowing* competence to *use representations*? It might be "only" a matter of practical – not logical – necessity that one acquire this special ability via the external, social route, but that fact – if it is one – might still be the key to understanding how it is possible at all. It might, for instance, be the key to understanding the general distinction I have drawn (1969) between the personal and subpersonal levels. A reminder may be in order: parsing sentences is not a personal-level activity for many of us; it is something few of us ever do except on those rare occasions when we discuss niceties and perplexities of grammar in an academic setting; at the subpersonal level, in contrast, parsing sentences is a phenomenon that occurs *within* us whenever we follow a conversation or read with comprehension. We must be careful not to confuse the two phenomena, and in particular not to assume that a good model of the former, rare phenomenon is also a good model of the latter, ubiquitous phenomenon. In the present context we may ask when, if ever, animals engage in personal-level activities at all, let alone personal projects of metarepresentation.

Let me propose a case in which we can see the philosophical sleight-of-hand happening right in front of our eyes: a puzzle is masked by our accepting an invitation to treat a curious phenomenon as unproblematically falling into our standard, human, folk-psychological categories. Many years ago. Bertrand Russell made a wry observation: "Animals studied by Americans rush about frantically, with an incredible display of hustle and pep, and at last achieve the desired result by chance. Animals observed by Germans sit still and think, and at last evolve the situation out of their inner consciousness" (Russell, 1927, pp. 32–33). Wolfgang Köhler's (1925) early experiments with chimpanzees were the inspiration for Russell's witticism, which helps to perpetuate a common misunderstanding. Köhler's apes did not just sit and think up the solutions. They had to have many hours of exposure to the relevant props – the boxes and sticks, for instance – and they engaged in much manipulation of these items. Those apes that discovered the solutions – some never did – accomplished it with the aid of many hours of trial-and-error manipulating.

Now were they *thinking* when they were fussing about in their cages? What were they manipulating? Boxes and sticks. It is all too tempting to suppose that their external, visible manipulations were accompanied by, and driven by, internal, covert manipulations – of thoughts about or representations of these objects, but succumbing to this temptation is losing the main chance. What they were attending to, manipulating and turning over and rearranging, were boxes and sticks, not thoughts.

They were *familiarizing themselves* with objects in their environments. What does that mean? It means that they were building up some sort of perceptuo-locomotor structures tuned to the specific objects, discovering the affordances of those objects, getting used to them, making them salient, and so forth. So their behavior was not all that different from the incessant trial-and-error scrambling of the behaviorists' cats, rats and pigeons. They were acting in the world, rearranging things in the world – without any apparent plan or insight or goal, at least at the outset.

Animals at all levels are designed to tidy up their immediate environments, which are initially messy, confusing, intractable, dangerous, inscrutable, hard to move around in. They build nests, caches, escape tunnels, ambush sites, scent trails, territorial boundaries. They familiarize themselves with landmarks. They do all this to help them keep better track of the things that matter – predators and prey, mates, and so forth. These are done by "instinct": automatized routines for improving the environment of action, making a better fit between agent and world.

This wise husbandry of one's own behavioral territory is economically focussed on the most important and ubiquitous features. Pre-eminent among these portions of the environment is the agent's own body, of course, always present, its condition always intensely relevant. Animals instinctively groom themselves and engage in behaviors that are apparently designed (although they need not realize this) to repair flaws and maintain and improve their coordination, muscle tone, and, in effect, to familiarize themselves with their own bodies. A part of the body that must not be overlooked in this maintenance and improvement schedule is the brain. It, too, can become messy, confusing, inscrutable, an overwhelmingly complex arena of action. So we should expect animals to be instinctually equipped to engage in mindless, automatic routines that tidy up their own brains.

We should especially expect it in *Homo sapiens*, whose huge brains are so plastic, so inundatable, so at the mercy of invading memes and memories. Resource management for a young human brain is, I think, a major task, and we should expect it to be accomplished by activities that are rooted, at the outset, in our biology, in our "instincts," but which also get enhanced in major ways by techniques that are themselves part of the influx of new resources.

3. Machines Made from Found Objects

Noam Chomsky has often said that birds do not have to learn their feathers and babies do not have to learn their language. I think there is a better parallel between birds and language: a child acquiring language is like a bird building a nest; it is a matter of "instinctual" or "automatic" resource-enhancement, taking found objects and constructing something of great biological value – part of what Dawkins (1982) calls the extended phenotype – which blurs the boundary between an organism (or agent) and the environment in which it must act.

The primary found objects, of course, are words, which, like the blacksmith's legendary tools, are tools for making more tools. As Andy Clark puts it, "The linguistic constructions, thus viewed, are a new class of objects which invite us to develop new (non-language-based) skills of use, recognition, and manipulation. Sentential and nonsentential modes of thought thus coevolve so as to complement, but not replicate, each other's special cognitive virtues" (1997, p. 211). It is because the lions cannot talk to each other that they also cannot come to use tokens of other sorts to represent, non-linguistically. And it is by that indirect route, I think, that we come to construct our minds. Here is a little fantasy about the Planet of the Baboons. The baboons that inhabit this planet are approached one day by an alien technocracy and offered an amazing prosthesis: an artifact that will permit a sort of time travel, far into the past and even into the future, and a sort of time compression: tasks that normally took days or weeks could be accomplished in a split second. What a boon these baboons were being offered! – but of course they could not even understand the offer, being baboons. We human beings can understand the offer, however, because we have already accepted it. We have already received the prosthetic extension of our brains that permits us to play such glorious tricks with time: we call it language.

First consider time "travel": Unlike the baboons, who cannot even conceive of *10 years ago*, and who may not even be capable of recollecting the specific events of their own past experience that have shaped their current dispositions,[4] we can conceive of the distant past, and use accurate information about events that happened centuries ago to guide our current projects. We can also see accurately into the future, predicting not just regular patterns such as nightfall and daybreak, and the coming winter (a trick that is in some regards within the competence of many animals and even plants), but such one-off events as the much anticipated millennial celebrations around the world, and, somewhat farther in the future, thank goodness, the extinguishing of the sun some billions of years hence. No non-human creature has a clue about any of that. Their time horizons may stretch for some limited purposes from seconds to hours to a year or two (think of the faithful biennial return of the albatross to its mate), but aside from that they have no conception. There is some remarkable evidence to suggest that elephants have some inkling of their own mortality, but it is equivocal. Our time horizons, unequivocally, extend to the point of evaporation; we can even think about – if not yet think about very well – the question of whether time itself has a beginning or end.

Second, consider time compression: We can teach a child, in a few seconds, lessons that animal parents have to drill into their offspring. Even in the highly specialized cases of learning what foods to eat and not to eat, where the Garcia effect and similar special-purpose varieties of one-shot learning have been found, animal parents have scant control over *which* lesson they can teach.

Consider, as a thought-experiment, the problem of a mother dog needing to warn her puppies not to attempt to eat the bright orange toads, which are poisonous. Not being able to raise the subject in conversation, she must wait till such a toad is in the offing, or perhaps seek one out for purposes of instruction, and then whenever the puppies approach it, she must bark or otherwise ward them off. It would be a form of operant conditioning, evolutionarily tuned, no doubt, so that the behavior shaping might be much swifter than what can be accomplished by "ecologically invalid" scientists in laboratories, but still vulnerable to the same ambiguities and indeterminacies.[5]

To dramatize the problem we might imagine the puppies *asking themselves* "Is it just *this* orange toad, or orange toads that hop like this one, or small brightly colored moving things, or orange things that smell like this, or ... ?" There are only two ways of answering these questions for the puppies: letting evolution answer them (by relying on whatever generalization-proclivities are built in), or varying the circumstances in further laborious training to clarify the boundaries of the classes of positive and negative stimuli. Can a mother dog learn, and teach to her young, that the food shaped and colored like hearts and spades, but not clubs and diamonds, is to be avoided? I do not know what empirical studies may have shown about the limits on such instruction – I think it is an interesting question worth pursuing, if it has not already been answered.

But we must not loose sight of the obvious fact that the puppies cannot literally (floridly) ask themselves these questions, lacking language. It is far from clear, in fact, that the mother, also lacking language, can even frame for herself the project of teaching anything so specific to her young. Her project, we may suppose, is to replicate in her young the disposition vis-à-vis orange toads that she acquired from her mother, but we must not impose our language-borne distinctions on the characterization of that disposition. For instance, in all likelihood, she has no way – and no need for a way – of distinguishing between passing along the generalization *in sensu composito*:

> Believe, my young, the following universal quantification: For all *x*, if *x* is an orange toad, ingesting *x* is to be avoided.

and passing along the general lesson *in sensu diviso*:

> If you ever encounter an orange toad, my young, believe at that moment: ingesting *this* is to be avoided.

The latter is the general disposition to have particular, perception-anchored beliefs about particular encountered toads; the former is the more intellectual state of mind of deeming true a universally quantified proposition about orange toads in general. In the normal course of canine affairs, the difference is not apt to loom large enough to make a difference, but in human affairs, it can be readily discerned in special circumstances. Small-town Tom, knowing everybody in town, believes all the town's Republicans are mean-spirited *in sensu diviso* (thus would he sort them, *seriatim*, if asked to list the mean-spirited). However, not knowing the political affiliations of all his fellow citizens – or not knowing whether or not he knew all the people in town – he would sincerely express agnosticism when given the generalization *in sensu composito* for assent or dissent. The latter expresses a proposition that is news to him even though his sorting behavior would reliably conform to the generalization. There are things you can do with the proposition – such as pass it along, verbally, or use it as a premise in a formal argument – that you cannot do with the sorting disposition alone. You can reflect upon it, for instance, and ask yourself what are the true boundaries of the class of the universally quantified predicate (the sort of questions the puppies cannot ask, even if their experience partially answers them *de facto*). It has often seemed innocuous to attribute general beliefs to animals on the basis of their "sorting" behavior without noting the possibility that a giant step may be concealed in this usage, the step from implicit to explicit generalization. That step may require the special thinking tools that only a natural language can provide.

What sort of mind do you need in order to acquire language in the first place? (Why will not a baboon's or chimp's mind be enough?) That is one question to which we still do not have a good answer, though the ground is littered with clues. A different question: What are the special talents of the sort of mind you acquire once you have language installed? Ray Jackendoff has recently expressed to me a striking way of answering it: we human beings can transform ourselves on a moment's notice into a somewhat different "machine," taking on new projects, following new rules, adopting new policies (personal communication, 1997). When psychologists devise a new experimental setup or paradigm in which to test such non-human subjects as rats or cats or monkeys or dolphins, they often have to devote dozens or even hundreds of hours to training each subject on the new tasks. Human subjects, however, can usually just be told what is desired of them. After a brief question-and-answer session and a few minutes of practice, we human subjects will typically be as competent in the new environment as any agent ever could be. Of course, we do have to *understand* the representations presented to us in these briefings

We are transformers – that is what a mind is, as contrasted with a mere brain. A chameleonic transformer. A virtual machine for making more virtual machines. And where are they, these virtual machines? Centered on a brain, to be sure, but not explicable without looking outside the brain into the world. Obviously some brains might be more amenable to being turned into powerful minds than others – differences in the operating system, you might say. The role that these differences might play is highly malleable, however, and may be largely eliminable. We let the myopic wear glasses; we may let the forgetful take their books along with them – why not? If we allow paper and pencil, why not a slide rule, why not a calculator, why not a colleague or a brains trust, when you get right down to it? Give me a choice between a not-too-swift Senator who has the wit and good taste to surround himself with high-powered advisors, and a brilliant do-it-myselfer who probably does not know his own limits, and I may well vote for the former. It is this distribution of the tasks of intelligence that makes our minds so much more powerful than all other animal minds.

Notes

1 Andy Clark proposed (at a Santa Fe Institute workshop in May, 1996) some more stringent requirements for "robust" representation, requiring "surrogates" that are specifically "manipulated" (for instance, in "forward models" of the sort one can find in both engineering and animal motor-control systems). This can be seen to be a proposal to split the difference, in effect, requiring

manipulanda *of sorts*, but not requiring the manipulation to be a personal-level, accessible, activity. This is a very tempting suggestion, I think, but I do not yet see how to follow it up.

2 Clark discusses "thinking about thinking" as a "good candidate for a distinctively human capacity" (1997, pp. 208–209).

3 The scare-quotes are to remind us that maybe this is not robust, or florid, thinking at all, the sort that involves manipulation of surrogates. Some participants at the Vancouver conference took me to be claiming that there was no evidence for metarepresentation *of any sort* without the prior establishment of natural language, but my point was rather to warn against the assumption that this variety of apparently higher-order cognition is all there is to meta-representation.

4 I have been challenging ethologists for several years to provide clear and persuasive evidence of episodic memory in non-human animals. The ethological and psychological literature, inspired by Tulving's (1983) work, treats episodic memory as a well-recognized category, but so far as I can see, there is a crucial equivocation in the discussions. True episodic memory is a tricky and sophisticated phenomenon. The dog that buries the bone and returns to it the next day does *not* show episodic memory; it merely shows that it has an expectation, engendered by a single episode of burying, that there will be something good to be found there. It may or may not be able to accompany its digging with an actual episode of recollection. Learning from a single episode – one-shot learning – is importantly unlike learning via lengthy conditioning (what I call ABC learning in *Kinds of Minds* and "Labeling and Learning") but it is not the same as episodic memory. We must not endow animals with a capacity for *recollection* just because they exhibit one-shot learning.

5 Dan Sperber has suggested a natural ramp up which learning of this sort could proceed, beginning with what might be call impromptu observation of another (by an animal that has rich metapyschological powers to begin with), and leading by gradual steps to directed teaching, all without benefit of language. I wonder if this can be successfully modeled in a computer simulation – a nice new toy problem for artificial life.

References

Baron-Cohen, Simon (1995). *Mindblindness: An essay on autism and theory of mind.* Cambridge:, MA: MIT Press.

Brooks, Rodney (1991). Intelligence without representation. *Artificial Intelligence Journal 47*, 139–159.

Clark, Andy (1997). *Being there.* Cambridge, MA: MIT Press.

Dahlbom, Bo, & Janlert, Lars-Erik (1996). *Computer future.* Unpublished book manuscript.

Darwin, Charles (1871). *The descent of man.* New York: Appleton.

Dawkins, Richard (1982). *The extended phenotype.* Oxford and San Francisco: Freeman.

Dennett, Daniel (1969). *Content and consciousness.* London: Routledge & Kegan Paul.

Dennett, Daniel (1993). Labeling and learning. *Mind and Language 8*, 540–548.

Dennett, Daniel (1996). *Kinds of minds.* New York: Basic Books.

Humphrey, Nicholas (1986). *The inner eye.* London: Faber and Faber.

Köhler, Wolfgang (1925). *The mentality of apes.* New York: Harcourt Brace and World.

Mithen, Steven (1996). *The prehistory of the mind.* London: Thames and Hudson.

Premack, D., & Woodruff, G. (1978). Does the chimpanzee have a theory of mind? Behavioral and Brain Sciences 1: 515–526.

Russell, Bertrand (1927). *An outline of philosophy,* London: Allen & Unwin.

Sperber, Dan (1996). Personal communication, in setting the topic for the 10th conference of Vancouver Studies in Cognitive Science, at which the papers in this volume were presented.

Tulving, Endel (1983). *Elements of episodic memory.* Oxford: Clarendon Press.

Chapter 3

The Mind beyond Itself

Robert A. Wilson

1. Individualism: What It Is and Why Care

Individualism is a view about how mental states are taxonomized, classified, or typed and, it has been claimed (by, e.g., Stich, 1983; Fodor, 1980), that individualism constrains the cognitive sciences. Individualists draw a contrast between the psychological states of individuals and their physical and social environments. Psychological states are not just "in the head" but the distinction between what is inside the head and what is outside of it is of taxonomic and explanatory significance for cognitive science. Individualism is thus sometimes called "internalism," and its denial "externalism."

One formulation of individualism is *methodological solipsism*, most often associated in contemporary discussions with Putnam (1975), who attacks it, and Fodor (1980), who defends it. Methodological solipsism is the doctrine that psychology ought to concern itself only with *narrow* psychological states, where these are states that do not presuppose "the existence of any individual other than the subject to whom that state is ascribed" (Fodor, 1980, p. 244). An alternative formulation of individualism offered by Stich (1978; 1983), the *principle of autonomy*, says that "the states and processes that ought to be of concern to the psychologist are those that supervene on the current, internal, physical state of the organism" (Stich, 1983, pp. 164–165). To put it in plain terms, organisms that do not differ in their "current, internal, physical state" cannot differ in the mental states they have, and so the taxonomies we formulate for psychological explanation should lead us to ascribe the same states to those individuals.

Part of the attraction of individualism for many philosophers is its perceived connection to functionalism in the philosophy of mind. Those committed to functionalism as a view of the mind liberal enough to countenance the multiple realization of mental states have often seen a functionalist commitment to individualism as what makes such liberalism compatible with a thorough-going materialism. The idea is that by

31

characterizing mental states in terms of individualistically individuated perceptual inputs, other mental states, and behavioral outputs, one can view mental states as states of an organism's central nervous system, even if they are not type identical with such states. And that should be materialism enough. Even allowing for the multiple realization of mental states in different physical states, physically identical individuals must be functionally identical and, given functionalism, functionally identical individuals must have the same psychological states. Thus, physically identical individuals must be psychologically identical – hence, individualism.

Another attraction of individualism, particularly for practicing cognitive scientists (who rightly point out the unlikelihood of encountering physically identical individuals), is its perceived connection to the representational theory of mind, which holds that we interact with the world perceptually and behaviorally through internal mental representations of how the world is (as the effects of perceiving) or how the world should be (as instructions to act). Provided that the appropriate, internal, representational states of the organism remain fixed, the organism's more peripheral causal involvement with its environment is irrelevant to cognition, since the only way in which such causal involvement can matter to cognition is by altering the mental states that represent that environment.

Many of the arguments for, and many of those against, individualism in the philosophical literature have drawn on general considerations from metaphysics, epistemology, and the philosophy of mind, of language, and of science. For example, it has been claimed by Ned Block (1986) and Jerry Fodor (1987, chap. 2) that denying individualism involves making a mystery (perhaps, more of a mystery) of mental causation, since to do so would be to posit causal mechanisms governing the operation of mental states that can vary without any corresponding variation in an individual's brain states. To take another example – deriving again from Fodor but accepted by many others including Crane (1991), McGinn (1991), and Owens (1993) – individualism in psychology is simply an instance of a general constraint on scientific taxonomy : taxonomic individuation in science must be "by causal powers," where an object's causal powers are determined by its intrinsic, physical states. I have argued elsewhere (e.g., Wilson, 1995, chaps. 2, 5–6) that all such arguments are unsound, and have called into question whether there are any general, *a priori*, valid arguments for individualism.

Given the sweeping range of philosophical issues that the debate over individualism raises, those with more empirical interests in the mind might well maintain a sceptical distance from the fray here. But cognitive scientists should care about this debate over individualism because (1) as I have suggested above, many are antecedently committed to individualism, seeing it as a trivially correct view of psychology, (2) this commitment is reflected in, and even structures, the range of research questions, approaches, and outcomes deemed relevant to the cognitive sciences, and (c) individualism is false. In short, those with a sustained, empirical interest in the mind should care about individualism for much the reason that psychologists in the 1950s should have cared about *behaviorism*: it represents a view of what is important to progress in cognitive research that is mistakenly motivated and normatively questionable.

2. Individualism in Cognitive Science

To give the flavor of the sort of individualistic tendencies that pervade much cognitive science, consider the following quotation from Ray Jackendoff:

> Whatever the nature of *real* reality, the way reality can look *to us* is determined and constrained by the nature of our internal mental representations ... Physical stimuli (photons, sound waves, pressure on the skin, chemicals in the air, etc.) act mechanically on sensory neurons. The sensory neurons, acting as transducers in Pylyshyn's (1984) sense, set up peripheral levels of representation such as retinal arrays and whatever acoustic analysis the ear derives. In turn, the peripheral representations stimulate the construction of more central levels of representation, leading eventually to the construction of representations in central formats such as the 3D level model. (Jackendoff, 1992, pp.159–161)

Jackendoff calls this view the "psychological" (versus philosophical) vision of cognition and its relation to the world and it is perhaps unsurprising that Jackendoff's scepticism about the "philosophical" vision parallels the disdain for "philosophical" approaches to language that Chomsky (e.g., 1991; 1995) expresses in his distinction between the "I-language" and the "E-language" and his insistence that only the former is suitable as an object of scientific study. To take a third example of an individualistic perspective on cognition, consider this extract from the Foreword to Simon Baron-Cohen's *Mindblindness*, written by Leda Cosmides and John Tooby.

> Although it is a modern truism to say that we live in culturally constructed worlds, the thin surface of cultural construction is dwarfed by (and made possible by) the deep underlying strata of evolved species-typical cognitive construction. We inhabit mental worlds populated by the computational outputs of battalions of evolved, specialized neural automata. They

segment words out of a continual auditory flow, they construct a world of
local objects from edges and gradients in our two-dimensional retinal ar-
rays, they infer the purpose of a hook from its shape, they recognize and
make us feel the negative response of a conversational partner from the roll
of her eyes, they identify cooperative intentions among individuals from
their joint attention and common emotional responses, and so on.
(Cosmides and Tooby, 1995, pp. xi–xii)

While Cosmides and Tooby clearly do assign the environment of the organism a role in the evolutionary history of species-typical capacities,
the cognitive capacities themselves are individualistic. In all three cases,
the idea is that we should investigate the mind and its functions by
bracketing the world to which it is connected; the taxonomies we derive
from such a methodology will be individualistic.

One way to argue that individualism is a mistaken view of taxonomy and explanation in cognitive science would be to reject – lock, stock,
and barrel – research programs that adopt an individualistic view. This
is not my way. Rather, my general strategy is to accept the insights that
such research programs offer but show how they can and should be di-
vorced from a commitment to individualism. In this chapter, I will deploy this strategy with respect to metarepresentation by proposing that
the metarepresentational systems that we possess and use are not individualistic but *wide*. There are two basic ideas.

The first is that metarepresentation inherits its width from the mental representations that are its objects. The second is that metarepresentation often involves operating on both internal *and* external symbols,
and this suggests that our cognitive systems extend beyond the heads
that house them. Before turning to this argument, I want to draw attention to two entrenched views, the first about psychological capacities
and the second about mental representation, that are incompatible with
the position I shall advocate.

3. Minimal Reductionism
and the Encoding View

The first of these views is *minimal reductionism*, the view that psychological capacities are nothing over and above capacities of the brain and central nervous system. We can see how minimal reductionism supports individualism by considering a standard way of interpreting the familiar
method of homuncular functional decomposition (HFD) and how it applies to metarepresentational cognitive abilities.

HFD with respect to cognition begins with some initial cognitive capacity, C, characterized at level n, which both requires intelligence and

is representational (e.g., problem-solving, recall, visual word recognition, mind-reading), decomposes C into constituent capacities $c_1 \ldots c_j$ at level $n-1$, and then re-applies this initial step recursively to $c_1 \ldots c_j$ until one reaches operations that are neither intelligent nor representational. Materialists have typically assumed that a relation of *realization* exists between any pair of adjacent levels, such that capacities specified at level n-1 provide a realization of those specified at level n. Realization is *determinative* in the following sense: where some object, process, event, or capacity A determines B, the presence of A is sufficient for the presence of B. Given that the properties posited at the most basic homuncular level, b, are individualistic, and that b provides a realization of properties specified at level $b+1$, such properties must also be individualistic. Since in moving from $b+1$ to n the same is true of each pair of adjacent levels, the properties specified at n must also be individualistic. Given that *metarepresentational* states are higher-order mental states that refer to, or control, other (in the first instance, first-order) mental states, they, too, inherit their individualistic character from those lower-order mental states.

To put this point another way, since the capacities at any level m are realized by those at level $m-1$, there is nothing *more* to instantiating the former than instantiating the latter, since realization is a determinative relation. This minimal reductionism allows us to understand HFD as a materialist or physicalist view, for it is clear that deploying this strategy of explanation does not require positing anything in addition to physical – in this case, neural – stuff.

The second apparently harmless view that supports individualism is a familiar view of mental representation, which I shall call the *encoding view* of mental representation. Simply put, it is the view that to have a mental representation, M, is to encode information about some object, property, event, or state of affairs m. A well-known version of the encoding view is the picture or copy theory of mind, where to have a mental representation of m is to have a mental picture or image of m in your head, where the picture is "of M" just because it looks like m. A version of the encoding view prevalent in cognitive science is the language-of-thought hypothesis, according to which to have a mental representation of m is to have a token in your language of thought, M, that stands for or refers to m. Unlike the copy theory of mental representation, this view requires no resemblance between the representation and the represented. On either view, because mental representations encode information about the world, cognitive scientists can (and should) explore the properties of these representations rather than the relationships that exist between organisms and environments. This is particularly clear in the case of metarepresentation, where the object of the cognitive process is itself some internal, mental representation.

I shall argue that psychological capacities are sometimes something over and above capacities of the brain and central nervous system – thus, minimal reductionism is false – and that mental representation should not be thought of exclusively as the encoding of information – thus, the encoding view is mistaken. I shall show how this view applies to metarepresentation. Furthermore, I think that the threat of two types of regress is more serious for individualistic (versus non-individualistic) accounts of metarepresentation, a view I express as a mere opinion in this paper; in the next section, I briefly gesture at the sorts of regresses I have in mind.

4. An Aside: Metarepresentation
and the Threat of Regress

There are two directions – "up" and "down" – in which accounts of the mind in general and metarepresentation in particular threaten to invoke an infinite regress. The downwards threat of an infinite regress in de-composing psychological capacities is familiar: it is the threat of never quite managing to exorcise the homunculus in the head and thus failing to provide an adequately mechanistic account of the mind. In accounts of metarepresentation, the threat is to end up with a decomposition of metarepresentational capacities that is itself metarepresentational in na-ture. The threat "upwards" is the threat of a never-ending story and it arises in attempting to account for mental states and operations that ap-pear to be complexes of simpler mental states and operations. Clearly, as views of a type of higher-order mental operation, accounts of metarepresentational capacities face this threat. It arises, for example, in Gricean accounts of verbal communication, where there appears to be an intricately nested hierarchy of mental states (intentions, beliefs, de-sires) that are encoded by speaker and hearer. This threat also arises in attempting to account for knowledge that is "implicit" in terms of inac-tive encodings in the brain, which may or may not be metarepresenta-tional. The problem here is not one of failed homuncular exorcism but of failed finitude.

Why should these threats of regress be more serious given individ-ualism? Consider the case of metarepresentation. In the case of the threat downwards, individualism makes it more likely that we will, in effect, posit a "metarepresentation box" (whether or not it has that name), that is, an undischarged homunculus that itself is metarepresentational. In the case of the threat upwards, the tie between individualism and the encod-ing view of representation makes it tempting for individualists to ascribe what are essentially implicit and context-sensitive metarepresentational abilities as due solely or primarily to the exercise of internal capacities.

5. Two Ways of Being Wide-Minded: Taxonomic and Locational width

Let me distinguish two ways in which a mind can be wide. The first is familiar, at least to philosophers, and relatively unproblematic in its application to metarepresentation. The second is less familiar and might be thought to be precisely the sort of view that individualists have been concerned (rightly, one might add) to warn us away from. However, the gap between these two ways to be wide-minded is not as great as might be thought and those interested in metarepresentation should attend to both types of width.

Since the distinction between narrow and wide mental states is one drawn with respect to how psychological states should be individuated or taxonomized, it is natural to think of wide psychological states as those psychological states, located in the organism's head, whose taxonomy presupposes reference to features of that organism's social or physical environment. Thus, though an organism's beliefs and other mental representations are located in its head, when we individuate them *as* beliefs, we do so by reference to their *content* or *intentionality*; this typically involves reference to the world beyond the organism's head (or, more generally, body). When we say that a given vervet monkey emits a certain type of alarm call because it believes that there is a leopard about, we are not giving an individualistic characterization of that monkey's mental state; it is not individualistic in the strict sense specified above because it is possible for an individual in a radically different environment to fail to have that belief, *even if* that individual were, by hypothesis, molecularly identical to the vervet in our example. (Suppose that vervets had evolved in environments where tigers fill the ecological niche that leopards, in fact, fill.) Whether there is some notion of "narrow content" with which we can reconcile this apparent rift between folk psychology and individualism is philosophically contentious.

Call the type of wideness of mind above *taxonomic width*. Apart from being taxonomically wide, psychological states may also fail to be narrow by being *locationally wide*. That is, the cognitive states of an individual may be wide because the cognitive system to which they belong is not fully instantiated or located in that individual. I have previously defended the related idea that some of the computational states that organisms instantiate are locationally wide in just this sense: they belong to wide computational systems, computational systems that extend beyond the boundary of the individual, and inherit their width from that of the system of which they are a part (see Wilson 1994; 1995, chap. 3). A simple example is that of arithmetic done with pencil and paper, where the calculations performed involve operations on mental symbols in the head as well as on written symbols on the page. Here the relevant representational system extends beyond the boundary of the individual performing the calculation.

Given that metarepresentational states are mental states located in an individual's head whose content is another mental state, then if those mental states are *taxonomically* wide, so too are the corresponding metarepresentational states. That is, taxonomic width (like taxonomic narrowness) is inherited up the homuncular hierarchy, in this case from the first-order states of folk psychology to the metarepresentational states that operate on them. Alternatively, if the mental states that are the object of one's metarepresentational states are located somewhere other than within the boundary of one's body, then those metarepresentational states are *locationally* wide, since the metarepresentational loop they form extends beyond oneself. In either case, minimal reductionism is false: in the former case, because the kinds of metarepresentational capacities we have are determined by factors outside of the head; in the latter case, because our metarepresentational systems themselves extend into the world.

6. Locational Width and
the Locus of Control

Metarepresentations are usually thought of as mental representations of other mental representations. This might make the idea of locationally wide metarepresentations seem a contradiction in terms, for the idea that organisms capable of higher-order mental representations instantiate locationally wide cognitive systems seems to fly in the face of the internal locus of control that such organisms have. In fact, we can distinguish between organisms that are increasingly sophisticated in their cognitive abilities – reactive, enactive, and symbolic organisms – in terms of where the locus of control for their cognitive systems lies, as shown in Table 1.

As Table 1 makes clear, talk of "types of organisms" here is merely a graphic way of talking about types of cognitive systems. As we move

Locus of Control	Type of Organism or Representational System	Example in Humans
environmental	reactive	reflexes
bodily	enactive	mimetic skills
cranial	symbolic	beliefs, desires

Table 1. Locus of Control and Representational Type

from reactive through enactive to purely symbolic cognitive systems, we have a shift in the locus of control from the environment through the body to the mind. Given that this is so, how can the idea of locational width get purchase in thinking about creatures with metarepresentational (and thus symbolic) capacities?

The basic answer is that there are a variety of metarepresentational processes whose locus of control is internal but whose cognitive loop extends into the world beyond the organism to whom they belong. Symbolic representational systems with an internal locus of control can be both locationally and taxonomically wide. Consider two ways to develop this answer.

First, let us return to the idea that mental states are realized as physical states of the brain. Consider humans, who possess reactive, enactive, and symbolic cognitive systems. What is it, then, that constitutes a realization[1] of their various cognitive capacities? In the case of "purely mental" capacities, it is the brain and, more particularly, the cognitive arrangement of the brain. In the case of what I shall call *enactive bodily skills*, such as rehearsing a tennis stroke or flossing one's teeth, it is the parts of the brain responsible for planning and executing motor control and the relevant parts of one's body. In the case of what I shall call *wide symbol systems*, involving conventionally established codes and symbols, it is the brain plus the physical tokens of the corresponding external symbols. In short, creatures like us, who possess cognitive systems with an internal locus of control, can also instantiate cognitive capacities with core realizations that are either internal, bodily, or world-involving (see Table 2).

Table 2 should help to clarify a point that I intimated at the end of section 5: the locational width of world-involving cognitive capacities is incompatible with minimal reductionism about cognition in general. It should also indicate what is problematic about the encoding view of mental representation, for neither in the case of enactive, bodily skills nor in that of world-involving capacities do parts of the brain encode for the other constituents of the realization of that capacity. Rather, in both cases what is inside the head and what is outside of it are related as parts of an integrated whole, with information flowing between those parts.

Cognitive Capacities in Symbol-Using Creatures	Realization of the Capacity
purely internal	internal cognitive arrangement of the brain
enactive bodily	cerebral + bodily configuration
world-involving	cerebral arrangement + external symbol tokens

Table 2. Cognitive Capacities and Their Realizations

		Locus of Control	
		Internal	**External**
Wide	Locational	arithmetical abilities animal navigation (Gallistel 1990)	cyborg cognition, e.g., human navigation (Hutchins 1995)
	Taxonomic	folk psychology	sustained manipulation of others
Narrow		most subpersonal psychology and cognitive science	stimulus-bound perceptual performance

Table 3. Some Examples of Narrow and Wide Psychology

Second, suppose we simply distinguish between the case where the locus of control is internal to the organism and that in which the locus of control is external. That, together with the distinction between taxonomic and locational width, gives us four possible types of wide cognitive systems. I think that there are examples of each of these types of cognitive system (see Table 3), despite the fact that the bulk of cognitive science has been conceived of as involving only narrow cognitive systems.

In the remainder of this chapter, I shall indicate how the distinctions summarized in Tables 2 and 3 illuminate contemporary work with a metarepresentational edge. Central to these illustrations is the idea that we should locate some of the psychological capacities typically identified as "purely internal" (in Table 2) and as "narrow" (in Table 3) elsewhere in the respective tables.

7. Memory

A focus of current debates over memory has been the relationship that research into memory bears to everyday memory; my illustrations of the ways in which memory is neither "purely internal" nor "narrow" are made with this focus in mind. In particular, debates over the classic "storehouse" model of memory and alternatives to it suggest ways of extending our traditional conception to show how memory itself is wide.

First, Koriat and Goldstein (1996) propose that two metaphors have structured research into memory over the last 100 years: the familiar storehouse metaphor, and what they call the "correspondence metaphor," according to which it is of the essence of memory to correspond to some past state of affairs, rather than simply to act as a storehouse for readily identifiable chunks of data. This characterization of the alternative view to the dominant conception of memory invokes a taxonomically wide conception of memory. That is, what individuates memory in general from other types of cognitive processes (e.g., imagination, fantasy, wishes) is the relationship memory bears to past, experienced states of affairs in the world. Moreover, on this view, what individuates a particular memory from others is, at least in part, what it is a memory of or about – that is, its intentionality. This represents a second way in which use of a correspondence metaphor relies on a taxonomically wide conception of memory.

Second, and by contrast, consider Neisser's (1996) claim that the underlying metaphor that structures research into "real-life" memory is one of "remembering as doing." On this view, such research may even adopt a *locationally* wide conception of memory since it views memory as performative or enactive, where what is enacted does not simply stop at the skin but involves engaging with the world through cognitively significant action. To adapt Neisser's own examples, to tell a joke or recite an epic tale is not simply to make certain mouth and body movements but to "impress and entertain" an audience. One way to state this point is to say that, if memory is a bodily, enactive skill and those skills are individuated widely, then memory is taxonomically wide. But, we might also conceive of such memory itself as extending into the world through the way in which it engages with and appropriates external systems, treating them in just the way that internal symbols are treated.

The idea that procedural memory may involve doing things with one's body, while itself old hat, does suggest an idea that seems more novel: that one may remember *by doing things with one's environment*. Perhaps even this idea is old hat; after all, we all know that we can use environmentally cued mnemonics, such as tying a piece of string around one's finger or leaving a note on the refrigerator. My suggestion is that, apart from these promptings to remember, there are ways of remembering that involve a sustained, reliable, causal interaction between an organism and its symbolic environment. The magnitude of our symbol-laden environments should be taken seriously and to do so is to see the mind as extending beyond itself, that is, as being constituted by such symbols and thus as locationally wide.

This wide perspective is most compelling in cases in which systems of external symbols come to change in significant ways the cognitive capacities of individuals who interact with them. Most striking here are cases in which an organism, such as a bonobo, develops in a symbol-enriched environment and subsequently displays massively increased symbolic capacities (Savage-Rumbaugh & Lewin, 1994). For example, given Kanzi's actual developmental environment, Kanzi plus a 256-

symbol keyboard forms a cognitive system with memory and other cognitive capacities that far exceed those of just Kanzi. (Much the same holds true of Alex, Irene Pepperberg's African grey parrot.) My point here is not the trivial one that enriched environments can produce smarter "critters"; rather, it is that what makes at least some "critters" smart is their being part of wide cognitive systems. Again, we have the mind beyond itself.

Neither the case of taxonomic width nor that of locational width involves viewing memory as having an external locus of control. Indeed, maintenance of an internal locus of control would seem crucial in such cases in order to explain the sense in which a person's memories are *that person's* memories rather than a part of some collective memory or (worse) free-floating cognitive flotsam.[2] We do, of course, have forms of external memory storage, such as diaries, which, while deriving from, and often recording, in part, an individual's mental life, can exist beyond the life of their author and come to be accessed as a form of memory by others. Further, each time any one of us speaks or writes in a communicative context, we create tokens of external symbols that constitute a common symbol pool from which each of us draws. To be sure, acts of communication always involve the internal mental representations each of us houses but my point is that they also involve *in just the same sense* public and shared representations that are not the province of any one mind. In many such cases, the locus of control may be internal to the speaker (in uttering) and to the hearer (in listening) but I see no incoherence in the idea that the locus of control may be outside of the head. Cases of fluent reading (e.g., speed reading) and manipulation (see §9, below) may best be viewed as examples in which this actually occurs.

Column 3 of Table 4 presents an extension of Table 2 that summarizes these ideas. As that table indicates, enactive, procedural memory that is locationally wide is an extension of traditionally conceived procedural memory, just as external memory is an extension of traditionally-conceived long-term memory. In both cases, we have a conception of memory that takes the mind beyond itself.[3]

If the view of memory as locationally wide provides a fruitful extension of traditional conceptions of memory, then it is obvious how metarepresentation itself may be either taxonomically or locationally wide: it is wide in one of these senses just when some of the representations on which it operates are locationally wide in the corresponding sense. In such cases, metarepresentational capacities are, indeed, something over and above capacities of the brain and central nervous system (minimal reductionism is false); and metarepresentation is not simply the encoding of information about other internal mental states but the formation of metarepresentational loops beyond the head in which segments of those loops are realized.

Cognitive Capacities in Symbol-Users	Realization of the Capacity	Adding Memory	Adding Theory of Mind	Adding Culture
purely internal	architectural + non-architectural features of the brain	traditional forms of memory, e.g., declarative/ procedural, LTM/STM	bare-bones FP	mental image of God? moral intuitions?
bodily, enactive	cerebral + bodily configuration	extension of procedural memory	full-blown FP	dance, played melody
world-involving	internal + external symbol tokens	extensions of other forms of memory to include external symbol systems	narrative engagement, sustained deceit and manipulation	street signs, maps, instruments and tools

Table 4: Adding Memory, Theory of Mind, and Culture

8. Theory of Mind

We are mindreaders. The explosion of work over the last 15 years in both cognitive development and primatology exploring the developmental and evolutionary origins of this ability has largely construed the capacity itself as a theory of mind, a theory that attributes folk-psychological states to agents and that allows one to predict and explain an agent's behavior in terms of the relationships between those states, perception, and behavior. I want to focus my discussion of the theory of mind on the end-state of these ontogenetic and phylogenetic processes, the folk psychology that we end up sharing and relying on in everyday life, beginning with what we can think of as our bare-bones folk psychology, the psychology of belief and desire.

The capacity that normal human adults have to ascribe belief and desire to one another is both locationally narrow and taxonomically wide. It is locationally narrow because the realization of the capacity is purely internal to the individual who has the capacity. On the other hand, it is taxonomically wide because beliefs and desires are individuated, in part, by their intentional content – that is, what they are about – and such content is wide. This is so whether one thinks that this ascriptive ability operates via a theory or via acts of imaginative simulation. Matters are less straightforward, however, when one considers both the full-blown capacities that we have for engaging in folk-psychological explanation and some of our more advanced deployments of folk psychology.

First, take full-blown folk psychology, which posits not only beliefs and desires but a whole range of psychological states, such as emotions (anger, elation, fear), moods (restless, aroused, inattentive), and sensations (of pain, of experiencing red, of tickling). Although these additional states are by no means homogenous, it is much less plausible to think that the realization of the capacity to ascribe them is purely internal than in the case of belief and desire. That is because these states have a felt component, whether it be experiential or bodily (or both), and it is difficult to see how one could accurately and reliably ascribe such states to others without knowing what they were like in one's own case. Further, such knowledge itself is procedural and has a bodily realization in that it involves not simply having one's brain in some internal state but, at least, having one's brain and body in a certain state.

Prima facie, this would seem to make a simulation view more plausible than a theory view of full-blown folk psychology, since it is easier to see how such experience can be integrated into simulation-based ascription than into theory-based ascription. The most obvious ploys for proponents of the theory view of folk psychology are to argue that (1) full-blown folk psychology can be reduced to bare-bones psychology, or (2) however important experiential and bodily aspects are to the acquisition of folk psychology, they do not form part of its realization, which is purely internal. While argument (1) appeals to minimal reductionism, argument (2) employs the encoding thesis, and so the plausibility of each of these responses will depend, in part, on the plausibility of these two views.

My claim, then, is that the move from bare-bones to full-blown folk psychology involves a shift from a purely internal mental capacity to a bodily enactive skill. I also want to suggest that some of our most sophisticated deployments of folk psychology – such as understanding a complicated narrative about the mental lives of others and manipulating another's full-blown folk psychology – involve a symbolic capacity that is world-involving. In such cases, folk psychology starts to look not just taxonomically but also locationally wide.

Consider narrative engagement that involves understanding the full-blown folk psychology of characters in a literary, dramatic, or cinematic genre. To understand, say, a novel such as *Pride and Prejudice* or *Bleak House* one must not only ascribe full-blown folk-psychological states to the characters in the novel but also understand those characters' (partial) views of the world, a world that naturally includes other people. As you read deeper into the novel, you must, of course, modify your representations of the folk-psychological representations that each character has. But since the metarepresentational load here increases dramatically with the complexity of the portrayal of the characters and their relationships to one another, it is no surprise that even partial expertise typically involves knowing how to find one's way about in the novel; it involves knowing how to locate and identify the folk-psychological representations that respective characters have and the signs of these in the novel itself. Here the representations that are the object of your own representations are located somewhere other than in your own head. In short, this understanding involves constructing a metarepresentational loop that extends beyond the head and into the minds of the fictional characters with whom you are engaged.

Much the same is true of appreciating the full-blown folk psychology of real people, especially those to whom you are close. Our (meta)representations of the mental lives of companions and friends are more sophisticated not simply because of the added internal complexity such representations have in our own heads but also because they index richer mental representations in the minds of one's companions than those in the minds of strangers. Rather than simply encoding information about these mental representations, we engage and interact with them and, in so doing, extend the system of mental representations to which we have access beyond the boundary of our own skins. As with our reliance on cognitive artifacts to bear some of the representational load carried during a complicated cognitive task, here we exploit rather than replicate the representational complexity of our environments. But unlike at least some such tasks (e.g., navigating a vessel or an aircraft, to take an example from Hutchins, 1995), we individuals remain the locus of representational control, with our interactions with external representations augmenting our internal representational systems.

Both the case of narrative engagement and that of locationally wide, full-blown folk psychology involve metarepresentational capacities whose locus of control is still, by and large, internal. Cases in which there is sustained deception that involves folk-psychological manipulation of an individual or those involving an individual's blind trust in the views of others are plausibly viewed as operating with a locus of control that is external to that individual. As with these other forms of locationally wide folk-psychological systems, the cognitive capacity here involves the world, with the relevant folk-psychological representations being located both inside and outside of a given individual's head. Considering just the perspective of the deceiver, manipulator, or person trusted, the locus of control here remains internal. But, from the perspective of the deceived, the manipulated, or the person trusting, their metarepresentational folk-psychological states are controlled by folk-psychological states beyond their own mind.

The fourth column of Table 4 summarizes how to fit theory of mind into the wide framework; looking ahead, the fifth column of that table does the same for culture.

9. Culture, Cognition, and Evolution

The ideas about memory and theory of mind that I have been floating question the peripheral or secondary role that individualists give to an organism's environment. In particular, I have argued that some of the metarepresentational capacities we have are world-involving rather than purely internal in that the realization base for the capacity extends beyond the boundary of the individual. The idea that external symbols come to form part of an individual's cognitive system is central to this argument. Culture represents a source for such symbols.

One general concessionary response to the above suggestions regarding memory and the theory of mind is to allow the world beyond the organism a role in a broader cultural understanding of metarepresentation but no such role in metarepresentational *cognition*. There are various ways to develop this idea, all of which ultimately turn on something like the encoding view of mental representation. For example, one might allow that certain cultural conditions are necessary (e.g., numerical systems) for specific cognitive capacities to emerge (arithmetical abilities) but deny that the cognitive capacities themselves are either taxonomically or locationally wide. Alternatively, one might see cultural innovations either as causes or effects of cognitive adaptations but never as constitutive of them. In either case, culture "beyond the head" is relevant to cognition only insofar as it becomes encoded by individual minds. These sorts of concessionary responses presuppose problematic and impoverished conceptions of culture and of the relation between culture, cognition, and evolution. I shall argue this point by exploring some of the broad options open to one in adopting a naturalistic approach to culture and its relationship to cognition and evolution.

Classic sociobiological theory (e.g., Wilson, 1975; 1978) attempted to account for "social behaviors" in a variety of animal species, including our own, through what I will call a *direct extension* (DE) model of evolutionary explanation.[4] That is, classic sociobiology took individual social behaviors as phenotypes and then applied the theory of natural selection to them, in effect explaining the persistence of those social behaviors as adaptations selected for their contribution to an organism's reproductive fitness. DE models construe heritability *genetically* and fitness *reproductively.* In addition, the theory of natural selection was typically understood by sociobiologists in terms of genic selection. This meant that genes for those social behaviors had been selected for their contributions to fitness, making sociobiological accounts individualistic about the causes of social behavior in something close to the sense in which most approaches to the mind within cognitive science have been individualistic.

Implicit in the sociobiological approach was an *aggregative* view of culture that corresponds to minimal reductionism about the mind: that cultural phenomena could be conceived of as the aggregation of individual social behaviors, and so are nothing over and above those individual acts. Thus, to take a classic example, the existence of "homosexual cultures" within certain societies was conceived of as an aggregation of individual agents who engaged in homosexual behavior. To explain cultural phenomena in evolutionary terms was simply to explain the behaviors of individual agents. Despite the recognition of various inadequacies in the sociobiological approach to "social behavior" (the anthropomorphism of its taxonomies; its omission of "the missing link" of psychology; an uncritical adaptationism; its insensitivity to philosophical questions about explanation), the aggregative conception of culture on which it relied is still predominant, particularly in other DE models of cultural evolution. And, like the genic version of sociobiology, alternative approaches to cultural evolution have remained individualistic in their orientation.

This seems clearest in the case of evolutionary psychology, which, when most akin to cognitive science (e.g., Tooby & Cosmides, 1992), attempts to identify "Darwinian algorithms" that underlie species-specific adaptations in an organism's cognitive architecture. Evolutionary psychology encapsulates a DE model of the evolutionary explanation of culture insofar as it construes the specific structures of the cognitive architecture as phenotypes that are selected for their contribution to reproductive fitness. While the process that maintains such phenotypes in the species – natural selection – is itself taxonomically wide and involves an external locus of control, the relevant phenotypes themselves are construed individualistically in that they are instantiated in brain structures taxonomized *computationally.*[5] Evolutionary psychology is aggregative about cultural phenomena just as classic sociobiology was, except that what is aggregated are not the individual social behaviors but the individual Darwinian algorithms underlying these.

Models of cultural evolution that rightly see culture related to (social) behavior through psychology need not and, in some cases, should not also adopt the aggregative and individualistic view of culture that prevails in DE models. This is both because DE models can themselves be wide and because there are alternative models of cultural evolution that make aggregativity and the accompanying individualism more difficult to sustain.

To take the former of these options first (and more briefly): DE models can be taxonomically or even locationally wide because the psychological capacities they purport to explain may be taxonomically or locationally wide. Many of an organism's adapted phenotypes are taxonomically wide (e.g., running faster than predators, being camouflaged, detecting prey effectively) and locationally wide (e.g., beavers + beaver dams, hermit crabs + the shells they inhabit, birds + the nests they build). Given that physical and behavioral phenotypes can be extended (*sensu* Dawkins, 1982), it is not clear why one should make an exception of psychological phenotypes; the idea that they are special in stopping at the skin relies on a dubious Cartesian separation between the physical and behavioral, on the one hand, and the psychological, on the other.

One reason for spending little time in pursuing wide options for DE models of cultural evolution is that DE models themselves are limited. The transmission of many aspects of culture (e.g., eating with a knife and fork, smoking, hand-shaking) has, at best, a tangential connection to reproductive fitness, and those whose promulgation *is* tied to reproductive fitness are often so tied only given the existence of wide cognitive capacities that are dependent upon culture. For example, while our capacities for sharing of food, selection of mates, and social exchange *do* bear a closer connection to reproductive success, each of these is a wide capacity (or, if you like, a narrow capacity whose adaptive significance lies in its being deployed in certain cultural environments rather than others). Likewise, I shall ignore what I call *heritability generalization* (HG) models, which add culturally mediated mechanisms of heritability (e.g., imitation, learning) to genetic mechanisms but maintain the reproductive fitness of individuals as the relevant notion of fitness. Instead, I want to comment on two other alternatives, each of which departs further from DE models than do HG models.

First are *fitness generalization* (FG) models, which as well as extending the mechanism for transmitting phenotypes also generalizes the notion of fitness. In these models there is a focus not simply on the reproductive fitness of individuals who carry certain memes but on the memes themselves and their "fitness," where this may conflict directly or indirectly with the reproductive fitness of individuals. The fitness of a meme is its capacity for transmission, where this clearly depends not only on its intrinsic properties and the cognitive architecture of individuals who transmit it, but also on features of the cultures in which the meme exists and the contexts in which it is expressed. To put it colloquially (but accurately), how catchy a meme is depends on who, how, where, and when it is expressed.

Second are what have been called *contagion* models of cultural evolution of the sort that Dan Sperber has defended over the last 10 to 15 years. Sperber's emphasis is on the ways in which the process linking cultural units is not one of replication but instead is *transformational* in its nature; this makes him sceptical of the notion of a meme, deriving as it does from that of a gene. As Sperber (1996) makes clear, there is dynamic interplay between mental and public representations in processes of cultural transmission and it is the inattention to the processes whereby mental representations are actually transmitted that gives FG models their superficial plausibility.

Although both FG and contagion models of cultural evolution give a central role to mental representations and the mental structures that underlie their processing, it is easy to see both as offering locationally wide accounts of the basic cultural units that are transmitted over time within a culture.[6] There are two ways in which these models posit locationally wide cognitive components of cultural transmission. The first is parallel to the way in which enactive procedural memory and external memory are locationally wide. These each involve extending the cognitive capacities of the mind of an individual. Likewise, we can see aspects of a culture as offering such an extension of an individual's cultural-processing hardware, the most obvious of which is technology in general and cognitive artifacts (maps, other people, computers) in particular. The second involves shifting the locus of control from the individual to some larger unit of which that individual is a part, as Hutchins (1995) has suggested is the case with human navigation. The final column of Table 4 makes these options more graphic.

Details about the cognitive architecture underlying the cognitive capacities that allow us to transmit cultural units will certainly take us part of the way, but both FG and contagion models identify more than the cognitive architecture as the "missing link" between behavior and fitness; included also are features of the resulting mental and external representations themselves (e.g., their rhythm), acquired and non-universal features of the mind (e.g., learning Chinese rather than English numerical systems), the availability of specific technological resources (e.g., the existence of particular writing systems), and non-representational facts about the structure of the cultures in which representations are transmitted (e.g., class structure, sexual division of labor). This makes the relationships between culture and cognition more complex than implied by the idea that the latter encodes the former and suggests a bidirectional causal relationship between the two that is incompatible with the aggregative view that individualists adopt.

Acknowledgments

Versions of this paper have been given at the Vancouver conference on metarepresentation in February 1997; to the Philosophy-Neuroscience-Psychology Program at Washington University, St. Louis in February 1998; and to the Centre for Advanced Studes at the University of Illinois, Urbana Champaign in March 1997. I am grateful for feedback from the audience in all three cases.

Notes

1 I should perhaps note that here, relying on Shoemaker's (1981) distinction between core and total realizations of mental states, I am asking a question about the core realization of various cognitive capacities. I have generalized this distinction elsewhere to argue that many "higher-order" states, including mental states, have a wide realization and that this has implications for both reductionist and non-reductionist views in the philosophy of mind. See Wilson (submitted).
2 This is not to suggest that being realized inside the head is sufficient for having an internal locus of control. Interesting, in this respect, is the discussion of George Graham and G. Lynn Stephens (1994) of psychopathologies that involve a feeling of a loss of control of the ideas that occur in one's own head.
3 I am indebted here to Merlin Donald (1991, esp. chap. 8) on the idea of external symbol storage and the conception of it as an extension to traditional conceptions of memory.
4 Although the name "direct extension" and the others that I use below are my own, the ideas are drawn and generalized from Elliott Sober (1991).
5 Of course, if the argument of my "Wide Computationalism" is correct (Wilson, 1994), then this inference from computationalism to individualism is invalid.

6 I doubt that this is Sperber's own view of either contagion or FG models of cultural evolution. In a number of places (e.g., Sperber, 1996, pp. 62, 96–97), Sperber himself indicates that intraindividual representations have some sort of priority over public representations in thinking about culture, the former being "psychological" and the latter "ecological."

References

Block, Ned (1986). Advertisement for a semantics for psychology. In P. French, T. Vehling, & H. Wettstein (Eds), *Midwest studies in philosophy: Vol.10. Philosophy of mind*. Minneapolis, MN: University of Minnesota Press.

Chomsky, Noam (1991). Linguistics and adjacent fields: A personal view. In A. Kasher (Ed.), *The Chomskyan Turn*. Cambridge, MA: Basil Blackwell.

Chomsky, Noam (1995). Language and nature. *Mind 104*, 1–61.

Cosmides, Leda,& Tooby, J. (1995). Foreword to S. Baron-Cohen, *Mindblindness*. Cambridge, MA: MIT Press.

Crane, Tim (1991). All the difference in the world. *Philosophical Quarterly 41*, 1–25.

Dawkins, R. (1982). *The extended phenotype*. Oxford: Oxford University Press.

Donald, M. (1991). *Origins of the modern mind*. Cambridge, MA: Harvard University Press.

Fodor, J. A. (1980). Methodological solipsism considered as a research strategy in cognitive psychology. *Behavioral and Brain Sciences 3*, 63–73. Reprinted in his *Representations*. Sussex: Harvester Press, 1981.

Fodor, J. A. (1987). *Psychosemantics*. Cambridge, MA: MIT Press.

Gallistel, C. R. (1990). *The organization of learning*. Cambridge, MA: MIT Press.

Graham, G., & Stephens, G. L. (1994). Mind and mine. In their *Philosophical Psychopathology*. Cambridge, MA: MIT Press.

Hutchins, E. (1995). *Cognition in the wild*. Cambridge, MA: MIT Press.

Jackendoff, R. (1992). The problem of reality. In his *Languages of the mind*. Cambridge, MA: MIT Press.

Koriat, A., & Goldstein, M. (1996). Memory metaphors and the real-life/laboratory controversy: Correspondence versus storehouse conceptions of memory. *Behavioral and Brain Sciences 19*, 167–188.

McGinn, C. (1991). Conceptual causation: Some elementary reflections. *Mind, 100*, 573–586.

Neisser, Ulric (1996). Remembering as doing. *Behavioral and Brain Sciences 19*, 203–204.

Owens, J. (1993). Content, causation, and psychophysical supervenience. *Philosophy of Science 60*, 242–261.

Putnam, H. (1975). The meaning of "meaning." In K.Gunderson (Ed.), *Language, Mind, and Knowledge*. Minneapolis, MN: University of Minnesota Press. Reprinted in his *Mind, language, and reality*. New York: Cambridge University Press.

Savage-Rumbaugh, S., & Lewin, R. (1994). *Kanzi: The ape at the brink of the human mind*. New York: Wiley and Sons.

Shoemaker, S. (1981). Some varieties of functionalism. *Philosophical Topics 12* (1),

83–118. Reprinted in his *Identity, cause, and mind*. New York: Cambridge University Press, 1984.

Sober, E. (1991). Models of cultural evolution. In P. Griffiths (Ed.), *Trees of life*. Dordrecht, NL: Kluwer Academic Publishers. Reprinted in E. Sober (Ed.), *Conceptual issues in evolutionary biology* 2nd ed. Cambridge, MA: MIT Press, 1994.

Sperber, D. (1996). *Explaining culture*. Cambridge, MA: Basil Blackwell.

Stich, S. (1978). Autonomous psychology and the belief-desire thesis. *Monist 61*, 573–591.

Stich, S. (1983). *From folk psychology to cognitive science*. Cambridge, MA: MIT Press.

Tooby, J., & Cosmides, L. (1992). *The psychological foundations of culture*. In J. Barkow, L. Cosmides, & J. Tooby (Eds.), *The adapted mind*. New York: Oxford University Press.

Wilson, E. O. (1975). *Sociobiology*. Cambridge, MA: Harvard University Press.

Wilson, E. O. (1978). *On human nature*. Cambridge, MA: Harvard University Press.

Wilson, R.A. (1994). Wide computationalism. *Mind 103*, 351–372.

Wilson, R.A. (1995). *Cartesian psychology and physical minds: Individualism and the sciences of the mind*. New York: Cambridge University Press.

Wilson, R.A. (submitted). Two views of realization.

Chapter 4

Consider the Source: The Evolution of Adaptations for Decoupling and Metarepresentation

Leda Cosmides and John Tooby

The Cognitive Niche and Local Information

Humans are often considered to be so distinct a species that they are placed outside of the natural order entirely, to be approached and analyzed independently of the rest of the living world. However, all species have unusual or differentiating characteristics and it is the task of an evolutionarily informed natural science to provide a causal account of the nature, organization, origin, and function, if any, of such characteristics without exaggerating, mystifying, or minimizing them.

Yet, even when placed within the context of the extraordinary diversity of the living world, humans continue to stand out, exhibiting a remarkable array of strange and unprecedented behaviors – from space travel to theology – that are not found in other species. What is at the core of these differences? Arguably, one central and distinguishing innovation in human evolution has been the dramatic increase in the use of contingent information for the regulation of improvised behavior that is successfully tailored to local conditions – an adaptive mode that has been labeled the *cognitive niche* (Tooby & DeVore, 1987). If you contrast, for example, the food acquisition practices of a Thompson's gazelle with that of a !Kung San hunter, you will immediately note a marked difference. To the gazelle, what looks to you like relatively undifferentiated grasslands is undoubtedly a rich tapestry of differentiated food patches and cues; nevertheless, the gazelle's decisions are made for it by evolved, neural specializations designed for grass and forage identification and evaluation – adaptations that are universal to the species, and that operate with relative uniformity across the species range. In contrast, the !Kung hunter uses, among many other means and methods that are not species-typical, arrows that are tipped with a poison found on only one local species of chrysomelid beetle, toxic only during the larval stage (Lee, 1993). Whatever the neural adaptations that underlie this behavior, they were not designed specifically for beetles and arrows, but exploit these local, contingent facts as part of a computational structure that treats them as instances of a more general class.

Indeed, most species are locked in co-evolutionary, antagonistic relationships with prey, rivals, parasites, and predators, in which move and countermove take place slowly, over evolutionary time. Improvisation puts humans at a great advantage: instead of being constrained to innovate only in phylogenetic time, they engage in ontogenetic ambushes[1] against their antagonists – innovations that are too rapid with respect to evolutionary time for their antagonists to evolve defenses by natural selection. Armed with this advantage, hominids have exploded into new habitats, developed an astonishing diversity of subsistence and resource extraction methods, caused the extinctions of many prey species in whatever environments they have penetrated, and generated an array of social systems far more extensive than that found in any other single species.

This contrast – between local, contingent facts and relationships that hold over the species' range – is at the heart of what makes humans so different. To evolve, species-typical behavioral rules must correspond to features of the species' ancestral world that were both globally true (i.e., that held statistically across a preponderance of the species' range) and stably true (i.e., that remained in effect over enough generations that they selected for adaptations in the species). These constraints narrowly limit the kinds of information that such adaptations can be designed to use: the set of properties that had a predictable relationship to features of the species' world that held widely in space and time is a very restricted one. In contrast, for situation-specific, appropriately tailored improvisation, the organism only needs information to be applicable or "true" temporarily, locally, or contingently. If information only needs to be true temporarily, locally, and situationally to be useful, then a vastly enlarged universe of context-dependent information becomes potentially available to be employed in the successful regulation of behavior. This tremendously enlarged universe of information can be used to fuel the identification of an immensely more varied set of advantageous behaviors than other species employ, giving human life its distinctive complexity, variety, and relative success. Hominids entered the cognitive niche, with all its attendant benefits and dangers, by evolving a new suite of cognitive adaptations that are evolutionarily designed to exploit this broadened universe of information, as well as the older universe of species-extensive true relationships.

The hominid occupation of the cognitive niche is characterized by a constellation of interrelated behaviors that depend on intensive information manipulation and that are supported by a series of novel or greatly elaborated cognitive adaptations. This zoologically unique constellation of behaviors includes locally improvised subsistence practices; extensive context-sensitive manipulation of the physical and social environment; "culture," defined as the serial reconstruction and adoption of representations and regulatory variables found in others' minds through inferential specializations evolved for the task; language as a system for dramatically lowering the cost of communicating propositional information; tool use adapted to a diverse range of local problems; context-specific skill acquisition; multi-individual coordinated action; and other information-intensive and information-dependent activities (Tooby & Cosmides, 1992). Although social interactions may have played a role, we do not believe that social competition was the sole driving force behind the evolution of human intelligence (as in the Machiavellian hypothesis; Humphrey, 1992; Whitten & Byrne,1997). We certainly do believe that humans have evolved sophisticated adaptations specialized for social life and social cognition (e.g., Cosmides, 1989; Cosmides & Tooby, 1989; 1992), but what is truly distinctive about human life encompasses far more than the social. For example, the causal intelligence expressed in hunter-gatherer subsistence practices appears to be as divergent from other species as human social intelligence.

The benefits of successful improvisation are clear: the ability to realize goals through exploiting the unique opportunities that are inherent in a singular local situation yields an advantage over a system that is limited to applying only those solutions that work across a more general class of situation. What ten years of ordinary battle on the plains of Troy could not accomplish, one Trojan Horse could. The improvisational exploitation of unique opportunities also fits our folk intuitions about what counts as intelligence. As members of the human species, instances of intelligence excite our admiration precisely to the extent that the behavior (or insight) involved is novel and not the result of the "mindless" application of fixed rules. Indeed, it would seem that every organism would be benefitted by having a faculty that caused it to perform behaviors adapted to each individual situation. This raises a question: Why haven't all organisms evolved this form of intelligence? Indeed, how is this form of intelligence possible at all?

Elsewhere, we have written at length about the trade-offs between problem-solving power and specialization: general-purpose problem-solving architectures are very weak but broad in application, whereas special-purpose problem-solving designs are very efficient and inferentially powerful but limited in their domain of application (Cosmides & Tooby, 1987; Tooby & Cosmides, 1992). Thus, on first inspection, there appear to be only two biologically possible choices for evolved minds: either general ineptitude or narrow competences. This choice rules out general intelligence. Traditionally, many scholars have assumed that because human intelligence appears unprecedentedly broad in application, the human cognitive architecture's core problem-solving engines must themselves be general-purpose. This has led to a fruitless insistence that viable candidate models of this architecture be largely free of special-purpose machinery. This insistence has, in our view, obstructed progress toward an accurate model of the human psychological architecture. Because general-purpose problem-solvers are too weak to supply the problem-solving power evolved organisms need to carry out the array of complex and arduous tasks they routinely face, human intelligence cannot consist primarily of domain-general computational engines. Instead of achieving general intelligence through general-purpose mechanisms, there is another alternative: Cognitive specializations, each narrow in its domain of application, can be bundled together in a way that widens the range of inputs or domains that can be successfully handled. More general-purpose engines can be embedded within this basic design (because their defects when operating in isolation can be offset by implanting them in a guiding matrix of specializations). Moreover, other architectural features are required to solve the problems raised by the interactions of these heterogeneous systems, as discussed below (Tooby & Cosmides, 1990a; 1992; in press). This is the only solution that we can see to the question of how human intelligence can be broad in its range of application but also sufficiently powerful when applied (Sperber, 1996; Tooby & Cosmides, 1990a; 1992).

Even so, the costs and difficulties of the cognitive niche are so stringent that only one lineage, in four billion years, has wandered into the preconditions that favored the evolution of this form of intelligence. Natural computational systems that begin to relax their functional specificity run into, and are inescapably shaped by, savagely intense selection pressures. One of the greatest problems faced by natural computational systems is combinatorial explosion (for discussion, see Cosmides & Tooby, 1987; Tooby & Cosmides, 1992). Combinatorial explosion is the term for the fact that alternatives multiply with devastating rapidity in computational systems, and the less constrained the representational and procedural possibilities, the faster this process mushrooms. When this happens, the system is choked with too many possibilities to search among or too many processing steps to perform. Marginally increasing the generality of a system exponentially increases the cost, greatly limiting the types of architectures that can evolve, and favoring, for example, the evolution of modules only in domains in which an economical set of procedures can generate a sufficiently large and valuable set of outputs. This means that domain-specificity will be the rule rather than the exception in natural computational systems.

A second difficulty is that, from evolutionary and computational perspectives, it is far from clear how local improvisation could evolve, operate, or even be a non-magical, genuine cognitive possibility. A computational system, by its nature, can only apply rules or procedures to problems, and must do so based on its rule-based categorization of individual problems into more general classes, so that it knows which procedures to activate in a given situation.[2] Moreover, natural selection is a statistical process that tested alternative computational designs against each other, summing over billions of individual lives and test runs, taking place over thousands of generations. A gene (and its associated design feature) could only have been selected to the extent that it operated well against the statistical regularities that recurred across vast ancestral populations of events. That is, the iterated conditions that the adaptation evolved to deal with must have extended over enough of the species range, and for an evolutionary period that was long enough to spread the underlying genes from their initial appearance as mutations to near universality.[3] In consequence, adaptations can only see individual events in the life of the organism as instances of the large-scale evolutionarily recurrent categories of events that built them (Tooby & Cosmides, 1990a). So, if computational systems can only respond to situations as members of classes to which computational rules apply, and if evolution only builds computational adaptations that "see" individual situations as members of large scale, evolutionarily recurrent classes of events, how can there be a brain whose principles of operation commonly lead it to improvise behaviors that exploit the distinctive features of a situation? How could species-typical computational rules evolve that allow situation-specific improvisation at all – or at sufficiently low cost? We will address several of these questions elsewhere (Cosmides & Tooby, in press). In this chapter, we shall concentrate on only one set of engineering problems associated with the exploitation of contingent information – what we call the *scope problem*.

The Scope Problem

When hominids evolved or elaborated adaptations that could use information based on relationships that were only "true" temporarily, locally, or contingently rather than universally and stably, this opened up a new and far larger world of potential information than was available previously. Context-dependent information could now be used to guide behavior to a far greater extent than had been possible formerly. This advance, however, was purchased at a cost: The exploitation of this exploding universe of potentially representable information creates a vastly expanded risk of possible misapplications, in which information that may be usefully descriptive in a narrow arena of conditions is false, misleading, or harmful outside the scope of those conditions.[4] Exactly because information that is only applicable temporarily or locally begins to be used, the success of this computational strategy depends on continually monitoring and re-establishing the boundaries within which each representation remains useful. Are the beetle larvae that are used to poison arrows toxic at all times of the year? Once harvested and applied, how long does the poisoned arrow tip remain poisonous? If it is poisonous to humans, gazelles, and duikers, is it also poisonous to lions, cape buffalo, and ostriches? If these relationships are true here, are they true on foraging territories on the other side of the Okavango? If the first several statements from my father in answer to these questions turned out to be true, will the remainder be true also? Information only gives an advantage when it is relied on inside the envelope of conditions within which it is applicable. Hence, when considering the evolution of adaptations to use information, the costs of overextension and misapplication have to be factored in, as do the costs and nature of the defenses against such misapplication. Expanding the body of information used to make decisions is harmful or dangerous if the architecture does not and cannot detect and keep track of which information is applicable where, and how the boundaries of applicability shift (Tooby & Cosmides, in press).

Moreover, the problem is not simply that information that is usefully descriptive only within a limited envelope of conditions will (by definition) be false or harmful outside the scope of those conditions. The scope problem is aggravated by the fact that information is integrated and transformed through inferences. Information is useful to the extent that it can be inferentially applied to derive conclusions that can then be used to regulate behavior. Inferences routinely combine multiple inputs through a procedure to produce new information, and the value of the resulting inferences depends sensitively on the accuracy of the information that is fed into them. For example, the truth of the conclusion that it will be better to move to an area where there is more game is dependent on the proposition that there is more game in the new location, and on the implicit or explicit assumption that the necessary poisons for hunting can be obtained there as well.

Not only does inference combinatorially propagate errors present in the source inputs, but the resulting outputs are then available to be fed in as erroneous inputs into other inferences, multiplying the errors in successive chains and spreading waves. For example, if one wrong entry is made in a running total, all subsequent totals – and the decisions based on them – become wrong. This process has the potential to corrupt any downstream data-set interacted with, in a spreading network of compounding error. The more the human cognitive architecture is networked together by systems of intelligent inference, and the more it is enhanced by the ability to integrate information from many sources,[5] the greater the risk that valid existing information sets will be transformed into unreconstructable tangles of error and confusion. In short, the heavily inference-dependent nature of human behavior regulation is gravely threatened by erroneous, unreliable, obsolete, out-of-context, deceptive, or scope-violating representations.

For these reasons, the evolution of intelligence will depend critically on the economics of information management and on the tools of information management – that is, the nature of the adaptations that evolve to handle these problems. The net benefit of evolving to use certain classes of information will depend on the cost of its acquisition, the utility of the information when used, the damage of acting on the information mistakenly outside its area of applicability, and the cost of its management and maintenance. Because humans are the only species that has evolved this kind of intelligence, humans must be equipped with adaptations that evolved to solve the problems that are special to this form of intelligence.

Scope Syntax, Truth, and Naïve Realism

For these reasons, issues involving not only the accuracy but also the scope of applicability of the information that the individual human acquires and represents became paramount in the design and evolution of the human cognitive architecture. We believe that there are a large number of design innovations that have evolved to solve the specialized programming problems posed by using local and contingent information, including a specialized scope syntax, metarepresentational adaptations, and decoupling systems. Indeed, we think that the human cognitive architecture is full of interlocking design features whose function is to solve problems of scope and accuracy. Examples include truth-value tags, source-tags (self versus other; vision versus memory, etc.), scope-tags, time-and-place tags, reference-tags, credal values, operators embodying propositional attitudes, content-based routing of information to targeted inference engines, dissociations, systems of information encapsulation and interaction, independent representational formats for different ontologies, and the architecture and differential volatility of different memory systems. One critical feature is the capacity to carry out inferential operations on sets of inferences that incorporate suppositions or propositions of conditionally unevaluated truth value, while keeping their computational products isolated from other knowledge stores until the truth or utility of the suppositions is decided, and the outputs are either integrated or discarded. This capacity is essential to planning,

interpreting communication, employing the information communication brings, evaluating others' claims, mind-reading, pretense, detecting
or perpetrating deception, using inference to triangulate information
about past or hidden causal relations, and much else that makes the human mind so distinctive. In what follows, we will try to sketch out some
of the basic elements of a scope syntax designed to defuse problems intrinsic to the human mode of intelligence.

By a scope syntax, we mean a system of procedures, operators, relationships, and data-handling formats that regulate the migration of information among subcomponents of the human cognitive architecture.
To clarify what we mean, consider a simple cognitive system that we suspect is the ancestral condition for all animal minds, and the default condition for the human mind as well: naïve realism. For the naïve realist,
the world as it is mentally represented is taken for the world as it really
is, and no distinction is drawn between the two. Indeed, only a subset of
possible architectures is even capable of representing this distinction and,
in the origin and initial evolution of representational systems, such a distinction would be functionless. From our external perspective, we can say
of such basic architectures that all information found inside the system
is assumed to be true, or is treated as true. However, from the point of
view of the architecture itself, that would not be correct, for it would imply that the system is capable of drawing the distinction between true and
false, and is categorizing the information as true. Instead, mechanisms
in the architecture simply use the information found inside the system
to regulate behavior and to carry out further computations. Whatever information is present in the system simply is "reality" for the architecture.
Instead of tagging information as true or false – as seems so obvious to
us – such basic architectures would not be designed to store false information. When new information is produced that renders old information
obsolete, the old information is updated, overwritten, forgotten, or discarded. None of these operations require the tagging of information as
true or false. They only involve the rule-governed replacement of some
data by other data, just like overwriting a memory register in a personal
computer does not require the data previously in that register be catego-
rized as false. For most of the behavior-regulatory operations that representational systems evolved to orchestrate, there would be no point in
storing false information, or information tagged as false. For this reason,
there is no need in such an architecture to be able to represent that some
information is true: Its presence, or the decision to store it or remember,
it is the cue to its reliability. In such a design, true equals accessible.

With this as background, and leaving aside the many controversies
in epistemology over how to conceptualize what truth "really" is, we can
define what we will call *architectural truth:* information is treated by an
architecture as true when it is allowed to migrate (or be reproduced) in

an unrestricted or scope-free fashion throughout an architecture, interacting with any other data in the system with which it is capable of interacting. All data in semantic memory, for example, is architecturally true. The simplest and most economical way to engineer data use is for "true" information to be unmarked, and for unmarked information to be given whatever freedom of movement is possible by the computational architecture. Indeed, any system that acquires, stores, and uses information is a design of this kind. The alternative design, in which each piece of information intended for use must be paired with another piece of information indicating that the first piece is true, seems unnecessarily costly and cumbersome. Because the true-is-unmarked system is the natural way for an evolved computational system to originate, and because there are many reasons to maintain this system for most uses, we might expect that this is also the reason why humans – and undoubtedly other organisms – are naïve realists. Naïve realism seems to be the most likely starting point phylogenetically and ontogenetically, as well as the default mode for most systems, even in adulthood.

The next step, necessary only for some uses, is to have representations described by other data structures: metarepresentations (in a relaxed rather than narrow sense). For example, a cognitive architecture might contain the structure, *The statement that "anthropology is a science" is true*. This particular data structure includes a proposition (or data element) and an evaluation of the truth of the proposition (or data element).[6] However, such structures need not be limited to describing single propositions. Although it is common in talking about metarepresentations and propositional attitudes to depict a single representation embedded in an encompassing proposition, a single proposition is only a limiting case. A set of propositions or any other kind of data element can be bundled into a single unit that is taken, as a data packet, as an argument by a scope operator to form a metarepresentation. For example, the metarepresentation, *Every sentence in this chapter is false*, describes the truth value of a set of propositions[7] as easily as *The first sentence in this chapter is false* describes the truth value of a single proposition. Indeed, sometimes integrated sets of propositions governed by a superordinate scope operator might become so elaborated, and relatively independent from other data structures, that they might conveniently be called worlds. We think large amounts of human knowledge inside individuals exist inside data structures of this kind.

A sketch of the kind of cognitive architecture and operators we have in mind begins with a primary workspace that operates in a way that is similar, in some respects, to natural deduction systems (see Gentzen, 1969/1935; Rips, 1994; Cosmides & Tooby, 1996b), although it may include axiom-like elements, and many other differences, as well. Its general features are familiar: There is a workspace containing active data elements;

procedures or operators act on the data structures, transforming them into new data structures. Data structures are maintained in the workspace until they are overwritten, or if not used or primed after a given period of time, until they fade and are discarded. Products may be permanently stored in appropriate subsystems if they meet various criteria indicating they merit long-term storage, or warrant being treated as architecturally true. Otherwise, the contents and intermediate work products of the workspace are volatile, and are purged, as one adaptation for protecting the integrity of the reliable data stores elsewhere in the architecture. Data structures may be introduced from perception, memory, supposition, or from various other system components and modules. Some of the procedures and tags available in the workspace correspond to familiar logical operators and elements such as variable binding, instantiation, 'if' introduction and 'if' elimination, the recognition and tagging of contradictions, *modus ponens*, and so on. Some of the procedures are ecologically rational (Tooby & Cosmides, in press; Cosmides & Tooby, 1996a), that is, they correspond to licensed transformations in various adaptive logics (which may diverge substantially from licensed inferences in the content-independent formal logics developed so far by logicians). Indeed, many procedures consist of routing data structures through adaptive specializations such as cheater detection or hazard management algorithms (Cosmides, 1989; Cosmides and Tooby, 1997), with outputs placed back into the workspace: a process that resembles either calling subroutines or applying logical transformations, depending on one's taste in formalisms.[8] Deliberative reasoning is carried out in this workspace: while many other types of inference are carried out automatically as part of the heterogeneous array of specializations available in the architecture. Some areas of this workspace are usually part of conscious awareness, and most are consciously accessible.

The data sets in this system exist in structured, hierarchical relations,[9] which we will represent as indented levels. Data elements in the left-most position are in what might be thought of as the ground state, which means they are licensed to migrate anywhere in the architecture they can be represented. They may enter into inferences in combination with any other ground state data-structure, and (usually) may be permitted to interact with subordinate levels as well: They are architecturally true, or scope-free. Other elements are subordinated under ground state elements through scope operators. So, we might represent an architecturally true statement in the leftmost position, such as:

(1)   Anthropology is a science.

It is unmarked by the architecture, and is free to be stored or to be introduced into any other nondecoupled process in the architecture. A subordinated statement may be scope-limited, such as:

(2)   The statement is false that:

(3)   Anthropology is a science.

In this case, the scope operator (2) binds the scope within which the information of the data structure (3) can be accessed, so that (3) is not free to be promoted to the ground state or to be used elsewhere in the system. In contrast, the function of an explicit true tag in a statement description operator (i.e., *The statement is true that p*) would be to release the statement from previous scope-restriction, promoting it to the next leftmost level or, if it was originally only one level down, changing its status to unmarked or architecturally true.[10] Time and location operators operate similarly:

(4)   In ≠Tobe (!Kung for "autumn"),

(5)   the mongongo nuts become edible and plentiful.

Or,

(6)   At Nyae Nyae,

(7)   there are chrysomelid beetles suitable for making
           arrow poison.

Scope operators define, regulate, or modify the relationships between sets of information, and the migration of information between levels. They involve a minimum of two levels, a superordinate (or ground) and subordinate level. In these cases, the subordinate propositions cannot be reproduced without their respective scope-tags, which describe the boundary conditions under which the information is known to be accurate, and hence which license their use in certain inferences but not others. As with classical conditioning, we expect that additional mechanisms are designed to keep track of the reality of the scope boundaries; e.g., observing a lack of contingency outside the boundaries may eventually release the restriction. Thus, (6)–(7) may be transformed into (7) for an individual whose travels from camp to camp are typically inside the beetle species' range. Conversely, architecturally true statements like (1) can be transformed by a scope operation into something scope-limited, as new information about its boundary conditions is learned. A time-based scope transformation would be:

(8)   It is no longer true that

(9)   anthropology is a science.

Scope operators regulate the migration of information into and out of subordinated data sets, coupling (allowing data to flow) and decoupling them according to the nature of the operator and the arguments it is fed. They bind propositions into internally transparent but externally regulated sets. In so doing, they provide many of the tools necessary to solve the problems posed by contingent information. By imposing bounds on where scope-limited information can travel (or what can access it), it allows information to be retained by the system and used under well-specified conditions, without allowing it to damage other reliable data-sets through inferential interaction. We will call representations that are bound or interrelated by scope operators *scope-representations* or *S-representations*.

Since computational features evolve because they enhance behavioral regulation, it is worth noting that these innovations markedly increase the range of possible behaviors open to the organism. In particular, one major change involves *acting as if*. The organism would be highly handicapped if it could only act on the basis of information known to be true or have its conduct regulated by architecturally true propositions, although this was likely to be the ancestral state of the organism. With the ability *to act as if p*, or *to act on the basis of p*, the organism can use information to regulate its behavior without losing any scope-represented restrictions on the nature of the information, or without necessarily losing a continuing awareness that the information acted on is not, or might not be, true. Conditions where such a behavioral-representational subsystem are useful include the many categories of actions undertaken under conditions of uncertainty (e.g., we will assume they got the message about the restaurant; or we will act as if there is a leopard hiding in the shadows of the tree), actions with respect to social conventions or deontic commitments (which are by themselves incapable of being either true or not true, at least in an ordinary sense; e.g., *Elizabeth is the rightful Queen of England; it is praiseworthy to make the correct temple sacrifices*), adapting oneself to the wishes of others, hypothesis testing, and so on.[11] Pretense (Leslie 1987) and deception (Whiten & Byrne, 1997) are simply extensions of this same competence, in which the agent knows the representations on which she is acting are false. These are simply the limiting cases rather than the defining cases. In order to get coordinated behavior among many individuals, and the benefits that arise from it, it is necessary to agree on a set of representations that will be jointly acted upon – a reason why social interaction so often involves the manufacture of socially constructed but unwarranted shared beliefs. Structures of representations can be built up that can be permanently consulted for actions without their contents unrestrictedly contaminating other knowledge stores.

Credal values and modals (*it is likely that p; it is possible that p; it is certain that p*) allow the maintenance and transformation of scope-marked information bound to information about likelihood and possibility – regulatory information that often changes while the underlying propositions are conserved. Propositional attitude verbs (e.g., think, believe, want, hope, deny) are obviously also a key category of scope-operator, as we will discuss.

Supposition, Counterfactuals and Natural Deduction Systems

What makes such a system resemble, to a certain extent, natural deduction systems is the presence of scope-operators such as supposition, and the fact that these operators create subdomains or subordinate levels of representation, which may themselves have further subordinate levels, growing into multilevel, tree-like structures. Supposition involves the introduction of propositions of unevaluated or suspended truth value, which are treated as true within a bound scope, and then used as additional content from which to combinatorially generate inferential products. The operator "if," for example, opens up a suppositional world: for instance, *I am in my office this afternoon. If students believe I am not in my office this afternoon, then they won't bother me. If I close my door, and leave my light off, they will believe I am not here.* The contents of this suppositional world are kept isolated from other proposition-sets, so that true propositions are not intermixed and hence confused with false ones (e.g., *I am not in my office*) or potentially false ones (e.g., *they won't bother me*). Any number of subordinate levels can be introduced, with additional subordinate suppositions or other scope operations. A key feature of such a deduction system is the restricted application of inferences. Inferences are applied in a rule-governed but unrestricted fashion within a level – e.g., *students believe I am not in my office this afternoon*, therefore, *they won't bother me* – but not across levels – e.g., there is no contradiction to be recognized between *I am in my office this afternoon*, and the proposition *I am not in my office this afternoon*, because they are at different levels in the structure. Contents are architecturally true with respect to the level they are in and may enter into inferences at that level, while remaining false or unevaluated with respect to both the ground state of the architecture and other intermediate superordinate levels. Certain propositional attitudes (e.g., "believe" as opposed to "know") also decouple the truth value of the propositions ("I am not in my office") that are embedded in encompassing statements, a process that can be dissected computationally. Paradoxically, an architecture that only processes true information is highly limited in what it can infer, and most forms of human discovery by reasoning involve supposition. While some cases are famous (10), normal cases of suppositions are so numerous that they permeate our thoughts in carrying out routine actions in our daily lives (11).

(10) Suppose I threw this rock hard enough that the earth fell away in its curvature faster than the rock's downward ballistic took it?

(11) What if I hold my airline ticket in my teeth while I pick up the baby with my right arm and our bags with my left arm?

Supposition is a scope operation that suspends truth-values for all successive computations that result from taking the supposition as a premise. For example, (12) suspends the truth-value of (13):

(12) Suppose my wife, Desdemona, was unfaithful with Cassio.

(13)　　　Then Cassio, whom I thought was my friend,
　　　　　has betrayed me.

Suppositions and their entailments remain internally interrelated and generative but isolated from the rest of the data in the architecture. If (13) were allowed to escape its scope-restriction to enter into ground-state originating inferences, the effects would be disastrous. Othello would have (13) as part of his uncritically accepted semantic store of propositions, without it being warranted (or "true" within the decoupled world of Shakespeare's *Othello*).[12] Nevertheless, S-representations like (12)–(13) allow many types of useful and revelatory reasoning to proceed – everything from proof by contradiction to the construction of contingency plans. Additionally, suppositions contain specifications of when subordinate deductions can be discharged. This occurs when other processes produce a true proposition that duplicates that supposition. Evidence establishing (12) as true discharges the supposition, promoting (13) to architectural truth and stripping it of its scope restrictions.

Actions can also discharge suppositions – a key point. Consider a hominid considering how to capture a colobus monkey in a tree. An architecture that cannot consider decoupled states of affairs is limited in the behaviors it can take (e.g., close distance with monkey). This may often fail because of the nature of the situation. For example, consider the situation in which there is a branch from the tree close to the branch of a neighboring tree. In this situation, the hominid confronts the following contingencies: If he climbs the trunk, then the monkey escapes by the branch. If he climbs across the branches, then the monkey escapes by the trunk. If, before taking action, the hominid suppositionally explores the alternative hunt scenarios, then it will detect the prospective failure. Moreover, given alternative inferential pathways leading to failure, the hominid, armed with the inferential power of supposition (and various other inferential tools, such as a model of the prey mind and a theory of mechanics), may then begin to consider additional courses of action suppositionally, reasoning about the likely consequences of each alternative.

Suppose there were no branch on the neighboring tree; then it could not be used as an escape route. Suppose, before I initiate the hunt by climbing up the trunk, I break that branch; then it could not be used as an escape route. If I then go up the trunk, the monkey cannot escape. The hunt will be a success. End search for successful outcome. Transform suppositional structure into a plan.

Conveniently for planning and action, the conditions for discharging a supposition specify the actions that need to be taken to put that aspect of the plan into effect, and the tree structure of suppositions provides the information about the order of the causal steps to be taken. Hominids armed with suppositional reasoning can undertake new types of successful behaviors that would be impossible for those whose cognitive architectures lacked such design features. It allows them to explore the properties of situations computationally, in order to identify sequences of improvised behaviors that may lead to novel, successful outcomes. The restricted application of inferences to a level, until suppositions (or other scope-limitations) are discharged is a crucial element of such an architecture. The states of affairs under the scope of a specific supposition are not mistaken for states of affairs outside that supposition: superordinate and subordinate relationships are kept clear until their preconditions can be discharged (as when an action is taken).

Like a clutch in an automobile, supposition and other scope operators allow the controlled engagement or disengagement of powerful sets of representations that can contain rich descriptions and acquired, domain-specific inference engines that can be applied when their preconditions are met. These operators provide vehicles whereby information that may or may not be counterfactual can be processed without the output being tagged as *true* and stored as such. Because contingent information can change its status at any time, with any new change in the world, it is important to have tools available that can take architecturally true information and scrutinize it. For example, the workspace that contains proposition p may benefit from demoting p into the scope-representation, *It appears that p*. Proposition p can still provide the basis for action, but can now be subjected to inferential processes not possible when it was simply a free representation at ground state. Demotion into a scope-representation brings a representation out of architectural truth and into a new relationship with the primary workspace. Because of this feature of the human cognitive architecture, humans can contingently refrain from being naïve realists about any specific data structure, although presumably we will always be naïve realists about whatever happens to be in the ground state in the workspace at any given time.[13]

Some operators are recursive, and some types of subordinated data structures can serve as the ground for further subordinated structures, leading potentially to a tree structure of subordinated and parallel relations whose length and branching contingencies are restricted only by performance limitations of the system. For example:

(14) Chagnon was under the impression that

(15)   Clifford has claimed that

(16)   most anthropologists believe that

(17)   the statement is false that:

(18)   anthropology is a science. [and]

(19)   quantum physicists have demonstrated that:

(20)   science is only an observer-dependent set of arbitrary subjective opinions.

Extensive thinking about a topic can produce structures too elaborate to be placed, in their entirety, into the workspace, and which are therefore considered in pieces. The cultural development of memory aids such as writing have allowed an explosion of conceptual structures that are larger than what our ancestors would have routinely used.

Scope operators greatly augment the computational power of the human cognitive architecture compared to ancestral systems lacking such features. One advantage of an architecture equipped with scope operators is that it can carry out inferential operations on systems of inferences of unevaluated or suspended truth value, while keeping their computational products isolated from other knowledge stores until the truth or utility of the elements can be decided. If they were not kept isolated, their contents would enter into inferences with other data-structures in the architecture, often producing dangerously false but unmarked conclusions (e.g., *science is only a set of arbitrary subjective opinions* would be disastrous guidance for someone who has to choose a medical strategy to arrest an epidemic in a developing country). Fortunately, (14) decouples the uncertain information in (15)–(20) from the rest of the architecture, but allows the information to be maintained, and reasoned about, within various lawful and useful restrictions specified in the scope operators. The structure (14)–(20) is free to migrate through the system as a bound unit, entering into whatever licensed inferences it can be related to, but its subordinate elements are not.

Within subordinate levels (15)–(20), similar scope operations structure the inferences that are possible. The operator "demonstrate" assigns the value "true" to the subordinate element (20: *science is only . . .*), allowing its contents to be promoted to the next level. Within that level, it is treated as true, although it is not true above that level or outside of its scope-circumscription. The operator that governs that level – "claim" –

prevents it from migrating independently of the metarepresentation it is bound to (*Clifford has claimed that . . .*). Both (16) plus entailments and (19) plus entailments are true within the world of Clifford's claims, and are free to inferentially interact with each other, along with (20), as well as with any other of Clifford's claims that turn up. Indeed, one can say that a representation is true with respect to a particular level in a particular data-structure; any level can function as a ground level to subordinate levels. A data-structure is scope-conditionally true when it is permitted by the architecture to interact with any other information held within the same or subordinate levels of that data-structure.

Source, Error Correction, and the Evolution of Communication

Different scope operators obviously have different regulatory properties, and hence different functions. *Claim, believe,* and *demonstrate,* for example, require source tags as arguments, as well as conveying additional information – i.e., publicly assert as true that *p*; privately treat as architecturally true that *p*; publicly establish the truth that *p*, respectively. Source tags are very useful, because often, with contingent information, one may not have direct evidence about its truth, but may acquire information about the reliability of a source. If the sources of pieces of information are maintained with the information, then subsequent information about the source can be used to change the assigned truth-status of the information either upwards or downwards. For example, one may not assign much credal value to what most anthropologists believe (16), or one may discover that Clifford in particular is highly unreliable (15), while having a solid set of precedents in which Chagnon's impressions (such as 14–20) have proven highly reliable, despite the fact that he himself is unwilling to evaluate his impressions as trustworthy. Sources may include not only people but also sources internal to the architecture, such as vision, episodic memory, a supposition, previous inference, and so on. Thus, humans can have the thought "My eyes are telling me one thing, while my reason is telling me another."

In general, our minds are full of conclusions without our having maintained the grounds or evidence that led us to think of them as true. For a massively inferential architecture like the human mind, each item can serve as input to many other inferential processes, whose outputs are inputs to others. To the extent that the s information is sourced, or its grounds and derivation are preserved in association with the data, then new data about the grounds can be used to correct or update its inferential descendants. To the extent that the information is not sourced or its process of inferential derivation is not preserved in association with it, then it cannot be automatically corrected when the grounds for belief are corrected. Indeed, our minds are undoubtedly full of erroneous inferential products that were not corrected when their parent source information was updated, because they could no longer be connected with their derivation. Because source tags, and especially derivations, are costly to maintain, mechanisms should monitor for sufficient corroboration, consistency with architecturally true information, or certification by a trusted source: If or when a threshold is reached, the system should no longer expend resources to maintain source information, and it should fade. This is what makes trust so useful (one does not need to keep the cognitive overhead of scope-processing communication) but so dangerous (one cannot recover and correct all of the implanted misinformation). After all, what is important about an encyclopedia of (accurate) knowledge about the world is the facts themselves: not who told them to you, what their attitude towards them was, or when you learned them. Typically, once a fact is established to a sufficient degree of certainty, source, attitude, and time tags are lost (Sperber, 1985; Tulving, 1983; Shimamura, 1995). For example, most people cannot remember who told them that apples are edible or that plants photosynthesize.[14] Moreover, an encyclopedia is most useful when the facts can cross-reference one another, so that each can support inferences that may apply to others, thereby adding further, inferred facts to the body of knowledge (e.g., "Mercury is a poison"; "Tuna has high levels of mercury"; therefore "people who eat tuna are ingesting poison"). This means that truth conditions must not be suspended for facts in semantic memory, and the scope of application for any truth-preserving inference procedures must be relatively unrestricted within the encyclopedia, such that facts can "mate" promiscuously to produce new, inferred facts.

Source tagging, source monitoring, and the scope-limitation of information by person must have played a critical role in the evolution of human communication and culture. Evolutionary biologists have long been aware that different organisms will have conflicting fitness interests and that this poses problems for the evolution of communication (Krebs & Dawkins, 1984). Information transmitted from other organisms will only be designed to be transmitted if it is in their interests, which opens up the possibility that each signal may be either deceptive or simply erroneous. The capacity to receive and process communication could not evolve if the interpretive process simply treated the communicated information as architecturally true, or unmarked, because deceptive exploitation would reduce the signal value to zero in most cases (see Sperber, this volume, for an analysis of how this adaptive problem may have led to the emergence of logical abilities deployed in the context of communication). The same argument holds true for culture-learning adaptations as well. Culture could not have evolved without the co-evolution of a representational immune system to keep the acquirer from adopting too many false or exploitive cultural elements (Sperber, 1985; Tooby & Cosmides, 1989). Source tagging and scope syntax are crucial to this process. Take, for example:

(21) Fagles argues that

(22)   Homer says that

(23)   Odysseus told Achilles that

(24)   he ought to be happy among the dead.

This structure uses communicative terms that attribute representations to sources, and that in so doing, clearly suspends their truth relations. This is just what one would expect of a scope-syntactic system that is well-designed for processing communication, while not being at the mercy of erroneous or deceptive messages.

Gerrig & Prentice (1991) have provided some empirical support for the notion that representations that are inconsistent with present knowledge are decoupled from representations that are consistent with it. After having read a story that contained statements like "Most forms of mental illness are contagious" subjects were asked to judge the truth "in the real world" of certain target statements. Regardless of retrieval context, they were faster at judging the inconsistent statements than the consistent ones, indicating that inconsistent ideas were stored separately from semantic memory. Judgments were even faster when the retrieval context suggested that the questions asked would be drawn from the story they had heard, lending some support to the idea that inconsistent information retains a source tag (in this case, the story-telling experimenter) that can be used for rapid retrieval.

Even more basically, Sperber has persuasively argued that the inferential nature of communication itself requires the on-line metarepresentational processing of language in order for interpretation to be successful (Sperber & Wilson, 1986; Sperber, 1985; 1996; this volume). Sperber (1985) has also proposed that metarepresentations as a data-format may be an adaptation to pedagogy, to deal with the problems posed by the long-term maintenance of information that is only partially comprehended.

Since Frege, philosophers have been aware that propositional attitudes suspend semantic relations such as truth, reference, and existence (Frege, 1892; Kripke, 1979; Richard, 1990). Frege noticed, for example, that the principle of substitution of co-referring terms breaks down when they are embedded in propositional attitudes (i.e., one can believe that Batman fights crime without believing that Bruce Wayne fights crime). Or, consider the statement:

(25) Shirley MacLaine believes that

(26)   she is the reincarnation of an Egyptian princess
            named Nefu.

This can be true without Nefu ever having existed and without it being
true that Shirley is her reincarnation. The propositional attitude verb *believe* suspends truth, reference, and existence in (26), fortunately decoupling (26) from the semantic memory of those who entertain this statement. However, rather than being quirks, problems, and puzzles, as
philosophers have often regarded them, it seems clear that such suspen-
sions are instead adaptations – design features of a computational architecture designed to solve the problems posed by the many varieties of
contingent information exploited by our ancestors and by the interrela-
tionships among sets of contingent information. Humans perform these
operations effortlessly and easily acquire words and grammatical forms
that correspond to various operators implementing these procedures.
Indeed, it seems likely that these features are species-typical, reliably developing features of the human cognitive architecture, because it seems
very difficult to conceive how they could plausibly be learned (in the domain-general, general-purpose sense).[15]

Development, Decoupling, and the Organizational
Domain of Adaptations

Decoupling and scope syntax also offers insight into some aspects of
how cognitive adaptations develop. Genes underlying adaptations are
selected so that, in development, genes and specific, stable aspects of the
world interact to cause the reliable development of a well-designed adaptation (Tooby & Cosmides, 1992). This means that information and
structure necessary for the proper development of an adaptation may
be stored in the world as well as in the genome, and that selection will
shape developmental programs to exploit enduring features of the
world. This allows adaptations to be far more elaborate than could be
managed if all of the necessary information had to be supplied by the
genome. What is likely to be genetically specified in adaptations is an
economical kernel of elements that guides the construction and initial-
ization of the machinery through targeted interactions with specific
structures, situations, or stimuli in the world. This means that aesthetic
motivations may be a necessary guidance system for the development
of each adaptation – that is, motivations to detect, seek, and experience
certain aspects of the world may be evolved design features, present to
help adaptations become organized into their mature form. Consequently, a computational system may operate not just to perform its

proper function on-line (e.g., the visual system performing useful scene analysis, the language system generating utterances for communicative purposes), but may operate in an organizational mode as well, designed to develop a better organization for carrying out its function (e.g., looking at sunsets to calibrate the visual system; babbling or speaking in order to develop a more effective language system). Thus, one might want to distinguish, in addition to the proper, actual, and cultural domains of an adaptation, what one might call its organizational domain, which consists of the conditions of operation for the adaptation that serve to organize the adaptation. Thus, a hunter-gatherer child might throw rocks at randomly chosen targets, developing her projectile skills outside of the context of hunting. On this view, aesthetics are aspects of the evolved components of the adaptation, designed to organize the adaptation in preparation for the performance of its function.

Now, much of the time, an adaptation may be improving its efficacy while it is performing its function in the actual situation for which the adaptation was designed, but the presence of scope and decoupling syntax offers the possibility of broadening the contexts of organization. Through scope syntax and other design features, activities that organize an adaptation can be liberated from the constraints of having to encounter the actual task, which may be very limited, dangerous, or simply not contain the informative feedback or revelatory data necessary by the time the organism needs the adaptation to be functioning well. For example, playing tag may develop flight skills that could not be advantageously developed purely in the context of actual instances of escape from a predator. The emancipation of the organizational domain from the proper domain of an adaptation can take place, if there is an abstract isomorphism between elements in the organizing experience and elements in the adaptive task, and if there are adaptations that can

(a) detect activities embodying this isomorphism;

(b) extract the organizing information present in them, and

(c) decouple the aspects of the organizational domain that are irrelevant or noncongruent from being processed by the adaptation as true or relevant for its development (e.g., although my father chases me, my father is not a predator with respect to me).

This last element is crucial: Not all parts of the experience are registered or stored, and the ability to decouple the processing of some inputs while preserving others is essential to the functioning of such a system.

It is important to recognize that this isomorphism can be very abstract and decontextualized, making some aesthetically driven activities seem very bizarre and nonfunctional when, in fact, they may have evolved to promote computational development. Because humans have many more computational adaptations, which require data-based elaborations from the world to fuel them, one might expect aesthetics to play a far larger role in human life than it does in the life of other species. Humans, being social and communicative organisms, can greatly increase their rate of computational development because individuals are no longer limited by the flow of actual experience, which is slow and erratic in comparison with the rapid rate of vicarious, contrived, or imagined experience. So, vicarious experience, communicated from others, should be aesthetically rewarding. But what could possibly be useful about fictive, counterfactual, or imagined worlds – that is, about false or indeterminate information? We will return to the case of fiction at the end of the paper.

Theory of Mind and the
Prediction of Behavior

One domain of critical importance to the success of organisms is understanding the minds of other organisms, such as conspecifics, predators, and prey, and it is plausible that humans have evolved computational specializations for this purpose. There is now considerable evidence that the human cognitive architecture contains computational machinery that is designed to infer the mental states of other people – their beliefs, desires, emotions, and intentions – and to use these to predict and explain their behavior (for a review, see Baron-Cohen, 1995). This machinery produces the *intentional stance* (Dennett, 1987), a mode of causal explanation based on mental states. For example, in answer to the question, "Why did Nike open the box?" most people over the age of three would consider "Because she *wanted* chocolate and *believed* there was chocolate in the box" a full and adequate response, even though Nike's mental states – her beliefs and desires – are the only causes mentioned.[16]

Designing a computational device that can predict behavior on the basis of beliefs presents certain problems: Not only does the machine need to infer the content of propositions in another person's head, but it needs to remember which person's head the proposition is in, what that person's attitude toward the proposition is (does the person *believe* X, *doubt* X, *imagine* X?), and when the person had that attitude. At the same time, it is important that the organism's *own* behavior be based on true beliefs about the world. This will not happen if other people's beliefs (a mixture of true and false propositions) are stored as "true." So the architecture needs to file memories specifying the content of other people's beliefs separately from its own mental encyclopedia of facts about the world.

Carefully noting these computational requirements, Leslie and his colleagues have proposed that the content of other people's beliefs – that is, the content of a (potentially counterfactual) proposition – is embedded in a special kind of data format, the M-representation (a kind of metarepresentation) (Leslie, 1987; Frith, Morton, & Leslie, 1991; Leslie & Frith, 1990). M-representations are a particular type of scope-representation that evolved specifically for the purpose of modeling other minds. The M-representation has a number of design features that solve the problems listed above, thereby making it particularly useful for understanding and predicting an agent's behavior. These features are as follows.

(a) An *agent slot*. This is a variable that represents *who* it is that believes (doubts, imagines, etc.) that *X*. In Leslie's example "Mommy is pretending that the banana is a telephone," "Mommy" fills the agent slot. In locating this in the broader landscape of scope-representations, we would say that the *agent slot* is one form of *source tag*. The specific arguments required for a scope representation obviously depend on the specific kind of scope representation (some require a source tag; some require that the source tag be an agent, etc.).

(b) An *attitude slot*. This variable specifies the attitude that the source (the agent) has to the information represented in *X*: whether the agent *is pretending* that *X*, *believes X*, *doubts X*, *imagines X*, and so on. For scope-representations, this corresponds to the *relationship slot*, which defines the relationship (and scope-restrictions) between two or more sets of representations.

(c) An *anchor*. In the case of pretense and beliefs (and perhaps other attitudes), there is an anchor: a primary representation (i.e., a representation of a real entity or state of the world) to which the embedded proposition refers. A fuller version of an M-representation in which Mommy's act of pretense could be stored would be [Mommy]–[is pretending (of the banana)]–[that it is a telephone]. The anchor is "the banana": It is the primary representation to which the decoupled proposition, "it is a telephone," refers. Different scope-operators take different numbers of arguments: In this case of pretense, there are two ground state representations, "Mommy" and the "banana," related to the decoupled proposition.

(d) A *proposition slot*. This is where the content of the belief or desire is stored ("It is a telephone".) For scope-representations, the proposition slot can include any number of propositions, and potentially any number of levels.

To this, we would also add

(e) A *time tag*. There must be a tag specifying *when* the agent held the attitude toward the proposition. After all, "Nike believes *X*," "Nike used to believe *X*," and "(after she sees *Y*) Nike will believe *X*" all specify different mental states.

In addition to these formatting properties, an M-representation has several other closely related features, which are also necessary if an organism is to represent (potentially false) beliefs yet still behave adaptively.

(a) *Suspending semantic relations.* Propositions stand in certain relationships to one another, such as contradiction, equivalence, or mutual consistency. For example, "the chocolate is in the box" implies certain other propositions, such as (1) "there is a chocolate" (*existence*); (2) "the chocolate is not outside the box" (*truth*); and (3) (if the chocolate being referred to is a Toblerone), "a Toblerone is in the box" (*reference*). Embedding the same proposition within the agent-attitude-proposition format of an M-representation takes that proposition out of circulation by suspending its normal truth relations. For example, "Nike *believes* the chocolate is in the box" can be a true statement, even if, unbeknownst to Nike, (1) someone has already eaten the chocolate (i.e., it no longer exists; *existence* relations suspended); and (2) the chocolate is not in the box (*truth* relations suspended). Moreover, if Nike does not realize the chocolate at issue is a Toblerone, she could simultaneously believe "the chocolate is in the box" and "there is no Toblerone in the box" (i.e., substituting "Toblerone" for "chocolate" is no longer truth preserving: *reference* relations suspended). As these situations show, to make adaptive choices, the system needs simultaneously to represent two parallel tracks: the actual state of the world versus Nike's beliefs about the world. Suspending truth relations for beliefs is necessary if both tracks are to be represented accurately.

(b) *Decoupling.* By virtue of being embedded in an M-representation, a proposition is "decoupled" from semantic memory. That is, it is not stored as "true." For example, the child who represents her mother as *pretending* that the banana is a telephone does not store as true "the banana is a telephone." As a result, she does not become confused about the properties of bananas or telephones.

(c) *Restricted application of inferences.* As Leslie and Frith note in the case of pretense, "Decoupling creates an extra level within the representation ... [Inference mechanisms] respect the levels and apply to them one at a time" (Leslie & Frith, 1990, p. 129). For example, they point out that (27) "The cup is full" and (28) "I pretend the cup is full" are both sensible propositions, whereas (29) *"The empty cup is full" involves a contradiction and (30) *"I pretend the cup is both empty and full" is strange. This is because the M-representation has a superordinate level and a subordinate level, which they call the upstairs and downstairs levels. So for (28), which translates into mentalese as "I pretend (of the empty cup) [it is full]," logical inference mechanisms cannot detect a contradiction at either the upstairs level – "I pretend (of the empty cup) [X]" or at the downstairs level – [it is full]. For sentence (30) – "I pretend (of the cup) [it is both empty and full]" – no contradiction is detected at the superordinate level ("I pretend (of the cup) [X]"), but a contradiction is detected at the subordinate level ([it is both empty and full]).

Note that none of these design features are necessary for propositions stored in semantic memory. However, as discussed earlier, all three of these properties are widespread, basic features of scope syntax, appearing in many system components, including, but not limited to, theory of mind contexts. We wish to particularly emphasize the importance of the restricted application of inferences, which is a crucial property of scope representations, as in the supposition processing outlined above. We want to underline that it is not an oddity or byproduct of either pretense or of ToMM, but is a core set of computational adaptations essential to modeling the minds of others accurately. When applied solely at the subordinate level, valid inferences can be made about other beliefs the agent holds at that level. For example, if Nike *believes* "the chocolate is in the box," then she also believes "the chocolate is not outside the box" and "there is a chocolate." These inferences about Nike's *beliefs* hold even if the chocolate is gone, that is, even if the premise ("the chocolate is in the box") is false. When applied solely to the superordinate or ground level, valid inferences can be made about the agent because semantic relations (reference, existence, truth) are suspended only for the embedded proposition, not for the scope-representation as a whole. For example, because an M-representation is itself a proposition, reference/identity relations allow substitution inferences, such as "Nike believes something," or (pointing to Nike) "That girl believes there is a chocolate in the box," or "Leda and John's daughter believes there is a chocolate in the box." In other words, the full power of whatever parts of propositional logic are implemented in the human mind can be brought to bear as long as the levels are kept separate for the purposes of inference making.

Beyond Modeling Other Minds

Predicting the behavior of other people is a critical adaptive problem for humans, and some scholars have proposed that mind-reading was the adaptive problem that drove the emergence of the distinctively human form of intelligence. We think this is very plausible, but far from certain, because mind-reading is not the only adaptive problem that poses computational requirements involving scope syntax. Many abilities critical to the cognitive niche require representations with scope-processing properties. We think that M-representations are one particular and important form of scope-representation, built out of various elements of scope-syntax. However, scope-representations of various permutations, often sharing many properties with M-representations, appear to play a key role in a wide variety of cognitive processes that create the distinctive form of intelligence one finds in our species. This includes our ability to engage in long chains of suppositional reasoning; our practical ability to craft tools that take advantage of facts that are true only contingently, rather than universally; and our ability to remember a personal past.

On this view, there is a close relationship – both conceptual and empirical – between decoupling, source monitoring, specifying an agent's attitude, and memory tags specifying source, time, and place. They are all key features of a scope syntax, required by many different cognitive niche abilities. To illustrate how they cluster – and some of their permutations – we shall consider a variety of different types of representation, and ask the following about each in turn:

(a) Does the representation need to be decoupled from semantic memory to prevent the corruption of data structures (i.e., to prevent what Leslie (1987) calls *representational abuse*)?

(b) Is it necessary to monitor where the representation originated (its source)?

(c) Is it necessary to store an agent's attitude toward the representation?

(d) When stored in memory, does the representation need a source tag? a time tag? a place tag?

We think that the answer to these questions is "yes" for a number of adaptive information-processing problems beyond modeling other people's beliefs. Some other adaptive information-processing problems that require the same kind of computational solution include certain kinds of goals and plans (Frith, 1992); simulations of the physical world; pedagogy (Sperber, 1985); episodic memories;[17] simulations of social interactions that have not yet happened; understanding story-telling; representing one's own beliefs when these are not yet confirmed; and representing one's own beliefs when their truth is in question. (Dreams pose similar, though different, problems, and therefore present an interesting contrast in which decoupling is accomplished via the volatility and purging of the memory trace.)

We propose that scope-representations (S-representations) are involved in each of these activities, and briefly review evidence that implicates them. There are obviously many different species of S-representation – e.g., S-representations designed for simulating the physical world may differ in certain respects from those designed for simulating social interactions. But evolution is a conservative process. Once a design that satisfies a particular set of computational requirements exists, natural selection can engineer solutions to new adaptive information-processing problems that pose similar requirements more quickly by modifying the existing design than by creating totally new designs from scratch. Consequently, even if there are different species of scope-representation, we expect that they will share certain important properties, and perhaps even share certain computational components. Indeed, Christopher Frith has proposed that there is computational machinery common to all metarepresentations, and that this common machinery is selectively damaged in schizophrenia, explaining many of this disorder's otherwise puzzling symptoms and signs (Frith, 1992; Frith and Frith 1991). Parts of our argument were inspired by his observations and theoretical analyses. One way that we will test the adequacy of our own view of the role of scope-representations is by applying it to episodic memory. This application yields testable predictions about which memory systems should be impaired in schizophrenia.

Representations of Goals

In this section, we consider representations of goals. Obviously, not all behavior that looks goal-directed involves representations of goals. For example, ticks have a circuit directly linking chemoreceptors to motor neurons, so that the smell of butyric acid causes the tick to drop from a tree. Because butyric acid is emitted only by mammals, this circuit usually results in the tick landing on a mammalian host, whose blood it then drinks. The design of this circuit makes the tick's behavior functionally goal-directed. Yet it involves no explicit representation of a goal state.

In addition to embodying circuits that only appear, by virtue of their design, to be goal-driven, the human cognitive architecture is also capable of representing goal states – such as "I want to have dinner at Downey's, on State Street" – and then devising plans to achieve these goals. The adaptive function of such representations is to regulate one's own behavior – an adaptive function different from Baron-Cohen's Intentionality Detector (1995) or Leslie's ToMM System 1 (1994), which are designed to infer other people's goals for the purpose of predicting and explaining their behavior. As a result, there are many differences in design. For example, whereas the Intentionality Detector infers goals on the basis of external cues, such as self-propelled motion or eye direction, individuals can formulate goals of their own without having to infer them on the basis of observations of their own behavior. Nevertheless, the ability to represent one's own goals – and remember them – while still

engaging in adaptive behavior poses a number of computational requirements that are similar to those for representing other people's beliefs.

What Are the Computational Requirements?

(1) Decoupling

The goal represents a state of the world that is not yet true of the world.
Without decoupling, goals would be stored as true states of the world.
Indeed, we sometimes find ourselves confused as to whether we did
something or only entertained it as a goal. These are cases when the decoupling of the representation has failed.

(2) Source Tag

When I look out the window and see the ocean, the source of that representation is assigned by my mind to "the outer world" (see *Simulations*,
below). But a goal representation cannot have the outer world as a
source: Goals cannot be observed in the environment because they are
not (by definition) states of the world that have already occurred. More
importantly, only agents are capable of having goals, and the agent – the
source of the goal representation – needs to be specified. The source of
a goal representation is either (a) my own mind; or (b) someone else's
mind. Moreover, if the source is someone else's mind, (c) was it the mind
of Person A or Person B? Only goal representations whose ground level
has a "self" source tag ($goal_{self}$) should be readable by mechanisms for
planning and producing one's own motor responses. (Obviously, we are
capable of taking other people's goals into account in formulating our
own; hence goal representations with an "other" source tag – $goal_{other}$ –
must be readable by those systems that formulate own-goal representations). We expect, however, that there is an important distinction to be
made between an implicit source tag of self, computationally present because of the representation's location in a motivational specialization,
and an explicit representation in a format common to other representations of social agency.

   If the source of the goal were not specified, delusions would ensue
(Frith, 1992). If the "self" source tag were lost, the content of the goal
would escape its normal scope-processing tag, perhaps being experienced as an order. "I want to [kiss that girl]" would be experienced as
"Kiss that girl". If the "other" source tag were lost, the same thing would
happen: "He wants to [kiss that girl]" would be experienced as a voice-
less order, "Kiss that girl" or might reacquire an implicit source tag. If
source tags were switched, *He wants to kiss that girl* might be remembered
as *I want to kiss that girl*. As Frith points out, all of these things can happen
in schizophrenia (Frith, 1992, p. 127). In schizophrenia, source monitoring is impaired (Frith, 1992), although it is not clear whether the mal-

function involves the machinery that reads source tags or the adhesion of the source tags themselves. Aberrations in source monitoring also appear to occur under hypnosis: the hypnotist suggests that certain goals originate with the subject.[18]

(3) Attitude Slot

For the representation to be useful, the agent's attitude toward the goal needs to be specified. The agent may *consider* (the goal), *want* (the goal to be realized), *intend* (to cause the goal to be realized), *decide to drop* (the goal), and so on.

(4) Memory Requirements

Storing a goal that has not yet been realized may be thought of as remembering the future (Ingvar, 1985) or, more precisely, remembering a possible (or subjunctive) future. A goal representation needs a time tag (e.g., "I would like X to happen"), so that any system that reads this representation can tell whether the goal has been realized yet, and modify its own functioning accordingly. For example, a planning system should only take goals$_{self}$ with a "future" tag on them as input; if it registered a past tag on the goal, presumably the planning system would abort operations based on that goal. Naturally, the source and attitude must also be remembered, in addition to the content. As time passes, one would expect goals that have already been realized to eventually lose their source tags and be stored in semantic memory as states of the world (unless the source of the goal is somehow relevant to one's social situation; see section on episodic memory).

(5) Restricted Scope of Inferences

Suspension of truth relations is necessary for the content of a goal$_{self}$ or a goal$_{other}$. The reason is related to that for beliefs but differs somewhat. In the case of beliefs, the suspension of truth relations is necessary because it is possible that the content of the belief is false: you need to be able to make accurate inferences about what other beliefs the person might hold, even if these are premised upon a belief you know to be false. Unlike a belief, however, a goal cannot, strictly speaking, be false. In the case of a goal – whether it is a goal$_{self}$ or a goal$_{other}$ – suspension of truth relations is necessary because the content of the goal specifies a state of affairs that *does not yet exist*. It specifies a possible world. Goal representations need a subordinate and superordinate level as well, so that inferences are restricted in their scope of application to only one level at a time. When applied subordinately, to the content of the goal itself, this allows one to reason suppositionally about possible worlds, and to make inferences about other goals, plans, and intentions that one might formulate. When applied superordinately, to a representation of the agent who has an attitude toward the goal, this allows one to make inferences about the real world (e.g., "Nike wants X" implies "John and Leda's daughter wants X").

(6) Relationship to Other Representation Systems

One would expect goal representations to be read by (1) simulation systems, (2) planning systems, and (3) a self-monitoring system. (The latter is a system designed to detect certain inner states, creating representations of these states that can then be acted on by other inferential systems, as when one reflects on one's own goals, plans, intentions, and thoughts; see Johnson, Hashtroudi, & Lindsay, 1993; Frith, 1992.) The machinery that formulates goal$_{self}$ representations must take input from motivational systems and from the planning system (formulating plans often requires the formulation of sub-goals); it must also be able to access semantic memory (because facts about the world are relevant to deciding on goals).

What Is the Solution?

One way to satisfy these requirements is to store the content of a goal in a scope-representation similar to an M-representation. The goal S-representation is decoupled from semantic memory, tagged with a source, attitude, and time scope, suspends truth relations for the goal content (but not reference), and has a ground and subordinate level such that inferences are applied to only one level at a time.

Representations of Plans

What Are the Computational Requirements?

(1) Decoupling

A plan represents a sequence of actions that can achieve a goal (or, more precisely, were chosen because it is believed that they can achieve a goal). The goal is not yet true of the world. The sequence of actions has not (yet been) carried out. Without decoupling, a plan could be stored as actions already carried out. Again, a prospect would be stored in semantic memory as a reality.

The issues relating to the source tag, the attitude slot, the memory requirements, and the restricted scope requirements closely parallel those for goal representations. Of course, suspension of truth relations is necessary for the content of a plan because it is a sequence of actions that has not yet occurred, and may not occur. Like goals, plan representations need superordinate and subordinate levels, so that inferences are restricted in their scope of application to only one level at a time. When applied downstairs, to the content of the plan itself, this allows one to reason suppositionally about possible chains of actions, and to make inferences about other goals, plans, and intentions that the agent might have. When applied upstairs, to a representation of the agent who has an attitude toward the plan, this allows one to make inferences about the real world (again, "Nike plans to X" implies "John and Leda's daughter plans to X"). Moreover, each necessary step in the plan creates another suppositional subdomain (*if x, then y; if y, then z*), whose execution must be completed before its contents are discharged, and the next step of the plan can be promoted and executed.

(2) Relationship to Other Representation Systems

A plan representation must be linked to the motor system in two ways. First, the plan needs linkages that generate the requisite sequence of motor actions – plans cause willed actions. Second, the plan must suppress the stimulus-driven action system (Frith, 1992), as discussed below. Because plan representations are formed in order to realize goals, they must also be linked to goal representations, and to the factual database of semantic memory. They should, in addition, be linked to simulation systems (see below).

What Is the Solution?

These computational requirements are almost identical to those for a goal representation. They can be satisfied by storing the content of the plan in a scope-representation specialized for the task: a representation that is decoupled from semantic memory, tagged with a source, attitude, and time scope, suspends truth relations for the plan's content, and has hierarchical levels such that inferences are applied to only one level at a time, or actions are taken in proper sequence.

The fact that plans must be linked to the motor system creates additional functional requirements that have interesting consequences. It is obvious that there must be ways to transform plans into actions. What is less obvious is that there needs to be a system whereby a plan scope-representation can inhibit stimulus-driven actions.

Based on neuropsychological evidence from a number of different disorders, Frith argues that the human cognitive system is constructed such that "there are two major sources of action. Some actions are carried out directly in response to environmental stimuli. Others are seemingly spontaneous and self-initiated" (Frith, 1992, p. 43). A stimulus driven action originates in perception: "perception → stimulus intention → action → response." (Frith, 1992, p. 46). A willed action originates in goal and plan representations: "goals/plans → willed action → responses"

(Frith, 1992, p. 46). This is supported by various disconnection syndromes. In Parkinson's disease, for example, plans and willed intentions are formed, but they do not generate action representations. In the negative cycle of schizophrenia, a person may be able to engage in stimulus-driven actions, but has difficulty translating a plan representation into a willed intention, resulting in poverty of action or perseveration.[19] In the positive cycle, a person may have difficulty inhibiting stimulus-driven actions, resulting in incoherence of action.

The system that allows plan representations to *inhibit* stimulus-driven actions can be neurologically compromised by any number of disorders and conditions: (1) frontal lobe damage (see Duncan, 1995, on "goal neglect," in which the goal is remembered but behavior is driven by external stimuli rather than by a representation of a plan that would achieve the goal; see also Shimamura, 1995, on inhibitory gating); (2) damage to anterior cingulate gyrus (a frontal structure; Posner & Raichle, 1994; Devinsky, Morrell, & Vogt, 1995; for supporting Position Emission Tomography (PET) results, see Pardo, Pardo, Janer, & Raichle, 1990); (3) conditions in which the stimulus-driven action system is intact, yet difficult to override, such as schizophrenia (Frith, 1992); and, possibly, (4) Tourrette's syndrome (Baron-Cohen, Robertson, & Moriarty, 1994; Baron-Cohen, Cross, Crowson, & Robertson, 1994). The ability to *construct* plans can be impaired by (1) frontal lobe damage (Frith, 1992); (2) anterior cingulate damage (Devinsky, Morrell, & Vogt, 1995), and (3) schizophrenia (Frith, 1992). The ability to *carry out* plans can be impaired by (1) frontal lobe damage, particularly when there is cingulate damage, as in akinesis and mutism (Damasio & Van Hoesen, 1983; Devinsky, Morrell, & Vogt, 1995; Duncan, 1995; Frith, 1992); (2) Parkinson's disease (Frith, 1992; Goldberg, 1985); (3) hypnosis, which creates a dissociation between plans and actions (Bowers, 1977; Hilgard, 1977); and (4) depression. It is interesting that a number of these conditions involve improper levels of dopamine (Parkinson's, schizophrenia, Tourrette's and, sometimes, depression).[20]

Information about how a plan representation can be neurologically compromised is relevant to our argument that scope-representations are involved in a number of cognitive processes. As you will see, other cognitive-niche abilities can be compromised by damage to the same brain regions and by the same syndromes. This is what one would expect if scope-representations were involved not only in beliefs, but in goals, plans, simulations, episodic memory, and so on. It suggests that some of these brain regions may be evolutionarily more recent adaptations to the cognitive niche, and that they are damaged more easily than other cognitive systems because the shorter evolutionary time-depth means less time in which selection could operate to debug them.

Representations of *Simulations* of the Physical World

In his William James Lectures, Roger Shepard posed the question: Why have thought experiments been so fruitful in physics? Why should our ability to imagine the world ever generate knowledge that corresponds to reality? (Shepard, 1994). Through experiments on apparent motion, "mental rotation," and related phenomena, Shepard and his colleagues have shown that representations of the movement of objects are constrained by procedures that reflect evolutionarily long-enduring properties of the world – even when these representations occur in the absence of an external stimulus. Consequently, this system represents translations and rotations that are, in many ways, functionally isomorphic to the translations and rotations of rigid objects through three-dimensional space (e.g., Shepard, 1984; 1987).

In other words, the mental models it produces reflect the world with some accuracy. That is why thought experiments can be useful: We have an analog representational system for simulating the movements of real world objects and the "motion" of these imagined objects is constrained in the same ways as the motion of real objects (Shepard 1984, 1987). Shepard calls these simulations "internally driven hallucinations," to contrast them with perceptual representations, which he calls "externally driven hallucinations." Both are constructed using a great deal of inferential machinery (hence "hallucinations," to remind one that the world is never perceived absent an inferential construction). The main difference between them is that perceptions are prompted by the world external to a person's mind whereas simulations are prompted by other internal representations.

Other researchers have focused on how infants (and adults) represent perceived objects and their movement – externally driven hallucinations – and have shown that the ways in which people conceive of objects and model their interactions is governed by a rich set of interlocking principles, which Leslie has dubbed a "theory of bodies" (ToBy) (e.g., Baillergeon, 1986; Leslie, 1988; 1994; Shepard, 1984; Spelke, 1988; 1990; Talmy, 1988). The conclusions of this work dovetail quite closely with Shepard's work on mental simulations, suggesting that ToBy provides constraints on both perceptual representations and mental simulations of the physical world (Brase, Cosmides, & Tooby, 1996).

In our view, this simulation system did indeed evolve to do physical thought experiments: those that might help a tool-using and environment-manipulating primate to imagine ways in which new tools can be developed, existing tools can be applied to specific situations, and environments can be physically modified. Simulations provide a way of forecasting how physical objects will interact before they actually do. Time may be lacking for a series of dry runs and, in any case, time, materials, and energy can be saved by doing mental experiments prior to physical experiments. Simulations may also allow one to avoid disastrous situations (such as being in the path of an impending rock slide) or take advantage of fortuitous ones (such as cleaning something by leaving it outside during a rainstorm).

From this standpoint, the fact that simulations of objects and their movement are constrained in the same way as real objects is critical: the thought experiments would be useless otherwise. Nevertheless, one would expect simulation systems to have certain properties that perceptual representations lack.

What Are the Computational Requirements?

(1) Decoupling

A simulation represents the ways in which objects can interact physically. These physical interactions have not happened in the real world. Without decoupling, a simulation could be stored as something that happened.

(2) Source Tag

Simulations are not externally derived through perception: They do not represent actual states of the world. They have an internal source, the mind of the agent who is doing the simulation. It is an internally driven "hallucination" (Shepard, 1984) and, therefore, needs a source tag to keep it identified once it is output from the simulation system.

(3) Credal Value and Memory Requirements

Storing a simulation is equivalent to remembering a potentiality. Simulations may be associated with different levels of certainty: a simple interaction among objects (e.g., that one billiard ball will launch another after hitting it) might be tagged with a higher degree of certainty than a complex one (e.g., that hitting the corner of one billiard ball will put enough spin on it to make it bounce off a side wall and hit two balls at the other end of the table, knocking one into the corner pocket). A simulation tagged with a high level of certainty might be marked as "timeless," rather than having a past, present, or future tag. After all, the laws of physics do not change over time; something that is true of the physical world now – e.g., that a sharp edge can be struck from flint – will always be true.

(4) Restricted Scope of Inferences

Simulation representations depict hypothetical transformations of objects in space and time and, thus, sequential transformations are suppositions with ordered hierarchical relations, describing states of the system at various points in time.

(5) Relationship to Other Representation Systems

For a simulation to occur, stored object representations must be retrieved – presumably from the Perceptual-Representational System (PRS) (Schacter, 1995) and perhaps from semantic memory – and placed into the simulation buffer. This buffer would be a form of working memory. The system that retrieves the object representations would control what interacts with what (and when) during the simulation, but not how the interaction proceeds. That would be governed by ToBy. The output of the simulation system would inform the planning system (e.g., on how to make a tool) as well as the goal system (creating, e.g., the realization that the goal of making a particular tool is feasible). It can also inform the motor system, allowing one to anticipate the future (e.g., to jump out of the way or to strike a stone from one angle rather than another.)

What Is the Solution?

The simulation must be conducted in a buffer that is decoupled from semantic memory. Something resembling an M-representation – [self]-[wants to know]-(about objects X, Y, Z)-[how they will interact] – might govern what gets simulated – i.e., it would retrieve appropriate object representations from the PRS and semantic memory systems and deposit them in the decoupled buffer. ToBy would conduct the simulation. The output would also be tagged with a degree of certainty.

Working memory, in the sense that Baddeley (1995) uses the term, would appear to meet these requirements. The *visuospatial sketchpad*, which Baddeley describes as a "slave system" of working memory (the other slave system being a phonological loop), is the decoupled buffer in which simulations depicting objects moving in space and time are conducted. The executive controls the contents of the sketchpad, i.e., determines what objects are placed in the visuospatial sketchpad. Simulations in the sketchpad – such as mental rotation – are governed by ToBy, which causes the simulations to reflect long-enduring properties of the world (e.g., Shepard, 1984; Leslie, 1988; 1994). (Hegarty has also suggested that there is a kinesthetic sketchpad for simulating body motions; personal communication).

In this view, there are a number of ways in which the simulation system could be damaged.

(a) The integrity of the buffer itself could be compromised. Insofar as the buffer uses parts of the visual system to represent space, damage to the visual system will cause damage to the buffer (Farah,

Soso, & Dasheiff, 1992; Kosslyn, Alpert, Thompson, et al., 1993; Kosslyn, 1994). Processes of visual attention appear to be involved in the "inspection" of mental images; patients with right parietal lesions who show neglect of the left half of their visual field, also neglect the left half-space when they form visual images (Bisiach & Luzzatti, 1978).

(b) The operations of ToBy or related specializations could be compromised. A suggestive, though not definitive, case is that of L.H., an agnosic who is impaired in his ability to form visual images of living things but not of non-living things (Farah, 1990).

(c) The executive, which is hypothesized to be responsible for providing input to the simulation buffer, could be impaired. Frontal-lobe damage causes impairments to executive functions and can impair one's ability to make plans. It is possible that impairments in the executive's ability to place object representations into the simulation buffer may be responsible for some of these cases. Left hemisphere damage is also known to affect imagery-control processes (Farah, 1984).

(d) The decoupler – the system that keeps the contents of the simulation buffer separate from semantic memory – could be compromised. For example, patients who have had a cingulectomy (to control obsessive compulsive disorder [OCD]) confabulate: They have unusually vivid mental experiences, which are mistaken for perceptions (in other words, there is a misattribution of the source, which is experienced as external rather than internal). These patients use their powers of inference to correct these misattributions. For example, one such patient thought he had had tea with his wife, when in fact he had only imagined it: "I have been having tea with my wife ... Oh, I haven't really. She's not been here today ... The scene occurs so vividly, I can see the cups and saucers and hear her pouring out" (Whitty & Lewin, 1957, p. 73; see Johnson, Hashtroudi, & Lindsay (1993) for discussion).

There are, of course, social, biological, and psychological simulations as well as physical simulations and admixtures. Reports from patients who have had a cingulectomy, as well as normal experience, suggest that although various simulation processes may differ in what specializations they invoke to carry out specific inferential steps (ToBy, ToMM, or a theory of human nature, ToHN, etc.), they may share some common buffers and representational machinery. Nevertheless, the principles should be similar to what we have sketched above.

Representations of Integrated Simulations and Fiction

The emergence of pretend play in children at 18 months of age, and a consideration of its computational requirements, was the basis of Leslie's initial proposals about the existence, format, and properties of M-representations (Leslie 1987). Moreover, the virtual absence of imaginative activities and pretend play is one of three impairments used to diagnose autism (Frith, 1989). In spite of the universality of pretend play, the apparent presence of a mechanism designed to cause it, and the existence of a disorder that selectively impairs it, little attention has been paid to what its adaptive function might be. The same is true of general imaginative simulations. If these are written down or shared, we call them fiction. There are two distinct functional questions raised by these activities. First, what is the function of generating imagined sets of propositions? Second, what (if any) is the function of attending to such representations, when others express them to you? Of course, many have advocated the idea that simulations are useful models developed to guide behavior (Shepard, 1994), and this seems highly plausible and likely to be a major explanatory factor. However, people often imagine obviously and blatantly false situations, which could play no realistic role in planning. Pretense is also often extravagantly at variance with ordinary reality. Of course, these could be functionless byproducts or susceptibilities of a system for practical simulation and planning.

However, we think there is another hypothesis worth considering. As previously discussed, imaginative activities may have the evolved function of organizing and elaborating computational adaptations that require exposure to certain inputs in order to develop properly, and the aesthetic motivations governing which inputs are sought, the way they are processed, what elements are decoupled, and where the outputs are routed may all be governed by a suite of evolved design features selected to implement this function. If this is true, one can supply inputs for oneself through imagination or one can seek out social and cultural products, such as narratives, that provide rich inputs that help to organize adaptations such as ToMM, adaptations for social interaction, and so on, as well as motivational and emotional adaptations. Still, how can imaginary, false, or counterfactual inputs possibly be useful?

One way is in fleshing out the motivational system, in which imagery or stories become the occasions for releasing information bound in some formats so that it becomes available to other subsystems (Tooby & Cosmides, 1990a). The human mind contains decision and evaluation rules that initially evolved to be triggered by actual exposure to biologically meaningful situations, and which can therefore be elicited by cues indicating the presence of the situation (e.g., fangs, smiles, running sores, sexual possibility, enemy ambush, death of a child). We have argued that imagery allows these ancestral systems to be tapped without the need to wait until one encounters the real situation, greatly augmenting the power of the motivation and planning functions (Tooby & Cosmides, 1990a). This would allow prospective courses of action to be evaluated using the same circuits as would be activated if the event were actually to occur. Using imagery and vicarious experience to evoke these systems (with appropriate decoupling) would provide motivational adaptations with a rich array of weightings for events. For example, imagining the death of your child can evoke something of the emotional state you would experience had this actually happened, activating previously dormant algorithms and making new information available to many different mechanisms. Even though you have never actually experienced the death of a child, for example, an imagined death may activate an image-based representation of extremely negative proprioceptive cues that instruct the planning function on the proper valence and intensity of motivational weightings. Instead of Aristotle's notion of catharsis, an alternate view would be that fictionally triggered emotion is a re-weighting process of the motivational system.

Story-telling is ubiquitous across cultures, and people are interested in stories even when they are told in advance that they are not true. Indeed, people are relatively indifferent to the truth of a narrative, compared to its other aesthetic qualities. This is consistent with the hypothesis that the evolved aesthetics guiding human attention are looking for input useful in organizing adaptations, but that they can recognize cues of useful inputs independent of the truth value of the total set of propositions involved. With socially supplied narratives, one is no longer limited by the flow of actual experience, slow and erratic compared to the rapid rate of vicarious, contrived, or imagined experience. "False" inputs incorporate many elements that are true or informative, and also provide occasions that activate procedures that build valuable higher-level structures (such as forms of social manipulation that one has not encountered first hand). "False" accounts may add to one's store of knowledge about possible social strategies, physical actions, and types of people, in a way that is better than true, accurate, but boring accounts of daily life. This does not mean that falsehoods are, other things being equal, preferred. True narratives about relevant people and situations – "urgent news" – will displace stories, until their information is assimilated, and the organizational demand of adaptations that need to be computationally fed in a decoupled fashion resumes.

Whether it is an adaptation or a byproduct of adaptations, our ability to think about fictional worlds poses a familiar set of computational problems.

What are the Computational Requirements?

(1) Decoupling

Stories may not be true – either in full or in part – even when the teller claims to be recounting events that actually happened. People tell stories for many different reasons other than to impart true information – including, sometimes, in an attempt to manipulate the hearer (Sugiyama, 1996). Thus, even stories that purport to be true ought to be treated with caution. But when a story is explicitly labeled as fictional, the propositions therein are false (by stipulation). Without decoupling, a fiction would be stored as a reality.

(2) Source Tag

Only an agent can be the source of a story, and the source of a representation of a fictional world needs to be specified if one is to avoid confusion and manipulation. It matters whether the source of a fiction is (a) my own mind, or (b) someone else's mind. Given that people have a wide variety of reasons for telling stories, a mechanism designed to treat information originating with other people with caution should also specify whether the source of the fiction is the mind of Person A or Person B.

(3) Attitude Slot

There is a difference between false beliefs and fiction. In the first case, the agent *believes* that the propositions recounted are true. In the second case, the agent *is providing* propositions regardless of their truth value. And, in fiction explicitly labeled as such, the teller *intends* that the hearer *believe* that the teller is providing false representations, but that the teller intends them to form a coherent narrative.

(4) Memory Requirements

Storing a story is similar to storing a false belief, but with different arguments in the attitude slot. In the case of a person who purported to be telling the truth but instead was knowingly telling a fiction, the time tags might be multiply embedded: "Kurt *was pretending* that [Story X] was true but he *believed* it was false and, now that we caught him, he *is no longer pretending* that it is true." Stories that turn out to be true may lose their scope-restrictions and their contents may be allowed to interact freely with encyclopedic knowledge. But, those explicitly labeled as fiction (e.g., *Little Red Riding Hood*) ought never to be retired without a source tag. The specificity of the source tag may be degraded, from (say) "*Mother* told me [story X]" to "*Someone* told me [story X]," but one would expect a fiction to remain decoupled and, insofar as source tags are an important part of a self-monitoring system (Frith, 1992; Johnson,

Hashtroudi, & Lindsay, 1993; Kunzendorf, 1985–1986), one would expect them to be retained in some form as well.

(5) Restricted Scope of Inferences

Suspension of truth relations is necessary for fictional worlds. This fact is directly reflected in the phrase "suspending disbelief," a state people recognize as essential to entering a fictional world. Representations of stories require hierarchical levels so that inferences are restricted in their scope of application to one level at a time. When applied to the content of the story itself, we are able to make all the ordinary implicit inferences necessary to understand the goals, intentions, beliefs, and motivations of the characters in the story. When applied superordinately to a representation of the agent who is telling the story, one can make inferences about the real world and the agent (e.g., "Mother dislikes wolves.")

(6) Relationship to Other Representation Systems

The falsity of a fictional world does not extend to all of the elements in it, and useful elements (e.g., Odysseus' exploits suggest that one can prevail against a stronger opponent by cultivating false beliefs) should be identified and routed to various adaptations and knowledge systems. One thing does seem likely: The fact that fiction can move people means that it can serve as input to whatever systems generate human emotions and motivation.

What Is the Solution?

These computational requirements are similar to those required for pretend play, which was Leslie's basis for developing his model of the M-representation. Consequently, one would expect the content of stories to be stored in an M-representational system: a representation that is decoupled from semantic memory, tagged with a source, attitude, and time scope, suspends truth relations for the story's content, and has ground and subordinate levels such that inferences are applied to only one level at a time. If the hypothesis that these activities function to organize adaptations in development is true, then there should be a set of associated aesthetic systems, isomorphism detectors, and output-routing systems as well (as described earlier in the paper, pp. 73–74).

Potts, St. John, & Kirson (1989) report memory-retrieval experiments suggesting that representations of fiction are indeed decoupled from representations in semantic memory. Each subject read a story about unfamiliar wildlife. Half of the group was told that the information in the story was all true and had been verified from reference books; the other half was told that most of the information in the story was fictional and had been made up for the purposes of conducting the experiment. When the retrieval context cued subjects that they were being asked to retrieve information from a particular *source* – the story they had been told – subjects who had been told the story was fictional verified statements faster than those who had been told it was true. This makes sense if information one believes to be fictional is stored in a decoupled scope-representation with a source tag, whereas information one believes to be true is stored in semantic memory without a source tag. Similarly, when the retrieval context cued subjects that they were being asked about real-world knowledge, those who had been told the story was true verified sentences slightly faster than those who had been told it was fictional. On our account, retrieving the fictional information would take longer in this condition because the context cued subjects to search semantic memory; to find information that is stored in a fiction scope-representation, they would have to switch their search to a different, decoupled memory system (see Gerrig & Prentice, 1991, for similar results). In other words, the results suggest that information from fiction is stored separately from true information ("compartmentalized", to use Potts, St. John, & Kirson's [1989] preferred term) and that it is clearly marked with a source tag, which can be accessed in retrieval.

It is not clear whether there are neuropsychological deficits that selectively knock out a person's ability to understand fiction without simultaneously knocking out other imaginative activities. But autism does seem to be an example of a developmental disorder that selectively impairs the imagination. A great deal of research is currently going on to track down the brain systems involved (Baron-Cohen, Ring, Moriarty, et al., 1994; Fletcher, Happe, Frith, et al., 1995; Stone, Baron-Cohen, & Knight, in press). Most evidence so far points to the frontal lobes, although there is still controversy over exactly which locations (dorsolateral, orbitofrontal, etc.) are involved.

Representations of a Personal Past: Episodic Memory

Tulving (1995) argues that there are at least five functionally distinct memory systems. Semantic memory is one of the five; episodic memory is another (Tulving, 1993a; 1995). Perhaps the best way to convey the difference between the two is to quote Tulving himself.

> Semantic memory registers, stores, and makes available for retrieval knowledge about the world in the broadest sense: If a person knows something that is in principle describable in propositional form, that something belongs to the domain of semantic memory. Semantic memory enables individuals to represent states, objects, and relations in the world that are not present to the senses ... Episodic memory is memory for

personally experienced events . . . It transcends semantic memory by being ego-centered: its contents include a reference to the self in subjective
space/time. Its operations are subserved by a neurocognitive system *specialized* for that purpose. The owner of an episodic memory system is capable not only of mental space travel but also mental time travel: it can
transport itself at will into the past, as well as into the future, a feat not
possible for those who do not possess episodic memory. (Tulving 1993a,
p. 67; italics in the original)

Note that episodic memory is not equivalent to autobiographical knowledge. Autobiographical knowledge can be stored in either episodic or
semantic memory. This is captured by the distinction between remembering and knowing: "I recall seeing the Grand Canyon" (episodic) versus "I know that I saw the Grand Canyon" (semantic). Tulving further
points out that the nature of conscious awareness (*qualia*) that accompanies retrieval of information differs for episodic and semantic memory.
Episodic retrieval is accompanied by autonoetic awareness, "a distinctive, unique awareness of re-experiencing here and now something that
happened before, at another time and in another place. The awareness
and its feeling-tone is intimately familiar to every normal human being"
(Tulving, 1993a, p. 68). Semantic retrieval is accompanied by noetic
awareness, "the kind of awareness that characterizes thinking about
other facts of the world" (Tulving, 1993a, p. 68).

In this view, the episodic system is different from the semantic system because the computational requirements of a system that can remember a personal past are very different from those of a system for storing and retrieving general knowledge. General knowledge (a) need not
come from one's own perceptual experience, (b) does not require a
source tag, and (c) if it initially has a source tag, that usually fades with
time, as the proposition is increasingly well-validated by converging
sources of evidence. Moreover, general knowledge (d) need not refer to
the past (it can be about time-invariant properties of the world, such as
that the sun rises every day), (e) needs to be retrievable for use at any
time and in a wide variety of circumstances, and (f) its retrieval should
be relatively independent of the context in which the information was
learned (e.g., it would be inefficient if we could only retrieve the fact that
plants need sun to grow by first remembering who it was who first
taught us about plants.)

At this point, a considerable body of data from experimental psychology and cognitive neuroscience supports the hypothesis that the design of episodic memory differs from that of semantic memory: that they
form two functionally distinct systems (for reviews, see Nyberg & Tulving, 1996; Schacter & Tulving, 1994; Tulving, 1995; 1998). Far less attention has been paid, however, to *why* humans should have a functionally

distinct, episodic memory system: that is, to what its adaptive function is. Why should this system have evolved in our species? What can a person with episodic memory do that would be impossible for a person without episodic memory?

This question has only begun to be explored but there are a number of possibilities. For example, episodic memory may have evolved to handle the social world. Many social interactions have game-like properties, and to act in an adaptive manner, many strategies require that histories of interaction be stored, as well as the present state of play. We think three of the more interesting functions of episodic memory involve (1) re-evaluating conclusions in light of new information, (2) judging the credal value of information, especially that derived from other people, and (3) bounding the scope of generalizations. To illustrate, we give examples involving judgments of other people's character (see Klein, Cosmides, Tooby, & Chance, submitted) but the argument applies equally to nonsocial judgments.

It is known that people form generalizations about their own personality (e.g., "I am usually friendly") and that of other people (e.g., "Donna is usually shy"), which are stored in semantic memory (Klein & Loftus, 1993). After such a trait summary has been made, what can be gained by retaining the database of episodes – in quasi-perceptual form and with source tags – on which the summary was based?

(1) Re-evaluating Conclusions

New information may cause previous episodes to be re-interpreted, drastically changing one's judgments of a person or a situation. Fred's friendly willingness to help you with household repairs may take on different significance if you learn that he is attracted to your wife. If episodes were lost after they had been analyzed to form a summary judgment of Fred's character, re-evaluating his past actions in light of new information about his intentions and values would be impossible.

Keeping a database of episodes is helpful even when a drastic re-interpretation of previous events is not called for. Judgments can be revised in light of new information. If a judgment that "Fred is usually friendly" was based on 30 episodes, an unfriendly act by Fred should have less impact on it than if it had been based on three episodes (Cosmides & Tooby, 1996a; see also Sherman & Klein, 1994). Without the original database, it is difficult to know whether new, inconsistent information should change one's summary judgment and, if so, by how much. Moreover, new reference classes can be formed to answer new questions. Suppose you need to decide whether your best friend would make a good employee – something you had never considered before. If a database of richly encoded episodes exists, it can be sifted for events relevant to making such a judgment.

(2) Evaluating Credal Value

Maintaining source information allows one to evaluate the credal value of stored information. Noting that (a) confidence ratings are positively correlated with judgments that one has "remembered" a fact (as opposed to having simply "known" it) and (b) amnesic patients lack a subjective sense of certainty about knowledge that they do, in fact, possess, Tulving suggested that the adaptive value of the autonoetic consciousness associated with episodic memory "lies in the heightened subjective certainty with which organisms endowed with such memory and consciousness believe, and are willing to act upon, information retrieved from memory ... [leading] to more decisive action in the present and more effective planning for the future" (Tulving, 1985, p. 10). Information derived from perception should be assigned a higher credal value than information derived from other people. This would explain why we might have a memory system that allows retrieval of engrams with a quasi-perceptual format: Preserving perceptual information allows one to "re-experience" – to retrieve a broad-band encoding of the original event in which a piece of information was encountered or from which it was inferred. The benefit of this is even stronger for humans, who get such a large proportion of their information from others. Most organisms acquire all of their (non-innate) knowledge through their own senses and, so, have less need for a system that discriminates between perceptually derived information and information from other sources.

For a species that subsists on information, much of it supplied by other people, judging how reliable that information is can be a matter of life and death. For example, the !Kung San, a hunter-gatherer group in the Kalahari desert of Botswana, distinguish sharply between the following four kinds of evidence: (1) "I saw it with my own eyes"; (2) "I didn't see it with my own eyes but I saw the tracks. Here is how I inferred it from the tracks"; (3) "I didn't see it with my own eyes or see the tracks but I heard it from many people (or a few people or one person) who saw it"; (4) "It's not certain because I didn't see it with my eyes or talk directly with people who saw it" (Tulkin & Konner, 1973, p. 35).

Assessing credal value is particularly important in navigating the social world. Often informants have agendas that bias or distort the information they communicate to you. Imagine that Eve, who immediately befriended you when you started your new job, told you many terrible things about another co-worker, Adam. Much later, you find out that she has been stalking him ever since he broke up with her a year ago. As a result, you realize that the stories you heard from Eve might well be untrue. In forming an impression of Adam, you integrated information from many sources. But one of these sources turned out to be unreliable: Eve has sowed the seeds of data corruption.

How can you update your judgments about Adam? Which of your trait summaries for Adam are still reliable, and which are not? A database of episodic memories would allow you to re-evaluate your judgments about Adam. Your "Adam database" would include episodes in which you had interacted with Adam yourself, episodes in which other people told you things about Adam, and episodes in which Eve told you stories about Adam. Because all these episodes have source tags, you can "consider the source": you can sort through your database and decide which judgments were based on sound information and which were colored by Eve's distortions. Had the episodes on which your judgments of Adam's character were based been lost, there would be no way to repair the corrupted segments of your semantic store. The ability to judge and re-evaluate the credal value of other people's communications is essential in an organism with language.

(3) Bounding the Scope of Generalizations

For quick decisions, it can be convenient to have summary judgments stored in semantic memory (Klein & Loftus, 1993; Klein, Cosmides, Tooby, & Chance, under review). But, there is a trade-off between speed and accuracy because information about particularities is inevitably lost in any generalization. Keeping an independent store of episodes allows the scope of a summary judgment – the circumstances under which it does, and does not, apply – to be specified. A trait summary such as "He is rarely honest" or "I am usually friendly" gives information about behavior under "average" circumstances, but it does not tell you under what circumstances the person's behavior deviates from average. In deciding how to behave, one is always facing a *particular* situation.

Imagine your semantic memory has an entry on Vanessa: "Vanessa is usually calm." You are planning what you hope will be a relaxed dinner party with some friends who are political activists of a different persuasion than Vanessa. Access to appropriate episodic memories can bound the scope of your semantic summary. Recalling that "Vanessa is usually calm – except those times we talked about abortion" may alter your decision about whom to invite. (Indeed, if there is a pattern to the exceptions, a summary of the exceptions might eventually be made as well and stored as an if-then proposition about the conditions under which Vanessa can be expected to become tense (Wright & Mischel, 1988).

Note that each of these three adaptive functions requires representations that are held separately from semantic memory, and that specify both the source of the information and the source's attitude toward it.

What are the Computational Requirements?

(1) Decoupling

The information in episodes is regulated and may be either isolated from other information structures, repressed, or activated and employed. It is regulated by time and space tags and does not necessarily have scope-unlimited implications: "At the time his wife became sick, we were not friends," rather than "We are not friends."

(2) Source Tag

The source of episodic memory representations is always the self, but also includes time and place tags. *When encoded*, the information was externally derived through perception and proprioception (the embedded knowledge represents a state of world *as perceived by the self*), so the encoding source tag should be $self_{external\ world}$. *When retrieved*, the memory has an internal source (one's own mind), so the source tag should be $self_{own\ mind}$. Without the $self_{external\ world}$ source tag, an episodic memory would not be a memory of having actually experienced something through perception. Even if it retained quasi-perceptual detail, there would be no way to tell whether it originated in perception or through someone else's account prompting mental imagery in the simulation system. The time and place tags allow the reconstruction of the state of play at the time of the event: for example, "Was he cool after you treated him unkindly, or before"? In fact, the scope tags identify when his change in attitude occurred by virtue of its position order of relevant social events rather than by reference to some other measure of time.

The information embedded in the episodic representation might itself have a source tag: "*I* recall that, at the water cooler, Eve told me that [Adam stole from the company]." Without such source tags, one could not distinguish which information was derived from one's own perceptual experiences and which was told to one by other people. Evaluating credal value and re-interpreting the meaning of past events would be impossible.

(3) Attitude Slot

According to Tulving, one has specific propositional attitudes toward the content of an episodic memory, which can be either "I *experienced* [the episode depicted]" or "I *am re-experiencing* [the episode depicted] *right now*." This is a defining element distinguishing an episodic memory from a semantic memory. Events stored in episodic memory are *remembered*, *recalled*, or *recollected*; those stored in semantic memory are merely known.

(4) Memory Requirements

To have a personal past, one must (a) store the episode, which is equivalent to remembering the past (i.e., there is a time tag); (b) store the source of the experience (i.e., have a self-source tag attached to the engram), and (c) store the source of a linguistically transmitted proposition, in the case of an episode in which someone told you something.

(5) Relationship to Other Representation Systems

Episodic memories can be a source of input to many different kinds of decision rules. They may sometimes be retrieved in tandem with representations from semantic memory, for example, to bound the scope of a generalization (Klein, Cosmides, Tooby, & Chance, under review). They can be used to assess the credal value of propositions originating with others (e.g., re-evaluations after betrayal) or originating from the self (e.g., Did I see him with my own eyes? Did I just hear the rustling in the leaves and assume that it was him?).

What Is the Solution?

These computational requirements can be met by storing an episode in a specific kind of scope-representation, i.e., a representation that is regulated or decoupled from semantic memory, has a source tag (own experience, time X, location Y), has an attitude slot (= *experienced* or *am re-experiencing*), has a time tag (a place in a chronology), and has a place tag. Moreover, for any propositional content originating with another person, the episodic M-representation can include an embedded source tag indicating that person and his attitude toward the proposition. In retrieval, dissociations between the episodic memory system and semantic memory system have been documented many times.

Moreover, episodic memory is impaired by some of the same brain areas and syndromes as other functions that we have argued involve scope-representations. For example:

(a) In classic amnesic syndrome, semantic information is largely intact but the person cannot recall any personal episodes. Sometimes the person cannot recall episodes from before the accident that caused the amnesia (retrograde amnesia) and sometimes the person cannot recall episodes that occurred after the accident (anteriograde amnesia). This underscores the fact that episodic memories come with time tags that place them in a chronology or sequence. Some amnesiacs mistake things they imagined for things they actually experienced, creating confabulated, pseudomemories (e.g., Wilson & Wearing, 1995) – exactly what one would expect if decoupling were compromised.

(b) Frontal lobe damage selectively impairs episodic memory. Free re-
     call is most impaired, then cued recall, then recognition memory
     (Wheeler, Stuss, & Tulving, 1995). In other words, frontal lobe dam-
     age particularly impairs retrieval that depends on having intact
     and/or accessible source, time, and place tags. (In free recall, these
     are the *only* basis on which the memory can be retrieved; cued recall
     and recognition memory provide "external" perceptual prompts,
     such that the memory could, in principle, be accessed through its
     embedded content, circumventing the need to retrieve via source,
     time, and place tags.) Frontal lobe damage is known to cause source
     amnesia (Janowsky, Shimamura, & Squire, 1989), and to impair
     memory for temporal order of events (Shimamura, 1995).

(c) Dissociations occur in new learning as well. K.C., the amnesic stud-
     ied by Tulving, can learn new semantic information but he cannot
     remember any of the episodes in which he learned it (Hayman,
     Macdonald, & Tulving, 1993).

(d) This extends to learning about one's own personality. After the ac-
     cident that rendered him amnesic, K.C.'s personality changed. But
     it turns out that he has trait summaries of the new personality, even
     though he has no access to the episodes on which the summaries
     were (presumably) based (Tulving, 1993b).

(e) Knowlton, Mangels, & Squire (1996) demonstrated what is argu-
     ably a double dissociation between episodic and semantic memory.
     Patients with Parkinson's disease were not able to learn a probabi-
     listic rule, but they were able to recall the episodes that were the ba-
     sis for learning in other subjects. Amnesics were able to learn the
     rule, but were not able to recall any episodes.

(f) PET studies suggest that episodic retrieval differentially engages
     the right hemisphere (including the right prefrontal cortex) whereas
     semantic retrieval differentially engages the left hemisphere (Ny-
     berg, Cabeza, & Tulving, 1996; Tulving, 1998).

(g) In normal, brain-intact subjects, one can create functional dissocia-
     tions between episodic and semantic memory. Retrieving trait sum-
     maries primes episodes that are inconsistent with the summary, but
     not those that are consistent with it (Klein, Cosmides, Tooby, &
     Chance, under review). This is what one would expect if one func-
     tion of keeping a database of episodic memories was to allow one
     to bound the scope of generalizations.

If we are correct in positing that episodic memories are stored in scope-
representations resembling M-representations, then three predictions

follow: (1) Episodic memory should be impaired in individuals with autism (because individuals with autism cannot form M-representations;
e.g., Baron-Cohen, 1995; Leslie, 1987; Leslie & Thaiss, 1992). (2) Episodic
memory should not emerge in children until they are capable of forming
M-representations. (3) Episodic memory should be impaired in individuals with any condition that damages the machinery that produces M-
representations.

Studies of episodic memory in autism are just beginning, but preliminary results by Klein, Chan, & Loftus (under review) support the
first prediction. Regarding the second prediction, we note that so-called
"childhood amnesia" lasts until one is 3 to 4 years of age (Sheingold &
Tenney, 1982; White & Pillemer, 1979; Perner, 1991) – approximately the
time that children start to pass the false-belief task (a standard test of a
mature ability to form M-representations; see Baron-Cohen, 1995).
Moreover, the lack in preschool age children of a fully mature system for
source tagging and forming multiply-embedded M-representations
would explain an otherwise curious fact about their memories: They
come to believe that they actually experienced events that never happened, if they are asked about these (fictitious) events repeatedly (Bruck
& Ceci, 1999). Evidence for the third prediction will be presented below,
in the context of schizophrenia.

Schizophrenia: A Test Case

If goals, plans, simulations, episodic memories, other people's beliefs,
fiction, and so on are stored in, or regulated by, scope representations
resembling M-representations, then an impairment to the M-
representational system should disrupt these functions. For example,
any condition that interferes with decoupling and source monitoring,
and that impairs one's ability to make inferences about the attitude slot
or contents of an M-representation, should lead to the corruption of semantic memory files. Semantic memory would store as true: fiction, false
beliefs (originating in the self or others), unrealized goals and plans, and
so on. A dysfunction in the machinery that produces or reads M-representations should impair episodic memory retrieval. Impaired links between M-representations and other representation systems – e.g., the
ability of metarepresentations to suppress stimulus-driven actions –
should lead to difficulties in communicating, controlling simulations,
planning, and in executing actions specified by a plan, such as shifting
from one M-represented goal to another.

The question is: Is there any syndrome or disease process that involves a breakdown of machinery necessary for producing, reading, or
maintaining the integrity of metarepresentations?

Christopher Frith has argued – compellingly, in our view – that schizophrenia is a late-onset breakdown of a metarepresentational system (Frith, 1992). We cannot do justice to his argument and data in this chapter, but Table 1 gives a sense of how it accounts for some of schizophrenia's most distinctive symptoms. In Frith's view, goals and plans are metarepresented, and his book presents lucid accounts of how schizophrenia would cause disruptions in goals, plans, and inferences about other minds.

If our prior claims about what gets metarepresented are true *and* schizophrenia is caused by an impairment of a metarepresentational system, then what would this predict about memory in schizophrenia?

(a) If episodic memories are stored in metarepresentations, then schizophrenics should have episodic memory impairments.

(b) If intact metarepresentational ability is necessary to prevent data corruption, then one should see symptoms of impaired semantic memory in schizophrenics.

(c) If the executive component of working memory uses metarepresentations, then it should be disrupted in schizophrenia.

(d) Memory systems that do not depend on metarepresentations should be unaffected.

After making these predictions, we found that the literature on schizophrenia contained data that bears on them. Schizophrenia does indeed cause episodic memory impairment. According to McKenna, Mortimer, & Hodges, for example, "the existence of episodic memory impairment in schizophrenia is well established. [It is] selective and disproportionate to the overall level of intellectual impairment ... [In schizophrenia] episodic memory is not only impaired but seems to be emerging as the leading neuropsychological deficit associated with the disorder" (McKenna, Mortimer, & Hodges, 1994, pp. 163, 169).

There is also evidence that semantic memory becomes corrupted in schizophrenia. In sentence verification tasks, which require retrieval of general knowledge from semantic memory, schizophrenics (a) are slower than normals (two-thirds fall outside normal range), (b) make more classification errors than normals, and (c) usually (but not always) misclassify false statements as true (McKenna, Mortimer, & Hodges, 1994). The last feature is perhaps the most interesting as it is exactly the kind of representational corruption that one would expect from a dysfunction of a metarepresentational system. The purpose of decoupling is to allow one to represent false beliefs, fictions, and not-yet-existing states of affairs separately from the database of true propositions stored in semantic memory. Damage to a decoupling system would therefore

Table 1: Symptoms of Schizophrenia Related to Impairment of the Metarepresentation System

Impaired source monitoring

- *thought insertion*: experience internally generated thoughts as originating from external agent (*"auditory" hallucinations*)

- *delusions of control*: experience own actions as having been caused by external agent rather than by self

Impaired ability to infer intentions, attitudes, and/or content of beliefs – other people's and one's own

- *delusions of reference*: (falsely) believe other people's communications are aimed at self

- *paranoia*: false beliefs about other people's beliefs and intentions

- *difficulty in communicating*: cannot infer relevance

Impaired ability to plan and/or execute plans in action

- incoherent speech

- lack of volition

- psychomotor slowness

(based on Frith, 1992)

---

cause false propositions to be stored as true, resulting in more misclassifications of this kind. (Alternatively, a breakdown in the system that allows one to understand that beliefs can be false might cause a response bias towards accepting sentences as true.)

The following phenomena are also plausibly interpreted as resulting from corruption of semantic memory: (a) formal thought disorders (ideas that appear disordered to an outside observer can result from false information; to see this, consider what the child in Leslie's example might say if she really did think that telephones were edible and yellow, or that fruit could serve as a transmitter of voices); (b) a "tendency for concepts to become pathologically large, their boundaries loose and blurred, and their content accordingly broad, vague, and overlapping" (McKenna, Mortimer, & Hodges, 1994, p. 176); and (c) exaggerated semantic priming (McKenna, Mortimer, & Hodges, 1994.[21]

Damage to a metarepresentation system should also have sequelae for working memory. We posited that the executive component of working memory uses metarepresentations to select content for input into other systems (such as the visuospatial sketchpad). If we are correct, then schizophrenia should impair the executive component of working memory, but not its slave systems (except insofar as their functions depend on an intact executive). There is, indeed, evidence of deficits in the executive (McKenna, Clare, & Baddeley, 1995), while the functioning of the articulatory loop is normal as well as verbal and non-verbal short-term and primary memory.

More generally, damage to the metarepresentational components of the system should leave any memory system that is not scope-regulated relatively intact. This does seem to be the pattern in schizophrenia. The procedural memory system (responsible for conditioning, storage of automated motor sequences, and habits) and the perceptual-representational system (responsible for object recognition and implicit priming) both appear to be intact in people with schizophrenia. In fact, McKenna, Clare, & Baddeley (1995) found that the pattern of memory impairment in schizophrenia is similar to the pattern in classic amnesic syndrome – except that there is evidence of some semantic memory corruption in schizophrenia. In the classic amnesic syndrome, there is (a) impaired episodic memory, (b) impairments in executive functions of working memory, (c) intact working-memory slave systems (articulatory loop, visuospatial sketchpad), (d) intact procedural memory, (e) intact PRS memory (implicit priming), and (f) intact semantic memory. This is the same pattern as found in schizophrenia, with the exception of the semantic memory. In amnesia due to head injury, there is no reason to think that inferences about metarepresentations would be impaired. Hence, there is no reason to expect corruption of semantic memory.

Conclusions

Behaviorally, humans are the strangest species that we have encountered so far. How did we get this way? The hypothesis that the ability to form metarepresentations initially evolved to handle the problems of modeling other minds (Leslie, 1987; Baron-Cohen, 1995) or the inferential tasks attendant to communication (Sperber, 1996; this volume; Sperber & Wilson, 1986) is very plausible, and our thinking is heavily indebted to this body of work. Still, the problems handled by metarepresentations, scope syntax, and decoupling are so widespread, and participate in so many distinct cognitive processes, that it is worth considering whether they were also shaped by selection to serve a broader array of functions – functions deeply and profoundly connected to what is novel about hominid evolution.

The central engine that has driven humanity down its unique evolutionary path may have been selection for computational machinery that allowed our species to enter what we have called the cognitive niche: that is, machinery that radically increased our ability to extract and exploit information that is local, transient, and contingent, wringing inferences from it that permit us to devise plans of action and behavioral routines that are successfully tailored to local conditions. For humans to enter, survive in, and take advantage of this strange new world of uncertain representations and the inferences that can be drawn from them, the human cognitive architecture had to evolve cognitive adaptations that solve the special problems that it posed. Because this new type of information is only applicable temporarily, locally, or contingently, the success of this computational strategy depends on the existence of machinery that ceaselessly locates, monitors, updates, and represents the conditional and mutable boundaries within which each set of representations remains useful. The problem of tracking the applicable scope of information is magnified by the fact that inference propagates errors, given that contingent information is often wrong outside its envelope of valid conditions. An error in the information that serves as input to an inference program will often lead to errors in the output, which may then be fed as input into yet other inference programs. As a result, a defective representation has the power to infect any data set with which it subsequently interacts, damaging useful information in contagious waves of compounding error. Inference is more powerful to the extent that information can be integrated from many sources, but this multiplies the risk that valid existing information sets will be progressively corrupted. Hence, the novel evolutionary strategy of using contingent information and densely networked inferential processing to regulate behavior could only evolve if natural selection could devise computational methods for managing the threat posed by false, unreliable, obsolete, out-of-context, deceptive, or scope-violating representations. Cognitive firewalls – systems of representational quarantine and error correction – have evolved for this purpose. They are, no doubt, far from perfect. But without them, our form of mentality would not be possible.

In this chapter, we have attempted to sketch out a few elements of the large series of specialized computational adaptations that we believe evolved to handle these problems. These include elements of a scope syntax, the regulated decoupling and recoupling of data structures, and metarepresentations. The basic elements of scope syntax must be built into the evolved architecture of our species because (i) there is a combinatorially infinite array of possible scope systems (e.g., ways of dividing up information into subsets, and procedures for regulating their permitted interactions), (ii) there are no observable models to which one can compare the output of a scope syntax for the purpose of modifying it so that it will perform more adaptively, and (iii) the problem of attributing computational success or failure to the scope-regulating design features responsible appears to be intractable, given that inferential networks are complex and that there is an open-ended set of variations that could be introduced ontogenetically. It remains, however, very likely that evolved developmental programs (as opposed to machinery invented *de novo* during ontogeny) can establish new boundaries and patterns of connection and dissociation over the course of the lifespan (as when, e.g., the representations produced by a wandering eye are disconnected from, and therefore cease to influence, or interfere with, higher levels of visual processing).

We are agnostic about whether the evolution of metarepresentational, scope-syntax, and decoupling machinery that subserves mind-reading and social interaction was a precondition for entering the cognitive niche, or whether the mind-reading machinery evolved after, or in tandem with, the machinery that accomplishes these functions in the other domains we discussed. That question can only be answered by a combination of (1) comparative studies of mindreading, planning, and other scope-regulated abilities in species that vary in the extent to which their evolutionary history involved complex social interaction and tool use and (2) close analysis in humans of the design features that accomplish scope-regulation in different domains, to see exactly how computationally similar they really are.

Many questions about the architecture that accomplishes scope-regulation are wide open. It is not clear, for example, whether the same neural system implements source tags, decoupling, and scope regulation for disparate cognitive activities, or whether different circuits with similar functional properties have been duplicated (and, perhaps, modified by selection) in different parts of the brain. Demonstrations by Leslie & Thaiss (1992) and by Charman & Baron-Cohen (1993) that one can lose the ability to reason about mental representations while retaining quite parallel abilities to reason about nonmental representations (such as photographs, models, and maps) suggests neural parallelism. In contrast, Christopher Frith's (1992) analysis of a patterned breakdown of metarepresentational abilities in schizophrenia (and some of our additions to his analysis) suggest that at least some of the requisite neural circuitry might be shared across functions. Another architectural question that remains open is the extent to which decoupling and scope-regulation are handled by explicitly syntactic features of cognitive operations (e.g., by source tags and operators within a deliberative reasoning system). In some cases, the same decoupling functions might be handled by neural independence, that is, by an architecture in which the outputs of certain imaginative, planning, or memory functions are quarantined from semantic memory or other representational systems by virtue of their being located in physically separate subsystems, without machinery that allows their outputs to become inputs to the systems that they could corrupt.

The exploration of the properties of scope management is just beginning and it would be premature to claim that any such proposals about the architecture have yet been established. Still, we believe that much that is so distinctive and otherwise puzzling about the human mind – from art, fiction, morality, and suppositional reasoning to dissociative states of consciousness, imaginary worlds, and philosophical puzzles over the semantic properties of propositional attitudes to the function of aesthetic sensibilities and the improvisational powers of human intelligence – are attributable to the operation of these adaptations. Further investigation of these issues seems to hold substantial promise.

Acknowledgments

This paper owes a deep intellectual debt to Alan Leslie for his work on pretense, propositional attitudes, and decoupling; to Dan Sperber for his work on metarepresentations and communication; and to Christopher Frith for his work on schizophrenia. We also wish to warmly thank Paul Hernadi, Michelle Scalise Sugiyama, and Francis Steen for their many illuminating thoughts about the nature of fiction. We thank the James S. McDonnell Foundation, the National Science Foundation (NSF Grant BNS9157-449 to John Tooby), and the UCSB Office of Research (through a Research across Disciplines grant: Evolution and the Social Mind) for their financial support.

Notes

1 Although some successful improvisations may be conserved across multiple lifespans and spread across many individuals, they still are very rapid with respect to the time it takes selection to operate.

2 By rules or procedures, we only mean the information-processing principles of the computational system, without distinguishing subfeatural or parallel architectures from others.

3 or stable frequency-dependent equilibria.

4 Indeed, the world outside the local conditions may be commonly encountered and, depending on how narrow the envelope of conditions within which the information is true, scope-violating conditions are likely to be far more common than the valid conditions.

5 i.e., to be de-encapsulated

6 There is no need, in particular, for the data-structure to be a sentence-like or quasi-linguistic proposition. For most purposes, when we use the term

"proposition" throughout this chapter, we are not commiting ourselves to quasi-linguistic data-structures – we will simply be using it as a convenient short-hand term for a data-element of some kind.

7 While not everyone would accept this as a metarepresentation, we think that such a rejection was a convenient rather than an accurate way of dealing with such problems as referential opacity.

8 Various operators and features of the workspace provide the intuitions that logicians have elaborated into various formal logics – the elaboration taking place through the addition of various elements not found in the workspace, the attempt simultaneously to impose self-consistency and conformity to intuition, and the removal of many content-specific scope-operators. For the human architecture itself, there is no requirement that the various procedures available to the workspace be mutually consistent, only that the trouble caused by inconsistency be less than the inferential benefits gained under normal conditions. Task-switching and scope-limiting mechanisms also prevent the emergence of contradictions during ordinary functioning, which makes the mutual consistency of the architecture as an abstract formal system not relevant. Mental-logic hypotheses for human reasoning have been rejected empirically by many on the assumption that the only licensed inferences are logical. We believe that the content-sensitivity of human reasoning is driven by the existence of domain-specific inference engines, which coexist beside operators that parallel more traditional logical elements.

9 There are, as well, heterarchical relations, governed by rules for data incorporation from other sources.

10 Promotion is equivalent to Tarskian disquotation with respect to the next level in the architecture.

11 Indeed, this kind of architecture offers a computational explanation of what kind of thing deontic ascriptions are: decoupled descriptions of possible actions and states of affairs, of suspended truth value, connected to value assignments of the possible actions.

12 Such an architecture explains how humans process fictional worlds without confusing their environments and inhabitants with the real world.

13 We think that ground state representations are present in consciousness, but are not automatically the objects of consciousness – that is, we are not automatically reflectively conscious of these data structures, although they can easily be made so. Data-structures in the ground state must be demoted to become the object of inferential scrutiny. Indeed, we think that the function of the architectural component that corresponds to one referent of the word consciousness is to be a buffer to hold isolated from the rest of the architecture the intermediate computational work products during the period when their truth-value and other merits are unevaluated. This explains why consciousness is so notoriously volatile.

14 A ubiquitous phenomenon, familiar to professors, is that when students deeply assimilate the knowledge being taught, they often forget who taught it to them, and feel compelled to excitedly share what they have learned from their teachers with their teachers.

15 We are not claiming that every propositional attitude term, for example, is reliably developing or "innate." We consider it more plausible that there is

an evolved set of information-regulatory primitives that can be combined to produce a large set of scope-operators and scope-representations.

16 What other causes could there be? One taking a *physical stance* might mention muscle contractions and force; one taking a *design stance* might mention the evolution of food seeking mechanisms; a behaviorist taking a *contingency stance* might mention a history of reinforcement; an astronomer might mention the Big Bang as a necessary (though not sufficient) cause; and so on.

17 Perner (1991) states that episodic traces are engrams with a metarepresentational comment regarding how the information was obtained. This is not quite an M-representation in Leslie's sense (see Perner, 1991, p. 35). However, Perner does not argue that episodic traces are metarepresentational because this is the only way that certain computational requirements can be met.

18 It is not clear why this is possible. The framework of Johnson, Hashtroudi, & Lindsay (1993) emphasizes inference in source monitoring; in this view, proprioceptive feedback may be critical to source monitoring, and the deep relaxation of hypnosis may interfere with proprioception (see also Kunzendorf (1985–1986) for a view more closely related to source tagging). It should also be noted that individuals differ in their hypnotic susceptibility – in their ability to enter "dissociative" states. It would be interesting to find out whether hypnotic susceptibility were related to individual differences in source monitoring or in decoupling. Two of the few things that correlates with hypnotic susceptibility is the tendency to become engrossed in movies or books, and vividness of imagery – both of which are plausibly related to scope-representational abilities (see sections on Fiction and Simulations).

19 Frith argues that perseveration occurs when the person knows a response is required of him but has trouble generating willed actions. Because the person either cannot form plans or cannot transform them into willed intentions, he simply repeats the last thing.

20 It is also interesting to note that dopamine is an inhibitory neurotransmitter. It is reasonable to assume that stimulus-driven action systems are evolutionarily more ancient than systems that allow the formation of plans and willed intentions; moreover, excitatory neurotransmitters, which open ion gates, are far more common than inhibitory ones. Plan S-representations would be part of an evolutionarily more recent system, which is designed to inhibit the more ancient stimulus-driven action system when a plan is to be enacted. A straightforward way of doing so would be through an inhibitory neurotransmitter, that is, one that operates by closing ion gates.

21 Seeing a semantically related word speeds time to classify a string of letters as word or non-word; this is known as semantic priming. Having pathologically large concepts means a wider variety of words will be seen as semantically related. This would lead to "exaggerated semantic priming" in schizophrenics. Indeed, schizophrenics with other evidence of formal thought disorder show exaggerated priming compared to controls.

References

Baddeley, A. (1995). Working memory. In M. S. Gazzaniga (Ed.), *The cognitive neurosciences* (pp. 755–764). Cambridge, MA: MIT Press.

Baillergeon, R. (1986). Representing the existence and the location of hidden objects: Object permanence in 6- and 8-month old infants. *Cognition 23*, 21–41.

Baron-Cohen, S. (1995). *Mindblindness: An essay on autism and theory of mind.* Cambridge, MA: MIT Press.

Baron-Cohen, S., Cross, P., Crowson, M., & Robertson, M. (1994). Can children with Tourette's Syndrome edit their intentions? *Psychological Medicine 24*, 29–40.

Baron-Cohen, S., Leslie, A., & Frith, U. (1985). Does the autistic child have a "theory of mind"? *Cognition 21*, 37–46.

Baron-Cohen, S., Ring, H. Moriarty, J., Schmitz, B., Costa, D., & Ell, P. (1994). Recognition of mental state terms: Clinical findings in children with autism and a functional neuroimaging study of normal adults. *British Journal of Psychiatry 165*, 640–649.

Baron-Cohen, S., Robertson, M., & Moriarty, J. (1994a). The development of the will: A neuropsychological analysis of Gilles de la Tourette's Syndrome. In D. Cicchetti and S. Toth (Eds.), *The self and its dysfunction: Proceedings of the 4th Rochester symposium.* Rochester, NY: University of Rochester Press.

Bisiach, E., & Luzzatti, C. (1978). Unilateral neglect of representational space. *Cortex 14*, 129–133.

Bowers, K. S. (1977). *Hypnosis for the seriously curious. New York: Jason Aronson.*

Brase, G., Cosmides, L., & Tooby, J. (1998). Individuation, counting, and statistical inference: The role of frequency and whole object representations in judgment under uncertainty. *Journal of Experimental Psychology: General 127* (1), 1–19.

Bruck, M., & Ceci, S. (1999). The suggestibility of children's memory. *Annual Review of Psychology 50* 419–439.

Charman, T., & Baron-Cohen, S. (1993). Understanding photos, models, and beliefs: A test of the modularity thesis of theory of mind. *Cognitive Development 10*, 287–298.

Cosmides, L. (1989). The logic of social exchange: Has natural selection shaped how humans reason? Studies with the Wason selection task. *Cognition 31*, 187–276.

Cosmides, L., and Tooby, J. (1987). From evolution to behavior: Evolutionary psychology as the missing link. In J. Dupré (Ed.), *The latest on the best: Essays on evolution and optimality.* Cambridge, MA: MIT Press.

Cosmides, L., & Tooby, J. (1989). Evolutionary psychology and the generation of culture, Part II. Case study: A computational theory of social exchange. *Ethology and Sociobiology 10*, 51–97.

Cosmides, L., &Tooby, J. (1992). Cognitive adaptations for social exchange. In J. Barkow, L. Cosmides, and J. Tooby (Eds.), *The adapted mind: Evolutionary psychology and the generation of culture.* New York: Oxford University Press.

Cosmides, L., & Tooby, J. (1996a). Are humans good intuitive statisticians after all? Rethinking some conclusions of the literature on judgment under uncertainty. *Cognition 58*, 1–73.

Cosmides, L., & Tooby, J. (1996b). A logical design for the mind? Review of *The psychology of proof*, by Lance J. Rips (1994, MIT Press). *Contemporary Psychology 41* (5), 448–450.

Cosmides, L., & Tooby, J. (1997). Dissecting the computational architecture of social inference mechanisms. In *Characterizing human psychological adaptations* (Ciba Foundation Symposium Volume #208). Chichester: Wiley.

Cosmides, L., & Tooby, J. (in press). Unraveling the enigma of human intelligence: Evolutionary psychology and the multimodular mind. In R. J. Sternberg & J. C. Kaufman (Eds.). *The evolution of intelligence*. Hillsdale, NJ: Erlbaum.

Ceci, S. (1995). False beliefs: Some developmental and clinical observations. In D. Schacter (Ed.), *Memory distortions* (pp. 91–125). Cambridge, MA: Harvard University Press.

Damasio, A., & Van Hoesen, G. (1983). Focal lesions of the limbic frontal lobe. In K. Heilmman & P. Satz (Eds.), *Neuropsychology of human emotion* (pp. 85–110). NY: Guilford Press.

Dennett, D. (1987). *The intentional stance*. Cambridge, MA: MIT Press.

Devinsky, O., Morrell, M., & Vogt, B. (1995). Contributions of anterior cingulate cortex to behaviour. *Brain 118*, 279–306.

Duncan, J. (1995). Attention, intelligence, and the frontal lobes. In M. S. Gazzaniga (Ed.), *The cognitive neurosciences* (pp. 721–733). Cambridge, MA: MIT Press.

Farah, M. (1984). The neurological basis of mental imagery: A componential analysis. *Cognition 18*, 245–272.

Farah, M. (1990). *Visual agnosia: Disorders of object recognition and what they tell us about normal vision*. Cambridge, MA: MIT Press.

Farah, M., Soso, M., & Dasheiff, R. (1992). Visual angle of the mind's eye before and after unilateral occipital lobectomy. *Journal of Experimental Psychology: Human Perception and Performance 19*, 241–246.

Fletcher, P., Happe, F., Frith, U., Baker, S., Dolan, R., Frackowiak, R., & Frith, C. (1995). Other minds in the brain: A functional imaging study of "theory of mind" in story comprehension. *Cognition 57*, 109–128.

Frege, G. 1892. On sense and reference. In P. Geach & M. Black (Eds.), *Translations of the philosophical writings of Gottlob Frege*. Oxford: Blackwell.

Frith, C. (1992). *The cognitive neuropsychology of schizophrenia*. Hillsdale, NJ: Erlbaum.

Frith, C., & Frith, U. (1991). Elective affinities in schizophrenia and childhood autism. In P. E. Bebbington (Ed.), *Social psychiatry: Theory, methodology, and practice*. London: Transaction.

Frith, U. (1989). *Autism: Explaining the enigma*. Oxford: Basil Blackwell.

Frith, U., Morton, J., & Leslie, A. (1991). The cognitive basis of a biological disorder: Autism. *Trends in Neuroscience 14*, 433–438.

Gentzen, G. (1969). Investigations into logical deduction. In M. E. Szabo (Ed.), *The collected papers of Gerhard Gentzen* (pp. 405–431). (Original work published 1935.)

Gerrig, R., & Prentice, D. (1991). The representation of fictional information. *Psychological Science 2*, 336–340.

Goldberg, G. (1985). Supplementary motor area structure and function: Review and hypotheses. *Behavioral and Brain Sciences 8*, 567–616.

Hayman, C., Macdonald, C., & Tulving, E. (1993). The role of repetition and associative interference in new semantic learning in amnesia: A case experiment. *Journal of Cognitive Neuroscience 5*, 375–389.

Hilgard, E. (1977). *Divided consciousness: Multiple controls in human thought.* New York: Wiley.

Humphrey, Nicholas (1992). *A history of the mind.* New York: Simon and Schuster.

Ingvar, D. (1985). Memory of the future: An essay on the temporal organization of conscious awareness. *Human Neurobiology 4*, 127–136.

Janowsky, J., Shimamura, A., & Squire, L. (1989). Source memory impairment in patients with frontal lobe lesions. *Neuropsychologia 27*, 1043–1056.

Johnson, M., Hashtroudi, S., & Lindsay, D. (1993). Source monitoring. *Psychological Bulletin 114*, 3–28.

Klein, S., Chan, R., & Loftus, J. (under review). Independence of episodic and semantic self-knowledge: The case from autism.

Klein, S., Cosmides, L., Tooby, J., & Chance, S. (under review, 1999). Decisions and the evolution of memory: multiple systems, multiple functions. *Psychological Review.*

Klein, S., & Loftus, J. (1993). The mental representation of trait and autobiographical knowledge about the self. In T. Srull & R. Wyer (Eds.), *The mental representation of trait and autobiographical knowledge about the self:* Vol. 5. *Advances in Social Cognition.* Hillsdale, NJ: Erlbaum.

Knowlton, B., Mangels, F., & Squire, L. (1996). A neostriatal habit learning system in humans. *Science 273*, 1399–1402.

Kosslyn, S. (1994). *Image and brain: The resolution of the imagery debate.* Cambridge, MA: MIT Press.

Kosslyn, S., Alpert, N., Thompson, W., Maljkovic, V., Weise, S., Chabris, C., Hamilton, S., Rach, S., & Buonanno, F. (1993). Visual mental imagery activates topographically organized visual cortex: PET investigations. *Journal of Cognitive Neuroscience 5*, 263–287.

Krebs, J. R., & Dawkins, R. (1984). Animal signals: Mind reading and manipulation. In J. R. Krebs & N. B. Davies, *Behavioural ecology: An evolutionary approach* (2nd ed.) (pp. 380–402). Oxford: Blackwell.

Kripke, S. (1979). A puzzle about belief. In A. Margalit (Ed.), *Meaning and Use.* Dordrecht: Reidel.

Kunzendorf, R. (1985–1986). Hypnotic hallucinations as "unmonitored" images: An empirical study. *Imagination, Cognition and Personality 5*, 255–270.

Lee, R. B. (1993). *The Dobe Ju/'hoansi.* (2nd ed.). New York: Holt, Reinhart, & Winston.

Leslie, A. (1987). Pretense and representation: The origins of "theory of mind." *Psychological Review 94*, 412–426.

Leslie, A. (1988). The necessity of illusion: Perception and thought in infancy. In L. Weiskrantz (Ed.), *Thought without language* (pp. 185–210). Oxford: Clarendon Press.

Leslie, A. (1994). ToMM, ToBy, and Agency: Core architecture and domain specificity. In L. Hirschfeld & S. Gelman (Eds.), *Mapping the mind: Domain specificity in cognition and culture.* New York: Cambridge University Press.

Leslie, A., & Frith, U. (1990). Prospects for a cognitive neuropsychology of autism: Hobson's choice. *Psychological Review 97*, 122–131.

Leslie, A., & Thaiss, L. (1992). Domain specificity in conceptual development: Neuropsychological evidence from autism. *Cognition 43*, 225–251.

McKenna, P., Clare, L., & Baddeley, A. (1995). Schizophrenia. In A. Baddeley, B. Wilson, & F. Watts (Eds.), *Handbook of memory disorders*. New York: Wiley.

McKenna, P., Mortimer, A., & Hodges, J. (1994). Semantic memory and schizophrenia. In A. David & J. Cutting (Eds.), *The neuropsychology of schizophrenia*. Hove, Sussex: Erlbaum.

Nyberg, L., & Tulving, E. (1996). Classifying human long-term memory: Evidence from converging dissociations. *European Journal of Cognitive Psychology 8*, 163–183.

Nyberg, L., Cabeza, R., & Tulving, E. (1996). PET studies of encoding and retrieval: The HERA model. *Psychonomic Bulletin and Review 3*, 135–148.

Pardo, P., Pardo, K., Janer, W., & Raichle, M. (1990). The anterior cingulate cortex mediates processing selection in the Stroop attentional conflict paradigm. *Proceedings of the National Academy of Sciences (USA) 87*, 256–259.

Perner, J. (1991). *Understanding the representational mind*. Cambridge: MIT Press.

Posner, M., & Raichle, M. (1994). *Images of mind*. New York: Freeman.

Potts, G., St. John, M., & Kirson, D. (1989). Incorporating new information into existing world knowledge. *Cognitive Psychology 21*, 303–333.

Richard, M. (1990). *Propositional attitudes: An essay on thoughts and how we ascribe them*. Cambridge: Cambridge University Press.

Rips, Lance J. (1994). *The psychology of proof: deductive reasoning in human thinking*. Cambridge, MA: MIT Press.

Schacter, D. (1995). Implicit memory: A new frontier for cognitive neuroscience. In M. Gazzaniga (Ed.), *The cognitive neurosciences* (pp. 815–824). Cambridge, MA: MIT Press.

Schacter, D., & Tulving, E., Eds. (1994). *Memory systems 1994*. Cambridge, MA: MIT Press.

Sheingold, K., & Tenney, Y. (1982). Memory for a salient childhood event. In U. Neisser (Ed.), *Memory observed* (pp. 201–212). San Francisco: W. H. Freeman.

Shepard, R. N. (1984). Ecological constraints on internal representation: Resonant kinematics of perceiving, imagining, thinking, and dreaming. *Psychological Review 91*, 417–447.

Shepard, R. N. (1987). Evolution of a mesh between principles of the mind and regularities of the world. In J. Dupré (Ed.), *The latest on the best: Essays on evolution and optimality* (pp. 251–275). Cambridge, MA: MIT Press.

Shepard, R. (1994). The mesh between mind and world. The William James Lectures, Harvard University, Cambridge, MA.

Sherman, J., & Klein, S. (1994). Development and representation of personality impressions. *Journal of Personality and Social Psychology 67*, 972–983.

Shimamura, A. (1995). Memory and frontal lobe function. In M. S. Gazzaniga (Ed.), *The cognitive neurosciences* (pp. 803–813). Cambridge, MA: MIT Press. .

Spelke, E. (1988). The origins of physical knowledge. In L. Weiskrantz (Ed.), *Thought without language* (pp. 168–184). Oxford: Clarendon Press.

Spelke, E. (1990). Principles of object perception. *Cognitive Science 14*, 29–56.

Sperber, D. (1985). Anthropology and psychology: Towards an epidemiology of representations. The Malinowski Memorial Lecture, 1984. *Man (N.S.) 20*, 73–89.

Sperber, Dan. (1996). *Explaining culture: A naturalistic approach.* Oxford and Cambridge, MA: Blackwell.

Sperber, D. (this volume). Culture and the epidemiology of meta-representations. *Tenth Annual Vancouver Cognitive Science Conference,* Simon Fraser University, Vancouver, Canada.

Sperber, Dan, & Wilson, Deirdre (1986). *Relevance: Communication and cognition.* Oxford: Blackwell.

Steen, F. (personal communication). Dept. of English, University of California, Santa Barbara.

Stone, V., Baron-Cohen, S., & Knight, R. (in press). Does frontal lobe damage produce theory of mind impairment? *Journal of Cognitive Neuroscience.*

Sugiyama, M. Scalise (1996). On the origins of narrative: Storyteller bias as a fitness-enhancing strategy. *Human Nature 7,* 403–425.

Symons, D. (1993). The stuff that dreams aren't made of: Why wake-state and dream-state sensory experiences differ. *Cognition 47,* 181–217.

Talmy, L. (1988). Force dynamics in language and cognition. *Cognitive Science 12,* 49–100.

Tooby, J., & Cosmides, L. (1989). Evolutionary psychology and the generation of culture, Part I. Theoretical considerations. *Ethology & Sociobiology 10,* 29–49.

Tooby, J., & Cosmides, L. (1990). The past explains the present: emotional adaptations and the structure of ancestral environments. *Ethology and Sociobiology 11,* 375–424.

Tooby, J., & Cosmides, L. (1992). The psychological foundations of culture. In J. Barkow, L. Cosmides, & J. Tooby (Eds.), *The adapted mind: Evolutionary psychology and the generation of culture.* New York: Oxford University Press.

Tooby, J., & Cosmides, L. (in press). Ecological rationality and the multimodular mind: Grounding normative theories in adaptive problems. In J. Tooby & L. Cosmides, *Evolutionary psychology: Foundational papers.* Foreword by Steven Pinker. Cambridge, MA: MIT Press.

Tooby J., & DeVore, I. (1987). The reconstruction of hominid behavioral evolution through strategic modeling. In W. Kinzey (Ed.), *Primate Models of Hominid Behavior.* New York: SUNY Press.

Tulkin, S., & Konner, M. (1973). Alternative conceptions of intellectual functioning. *Human Development 16,* 33–52.

Tulving, E. (1983). *Elements of episodic memory.* Oxford: Oxford University Press.

Tulving, E. (1985). Memory and consciousness. *Canadian Psychology/ Psychologie Canadienne 26,* 1–12.

Tulving, E. (1993a). What is episodic memory? *Current Perspectives in Psychological Science 2,* 67–70.

Tulving, E. (1993b). Self-knowledge of an amnesic individual is represented abstractly. In T. Srull & R. Wyer (Eds.), *The mental representation of trait and autobiographical knowledge about the self:* Vol. 5. *Advances in social cognition.* Hillsdale, NJ: Erlbaum.

Tulving, E. (1995). Organization of memory: Quo vadis? In M. S. Gazzaniga (Ed.), *The cognitive neurosciences* (pp. 839–847). Cambridge, MA: MIT Press.

Tulving, E. (1998). Brain/mind correlates of human memory. In M. Sabourin & F. Craik (Eds.), *Advances in psychological science:* Vol. 2. *Biological and cognitive aspects.* Hove, Sussex: Erlbaum.

Wheeler, M., Stuss, D., & Tulving, E. (1995). Frontal lobe damage produces episodic memory impairment. *Journal of the International Neuropsychological Society 1*, 525–536.

White, S., & Pillemer, D. (1979). Childhood amnesia and the development of a socially accessible memory system. In J. Kihlstrom & F. Evans (Eds.), *Functional disorders of memory* (pp. 29–73). Hillsdale, NJ: Erlbaum.

Whiten, Andew W., & Byrne, Richard W. (1997). *Machiavellian intelligence II: Extensions and evaluations.* Cambridge: Cambridge University Press

Whitty, C., & Lewin, W. (1957). Vivid day-dreaming: An unusual form of confusion following anterior cingulectomy. *Brain 80*, 72–76.

Wilson, B., & Wearing, D. (1995). Prisoner of consciousness: A state of just awakening following herpes simplex encephalitis. In R. Campbell & M. Conway (Eds.), *Broken memories: Case studies in memory impairment* (pp. 14–30). Cambridge, MA: Blackwell.

Wright, J. C., & Mischel, W. (1988). Conditional hedges and the intuitive psychology of traits. *Journal of Personality and Social Psychology 55*, 454–469.

Chapter 5

Metarepresentations in an Evolutionary Perspective

Dan Sperber

Just as bats are unique in their ability to use echo-location, so humans are unique in their ability to use metarepresentations. Other primates may have some rather rudimentary metarepresentational capacities. We humans are massive users of metarepresentations and of quite complex ones at that. We have no difficulty, for instance, in processing a three-tiered metarepresentation such as that in example (1).

(1)   Peter thinks that Mary said that it is implausible that pigs fly.

The fact that humans are expert users of metarepresentations, is, I would argue, as important in understanding human behavior as the fact that bats are expert users of echo-location is in understanding bat behavior.

How has the human metarepresentational capacity evolved? In order to contribute to the ongoing debate on this question, I will focus on three more specific issues:

(i)   How do humans metarepresent representations?

(ii) Which came first, language or metarepresentations?

(iii) Do humans have more than one metarepresentational ability?

How Do Humans Metarepresent Representations?

Metarepresentations are representations of representations but not all representations of representations are metarepresentations in the relevant sense. The human metarepresentational capacity we are interested in here is, first and foremost, a capacity to represent the *content* of representations. Consider:

(2) (a) Bill had a thought.

     (b) This claim is often repeated.

Statements (2a) and (2b) are about representations but they do not in any way represent their contents. They are not metarepresentations in any useful sense. One can imagine a biological or artificial device that could detect the presence of representations but not at all their content properties. It could detect, say, mental representations by being sensitive to the appropriate manifestations of brain activity or it could detect public representations such as utterances by being sensitive to their phonetic properties. Such a device, lacking access to the content properties of the representations it would represent, would not have a metarepresentational capacity in the sense intended. Consider:

(3) (a) Mary is hypochondriac.

    (b) Henry is always complaining.

    (c) John is a creationist.

    (d) This claim is slanderous.

Statements (3a) through (3d) do attribute a more or less specific tenor to representations they are directly or indirectly about. Thus, (3a) is true only if Mary tends to form unwarranted beliefs the gist of which is that she is seriously ill; (3b) is true only if Henry is making claims to the effect that certain things are not the way they ought to be; (3c) is true only if John accepts the central tenets of the creationist doctrine; (3d) is true only if the claim, to which reference is made, attributes to some agent some undesirable property. Representations (3a) through (3d) do state or imply something about the content of some representations, although they do not articulate the contents of these representations. They are metarepresentational only in a rudimentary way.

There may be animals capable of detecting the presence and tenor of some mental representations in others but who do so by means of unstructured representations. Thus, an animal might detect the fact that a conspecific wants to mate and represent this by means of a single unarticulated symbol *wants-to-mate* as in statement (4a). Similarly an animal might detect the fact that a conspecific has been suitably impressed with some display of strength and represent this by means of a single unarticulated symbol *knows-that-I-am-stronger-than-him* as in statement (4b).

(4) (a) He wants-to-mate.

    (b) He knows-that-I-am-stronger-than-him.

Such animals would possess a very rudimentary metarepresentational capacity lacking compositionality and recursion. They could only metarepresent a short and fixed list of representations.

Imagine a species with quite limited cognitive capacities. The contents of its mental representations belong to a limited repertoire: "there is a predator (at a certain location)"; "there is a prey"; "there is a mating partner," and so forth. Suppose it were advantageous for members of this species to be capable of representing some of the mental states of their conspecifics. Then, a rudimentary metarepresentational ability of the kind that I have just evoked might evolve.

Consider now a species with rich cognitive capacities, capable of forming and of using in its behavior mental representations of indefinitely varied contents. Suppose again that it were advantageous for members of this species to be capable of representing indefinitely many of the mental states of their conspecifics. A rudimentary metarepresentational ability of the kind just considered would not do this time since it would be sufficient to represent only a narrow and fixed subset of the indefinitely varied mental representations of the members of the species.

Another way to put the same point is this. Consider first the case of a species with a system of internal representations consisting, roughly, of a small list of representation types that can occasionally be tokened (and indexed to the situation). Then, the internal representations of members of this species could be metarepresented by means of a rudimentary metarepresentational system with a different mental symbol for each metarepresentable representation type. Consider now a species with system of internal representations that is – or is equivalent to – a mental language with compositionality and recursion. Then, the internal representations of members of this species could be metarepresented only by means of metarepresentational system consisting in – or equivalent to – a meta-language no less rich than the language the expressions of which it serves to metarepresent. If, moreover, several levels of metarepresentation are possible, as in statement (1) above, the metarepresentational system must equally rich or richer at each level. The only cost-effective way to achieve this is to have the expressions of the object-language do double service as expression of the meta-language (or, if n levels of metarepresentation are possible, do $n+1$-tuple service). A full-fledged metarepresentational capability such as that found in human languages and in human thinking is based on the possibility of interpreting any expression-token as representing another token of the same expression or the expression-type or, more generally, some expression type or token it resembles in relevant respects. Thus, in examples (5a) through (5e) the expressions italicized represent not the state of affairs that they describe but representations (mental, public, or abstract) the contents of which they serve to render.

(5) (a) Bill thought that *the house was on fire.*

(b) The claim that $2 + 2 = 4$ is often repeated.

(c) Mary believes that *she is seriously ill.*

(d) Henry is complaining that *life is too short.*

(d) John believes that *God created the world.*

(e) The claim that *John is a creationist* is slanderous.

Examples (1) and (5a) through (5e) are linguistic but I take it that humans are capable of entertaining their mental equivalent. In other words, expressions in the internal system of conceptual representations (however close or distant from natural language this system might be) can serve to represent expression types or tokens that they resemble in relevant respects (and identity is best seen here as just a limiting case of resemblance; see, Sperber & Wilson, 1995, chap. 4).

Imagine an organism endowed with a rich internal system of conceptual representations but without the ability to use these "opaquely" or metarepresentationally, that is, as iconic representations of other representations (types or tokens). Could such an organism *learn* to do so? Think of what is involved. The organism has no more knowledge of its internal representations *qua* representations than it has of its patterns of neural activities. Its representations are wholly transparent to it. Such an organism might be capable of representing, say, the fact that it is raining but never of representing the fact that it is representing the fact that it is raining.

It is hard to imagine what combination of external stimulations and internal dispositions might ever cause individual organisms of this type to become capable of using their repertoire of mental representations in order to represent not what these representations transparently represent but, in virtue of resemblance relationships, to represent opaquely other representations. This seems as implausible as learning to guide one's spontaneous movement by means of echo-location in the absence of a genetically determined domain-specific disposition. Such abilities speak of biological and evolutionary rather than cognitive and developmental transitions. I am, of course, aware of the relative weakness of "hard-to-imagine-otherwise" arguments. Still, if you are arguing that a full-fledged metarepresentational ability is something learnt (in the sense of learning theory) and do not illuminate how this learning might take place, then you are signing a huge promissory note the equivalent of which has never been honored. If, on the other hand, you assume that a metarepresentational ability is a biological development, the promissory note you are signing is more modest: there are well-understood biological developments of much greater complexity.

Which Came First: Language or Metarepresentations?

Language – rather than metarepresentational ability – is usually taken to be the most distinctive feature of the human species. The two are clearly linked as natural languages serve as their own meta-language and thus incorporate a full-fledged metarepresentational capacity. Linguistic utterances are public representations and typical objects of mental metarepresentation. Speakers, in intending an utterance, and hearers, in interpreting an utterance, mentally represent it as a bearer of specified content, that is, they metarepresent it.

Language and metarepresentations are made possible by biologically evolved mental mechanisms, which, it has been argued in both cases, are domain-specific. Noam Chomsky arguing for a domain-specific language faculty (e.g., Chomsky 1975, 1980) introduced the very idea of domain-specificity to the cognitive sciences. The idea of metarepresentations became familiar in cognitive science through work on naïve psychology or "theory of mind." In suggesting, in their article, "Does the chimpanzee have a theory of mind?" that the ability to attribute mental states to others was also found among non-linguistic animals, Premack and Woodruff were implying that this ability, at least in its simpler forms, is independent of language (Premack and Woodruff, 1978; see also, Premack, 1988). Developmental psychologists have argued that theory of mind is based on a domain-specific mental module (Leslie 1987; 1994; Baron-Cohen 1995).

If one accepts, as I do, the existence of two dedicated mental mechanisms, one for language, the other for metarepresentations, it seems reasonable to assume that, in humans, they have co-evolved. While the fully developed version of each of these two mechanisms may presuppose the development of the other, it still makes sense to ask which of these two, the linguistic or the metarepresentational, might have developed first to a degree sufficient to bootstrap the co-evolutionary process. At first blush, the language-first hypothesis seems quite attractive – and has attracted, for instance, Daniel Dennett (1991).

The hypothesis that the language faculty evolved first may seem, moreover, to offer a way of explaining how a metarepresentational ability might emerge in individual cognitive development, even in the absence of a biologically evolved specialized disposition. Linguistic communication fills the environment with a new kind of object – utterances, that is, public representations. Utterances can be perceived, attended to, thought about, just as any other perceptible object in the environment. At the same time, they are representations, they have meaning, content. It may seem imaginable, then, that children, finding linguistic representations in their environment, grasp the representational character of these utterances because they are linguistically equipped to assign them content and, as a result, develop an ability to represent representations *qua* representations. This acquired metarepresentational ability would apply first to linguistic utterances and, then, would extend to other types of representations, in particular mental representations.

This hypothesis loses much of its appeal under scrutiny. Spelling it out results in a worrisome dilemma. On the one hand, we can argue that ancestral linguistic communication, though presumably simpler in many respects, was based on the same kind of communicative mechanism as modern linguistic communication. If so, it presupposed metarepresentational ability and, therefore, could not precede it. On the other hand, we can argue that ancestral linguistic communication was strictly a coding-decoding affair like other forms of non-human animal communication. There is then no reason to assume that our ancestors had the resources to become aware of the representational character of their signals anymore than bees or vervet monkeys do.

When we, modern humans, communicate verbally, we decode what the words mean in order to find out what the speaker meant. Discovering the meaning of a sentence is just a means to an end. Our true interest is in the speaker's meaning. A speaker's meaning is a mental representation entertained by the speaker that she intends the hearer to recognize and to which she intends him to take some specific attitude (e.g., accept as true). Verbal understanding consists in forming a metarepresentation of a representation of the speaker (in fact, a higher-order metarepresentation since the speaker's representation is itself a metarepresentational intention). Moreover, there is a systematic gap between the sentence's meaning and the speaker's meaning. Sentences are typically ambiguous and must be disambiguated; they contain referring expressions the intended referent of which must be identified; they underdetermine the speaker's meaning in many other ways. Linguistic utterances fall short, typically by a wide margin, of encoding their speaker's meanings. On the other hand, utterances are generally good pieces of evidence of these meanings. Inference to the best explanation of the speaker's linguistic behavior generally consists in attributing to her the intention to convey what actually was her meaning in producing her utterance. Linguistic comprehension is an inferential task using decoded material as evidence. The inferences involved are about the speaker's meaning, that is, they are aimed at metarepresentational conclusions.

If the ability to communicate linguistically had preceded the ability to use metarepresentations, then this pre-metarepresentational, ancestral verbal ability would have been radically different from the kind of verbal ability we modern humans use, which is metarepresentational through and through. The ancestral language would have been a coding-decoding affair as are the many forms of non-human animal communication of which we know. This, in itself, is an unattractive speculation since it implies a radical change in the mechanism of human linguistic communication at some point in its evolution.

Even more importantly, there is no reason to assume that a decoding animal experiences or conceptualizes the stimulus it decodes as a representation: for non-human animals, coded communication and attribution of mental states to others are two unrelated capacities (the second apparently much rarer than the first). What seems to happen, rather, is that the decoding of the stimulus automatically puts the animal in a specific cognitive, emotional, or motivational state appropriate to the situation. For instance, the decoding of an alarm signal typically triggers a state of fear and activates escape plans. It would be quite unparsimonious to hypothesize that the decoding animal is able to recognize the signal as a signal endowed with meaning. It is more sensible (and the burden of proof would be on whoever maintained otherwise) to assume that, to communicators who merely code and decode, signals are transparent. Such signals play a role comparable to that of proximal stimuli in perception; they occur at an uncognized stage of a cognitive process.

If our ancestors were such coders-decoders and had no evolved disposition to metarepresent, then there is no sensible story of how the presence of utterances in their environment would have led them to discover their representational character, to metarepresent their content, and to use for this their own mental representations in a novel, opaque, manner. Out goes the hypothesis that language developed first.

What about the hypothesis that metarepresentations developed first? A metarepresentational and, more specifically, a metapsychological ability may be advantageous and may have evolved on its own. This has been convincingly argued in much recent literature on "Machiavellian intelligence" (Byrne & Whiten, 1988; Whiten & Byrne, 1997). The ability to interpret the behavior of intelligent conspecifics not just as bodily movement but as action guided by beliefs and desires gives one a much-enhanced predictive power. Predicting the behavior of others helps to protect oneself from them, to compete successfully with them, to exploit them, or to co-operate more profitably with them. A metarepresentational ability is plausible as an adaptation quite independently of communication.

Moreover, a well-developed metarepresentational ability makes certain forms of communication possible quite independently from any code or language. Organisms with metarepresentational abilities live in a world where there are not only physical facts but also mental facts. An individual may form beliefs or desires by emulating those it attributes to another individual. An individual may want to modify the beliefs and desires of others. It may want others to become aware of its beliefs and desires and to emulate these. Let me illustrate. Imagine two of our hominid ancestors, call one Mary and the other Peter.

First scenario

Mary is picking berries. Peter happens to be watching Mary. He infers from her behavior that she believes that these berries are edible and, since he assumes she is knowledgeable, he comes to believe that they are. Peter is using his metarepresentational ability to form new beliefs not just about Mary's mental representations but also about the state of affairs Mary's representations are about. He comes to "share" a belief of Mary's. Mary, however, is unaware that Peter is watching her and she has no desire to affect his beliefs. Peter in this case has a first-order metarepresentational belief:

> Mary believes
>
> > that these berries are edible

Second scenario

Mary is aware that Peter is watching her and that he is likely to infer from her behavior that the berries are edible, and she intends him to draw this inference. Her behavior has now two goals: collecting berries and affecting Peter's beliefs. Peter, however, is unaware of Mary's intention to affect his beliefs. In an interestingly different scenario, Mary could believe that the berries are *in*edible and pick them in order to deceive Peter. In either case, Mary has a first-order metarepresentational intention:

> That Peter should believe
>
> > that these berries are edible!

Third scenario

Peter is aware that Mary is picking berries with the intention that he should come to believe that these berries are edible. Mary, however, is unaware of Peter's awareness of her intention. How should Peter's awareness of Mary's intention affect his willingness to believe that the berries are edible (and to fulfil, thereby, Mary's intention)? If he believes that she is trying to be helpful to him by informing him that the berries are edible, this will give him extra reason to accept that they are. If, on the other hand, he mistrusts her, being aware of her informative intention will be a reason not to fulfil it. In either case, Peter has a second-order metarepresentational belief:

> Mary intends
>
> > that he should believe
> >
> > > that these berries are edible.

Fourth scenario

Mary intends that Peter should be aware of her intention to inform him that the berries are edible. She has, then, not one but two informative intentions: a first-order informative intention that Peter should believe that the berries are edible and a second-order informative intention that Peter should be aware of her first-order informative intention. What reasons might she have to have the second-order informative intention? As mentioned above, Peter's awareness of Mary's first-order informative intention, provided he trusts her, may give him an extra reason to believe her. In other words, the fulfillment of the second-order informative intention may contribute to the fulfillment of the first-order informative intention. The second-order informative intention is, of course, a third-order metarepresentation to the effect:

That Peter should believe

that Mary intends

that he should believe

that these berries are edible!

Fifth scenario

Peter is aware that Mary intends him to be aware of her informative intention. He has a fourth-order metarepresentational belief:

Mary intends

that he should believe

that she intends

that he should believe

that these berries are edible.

Peter might come to have this belief when he notes that Mary is ostensively making sure that he is paying attention to her behavior by, say, establishing eye contact with him, picking the berries in somewhat formal manner, and so forth. Mary's first-order informative intention is now an "overt" (Strawson, 1964) or "mutually manifest" (Sperber & Wilson, 1995). We have reached a level where communication proper occurs, though no code or language is involved.

Once the level of metarepresentational sophistication of our fifth scenario is reached, a dramatic change indeed occurs. Whereas before,

in order to fulfil her first-level informative intention, Mary had to engage
in behavior – picking the berries – that was best explained by attributing
to her the belief that the berries were edible and the desire to collect the
berries, she can now resort to symbolic behavior, the best explanation of
which is simply that she is trying to fulfil an informative intention, her
desire to inform (or misinform) Peter that the berries are edible. Instead
of actually picking the berries, she might, for instance, mime the action
of eating the berries.

Typically, symbolic behavior such as miming has no plausible explanation other than that it is intended to affect the beliefs or desires of
an audience. This generally is the one effect of such a behavior that could
clearly have been intended by the agent. Thus. for Mary to mime eating
the berries does not feed her, does not help her in any easily imaginable
way, except through the effect it has on Peter. Her miming behavior triggers in Peter's mind, through the perception of a resemblance between
the miming behavior and the behavior mimed, the idea of eating the berries. Moreover, if it is at all relevant to Peter to know whether or not the
berries are edible, Mary's behavior suggests that they are. Provided that
Peter sees this miming behavior as intended by Mary to inform him of
an informative intention of hers, he is justified in assuming that the very
idea triggered in his mind was one Mary wanted him to entertain, elaborate and accept.

The same result achieved by miming could, provided Peter and
Mary shared an appropriate code, be achieved by means of a coded signal or by means of some combination of iconic and coded behavior. Suppose Mary and Peter shared a signal meaning something like "good."
Mary might point to the berries and produce this signal, again triggering
in Peter's mind the idea that the berries were good to eat, doing so in an
manifestly intentional manner and, therefore, justifying Peter in assuming that she intended him to believe that the berries were edible.

Note that, if Mary used the coded symbol "good" in this way, she
would, nevertheless, be very far from *encoding* her meaning that these
berries are edible. She would merely be giving evidence of her intention
to cause Peter to come to accept this meaning as true. The use of coded
signals as part of the process of communication is no proof that the communication in question is wholly, or even essentially, of the coding-
decoding kind.

Metarepresentational sophistication allows a form of inferential
communication independent of the possession of a common code. This
type of inferential communication, however, can take advantage of a
code. It can do so even if the signals generated by the code are ambiguous, incomplete, and context-dependent (all of which linguistic utterances actually are). By triggering mental representations in the audience,
coded signals provide just the sort of evidence of the communicator's

informative intention that inferential communication requires, even if they come quite short of encoding the communicator's meaning.

To conclude this section, there is a plausible scenario where a metarepresentational ability develops in the ancestral species for reasons having to do with competition, exploitation, and co-operation and not with communication *per se*. This metarepresentational ability makes a form of inferential communication possible initially as a side effect and, probably, rather painstakingly at first. The beneficial character of this side effect turns it into a function of metarepresentations and creates a favorable environment for the evolution of a new adaptation, a linguistic ability. Once this linguistic ability develops, a co-evolutionary mutual enhancement of both abilities is easy enough to imagine.

Do Humans Have More than One Metarepresentational Ability?

Current discussions have focused on the metapsychological use of a metarepresentational ability to represent mental states, the beliefs and desires of others and of oneself. Humans, however, metarepresent not just mental representations but also public representations and representations considered in the abstract, independently of their mental or public instantiation. The three types of metarepresented representations are simultaneously illustrated in (1) and individually highlighted in (6a) through (6c).

(1)   Peter thinks that Mary said that it is implausible that pigs fly.

(6) (a) Peter thinks that *Mary said that it is implausible that pigs fly*.

     (b) Mary said that *it is implausible that pigs fly*.

     (c) It is implausible that *pigs fly*.

In example (6a), the italicized phrase metarepresents a mental representation of Peter's, in (6b), it metarepresents an utterance, that is, a public representation of Mary's, and in (6c), it metarepresents a representation considered in the abstract (as a hypothesis), independently of whoever might entertain or express it.

Representations considered in the abstract are reduced to their logical, semantic, and epistemic properties: they may be true or false, self-contradictory or necessarily true, plausible or implausible, standing in relationships of entailment, of contradiction, of warrant, of being a good argument one for the other, of meaning similarity, and so forth. They may be normatively evaluated from a logico-semantic point of view (and also from an aesthetic point of view).

Mental and public representations have the same content properties as their abstract counterparts – or arguably, abstract representations are nothing but the content properties of concrete representations, abstracted away. Mental and public representations also have specific properties linked to their mode of instantiation. A mental representation occurs in one individual; it is causally linked to other mental and non-mental states and processes of which the individual is wholly or partially the locus. A mental representation can be sad or happy, disturbing or helpful; it can be normatively evaluated in psychological terms as poorly or well reasoned, as imaginative, as delusional, and so on. A public representation typically occurs in the common environment of two or more people; it is an artifact aimed at communication. It exhibits such properties as having a certain linguistic form, as being used to convey a certain content in a certain context, as attracting more or less attention, as being more or less comprehensible to its intended audience, and so on. It can be normatively evaluated from a communicative point of view as sincere or insincere, intelligible or unintelligible, relevant or irrelevant.

The properties of these three types of representations – mental, public, and abstract – do not constitute three disjoint sets and are not always easy to distinguish. Mental and public representations have the logico-semantic properties of their abstract counterparts. A belief or an utterance is said, for instance, to be true or false when its propositional content is. Public representations serve to convey mental representations and have, at least by extension, some of the properties of the mental representations they convey. An utterance is said, for instance, to be imaginative or delusional when the thought it expresses is. Still, many properties are best understood as belonging essentially to one of the three types of representation and as belonging to another type of representation, if at all, only by extension, in virtue of some relational property that holds between them (such as the relationship of expression that holds between an utterance and a thought).

There is no question that we modern humans can attend in different ways to these three types of representations. We can attribute mental states, interpret public representations, and reflect on the formal properties of abstract representations. Are these performances all based on a single metarepresentational ability or do they, in fact, involve different competencies? In the latter case, is it plausible that these competencies might each be a distinct evolved adaptation? Could there be several metarepresentational "modules"? In the literature of evolutionary psychology, on the one hand, and in the literature of developmental psychology, on the other, the only metarepresentational adaptation envisaged is a metapsychological "theory of mind," the main function of which is to predict the behavior of others. Even a peculiar behavior such as collective pretend play, which involves essentially the creation and manipulation of public representations, is often treated as a regular use of "theory of mind."

What does a metarepresentational ability whose function is basically metapsychological do? What kind of inferences does it draw? Which properties of representations does it attend to? It draws inferences from situation and behavior to mental states as in examples (7a) through (7c), from mental states to other mental states as in examples (8a) and (8b), and from mental states to behavior as in examples (9a) and (9b).

(7) (a) There is a predator just in front of A.
         Therefore, A knows that there is a predator just in front of it.

    (b) A is panting.
         Therefore, A wants to drink.

    (c) A is running, occasionally looking behind its back.
         Therefore, A is trying to escape.

(8) (a) A knows that there is a predator just in front of it.
         Therefore, A is afraid of the predator.

    (b) A wants to drink.
         Therefore, A wants to find some water.

(9) (a) A is afraid of the predator.
         Therefore, A will try to escape.

    (b) A wants to find some water.
         Therefore, A will go to the river.

A metapsychological ability assumes that others have some basic knowledge and basic drives, and attributes to them specific beliefs and desires derived through perception and inference. Does such an ability, with the kind of power we are entitled to grant it on evolutionary and developmental grounds, suffice to explain the kind of metarepresentational processes we engage in when we interpret public representations, in particular utterances, or when we attend to the formal properties of abstract representations?

A comprehension module?

Comprehension (or its pragmatic layer) is an inferential process, using as input the output of linguistic decoding and aiming at discovering the speaker's meaning. Comprehension consists, therefore, in inferring a mental state (an intention of a specific kind) from behavior (an utterance). It might seem that this is precisely the kind of result a metapsychological ability should be able to achieve. In the story above of Mary, Peter, and the berries, I tried to illustrate how, in principle, a multileveled metapsychological ability might make inferential communication possible. The communication achieved between Mary and Peter in the fifth scenario showed metarepresentational prowess. In modern humans, however, comparable or greater metarepresentational achievements have become routine and we communicate at great speed much more complex contents than Mary and Peter ever could. This is a first reason to hypothesize that a more specialized adaptation aimed at comprehension has evolved. A second reason has to do with the pattern of inference from observed behavior to attributed intention.

In the simplest case, behavior (say, throwing a stone) is observed to have several effects (making a noise, casting a moving shadow, killing a bird). One of these effects (killing a bird, as it might be) can be seen as desirable to the agent. It is then inferred that the agent performed the behavior with the intention of achieving this desirable effect. Inferring intentions is somewhat harder when the behavior fails to achieve its intended effect. Say the bird is merely frightened away rather than killed. Competent attributers of mental states will nevertheless recognize that throwing the stone could have killed the bird and that the agent could expect this effect (with greater or lesser confidence). They will then infer that this unachieved effect was the one intended.

In the case of attributions of a speaker's meaning, these standard patterns of inference (from behavior to intention through identification of a desirable actual or failed effect) are not readily available. The essential effect intended by a speaker, that is, comprehension of her meaning, cannot be achieved without the very recognition of her intention to achieve this effect. The intended effect cannot, therefore, be independently observed to occur and then be recognized as desirable and presumably intentional. Nor does it make sense to imagine that the comprehender might recognize as the effect intended an effect that might plausibly have occurred but that, in fact, failed to do so, since the recognition of the intended effect would secure its occurrence.

There are, in the literature, two basic ways of solving the puzzle raised by inferential comprehension. The first way is Grice's (1989). It aims at showing a way around the difficulty while remaining within the limits of standard belief-desire psychology. It consists in assuming that the decoding of the linguistic signal provides a default assumption regarding the speaker's meaning. By default, the speaker is assumed to mean what the sentence she utters means. This default assumption can be inferentially complemented or otherwise corrected when there is a mismatch between it and general assumptions about standing goals that the speaker is presumed to aim at in her verbal behavior, goals codified by Grice in terms of his Co-operative Principle and Maxims. Such inferential correction involves a form of metarepresentational reasoning about the speaker's intentions in which not only the conclusion (an attribution of meaning to the speaker) but also some of the premises are metarepresentational. For instance, in the case of a metaphor such as example (10), the hearer is supposed to reason somewhat as in (11):

(10)   John is a soldier.

(11) (a)   The speaker seems to have said that John is a soldier.

 (b)   The speaker does not believe and knows that I know that he does not believe that John is a soldier.

 (c)   The speaker is respecting the Co-operative Principle and, in particular, is trying to be truthful.

 (d)   Therefore, the speaker could not mean that John is a soldier.

 (e)   The speaker must be trying to convey a closely related meaning compatible with the presumption that the speaker is co-operative.

 (f)   By inference to the best available explanation, the speaker means that John is like a soldier: he is devoted to his duty, obedient to orders, and so on.

It is as if, by flouting the maxim of truthfulness, the speaker deliberately failed to achieve a certain effect, thus suggesting that the truly intended effect is in the vicinity of the overtly failed one.

As this example illustrates, Gricean pragmatics can be seen as an account where the inferential part of comprehension consists in applying common-sense psychology to verbal behavior. If Grice were right, a general metapsychological ability, together with a presumably socially acquired knowledge of the Co-operative Principle and the Maxims, would be sufficient to account for inferential comprehension.

Gricean pragmatics might seem attractively parsimonious since it does not require any specialized comprehension ability. The economy in terms of the number of mental devices one may be led to postulate, however, is more than offset by the cumbersome character of the inferences that Gricean pragmatics necessitates every time a speaker's meaning diverges from sentence's meaning (and we have argued that it *always* so diverges). Do we really have, in the case of implicature, of indirect speech acts, of metaphor, or of irony, to reflect on what the speaker knows we know she knows, on what respecting the maxims requires of her, on what she might mean and not mean? Does it take more effort and hence longer to process such utterances? (The answer is no; see Gibbs, 1994; this volume). Do we want to attribute to young children these complex inference patterns or to deny them the ability to comprehend metaphor and other forms of so-called indirect speech? As a rational reconstruction of how inferential comprehension might be possible, Grice's account, though not without problems, is certainly appealing. As a psychologically realistic account of the mental processes actually involved in comprehension, it is much less so.

Though we owe a great deal to Grice's inspiration, Deirdre Wilson and I have criticized his pragmatics and, among other aspects, this account of metaphor. We have developed relevance theory as another way to solve the puzzle raised by inferential comprehension (Sperber and Wilson, 1995). In relevance theory, we assume that comprehension follows a very specific inferential pattern suited for the discovery of the informative intentions of communicators. We define the relevance of a cognitive input to an individual as a positive function of the cognitive effects achieved by processing this input and as a negative function of the amount of effort involved in this processing. We argue that every utterance (and, more generally, every communicative act) conveys a presumption of its own relevance. We show that this justifies the following inferential procedure: follow a route of least effort in constructing an interpretation – taking the very fact that an element of interpretation comes first to mind as an argument in its favor – until the effects achieved are sufficient to warrant the presumption of relevance conveyed by the utterance, and then stop. To illustrate briefly: given the context, utterance (10) might be capable of activating in the mind of the hearer the ideas in (11a) through (11g) in that order.

(10)   John is a soldier.

(11) (a) John is devoted to his duty.

     (b) John willingly follows orders.

     (c) John does not question authority.

     (d) John makes his own the goals of his team.

     (e) John is a patriot.

     (f) John earns a soldier's pay.

     (g) John is a member of the military.

Suppose that the utterance, when interpreted as conveying (11a) though (11d), satisfies the expectations of relevance it has itself raised. Then, we predict that the interpretation will stop at this point and that (11g), that is, the literal interpretation will not even be considered. In another context, the order in which the elements of interpretation might come to the mind of the hearer would be different and the stopping point might be such that the overall interpretation would include (11g) and be literal. Suppose, for instance, that "John is a soldier" was said in response to the question "What does John do for a living?" Then (11a through (11g) would probably be accessible in the reverse order, from (11g) through (11a). The hearer, moreover, would likely stop at (11f) or (11e). The resulting interpretation (11g) through (11e) would be literal and not even overlap with the metaphorical interpretations (11a) through (11d) of the same sentence uttered in a different context. In all cases, however, the comprehension procedure is the same: follow the path of least effort until adequate relevance is achieved. This may yield a literal, a loose, or a metaphorical interpretation without the comprehender having to take notice of the type of interpretation achieved.

The *conclusion* of such a process of interpretation is an attribution of a meaning to the speaker and, hence, a metarepresentation. Nevertheless, the *premises* in the inference process need not be metarepresentational. This procedure, therefore, can be followed by a relatively unsophisticated metarepresenter, for instance by a young child capable, as young children are, of comprehending metaphor. On the other hand, how would the child or, for that matter, the adult discover this procedure and recognize that it is a reliable means to infer a speaker's meaning? A plausible answer is that this procedure is not individually discovered but is biologically evolved. It is an evolved module.

The relevance-based comprehension procedure could not be soundly applied to the discovery of non-communicative intentions. Non-communicative behavior carries no presumption of relevance to possible observers. The order in which elements of interpretation come to the mind of the observer has no particular epistemic value. There is no level where, expectations of relevance being satisfied, the observer is thereby justified in believing that his interpretation of the agent's intention is complete.

What could be the relationship between a relevance-based comprehension module and a more general metapsychological module? The former might be a sub-module of the latter, in the manner in which linguistic acoustic abilities are a sub-module of general acoustic abilities. Speech sounds are sounds and their perception recruits the hearing system. At the same time, speech sounds are, from birth onwards, attended and processed in a proprietary way. Similarly, the recognition of communicative intentions might be a biologically differentiated and stabilized sub-system of human naïve psychology.

A "Logical" Module?

Is the human metapsychological ability enough to explain the human ability to attend to formal and, in particular, to logical properties of representations? A metapsychological ability attributes inferences to others. Inferences must, on the whole, respect logico-semantic relationships such as entailment or warrant – that is, relationships holding among representations in the abstract – or else they are not truly inferences. Successful attribution of inferences to others must also respect these relationships. Still, if we suppose that the organisms to which mental states are attributed have quite limited inferential abilities, then the attributing organisms – the metapsychologists – need attend only to a few logical relationships. Moreover, this attention need not be reflective. That is, the metapsychologists need not be logicians, thinking about logical relationships; it is enough that they themselves be able to make, off-line so to speak, the inferences they attribute. (This is sometimes presented as the simulation view but there is a weak and sufficient version of it that is equally compatible with the simulation view, *à la* Goldman and with the theory-of-mind view, *à la* Leslie.)

The type of metapsychological competence that is likely to be an evolved adaptation is unlikely to explain the modern human ability to attend to abstract representations and, in particular, to do formal logic. However, it is dubious that such an ability is widely shared. It might be just a skill acquired with some difficulty by a minority of people in scholarly institutions.

In fact, psychologists favorable to an evolutionary point of view have expressed doubts as to the existence of a genetically determined domain-general "logical ability." If by a "logical ability" what is meant is a unitary, domain-general ability that would govern all human inferences, then indeed, positing such an ability would go against well-known evolutionary arguments for the domain-specificity of mental mechanisms (see Sperber, 1996, chap. 5). On the other hand, if we think of the kind of logical ability that is involved in formulating or evaluating arguments, far from being domain-general, this is a highly domain-specific metarepresentational ability: its domain is some specific properties of abstract representations. An appearance of domain-generality might come from the fact that the representations that such a device would handle could be representations of anything. The device, however, would just attend to some formal properties of these representations, independent of what they happen to represent, and would be as specialized as, say a grammar-checker in a word-processor, which is able to process statements about anything but is obviously not domain-general for all that.

Still, what is the plausibility, from an evolutionary point of view, that a logical module specialized in checking the validity of arguments would have evolved? It might seem low but let me speculate and offer an argument why such a logical module with a fairly specific function is not so implausible.

Though the conclusion is quite different, the structure of my argument is parallel to Leda Cosmides's argument on cheater detection (Cosmides, 1989). She draws on the neo-Darwinian argument according to which "reciprocal altruism" is unstable unless there is some form of control for cheating since, otherwise, cheaters would be more successful until there were not enough genuine altruists left to be cheated. In the case of complex forms of reciprocal exchange, as found among humans, the prevention of cheating is an elaborate cognitive task that is likely, Cosmides argues, to have caused the evolution of an ad hoc adaptation, a cheater-detection mechanism. As usual, it is an open question as to whether the adaptation that handles the problem is precisely calibrated for the task or is, in fact, a narrower or, on the contrary, a larger ability that was still the best biologically available solution for the task. (I do not want to discuss Cosmides's basic argument, which I find illuminating, but to draw inspiration from it; for a critical discussion of her use of the selection task to provide empirical evidence for this argument, see Sperber, Cara & Girotto, 1995).

Communication is a form of co-operation that seems particularly advantageous for animals that depend as much as humans do on their cognitive resources. Instead of being restricted in one's knowledge to the products of one's own experiences and thinking, communication makes experience and thinking available by proxy. Alas, as with other forms of co-operation, communication makes one also vulnerable to misinformation, deception, and misguidance. Of course, one could protect oneself from the harms of deception by being systematically mistrustful but one would lose, by the same token, the benefits of communication. Communication is advantageous only if it is paired with mechanisms that ensure the proper calibration of trust. It is even more advantageous if, while protected from the deception of others without being overprotected, you can penetrate their protection and deceive them.

The human reliance on communication is so great, the risks of deception and manipulation so ubiquitous, that it is reasonable to speculate that all available cost-effective modes of defense are likely to have evolved. There are several such modes. One is to be discriminating about whom to trust and to accept authority quite selectively. Clearly, humans do this. Another is to be sensitive to subtle signs of deceptive intent, to read the relevant attitudinal and emotional signs. These safeguards can be breached, as they are by professional swindlers who typically "look absolutely trustworthy."

I want to focus on yet another possible protective mechanism against misinformation: check the consistency of the information communicated – both its internal consistency and its consistency with what you already believe. As anybody who has ever tried to lie knows, the liar's problem is to maintain consistency, both internally and contextually. An organism that drew its knowledge only from its senses and a few reliable inferential routines would probably waste energy in checking the consistency of the information it acquired. Inconsistencies in perception-based information occur but they are rare, and trying to eliminate them may not be worth the cost. For richly communicating animals like us, eliminating inconsistencies may not only be worth the cost but, indeed, literally life-saving.

For this reason, I hypothesize the emergence of an ability to check for consistency and to filter incoming information on this basis. But, this is only the first blow in the persuasion counter-persuasion arm race. More advantageous than merely protecting yourself from misinformation is to combine this with the ability freely to inform and misinform others, to persuade them of what it is in your interest to persuade them of, whether true or false. Persuaders addressing consistency-checkers cannot do better than display the very consistency – or, at least, the appearance of it – for which their audience is likely to check. Communicators now express not only the propositions they want their audience to accept but also arguments to accept these propositions and the very argumentative structure that leads to the intended conclusion. The language is enriched with logical terms ("and," "or," "if," etc.) and para-logical terms ("therefore," "but," "since," "although," "even," etc.) that display the real or alleged consistency and logical force of the communication.

The next stage in the persuasion counter-persuasion arm race is the development of the ability to scrutinize these argumentative displays and to find fault with them. In other terms, I am surmising, on evolutionary grounds, the development of a very special kind of "logical," or logico-rhetorical ability. It is special in that it attends to logical relationships, not *per se* nor for the sake of the benefits that good reasoning can give the individual thinker, but, on the one hand, as a means to filter communicated information and, on the other hand, as a means to penetrate the filters of others. Such a speculation has experimentally testable implications. It predicts, for instance, that logically equivalent tasks will yield significantly better performance when they are presented in a context where subjects are scrutinizing arguments plausibly aimed at persuading them than when they are evaluating these arguments in the abstract (as happens in most experimental tasks).

Conclusion

My aim in the present chapter has been to discuss the possibility that humans might be endowed, not with one, but with several evolved metarepresentational abilities. I have considered argument as to why, beside the standard metapsychological ability, they might have a comprehension module aimed at the on-line interpretation of utterances and a logico-argumentative module aimed at persuading others while not being too easily persuaded themselves. If there are, indeed, three such metarepresentational modules, the obvious next step would be to envisage their evolution not separately but, much more systematically than I have done here, as a case of co-evolution involving also the "language instinct," and – dare I say it? – consciousness.

Acknowledgments

I am grateful to Steven Davis, Gloria Origgi, and Deirdre Wilson for their useful comments on earlier versions of this chapter.

References

Baron-Cohen, Simon (1995). *Mindblindness: An essay on autism and theory of mind.* Cambridge, MA: MIT Press.

Byrne, Richard, & Whiten, Andrew, Eds. (1988). *Machiavellian intelligence.* Oxford: Clarendon Press.

Chomsky, Noam (1975). *Reflections on language.* New York: Random House.

Chomsky, Noam (1980). *Rules and representations.* New York: Columbia University Press.

Cosmides, Leda (1989). The logic of social exchange: Has natural selection shaped how humans reason? Studies with Wason Selection Task. *Cognition* 31, 187–276.

Dennett, Daniel (1991). *Consciousness explained.* Boston: Little, Brown.

Gibbs, Raymond (1994). *The poetics of mind.* Cambridge : Cambridge University Press.

Grice, Paul (1989). *Studies in the way of words.* Cambridge, MA: Harvard University Press.

Leslie, Alan (1987). Pretense and representation: The origin of "theory of mind." *Psychological Review 94,* 412–426.

Leslie, Alan (1994). ToMM, ToBY, and Agency: Core architecture and domain specificity. In L. A. Hirschfeld & S. A. Gelman (Eds.), *Mapping the mind: Domain specificity in cognition and culture* (pp. 119–148). New York: Cambridge University Press.

Premack, D (1988). "Does the chimpanzee have a theory of mind?" revisited. In Richard Byrne and Andrew Whiten (Eds.), *Machiavellian intelligence* (pp. 161–179). Oxford: Clarendon Press.

Premack, D., & Woodruff, G. (1978). Does the chimpanzee have a theory of mind? *The Behavioral and Brain Sciences 1,* 532–526.

Sperber, Dan (1996). *Explaining culture: A naturalistic approach.* Oxford: Blackwell.

Sperber, Dan, Cara, Francesco, & Girotto, Vittorio (1995). Relevance theory explains the selection task. *Cognition 57,* 31–95.

Sperber, Dan, & Wilson, Deirdre (1995). *Relevance: Communication and cognition.* Oxford: Blackwell. (Original work published in 1986.)

Strawson, R. (1964). Intention and convention in speech acts. *Philosophical Review* 73, 439–460.

Whiten, Andrew, & Byrne, Richard (1997). *Machiavellian intelligence II: Extensions and evaluations.* Cambridge: Cambridge University Press.

Chapter 6

Chimpanzee Cognition and the Question of Mental Re-representation

Andrew Whiten

Introduction

Metarepresentation is a mental capacity of enormous significance for our species. Children's grasp of other peoples' mental life is remarkable even within their first few years, and many writers have argued that – like the equally remarkable ease of first-language acquisition – a high degree of inherited preparedness must exist. This developmental priority itself suggests that metarepresentational capacities are of great functional significance for humans, a conclusion additionally underlined by the often crippling social difficulties experienced by autistic individuals who manifest delays in specific kinds of metarepresentational activity (Baron-Cohen, 1995; Baron-Cohen, Leslie, & Frith, 1985; Leslie, 1987; 1991). Although there are many controversies within the burgeoning literature on the development of children's metarepresentational abilities (e.g., Bogdan, 1997; Carruthers & Smith, 1996a; chapters in Carruthers & Smith, 1996b; chapters in Lewis & Mitchell, 1994; Mitchell & Lewis, 1994; Perner, 1991), there is a consensus that these abilities have multiple ramifications in cognition, communication and social competence (Baron-Cohen, Tager-Flusberg, & Cohen, 1993; Lewis & Mitchell, 1994).

A natural question thus arises as to how such abilities evolved, and from what they evolved. This is the subject of the present chapter. Does a study of our closest living ape relatives suggest that our common ancestor had abilities which can properly be called "metarepresentational"? If not, what of capacities which may have acted as precursors, or foundations on which a distinctive human potential has got constructed in the course of hominid evolution?

The answer to such questions is going to depend not only on the nature of ape minds, but on our methods for understanding them. It will also depend on our definitions and conceptions of what nonverbal metarepresentation would look like. Likewise, we need to assess which characteristics of "full-blown" metarepresentation are shared with simpler cognitive processes that may be precursors to it, ontogenetically or phylogenetically. We must address these rather tricky conceptual and definitional questions before reviewing the relevant findings.

What Might Nonverbal Kinds of Metarepresentation Look Like?

The term 'metarepresentation' has already been used in some quite different ways (Perner, 1991, p. 60; Whiten & Perner, 1991). In developmental psychology, this has meant that it could be true to say that a young child is capable of "metarepresentation" in one sense, but not yet in another, more "advanced" sense. It is essential to distinguish these and acknowledge which sense one is using on any one occasion. This is equally true where the subjects are non-human primates.

Although it is not the only distinction that can be usefully drawn within the idea of metarepresentation, the one I shall focus on here has emerged in the different usages of Alan Leslie and Josef Perner, and exchanges between them. In both cases, the term has been used to denote *representation of a representation*, or in other words a *second-order representation*: indeed, that much would appear to be inherent in any use of the term 'metarepresentation'. In this chapter we shall principally be interested in the case where both the primary representation and the second-order representation of it are mental, rather than physical representations like photographs.

Kinds of Metarepresentation

The two main meanings of 'metarepresentation' we need to discriminate can be described as follows, the difference lying in an additional phrase extending the second alternative.

Sense (1) A mental representation of a mental representation

Sense (2) A mental representation of a mental representation *as a representation*

At first sight, this may appear an abstruse distinction but it is important. I see the first sense as that in which the expression "metarepresentation" was used by Leslie (1987) in analyzing the origins of a theory of mind in young children, as early as in their second year. The second sense was distinguished by Perner (1988; 1991) and applied to older children once they showed evidence of discriminating false beliefs in others. We need to unfold these distinctions in a little more detail before talking about apes, and we must start by looking at the building-block concept of *representation*.

Representation

Leslie took his sense of representation from the "information processing or cognitivist, approach to cognition and perception" (1987, p. 414). Consistent with this framework, Leslie argued that

> the basic evolutionary and ecological point of internal representation must be to represent aspects of the world in an accurate, faithful and literal way, in so far as this is possible for a given organism. Such a *basic* capacity for representation can be called a capacity for *primary representation*. Primary representation is thus defined in terms of its direct semantic relation with the world. (Leslie, 1987, p. 414)

Accordingly, Leslie took *perception* to be one major manifestation of primary representation. One reason this makes sense is that even the "simple" act of perception involves the construction of a (neural) code which is physically quite different from the object of perception. As we well know, to "see" a tree involves more than taking a "mental photograph" as if with a pinhole camera: it involves an active process of interpretation and construction, terminating in a pattern of neural activity, the function of which is to "stand for" a tree. That perception is inherently representational is underlined by the existence of visual illusions, which as Gregory (1966/1996) has shown, are very much like "hypotheses" about the world, in which our neural states may oscillate between two different interpretations or representations of the same visual input.

This relatively broad sense of the term 'representation' is the one my own treatment shares. However, others use it in much more constrained ways. 'Representation' is a term used in certain developmental and comparative literature, particularly following Piaget's writings, to denote only a small subset of what is labelled representation in cognitive science generally; specifically, the ability to remember objects or events so as to operate on them cognitively when they are absent (see, e.g., Parker, 1990). Talking of great apes, Byrne suggested that "their various accomplishments both in social and technical problem solving, suggest that they – like humans, but unlike monkeys and most animals – have a representational understanding of the world . . . in everyday terms, they can think" (Byrne, 1997, p. 297). Perner (1988) suggested denoting this kind of usage of the term "re-presentation," a convention that would perhaps be helpful if it were universally adopted. However, is not the idea of 're-presenting' an aspect of reality the reason why we have the term "representation" in the first place? In the case of primary representation as used by Leslie, for example, a seen tree is a real tree (re)-presented in the mind. Remembering the broad sense in which I am defining representations, let us turn to representations of representations.

Metarepresentation: Senses (1) and (2)

Whether we apply the broad or the narrow meaning of 'representation' will drastically affect what we shall count as representing another's representations. According to the general cognitive-science usage I described above, an individual (I will call such an individual a "mindreader") who mentally represents *the seeing of a tree* by another individual is manifesting metarepresentation in Sense (1) noted above.

For Perner, metarepresentation should be more than this, and it is largely to Perner that we owe Sense (2) as defined above. For Perner, the criterion is that the mindreader "understands that the mind represents" (1991, p. 10). And since the most fundamental defining feature of representation is the prospect of *misrepresenting* reality, the criterion is operationalized when an individual comes to attribute *false beliefs* to another, as revealed in the now-famous "unexpected transfer" tests pioneered by Wimmer & Perner (1983) and Baron-Cohen, Leslie, & Frith (1985). It is in this sense that the mindreader represents representations *as representations*: that is, the mindreader represents the "representing relationship" between mind and reality, which incorporates the possibility of false representation. It seems appropriate to distinguish Sense 2 as *conceptual*: now, the mindreader can be said to have a concept of what mental representation and misrepresentation are.

This level of metarepresentation is one object of study in my ongoing primate experiments. However, until this year, attribution of false belief was the subject of only two reports in the literature, both resting upon only one-off tests with single subjects, and accordingly ambiguous results (Premack, 1988; Savage-Rumbaugh, 1997). In the present chapter, the focus instead will be on what has been distinguished above as Sense (1), an issue on which more empirical work has been done. Perner (1991) has proposed distinguishing the most advanced forms of this level of representational capacity as "secondary representation" rather than metarepresentation. I followed this usage and Perner's underlying rationale in a recent analysis of our current understanding of ape cognition in this area (Whiten, 1996a) and I shall refer to it again further below. However, I have introduced the notion of 're-representation' into the title of the present chapter, rather than 'secondary representation'. I think this may be a more apt label for what I want to examine as underlying the behavioural phenomena I am going to describe. I will return to a comparison of the concepts of secondary representation and re-representation later, but I will explain what I mean by re-representation next.

Metarepresentation and Re-representation

Consider the case where Tom thinks Samantha knows which of two locations contains hidden food, and on this basis he correctly predicts her success in finding it. This is because Tom saw Sam watch the food being hidden. This is a case of second-order representation, since Tom mentally represents Sam's representation of the food's location. However, let us suppose it is not metarepresentation in Sense (2), because Tom does not yet know that false beliefs exist (children attribute several other states of mind before false belief – e.g., Wellman, 1990). From Perner's perspective it is not appropriate to say Tom represents *Sam's representation* – Tom does not even know what a representation is, so he cannot represent Sam's representation *as a representation*.

If we add to this the obvious consideration that Tom is not indulging in telepathy and so has no direct access to Sam's representation of the situation, I suggest the term *re-representation* is perhaps more felicitous for describing what is happening in Tom's brain. Given there is no telepathy, Tom's brain must be classifying certain observable behavioural and environmental patterns – Sam watching the food being hidden in a particular container – as having the properties to which we attach the term "knowing." This is a case of *re-representation* in that Sam's representation gets *re*-represented, in its essential elements (i.e., those we would describe as Sam *knowing where the food is*) in Tom's brain, allowing Tom to make good predictions about Sam's behaviour: but this could be so even when it would be misleading to say that "Tom represents Sam's representations" because Tom lacks a concept of representation (i.e. Sense (2) of metarepresentation does not apply; e.g., Tom may not appreciate that Sam could *mis*-represent where the food is hidden).

We should also note that the process of re-representation does not necessarily require that Tom conceive of "mental states" that have such properties as being *internal, subjective, non-real* or *hypothetical*, all of which Wellman (1990; 1991) noted as coming to be ascribed in talk about states of mind once children have developed a rich enough language. In the most basic case of re-representation, Tom may need only to recognize the appropriate behaviour-situation patterns to classify Sam as being in a certain state (such as that which corresponds to "knowing" in the example above), so that critical features of Sam's mental representations get re-represented in Tom's brain. How this would work is best considered further with respect to evidence for particular cognitive capacities shown by both chimpanzees and humans, and thus, through inference, by ancestors the species share. We start with imitation.

Imitation

Imitation and Re-representation

Imitation is a promising candidate for manifestation of re-representation, because in a case of Tom imitating Sam, the representation which in Sam's brain guided Sam's act, is re-created (re-represented) in Tom's brain well enough that Tom looks to be doing an act with some resemblance to Sam's. Thus, as Sperber put it in drawing the link between mental representations and cultural transmission, "an idea, born in the brain of one individual, may have, in the brains of other individuals, descendants that resemble it" (1996, p. 1). In the case of imitation, the idea or representation at stake can be regarded as some kind of plan or program for the behaviour (Byrne, 1994; Whiten & Byrne, 1991; Whiten & Ham, 1992). Of course, such a process is unlikely to entail perfect replication. "Representations are transformed almost every time they are transmitted" (Sperber, 1996, p. 25). This is why Whiten and Ham (1992, p. 250) defined imitation as occurring when "B learns from A *some part* of the form of a behaviour" – by its very nature imitation is selective.

As explained earlier, this does not require that Tom, in imitating Sam, be seen as somehow directly "reading the mind" of Sam, nor that Tom has some understanding of the nature of representation: but like all mindreading done without benefit of telepathy, it will require an ability to *process information about others' actions and circumstances in special ways.* In seeing the relevant structure to be imitated, an imitator is inherently performing some level of analysis of what is going on in the mind of the model. This is necessary for the requirement to translate between the perspective-of-action of another and of oneself. However, as imitation varies in cognitive complexity within and between species, the sophistication of re-representation will vary, too, some levels approaching more closely the phenomena typically referred to as metarepresentation. We will shortly examine some of these in chimpanzees.

Consistent with such thoughts about imitation, several authors have examined possible links between imitation and "mindreading" (in the conventional sense of attributing mental states) in recent years. Whiten and Byrne (1991) noted that, although the evidence is controversial, several authorities have concluded that the evidence for both imitation and mindreading is stronger in the great apes (with whom we shared a common ancestor a few million years ago – about 5 to 7 Myr in the case of the chimpanzee) than in monkeys (with whom we shared more distant ancestors of the order of 30 Myr ago). That other aspects of cognition such as pretend play and mirror self-recognition fit this pattern too suggests the exciting possibility that all may be explained by some fundamental underlying cognitive capacity that has evolved in apes and that formed a platform for the later evolution of advanced metarepresentation in hominids (Suddendorf, 1998; 1999; Whiten, 1996a; Whiten & Byrne, 1991). This is discussed further below. Whiten and Byrne also pointed out that the signs of a phylogenetic correlation between imitation and mindreading raised a prediction worth exploring, that autistic individuals with deficits in mindreading might also have difficulties with imitation (see Whiten & Brown, 1999).

Coincidentally, in 1991 Rogers and Pennington published the first full review of studies of imitation in autism, and concluded that most studies did indeed find a deficit. Accordingly, they went on to elaborate a theory of the development of a theory of mind – and its malfunctioning in autism – in which imitative capacities played a foundational role. They proposed that the basis of what goes wrong in autism lies in impairment of a capacity for "formation/co-ordination of specific self-other representations" (1991, p. 152); in other words, the ability to translate between the representational perspectives of self and others. They suggested that from this a cascade of problems arises, beginning with impaired imitation and proceeding to other capacities, including theory of mind. The reference to "self-other representations" alerts us to the fact that such ideas may have relevance for the later emergence of the functions described as "metarepresentational" by workers like Leslie and Perner.

Additionally, Meltzoff and Gopnik (1993) have suggested that imitation in infancy may provide a device that facilitates the beginnings of mentalism, because in exercising heavily pre-prepared capacities to copy others' actions, infants are able to connect up seen behaviours (of others) with corresponding internal states such as feelings and plans (their own, when they imitate those seen behaviours); and this is very much what mindreading has to do – construct states of mind on the basis of observations of behaviour and other public events. Meltzoff and Gopnik's idea can be seen as one hypothetical scenario for the early phases of the developmental cascade proposed in Rogers and Pennington's analysis.

Lastly, it can be argued that one of the two main theories about how mindreading gets done should be expected to share particular links with imitation. This is the "simulation theory," so called because it posits that the mindreader guesses what will be going on in others' minds by simulating them. Such a mindreader in effect "puts themselves in the other's shoes" and from the way their own mind would operate in the situation faced by the other, constructs hypotheses about the other mind. Any simulation is, of course, a kind of copy or imitation of something else, so it is a natural inference that if simulation is important in mindreading, it might share cognitive resources with imitative processes,[1] and/or build on them developmentally. This subject is dealt with in detail by Goldman in this volume (and see also Mitchell, 1994). However, we must also note that others who see a developmental link between imitation and mindreading favour mindreading theories quite different to the "simulation" one (e.g., Gopnik & Meltzoff, 1997). I am not going to attempt to adjudicate between these alternatives here. Perhaps the fact that workers espousing such very divergent theories of mindreading are nevertheless eyeing links with imitation suggests that some fundamental connection of this kind deserves our further attention.

With these theoretical ideas in mind, we can examine some of the imitative capacities of chimpanzees, and then return to the question of how they relate to operations of re-representation and metarepresentation.

Imitation in Chimpanzees

In recent years, the study of imitation in animals has been both rejuvenated and cast into considerable turmoil (see Heyes & Galef, 1996, for a recent compilation). A variety of new methods and conceptual approaches applied to different species have generated claims as surprising to received wisdoms as that imitation is unproven in wild chimpanzees (Tomasello, 1990; 1996) or indeed in primates generally (Heyes, 1993b; 1998). In contrast, others have argued that apes, at least, have shown quite sophisticated forms of imitation (e.g., Miles, Mitchell, & Harper, 1996; Russon, 1997). There is not the space here to offer a comprehensive comparative analysis that does justice to this now-complex literature. I will instead summarize those positive findings which make fairly clear what chimpanzees *can* copy, emphasizing several aspects relevant to the complexity of re-representation.

(1) Functional Acts   One rigorous test we have developed is a naturalistic re-creation of the complex acts of food "processing" that wild primates sometimes have to do – peeling, poking, tearing and so on, to get into naturally protected foods like shelled fruits. Each subject watches a model open an "artificial fruit'" using one of two alternative techniques and we then measure the extent to which this biases the subject's own subsequent attempts in matching ways (Whiten, Custance, Gomez, Teixidor, & Bard, 1996). In such tests, chimpanzees show evidence of imitation but are typically quite selective in what they copy. For example, after watching a model who pokes a rod out of the way rather than an alternative model who pulls and twists it out, they may be more likely to poke it yet may do so by applying their own battery of approaches, like using their thumb or a stick. One might say that it is as if they read a certain level of copyable goal into the act ("get the rod poked out") but display intelligent flexibility in the way they construct their copy. However, an alternative hypothesis making no reference to reading of goals is that they perceive just that "poking gets the rod out." To differentiate these hypotheses, different experiments are required, such as that in which Meltzoff (1995) showed that human infants would extend their imitations to complete the acts that the model's behaviour had been aimed at but that were not actually achieved. Such experiments have not yet been published for apes, although they are being attempted.

(2) Sequential and Hierarchical Structures   Our artificial fruit has been designed so that the elements can be dealt with in different sequential

orders. Whiten (1998b) showed that after several observations, chimpanzees came to copy the sequential structure they had observed. What is of interest in the present context is that what they are copying is essentially the plan or schema that guides the models' performance. To be sure, these chimpanzees are watching behaviour and not mind; the point is that they are able to read in that behaviour an interesting aspect of mind, namely the specifying of sequential structure of component elements – and this gets re-represented in the mind of the imitator. How widespread in animals this ability is as yet we do not know; this is the first study to apply the test.

Byrne and Russon (1998) have hypothesized that apes and perhaps other animals may be able to discern and copy not only sequential but also hierarchical plans such as those underlying skilled actions. To discover if this is true requires a more complex test. We have now extended the sequence-testing approach to this, showing that 3-year old children copy such hierarchical plans (Whiten, 1999) but this has yet to be applied to apes.

(3) Unseen Body Parts   Custance, Whiten, & Bard (1995; Whiten & Custance, 1996) performed a rigorous replication of an earlier approach by Hayes and Hayes (1952) that has come to be called "Do-as-I-Do" (DAID), or "Simon says." Using a number of training actions, researchers encourage the subject, on a signal like "do this," to mimic whatever act the experimenter performs. Subjects are then tested on novel actions, of which Custance et al. (1995) used 48. The two young chimpanzees tested both achieved significant matching. What is of interest in the present context is that these youngsters were as able in copying actions they could not see (touching body parts they could not see, facial actions) as those they could see. In these cases, the re-representation involved does not rely on seeing a visual resemblance between other's acts and one's own, but translating between acts observed in others and the "felt" (i.e., kinaesthetically represented) equivalent in oneself (Heyes, 1993b; Mitchell, 1994). Recall that this linkage was the one Meltzoff and Gopnik (1993) proposed as a basis for the origins of children's mindreading. One possibility they suggested was that this kind of (re-representational) ability could mediate empathy. An obvious speculation that follows is that a linkage between visual-kinaesthetic matching and empathy might also obtain for chimpanzees. However, note that pigeons have been shown to imitate a model who operates a treadle either with their beak (which although they may be able to "see" it, clearly looks very different to the model's beak) or their foot (Zentall, Sutton, & Sherburne, 1996), so at least within the limits of well-rehearsed actions like this, the phenomenon may by a feature of avian and mammalian imitation.

(4) A Concept of Imitation?   It seems that the DAID test described above will only work if the subject can grasp something like a concept of imitation ("I am to *imitate* this new action presented") (Whiten, in press). This seems to imply a very general mental "set" that can map between the behavioural potentials of others and oneself, of the kind that could prepare the imitator to attend to targets of mindreading like others' attention and goals. It is therefore of interest that DAID evidence is available only for great apes amongst the primates (chimpanzees, as above; orang-utans, Miles et al., 1996; gorillas, Tanner & Byrne, 1998) – although admittedly only one (negative) attempt appears to have been made with a monkey (Mitchell & Anderson, 1993).

(5) Delayed Imitation   Tomasello, Savage-Rumbaugh, & Kruger (1993) found that when imitation followed almost immediately on an observed action, chimpanzees and young children performed at similar imitative levels: however, in tests involving a 24-hour delay, chimpanzees gave much stronger imitative responses than the children. Clearly, the re-representation process in this case is robust with respect to storage over periods this long and presumably longer.

(6) Novel Acts   Chimpanzees have been reported to imitate novel acts (Whiten & Ham, 1992 for a review) but we lack a good, systematic means of describing and measuring novelty. How "novel" is novel? As Whiten and Custance (1996) argued, imitated actions are unlikely to be completely novel, but instead will be derived from some abilities already in the repertoire. However, experimental studies have reported imitation which seems to parallel that expected in "novel" situations in natural conditions, such as opening a new fruit (Whiten et al., 1996) or using a new tool (Tomasello et al., 1993). In the latter study, subjects copied a wide range of relatively arbitrary actions done with objects, and this may be one way in which chimpanzees differ from various other non-primates that have imitated in experimental tests. In the latter, the actions have been both simple and few, as in the pigeon example of stepping or pecking a treadle, mentioned earlier. It looks as if chimpanzees, by contrast, have a relatively "open" copying system that can re-represent many different kinds of action schema. However, this remains to be systematically demonstrated.

Imitative re-representation of these kinds resembles mindreading in general insofar as it involves translating between the perspective of another and of oneself: to imitate, as to mindread, is to "stand in the other's shoes." I have attempted to draw out the ways in which, as imitation becomes sophisticated in the ways it is in chimpanzees, it involves re-representing processes which could well pave the way in both evolution and development for the construction of metarepresentations in both Senses (1) and (2). We now turn to "mindreading" proper.

Mindreading

Unlike imitation, a case of mindreading like "I know what you're thinking!" does not appear to require a lengthy explanation as to how it may qualify as a case of re-representation. If we read what is in another individual's mind, we shall be (re)representing, in our own mind, their mental representations. Examples of the representations we might read include their perceptions, knowledge, actions plans, intentions, and desires.[2]

However, when we get down to examining particular candidate cases of mindreading, particularly in nonverbal or preverbal organisms like chimpanzees and infants, the criteria for identifying mindreading and re-representation are not so self-evident. This is because when we study a candidate non-verbal mindreader in relation to another individual whose mind may be being read, we do not witness telepathy: however advanced the mindreader, they must read mind through observations of the behaviour and situation of the other; and we as scientists in turn can only conclude they are reading mind, or evidencing re-representation, by recording their capacity to make such discriminations. If all mindreading operates through such observables, the distinction between mentally representing another's representations, and representing their observable behaviour / situation, is not going to be an obvious or straightforward one (Whiten, 1996b). Let us first look at some recent experiments on what chimpanzees *do* discriminate. We can then consider for each set of findings what shall count as evidence of nonverbal re-representation.

The studies summarized below were undertaken at the Language Research Center of Georgia State University. Some of the chimpanzees at this facility are involved in "ape language" studies (Savage-Rumbaugh, 1986), some are not: but all live rich social lives in interaction with other chimpanzees and humans. Their social and physical situation makes them excellent subjects for studies of sophisticated aspects of social cognition. The experiments described below are selected from a series of "mindreading" and imitation studies, some of which focus on chimp-chimp interaction (e.g., staged deception) and others of which examine evidence of chimpanzee reading of human mind. What follows are examples of the latter, which happen to be at a more advanced stage of analysis.

Discrimination of States of Knowledge versus Ignorance in Chimpanzees

In a recent study, an approach pioneered by Gomez and Teixidor (1992: see Gomez 1996 and 1998 for details) was modified and applied in experiments with 3 chimpanzees: two adult males (Austin and Sherman) and one adolescent female (Panzee). All these subjects had previously been involved in language studies, in which they had learned to communicate with humans by selectively touching different keys in visual displays. In the course of this they had acquired "pointing" gestures which are not a natural part of chimpanzee behaviour in the wild, but which do seem to emerge without explicit training in some apes who undergo intensive interaction with humans (e.g., Call & Tomasello, 1994; Gomez, 1996). In the present study, a "point" did not need to look like the human version in which the index finger is extended and the other digits folded back (although Panzee did tend to point with the index finger extended beyond the others). It was sufficient that a gesture was used to direct a human's attention selectively at one object rather than another.

During the experiment, the chimpanzee subject was isolated from other chimpanzees in a large cage. The subject could see human interactors through the cage mesh and through a large window. Baseline, pre-experimental trials proceeded as follows. Experimenter A (the Hider) approached the cage with an attractive food item, took a key hanging in front of the cage, opened one of two boxes lying there a meter apart, put the food in it and, having locked the padlock again, put the key back on its hook and left. Experimenter B (the Helper) entered a minute or two later, stood between the boxes, looked at the chimpanzee subject and said, "Okay, Panzee (or appropriate name)." In the first few baseline trials, the Helper additionally invited the subject to indicate one of the boxes by reaching one hand to each and saying, "Which box?" All subjects immediately responded appropriately and the Helper then took the key, unlocked the box and gave the food to the subject. After a few trials, the Helper needed only stand between the two boxes on entering and the subject would indicate the baited box.

Panzee received 100 of these baseline trials. Experimental trials, together with further controls, were interspersed amongst the last 80 of these baseline trials. In an experimental trial, it was the Helper, instead of the Hider, who entered bearing food. Like the Hider, the Helper unlocked one box, baited it, put the key back on its hook, and left. A minute or two later, the person who was usually the Hider entered. In the first of such trials, Panzee pointed to the baited box, apparently assuming that the Helper and Hider had just changed roles. The Hider, ignoring this, took the key from its hook and, jingling it so it was obvious to the subject what he was doing, took the key to a novel location visible to the subject and left it there. In 10 experimental trials, 7 different locations were used, with 3 locations being used twice. New locations included a stool behind the far side of the cage, a fire-extinguisher hook to the right of the cage and a bolt behind where the Hider and Helper usually stood with the boxes.

It will be apparent that in experimental trials the epistemic status of the Helper was reversed with respect to the usual situation obtaining in the baseline situation. In baseline trials the Helper was knowledgeable about the location of the key, which was always in its habitual position (the first 20 baseline trials established this as routine), but they were ignorant of which box was baited. In the experimental trials, by contrast, the Helper knew which box was baited (because they had done the baiting themselves), but they did not know the whereabouts of the key, because they were absent when the Hider moved it. The critical question was whether the subject would recognize that in experimental trials the Helper needed information on the whereabouts of the key rather than the choice of box.

Panzee's response was quite startling. In the very first experimental trial, in which the key was put behind the cage, she sat near it, and as the Helper arrived, pointed to it. In the first 9 experimental trials, she likewise indicated the new location of the key.

This behaviour was thus consistent and quite different to that in the baseline trials. However, Panzee did point to the key, as well as the box, in 13 of the 100 baseline trials. One possible interpretation of this behaviour is that she was not *informing* a human perceived as ignorant (needing information), but rather signalling to them to *encourage* them to act on a useful part of the environment (such that we might paraphrase her communication as proto-imperatives: "Get that key" and "Open that box"). Under this interpretation, moving the key in experimental trials so that it was further from the experimenter could have led Panzee to be keener to signal "Get the key." For this reason, an additional series of controls was run, also interspersed amongst the last 80 baseline trials. In these, the Helper entered, opened both boxes (leaving their padlocks loose) and moved the key to a new location. He then left. The Hider then entered, baited one of the boxes, locked both boxes and left without needing to handle the key at all. In these control trials, the key was thus moved to a new location just as it was in experimental trials, yet epistemically the Helper was in the same situation as baseline trials, knowing the whereabouts of the key but not which box to open. Significantly, in all but 2 trials, Panzee indicated only the correct box and not the new key location.

In a prior study which inspired this experiment, Gomez (1996) reported that an orang-utan likewise came to preferentially indicate the new location of the key, rather than (as had been appropriate in baseline trials) the correct one of two baskets. However, she did not do this in the first six trials: in these she began to point to the key only after the human had begun to search in the (incorrect) old location. Then she began quite consistently to point to the key first. Gomez comments that this performance was impressive insofar as "a relatively brief exposure to the consequences of false-belief situations seemed to lead to the development of some understanding" (Gomez, 1996, p. 340). The two other subjects in the present experiment, Austin and Sherman, passed through similar phases, shifting from pointing to the key only after the Helper began to search in the wrong location, to providing the required information from the start. As reported above, Panzee, by contrast, made the critical distinctions from the start, so for her there was no possible role for trial-and-error discovery of the optimal strategy during the experiment.

In sum, Panzee entered the experiment with a capacity already in place to discriminate those occasions on which the Helper was ignorant from those in which he was knowledgeable about the key location. She appeared to appreciate that in the ignorant condition, he needed information and she supplied it to him. There is thus an important sense in which she must be said to be evidencing re-representation: those of her representations which informed her pointing actions discriminated between representational states of the Helper in which the location of the key was respectively known or unknown. As noted in the early part of this paper, this does not imply metarepresentation in strong Sense (2): it does not imply that Panzee has concepts of representation or misrepresentation. Nor does it require that Panzee has any idea about a causal role for states which are "internal," "subjective," "non-real," or "hypothetical" (recall my earlier reference to Wellman, 1990, p. 20), which is what some authorities might feel mental metarepresentation should entail. Of course, it does not argue that she definitely does *not* see the distinction in this way: but what it does seem to imply is that, Panzee *in effect* must be re-representing the relative ignorance / knowledge state the helper is in, although she does it, of course, by discriminating those observables you and I would use to discriminate what we would call "knowledge" and "ignorance" in the Helper, such as whether an individual is present or absent when a critical object is moved to an unexpected location.

These are not the first experiments to investigate the ability of chimpanzees to discriminate between states of ignorance and knowledge in others. Previous attempts have produced a mixture of positive (Premack, 1988; Povinelli, Nelson, & Boysen, 1990) and negative results (Povinelli, Rulf, &Bierschwale 1994). But the positive ones, under close scrutiny, are vulnerable to the explanation of fast learning of non-psychological cues ("Avoid the person with the covering over their head, choose the other one to help you find the hidden food") (Heyes, 1993a; Povinelli, 1994; Whiten, 1993a). In addition, in one extensive investigation, young chimpanzees showed a poor understanding of the conditions of "seeing," warranting scepticism about the possibility they would recognize seeing-knowing linkages (Povinelli & Eddy, 1996a). This would suggest that Panzee's performance represents a rather exceptional case, perhaps reflecting the impact of her intensive experience of human enculturation. Alternatively it can be argued (paralleling similar debates over the role of enculturation in the ontogeny of imitation – Tomasello et al., 1993; Whiten, 1993b) that the richness of her social life may have recreated critical aspects of that experienced by wild chimpanzees, to a greater extent than for subjects in other experiments, who may, in some cases, have been reared in socially unchallenging captive conditions. Only further studies will clarify this.

Attending to What Others Attend to

Joint attention is of particular interest with respect to "borderlines," where apes or infants begin to act in ways which indicate they are mentally re-representing. This is partly because, unlike the knowledge / ignorance distinction, which rather obviously falls within the scope of mental representation, "attention" lies in a relatively grey area. At one level it can just refer to looking behaviour: to say I am attending to one object rather than another may mean only that my gaze falls on it. On the other hand, to recognize that someone may need to *notice* something before they can know about it or act on it in certain ways is to take account of a representational aspect of their psychology. Accordingly, Baron-Cohen (1991; 1995) has suggested that the operation of a capacity for shared attention in the human infant's second year is an important precursor to a later-emerging representational theory of mind – two developmental stages which probably map to the way I have distinguished metarepresentation in Senses (1) versus (2). Evidence supporting Baron-Cohen's model of the mindreading system comes from the sequence observed in normal development and the deficits and delays observed in autism. Failure to establish joint attention appears to predict later problems in attributing false beliefs, which tend to be associated with autism (Baron-Cohen, 1995; Baron-Cohen, Allen, & Gillberg, 1992).

The establishment of joint attention also shares some of the characteristics of imitation and thus underlines some of the discussions about the nature of re-representation discussed earlier. If one individual attends to a given object, and a second individual manages to share that attentional focus, there is an obvious sense in which they are actually imitating the other – they are "doing the same thing," with respect to the same locus; however, as in the case of imitation of other manual or bodily actions, successful joint attention involves *translating* from the action-perspective of the other to one's own.

The human infant's capacity for establishing joint attention provides the starting point for the ape study summarized here (see also Whiten, 1998a). By the time they are 18 months old, human infants can not only track another's visual attention, but can somehow integrate the utterances and attentional focus of another person so as to learn new names for objects that this person has talked about (Baldwin, 1993). This led Baldwin and Moses to argue that "by the beginning of the second year, infants have a dawning appreciation of the mentalistic significance of attentional information as in index of the other's psychological engagement and referential intentions" (1994, p. 150), because this is what is required for infants to connect up what the other is saying and the phenomenon in the world they are attending to, and thus talking *about*. Baldwin and Moses suggest that "between 12 and 18 months of age a fledgling understanding of attention as something like a psychological spotlight that can be intentionally directed at external objects and events has begun to emerge" (1994, p. 151).

Since I was working with apes who could also name objects using their keyboards (each "name" is an abstract symbol on a specific key – a "lexigram"), I conducted a related series of experiments on joint attention. The basic design of the first experiment was extremely simple, and depended on the fact that these apes are typically asked for the name of an object by physically tapping it and/or holding it up before them. For the experiment, a number of objects which the ape could name by lexigram were suspended between the subject and the human experimenter in an archlike arrangement (Whiten, 1998a). The experimenter then called the subject's name to get their attention, and turned to look at one of the objects, asking "what's that?" This was a new experience for the two subjects studied, Austin and Sherman. The question in this experiment was whether this would make immediate sense to the ape, or be a meaningless question, such that the ape would simply wait for some object to be physically highlighted, and / or would respond randomly.

In the event, both subjects named the first four objects presented almost perfectly, and continued in this fashion when the objects were rearranged and the questions repeated. Already at this stage of the study, they correctly named the objects well above chance levels. Thus, the answer to the first question was positive: it seemed natural to these apes to identify as the object of the experimenter's question the object upon which the experimenter's visual attention was focused. This suggests that the apes are interpreting gaze as the kind of psychological spotlight referred to by Baldwin and Moses, which can be used to identify the referent of the gazer's utterances. Put in the terms of this chapter, as expressed earlier with respect to the reading of knowledge and ignorance, the apes appear to be re-representing – that is, mentally representing the referential focus of the experimenter.

Further experiments have explored the scope of this 'joint referential space' which ape and experimenter can share. This is important because one of the ways in which mindreading can be distinguished from "mere behaviour reading" lies in the extent to which a state of mind is fluently read across different contexts, an idea discussed at length elsewhere under the heading of "mental states as intervening variables" (Whiten, 1993a; 1994; 1996b; Dennett, 1996). In the case of attention, the idea here would be that reading attention as a "state of mind" means that the mindreader recognizes that state as the unifying attribute of many different physical observables (e.g. pointing at, naming, gazing intently at), which in turn can be used to make many different predictions and interpretations of the attender's further actions (such as what object they are talking about, what they want, and so on).

Accordingly, further experiments have shown that the chimpanzees interpret the experimenter's actions in a similar way to that described above if (1) the object attended to is behind the ape, so they cannot immediately see it but have to turn to do so; or (2) the experimenter turns his back on the ape and asks about objects now in front of both experimenter and ape. In this last case the ape can only see the back of the experimenter's head, but seems to "read" a similar significance to that derived from viewing the experimenter's eyes and face. However if the experimenter faced the subject and used only eye movements (rather than the usual eye and head movements) to focus on a target, subjects' performance dropped to chance levels. This seems consistent with the findings of a suite of experiments conducted by Povinelli & Eddy (1996a), which found that chimpanzees made surprisingly little use of specific cues about the eyes (e.g., open versus closed) in choosing which of two partners to communicate with to elicit help in obtaining food rewards. The results as a whole suggest a curious mixture of reading attentional focus as a representational state across physically quite diverse expressions of it, together with a lack of finesse about details of what the eyes are doing specifically.

Pretence

The focus of Leslie's (1987) influential paper on metarepresentation was links between the nature of pretence and theory of mind. Probably many reading this book will be familiar with the paper, and if not they are encouraged to assimilate it. From it I have earlier derived and discussed links between imitation, mindreading and pretence in some depth (Whiten & Byrne, 1991; Whiten, 1996a). Accordingly, I shall here attempt only to highlight key points, adding one interesting new observation of relevance.

Leslie suggested that in the pretend play of 2-year-old children we may see the earliest signs of the metarepresentational ability that eventually develops into the core of the child's theory of mind. Leslie's rationale began by pointing out that in such a case as pretending that an empty cup contains juice, a child cannot simply be "representing the cup as full." To avoid becoming hopelessly confused about reality, the child must maintain a primary representation of the true status of what is being pretended about (e.g., an empty cup) along with a pretend representation derived from this (a full cup). Thus, pretend representations are second-order representations of primary representations of reality, and

Leslie referred to them as metarepresentations. That this is an appropriate conclusion has been disputed, notably by Perner (1991), who, preferring the Sense (2) of metarepresentation outlined at the opening to this chapter, saw metarepresentation as too sophisticated an ascription for the 2-year-old child engaged in pretence. Readers are directed to Harris (1994); Harris, Lillard, & Perner (1994); Lillard (1994); Perner, Baker, & Hutton (1994); Suddendorf (1999); and Whiten (1996a) for further discussion and debate on this. Here, I shall note only that if we stick to Sense (1) of metarepresentation and ask whether some kind of re-representation is involved in pretence, the answer seems to be "yes." All pretence appears to involve a cognitive manipulation of already existing primary representations.

If early pretence is truly a metarepresentational precursor to a full-blown theory of mind, deficits in the former should be associated with deficits in the latter. That this is seen in autism was interpreted by Leslie (1987) as supporting his case. Turning to animal cognition, the empirical prediction would be that associated with the imitative and mindreading evidence of re-representation would be signs of pretence. However, as Leslie (1987) made clear, we need to apply quite severe criteria for the kind of pretence of interest. If a child is suspected to be pretending an empty glass is full of juice, strong evidence that the child is truly operating with secondary representations, cognitively marked as pretence, is obtained if the child can generate logical implications from those representations. For example, we jog the child's arm so the pretend juice should "spill"; if the child then acts as if mopping up the spillage, we have good evidence the child is truly pretending, and not just acting out some convention she has learned, or has simply not noticed the glass is empty. Do we see anything like this in chimpanzees?

There are two sources of relevant evidence. The first concerns pretend play, the same category considered by Leslie. Here, the most compelling cases come from chimpanzees living with humans, surrounded by human artefacts. Ethologists studying chimpanzees in the wild may sometimes suspect pretence (Goodall, 1986) but it is difficult to tell, because the chimpanzees are generally doing things in the species' general repertoire, operating with materials surrounding them every day. In the richness of a human environment, the novel response required by Leslie's criteria can become more tangible. There are just a handful of resulting observations in the literature, summarized by Whiten and Byrne (1991) and Whiten (1996a). The best illustration continues to be that described by Hayes (1951) in which a young chimpanzee, Viki, on several occasions acted as if dragging an imaginary pull-toy (she also had real ones). The most remarkable observation was that when the string appeared to get tangled around something, Viki acted as if she had thus got stuck and made motions as if untangling the string.

Until recently, all such observations have come from captive animals, as noted above. However, Wrangham in Wrangham and Peterson (1996) described an intriguing case in wild chimpanzees. An adult male, Kakama, carried a small log as if it were an infant. The male took the log up a tree, placed it in a series of nests he made and manipulated it in ways that mothers are sometimes seen to do with their infants. He continued to carry it later. Mindful that his interpretation that the male was pretending the log was an infant was fanciful, Wrangham kept his observation to himself. However, returning to the field at a later time, he found that his Ugandan field assistants had not only made a similar observation but also interpreted it in the same way, collecting the new log and displaying it in camp with a label, "Kakama's toy baby."

Apart from pretend play, the other kind of evidence relevant to pretence in primates is deception. Whiten and Byrne (1988) collated data contributed by field primatologists describing *tactical deception*, in which the perpetrator shows behaviour borrowed from its normal, honest context, performing it in a context in which others are misled. By far the largest corpus of records concerned chimpanzees, a finding amplified in a second survey that generated a total of 253 records (Byrne & Whiten, 1990). However, as in pretend play, if we are interested in re-representation of reality we need to ask whether the perpetrators of such deception are operating in a "pretend" mode, showing appropriate adjustments of behavior to maintain the pretence appropriately in the face of novel events. A possible case of this occurred when the bonobo Kanzi hid a key, later retrieving it and escaping from his enclosure (Savage-Rumbaugh & McDonald, 1988). In the interim, Savage-Rumbaugh searched for the key. When invited to help, Kanzi went through the appropriate searching motions – in other words, pretending to search (at a time when, because of his earlier and later acts, it seems evident he had a clear primary representation of reality that would making searching needless from his own point of view). However, as with pretend play, such detailed records are relatively rare and because they are so opportunistic they tend not to be backed up by video records or the possibility of inter-observer reliabilities. Pretence seems so inherently spontaneous that (unlike phenomena like imitation) it does not lend itself to experimental testing. Thus these few observations tantalizingly suggest that chimpanzees may be capable of the relevant kinds of pretence, but do not substantiate it. Perhaps the fact that the evidence is so thin and fragile is simply telling us that chimps are not sophisticated pretenders; certainly, pretence does not leap out at us when we watch young chimpanzees playing, as it does when we watch 2-year-old children. However, I think it more appropriate to conclude that at present we cannot be sure of the true situation, for few observers have so far recognized what criteria they really need to be watching for and recording.

Summary and Conclusions

Re-representation, Secondary Representation, Metarepresentation

I have outlined aspects of chimpanzee cognition that are relevant to the existence of what I called re-representation – mental representations whose content derives from other mental representations either in one-self or in others. Phenomena generally described as mindreading are classic examples of this. Additionally I suggested that imitation fits the bill because in imitation a representation in one mind gets copied into another mind (with varying degrees of fidelity – but all varieties of re-representation may risk loss of information). Finally, in pretence, reality is re-represented in a pretend form.

I am presenting re-representation as the most basic form of metarepresentation. Some authorities will be unhappy with that, as in the case where they prefer the definition of metarepresentation I described at the outset as Sense (2). However, more important than agreement on whether these phenomena fall neatly in or out of the complex concept of metarepresentation is the proposition that they share interesting features with it. Those who would exclude the phenomena I have outlined from their (presumably more advanced) conception of metarepresentation may nevertheless wish to consider the role that these phenomena may have in attainment of metarepresentation as they define it, from both an ontogenetic and evolutionary perspective. As we have noted, developmental psychologists have already suggested that advanced metarepresentational abilities seen in 4-year-old children have potential precursors in pretend play in the second year, and / or in joint attention and imitation in even earlier phases of infancy.

As mentioned above, I had earlier adopted Perner's (1991) concept and terminology of *secondary representation* as the hypothesized kind of process (metarepresentation "sense-1") underlying the mindreading, imitation and pretence examplars I am discussing (Whiten, 1996b). Interestingly, Suddendorf (1998, 1999) has independently come to very similar conclusions, working from Perner's scheme and relating it to phylogenetic patterns in cognition including mindreading, pretence and imitation, as well as other phenomena (as did Whiten & Byrne, 1991; and see also Gallup, 1982). Such convergencies of thought offer strong support that these ideas about secondary representation may be on the right lines. However, I need to say why, in a field overrun with terminology, I have here preferred another expression, "re-representation." [3]

First, I should clarify the fact that in using "secondary representation" (Whiten, 1996a) I was not disputing Leslie's analysis (as Perner did); rather, I was acknowledging the distinction between metarepresentation Sense (1) and Sense (2), as discriminated earlier in this chapter, and using 'secondary representation' as a convenient label consistent with Sense (1). I thought it could then be clearer to suggest (as does Suddendorf, 1999) that ape data appeared consistent with secondary representation, rather than to use the term 'metarepresentation' (with its ambiguous two meanings) as had Whiten and Byrne (1991).

By referring here to re-representation, however, I am aiming to expand the hypothesis about what cognitive components are fundamentally related, beyond the term "secondary representation" and the connotations Perner attaches to it. What the concept of re-representation emphasizes, as used throughout this chapter, is that we are talking of some variant of second-order representation in all cases. One important aspect of this is to encompass what is shared not only between mindreading and pretence (a linkage analyzed by both Leslie 1987 and Perner 1991) but also with imitation (to which attention has been drawn by others concerned with the origins of mindreading, like R. Mitchell, Meltzoff, Gopnik, Rogers and Pennington, discussed earlier, as well as by Goldman in this volume). Another, related feature of re-representation is that it points to the continuity that exists between the mindreading achievements of the 2-year-old and the 5-year-old child. Perner describes the core of secondary representation in the 2-year-old as handling "multiple models" of reality, which describes the hypothetical constructions of pretence well but is less successful is denoting that mindreading even at this stage is a second-order representational process in which others' states of mind get re-represented in the mindreading child's mind – it is just that at a later stage of development, more sophisticated states (false beliefs) will be recognized.

The Ontogenetic and Phylogenetic Patterns

The hypothesis in my earlier paper (Whiten, 1996a) and in Suddendorf (1999) was that, in the same way that an ontogenetic stage of secondary representation encompasses a suite of cognitive achievements, so too with a phylogenetic stage associated with the evolution of great apes. Since these achievements have been hypothesized to be important in the emergence of more sophisticated metarepresentation in later stages of human development, such abilities existing in the ancestors we share with apes could have also played pivotal roles in the evolution of these human metarepresentational capacities. At present, empirical data are sufficient to support the development of this hypothesis about the ape mind, but not adequate to test it; on this score little more can be said to add to the findings reviewed in my 1996 paper. In the present chapter I have been concerned instead with discussing how these various capacities relate to the notion of metarepresentation. Accordingly I end with only the briefest summary of the status of current evidence.

Taking pretence first, the evidence is thinnest for this category. There appears little scope for experimentation to clarify the situation, but it is to be hoped that analyses like the present chapter and related papers will stimulate observers to record the critical data required.

By contrast, the evidence concerning recognition of states of mind by chimpanzees continues steadily to accumulate, with a greater variety of researchers becoming involved than in the early 1990s (Heyes, 1998; Povinelli, 1996; Whiten, 1997; 1998a, for reviews). Consistent with the idea that apes may be able to mindread at levels corresponding to early childhood are positive results concerning the recognition of intention (Call & Tomasello, 1998) and attention (Povinelli & Eddy, 1996b; Whiten study described in subsection "Attending to What Others Attend to," above), and negative results concerning the much more advanced ability of attributing false beliefs (Call & Tomasello, in press). On the developmentally intermediate issues of discriminating ignorance and knowledge states and the seeing-knowing linkage, there are contradictory negative and positive results (Boysen, 1998; Povinelli & Eddy, 1996a).

The position on imitation is different, because although some data clearly show chimpanzee imitation, as reviewed above, there are also surprising negative findings (Tomasello, 1996, for a review). At the same time, there is evidence for various kinds of imitation in other birds and mammals (although little for monkeys: Custance et al., 1999). The interpretation I favor is that, because of this phylogenetic distribution, imitation is an interesting candidate for the earliest of the evolutionary stages through which re-representation became more complex. Chimpanzees' imitation appears to have become particularly sophisticated in the re-representations it can perform, as discussed above. This suggests that our common ancestor with the chimpanzee had advanced imitative capacities that may have been elaborated into other re-representational abilities in the hominid lineage.

Notes

1 Neurons that respond similarly to actions of one's self and others (e.g., a similar hand movement) have been called "monkey see, monkey do" cells, raising the prospect that they may be implicated in imitation (Carey, 1996; Carey, Perrett, & Oram, 1997). Interestingly, with respect to the present discussion, Gallese and Goldman (1998) have argued that such cells (which they call "mirror neurons") may function in mindreading by simulation.

2 In the developmental literature, it is sometime implied that certain mental states are non-representational. For example, Wellman (1990; 1991) argues this for states of desire. I, and at least some philosophers (Campbell, 1992), find this puzzling. If we take Wellman's example of recognizing that another individual has a desire for an apple, it would seem difficult to represent this without denoting that the desire is about (and thus has embedded in it a representation of) the apple (rather than a pear, or perhaps some other apple).

3 The term 're-representation' is also used by Karmiloff-Smith (1992). Karmiloff-Smith proposes that "a specifically human way to gain knowledge is for the mind to exploit internally the information that it has already stored (both innate and acquired), by redescribing its representations or, more precisely, by iteratively re-representing in different representational formats what its internal representations represent" (pp. 15–16). Implicit information is first re-represented as explicit knowledge, which involves compression to a more abstract representation. This in turn may be re-represented through higher explicit levels, the highest of which support verbal report of what is represented. How does this scheme relate to "re-representation" as I have used it? The crucial scope of Karmiloff-Smith's analysis appears to be processes of re-representation occurring within the individual. For this reason, our perspectives appear to align (and with Leslie's too) in the case of pretence; the concept of primary representations being re-represented as pretence representations seems to correspond to implicit representations of reality being re-represented as explicit pretended representations. However, it is less clear how Karmiloff-Smiths' model maps to re-representations that are inter-individual, like mindreading and imitation, because it is not apparent how (or if) these processes of re-representation should always correspond to a step up Karmiloff-Smith's hierarchy.

References

Baldwin, D. A. (1993) Infants' ability to consult the speaker for clues to word reference. *Journal of Child Language 20*, 395–418.

Baldwin, D. A., & Moses, L. J. (1994). Early understanding of referential intent and attentional focus: Evidence from language and emotion. In C. Lewis & P. Mitchell (Eds.), *Children's early understanding of mind* (pp. 133–156). Hillsdale, NJ: Erlbaum.

Baron-Cohen, S. (1991). Precursors to a theory of mind: Understanding attention in others. In A. Whiten (Ed.), *Natural theories of mind* (pp. 233–251). Oxford: Basil Blackwell.

Baron-Cohen, Simon (1995). *Mindblindness: An essay on autism and theory of mind.* Cambridge, Mass.: Bradford/MIT Press.

Baron-Cohen, S., Allen, J., & Gillberg, C. (1992). Can autism be detected at 18 months? The needle, the haystack and the CHAT. *British Journal of Psychiatry 161*, 839–843.

Baron-Cohen, S., Leslie, A. M., & Frith, U. (1985). Does the autistic child have a 'theory of mind'? *Cognition 21*, 37–46.

Baron-Cohen, Simon, Tager-Flusberg, Helen, & Cohen, Donald J., Eds. (1993). *Understanding other minds: Perspectives from autism.* Oxford: Oxford University Press.

Bogdan, Radu (1997). *Interpreting minds: The evolution of a practice.* Cambridge, MA: MIT Press.

Boysen, S. T. (1998, August). Attribution processes in chimpanzees: heresy, hearsay or heuristic? Paper presented at the 17th Congress of the International Primatological Society, Antananarivo, Madagascar.

Byrne, R. W. (1994). The evolution of intelligence. In P. J. B. Slater & T. R. Halliday (Eds.), *Behaviour and Evolution* (pp. 223–265). Cambridge: Cambridge University Press.

Byrne, R. W. (1997). The technical intelligence hypothesis: An additional evolutionary stimulus to intelligence? In A. Whiten & R.W. Byrne (Eds.), *Machiavellian intelligence II: Extensions and evaluations* (pp. 289–311). Cambridge: Cambridge University Press.

Byrne, R. W., & Russon, A. E. (1998). Learning by imitation: A hierarchical approach. *Behavioral and Brain Sciences 21*, 667–721.

Byrne, R. W., & Whiten, A. (1990). Tactical deception in primates: The 1990 database. *Primate Report 27*, 1–101.

Call, J., & Tomasello, M. (1994). Production and comprehension of referential pointing by orangutans (*Pongo pygmaeus*). *Journal of Comparative Psychology 108*, 307–317.

Call, J., & Tomasello, M. (1998). Distinguishing intentional from accidental actions in orangutans (*Pongo pygmaeus*), chimpanzees (*Pan troglodytes*), and human children (*Homo sapiens*). *Journal of Comparative Psychology 112*, 192–206.

Call, J., & Tomasello, M. (in press). A non-verbal false belief task: The performance of children and great apes. *Child Development.*

Campbell, J. (1992). Paper presented at New College Interdisciplinary Conference on Mindreading, Oxford.

Carey, D. P. (1996). "Monkey see, monkey do" cells. *Current Biology 6*, 1087–1088.

Carey, D. P., Perrett, D., & Oram, M. (1997). Recognising, understanding and reproducing action. In F. Boller & J. Grafman (Eds.), *Handbook of Neuropsychology*: Vol. 11. Elsevier Science, B.V.

Carruthers, P., & Smith, P. K. (1996a). Introduction. In P. Carruthers & P. K. Smith (Eds.), *Theories of theories of mind* (pp. 1–8). Cambridge: Cambridge University Press.

Carruthers, Peter, & Smith, Peter K. (1996b). *Theories of theories of mind*. Cambridge: Cambridge University Press.

Custance, D. M., Whiten, A., & Bard, K. A. (1994) The development of gestural imitation and self-recognition in chimpanzees (*Pan troglodytes*) and children. In J. J. Roeder, B. Thierry, J. R. Anderson & N. Herrenschmidt (Eds.), *Current primatology: Selected proceedings of the 14th congress of the International Primatological Society, Strasbourg: Vol. 2. Social development, learning, and development* (pp. 381–387). Strasbourg, France: Université Louis Pasteur.

Custance, D. M., Whiten, A., & Bard, K. A. (1995). Can young chimpanzees imitate arbitrary actions? Hayes and Hayes (1952) revisited. *Behaviour 132*, 839–858.

Custance, D. M., Whiten, A., & Fredman, T. (1999). Social learning of a two-action artificial fruit task in capuchin monkeys. *Journal of Comparative Psychology 113*, 1–11.

Dennett, Daniel C. (1996). *Kinds of minds*. Cambridge, MA: Bradford Books.

Gallese, V., & Goldman, A. (1998). Mirror neurons and the simulation theory of mind-reading. *Trends in Cognitive Sciences 2*, 493–501.

Gallup, G. G. (1982). Self-awareness and the evolution of mind in primates. *American Journal of Primatology 2*, 237–248.

Gomez, J.-C. (1996). Nonhuman primate theories of (nonhuman primate) minds: some issues concerning the origins of mindreading. In P. Carruthers & P. K. Smith (Eds.), *Theories of theories of mind* (pp. 330–343). Cambridge: Cambridge University Press.

Gomez, J.-C. (1998). Assessing theory of mind with nonverbal procedures: Problems with training methods and an alternative "key" procedure. *Behavioral and Brain Sciences 21*, 119–120.

Gomez, J.-C., & Teixidor, P. (1992, August). Theory of mind in an orangutan: A nonverbal test of false-belief appreciation? Paper presented at the 14th Congress of the International Primatological Society, Strasbourg, France.

Goodall, Jane (1986). *The chimpanzees of Gombe: Patterns of behaviour.* Cambridge, MA: Harvard University Press.

Gopnik, Alison, & Meltzoff, Andrew (1997). *Words, thoughts and theories.* Cambridge, MA: MIT Press.

Gregory, Richard (1996). *Eye and brain,* 5th ed. London: World University Library. (Original work published 1966.)

Harris, P. L. (1994). Understanding pretence. In C. Lewis & P. Mitchell (Eds.),*Children's early understanding of mind: Origins and development* (pp. 235–259). Hove, Sussex: Erlbaum.

Harris, P. L., Lillard, A., & Perner, J.(1994). Triangulating pretence and belief. In C. Lewis & P. Mitchell (Eds.), *Children's early understanding of mind: Origins and development* (pp. 287–293). Hove, Sussex: Erlbaum.

Hayes, Catherine (1951). *The ape in our house.* New York: Harper & Row.

Hayes, K. J., & Hayes, C. (1952). Imitation in a home-reared chimpanzee.*Journal of Comparative Psychology 45*, 450–459.

Heyes, C. M. (1993a). Anecdotes, training, trapping and triangulating: Do animals attribute mental states? *Animal Behaviour 46*, 177–188.

Heyes, C. M. (1993b) Imitation, culture and cognition. *Animal Behaviour 46*, 999–1010.

Heyes, C. M. (1998). Theory of mind in nonhuman primates.*Behavioral and Brain Sciences 21*, 101–148.

Heyes, C. M., Dawson, G. R., & Nokes, T. (1992). Imitation in rats: Initial responding and transfer evidence. *Quarterly Journal of Experimental Psychology 45b*, 59–71.

Heyes, Celia M., & Galef, Bennett G., Jr., Eds. (1996). *Social learning in animals: The roots of culture.* London: Academic Press.

Karmiloff-Smith, Annette (1992). *Beyond modularity: A developmental perspective on cognitive science.* Cambridge, MA: MIT Press.

Leslie, A. M. (1987). Pretense and representation in infancy: The origins of "theory of mind." *Psychological Review 94*, 84–106.

Leslie, A. M. (1991). The theory of mind impairment in autism: Evidence for a modular mechanism of development? In A. Whiten (ed.) *Natural theories of mind: Evolution, development and simulation of everyday mindreading* (pp. 63–78). Oxford: Basil Blackwell.

Lewis, Charlie, & Mitchell, Peter, Eds. (1994). *Children's early understanding of mind: Origins and development.* Hove, Sussex: Erlbaum.

Lillard, A. (1994). Making sense of pretence. In C. Lewis & P. Mitchell (Eds.),*Children's early understanding of mind: Origins and development* (pp. 211–234). Hove, Sussex: Lawrence Erlbaum.

Meltzoff, A. N. (1995). Understanding the intentions of others: Re-enactment of intended acts by 18-month-old children. *Developmental Psychology 31*, 838–850.

Meltzoff, A. N. & Gopnik, A. (1993). The role of imitation in understanding persons and developing a theory of mind. In S. Baron-Cohen, H. Tager-Flusberg & J. D. Cohen (Eds.), *Understanding other minds: Perspectives from autism.* Oxford: Oxford University Press.

Miles, H. L., Mitchell, R. W., & Harper, S. E. (1996). Simon says: The development of imitation in an enculturated orangutan. In A. E. Russon, K. A. Bard, & S. T. Parker (Eds.), *Reaching into thought: The minds of the great apes* (pp. 278–299). Cambridge: Cambridge University Press.

Mitchell, P., & Lewis, C. (1994). Critical issues in children's early understanding of mind. In C. Lewis & P. Mitchell (Eds.), *Children's early understanding of mind: Origins and development* (pp. 1–16). Hove, Sussex: Erlbaum.

Mitchell, R. W. (1994). The evolution of primate cognition: simulation, self-knowledge, and knowledge of other minds. In D. Quiatt & J. Itani (Eds.), *Hominid culture in primate perspective* (pp. 177–232). Colorado: University Press of Colorado.

Mitchell, R. W., & Anderson, J. R. (1993). Discrimination learning of scratching, but failure to obtain imitation and self-recognition in a long-tailed macaque. *Primates 34*, 301–309.

Moore, B. R. (1992). Avian movement imitation and a new form of mimicry: tracing the evolution of a complex form of learning. *Behaviour 122*, 231–262.

Parker, S. T. (1990). Origins of comparative developmental evolutionary studies of primate mental abilities. In S. T. Parker & K. R. Gibson (Eds.), *"Language" and intelligence in monkeys and apes: Comparative developmental perspectives* (pp. 3–64). Cambridge: Cambridge University Press.

Parker, S. T., & Gibson, K. R., Eds. (1990). *"Language" and intelligence in monkeys and apes: Comparative developmental perspectives.* Cambridge: Cambridge University Press.

Perner, J. (1988). Developing semantics for theories of mind: From propositional attitudes to mental representation. In J. W. Astington, P. L. Harris, & D. R. Olson, (Eds.), *Developing Theories of Mind* (pp. 141–172). Cambridge: Cambridge University Press.

Perner, Josef (1991). *Understanding the representational mind.* Cambridge, MA: Bradford.

Perner, J., Baker, S., & Hutton, D. (1994). The conceptual origins of belief and pretence. In C. Lewis & P. Mitchell (Eds.), *Children's early understanding of mind: Origins and development* (pp. 261–286). Hove, Sussex: Erlbaum.

Povinelli, D. J. (1994). Comparative studies of mental state attribution: A reply to Heyes. *Animal Behaviour 48*, 239–241.

Povinelli, D. J. (1996). Chimpanzee theory of mind? The long road to strong inference. In P. Carruthers & P. K. Smith (Eds.), *Theories of theories of mind* (pp. 293–329). Cambridge: Cambridge University Press.

Povinelli, Daniel. J., & Eddy, Timothy J. (1996a). What young chimpanzees know about seeing. *Monographs of the Society for Research in Child Development 61* (2, Serial No. 247).

Povinelli, Daniel. J., & Eddy, Timothy J. (1996b). Chimpanzees: Joint visual attention. *Psychological Science 7*, 129–135.

Povinelli, D. J., Nelson, K. E., & Boysen, S. T. (1990). Inferences about guessing and knowing by chimpanzees (*Pan troglodytes*). *Journal of Comparative Psychology 104*, 203–210.

Povinelli, D. J., Rulf, A. B., & Bierschwale, D. T. (1994). Absence of knowledge attribution and self-recognition in young chimpanzees (*Pan troglodytes*). *Journal of Comparative Psychology 108*, 74–80.

Premack, D. (1988). Does the chimpanzee have a theory of mind, revisited. In R. W. Byrne & A. Whiten (Eds.), *Machiavellian intelligence: Social expertise and the evolution of intellect in monkeys, apes and humans* (pp. 160–179). Oxford: Oxford University Press.

Rogers, S. J., & Pennington, B. F. (1991). A theoretical approach to the deficits in infantile autism. *Development and Psychopathology 3*, 137–162.

Russon, A. E. (1997). Exploiting the expertise of others. In A. Whiten & R. W. Byrne (Eds.), *Machiavellian intelligence II: Evaluations and extensions* (pp. 174–206). Cambridge: Cambridge University Press.

Savage-Rumbaugh, E. Sue (1986). *Ape language: From conditioned response to symbol*. New York: Columbia University Press.

Savage-Rumbaugh, E. S. (1998). Why are we afraid of apes with language? In A. B. Scheibel & J. W. Schopf (Eds.), *The origin and evolution of intelligence* (pp. 43–69). Sudbury, MA: Jones and Bartlett.

Savage-Rumbaugh, E. S., & McDonald, K. (1988). Deception and social manipulation in symbol-using apes. In R. W. Byrne & A. Whiten (Eds.), *Machiavellian intelligence: Social expertise and the evolution of intellect in monkeys, apes and humans* (pp. 224–237). Oxford: Oxford University Press.

Sperber, Dan. (1996). *Explaining culture: A naturalistic approach.* Oxford: Blackwell.

Suddendorf, T. (1998). Simpler for evolution: secondary representation in apes, children and ancestors. *Behavioral and Brain Science 21*, 131.

Suddendorf, T. (1999). The rise of the metamind. In M. C. Corballis & S. E. G. Lea (Eds.), *The descent of mind*. Oxford: Oxford University Press.

Tanner, J., & Byrne, R. W. (1998). Imitation in a captive lowland gorilla: A spontaneous experiment. Unpublished manuscript, University of St Andrews, Fife, Scotland.

Tomasello, M. (1990). Cultural transmission in the tool use and communicatory signaling of chimpanzees? In S. T. Parker & K. R. Gibson (Eds.), *"Language" and intelligence in monkeys and apes: Comparative developmental perspectives* (pp. 274–310). Cambridge: Cambridge University Press.

Tomasello, M. (1996). Do apes ape? In C. M. Heyes & B. G. Galef, Jr. (Eds.), *Social learning in animals: The roots of culture* (pp. 319–346). London: Academic Press.

Tomasello, M., Savage-Rumbaugh, E. S., & Kruger, A. (1993). Imitative learning of actions on objects by children, chimpanzees and enculturated chimpanzees. *Child Development 64*, 1688–1705.

Wellman, Henry. M. (1991). *The child's theory of mind*. Cambridge, MA: Bradford.

Wellman, H. M. (1990). From desires to beliefs: Acquisition of a theory of mind. In A. Whiten (Ed.), *Natural theories of mind: Evolution, development and simulation of everyday mindreading* (pp. 19–38). Oxford: Basil Blackwell.

Whiten, A. (1993a). Evolving a theory of mind: The nature of non-verbal mentalism in other primates. In S. Baron-Cohen, H. Tager-Flusberg, & D. J. Cohen (Eds.), *Understanding other minds* (pp. 367–396). Oxford: Oxford University Press.

Whiten, A. (1993b). Human enculturation, chimpanzee enculturation and the nature of imitation. Commentary on *Cultural learning*, by M. Tomasello et al. *Behavioral and Brain Sciences* 16, 538–539.

Whiten, A. (1994). Grades of mindreading. In C. Lewis & P. Mitchell (Eds.), *Children's early understanding of mind: Origins and development* (pp. 47–70). Hove, Sussex: Erlbaum.

Whiten, A. (1996a) Imitation, pretence and mindreading: Secondary representation in comparative primatology and developmental psychology? In A. E. Russon, K. A. Bard, & S. T. Parker (Eds.), *Reaching into thought: The minds of the great apes* (pp. 300–324). Cambridge: Cambridge University Press.

Whiten, A. (1996b). When does smart behaviour reading become mindreading? In P. Carruthers & P. K. Smith (Eds.), *Theories of theories of mind* (pp. 277–292). Cambridge: Cambridge University Press.

Whiten, A. (1997). The Machiavellian mindreader. In A. Whiten and R. W. Byrne (Eds.), *Machiavellian intelligence II* (pp. 144–173). Cambridge: Cambridge University Press.

Whiten, A. (1998a). Evolutionary and developmental origins of the mindreading system. In J. Langer & M. Killen (Eds.), *Piaget, evolution and development* (pp. 73–99). Hove, Sussex: Erlbaum.

Whiten, A. (1998b). Imitation of the sequential structure of actions in chimpanzees (*Pan troglodytes*). *Journal of Comparative Psychology* 112, 270–281.

Whiten, A. (1999). Imitation of sequential and hierarchical structure in action: Experimental studies with children and chimpanzees. *Proceedings of the Artificial Intelligence and Simulation of Behaviour Convention*, Edinburgh, April 1999, 38–46.

Whiten, A. (in press). Primate culture and social learning. *Cognitive Science.*

Whiten, A., & Brown, J. D. (1999). Imitation and the reading of other minds: Perspectives from the study of autism, normal children and non-human primates. In S. Braten (Ed.), *Intersubjective communication and emotion in ontogeny: A sourcebook.* Cambridge: Cambridge University Press.

Whiten, A., & Byrne, R. W. (1988). Tactical deception in primates. *Behavioral and Brain Sciences 11*, 233–273.

Whiten, A., & Byrne, R. W. (1991). The emergence of metarepresentation in human ontogeny and primate phylogeny. In A. Whiten (Ed.), *Natural theories of mind: Evolution, development and simulation of everyday mindreading* (pp. 267–281). Oxford: Basil Blackwell.

Whiten, A., & Custance, D. M. (1996). Studies of imitation in chimpanzees and children. In C. M. Heyes & B. G. Galef, Jr. (Eds.), *Social learning in animals: The roots of culture* (pp. 291–318). London: Academic Press.

Whiten, A., Custance, D. M., Gomez, J.-C., Teixidor, P., & Bard, K. A. (1996). Imitative learning of artificial fruit processing in children (*Homo sapiens*) and chimpanzees (*Pan troglodytes*). *Journal of Comparative Psychology 110*, 3–14.

Whiten, A., & Ham, R. (1992). On the nature and evolution of imitation in the animal kingdom: Reappraisal of a century of research. In P. J. B. Slater, J. S. Rosenblatt, C. Beer, & M. Milinski (Eds.), *Advances in the study of behaviour*, Vol. 21 (pp. 239–283). New York: Academic Press.

Whiten, A., & Perner, J. (1991). Fundamental issues in the multidisciplinary study of mindreading. In A. Whiten (Ed.), *Natural Theories of Mind* (pp. 1–17). Oxford: Basil Blackwell.

Wimmer, H., & Perner, J. (1983). Beliefs about beliefs: Representation and constraining function of wrong beliefs in young children's understanding of deception. *Cognition 13*, 103–128.

Wrangham, Richard, & Peterson, Dale (1996). *Demonic males: Apes and the origins of human violence*. London: Bloomsbury.

Zentall, T. R., Sutton, J.E., & Sherburne, L. M. (1996). True imitative learning in pigeons. *Psychological Science 7*, 343–346.

Metarepresentation
in Mind

Chapter 7

The Mentalizing Folk

Alvin I. Goldman

1. Multiple Questions

Ordinary people are mentalizers. The folk not only have mental states, but they represent themselves – both self and others – as having mental states. Many of these mental states (e.g., beliefs and desires) represent how the world is or ought to be. By representing themselves as having such first-order representational states, the folk engage in second-order representation, or metarepresentation. The class of representations is not exhausted, of course, by mental states; linguistic utterances and inscriptions are also representations though not mental ones. The representation of mental representation is a big enough topic for a single chapter, however, and it is all that I shall bite off here.

Restricting ourselves to mental metarepresentation, there remains a wide array of questions to which philosophers and cognitive scientists devote their attention. I divide the central questions into three main groups.

(1) Questions about the contents of mental concepts

What concepts do the folk have of mental representations? How do they conceptualize or represent to themselves such states as belief, desire, intention, and the other mental attitudes? What properties do they endow these states with, in their fundamental grasp of them? These questions should be contrasted with questions about the essential nature of mental states. As far as scientific ontology is concerned, mental states might turn out to be neural states. But scientifically and philosophically untutored people presumably do not conceptualize beliefs and desires as neural states. How do they conceptualize them?

(2) Questions about processes of mental-state attribution

The folk not only possess mental-state concepts, but they deploy these concepts with some frequency, ascribing specific instances of these concepts both to self and others. A person may ascribe to herself a desire that *p*, or ascribe to another a belief that *q*. How do they go about selecting these specific ascriptions? What evidence and inferential procedures do they use, or what techniques, routines, or heuristics are deployed? Since mental attitudes are ascribed both to self and others, and since these ascriptions may involve different evidence and different routines, there are two questions to be asked: What procedures are used in making first-person attributions, and what procedures are used in making third-person attributions?

(3) Questions about the development or acquisition of mentalizing skills

What are the sources and antecedents of people's mentalizing facility? What native endowments underpin this cognitive skill, and what modes of maturation or learning generate full competence at mentalizing or metarepresentation? Issues about acquisition are the core issues for many developmental psychologists. As a philosopher, however, I am principally interested in the first two sets of questions. Acquisition is of interest to me only insofar as it sheds light on answers to the first two sets of questions.

I shall not try to answer any of these questions in full detail, but some of the principal answers currently on offer will be reviewed and evaluated, and I shall place my own position against the background of these competing answers. I shall begin by examining the collection of approaches grouped under the heading "theory-theory" (TT), approaches that jointly comprise the dominant perspective on mentalizing. Each of these approaches will be faulted, either for empirical implausibility or for failure to answer some of the core questions about mentalizing. I shall then turn to the approach I find most compelling, a version of the "simulation" theory flavored with an infusion of introspectionism.

2. Theory-Theories

Many researchers claim that the folk (i.e., adult folk) have a rudimentary theory of mind, a theory that gets deployed in mental-state attribution, explanations of actions in terms of mental states, and so forth. A related claim is that mental-attitude concepts are understood wholly in terms of this folk theory. The contents of mental concepts can only be spelled out properly in terms of the theory in which they are embedded.

2.1 Philosophical Functionalism

The earliest version of TT originated with philosophers of mind (Sellars, 1963; Lewis, 1972), who were largely interested in the analysis of mental-state concepts. Their leading idea was borrowed from positivist philosophers of science, the idea that theoretical, non-observational concepts in science are definable by means of lawful relationships to observables.

They claimed that mentalistic words like 'desire' and 'belief' are definable in terms of laws relating the intended inner states to stimulus inputs, other inner states, and behavioral outputs. Since these laws are
supposedly possessed and deployed by the folk themselves, not just by
scientists, this approach is sometimes called "commonsense functionalism" (Lewis, 1972; Block, 1980).

Commonsense functionalism is touted for its ability to account for
the layperson's facility at predicting and explaining the behavior of others. Laws permit users to infer behavior predictively or retrodictively
from a third party's mental states. They also permit users to infer mental
states from prior mental states or from stimulus conditions. So common-
sense functionalism purports to show how people attribute mental attitudes (viz., by means of inferences employing lawlike premises).

Three fundamental difficulties face this functionalist version of TT.
First, is there really a set of commonsense psychological laws that lay-
people deploy in prediction and explanation? Although philosophers of
mind provide a few examples of such laws, difficulties and obscurities
surround the attempt to state them carefully (Schiffer, 1987; Goldman,
1989). Furthermore, it is extremely doubtful that predictions are always
based on such laws. I have used Kahneman and Tversky's (1982) airport
example to illustrate this point. Given descriptions of two imaginary
travellers who both miss their flights, subjects were asked to predict
which traveller would be more disappointed. Ninety-six percent of the
subjects said that the traveller who barely misses his flight will be more
disappointed than the one who misses it by 30 minutes. Does this consensus result from all subjects' knowing a *law* about degrees of disap-
pointment? That is highly dubious (Goldman, 1989).

A second nest of problems for commonsense functionalism concerns
first-person attributions of mental states (Goldman, 1993a). Functionalism is poorly equipped to accommodate people's special access to their
own present attitudes. Since functionalism claims that desires, beliefs,
and intentions are understood purely in terms of their causal relations to
other states, and ultimately in terms of their causal relations to stimuli
and behavior, the only method of identifying one's current desires and
beliefs according to functionalism is by inference from stimuli and behavior. This seems clearly wrong. Surely I can tell that I currently intend
to cook shrimp for dinner without knowing any stimulus that has caused
this intention nor any behavior that has resulted from it. (I may not have
purchased any shrimp yet, nor performed any other item of shrimp-
oriented behavior.) Of course, functionalism does not say that a given
mental state always produces designated outcomes; it is only a *disposition*
or *propensity* to produce them *if* other inner and / or outer conditions are
ripe. But it is radically unclear how a person is supposed to be capable
of detecting a token state's dispositional or subjunctive properties. It is

therefore unclear how a person can actually go about using functionalist laws to classify their own mental states, especially to classify them in the seemingly "direct" fashion available to us. Functionalism's postulation of extensive conceptual connectivity among mental states also creates severe computational problems, specifically, the threat of combinatorial explosion (for details, see Goldman, 1993a). Thus, the functionalist story has many counts against it.

2.2 The Child Scientist Theory

Psychologists as well as philosophers use the label "theory of mind" for their approach to folk mentalization. But psychologists often mean something a bit different by "theory of mind," and the arguments they adduce for their position are certainly quite different. Several psychologists, however, present a version of TT with some similarities to functionalism. Wellman, Gopnik, and Perner all view folk mental concepts as theoretical constructs, introduced to provide causal explanations and facilitate predictions (Wellman, 1990; Perner, 1991; Gopnik, 1993; Gopnik & Wellman, 1992). They claim these concepts must be theoretical concepts because they undergo theoretical change just as theoretical concepts in science do. Their argument for the theoretical character of mental concepts rests on claims about the way these concepts change in early childhood development.

The hallmark of this group of psychologists is the view that the growing child is, in essence, a theoretical scientist. Gopnik and collaborators (Gopnik & Wellman, 1992; 1994; Gopnik, 1996; Gopnik & Meltzoff, 1997) view children's alleged transitions from one theory of mind to another as comparable to transitions in scientific theory (e.g., astronomy's theoretic transitions from Copernicus to Brahe to Kepler). Children's early concepts of perception, desire, and belief are said to be non-representational. This primitive form of mentalistic theory excludes the idea of misrepresentation (e.g., false belief). That is why, supposedly, 3-year-olds and younger children standardly fail the false-belief task: they do not yet have a concept of false belief. The richer, genuinely representational concept of belief only comes with the advent of a subsequent, 4-year-old theory.

This story of alleged transitions, however, including the subplot of conceptual deficit prior to 4 years of age, is empirically quite problematic. In recent studies concerning false-belief tasks, the earlier hypothesis of conceptual deficit prior to age 4 has been disintegrating. Clements and Perner (1994) found that children from 2 years 11 months demonstrated implicit understanding of false belief even when their explicit answers to false-belief questions failed to evince such understanding. Two papers by Freeman and colleagues strongly suggest that 3-years-olds' troubles with false-belief tasks rest on performance problems rather than on a conceptual deficit. Lewis, Freeman, Hagestadt, & Douglas (1994) found that preschoolers (including 3-year-olds) did better on false-belief tasks when they were allowed to go through a story twice rather than just once, presumably giving them needed help in reconstructing the protagonist's mental state from memory. The memory explanation for poor performance on false-belief tasks was further confirmed by Freeman and Lacohee's (1995) finding that children are better able to attribute prior false belief to themselves when an aid to memory is provided.

All of these studies shed doubt on the notion that young children have an early conception of belief (or "prelief," as Perner calls it) that lacks the notion of misrepresentation. What about other mental attitudes in young children? There, too, the story of early conceptual deficits seems to be falling apart with the help of more sophisticated experimental techniques. Consider the work of Meltzoff (1995) on young children's grasp of intention. Even 18-month-olds were found to have a grasp of misrepresentation in connection with intentions. In Meltzoff's experiments, infants observed adults "try" but fail to achieve unfamiliar effects with certain manipulanda (at least this is how the behavior would be described by an adult). The experimenter would pick up a stick-tool and "aim" to push a button with it, but the button was always missed. Would an infant interpret this behavior in goal-oriented terms, despite the fact that the goal was never fulfilled? Dramatically, the answer was "Yes." Eighteen-month-olds enacted the intended but failed attempts of the experimenter rather than the actual behavior. Thus, even children of 18 months have a preverbalized concept of intention that permits misrepresentation.

Compelling evidence of another variety against the child-scientist approach comes from studies of Williams Syndrome patients. Patients with Williams Syndrome are retarded, with an average IQ of about 50, and even adolescents and adults appear to be unable to undergo any of the forms of conceptual change associated with theory building (Johnson & Carey, 1996). Nonetheless, children with Williams Syndrome begin to explain actions in terms of beliefs and desires at about normal ages (Tager-Flusberg, 1994). This is powerful evidence against the notion that mentalizing is a product of a general theory-building capacity (Segal, 1996; Carey & Spelke, 1996).

In addition to this body of empirical counter-evidence, three theoretical considerations also speak against the child-scientist approach. First, as Leslie and Roth (1993) point out, the child-scientist approach sees the child not just as a theorist, but as a quite brilliant theorist. After all, the concepts of propositional attitudes are highly sophisticated and logically complex. But children do not appear to be brilliant theorists in all domains, which suggests that the development of mentalizing has different roots. Second, as Segal (1996) notes, the developmental pattern and end point of mentalizing are remarkably similar across individuals and apparently across cultures. This convergence would be surprising if each child, like a scientist, developed their own mentalizing theory, because in science different theorists do not normally converge so rapidly on the same theory (e.g., psychologists do not agree about how the mentalizing facility is acquired). Third, as Carruthers (1996) points out, scientists modify a theory when they come to believe that it is false, or at least believe that it makes false predictions. But the very young child-scientist cannot decide that her hitherto accepted theory of mind is false when, by hypothesis, her only concept of belief up until then precludes the idea of falsity! This is a basic incoherence in the child-scientist version of TT.

Finally, for those of us primarily interested in the first two (sets of) questions presented in section 1, the child-scientist version of TT has little to offer. This group of proponents of TT mainly argue that mental concepts must be theoretical constructs of some sort, and inferences deployed in applying these concepts must be theoretical inferences of some sort. They give us few specifics, however, about the exact content of the various mental concepts or the exact inferences used in applying them. From the point of view of our first two questions, little is provided by way of answers.

2.3 The Modularity Theory

Let us proceed, therefore, to another version of TT, the one advanced by Leslie (Leslie, 1987; 1994; Leslie & Thaiss, 1992; Leslie & Roth, 1993). Leslie claims that the ability to engage in mentalizing depends upon possession of a domain-specific mechanism, ToMM. This mechanism is an innate endowment of the human species and begins to develop in infancy. ToMM is an information processing device that computes data structures called metarepresentations. A metarepresentation makes explicit four kinds of information: (1) an attitude (e.g., belief, desire, pretense), followed by three arguments which specify, respectively, an agent, an anchor (some aspect of the real situation, e.g., that the agent is holding a banana), and an imaginary or pretend state (e.g., that the agent is holding a telephone). For example, a metarepresentation might be: Mother pretends (of) this banana (that) "it is a telephone."

Leslie claims that "having access to such data structures, together with the inferences they support, constitutes a tacit and intuitive theory of mind, or . . . a tacit theory of the specific "representational relations" (like *pretends, believes, wants*) that enter into the causation of agents' behaviour" (Leslie & Roth, 1993, p. 91). Elsewhere he says: "We will make no bones about the fact that we are on the side of theory-theory" (Leslie & German, 1995, p. 123). These and similar statements make it natural to place Leslie in the TT camp. But although Leslie himself classifies his approach (in these passages) as a version of TT, that does not make it so. Leslie and his collaborators clearly offer a cognitive science theory of

mentalizing, but a cognitive science theory of mentalizing is not necessarily a TT. Simulation theory is equally a cognitive science theory of
mentalizing (or aspires to be), but it is not a specimen of TT. Something
qualifies as a specimen of TT if it not only is itself a theory but ascribes
to the folk the possession and deployment of a theory. Despite occasional
pronouncements to the contrary, Leslie does not seem to attribute to the
folk the possession and deployment of a genuine theory, in an appropriate sense of "theory." Furthermore, it is unclear whether Leslie's approach tries to answer the first two questions on our original list,
whether in terms of theory possession or otherwise. But insofar as he
hints at answers to them, it is not obvious that the answers embody a TT.

One part of Leslie's work, as we have seen, involves a characterization of the "logic" of pretend representations. According to this logic, "primary" representations such as 'the cup is full' can be "decoupled" so as
to produce what philosophers call an opaque construction. Thus, there is
no contradiction – and the child understands that there is no contradiction
– in a representation of the form, 'I pretend (of) the empty cup (that) it is
full'. Obviously, this logic per se does not constitute a theory in the sense
of a set of lawlike principles used by the child for explanation and / or prediction. However, Leslie goes on to say that decoupled expressions can be
combined with real-world inferences to elaborate on pretend situations
(Leslie, 1994). For example, a real-world causal inference is: If a container
filled with liquid is upturned, then the liquid will pour out and make
something wet. This causal inference enables a pretend scenario to unfold.
If it is pretended of an empty cup that it is full, and if this cup is upturned,
then it is pretended of the cup that it pours liquid out and makes something wet. Leslie has presented this kind of scenario to children, and they
indeed respond by saying that a cup upturned over a play character's
head makes that character wet. Leslie further describes the children as inferring what the experimenter was pretending. So here Leslie addresses
the issue of inferring the mental states of others.

But has any such inference involved a *psychological theory possessed
by the child*? No evidence is presented to this effect. A child in Leslie's experiment may simply build on the experimenter's props and actions to
construct his own pretend scenario, and then infer that the experimenter
pretends likewise. If this is what the child does, it involves no psychological theory featuring psychological laws. (It may involve physical
laws, however, such as the upturning-causes-spilling "law" mentioned
above.) In fact, it sounds very much like the story a simulation theorist
would tell about this situation. In fact, Leslie himself concedes that the
simulation account is a perfectly acceptable fit with what the child does!

[I]f the child can infer that a cup containing water will, if upturned over
a table, disgorge its contents and make the table wet, then the same child

can also elaborate his own pretence or follow another person's pretence using the same inference . . . Now, if someone wants to call the above "simulation", then they can, but it adds little or nothing to the account to do so. (Leslie & German, 1995, p. 128)

The last sentence acknowledges that the simulation approach is quite compatible with this kind of case, a paradigmatic one in Leslie's studies.

The previous paragraph indicates that, while Leslie (sometimes) does address the second question posed in section 1, he has no evidence that specifically favors a TT answer to the question over a simulation theory (ST) answer. As to the first question raised in section 1, it does not seem as if Leslie answers it, or has the resources within his theory to answer it. Leslie does not explain how each separate attitude concept is represented, what the conceptual differences are, for example, between belief, desire, fear, and intention. Nor does his theory explain how a person classifies or identifies her own mental states (part of the second set of questions). Consider the judgment, "I currently desire a cookie." How does a person decide that he currently *desires* a cookie rather than *believes* that he will get a cookie? Leslie does not tell us.

2.4 Generic Theory-Theory

Another group of TT defenders defend it only in the most general or generic terms, without venturing to provide any details of folk theorizing. This is the approach of Stich, Nichols, and colleagues (Stich & Nichols, 1992; 1995; Nichols, Stich, Leslie, & Klein, 1996). These writers are deliberately noncommittal on the specific content of the folk theory: whether it involves laws (as in functionalism), theoretical constructs (as in science), or the like. They mean by 'theory' *any* kind of knowledge structure whatever – either "a body of rules or principles or propositions" (Stich & Nichols, 1992, p. 35). They define the field as a debate between TT and ST, and their chief aim is the negative one of disproving ST rather than providing a specific form of TT.

Their way of defining the issue, however, is actually a bit contentious. They often focus on only a "radical" version of ST that involves the wholesale exclusion of "knowledge" in favor of "ability" (Leslie & German, 1995). They insist that *any* use of information by subjects in the mentalizing process is incompatible with ST (Nichols et al., 1996). But these portraits of ST unduly restrict its range. While some friends of simulation might accept these renditions of their view, my own version of ST permits subjects to employ a modest or even substantial amount of information (as explained below). This allows a reasonable contrast between ST and TT, but rejects the framing of the debate as one of *some* information versus *no* information.

3. Introspection and First-Person Attribution

I turn now to my own, positive approach to mentalizing, beginning with the concepts of attitudinal states. I propose to take seriously the role of consciousness in our folk concepts of mental states. This proposal takes its point of departure from three assumptions that should be congenial to cognitive science.

(1) There is conscious experience.

(2) The occurrent, or activated, forms of the representational attitudes are often found in conscious experience.

(3) People, even children, have introspective access to these occupants of conscious experience.

With the dramatic growth of consciousness studies in contemporary cognitive science, assumption (1) should now be uncontroversial. Assumption (2) is also mild: it simply denies that conscious experience is exhausted by perceptions, feelings, and emotions. Tokens of the propositional attitudes (at least in their occurrent forms) are also found in experience. If anybody needs convincing that cognitive science regards certain representational states as conscious, consider the fact that memory researchers distinguish explicit from implicit memory by saying that the former involves conscious recollections (Schacter, 1989). Assumption (3) is also quite modest, simply saying that conscious events are open to a special form of access: introspective access. Elsewhere, I show that reliance on introspection is widespread in cognitive science, and not epistemologically objectionable (Goldman, 1997). So assumption (3) is not alien to cognitive science.

My hypothesis is that mental-state concepts such as desire, belief, and so forth are understood at least in part in terms of non-dispositional characteristics of conscious experience, characteristics that can be introspected by the subject of the experience. The most natural account of people's special access to their mental states is an account that posits some sorts of non-dispositional characteristics that are introspectively available to the subject and distinguishable from one another. My hypothesis is that such characteristics underlie the grasp of mental-state concepts.

To say that a characteristic of consciousness is introspectively accessible or discriminable is only to say that it *can potentially* be identified or discriminated, not that it is or will be identified on every (or any) occasion that it occurs. (The HOT theory of consciousness, by contrast, says that a state is conscious only if its subject actually has a higher-order thought about that state; see Rosenthal, 1992). In particular, I am not committed to any thesis of the infallibility or transparency of conscious

characteristics. Property detection requires appropriate conceptual facility, and this facility is not guaranteed by introspective accessibility. So
although an infant or child may experience beliefs, hopes, and desires,
the child may lack the conceptual facility to classify them in intentional
or representational terms. Once the child develops this conceptual facility, however, she can locate instantiations of these concepts squarely
within her conscious experience. In this sense, occurrent incarnations of
belief, desire, intention, and so forth are not "unobservables," contrary
to most theory-theorists (e.g., Leslie, 1994, p. 212).

It is important to appreciate that the introspective or "Cartesian"
story is perfectly compatible with the early development of metarepresentational concepts, even along lines that theory-theorists have
sketched. Leslie might be right, for example, to postulate an innate module which, when fully deployed, makes available the sort of conceptual
structures he postulates. He may also be right in claiming that autism
involves an impairment in ToMM that results in autistic children never
acquiring the postulated metarepresentional structures, or their not applying them, at any rate, to first-order mental states. This is all compatible with introspectivism. What introspectivism says is that acquiring
the concepts of mental representational states involves the task of latching these complex conceptual structures onto the right sorts of conscious
characteristics (i.e., latching the belief concept onto belief episodes, the
desire concept onto desire episodes, and so forth). Although people with
autism certainly experience belief episodes and desire episodes, they apparently have deficits in representing them as representations (i.e., as
states that can be true or false, fulfilled or unfulfilled, and the like). This
is compatible with an introspectivist approach.

Gopnik (1993; Gopnik & Wellman, 1992) argues that an introspectivist or privileged-access account of first-person attribution fails to explain certain errors of young children in self-ascription of beliefs. In the
Smarties task, 3-year-olds are asked what they thought was in the candy
box before it was opened. In fact, they thought it was candy. But one-
half to two-thirds mistakenly say they had originally thought there were
pencils (as they subsequently learned). Gopnik thinks that introspectivism cannot accommodate this finding because introspectivism is committed to first-person infallibility. But introspectivism is not committed
to infallibility; it can cheerfully grant that three-year-olds might lack a
mastery of propositional-attitude attribution, especially verbal mastery.
Moreover, in Gopnik's experiments, the target belief-episodes are in the
(recent) past, and hence are not open to immediate introspection. They
can only be recalled or not recalled. Memory explanations of errors in
these sorts of tasks are indicated by papers cited in section 2.2 above. It
is no objection to introspectivist accounts that young children have
memory difficulties even with recently experienced thoughts. When the

states are genuinely concurrent, however, the special access to one's own conscious experience readily accounts for the ease and accuracy of first-person attribution. No version of TT explains this ease and accuracy.

A different problem raised against the introspection-simulation approach is how it accounts for developmental differences across mental-state concepts. According to this approach, why is there a lag in deployment of belief as compared with desire in action explanations (Gopnik & Wellman, 1992; 1994)? There are several possible answers here. One might appeal to the comparative phenomenological salience of desire as compared with belief. If desire is more salient than belief, it may be easier for children to latch onto the concept of desire than the concept of belief. A very different explanation might invoke differences in the *language* of desire and belief. As Harris (1996) notes, there may be a social premium on the communication of desire that results in greater conversational deployment of the language of desire. A great deal of child-adult activity involves joint or collaborative action, the success of which depends on the communication of the desires of each. The focus on desires, with beliefs left unspoken, might explain the child's greater preoccupation with desire and mastery of the language of desire.

Many cognitive scientists are wary of regarding one's own conscious episodes as central to our grasp of psychological concepts. In addition to methodological worries about introspection, this denigration of the first-person perspective may stem from an evolutionary perspective. Identifying the mental states of others, as opposed to one's own mental states, has a clear selectional advantage. There is a definite biological benefit to be derived from accurate beliefs about the inner life of one's rivals, as a predictor of what they will do next. Given this selectional advantage, should we not expect mental concepts to be rooted in the behavioral features of others, not in our own conscious states? Humphrey (1983) points out a plausible connection between the two: nature might provide us the means of mindreading others via an ability to read our own minds and thereby simulate the minds of others.

> [A] revolutionary advance in the evolution of mind occurred when, for certain social animals, a new set of heuristic principles was devised to cope with the pressing need to model a special section of reality – the reality comprised by the behavior of other kindred animals. The trick that nature came up with was *introspection*; it proved possible for an individual to develop a model of the behavior of others by reasoning by analogy from his own case, the facts of his own case being revealed to him through examination of the contents of consciousness. (Humphrey, 1983, p. 30)

But are there not innate tendencies to detect mental states in others on a purely behavioral basis? And does this not support a third-person rather than first-person approach to the fundamental grasp of mental-state concepts? Baron-Cohen (1995) identifies several behavioral cues for mental states, and conjectures specialized innate mechanisms for exploiting those cues. An intentionality detector interprets self-propelled motion as a sign of goal or desire. An eye-direction detector detects the direction of another organism's eyes, and infers that that organism sees that thing (where seeing is a type of mental state).

I respond that the use of these behavioral cues is compatible with a first-person, introspective understanding of mental-state concepts. Baron-Cohen suggests this himself: "I assume that the infant obtains [the knowledge that eyes can see] from the simple contingencies of closing and opening its own eyes ... Although this knowledge is initially based on the infant's own experience, it could be generalized to an Agent by analogy with the Self" (Baron-Cohen, 1995, p. 43). Another possibility is innate cross-modal knowledge of mental states, analogous to the cross-modal knowledge discovered in infants by Meltzoff. Meltzoff and Moore (1983) found that newborn infants as young as 42 minutes can imitate such facial gestures as mouth-opening and tongue-protrusion. How do these infants correlate visual cues of the other's movements with motor/proprioceptive information about their own movements? They suggest an innate cross-modal matching between visual and proprioceptive information. I suggest that there may be a similarly innate matching between third-person behavior and mental states understood in introspective terms. The child may be innately disposed to interpret other creatures' self-propelled motion as stemming from a desire experience familiar from her own case.

My position here contrasts sharply with that of some other simulation theorists, notably Gordon (1992, 1995, 1996). Gordon tries to develop an account of first-person attribution that avoids any appeal to introspection or inner recognition. He proposes what he calls an "ascent routine" approach. The way a person answers the question, "Do you believe Mickey Mouse has a tail?" (Q_1) is to ask himself the question, "Does Mickey Mouse have a tail?" (Q_2). If the answer to Q_2 is Yes, then the presumptive answer to Q_1 is also Yes. The answer to Q_1 is No if either the answer to Q_2 is No or no answer is available. What attracts Gordon to this approach is that it allows one to get the answer to a question about oneself, and specifically about one's mental states, by answering a question that is not about oneself, nor about mental states at all (Gordon, 1996, p. 15). Gordon wisely avoids the implausible claim that ascent routines alone yield genuine, comprehending self-ascriptions of belief. Ascent routines yield such comprehension, he says, only when they are embedded within a simulation, or when relativized to a point of view. I find it difficult to understand, though, how the two elements combine to yield genuine, comprehending self-ascriptions of belief.

There is a further difficulty for the ascent routine approach: how can it account for self-attributions of attitudes other than belief? Consider hope, for example. Suppose someone is asked the question, "Do you hope that Team T won their game yesterday?" (Q_1). How is she supposed to answer that question using an ascent routine? Clearly she is not supposed to ask herself the question, "Did Team T win their game yesterday?" (Q_2), which would only be relevant to belief, not hope. What question is she supposed to ask herself? Gordon fails to address this, nor does he provide any reason to think that, for each attitude type, there is a distinctive non-mental question the response to which would provide an answer to the first-person attitude question. So his account is quite incomplete, restricted, as it is, to self-ascription of belief. Finally, Gordon does not really tell us, in cognitive terms, how people go about answering his de-mentalized questions (the Q_2 questions). Introspection may be required to answer these questions, and if so, Gordon has not really avoided the necessity of introspection for accurate first-person attribution.

4. Simulation and Third-Person Attribution

This section of the paper concerns the simulation theory (ST) alternative to the TT account of third-person attribution. Since my overall theory of attribution combines a simulation approach to third-person attribution with an introspectivist approach to first-person attribution, it is naturally called the *introspection-simulation* view.

The basic idea of ST is that ordinary folk can attribute representational states to others by first imaginatively adopting their perspective, and then seeing what further states would ensue. For example, to determine what decision or choice another person will make, you pretend to have the desires and beliefs that you antecedently take them to have (on independent grounds). These pretend desires and beliefs are fed as inputs into your own decision-making system, which is run "off-line." The output of the decision-making system does not lead you to action; rather, it is used as a basis to predict what the other person will do.

At the heart of the simulation hypothesis is the notion that pretend mental states have some sort of intimate similarity, or homology, to their non-pretend counterparts. That is how they can succeed, on many occasions at least, in generating the same outputs as the non-pretend states would do when fed into the same processing system. Pretend states are obviously not identical to their non-pretend counterparts. It is an empirical question, to be discussed below, just what the respects of similarity and dissimilarity turn out to be.

The simulation approach can be endorsed in various stronger or weaker variants. The strongest version would say that all third-person mental attributions by the folk involve the simulation routine. Weaker versions would say that some but not all attributions involve simulation. I have never endorsed the strongest version of the approach (see Goldman, 1989; 1992a), nor do I wish to do so here. I wish to endorse only the weaker and admittedly vague view that simulation plays an "important" role in third-person attribution. The precise extent of simulation must be determined by future empirical investigation.

It is noteworthy that many researchers who began in the TT camp, or still identify themselves as theory-theorists, have now moved over to a hybrid position, either explicitly or implicitly. So ST has already won numerous partial "converts." Perner, who began as an unqualified opponent of ST (Perner & Howes, 1992), now advocates a simulation-theory "mix" (Perner, 1996). Carruthers (1996) calls himself a theory-theorist but acknowledges a "limited" role for simulation. Similarly, Stich and Nichols, heretofore among the staunchest foes of ST, now propose a sort of theory-simulation hybrid (Stich & Nichols, 1997). Finally, although Leslie considers himself a theory-theorist, he makes substantial concessions to simulation in recent writing. He resists simulationism largely because he mistakenly thinks that it is inconsistent with metarepresentational *conceptual* structures. Leslie and German (1995) write as follows:

> In summary, we have few qualms about entertaining the idea that "simulation" may be one of the theory of mind related abilities. What these abilities have in common is that they use structured, systematic metarepresentational knowledge. Access to metarepresentations is required to define the problems to be solved, to initiate and guide the problem-solving process, to select relevant inputs for it, and to encode and interpret its intermediate and final results ... [S]imulation needs metarepresentation. (Leslie & German, 1995, p. 133)

Moderate simulationism, however, can cheerfully live with metarepresentational concepts. Appropriate concepts are certainly needed to make attitude attributions, and they are needed for simulation-based attributions as much as for theory-based attributions.

Furthermore, some forms of propositional knowledge are undoubtedly needed both to initiate and to accompany the simulation heuristic. First, to engage in successful simulation, the attributor needs information about the target agent's initial states on the basis of which accurate (initial) pretend states can be constructed. Second, while running a simulation, the pretend states must be represented or "tagged" as states of the target agent. At a minimum, this must be done at the beginning and at the end of the simulation process, if not concurrently during its run. Otherwise, how can the simulator know that the output of the process should be attributed to the target agent (e.g., Jones) rather than someone else?

Admitting the attributor's need for such knowledge or information does not compromise the fundamental distinctness of the simulation approach. ST contrasts with pure TT in its positive claim that some attribution processes involve attempts to *mimic* the target agent, and in its negative claim that denies the use of theoretical propositions, such as scientific laws, in these attributional activities. Let me be more explicit about these differences. TT maintains that all attribution employs the attributor's beliefs about the target's initial states (which include desires, beliefs, and so forth). The attributor's beliefs take the form: $B_a(D_t(p))$, $B_a(D_t(q))$, $B_a(B_t(r))$, $B_a(B_t(s))$, and so forth. These beliefs of the attributor, together with his belief in some (typically) nomological proposition(s) about folk psychology, $B_a(N)$, are fed into the attributor's theoretical inference mechanism (or a specialized module), which generates an output belief about a further mental state of the target. By contrast, the simulation heuristic allegedly works by starting with pretend states of the attributor. These pretend states are not supposed to be ordinary belief states, desire states, or the like, so let us distinguish them by an asterisk: $D_a^*(p)$, $D_a^*(q)$, $B_a^*(r)$, $B_a^*(s)$, and so forth. Although some of these states may be pretend belief states, others can be pretend mental states of any variety. To execute a simulation heuristic, the attributor feeds these pretend states into some cognitive mechanism of his, which operates on them and produces a suitable output. In general, the mechanism need not be a theoretical inference mechanism. To predict a target agent's decision, for example, the attributor feeds pretend desires and beliefs into a decision-making mechanism, which outputs a (pretend) decision. This decision is then predicted to be the target's decision. In the simulation heuristic, moreover, there is no need for any theoretical premise 'N'. The prediction is accomplished by running the attributor's own cognitive mechanism rather than by deploying a theoretical premise about the operational pattern of such a mechanism.

Having clarified the fundamental contrast between TT and ST, let me address a continuing source of resistance to ST. This stems from the Stich and Nichols contention that the simulation hypothesis is fundamentally at odds with the "dominant explanatory strategy" in cognitive science (Stich & Nichols 1992, p. 35), that it constitutes a "radical departure from the typical explanations of cognitive capacities" (Nichols et al., 1996, p. 39). I now want to turn attention to motivating the view that cognitive scientists should feel perfectly comfortable with the simulation hypothesis, because processes akin (in different ways) to mental simulation are already well established by empirical research. The processes I shall discuss in the next segment are not themselves instances of mind-reading (i.e., mental attribution) but acknowledgment of these processes should increase the scientific credibility of simulation as an approach to mind-reading.

The essence of third-person mental simulation, in my view, is the deliberate attempt to replicate or reproduce in oneself an event or sequence of events that occurs (or is thought to occur) in somebody else. Even in successful simulation, there may be important differences between the target events and the facsimile in one's own mind. Pretend beliefs and desires may differ in intrinsic as well as relational properties from natural, non-pretend beliefs and desires. But there must be important respects of resemblance if the simulation heuristic is to succeed in making accurate attributions and predictions. It is an open, empirical question, however, just what the points of similarity and dissimilarity may be. At the outset, we can distinguish "pretend" mental states from their "natural" counterparts by noting that, in central cases, the former are produced artificially by the simulator's act of will, or voluntary choice. Natural beliefs, desires, and other mental states arise spontaneously, not as a result of the subject's voluntary control.

The volitional source of simulation is something it shares with imagination. Seeing an elephant is having a visual experience of an elephant produced spontaneously and involuntarily by the visual system. Imagining an elephant, by contrast, is deliberately creating a vision-like experience of an elephant, at least in typical cases. Other cognitive resources beyond mere willing are undoubtedly utilized in generating a visual image of an elephant. For present purposes, however, it suffices to highlight the contrast between natural and artificial (voluntary) modes of producing the two events. Imagination also resembles simulation in that the facsimile event (the visual image of an elephant) does not share all cognitive properties with its counterpart (the actual seeing of an elephant). Exactly which properties are and are not shared is a question for cognitive science to resolve, but substantial neuropsychological commonalities are already well established (Currie, 1995; Farah, 1988; Kosslyn et al., 1993). For example, there are content specific interactions between imagery and perception: imaging an "H" affects detection of visually presented "H"s more than it affects detection of "T"s. And patients who suffer visual deficits from cortical damage suffer parallel imagery deficits as well.

For those who doubt that simulation events *ever* transpire, who doubt that such facsimile events should be countenanced by cognitive science, it is instructive to be apprised of such research findings. The existence of mental events that are deliberately produced facsimiles of other mental events is established by this imagery research, and their existence makes it more credible than it otherwise might be that mental attribution could consist of analogous facsimile events. Currie (1995) rightly emphasizes this parallel with mentalistic simulation.

Nichols et al. (1996) challenge Currie's linkage of simulation and visual imagery. If simulation is to account for visual imagery in a novel fashion, they argue, either a distinct pretend-input generator for imagery must be postulated, or the same device must be used as in the case of decision-making simulation. Neither of these assumptions, they claim, is plausible. If Currie means to be claiming that existing theories of visual imagery are simulationist, Nichols et al. deny this on the grounds that ST is committed to the "no information" assumption, whereas leading theories of visual imagery do appeal to an information base.

These criticisms do not seem very damaging to me. Although theory-theorists commonly postulate pretend-input generators in their expositions of ST, that is not really essential to ST. ST can hold that pretend states are generated by some voluntary marshalling of pertinent informational resources without as yet committing itself to either task-specific or task-general devices. The important point is that there are products that mimic "naturally" produced states, however exactly these are produced. Furthermore, it is no embarrassment to ST for it to acknowledge that the generation of such facsimile events partly involves information. The no-information assumption is one that TT proponents foist off on ST, not an assumption that ST proponents are bound (or ought) to accept.

A further striking parallel is presented by Currie and Ravenscroft (1997) in a treatment of motor imagery. Here too it is found that subjects can deliberately produce facsimiles of naturally produced, motor-controlling cognitions, where the facsimiles bear remarkable similarities to their targets. Let me briefly summarize some of the salient findings reported by Currie and Ravenscroft.

Sports psychologists have long recognized the ability of mental rehearsal to enhance athletic performance (Richardson, 1967). Athletes who mentally rehearse their performance show marked improvement over those who do not. In "internal" imagery, the athlete experiences sensations of both effort and movement, and this kind of imagery has a more marked effect than so-called "external" imagery, which is picturing oneself as a spectator might see one. This suggests the hypothesis that internal motor imagery is generated by deliberately or artificially running the motor system but without letting it generate its normal behavioral outcome. This hypothesis leads to a number of predictions. First, temporal and kinematic properties of movements should be reflected in motor imagery. Second, when damage to central parts of the motor cortex cause deficits in motor performance, it should also cause impairment in motor imagery. Third, motor control should be improved by motor imagery. Fourth, motor imagery should affect heart and respiration rates, since activating the motor areas of the brain affects these rates. Finally, the neural substrate of movement should overlap the substrate of motor imagery. All of these predictions are borne out to a remarkable extent, as Currie and Ravenscroft document.

Yue and Cole (1992) compared the increase in muscular strength among subjects who actually trained with the strength of subjects who merely generated the appropriate motor imagery. Remarkably, while actual training produced a 30% increase in maximal force, motor imagery produced a 22% increase. EMG recordings revealed that the subjects in the motor imagery condition did not make covert muscle contractions during imagery, so the explanation of the effect must be a central explanation. Concerning heart and respiration rate increases, Adams, Guz, Innes, & Murphy (1987) demonstrated that these changes must originate in the (central) motor system itself. When the motor system instructs the large muscles to begin vigorous action, a parallel signal is sent to the vegetative effectors. We might therefore expect an increase in both heart and respiration rates during motor imagery of vigorous exercise. This is precisely what is found. Decety, Sjoholm, Ryding, Stenberg, & Ingvar (1991) report that not merely did heart rate and respiration rate increase during imaged exercise, they increased in proportion to the imagined vigorousness of the exercise!

The foregoing material supports the existence of intentionally produced facsimiles of mental events but it does not address the use of any such facsimiles for interpersonal interpretation. To strengthen the plausibility of this hypothesis, I first adduce evidence of interpersonal *behavioral* imitation on the part of young children, and then argue that *mentalistic* imitation would be a natural extension or outgrowth of behavioral imitation.

As discussed earlier, Meltzoff and Moore established 15 to 20 years ago the existence of infant imitation of facial expressions (Meltzoff & Moore, 1983). In more recent work, they show how imitation is central to the infant's understanding of people (Meltzoff & Moore, 1995). Here, the authors provide evidence that 6-week-old infants use facial imitation to differentiate among individuals they encounter and to reidentify them. For example, on day 1 they saw a single adult demonstrate either mouth opening, tongue protrusion at midline, tongue protrusion to the side, or no oral movement (control). On day 2 the same adult first sat and presented a neutral face, then the assigned gesture was demonstrated again. The results showed both immediate imitation (when the gestures were shown) and imitation from memory (when the adult sat with a neutral face). Thus, infants were acting on their remembrance of things past. Meltzoff and Moore suggest that infants are using these gestural signatures to identify the individuals. As discussed earlier, Meltzoff (1995) has shown that by 18 months, children go beyond imitating the visible surface behavior of an adult to imitating acts that are intended but not executed. Thus, at this age, children's replication proclivities extend, as it were, into the adult's psychology, not simply to his surface behavior.

None of this demonstrates, of course, that children and adults go on to deploy a process of *mental* imitation, in which they try to interpret others' mental states through the medium of intentionally produced facsimiles in their own minds. (More precisely, models of mental simulation suggest that one intentionally initiates a sequence of mental events intended to mimic another mind, but the whole sequence is not under direct voluntary control. Later stages are controlled by whatever system operates on the initially generated inputs.) But we can say this much. Meltzoff's work suggests that the capacity for intentional imitation of behavior is an innate and fundamental capacity of human nature. Currie and Ravenscroft (1997) show that people have capacities for intentional production of mental facsimiles as well, at least facsimiles of their own mental states. It is not too dramatic a leap, therefore, to conjecture that people might intentionally deploy mental facsimiles to interpret the mental states of others, as ST proposes. The evidence at least warrants rejection of the claim that ST is a "radical departure" from accepted trends in cognitive science.

How can more direct evidence be obtained for or against mental simulation? One type of argument for the existence of mental simulation is the absence of pertinent theoretical information that could guide predictors to their conclusions. Undermining TT in this fashion would indirectly support ST, which is TT's only competitor. This was the type of argument I offered with the example of airline travellers (section 2.1, above). Another type of case is Harris's (1992) hypothetical example in which one person is asked to predict another's judgments of the grammaticality (or acceptability) of various sentences. Since members of the folk possess comparatively little theoretical knowledge of grammaticality, Harris plausibly contends that a person might execute this task by simulation, by making her own judgments and assuming that the other person would judge similarly. This is not a standard form of simulation, however, as Stich and Nichols (1997) rightly point out. Here the predictor places herself in the *actual* position of the predictee, rather than *pretending* to be in the predictee's situation.

A second general type of evidence in favor of ST might exploit what I regard as the basic difference between ST and TT. The difference consists in the fact that ST posits facsimile tracking of another person's mental states, at least on some occasions of third-person mental interpretation, whereas pure TT denies that this ever occurs. By "facsimile tracking" I mean the production, in the interpreter's own mind, of a sequence of states that resemble, in crucial cognitive respects, the intended target of interpretation or attribution. TT agrees, presumably, that interpretation and successful attribution typically involve some sort of tracking of the target's states, but in this case the tracking would be purely doxastic or intellectual. It would consist of a series of conjectures and / or beliefs about the mental states of the target, and in general these beliefs would not be facsimiles of their counterparts. Instead of replicating or emulating the mental activity of the target, the interpreter would be a pure observer or spectator. Given this difference between the views, some observable predictions might be deducible. Facsimile tracking should predict tell-tale feelings, behavior, or physiological symptoms that intellectual tracking would not predict. Of course, when the target mental activity is merely theoretical inference or decision making, even facsimile tracking would not predict any noteworthy physiological symptoms or unusual feelings. But facsimile tracking might predict such feelings where the target mental activity itself yields affect or other distinctive sensations. If a predictor engaged in tracking such a target herself undergoes facsimiles of such feelings, this might be evidence in favor of ST. So I have argued in linking ST with empathy (Goldman, 1992b; 1993b). For example, people asked to predict the feelings of the parents of a kidnapped child might themselves be found to have empathic emotional reactions, especially if the circumstances are described in detail. This would suggest that the predictors have engaged in simulative (role-taking) tracking of the parents' feelings, not merely intellectual tracking. If the tracking had been purely intellectual, why would the predictors themselves experience parallel emotions? A similar argument could be made for readers of a romantic novel who experience feelings parallel to those of the novel's heroine. And many people experience feelings of discomfort or queeziness when observing the pierced tongues or pierced lips of contemporary teenagers. Such feelings are readily explained on the assumption that the observer tracks the imagined experience of having the organ pierced, and tracks it in a simulative or replicative mode.

Nichols et al. (1996) reply that empathy can be explained in information-based terms. "Empathic responses might arise when the subject is reminded of events in her past similar to those of the object of empathy. So, for example, if your friend tells you that her dog has died, you might empathize with her via remembering the death of your own dog" (Nichols et al., 1996, p. 61). They even cite researchers on empathy who mention the memory explanation as one possibility (Hoffman, 1984; Eisenberg & Strayer, 1987). However, memory does not accommodate all cases. You can empathize with the parents of a kidnapped child even if you have never yourself suffered such a tragedy and therefore lack any such memory. Furthermore, even if memory does play a role in generating empathic affect, that is not incompatible with a simulation story. Perhaps memories simply assist the construction of a simulation, which then produces the affect. Remembering different wounds of your own might help you imagine your tongue or lip being pierced. This imagination might be necessary to elicit discomfort or queeziness. A purely factual memory of having suffered past wounds might not suffice to induce queeziness or discomfort. It has already been found, experimentally, that imaginative involvement plays a role in such matters. Stotland (1969) had subjects watch someone else whose hand was strapped into a machine, which was said to generate painful heat. Some subjects were instructed just to watch the man carefully, some to imagine the way he was feeling, and some to imagine themselves in his place. Using both physiological and verbal measures, the experimental results showed that the deliberate acts of imagination produced a greater response than the sole act of watching. All of this requires more detailed empirical research, but initial evidence seems to support a role for simulative tracking.

Among the attempts to produce experimental evidence against ST, the most widely discussed are Stich and Nichols' experiments based on considerations of "cognitive penetrability" (Stich & Nichols, 1992; Nichols et al., 1996). Stich and Nichols made the theoretical claim that, if ST is correct, then essentially what attributors "don't know about psychology won't hurt them" – that is, it will not lead to false attributions. If people's decision-making propensities have a quirky feature, theoretical ignorance of that quirk should not prevent simulative predictors of their decisions from predicting correctly, because as simulators they would just use the same psychological mechanisms, which should yield similar outputs given similar inputs. Stich and Nichols proceeded to study people's predictions of choice behavior shown by psychologists to be quirky, to see if the predictions accord with what ST (allegedly) implies. For example, Langer (1975) reported an experiment in which subjects who agreed to buy a ticket in a lottery were later offered an opportunity to sell their ticket. Langer found that subjects who were offered an opportunity to choose their own ticket set a significantly higher price than those who were simply handed a ticket when they agreed to buy one. Stich and Nichols performed an experiment (reported in Nichols et al., 1996) in which subjects saw videotapes of targets in a Langer-style situation and were then asked to predict their sell-back price. Some videotaped targets got to choose their own ticket while others were simply given tickets, and subjects were shown either the choice situation or the no-choice situation. Subjects viewing the choice version did not predict higher values than those viewing the no-choice version. Given the background theoretical assumption, Nichols et al. (1996) argued that this evidence undermines ST.

There are several reasons why these results are not decisive, however. First, the moderate form of ST that I endorse does not claim that *all* behavior prediction is simulation-based. So even if simulation was not used in the Langer-style task, this does not show that it is never used. Second, it is an open question, as I have emphasized, exactly which properties mental facsimiles share with their natural counterparts. Even the best simulation may not perfectly replicate its target. So it cannot be precluded that observer subjects in the experiment did engage in facsimile tracking but still failed to reproduce the price-setting behavior of their targets. Third, Kühberger, Perner, Schulte, & Leingruber (1995) failed on several occasions to replicate the original findings of Langer, and this raises doubts about all dimensions of this line of experimentation. Nichols, Stich and Leslie (1995) reply to Kühberger et al., but the dispute is far from settled. Finally, Heal (1996) has challenged the theoretical claim that misinformation cannot penetrate a predictor's simulation process. In response to Heal's challenge, Stich and Nichols (1997) now concede that it is a mistake to make the general claim that simulation is cognitively impenetrable. On the other hand, it is not clear how this helps an ST theorist explain what was happening in their Langer-style experiment, because it is not clear what belief might have penetrated the predictors' simulation process, if simulation is what they were using.

5. Conclusion

The inconclusiveness of the experiments just reviewed is typical of the experimental forays made thus far to decide between TT and ST. Pending more conclusive direct experimentation, the prospects for the two approaches must be judged by converging evidence from many sources of the kinds reviewed earlier. This evidence undercuts pure forms of TT and gives substantial support to ST, at least in the weak form that assigns simulation an "important" (not necessarily universal) role in third-person attribution. First, the detailed articulations of TT either face serious empirical problems or turn out on careful inspection not to be so clearly versions of TT rather than ST. Second, TT suffers from a failure to acknowledge or deal adequately with people's ability to attribute mental states to themselves in a distinctive manner. The introspection-simulation approach deals with this problem quite naturally. Third, evidence from several domains of cognitive research, including visual imagery, motor imagery, neonate imitation and empathy, make it highly plausible that people could have a skill at producing mental facsimiles that is deployed in interpreting the states of others. These kinds of evidence may be among the reasons why many of the most resolute critics of ST have recently moved toward a hybrid position, a position that is difficult to distinguish from weak simulationism. There is, no doubt, much work to be done to articulate ST with greater precision, and to fill in the developmental story in an ST-friendly way. At the present juncture, however, the prospects for ST look extremely bright.

Acknowledgments

I wish to thank Tim Bayne, Gregory Currie, Robert Gordon, Alan Leslie, Shaun Nichols, Joel Pust, Ian Ravenscroft, and Dan Sperber for helpful comments and feedback on earlier drafts of this paper.

References

Adams, L., Guz, A., Innes, J., & Murphy, K. (1987). The circulatory and ventilatory response to voluntary and electrically induced exercise in man. *Journal of Physiology 383*, 19–30.

Baron-Cohen, Simon (1995). *Mindblindness*. Cambridge, MA: MIT Press.

Block, N. (1980). Troubles with functionalism. In N. Block (Ed.) *Readings in philosophy of psychology: Vol. 1*. Cambridge, MA: Harvard University Press.

Carey, S., & Spelke, E. (1996). Science and core knowledge. *Philosophy of Science 63*: 515–533.

Carruthers, P. (1996). Simulation and self-knowledge: A defence of theory-theory. In P. Carruthers & P. Smith (Eds.), *Theories of theories of mind*. New York: Cambridge University Press.

Clements, N., & Perner, J. (1994). Implicit understanding of belief. *Cognitive Development 9*, 377–395.

Currie, G. (1995). Visual imagery as the simulation of vision. *Mind and Language 10*, 25–44.

Currie, G., & Ravenscroft, I. (1997). Mental simulation and motor imagery. *Philosophy of Science 64*, 161–180.

Davies, Martin, & Stone, Tony, Eds. (1995a). *Folk psychology*. Oxford: Basil Blackwell.

Davies, Martin, & Stone, Tony, Eds. (1995b). *Mental simulation*. Oxford: Basil Blackwell.

Decety, J., Sjoholm, H., Ryding, E., Stenberg, G., & Ingvar. D. (1990). The cerebellum participates in cognitive activity: Tomographic measurements of regional cerebral blood flow. *Brain Research 535*, 313–317.

Eisenberg, N., & Strayer, J. (1987). Critical issues in the study of empathy. In N. Eisenberg & J. Strayer (Eds.), *Empathy and its development*. New York: Cambridge University Press.

Farah, M. (1988). Is visual imagery really visual? Overlooked evidence from neurophysiology. *Psychological Review 95*, 307–317.

Freeman, N., & Lacohee, H. (1995). Making explicit 3-year-olds' implicit competence with their own false beliefs. *Cognition 56*, 31–60.

Goldman, A. (1989). Interpretation psychologized. *Mind and Language 4*, 161–185. (Reprinted in *Folk psychology*, by Martin Davies & Tony Stone, Eds., 1995, Oxford: Basil Blackwell.)

Goldman, A. (1992a). In defense of the simulation theory. *Mind and Language 7*: 104–119. (Reprinted in *Folk psychology*, by Martin Davies & Tony Stone, Eds., 1995, Oxford: Basil Blackwell.)

Goldman, A. (1992b). Empathy, mind, and morals. *Proceedings and Addresses of the American Philosophical Association 66* (3): 17–41. (Reprinted in *Mental simulation*, by Martin Davies & Tony Stone, Eds., 1995, Oxford: Basil Blackwell.)

Goldman, A. (1993a). The psychology of folk psychology. *Behavioral and Brain Sciences 16*, 15–28.

Goldman, A. (1993b). *Philosophical applications of cognitive science.* Boulder, CO: Westview Press.

Goldman, A. (1997). Science, publicity, and consciousness. *Philosophy of Science 64*, 525–545.

Gopnik, A. (1993). How we know our minds: The illusion of first-person knowledge of intentionality. *Behavioral and Brain Sciences 16*, 1–14.

Gopnik, A. (1996). The scientist as child. *Philosophy of Science 63*, 485–514.

Gopnik, Alison, & Meltzoff, Andrew (1997). *Words, thoughts, and theories.* Cambridge, MA: MIT Press.

Gopnik, A., & Wellman, H. (1992). Why the child's theory of mind really *is* a theory. *Mind and Language 7*, 145–171. (Reprinted in *Folk psychology*, by Martin Davies & Tony Stone, Eds., 1995, Oxford: Basil Blackwell.)

Gopnik, A., & Wellman, H. (1994). The theory theory. In L. Hirschfeld & S. Gelman (Eds.), *Mapping the mind.* New York: Cambridge University Press.

Gordon, R. (1992). The simulation theory: Objections and misconceptions. *Mind and Language 7*, 11–34. (Reprinted in *Folk psychology*, by Martin Davies & Tony Stone, Eds., 1995, Oxford: Basil Blackwell.)

Gordon, R. (1995). Simulation without introspection or inference from me to you. In Martin Davies & Tony Stone, Eds., *Mental simulation*. Oxford: Basil Blackwell.

Gordon, R. (1996). "Radical" simulationism. In P. Carruthers & P. Smith (Eds.), *Theories of theories of mind.* New York: Cambridge University Press.

Harris, P. (1992). From simulation to folk psychology. *Mind and Language 7*, 120–144. (Reprinted in *Folk psychology*, by Martin Davies & Tony Stone, Eds., 1995, Oxford: Basil Blackwell.)

Harris, P. (1996). Desires, beliefs, and language. In P. Carruthers & P. Smith (Eds.), *Theories of theories of mind.* New York: Cambridge University Press.

Heal, J. (1996). Simulation and cognitive penetrability. *Mind and Language 11*, 44–67.

Hoffman, M. (1984). Interaction of affect and cognition in empathy. In C. Izard, J. Kagan, & R. Zajonc (Eds.), *Emotions, cognition, and behavior.* New York: Cambridge University Press.

Humphrey, Nicholas (1983). *Consciousness regained.* New York: Oxford University Press.

Johnson, S., & Carey, S. (1996). Distinguishing knowledge enrichment from conceptual change: Evidence from Williams Syndrome. Unpublished paper, Department of Psychology, New York University.

Kahneman, D., & Tversky, A. (1982). The simulation heuristic. In D. Kahneman, P. Slovic, & A. Tversky (Eds.), *Judgment under Uncertainty.* Cambridge: Cambridge University Press.

Kosslyn, S., Alpert, N., Thompson, W., Maljkovic, V., Weise, S., Chabris, C., Hamilton, S., Rauch, S., & Buannano, F. (1993). Visual mental imagery activates topographically organized visual cortex: PET investigations. *Cognitive Neuroscience 5*, 263–287.

Kühberger, H., Perner, J., Schulte, M., & Leingruber, R. (1995). Choice or no choice: Is the Langer Effect evidence against simulation? *Mind and Language* 10, 423–436.

Langer, E. (1975). The illusion of control. *Journal of Personality and Social Psychology 32*, 311–328.

Leslie, A. (1987). Pretence and representation: The "origins" of theory of mind. *Psychological Review 94*, 412–426.

Leslie, A. (1994). Pretending and believing: Issues in the theory of ToMM. *Cognition 50*, 211–238.

Leslie, A., & German, T. (1995). Knowledge and ability in "theory of mind": One-eyed overview of a debate. In Martin Davies & Tony Stone, Eds., *Mental simulation*. Oxford: Basil Blackwell.

Leslie, A., & Roth, D. (1993). What autism teaches us about metarepresentation. In S. Baron-Cohen, H. Tager-Flusberg, and D. Cohen (Eds.), *Understanding other minds: Perspectives from autism*. Oxford: Oxford University Press.

Leslie, A., & Thaiss, L. (1992). Domain specificity in conceptual development: Neuropsychological evidence from autism. *Cognition 43*, 225–251.

Lewis, C., Freeman, N., Hagestadt, C., & Douglas, H. (1994). Narrative access and production in preschoolers' false belief reasoning. *Cognitive Development 9*, 397–424.

Lewis, D. (1972). Psychophysical and theoretical identifications. *Australasian Journal of Philosophy 50*, 249–258.

Meltzoff, A. (1995). Understanding the intentions of others: Re-enactment of intended acts by 18-month-old children. *Developmental Psychology 31*, 838–850.

Meltzoff, A., & Moore, M. (1983). Newborn infants imitate adult facial gestures. *Child Development 54*, 702–709.

Meltzoff, A., & Moore, M. (1995). Infants' understanding of people and things: From body imitation to folk psychology. In J. Bermudez, A. Marcel, & N. Eilan (Eds.), *The body and the self*. Cambridge, MA: MIT Press.

Nichols, S., Stich, S., Leslie, A., & Klein, D. (1996). Varieties of off-line simulation. In P. Carruthers & P. Smith (Eds.) *Theories of theories of mind*. New York: Cambridge University Press.

Nichols, S., Stich, S., & Leslie, A. (1995). Choice effects and the ineffectiveness of simulation. *Mind and Language 10*, 437–445.

Perner, Josef (1991). *Understanding the representational mind*. Cambridge, MA: MIT Press.

Perner, J. (1996). Simulation as explicitation of predication-implicit knowledge about the mind: Arguments for a simulation-theory mix. In P. Carruthers & P. Smith (Eds.), *Theories of theories of mind*. New York: Cambridge University Press.

Perner, J. & Howes, D. (1992). 'He thinks he knows'; and more developmental evidence against the simulation (role-taking) theory. *Mind and Language 7*, 72–86. (Reprinted in *Folk psychology*, by Martin Davies & Tony Stone, Eds., 1995, Oxford: Basil Blackwell).

Richardson, A. (1967). Mental practice: A review and discussion, parts I and II. *Research Quarterly 38*, 95–107; 262–273.

Rosenthal, D. (1992). Thinking that one thinks. In M. Davies and G. Humphreys (Eds.), *Consciousness*. Oxford: Blackwell.

Schacter, D. (1989). On the relation between memory and consciousness. In H. Roediger III & F. Craik (Eds.), *Varieties of memory and consciousness.* Hillsdale, NJ: Erlbaum.

Schiffer, S. (1987). *Remnants of meaning.* Cambridge, MA: MIT Press.

Segal, G. (1996). The modularity of theory of mind. In P. Carruthers & P. Smith (Eds.), *Theories of theories of mind.* New York: Cambridge University Press.

Sellars, W. (1963). Empiricism and the philosophy of mind. In his *Science, perception and reality.* London: Routledge.

Stich, S., & Nichols, S. (1992). Folk psychology: Simulation or tacit theory? *Mind and Language 7*, 35–71. (Reprinted in *Folk psychology,* by Martin Davies & Tony Stone, Eds., 1995, Oxford: Basil Blackwell.)

Stich, S., & Nichols, S. (1995). Second thoughts on simulation. In Martin Davies & Tony Stone, Eds., *Mental simulation.* Oxford: Basil Blackwell.

Stich, S., & Nichols, S. (1997). Cognitive penetrability, rationality and restricted simulation. *Mind and Language 12*, 297–326.

Stotland, E. (1969). Exploratory investigations of empathy. In L. Berkowitz (Ed.), *Advances in experimental social psychology,* Vol. 4. New York: Academic Press.

Tager-Flusberg, H. (1994). Theory of mind in young children with Williams Syndrome. Paper presented at the Biennial Meeting of the Williams Syndrome Association, San Diego.

Wellman, Henry (1990). *The child's theory of mind.* Cambridge, MA: MIT Press.

Yue, G., & Cole, K. (1992). Strength increases from the motor program: Comparison of training with maximal voluntary and imagined muscle contractions. *Journal of Neurophysiology 67*, 1114–1123.

Chapter 8

How to Acquire a
Representational Theory of Mind

Alan M. Leslie

The study of cognitive development is dominated by the view that concepts are essentially *packets of theory-like knowledge* (Carey, 1985; 1988; Keil, 1989). This view has emerged from a long tradition of viewing concepts as descriptions of one kind or another, though there have been and continue to be many variations and disagreements concerning the character of the associated knowledge (e.g., Murphy & Medin, 1985; for critical reviews of this tradition, see Fodor, 1998; Kripke, 1972; Laurence & Margolis, in press). The essence of this family of views is that the knowledge packet associated with the concept determines what in the world a given concept refers to or designates – it fixes what the concept is a concept of. For example, the concept DOG[1] might be associated with a knowledge structure that specifies "HAIRY, FOUR-LEGGED, ANIMAL, BARKS, WAGS TAIL . . ." If this specification captures the structure of the concept, DOG, then this is the specification you will need to know in order to possess the concept, for the following reason: this specification, when applied to the world, is what will selectively pick out the things that are *dogs* and thus link DOG with *dogs*.

The concept-as-knowledge view is so deeply entrenched that it is hard to see how there could be an alternative. The view has two powerful implications for conceptual development. First, the acquisition of a concept must be the acquisition of the critical knowledge that defines the concept. Second, the innateness of a concept must be the innateness of the critical knowledge that defines the concept.

The knowledge view of concepts will, perhaps, prove to be correct. To date, however, there is not a single concept for which a detailed model of the critical knowledge has been worked out and empirically substantiated; there is not a single concept whose acquisition or innateness has been understood. All conclusions, therefore, remain highly tentative.

Much of the most interesting work in cognitive development over the last 20 years has been concerned with abstract concepts, that is, with concepts that are not reducible to sensory transduction. Many abstract concepts are now thought to emerge early in development. Mental-state concepts, such as BELIEVE, DESIRE, and PRETEND, are among the most abstract we possess. It is striking that these concepts are routinely acquired by all normally developing children before they attend school and are even acquired by children who are mentally retarded. The verbal labels associated with these concepts are never explicitly taught yet are typically in use by children around their third birthday; by contrast, words for colors, a salient sensory property, very often are explicitly taught by parents but are typically not learned any earlier and are often learned later. Mental-state concepts provide a crucial challenge to our attempts to understand what is required for the acquisition and possession of abstract concepts. In our attempts to understand early emergence, one variant of the knowledge view of concepts has become popular; in this variant, critical knowledge is said to take the form of a *theory*. The concept BELIEF has been a central focus of these attempts.

At first sight, it is plausible that the acquisition of the concept BELIEF must be theory formation because how else can we come to know abstract things, if not by employing theories. The so-called theory-theory of BELIEF has gained a widespread credence (Gopnik & Meltzoff, 1997; Gopnik & Wellman, 1994; 1995; Perner, 1991; Wellman, 1990). However, I believe that current attempts to develop a theory-theory of BELIEF have foundered. In this chapter, I shall explore the reasons for these present difficulties. Because I have elsewhere written extensively on the relevant experimental evidence and developed an alternative framework to theory-theory (see, e.g., Leslie, in press), here I shall confine myself to examining the deeper motivations for theory-theory in order to say why I believe the entire enterprise is mistaken.

Three Versions of Theory-Theory

There seem to be about three versions of theory-theory currently active; they are not always clearly distinguished, though they need to be. The first is simply the idea that not all knowledge is sensory in character and that some knowledge is concerned with "understanding" the world. This seems sensible and true. To say that people acquire common-sense "theories" in this sense is just to say that they acquire abstract knowledge and opinion. For example, people develop opinions about the existence of ghosts (Boyer, 1994), the nature of consciousness (Flavell, Green, & Flavell, 1993), and the disposition of heavenly bodies (Vosniadou, 1994). People also develop opinions about circumstances that will cause beliefs to be false. If this is to be called a "representational theory of mind," then I shall argue that the concept BELIEF exists prior to the theory.

A second current version of theory-theory is more controversial. This view holds that routine early cognitive development and the process of scientific discovery both result in knowledge of "theories"; in particular, it is claimed that the child's "theory of mind" really *is* a theory. I shall discuss this version in the next section, Some Current Beliefs about Belief, where I conclude that it is not useful to insist that things that are merely theory-*like* really *are* theories.

The third version of theory-theory goes deeper than the first two because it tries to account for the nature and acquisition of concepts. In its most explicit and sophisticated form, developed by Carey (1985, 1988), fundamental structures of thought are said to depend upon ontological concepts, such as PHYSICAL OBJECT, LIVING THING, and so forth. The identity of an ontological concept is determined by the role it plays in a set of explanatory principles grasped by the child. A given set of explanatory principles is domain-specific and theory-like but, most importantly, constitutes the "packet of knowledge" that allows the child (or another user) to pick out just those things in the world to which the concept refers. Put more simply, a concept, DOG, for example, is possessed by grasping a certain common-sense theory, namely, the theory that tells the user what kind of thing a *dog* is. Acquiring this concept is acquiring the theory of what a *dog* is. If (knowledge of) a given theory is innate, then the associated concept will also be innate; if a given theory must be acquired, then the associated concept must be acquired (by acquiring knowledge of the theory). Perner (1991, 1995) has applied this framework to the concept, BELIEF. In his account, the child acquires the concept BELIEF by acquiring a theory of what *beliefs* are, namely, the theory that *beliefs are representations*. I discuss this version of theory-theory in a later section, Concept as Theory, pointing out that it requires the child to have much obscure knowledge for which there is no independent evidence and that, even so, it still fails to account for possession of the specific concept, BELIEF.

Some Current Beliefs about Belief

The empirical basis of the belief problem is as follows. Wimmer and Perner (1983) developed a test of false-belief understanding (the Maxi task) that the majority of six-year-old children could pass while four-year-old children performed at chance. Baron-Cohen, Leslie and Frith (1985) subsequently modified this task, simplifying it (the Sally and Ann task, see Figure 1). They found that the majority of normally developing four-year-old children passed this version. This study also found that a majority of mildly retarded children with Down's syndrome could pass the task but that children with autism, even those with normal IQs, failed. Subsequently, numerous studies have confirmed and extended these results (for reviews, see Happé, 1995; Leslie, in press). By age four, most normally developing children are demonstrably employing the concept BELIEF.

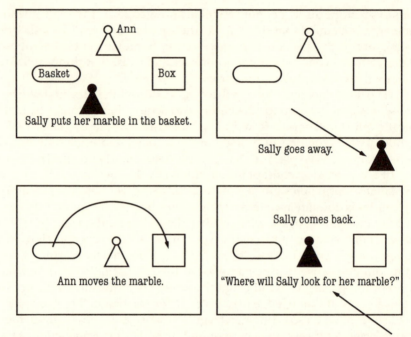

Figure 1. A standard test of false-belief attribution. In addition to the belief pre-diction question, children are asked two control questions, one to check that they remember where Sally put the marble and another to check they realize where the marble is currently. An alternative to the prediction question is the *think* question: Where does Sally think the marble is? Both prediction and think questions yield similar results with normally developing children and with chil-dren with developmental disorder. (After Baron-Cohen, Leslie, & Frith, 1985).

The Real-Theory-Theory

One version of theory-theory is that people, including children, "have theories." As I indicated, there is little in this claim to disagree with, in part because the notion of 'theory', especially when extended from sci-ence to common sense, is vague enough to cover almost any kind of knowledge and opinion.

Recently, however, the claim has been pushed to an extreme in which routine cognitive development and the process of scientific dis-covery are claimed to be essentially identical (e.g., Gopnik & Meltzoff, 1997; Gopnik & Wellman, 1995).[2] Although there is some disagreement within the theory-theory camp over whether the child-as-scientist claim relates to the *process* of development (denied by Wellman, 1990 and by Perner, 1995 but espoused by Gopnik and Wellman, 1995 and by Gopnik and Meltzoff, 1997) or only to the *outcome* of that process (Perner, 1995; Wellman, 1990), there appears to be agreement that it relates at least to the outcome. Gopnik and Wellman develop their claim by thinking of scientific theories as a species of psychological entity (Gopnik & Wellman, 1994; 1995). They are not concerned with the substance of any particular scientific theory but, rather, with the general psychological properties of that whole class of knowledge. From this point of view, they generate a list of critical properties. The critical properties of scientific theories are said to be abstractness, coherence, predictiveness, defeasibility, interpretation of evidence, and explanatoriness. Gopnik and Wellman then point to features of the child's theory of mind as it develops from about two to four years of age that illustrate each of these properties. They conclude that, therefore, what the child has acquired over this time really *is* a theory because these properties of a scientist's knowledge are also properties of a child's theory-of-mind knowledge.

The Case of Language

Unfortunately, the properties that Gopnik and Wellman (also Gopnik & Meltzoff, 1997) consider crucial to establishing their claim fail to distinguish knowledge entities that are indisputably real theories from knowledge entities that are merely theory-*like*. Consider the case of language. The left-hand panel of Figure 2 mentions an indisputably *real* theory of language, namely, the *Principles and Parameters* theory of generative linguistics (e.g., Chomsky & Lasnik, 1995). This theory is widely regarded as being a piece of *echt* science even by those who do not regard it as being true. Furthermore, it is undoubtedly the case that some people (certainly not me) possess real knowledge of this theory. So, here is a clear sense in which someone (i.e., Noam Chomsky) knows something and the something that he knows really *is* a theory.

The right-hand panel of Figure 2, by contrast, shows the psychological entities and mechanisms that (are postulated by the theory on the left to) embody the knowledge of language that people routinely possess, including regular people like me and my neighbor's child and not just special people like Chomsky. One of these entities is the grammar of English, in some way represented in my brain and in the brain of my neighbor's child. Another entity is Universal Grammar, which, according to the theory in the left-hand panel, is the entity, again in some way represented in the brain, that enabled me and my neighbor's child to acquire our knowledge of the grammar of English. Chomsky's brain in some way represents all the entities depicted in Figure 2.

Now, a mental grammar has often been described as an internalization of a theory of a language and the child's acquisition of a language has often been described as being like a process of theory formation. For example, Chomsky claims that, in acquiring knowledge of a language, "the young child has succeeded in carrying out what from the formal point of view . . . seems to be a remarkable type of theory construction"

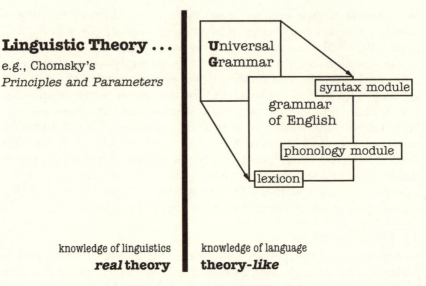

Linguistic Theory ...
e.g., Chomsky's
Principles and Parameters

Universal Grammar

syntax module

grammar of English

phonology module

lexicon

knowledge of linguistics
***real* theory**

knowledge of language
theory-*like*

Figure 2. The case of language illustrates the distinction between a scientific theory ('*real* theory') and psychological entities that are theory-*like*. Both can be represented in the brains of people who possess the relevant knowledge: knowledge of linguistics and knowledge of language, respectively. However, most people only have knowledge of language.

(Chomsky, 1957, p. 56). The entities or processes on the right side in Figure 2 can reasonably be described as theory-*like*. However, one would have to be *completely* blind to questions of mechanism to say that an internalized grammar really *is* a theory as Chomsky's *Principles and Parameters* is. Although almost nothing is known about the psychological basis of scientific knowledge, the best guess is that the child's knowledge of language is distinct from Chomsky's knowledge of linguistic theory in just about every respect that a psychologist might be interested in, including the mental representations involved, accessibility, penetrability, the timing, time course and process of acquisition, and the underlying brain systems. Such distinctions are missed if we say that both knowledge of linguistics and knowledge of language really *are* theories.

As noted earlier, Gopnik and Wellman argue that the child's theory of mind really *is* a theory because it meets a set of criteria derived from a characterization of real theories (Gopnik & Wellman, 1994, 1995; also Gopnik & Meltzoff, 1997). Unfortunately, for anyone interested in the above distinctions, these criteria also characterize the theory-like entities in the right panel of Figure 2 every bit as much as they characterize the *real* theory in the left panel. Theories postulate abstract entities that explain phenomena (Gopnik & Wellman, 1995, p. 260); the child's internalized grammar is thought to "postulate" abstract entities (e.g., categories like S and NP; properties of parse-tree geometry) that explain sentence structure. Theories exhibit coherence in a system of laws or structures (Gopnik & Wellman, 1995, p. 260); the child's internalized grammar is thought to be a system of interacting rules and representations that generate the structures of his language ("systematicity"). Theories make predictions "about a wide variety of evidence, including evidence that played no role in the theory's initial construction" (Gopnik & Wellman, 1995, p. 261); an internalized grammar allows the child to produce and comprehend novel sentences that "played no role in the [grammar's] initial construction" ("productivity"). Theories can be falsified by their predictions yet may be resistant to counter-evidence, may spawn auxiliary hypotheses, and so on (Gopnik & Wellman, 1995, p. 262–263); such phenomena in relation to the construction of an internalized grammar are much discussed in the language acquisition literature. Theories "produce interpretations of evidence, not simply descriptions ... of evidence" (Gopnik & Wellman, 1995, p. 262); internalized grammars produce interpretations of sound patterns in terms of meaning via intermediate levels of structure including phonology, morphology, and syntax, and not simply descriptions of the sounds themselves. Finally, although a "distinctive pattern of explanation, prediction, and interpretation" (such as we have noted above for grammar) "is among the best indicators of a theoretical structure" (Gopnik & Wellman, 1995, p. 262), it cannot distinguish a child's knowledge of language from Chomsky's knowledge of linguistic theory.

Modules and Theory-Theory

Gopnik and Wellman are not unaware that their criteria of "theory-hood" are too weak to do much work. In contrasting their theory-theory view with the innate-module view of the child's theory of mind, they note, "many kinds of evidence that are commonly adduced to support [theory-theory] or [modularity], in fact, cannot discriminate between the two ... the fact that the representations in question are abstract, and removed from the evidence of actual experience is compatible with either view" (Gopnik & Wellman, 1994, p. 282).

The failure to identify a *formal* basis for distinguishing between theory-like knowledge structures (such as might be found in modular systems) and knowledge of real theories should not be surprising. The philosophical project to develop a formal theory of what makes a set of beliefs into a scientific theory has long been abandoned as hopeless, as Gopnik and Wellman are aware. Many sets of beliefs, even the beliefs of perceptual systems, are abstract, coherent, predictive, explanatory, and offer interpretations that go beyond the evidence. There is no great harm in calling these systems "theories" or "theory-like." But it is hard to see what the point might be in arguing that these systems "really *are* theories" unless there is some definite way to distinguish them from systems that "really *aren't* theories" but are merely theory-like. However, there is no reason why one should expect science to be a natural kind.

Gopnik and Wellman advance one property of theories that, they say, discriminates theories from modules, namely, "defeasibility" (Gopnik & Wellman, 1994; see also Gopnik & Meltzoff, 1997). The notion of defeasibility in the philosophy of science refers to the willingness of a theorist to regard a proposition or theory as "negotiable" or revisable, for example, in the light of evidence. According to Gopnik and Wellman, this property of real theories is also a property of the common-sense theories that they attribute to children. Presumably, what they mean is simply that children's "real theories" are revisable rather than that children always *believe* that their theories are revisable. In any case, according to these authors, modules are not similarly "defeasible." In fact, Gopnik and Wellman go so far as to label modules "anti-developmental" (1994, p. 283), apparently because they believe that knowledge in modules cannot be revised. They are careful to point out that it is not the issue of innateness that divides theory-theory from modularity theory. Indeed, they hold that theory-theory needs to postulate innate theories, including in particular, an innate theory of mind. But these innate theories are not fixed for all time; they are defeasible and are often quickly revised by the child.

Even the property of defeasibility, however, does not discriminate between real theories and theory-like entities such as modules (see Stich & Nichols, 1998). It is hard to know why Gopnik and colleagues have come to believe that modules are fixed at birth, unrevisable, and anti-developmental. None of the major modularity theorists posit such properties. Take the Chomskean modules of Figure 2 (right panel) as an example. The module, Universal Grammar, has the job of "revising" itself in the light of the properties of the language(s) to which it is exposed. It does this by setting the values of a number of parameters. This, in turn, affects the nature of the grammar module that is constructed for a particular language. These modules learn and in the process revise themselves and no doubt will have mechanisms to recover from error. My point is not that Chomsky's proposal is correct but that, in proposing modular processes, Chomsky did not somehow overlook the fact that his modules were learning mechanisms. On the contrary, for Chomsky that was the whole point.

To take a rather different example of a module, consider Marr's "Object Catalogue" whose job is to recognize three-dimensional objects from arbitrary viewing points (Marr, 1982). A module that performs this job has to learn the three-dimensional shapes of literally tens of thousands of everyday objects and no doubt makes the occasional error-plus-revision along the way. Again, my point is not that Marr's theory is right but that, in making his proposal, Marr, as an important modularity theorist, was quite happy that his module could perform a prodigious feat of learning. Or, consider the lexicon that modularity theorists, like Fodor, often assume is a module (Fodor, 1983). Given that the adult lexicon contains many tens of thousands of items (Levelt, 1999) and that infant lexicons contain none, the lexicon must learn on a grand scale, with the occasional recovery from error (Carey, 1978).

Innate Theories and General Learning

Gopnik and colleagues claim that modules are anti-developmental. Perhaps they mean that the degree of defeasibility is too low, that "theories" can be *radically* revised while modules cannot. Wellman (1990) argues that the child's initial theory of belief is that "beliefs are copies of reality" and that this theory is soon revised to become the theory that "beliefs are representations of reality." Perhaps this is an example of the radical revision of which modules are supposed incapable. The issues here are far from clear. However, it does seem odd that children should have an innate theory that almost immediately requires radical revision and indeed that receives such revision within a year or two. If the necessary revisions to the innate theory become obvious to the average child between the ages of two and four years after applying his limited reasoning abilities to the morsel of idiosyncratic experience available in that time, why, with its vast experiential resources of biological time and whole populations, were these revisions not glaringly obvious to the processes of evolution or whatever Gopnik and colleagues assume bestowed the innate theory? Why does Nature not just bestow the revised "theory" and be done with it? These are interesting questions but, as Scholl and Leslie (1999b) point out, there is no reason to suppose that early theory of mind involves radical revision rather than plain learning. It is obvious why Nature should bestow a module (e.g., the lexicon) that will contain more information at the end of its life than it does at the start. It is far from clear, however, how the *representational* theory of belief contains *more* information than the *copy* theory of belief, rather than simply being a "better" theory. And, it is quite puzzling why Nature should bestow a false theory when she could have bestowed a true theory.

Perhaps, what Gopnik and colleagues really want to say about theories in comparison with modules is that theories are acquired by mechanisms of general learning whereas modules are mechanisms of specialized learning. Thus, someone acquiring knowledge of Chomsky's linguistic theories would have to employ mechanisms of general learning. Meanwhile, (according to Chomsky's theory) a child acquiring knowledge of language employs specialized modular learning mechanisms. There are many interesting issues here, which would take us too far afield to pursue. However, the case for purely general mechanisms in theory-of-mind development does not look good. Which general learning mechanisms might be involved? Presumably, exactly those that are used in building scientific theories. If that claim seems too strong, we can weaken it: if not those responsible for scientific creativity, then the mechanisms are those mechanisms involved at least in learning about scientific theories or, at the very least, those involved in learning about science at elementary levels of education. These mechanisms for "real" learning of science are highly sensitive to IQ: witness the large differences between individuals in their ability to benefit from science education. In fact, IQ tests were specifically designed to measure such differences in general or "academic" intellectual ability (Anderson, 1992). Mildly retarded individuals – e.g., those with IQs around 60 – have an extremely limited ability to acquire even elementary scientific ideas. Yet, we have known for some time that mildly retarded non-autistic individuals can pass standard false-belief tasks (e.g., Baron-Cohen et al., 1985; Happé, 1995). Early theory-of-mind development is substantially independent of intellectual level and, therefore, cannot depend solely upon general-purpose learning mechanisms. More recent evidence, some of it from unexpected sources, has further supported the modular nature of theory of mind (Hughes & Cutting, 1999; Langdon & Coltheart, 1999; Leslie, in press; Varley & Siegal, in press).

Articulating Theory-Theories

Before I leave this question, I want to remark upon one property that real theories always have. It is impossible to imagine a scientific theory that is not explicitly articulated in a natural or a formal language. For example, Chomsky's knowledge of *Principles and Parameters* theory is explicitly articulated in a number of books and articles. Those who claim knowledge of Chomsky's theory must also be able to formulate explicitly its propositions and, to the extent that they cannot do this, we deny them that knowledge. Translating this property into the "real theory-theory" framework, shouldn't we say that knowledge cannot really *be* a theory unless it is explicitly articulated in a declarative representation? This places a strong requirement upon knowledge that is to count as a real theory: it demands that the child be able to articulate, for example, his theory of belief. Is this too strong a requirement to place upon knowledge of a theory? It is, if we want to allow "implicit" knowledge of theories. I am very much in favor of implicit knowledge in theory-*like* entities and of leaving open to empirical investigation the question of which properties of a psychological entity are theory-like and which are not. That is the point of using *metaphors* – one gets to choose the properties in respect of which the metaphor does and does not hold. But, can Gopnik and colleagues claim that a psychological entity non-metaphorically, *really*, is a theory and then be allowed to pick and choose the properties in respect of which this is alleged to be true? I don't believe they can. However, I shall put aside my misgivings and not insist that the child be able to state (even) his "real" theories.

I will insist, however, that the theory-theorist be able to articulate the content of the child's theory – on the child's behalf, as it were. After all, the content of the child's theory forms the central substance of the claims made by the theory-theorist. As described by Gopnik and colleagues, it is hard to discern exactly what the child's theory of belief is. What is it exactly the child thinks when the child entertains his "representational theory of belief"? Surely, the child's theory cannot simply be that beliefs are representations. Why would that really *be* a theory? Both Gopnik and Wellman focus on what the younger child does *not* understand but say little to specify what the older child's view actually is. Among the theory-theorists, only Perner has addressed this important point. I discuss Perner's specific proposals in the next section, Concept as Theory, after I have outlined the third and most interesting strand of current theory-theory, which uses a theory analogy to provide an account of the semantics of abstract concepts.

Concept as Theory

From this point in the discussion, we shall no longer worry about whether a "theory" the child might have really *is* a theory. It will be enough if a piece of knowledge is merely theory-like. In this section, we shall be concerned principally with Perner's proposal and Perner is not, as far as I know, committed to the theory of mind really *being* a theory, in the sense of Gopnik and her colleagues. Perner (1991, 1995) is, however, committed, first, to the notion that a child acquires an explicit understanding of belief-as-representation, second, to the notion of conceptual change, and, third, to the idea that "each particular mental concept gets its meaning not in isolation but only as an element within *an explanatory network of concepts*, that is, a theory" (Perner, 1991, p. 109). He is, therefore, committed to the idea of concept-as-theory.

The basic idea behind concept-as-theory is as follows. With something as abstract as belief, the only way that you could think thoughts about beliefs is if you have a theory of what beliefs really are. Beliefs do not look like anything, they do not sound like anything, and they are not found in some specifiable location, and so forth, so how are you (or your cognitive system or brain) going to describe to yourself (or itself) what a belief is? An attractive answer is that you will need something like a theory to describe to yourself what a belief is. The theory has to be accurate enough in its description to ensure that the concept, BELIEF, which is embedded in the theory, does in fact refer to *beliefs* and not to something else. The description is what will determine what is picked out by the concept. So, if the description does a very bad job (of describing what a belief is) and instead describes, say, a desire or a toothache, then the associated concept will not in fact be a concept of *belief* but a concept of *desire* or *toothache*, as the case may be. So, the exact nature of the associated theory is vitally important because this is what determines both the sense of the concept and what its referent will be.

Moreover, on the concept-as-theory account, acquiring the concept, BELIEF, is acquiring the theory that says what kind of thing *belief* is. If the child has not acquired the theory, then he will not be in possession of the concept; if he acquires a theory that so badly describes *belief* that it instead describes *desire*, then the child will have acquired the concept DESIRE instead. It makes sense, then, on this version of theory-theory to pay a lot of attention to exactly what the child knows about *belief*. Because what he knows or doesn't know about *belief*, will determine what concept he has. To put it round the other way, you can discover what concept the child has by discovering what he knows or does not know about *belief*. But, before you can decide whether the state of the child's knowledge means that he possesses the concept BELIEF, you must first decide what the critical knowledge is that the child must possess. This means you must first decide what are the critical features of the adult concept BELIEF – what it is that we adults know about *belief* that makes our concept pick out just the things that are *beliefs*. If you are a theory-theorist, this critical adult knowledge must be our common-sense theory of what *beliefs* are. From the adult theory of *belief*, the developmental researcher derives a set of criteria that will be applied to the child's knowledge. If the child meets these criteria, he must possess the concept; if he does not, he must lack the concept. Hence the theory-theorist's interest in setting knowledge criteria for concept possession (Perner, 1991, chap. 5).

The Concept Dictionary Model

Abstract concepts, as I noted earlier, are widely supposed to be abbreviations for packets of knowledge. The concept-as-theory is one variant of this view. Imagine our repertoire of concepts as a dictionary – a long list of items, each made up of two parts, a concept on the left and an associated theory or definition on the right. Almost all the variance in theories of concepts has to do with the nature of the entries postulated for the right-hand side of the list: necessary and sufficient conditions (definitions), a stochastic function over features (prototypes), rules of inference, or theories. In every case, however, the entry on the right functions as some kind of a description of whatever the concept on the left denotes and, hence, the term 'Descriptivism' for this general view of concepts. A dictionary model might be held explicitly, in the sense that its entries are assumed to be mental symbols, or implicitly, in the sense that the entries are assumed to be merely emergent properties. Either way, possessing a given concept means having the correct entry for that concept in one's mental dictionary; using that concept (as the meaning of a word or as an element of a thought) is gaining access to the associated entry; and acquiring that concept means acquiring that entry.

Just as a real dictionary describes the meanings of words in terms of other words, so, in the dictionary model of concepts, it is assumed that the items on *both* the left and right sides of an entry are concepts. A concept is given a definition (or a prototype, theory, etc.) that itself is composed of concepts. For example, the entry for the concept DOG might give the definition, DOG = CANINE ANIMAL. In a prototype theory, DOG will be characterized as a stochastic function over properties such as HAIRY, FOUR LEGS, SLAVERS, BARKS, etc. A theory-theory might show an entry that makes critical reference to a dog being a LIVING THING. In all these cases, the descriptive entries are assumed to be made up of other concepts, such as CANINE, ANIMAL, HAIRY, LIVING THING, and so on, each of which will have its own entry with an associated description in the dictionary. That the descriptive entry is formed by other concepts is an especially natural assumption for the theory-theory, because it is hard to imagine how a theory could ever be stated without using concepts. In all dictionary-model accounts, but in theory-theory accounts in particular, possessing, using, and acquiring one concept depends upon possessing, using, and acquiring other concepts.

The dictionary model has a number of attractive features but it also has one major drawback. The everyday dictionary of words depends upon the fact that its user already knows the meanings of most of the words in the dictionary. If this were not true, the practice of defining one word in terms other words would go nowhere. A dictionary in an utterly foreign tongue offers no point of entry or exit. If we know none of them, we can never escape from the maze of words and the dictionary is useless. The same point applies to the dictionary model of concepts. If we come to know what a given concept is by learning its (theoretical, etc.) description, which is given in terms of other concepts, then we shall need already to possess those other concepts and be able already to pick out the things in the world to which they refer. But, those other concepts are known by way of their entries in the concept dictionary, and those entries comprise yet other concepts, and so on. Because this cannot, in fact, go on forever, there must be some concepts that are known, not by a describing entry in the dictionary but by some other route. These are usually called the primitive concepts. Primitive concepts provide the floor or ground upon which all other concepts stand are are ultimately defined. A primitive concept is not acquired by learning a description; otherwise, we are back in the maze. But, if there is a way to acquire a concept without learning a description, then the whole dictionary model is called into question. For this reason, dictionary models assume that primitive concepts are unlearned, i.e., innate.

With a highly abstract concept like BELIEF, the dictionary model creates a dilemma for theory-theory. Either BELIEF is primitive and innate or it is acquired. If it is innate, then either the concept is constituted by an associated theory or it is not. If BELIEF is established by an associated theory (and is innate), then knowledge of that theory too must be innate. If it is not so constituted, then BELIEF is an innate abstract concept that falls outside the scope of theory-theory. In which case, we shall want to know for which other theory-of-mind concepts theory-theory is irrelevant.

Alternatively, if BELIEF is acquired, then we have to ask what the other concepts are in the description the child has to acquire in order to possess BELIEF. Once we have an answer to that, we shall be obliged to ask the same question about each of those concepts. What are their associated theories? What are the concepts in those theories? We must press our inquiries until, finally, we get answers that contain only primitive concepts. When we reach the innate primitive concepts, each of those concepts will either fall outside the scope of theory-theory or be constituted by an associated innate theory.

We can now pinpoint the dilemma that BELIEF creates for theory-theory. When we pursue repeated rounds of asking which concepts make up the associated theory that establishes BELIEF, the answers can go in one of two directions. Either the concepts in the associated entries become less abstract than BELIEF or they become more abstract. If we assume they should be less and less abstract, we will end up describing BELIEF in behavioral terms. Theory-theorists correctly want to account for the mentalistic character of theory-of-mind concepts but cannot do this by characterizing children as behaviorists. Alternatively, if we assume, along with Perner, that the concepts in the associated entry for BELIEF are more abstract than BELIEF, we soon find ourselves chasing increasing numbers of increasingly abstract concepts, most of them quite obscure, while the possibility of accounting for their acquisition slips further from our grasp. Let us look at this more closely.

A Close-Up of the Representational Theory-Theory

Perner (1988, 1991) proposed that the four-year-old child comes to pass false-belief tasks by discovering the representational theory of mind and, in particular, the representational theory of belief. Younger children adhere to a different theory, namely, that people are "mentally connected to situations," a theory that is meant to preclude conceptualizing belief such that the content of a belief can be false. Older children then make a theoretical advance, discovering that beliefs are really representations; this advance creates a new concept, namely, BELIEF, and ushers in success on false-belief tasks.

When Perner originally proposed the representational theory-theory, his idea was that the child discovered that mental states were like other representations – like pictures or models, for example. "If we define representation ... as I have done, then we use the word "representation" to refer to the representational medium (more precisely the state of the medium). For instance, in the case of a picture it is the picture (medium) that is the representation and not the scene depicted on it (content)" (Perner, 1991, p. 280). The key development in the child's theory of mind was then said to occur at about the age of four years, when the child acquired the (supposedly adult-like and common-sense) theory that mental states have a "medium" and not just a content, that is, are internal representations. This, in turn, was said to be achieved by the child coming to "model models" by "work[ing] out the notion that something (referent) is apprehended (represented) as something (sense)" (Perner, 1991, p. 284).

Leslie and Thaiss (1992) then pointed out that the most natural supposition for a representational theory-theory is that children acquire a representational theory of belief by hypothesizing that beliefs are internal mental pictures. Sally puts the marble in her basket and makes a mental picture (or takes a mental photograph) of the marble in the basket (see Figure 1). Then she goes away with her mental picture. While she is away, naughty Ann discovers the marble and moves it from the basket to the box. Now, Sally is coming back! Where will she look for her marble? Answer: Sally will consult her mental picture, which will show that the marble is in the basket.

This idea is highly attractive for a number of reasons. First, it provides a series of thoughts that preschool children might actually have, avoiding obscure and ultra-abstract concepts. Second, it would explain how preschoolers come to have the concept BELIEF by learning about things, like pictures, that are visible, concrete objects rather than invisible "theoretical" constructs. Third, mother can show you pictures, she can point to them, count them, discuss and compare them with you; in short, she can tutor you about pictures in ways she cannot tutor you about beliefs. Finally, almost every picture or photograph you have ever seen is "false" or out of date, making them ideal for learning about their representational proprieties – about how something (you, now a big boy or girl) is represented as something else (a baby).

Coming to solve the false-belief task by way of a picture theory implies that understanding an out-dated picture is a sub-component of understanding an out-dated belief. If a picture-task is a component task, then it cannot possibly be harder than a false-belief task and, indeed, ought to be easier. Using tasks adapted from Zaitchik (1990), Leslie and Thaiss (1992) showed that understanding out-dated pictures is not easier and, in fact, is slightly harder, at least for normally developing children. For children with autism, Leslie and Thaiss showed that exactly the opposite is true (see also, Charman & Baron-Cohen, 1992; 1995). Understanding out-dated pictures is, therefore, neither a necessary nor a sufficient condition for passing a false-belief task. These findings are a blow to the idea that the child "works out" that beliefs have a "representational medium" (for further discussion, see Leslie & Thaiss, 1992; Leslie & Roth, 1993; Leslie, 1994/1995).

In light of these sorts of findings, Perner (1995) abandoned his original version of representational theory-theory. Rather than having to master a general theory of representation, the child is now said to employ a theory of representation specific to understanding beliefs.[3]

Perner draws upon Fodor's explication of the theoretical foundations of cognitive science for his new theory-theory. Fodor (1976; 1981a) argues that a propositional attitude, such as *believing that p*, should be understood as a "computational relation" between an organism and a mental representation expressing the proposition *p*. Fodor's account is intended as a scientific account of what propositional attitudes really are. Perner attributes knowledge of this account to the child with one modification: instead of the child conceptualizing the notion COMPUTATIONAL RELATION, Perner says that the preschooler uses the concept SEMANTICALLY EVALUATES. According to Perner (1995), in order to understand that *Sally believes that p*, (in the case that *p* is false), the child must construct the "metarepresentation," *Sally semantically evaluates a mental representation expressing the proposition that p* (see Figure 3).

The first thing to notice is that moving from a general theory of representation to a specific theory of mental representation deprives the theory of any independent evidence. Perner's version of 1991 could hope to draw upon independent evidence that children first understand the idea of representing something as something else in regard to external, public representations like pictures, maps or models and, then, project these ideas to internal mental states. But, as we saw above, the hoped-for independent evidence has evaporated. This has the disturbing consequence that the evidence supporting the idea that the child grasps *Sally semantically evaluates a mental representation expressing the proposition that p* is just the evidence that supports the idea that the child grasps *Sally believes that p*, namely, passing false-belief tasks. Therefore, there is, at present, no (independent) evidence to support the new theory-theory.

Let us remind ourselves of how Perner got to this position. He accepts the theory-theory account of concept possession: to possess the abstract concept BELIEF is to possess critical knowledge about *belief* and to acquire the concept is to acquire the critical knowledge. The critical knowledge in question is a theory of what *belief* is. In order to state the theory of *belief*, other concepts must be used. Therefore, the possessor of BELIEF must also possess these other concepts (the ones used to state the

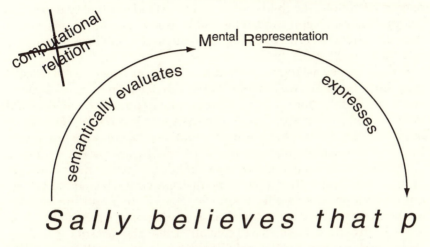

Figure 3. Perner's latest proposal borrows from cognitive science the idea that a belief is a relation to a mental representation. But, instead of referring to a computational relation, the preschool child's critical knowledge that establishes the concept BELIEF refers to a semantic-evaluation relation to the mental representation. If Gopnik views the child as "little scientist," Perner views the child as "little Fodor."

theory of *belief*). Rightly, Perner eschews the constraint that these other concepts must be *less* abstract than BELIEF. If, ultimately, BELIEF can be "cashed out as," or reduced to, sensory concepts, then theory-theory is not really required. Moreover, reduction would entail that the child's (and our adult) theory-of-mind concepts are fundamentally behavioristic and non-intentional. Rightly, though, theory-theory is committed to mentalism. But, in rejecting the reductionist route, Perner is forced to allow the theory-explicating concepts to be more abstract.

Perner is also forced to choose a theory of *belief* that might plausibly be true. The theory of *belief* that he requires has to explain how a thought containing the concept BELIEF actually picks out *belief* rather than something else, such as a desire, serious facial expressions, an earnest gesture, or some other property of a situation containing a person with a belief. If the child (e.g., the three-year-old) has the wrong theory, then his concept BELIEF* will pick out something different from our concept BELIEF. And, what theory can do the job of picking out *belief* other than our adult theory of what a *belief* really is?

There is, however, a heavy price for taking this approach. In order to discover and apply the foregoing representational theory of belief, the child must acquire the following concepts: SEMANTIC, EVALUATE, MENTAL, REPRESENTATION, EXPRESS, and PROPOSITION. The child must acquire these concepts because these are the concepts that state the critical theory of *belief*. Therefore, the child could not understand this theory unless she grasped these concepts. And, if the child did not understand this theory, then, according to Perner and the theory-theory, the child would not possess the concept BELIEF.

We began by asking how one difficult and obscure concept (BELIEF) is acquired but, now, we have six more, each of which is just as difficult and considerably more obscure. It is every bit as puzzling how the child might acquire any one of these six notions as it is puzzling how he acquires BELIEF. One answer might be that these six concepts are innate. But if we are willing to accept that answer, why are we not willing to accept that BELIEF is innate? If we are not willing to accept these new concepts as innate primitives, then each must, like BELIEF, be acquired by acquiring and possessing critical knowledge – i.e., by acquiring a theory of *semantic evaluation*, a theory of *mental*, a theory of *representation*, and so on. Each of these theories will spin off further abstract concept-theory cycles, with no end in plain sight. If, at this point, we balk at pursuing a theory-theory of concept possession and acquisition, the question inevitably arises why we did not do so earlier, at the first step, the decision to pursue a theory-theory of BELIEF.

Unfortunately, the situation for the "mental representation" theory-theory of *belief* is even worse than we have suggested so far. Fodor's formulation of propositional attitudes as computational relations to mental representations was designed to say what propositional attitudes are in general. It was not designed to describe *beliefs* specifically. Fodor's formulation, therefore, does not distinguish *beliefs* from other mental states such as *desires*, *hopes*, *pretends*, and so forth – all are computational relations to mental representations. Each attitude is assumed to involve a different kind of computational relation, putting it on the agenda for cognitive science to develop theories of each of the specific computational relations involved. This general description of propositional attitudes carries over into Perner's replacement of computational relation by a semantic-evaluation relation (Figure 3). All propositional attitudes "semantically evaluate" their "mental representations" – by definition, all propositional attitudes are attitudes to the truth of a proposition. So, even if the child did discover this obscure theory, it would still not provide her with the concept BELIEF but only with an undifferentiated concept of propositional attitude. The theory in Figure 3 will only tell the child about propositional attitudes in general, applying to *desires* and *pretends* equally as it applies to *beliefs*. It will even apply just as well to "*prelief*," the pretend-belief state that Perner, Baker, and Hutton (1994) suggest three-year-olds attribute to other people. What it will not do is tell the child specifically what a *belief* is.[4]

Can the theory-theory in Figure 3 be patched up so that it provides the child with a theory of what *belief* is (as opposed to *desire*, *pretense*, etc.)? The main problem is with the relation 'semantically evaluates'. Mental representations that express propositions will be a common feature in theories of *belief, desire, pretense, hopes,* and so on because Sally can desire that her marble be in the basket, can pretend that her marble is in the basket, or hope that her marble is in the basket, as well as believe that that is where it is (all the while the marble is in the box). What differs from case to case is the "mode" of evaluation. The obvious temptation, then, is to add a simple qualification: Sally semantically evaluates *with respect to believing* a mental representation. Certainly, this will do the job. By the same token, simply replacing 'semantically evaluates' with 'believes' will also do the job and for exactly the same reason, namely, the concept BELIEF is used. Unfortunately, this makes the theory-theory circular. *Belief* is *belief* and, most certainly, the child will acquire the concept BELIEF by acquiring the concept BELIEF. The challenge is to find a description without circularity that can do the job of picking out specifically *beliefs*. I doubt that this can be done.

Agenda for a Successful Theory-Theory

Here is a minimal agenda for a theory-theory of BELIEF. The first problem is to say, without circularity, what belief really is. Having made explicit the theory that constitutes the critical knowledge for concept possession, the next step is to provide independent evidence that the child does, in fact, acquire this critical knowledge. Finally, it must be shown that it is by acquiring this critical knowledge that the child acquires the target concept. Present accounts fall far short of achieving any of these goals.

Considerable obstacles lie in the way. I identified three sets of problems that face theory-theories of belief and, probably, theory-theories more generally. The first is the conceptual explosion caused by concepts having dictionary entries – that is, theories attached to each concept. Because theories are themselves composed of concepts, the number of concepts for which the theory-theorist must seek an acquisition account grows explosively. Secondly, because theory-theorists reject the idea that all abstract concepts reduce to statements formed solely of sensory concepts (you certainly cannot be a theory-theorist if you accept that doctrine), the concept explosion will involve the escalating obscurity of the concepts that are spun off (cf. Fodor, 1981b). Perner's proposals illustrate this nicely. On the first iteration alone, we move from worrying about BELIEF to worrying about SEMANTIC. And what is the theory, grasped by the child, that constitutes the concept SEMANTIC? I suspect that escalating obscurity is a general feature of theory-theories (for instance, DADDY = MALE REPRODUCER). Finally, the critical knowledge for BELIEF, conceptually rich and potent though it was in Perner's proposal, still fell short of the mark in specifying an exact description of BELIEF. This means that such a concept specification would not, in fact, do its critical job of specifically picking out *beliefs* but instead would pick out any and all propositional attitudes. Again, I suspect that this reflects a more general feature of theory-theory and that, unless one introduces circularity, the search for critical knowledge will only provide para-phrastic approximations that forever fall short of their target.

Current attempts to develop an acquisition theory-theory face a number of serious problems. Whether theory-theory can overcome these obstacles remains to be seen. In the meantime, alternative approaches should be vigorously explored.

Concept as Soap Molecule

One avenue to explore involves dropping the notion that the sense of a concept – its associated critical knowledge – determines its reference and, therefore, which concept it is. The referent of a concept must be determined somehow but stored knowledge is not the only conceivable way. In fact, it is far from clear how sense is supposed to determine reference. How does a concept fit to the world? Answer: a concept points to a stored description (of some sort); the description is laid against the world by the cognitive system and the things that fit the description are admitted to membership of the set of things in the concept category. But, if a description is itself composed of concepts, saying that a concept fits to the world via a description does not answer the question of how a concept fits to the world. It provides a postponement instead of an answer.

Historically, there used to be an answer that did not beg the question. Empiricist philosophers, like Hume (1740), argued that concepts fall into two major types: the sensory and the abstract (in his terminology, "impressions" and "ideas," respectively). Possession of the sensory concepts is provided directly by the structure of the sensory apparatus. That is, Hume assumed that the way a concept like RED referred or "locked" to the world did not entail applying knowledge of a description of *redness* (whatever that would be). The locking was provided by a mechanism, namely, the mechanisms of color vision. These mechanisms could be innate and provide an innate concept RED without our having to suppose that, therefore, some piece of knowledge or theory about *redness* is innate. An infant does not need a theory of *redness* if she possesses something else, namely, the mechanisms of color vision. Possession of the sensory concepts does not require knowing a dictionary definition or theory because these concepts refer to the appropriate property in the world via sensory mechanisms.

So long as all non-sensory (abstract) concepts reduce to descriptions composed entirely of sensory concepts, we have a general outline for how the sense of abstract concepts determines their reference. But, without that reductionist assumption about abstract concepts, we lack any idea how their sense could determine their reference. Theory-theory rightly rejects the notion that all abstract concepts reduce to sensory descriptions. But, as we saw, this raises a number of obstacles to understanding how certain abstract concepts can appear so early in life. These problems could be avoided if there were some way for an abstract concept to lock to the world other than through applying a description or "critical" knowledge. In the case of sensory concepts, such an alternative has seemed uncontroversial: a sensory concept is locked on target by a psychophysical mechanism. Can this idea be extended to abstract concepts, too?

The idea that certain abstract concepts might be acquired by way of a mechanism that locks on a specific target property in the world is certainly a wild idea. But, is it wild enough to be true? There is a philosophical tradition that has received far less attention than the mainstream Descriptivist accounts to which theory-theory is heir. This tradition has tried to develop causal theories of reference (e.g., Fodor, 1998; Kripke, 1972; Margolis, 1998; Putnam, 1975). The fundamental idea is that concepts bear information about a specific property not because of subjective knowledge but because of an entirely objective causal relation between the concept (as psychological entity) and a property ("in the world"). Such views stress the psychophysical duality of concepts. Like a soap molecule with one pole locked to oil and the other pole locked to water, a concept has one "pole" locked to the causal processes of a cognitive system and the other "pole" causally locked to the world. Instead of being lost in the endless maze of mutual inter-definition, the representational relation between concept and world is brought directly to the fore.

What is the role of knowledge in "conceptual psychophysics"? Knowledge about the referent of a concept is acquired and associated with the concept but this stored associated knowledge does not provide or constitute the sole locking mechanism for the concept. So, the knowledge is free to change without affecting what the concept designates.

But is it not true that we acquire new knowledge and that this new knowledge changes the way we think about something? Do we not learn about *beliefs* or *fathers* or *dogs* so that we come to see them in a new light? Most certainly we do. What is at stake is not whether we learn or whether that learning leads us to conceive of things in a new way. Rather, what is at stake is whether the referent of FATHER changes systematically in relation to our evolving ideas about what a *father* really is. According to the Descriptivist view (and theory-theory), it does. According to conceptual psychophysics, it does not. We can capture our intuition about changes in the way we conceive of things by distinguishing between concepts and conceptions. 'Concept' will refer strictly to the symbol-*cum*-reference-relation-to-a-property, while 'conception' will refer to any knowledge associated with the symbol. 'Conception' will capture what we know or believe about whatever the concept refers to. Since what we believe about something determines how it appears to us, we can retain the intuition that new knowledge changes how we think about things. What new knowledge will not do is change the meaning of our concepts.

In theory-theory, or any Descriptivist approach, the claim that a given (abstract) concept is innate entails that critical knowledge is innate. In a conceptual psychophysics framework, this entailment does not hold. A concept may be innate if at least one locking mechanism is innate (there does not have to be a unique or critical mechanism). The existence of innate knowledge remains an empirical question, of course, and it is even possible that innate knowledge may play a role in a given locking mechanism. However, innate knowledge is not necessary for innate concept possession. Likewise, in theory-theory or any Descriptivist approach, the acquisition of a given concept entails the acquisition of critical knowledge. Again, this entailment does not hold within a conceptual psychophysics approach. Acquiring a new concept will mean acquiring a lock on a new property.

It seems to me that a good way to study these questions empirically is concept by abstract concept. Although there are a great many concepts, it would be a great advance to have an account of how even a single abstract concept is innate or how it is acquired. There have already been suggestive findings. For example, Leslie and Keeble (1987) showed that six-month-old infants recognized a specifically causal property of events in which one object launched another by colliding with it. They proposed that infants' recognition was based upon a modular mechanism operating independently of general knowledge and reasoning to "provide information about the spatiotemporal and causal structure of appropriate events" and that "it could do this without having to know what a cause 'really' is" (Leslie & Keeble, 1987, p. 286). Such a mechanism allows the infant to attend to physical causation, to lock in the concept CAUSE and, then, to begin to learn about causal mechanisms from instances. The concept is prior to the "theorizing." There are also promising ideas concerning locking mechanisms for number concepts (see, e.g., Gallistel & Gelman, 1992) and faces (Johnson & Morton, 1991). Recently, Leslie, Xu, Tremoulet and Scholl (1998) have suggested an account of how the infant's concept of *object* gets locked without recourse to knowledge of a theory of objecthood (see also, Scholl & Leslie, 1999a). Finally, in the theory-of-mind domain, Leslie (1987) proposed a model of how the concept PRETEND is locked without assuming that the infant has critical knowledge of what pretending really is (see also, German & Leslie, 1999). In a similar vein, Leslie (in press) discusses the development of the concept BELIEF as part of a mechanism of selective attention.

So, How Do You Acquire a Representational Theory of Mind?

In the theory-theory account, the child discovers a theory of general (or alternatively, mental) representation that gives birth to the concept BELIEF and to success on false-belief problems. In this chapter, I have laid out a number of reasons that make me skeptical of this claim. In fact, I think the relationship between concept and theory is exactly the reverse. It is the possession of the concept BELIEF (plus a gradual increase in skill at employing the concept) that eventually gives rise to a common-sense representational theory of mind. As the child begins to enjoy increasing success at solving false belief problems, he will increasingly *notice* false beliefs and the circumstances that give rise to them. In an everyday sense, the child will then develop common-sense "theories" about how other people represent the world. For example, if Mary represents bananas as telephones, the child can model this fact as *Mary thinks bananas are telephones*. Or, if the child sees a dog chase a squirrel, which runs up tree *B*, while the dog goes barking up tree *A*, the child can "theorize" that *the dog is barking up the wrong tree because it thinks there is a squirrel up there*. In the limited manner of common-sense theory and opinion, this is a representational theory of the dog's mind. It should not be disappointing to find that the child's representational theory of mind is so mundane and epiphenomenal on the child's concept of *belief*. Although it's not much of a theory, being able to attend to and, consequently, learn about false belief situations – their causes, their consequences, and their uses – will bring vast dividends. Moreover, at least we know that children actually think thoughts like these. There is no evidence that children ever think thoughts of the sort in Figure 3.

Acknowledgments

I am grateful to the following friends and colleagues: Eric Margolis and Susan Carey for helpful discussions, and Jerry Fodor, Shaun Nichols, and Brian Scholl for helpful discussions and detailed comments on an earlier draft.

Notes

1 I use SMALL CAPS when referring to a concept as opposed to what the concept denotes (italicized). Normally, one could simply say that the concept is a psychological entity, while what it denotes is not, e.g., dog refers to dogs. But, in the case of mental-state concepts, what they denote are also psychological entities.

2 For critical discussion of this idea see Carey & Spelke (1996), Leslie & German (1995), and Stich & Nichols (1998).

3 Slaughter (1998) claims that the dissociation between children's performance on false-belief tasks and photographs tasks is predicted by Gopnik and Wellman's theory-theory on the grounds that "[a]lthough theory-building processes require general cognitive skills and resources, the resultant concepts, including mental representation, are held to be specific to the domain of folk psychology" (Slaughter, 1998, p. 330). It is hard to see what property of Gopnik and Wellman's views predicts that concepts or theories should be specific in this way. Certainly, the opposite is true of real theories, which strive for as much generality as possible. Indeed, the representational theory of mind is exactly the attempt to treat mental states as instances of something more general, viz., as representations. Without this generality, it is not obvious even what is meant by 'representational' in the phrase 'representational theory of mind'.

   Incidentally, Slaughter (1998) overlooks the fact that in her study she compared children's performance on a "modified" photographs task with an unmodified false-belief task. Just as it is possible to simplify false-belief tasks to make them easier for three-year-olds to pass, so it should be possible to simplify photograph tasks, too. Slaughter's results confirm this. According to the model from Leslie and Thaiss (1992), in making the comparison she did, Slaughter removed the only limiting factor that photograph tasks and false-belief tasks have in common, namely, what Leslie and Thaiss call "selection processing." The resulting lack of correlation in children's performance does not "call into question the ... model of development offered by Leslie," as Slaughter claims, but instead actually supports the model.

4 Fodor (personal communication, 1999) points out that *believing that p* cannot be the same thing as *evaluating or holding-true a representation that means that p*. Consider: I have in my hands a copy of Einstein's paper on Special Relativity. I have never read this paper and, to be honest, I do not have a clue about what it says. However, I know that the theory expressed in this paper is a cornerstone of modern physics, which, as far as I am concerned, means that it is true. Secondly, this bunch of paper I have in my hands is only a representation of Einstein's theory. So, I semantically evaluate (as true) this representation expressing the Special Relativity Theory. However, there is not a single proposition expressed in this paper that I have as a belief in the usual sense because I have no idea which propositions this paper expresses. But *whatever* they are, I hold them all to be true because I trust physicists to know what is what on this topic. But, when I think that Sally believes that *p*, the marble is in the basket, I think that she actually grasps that very proposition. The idea behind treating belief as a particular kind of computational relation is that an organism standing in such a relation will *thereby* grasp and believe the proposition expressed. Without that assumption, a computational account of belief will not work. However, as the example above shows, exactly this assumption fails for the semantic-evaluation relation. This is a further reason why substituting 'semantic evaluation' for 'computational relation' will not provide a theory of *belief*.

References

Anderson, M. (1992). *Intelligence and development: A cognitive theory.* Oxford: Blackwell.

Baron-Cohen, S., Leslie, A. M., & Frith, U. (1985). Does the autistic child have a "theory of mind"? *Cognition 21,* 37–46.

Boyer, P. (1994). Cognitive constrains on cultural representations: Natural ontologies and religious ideas. In L. A. Hirschfeld and S. A. Gelman (Eds.), *Mapping the mind: Domain specificity in cognition and culture* (pp. 391–411). Cambridge: Cambridge University Press.

Carey, S. (1978). The child as word learner. In M. Halle, J. Bresnan, & G. A. Miller (Eds.), *Linguistic theory and psychological reality.* Cambridge, MA: MIT Press.

Carey, S. (1985). *Conceptual change in childhood.* Cam bridge, MA: MIT Press.

Carey, S. (1988). Conceptual differences between children and adults. *Mind & Language 3,* 167–181.

Carey, S., & Spelke, E. (1996). Science and core knowledge. *Philosophy of Science 63,* 515–533.

Charman, T., & Baron-Cohen, S. (1992). Understanding drawings and beliefs: A further test of the metarepresentation theory of autism (Research Note). *Journal of Child Psychology and Psychiatry 33,* 1105–1112.

Charman, T., & Baron-Cohen, S. (1995). Understanding photos, models, and beliefs: A test of the modularity thesis of theory of mind. *Cognitive Development 10,* 287-298.

Chomsky, N. A. (1957). *Syntactic structures.* The Hague: Mouton.

Chomsky, N. A., & Lasnik, H. (1995). The theory of principles and parameters. In N. A. Chomsky, *The minimalist program* (pp. 13–127). Cambridge, MA: MIT Press.

Flavell, J. H., Green, F. L., & Flavell, E. R. (1993). Children's understanding of the stream of consciousness. *Child Development 64,* 387–398.

Fodor, J. A. (1976). *The language of thought.* Hassocks, Sussex: Harvester Press.

Fodor, J. A. (1981a). Propositional attitudes. In J. A. Fodor (Ed.), *Representations: Philosophical essays on the foundations of cognitive science* (pp.177–203). Cambridge, MA: MIT Press.

Fodor, J. A. (1981b). The present status of the innateness controversy. In J. A. Fodor (Ed.), *Representations: Philosophical essays on the foundations of cognitive science* (pp. 257–316.) Cambridge, MA: MIT Press.

Fodor, J. A. (1983). *The modularity of mind.* Cambridge, MA: MIT Press.

Fodor, J.A. (1998). *Concepts: Where cognitive science went wrong.* Oxford: Clarendon Press.

Gallistel, C. R., & Gelman, R. (1992). Preverbal and verbal counting and computation. *Cognition 44,* 43–74.

German, T. P., & Leslie, A. M. (1999). Children's inferences from *knowing* to *pretending* and *thinking.* Technical Report No. 51. Rutgers University Center for Cognitive Science.

Gopnik, A., & Meltzoff, A. N. (1997). *Words, thoughts, and theories.* Cambridge, MA: MIT Press.

Gopnik, A., & Wellman, H. M. (1994). The theory theory. In L. Hirschfeld and S. Gelman (Eds.), *Mapping the mind: Domain specificity in cognition and culture* (pp. 257–293). New York: Cambridge University Press.

Gopnik, A., & Wellman, H. M. (1995). Why the child's theory of mind really *is* a theory. In M. Davies & T. Stone, (Eds.), *Folk psychology: The theory of mind debate* (pp. 232–258). Oxford: Blackwell.

Happé, F. G. (1995). The role of age and verbal ability in the theory of mind task performance of subjects with autism. *Child Development 66*, 843–855.

Hughes, C., & Cutting, A.L. (1999). Nature, nurture, and individual differences in early understanding of mind. *Psychological Science 10*, 429–432.

Hume, D. (1740). *A treatise of human nature*. In A. Flew, *David Hume on Human Nature and the Understanding*. New York: Collier, 1962.

Johnson, M. H., & Morton, J. (1991). *Biology and cognitive development*. Oxford: Blackwell.

Keil, F. C. (1989). *Concepts, kinds, and cognitive development*. Cambridge, MA: MIT Press.

Kripke, S. A. (1972). Naming and necessity. In D. Davidson and G. Harman (Eds.), *Semantics of natural language* (pp. 253–355). Dordrecht: Reidel.

Langdon, R., & Coltheart, M. (1999). Mentalising, schizotypy, and schizophrenia. *Cognition 71*, 43–71.

Laurence, S., & Margolis, E. (1999). Concepts and cognitive science. In E. Margolis and S. Laurence (Eds.), *Concepts: Core readings*. Cambridge, MA: MIT Press.

Leslie, A. M. (1987). Pretense and representation: The origins of "theory of mind." *Psychological Review 94*, 412–426.

Leslie, A. M. (1994/1995). *Pretending* and *believing*: Issues in the theory of ToMM. *Cognition, 50*, 211–238. Reprinted in J. Mehler and S. Franck (Eds.), *COGNITION on cognition* (pp. 193–220). Cambridge, MA.: MIT Press.

Leslie, A. M. (in press). 'Theory of mind' as a mechanism of selective attention. In M. Gazzaniga (Ed.), *The Cognitive Neurosciences* (2nd Ed.). Cambridge, MA: MIT Press.

Leslie, A. M., & German, T. P. (1995). Knowledge and ability in "theory of mind": One-eyed overview of a debate. In M. Davies and T. Stone (Eds.), *Mental simulation: Philosophical and psychological essays* (pp. 123–150). Oxford: Blackwell.

Leslie, A. M., & Keeble, S. (1987). Do six-month-old infants perceive causality? *Cognition 25*, 265–288.

Leslie, A. M., & Roth, D. (1993). What autism teaches us about metarepresentation. In S. Baron-Cohen, H. Tager-Flusberg, and D. Cohen (Eds.), *Understanding other minds: Perspectives from autism* (pp. 83–111). Oxford: Oxford University Press.

Leslie, A. M., & Thaiss, L. (1992). Domain specificity in conceptual development: Neuropsychological evidence from autism. *Cognition 43*, 225–251.

Leslie, A. M., Xu, F., Tremoulet, P., & Scholl, B. (1998). Indexing and the object concept: Developing 'what' and 'where' systems. *Trends in Cognitive Sciences 2*, 10–18.

Levelt, W. J. M. (1999). Models of word production. *Trends in Cognitive Sciences 3*, 223–232.

Margolis, E. (1998). How to acquire a concept. *Mind & Language 13*, 347–369.

Marr, D. (1982). *Vision*. San Francisco: W. H.Freeman.

Murphy, G. L., & Medin, D. L. (1985). The role of theories in conceptual coherence. *Psychological Review 92*, 289–316.

Perner, J. (1988). Developing semantics for theories of mind: From propositional attitudes to mental representation. In J. Astington, P. L. Harris and D. Olson (Eds.), *Developing theories of mind* (pp. 141–172). Cambridge: Cambridge University Press.

Perner, J. (1991). *Understanding the representational mind*. Cambridge, MA: MIT Press.

Perner, J. (1995). The many faces of belief: Reflections on Fodor's and the child's theory of mind. *Cognition 57*, 241–269.

Perner, I, Baker, S., & Hutton, D. (1994). Prelief: The conceptual origins of belief and pretence. In C. Lewis and P. Mitchell (Eds.), *Children's early understanding of mind: Origins and development* (pp. 261–286). Hove, UK: Lawrence Erlbaum.

Perner, J., & Wimmer, H. (1988). Misinformation and unexpected change: Testing the development of epistemic state attribution. *Psychological Research 50*, 191–197.

Putnam, H. (1975). The meaning of 'meaning'. In K. Gunderson (Ed.), *Language, mind, and knowledge* (pp. 131–193). Minneapolis, MN: University of Minnesota Press .

Scholl, B. J., & Leslie, A. M. (1999a). Explaining the infant's object concept: Beyond the perception/cognition dichotomy. In E. Lepore & Z. Pylyshyn (Eds.), *What Is Cognitive Science?* (pp. 26–73). Oxford: Blackwell.

Scholl, B. J., & Leslie, A. M. (1999b). Modularity, development and 'theory of mind'. *Mind & Language 14*, 131–153.

Slaughter, V. (1998). Children's understanding of pictorial and mental representations. *Child Development 69*, 321–332.

Stich, S., & Nichols, S. (1998). Theory-theory to the max: A critical notice of Gopnik & Meltzoff's *Words, Thoughts, and Theories. Mind & Language 13*, 421–449.

Varley, R., & Siegal, M. (in press). A dissociation between grammar and cognition. *Nature.*

Vosniadou, S. (1994). Universal and culture-specific properties of children's mental models of the earth. In L. A. Hirschfeld and S. A. Gelman (Eds.), *Mapping the mind: Domain specificity in cognition and culture* (pp. 412–430). Cambridge: Cambridge University Press.

Wellman, H. M. (1990). *The child's theory of mind*. Cambridge, MA: MIT Press.

Wimmer, H., & Perner, J. (1983). Beliefs about beliefs: Representation and constraining function of wrong beliefs in young children's understanding of deception. *Cognition 13*, 103–128.

Zaitchik, D. (1990). When representations conflict with reality: The preschooler's problem with false beliefs and 'false' photographs. *Cognition 35*, 41–68.

Chapter 9

Metarepresentation and Conceptual Change: Evidence from Williams Syndrome

Susan Carey and Susan Johnson

1. Overview

Abnormal development sometimes provides a unique vantage point from which to view normal development. Data on autism has enriched our understanding of the normal development of a theory of mind (Baron-Cohen, 1995; Baron-Cohen, Leslie, & Frith, 1985; Frith, 1989). The analysis of data from deaf children who are late learners of American Sign Language has extended our understanding of normal language acquisition (Newport, 1990), and data from blind children has been brought to bear on the question of the role of visual input in language acquisition (Landau & Gleitman, 1985).

Here we present a case study of abnormal cognitive development, specifically, the acquisition of an intuitive theory of biology, by a population of people with mental retardation associated with Williams Syndrome (WS). This case study yields insights concerning several fundamental issues about cognitive development. It informs our understanding of the distinction between core knowledge and constructed knowledge and of that between knowledge enrichment and conceptual change. It suggests new hypotheses about the role of metaconceptual capacities in the processes that underlie conceptual change, and about the status of the 4-year-old's theory of mind as core knowledge or constructed knowledge.

2. Core Knowledge versus Constructed Knowledge

Many areas of study, from the beginnings of philosophy through to contemporary biological, psychological and cognitive sciences, lay claim to explaining the origin and acquisition of human knowledge. An account is sought of the processes through which adults come to represent the concepts, beliefs, and theories that articulate understanding of the social, biological, and physical world. An account of the development of human knowledge will include a specification of innate representational resources, and of the mechanisms (both learning and maturation) that take the infant beyond the initial state: so much is a truism agreed upon by all. Beyond this agreement, a vast space of options has been well articulated. Adherents of different positions battle over the proper characterization of the initial state (a Quinean perceptual similarity space vs. well-organized cognitive modules) and over the characterization of learning mechanisms sufficient to explain conceptual development (correlation detection, association, parameter setting, hypothesis testing, bootstrapping processes, and so on).

Fully engaging in these debates is beyond the scope of the present chapter. Here we endorse the attribution of rich initial knowledge to the infant (see Carey & Spelke, 1996; Carey & Gelman, 1991; and Hirschfeld & Gelman, 1994, for reviews of the evidence in favor of this position.) Further, the data indicate that initial knowledge is modular, organized by distinct cognitive domains. Following Spelke, Breilinger, Macomber, & Jacobson (1992), we call the domains of knowledge that emerge in early infancy, "core domains." One core domain includes knowledge of the physical world, with physical objects as the main entities it covers and with contact causality as its deepest explanatory device (e.g., Carey & Spelke, 1994; 1996; Leslie, 1994; Oakes & Cohen, 1995). Another core domain includes knowledge of the psychological world, centered on intentional agents, especially people and animals, as the entities it covers and on aspects of intentional causality (goal directedness, attentional and referential states) as its deepest explanatory devices (e.g., Woodward, 1988; Spelke, Phillips, & Woodward, 1995; Johnson, Slaughter, & Carey, 1998).

Carey and Spelke (1996) summarize the several respects in which core knowledge differs from later developing knowledge. Besides developing early, core knowledge is widely shared among other primates, and stable during development. Most important, core knowledge is cognitively shallow: it is close to perceptual knowledge in two ways. First, it is often highly modality-specific. For example, knowledge of a given regularity may support reaching but not drive visual attention, or vice versa (von Hosten, Vishton, Spelke, Feng, & Rosander, 1998; see Milner & Goodale, 1995, for evidence of similar cognitive architecture among adults). Second, the entities and causal principles that articulate core knowledge are identifiable from spatiotemporal analysis. For example, *object* is specified by cohesion and spatiotemporal continuity (Spelke, & Van de Walle, 1993) and *intentional agent* is specified by self-generated, irregular, contingently driven motion (Johnson et al., 1998).

Constructed domains, especially intuitive theories, differ from core domains in each of the above respects. They are later developing, not manifest in other primates, not constant during development, and cognitively deep, in the sense that long inferential chains mediate perceptual data and the theoretical entities they pick out. Describing the path through which children come to share the intuitive theories of the adults in their culture is an important part of characterizing cognitive development. Notable progress has been made in charting the development of intuitive mechanics, psychology (theory of mind), biology, cosmology, and theory of matter (Au, 1994; Carey, 1985; 1988; 1991; 1995; Gopnik & Wellman, 1994; Hatano & Inagaki, 1994; Keil, 1989; 1994; Leslie, 1994; Perner, 1991; Spelke, 1991; Vosniadu & Brewer, 1992; Wellman & Gelman, 1992). Intuitive theories in each of these domains are constructed by normally developing children within the age range of 4 to 10 years.

3. Knowledge Enrichment versus Conceptual Change

More controversially, we believe that another difference between core domains and constructed domains is that the acquisition of the latter often requires conceptual change (e.g., Carey, 1985; 1988; 1991; in press; Carey & Spelke, 1996). Conceptual change is implicated in those cases of theory development that involve incommensurability, and is, as it says, change at the level of individual concepts. A given theory at time 1, T1, and the descendent of that theory at time 2, T2, are incommensurable insofar as the beliefs of one cannot be formulated over the concepts of the other – that is, insofar as the two are not mutually translatable.

Not all theory development involves conceptual change; often theories are merely enriched as new knowledge accumulates about the phenomena in the domain of the theory. Theory enrichment consists of the acquisition of new beliefs formulated over a constant conceptual repertoire. Carey (1991) provides a summary of related analyses of conceptual change in the philosophical literature (Hacking, 1993; Kitcher, 1988; Kuhn, 1962; 1982), as well as a defense of the claim that normal cognitive development involves theory changes that implicate incommensurability.

Conceptual changes take several forms. Perhaps the most common is differentiation. In conceptual differentiations involving incommensurability, the undifferentiated parent concept from T1 no longer plays any role in T2. Examples include Galileo's differentiation of average from instantaneous velocity (Kuhn, 1977), Black's differentiation of heat from temperature (Wiser & Carey, 1983), and the child's differentiation of weight from density (Smith, Carey, & Wiser, 1985; Carey, 1991). Another common type is coalescence. In coalescences involving incommensurability, entities considered ontologically distinct in T1 are subsumed under a single concept in T2. Examples include Galileo's abandonment of Aristotle's distinction between natural and artificial motions (Kuhn,

1977) and the child's uniting of animal and plant into the new concept, *living thing* (Carey, 1985). Conceptual change may also involve the reanalysis of a concept's basic structure (such as the Newtonian reanalysis of weight from a property of objects to a relationship between objects). And finally, on the common treatment of concepts as having a core/periphery structure, changes in the concept's core constitute examples of conceptual change (Kitcher, 1988). See Carey (1988; 1991) for examples of each of these types of conceptual change in the course of normal cognitive development.

We would like to dispel, at the outset, several misunderstandings concerning the claim that cognitive development involves conceptual change. It is important to note that the difference between knowledge enrichment and conceptual change is not sharp. There are a variety of intermediate cases. Also, the analysis of conceptual change endorsed here is not that of Kuhn (1962) and Feyerabend (1962). These writers were committed to the existence of radical incommensurability, in which theories before and after conceptual change share no conceptual machinery. The incommensurability that occurs in the cases of historical and developmental theory building we have examined is what Kuhn (1982) called local incommensurability, incommensurability which implicates only some of the concepts that articulate successive theories. Finally, conceptual change does not occur suddenly. There is not a moment of gestalt shift. It takes time for concepts to change, sometimes centuries in the history of science, always years in the individual scientist or student or child engaged in knowledge restructuring (Kuhn, 1977; Gruber, 1974, on Darwin; Nersessian, 1992, on Maxwell 1992; Carey, 1985; 1991; Chi, 1992).

It is worth stepping back and considering what is being presupposed by the choice of the term "intuitive theory" rather than the more neutral "cognitive structure." We favor the former term, for we believe that intuitive theories play several unique roles in mental life. These include: (1) determining a concept's core (the properties seen as essential to membership in a concept's extension); (2) representing causal and explanatory knowledge; (3) supporting explanation-based inference. As Gopnik and Meltzoff (1997) emphasize, and we endorse, the mechanisms underlying theory development differ from those that underlie the acquisition of different types of conceptual structures.

It is an empirical question whether children represent intuitive theories, and whether knowledge acquisition in childhood involves the process of theory change. Those who talk of "intuitive theories," and "framework theories," are explicitly committing themselves to an affirmative answer to those empirical questions. This commitment does not deny that there are important differences between children as theorizers and adult scientists (hence the qualifier, "intuitive theories"). Children are not explicit theory builders. They are not aware they are constructing theories, they do not consciously compare theories, nor do they attempt to state them explicitly, let alone formalize them. In spite of these differences, the research enterprise in which this work is placed presupposes that there are a set of questions that can be asked, literally, of both scientific theories and intuitive theories, and which receive the same answer in both cases. Of course, the merit of this presupposition depends upon the fruitfulness of the research it generates. See, for example, the explicit comparison of conceptual change within thermal concepts in the history of science and conceptual change within concepts of matter in middle childhood (Carey, 1991; Smith, Carey, & Wiser, 1985; Wiser & Carey, 1983).

4. What Is at Stake?

The distinctions between core knowledge and constructed knowledge and between conceptual change and knowledge enrichment, along with the existence of conceptual change in childhood, raise fundamental descriptive questions for those of us who study cognitive development. First, which domains are core domains? For example, Gopnik and Meltzoff (1997) claim that the infant's intuitive mechanics built around the concept of permanent object is constructed knowledge, requiring conceptual change for its acquisition (see Carey & Spelke, 1996, for a counter-argument). Similarly, many have argued that the 4-year-old's theory of mind, a full belief/desire psychology, requires conceptual change for its acquisition (Gopnik & Meltzoff, 1997; Perner, 1991), and is thus a constructed domain. The study of Williams Syndrome we present below weighs in on the side of those who argue that the 4-year-olds' theory of mind is acquired by a process of enrichment of a core domain (e. g., Fodor, 1992). Second, and relatedly, which cases of knowledge acquisition involve incommensurability? Another way of putting the latter question: When are children's beliefs formulated over concepts incommensurable with ours? The preschool child tells us the sun is alive, or that buttons are alive because they keep your pants up. The preschool child tells us that it cannot be that statues are not alive, since you can see them. How are we to interpret these bizarre beliefs? Is the child saying something false, in terms of concepts shared with us? Or is the child saying something true, formulated over different concepts than those expressed by our use of the same terms? If the latter, are the child's concepts locally incommensurable with ours?

Finally, the existence of conceptual change, both in childhood and in the history of science, raises some of the very toughest challenges to an understanding of the sources of cognitive development. Many classes of learning mechanisms, which account for a major share of knowledge acquisition, consist in selection or concatenation over an existing conceptual base. These include hypothesis testing, parameter setting, association, correlation detection, and many others. These mechanisms suffice for knowledge enrichment. It is highly likely that additional learning mechanisms, of some other sort, are implicated in conceptual change.

5. Achieving Conceptual Change

Not everyone agrees that the processes that subserve conceptual change differ from those that subserve knowledge enrichment. For example, Churchland (1992), points out that simple connectionist systems restructure themselves during learning, and proposes that this process provides a good model of conceptual change. Connectionist systems, paradigm associative devices, also provide a good model of one class of enrichment mechanisms. Churchland denies, then, that there is a principled distinction between enrichment and conceptual change, or that distinct learning processes are required for each.

Those who take as a starting point that conceptual change requires different learning mechanisms from conceptual enrichment have described myriad specific bootstrapping processes that subserve conceptual change (Carey, in press; Carey & Spelke, 1994; Gopnik & Meltzoff, 1997; Nersession, 1992; Smith, Snir, & Grosslight, 1992; Wiser, 1988). The bootstrapping processes include the exploration of analogical mappings between domains, the exploration of limiting-case analyses, and a variety of abductive processes captured in metaphors such as Neurath's boat or Quine's chimney (Quine, 1960) or the familiar bootstrapping ladder that is kicked out from under when T2 is achieved.

6. Metarepresentation and Conceptual Change

In the case of adult scientists in the process of conceptual change, and in the case of some conceptual-change science curricula, such bootstrapping processes are typically under explicit metaconceptual control (see Nersessian, 1992, on Maxwell; or Smith et al., 1992; Wiser, 1988). Maxwell was well aware that he was engaged in theory building and consciously explored, over months of systematic work, an analogy between Newtonian mechanics and the electromagnetism phenomena discovered by Faraday. Similarly, in Smith's weight/density and Wiser's heat/temperature conceptual change curricula, students consciously explore the analogy between visual models that represent the mathematics of intensive and extensive quantities, on the one hand, and physical phenomena, on the other.

However, a two-line argument shows that explicit metaconceptual control of bootstrapping processes is not necessary for conceptual change. First, such explicit metaknowledge and executive control processes develop late, well into adulthood. Second, there are well-documented conceptual changes early in childhood. Three well-described cases of conceptual change that take place between the ages of 4 and 8 to 10 are: changes in the concept *animal* as part of the construction of an intuitive vitalist biology (see below), changes in the concept of weight as part of the construction of an intuitive theory of matter (Carey, 1991; Piaget & Inhelder, 1941; Smith, Carey, & Wiser, 1985), and changes in the concept of earth as part of the construction of an intuitive cosmology (Vosniadu & Brewer, 1992). Studies of intuitive epistemology indicate that children this young are notoriously unable to carry out, explicitly, metaconceptual evaluation of their knowledge. Comprehension monitoring abilities are poor before age 8 or so (Markman, 1985); children fail to notice and easily tolerate blatant contradictions in what they are reading or hearing. It is not until adolescence or later that children construct explicit concepts of consistency, contradiction, validity, evidence (e.g., Osherson & Markman, 1975; Kuhn et al. 1988).

However, even if conceptual change processes are not under explicit metaconceptual control, it seems likely they will recruit metarepresentational capacities. Many assume that conceptual change is at least sometimes triggered by attempts at maximizing consistency among beliefs, constructing coherent explanatory systems, minimizing contradictions between expected outcomes and actual states of affairs in the world. Indeed, Sperber (1994) argued that a variety of metarepresentational abilities, "semantic evaluative" abilities, are implicated in such processes underlying conceptual change. These include: the ability to evaluate semantic relations among representations such as consistency and contradiction, the ability to evaluate validity of inferences, the ability to evaluate evidence for beliefs, the ability to evaluate the reliability of sources.

Sperber argues that these semantic evaluative abilities require the metarepresentational machinery evident in the normally developing 4-year-old's theory of mind. While there is no doubt that 4-year-olds have a theory of mind (Gopnik & Meltzoff, 1997; Perner, 1991; Wellman, 1990) and therefore the representational format to evaluate propositions semantically, there is in fact no evidence that these semantic evaluation capacities come free with the 4-year-old theory of mind, nor that the 4-year-old's theory of mind is sufficient to make available the machinery to support conceptual change. The present case study will bear on these issues.

The distinction between metaconceptual knowledge, on the one hand, and metarepresentational capacities, on the other, bears dwelling upon. Those who speak of metacognition (e.g., Campione, Brown, & Ferrara, 1982) include both explicit, verbalizable, knowledge about cognition (metaknowledge) and also executive processes that strategically control the acquisition and deployment of knowledge (executive control). Take memory as an example. Metamemorial knowledge includes statable generalizations such as: organized material is easier to remember than unorganized material. Executive processes include the host of strategies that enhance encoding, rehearsal, and retrieval of information to be remembered.

Metarepresentational capacities, as Sperber uses the term, are part of basic representational format. Metarepresentational capacities allow a mental representation to be about a mental representation. Among them are the basic capacity to represent propositional attitudes such as "John believes that ghosts exist," or "Alice hopes that George will find them an apartment," and to consider the truth or falsehood of a proposition, in addition to the more complex capacities on Sperber's list.

Metarepresentational capacities, then, are necessary for metacognition, but the metacognitive knowledge and skills discussed in the developmental and retardation literature go beyond basic metarepresentational capacity in two ways. First, one may have any particular metarepresentational capacity, such as the ability to recognize a contradiction, without having the explicit knowledge of it – for example, without the explicit concept of a contradiction or the explicit idea that contradictions are undesirable. Second, the basic architecture that allows representation of representations does not guarantee any particular complex strategy useful in conceptual change, such as the capacity to recognize a visual instantiation of a mathematical formalism and to use it, as Maxwell did, as a stand-in for the formalism in exploring an analogical mapping between two domains, "because it is easier to think with" (Nersessian, 1992).

Late-developing, explicit metaconceptual knowledge and complex executive control processes undoubtedly play a role in the processes adult scientists deploy in the service of theory construction, including cases of conceptual change. Furthermore, the empirical status support for Sperber's hypothesis remains open. By age 4, children's theory of mind requires extensive metarepresentational capacities for its expression and deployment. Children of this age have explicit concepts of belief, false belief, appearance, reality, knowing, guessing, and intentional action, among others (e. g., Perner, 1991; Wellman, 1992). They are capable of imagining different points of view (level 2 perspective taking; Flavell, Everett, Croft, & Flavell, 1981) and specifying sources of their knowledge (perception vs. testimony, which modality of perception; O'Neill & Gopnik, 1991). Thus, even preschool children command an extensive set of metarepresentational tools to bring to bear on knowledge acquisition. The known examples of conceptual change in childhood (intuitive vitalism, theory of matter, intuitive cosmology) occur after age 4. Thus, it may be that Sperber is correct that metarepresentational capacities that are part of the 4-year-old's theory of mind are sufficient to support conceptual change.

Which metarepresentational capacities, if any, play a necessary role in the processes that subserve conceptual change? Are those that are embodied in the late preschoolers' rich theory of mind sufficient, or are later developing metacognitive knowledge and control strategies necessary? Or, as Churchland suggests, are enrichment processes alone sufficient to explain knowledge acquisition and restructuring? Here we explore these questions through a case study of a population of individuals with mental retardation, those with Williams Syndrome (WS), who achieve the late preschool child's theory of mind more or less on schedule, but who remain impaired on later developing metarepresentational skills even into adulthood. Do these individuals achieve the conceptual changes typical of normal developing 6- to 10-year olds?

7. Case Study: Williams Syndrome

Williams Syndrome (WS) is a neurodevelopmental disorder of genetic origin (Frangiskakis et al., 1996; Morris, 1994) that typically results in mental retardation as well as a variety of other physical problems including heart defects, metabolic problems of calcium and calcitonin, failure to thrive, hyperacusis, and characteristic facial and dental features (Williams, Barrett-Boyes, & Lowes, 1962; Jones & Smith, 1975; Udwin & Yule, 1990). Neuroanatomical studies of WS reveal no localized lesions in the neocortex, although there is evidence of reduced cerebral volume in general, together with unusual preservation of neocerebellum (Jernigan & Bellugi, 1990). Within the cognitive realm, researchers have documented a strikingly uneven cognitive profile resulting from WS, including, for instance, dissociations between good language and poor visuospatial skills (Bellugi, Birhle, Neville, Jernigan, & Doherty, 1993) and between preserved face recognition and other impaired aspects of spatial and visual reasoning and memory (Birhle, Bellugi, Delis, & Marks, 1989).

Williams Syndrome offers a particularly interesting arena to explore the contrast between knowledge enrichment and conceptual change, for individuals with WS also show preserved ability to acquire general encyclopedic and world knowledge, relative to other indicators of mental age (Levine, 1993). Furthermore, their performance on the Peabody Picture Vocabulary Test, a test of lexicon size that is sensitive to normal development into the fourth decade, is markedly better than predicted by full-scale IQ (Bellugi et al., 1993; Levine, 1993; Scott, Mervis, Bertrand, Klein, Armstrong, & Ford, 1994). Thus, individuals with WS have at least some learning mechanisms intact that are sufficient for knowledge enrichment. At issue is whether they also undergo conceptual change.

With respect to metacognitive capacities, Tager-Flusberg, Sullivan, & Zaitchik (1994) showed that as soon as children with WS could handle the language in terms of which the questions are posed (at about age 6), they succeeded on the standard false-belief-tasks diagnostic of the 4-year-old's theory of mind. However, in spite of relatively spared acquisition of the 4-year-old theory of mind, even older adolescents and adults with WS fail to achieve the normally developing 8-year-old's explicit conceptual understanding of human memory (Bertrand & Mervis, 1994). This last finding, of impaired metamemory knowledge, is consistent with the general literature on mental retardation (for reviews see Bebko & Luhaorg, 1998; Campione et al., 1982; Montague, 1998) and suggests that people with WS, like other individuals with mental retardation, will be found lacking in many aspects of metaknowledge and executive control processes, including comprehension monitoring, strategy invention and use, and the detection of contradictions and inconsistencies. Indeed, Bellugi et al. (1993) report an impairment in the performance of same/different judgments in adolescents with WS.

If there is no distinction between knowledge enrichment and conceptual change (as Churchland, 1992, suggests), then measures of knowledge acquired in some domain that is formulated over the concepts of T1 should predict degree of acquisition of T2, for any relevant T1 and T2, even in the case of individuals with WS. However, if distinct learning mechanisms are required for conceptual change, then it is possible that individuals with WS will fail to achieve it. In particular, with respect to metarepresentational abilities, if the 4-year-old theory of mind is sufficient, then adolescents and adults with WS should be limited only by domain-relevant knowledge (as suggested above). However, if other metacognitive knowledge or executive processes are necessary, we should see marked impairments in the capacity of individuals with WS to construct intuitive theories that require conceptual change.

Intuitive biology is a particularly appropriate conceptual domain to test for the knowledge achievements of people with WS. Biological knowledge depends minimally on either visuospatial or numerical abilities, both of which are implicated in WS (Bellugi et al., 1993; Frangiskakis et al., 1996). Furthermore, the domain of biology lends itself to general, encyclopedic knowledge. Many facts (e.g., that animals breathe) could plausibly be learned without having to first understand that animals belong to the ontology of living things, or without understanding the role of breathing in maintaining life (i.e., without being embedded in T2). The following anecdote is suggestive. SK, a 21-year-old woman with WS, with a verbal IQ of 69, could read, and particularly liked, novels about vampires, of which she had read several. When asked what a vampire is, she replied, "Oooh, a vampire is a man who climbs into ladies' bedrooms in the middle of the night and sinks his teeth into their necks." When asked why vampires do this, she was visibly taken aback – she hesitated and said, "I've never thought about that." She then thought for a long time before finally answering, "Vampires must have an inordinate fondness for necks."

SK's responses exemplify several aspects of the language of people with WS; they are syntactically well-formed and complex, and display conversational hooks (Reilly, Klima, & Bellugi, 1991), such as the drawn out "oooh" that began SK's description of vampires, and her exaggerated "inordinate," which is also an example of complex vocabulary used appropriately. But most interestingly from our point of view, SK's responses suggest that SK had indeed read several vampire books and had accumulated a store of information about vampires without ever constructing a concept of vampires as sucking blood, of being between dead and alive themselves, or of killing their victims and thereby creating new vampires. That is, this articulate 21-year-old with WS did not really know what a vampire is supposed to be, in just those deep conceptual respects that implicate the T2 intuitive biology of adults.

8. Intuitive Biology: Evidence That Its Construction Involves Conceptual Change

Consider the changes within the ontologically central concepts, *person* and *animal*, between ages 4 and 10. Older infants and preschoolers have an elaborate concept of person for reasoning about human behavior (for a review, see Spelke et al., 1996; Wellman & Gelman, 1992). Both also have a concept of animal (Carey, 1985; Mandler, Bauer, & McDonough, 1991; Wellman & Gelman, 1992). They distinguish animals from nonanimals, and use this distinction productively in similarity based inductive reasoning. Nevertheless, there is ample evidence that the preschooler's concepts of animal and person differ from the 10-year-old's, being embedded in very different framework theories (Carey, 1985; 1988; 1995).

According to Carey's analysis, the core of the preschooler's concept of animal is that of a behaving being, in essence a simplified variant on the prototypical behaving beings – people. The young child understands and interprets the body in terms of the role body parts play in supporting behavior. That is, the preschooler's concepts person and animal are embedded is in the core domain of intuitive psychology.

By the age of 10 (recent work has revised this estimate downward to closer to 6 or 7; see Carey, 1995, for a review), the child has constructed a new intuitive theory of biology, T2, with animal and plant coalesced into the single, core, ontological kind, living thing and people reanalyzed as one just one animal among many (Carey, 1985). Inagaki & Hatano (1993) characterize this new biology as a vitalist biology. Crider (1981) characterizes it as the container theory of the body. We characterize it as a theory of the life cycle and the role of bodily function in maintaining life.

For it to be true that there are conceptual changes within the concepts, *person* and *animal*, there must also be changes in a host of interrelated concepts. And indeed, there are. These include the differentiation of *not alive* into *dead, inanimate, unreal*, and *nonexistent* (Carey, 1985; 1988) and the differentiation of *family* into *biological family* and *social family* (Johnson & Solomon, 1997; Solomon, Johnson, Zaitchik, & Carey, 1996; but see also Springer & Keil, 1989; Springer, 1992; 1996). Others are the reanalysis of *death* from a behavioral interpretation to one based on the collapse of the bodily machine (Carey, 1985; Koocher, 1974; Nagy, 1948), and the reanalysis of *baby* from *small, helpless animal* to *reproductive offspring* (Carey, 1985; 1988; Goldman & Goldman, 1982). The core features of the concept *species kind* shift away from physical and behavioral characteristics toward origins of the animal (Keil, 1989; Johnson & Solomon, 1997).

In the domain of intuitive biology, this conceptual-change view has been challenged by an enrichment-only view (c.f. Atran, 1994; Coley, 1996; Keil, 1992; 1994; Springer, 1992; 1995; Springer & Keil, 1989; Wellman & Gelman, 1992). These two views share several assumptions. Both views allow for the enrichment of existing conceptual structures via inferential processes. For example, Springer (1995) suggested that children work out a core principle of biological inheritance (that babies' physical properties are derived from the mother) by inference over the learned premises: (1) babies grow in their mother's tummies; and (2) nothing external to the mother influences the baby while it is growing. Similarly, Carey (1985) suggested that young children use patterns of intercorrelated animal properties productively in similarity-based (inductive) inference. Furthermore, both views hold that preschoolers' knowledge is framed by genuine intuitive theories that determine ontological commitments, represent causal mechanisms, and constrain the child's interpretation of phenomena and the child's further learning in the domain.

However, according to the enrichment-only view, the core concepts encompassing animals and plants in the 10-year-old's theory are the same as those in the preschooler's theory. According to this view, new kinds may be discovered (e.g., aardvarks), but no new basic ontological concepts are constructed (e.g., *living thing* is already available); differentiations may occur (e.g., *dog* into *poodle, collie, terrier, . . .*) but none in which the previously undifferentiated concept no longer plays any role.

There are no changes in concepts' cores, no construction of new explanatory mechanisms. In short, there are no incommensurabilities between time 1 and time 2 and therefore there is no new T2 formulated over concepts not available in T1.

9. The Study

Drawing on the published literature and a reanalysis of Carey's (1985) position, Johnson and Carey (1998) constructed two batteries of developmentally sensitive tasks based on whether adultlike performance on each task in fact entails T2 (the adult intuitive biology). If there is no distinction between the processes that produce enrichment and those that produce conceptual change, then adultlike performance on any randomly chosen animal-based inference task should, on average, predict adultlike performance on any other, including those that depend upon the concepts of T2. One of the batteries (the T1/T2 Neutral Battery) requires concepts that could, on Carey's analysis, be expressed in T1; where the other (the T2-Dependent Battery) diagnoses the concepts of T2 that implicate conceptual change in their acquisition.

Our main hypothesis could have best been tested by matching participants with WS to normally developing participants on the basis of performance on one of the two batteries of tasks, then comparing their performances on the other battery to test for correspondence or lack thereof. We adopted an indirect route to this end. We reasoned that a test of lexical knowledge, such as the Peabody Picture Vocabulary Test-Revised (PPVT-R; Dunn & Dunn, 1981), would be a good predictor of performance on the first battery (T1/T2-Neutral Animal Knowledge battery), since lexical growth of the type tapped by the PPVT-R generally requires no conceptual change. That is, the harder items on the PPVT-R are harder just because they are rare; hard items are from the same ontological categories (tools, animals, vehicles, clothes, human physical or social interactions, human occupation, etc.) as are easier ones. All these categories are available to preschool children. In addition, the PPVT-R provides standardized scoring which allows fine-grained matches between participants with WS and normally developing participants predicted to have comparable general knowledge to the participants with WS. Furthermore, in order to maximize the chance that the participants with WS would possess T2, and that they would possess the general knowledge of typical 9- to 10-year-olds, we selected only those who performed at least as well as normally developing 9-year-olds on the PPVT-R (i.e., had PPVT-R mental ages of at least 9).

Three groups of participants were tested: 10 adolescents and adults with WS, an older group of 10 normally developing children individually matched to the participants with WS on the PPVT-R, and a younger group of 9 normally developing children. The participants with WS were between the ages of 10 and 32 years (average 24;3). Children in the matched control group were between 8 and 13 years (average 9;10) and those in the younger control group were between 5 and 7 (average 6;5). Children in both groups were selected such that their mental ages as measured by the PPVT-R were average given their chronological ages; 10;11 for the older group and 6;7 for the younger. The participants with WS had an average mental age of 11;5.

9.1 T1/T2-Neutral Animal Knowledge Battery

The tasks of the first battery, the T1/T2-Neutral Animal Knowledge battery, were built on the concepts of animal, animal properties, and animal parts, concepts found in both T1 (the core domain of psychology) and T2 (the constructed domain of vitalist biology). Although normal development of these concepts undoubtedly involves shifts in the core/peripheral properties of animals (Carey, 1985), Johnson and Carey (1998) argued that adultlike performance is, in principle, possible in the absence of that shift having occurred. This is because the basic scope of the animal category (excepting the role of person) is already firmly in place in T1 (Carey, 1985; Keil, 1989). There is nothing proposed by the enrichment-only view or the conceptual change view to prevent the acquisition or construction of new information predicated on these concepts through pure enrichment processes.

Take, for example, the property "breathing" as an observable bodily phenomenon of animals. The phenomenon of breathing itself can be interpreted in multiple ways. For instance, within the context of a biological theory (T2), breathing can be understood as a mechanism for maintaining life, by which a living organism exchanges oxygen and carbon dioxide with the surrounding air. The reasoning then goes, insofar as an organism has a life to maintain, it probably breathes in one way or another. On the other hand, in the context of a behavioral theory (Carey's T1), breathing can be understood as the simple act of taking air in and out of the nose and mouth – in this case, insofar as an organism has a nose or mouth, it probably breathes. Or even more simply interpreted, breathing is something people do, therefore insofar as an object is like a person, it is likely to breathe – leaving open entirely the dimension of similarity invoked.

Three tasks assessed knowledge built on the T1/T2-Neutral concepts of animal, animal parts and animal properties: attribution of bodily properties to animals and to non-living objects, the inductive projection of a novel property taught about people, and size of the animal lexicon.

Animal Lexicon

Preschool children (and perhaps even infants) have the concept *animal kind*. Adding new exemplars of kinds of animals to one's knowledge base, and learning their names, does not require conceptual change. To estimate the size of the animal lexicon, we asked participants to name as many members of the category animal as they could think of. Of course, if anything, such a production task underestimates the total number of animals known, since participants would surely retrieve many more animal names if cued with pictures, or verbal probes (e.g., zoo animals, sea animals, farm animals, pets, etc.). Each participant was assigned a score based on the total number of animal names produced, minus any repetitions and intrusions.

Attribution

This task assessed knowledge of the properties of animals, tapping both directly retrieved general knowledge and knowledge derived from similarity based inductive inference. It was modeled on those reported in Carey (1985; see also Inagaki & Hatano, 1987). The participant was asked a series of simple yes/no questions about each of several pictured objects from the categories of animals (people, dogs, birds, worms) and inanimate objects (computers, the sun, and rag dolls). (A plant [tree] was also included in the series, but responses to plant were scored as part of the T2-Dependent battery, for they tap whether plants have been analyzed as living things.) Four bodily properties of animals were probed of each object: breathes, has a heart, hears, and has babies. Knowledge that people have these properties is most likely directly retrieved from memory, but some decisions, for example, whether birds or worms have hearts, depend on inference. Participants were unlikely to have learned such facts explicitly. Indeed, most adults do not know for sure whether worms have hearts or not. Carey (1985) argues that such inferences are similarity based, reflecting the distribution of known properties of animals (see Osherson, Smith, Wilkie, Lopez, & Shafir, 1990). The questions about bodily properties were intermixed with filler questions designed to minimize response biases and to ensure that the task demands were within the capabilities of the participants.

Normal performance on the attribution of bodily properties is characterized by both general and developmental effects (Carey, 1985; Inagaki & Hatano, 1987). In general, normal participants at all ages use the distinction between animals and non-animals to constrain their inferences. Even children who hold T1 refrain from attributing animal properties to inanimate objects, including those they independently rate as highly similar to people (such as dolls or stuffed animals; Carey, 1985). There are, in addition, two developmental effects on the pattern of animal property attributions within the category of animal. Young children both attribute animal properties with decreasing frequency as the object becomes less similar to people, and they do so regardless of the particular property's identity. Adults, on the other hand, project some properties universally across the category animal (breathes, has babies), whereas others (has bones, hears, has a heart) come to be restricted to vertebrates only.

Performance on this task was assessed relative to both patterns of normal developmental change. First, we derived a measure that reflected the degree to which attribution of animal's properties fell off as a function of dissimilarity from people. A high score here reflects a rich knowledge base of facts about animals, and a lower score suggests the more immature inferences based on similarity to people. Second, we derived a score that reflected the differentiation among universal and restricted bodily properties in attribution to vertebrates and invertebrates. In normal development this difference score increases with age.

Both of these aspects of animal-based knowledge can be acquired within the framework of T1, hence the inclusion of this task in the T1/T2-Neutral battery.

Inductive Projection of a Novel Property
Taught about People

This was a similarity-based, inductive inference task from Carey (1985). Its purpose was to confirm that participants' knowledge was productive, and that the patterns generated in the attribution task were true inferences reflecting the role of the concept of animal in a participant's conceptual system (whether T1 or T2), as opposed to merely the recitation of a list of memorized facts. The use of a novel property ensured this.

Participants were taught a new word ("omentum"). They were told that one of the things in the world that has omentums inside them are people. Participants were shown where on a picture of a person you might expect to find an omentum. They were then asked to judge whether any of the objects used in the attribution task had omentums.

Each participant's performance on this task was captured by a difference score between the percentage of animals attributed omentums minus the percentage of inanimate objects attributed omentums. In normal development, performances on this task mirrors performances on induction tasks using familiar properties.

9.2 T2-Dependent Battery

The T2-Dependent battery was designed to tap concepts in the vitalist biology that are incommensurate with the preschoolers' T1, including *life, death, the body-machine, person-as-one-animal-among-many,* and *species kind* identity based on origins (Carey, 1985; Keil, 1989; Johnson &

Solomon, 1997). Unlike the tasks in the T1/T2-Neutral battery, we proposed that enrichment processes alone could not readily lead to concepts capable of supporting the adultlike (T2) performance, just because acquisition of these concepts requires conceptual change.

Five tasks were chosen that diagnose several of the conceptual changes within intuitive biology listed above. Seven basic measures were derived from the tasks.

Animism

Childhood animism is Piaget's (1929) term for the young child's propensity to claim that objects such as the sun, the moon, the wind, fire, cars, bicycles, and so forth are alive. Carey (1985) interpreted this phenomenon as reflecting the child's undifferentiated concept *living/existing/animate/real*, which the child has mapped onto the term "alive." It takes theory change within intuitive biology, not achieved during normal development until well into middle childhood, for these alternative interpretations of the word "alive" to be distinguished.

The animism task we administered was adapted from the standardized version of Laurendeau & Pinard (1962). The participant judged whether each of 20 objects drawn from the categories of animals, plants, inanimate natural kinds, and artifacts was alive. Participants were also asked to justify each judgment. The performance of each participant was scored in two different manners. First, judgments alone were analyzed for the percentage of inanimate objects correctly judged not alive. Second, the overall level of performance for each participant was scored based on patterns of judgments and the nature of explanations given (see Carey, 1985; Laurendeau & Pinard, 1962, for details). Participants were classified into Levels ranging from 0 (random judgments) through 6 (adult performance). Intermediate levels reflected different justification patterns. For example, Level 1 participants judged some inanimate objects alive and appealed to activity, utility or existence in their justifications, whereas Level 3 participants judged some inanimate objects alive and appealed to the capacity for autonomous motion in their justifications.

Death

This interview was adapted from those of Koocher (1974) and Nagy (1948) and diagnosed conceptual change in the child's concept of death. The preschool child has not yet differentiated two senses of "not alive" into *dead* and *inanimate* (Carey, 1985). This differentiation during middle childhood plays a role in the differentiation of the preschool child's undifferentiated concept *alive/animate/exists/real* which underlies the end of childhood animism. Preschool children interpret death in behavioral terms; a dead person has gone away, is somewhere else, never to return. Sometimes they see the dead person as having fallen into a sleeplike state. Adult understanding entails the construction of a body-as-biological-machine concept, in terms of which the concept of death is then reanalyzed. While properties such as absence remain important attributes of the dead even in the adult concept, they are derived from a new core concept centered around the biological notion of the breakdown of the bodily machine.

The death interview included a series of questions on the meaning of death and what happens specifically to a person and their body when they die. Four levels of understanding were identified in participants' responses. Level Minus 1: Death was described as the absence, departure, or altered sleeplike state of the dead person. Level 0: No evidence was offered for any interpretation of death. Level 1: Death was described as a cessation of behavioral processes such as talking, moving, or thinking. Level 2: Death was described as the cessation of bodily processes such as the heart beating, breathing, or the blood circulating. In cases where participants offered responses falling into more than one level, they were credited with the higher level.

Inductive Projection of a Novel Property
Taught about Dogs

Carey (1985) found that when a novel bodily property is predicated of dogs (or some other non-human animal), preschool children project that property to other animals less than when it is taught about people. The children are especially reluctant to project a novel property from a non-human animal to humans. For example, 4-year-olds project a novel property such as having an omentum from people to dogs around 75% of the time, but if the property were taught about dogs, the children project it to people less than 20% of the time (Carey, 1985). Normal 10-year-olds (and adults) project a novel bodily property with equal likelihood from dogs to people as from people to dogs. In the T2 of 10-year-olds, people and dogs apparently have equal status within the category animal, at least for the purposes of inferences about bodies. In the T1 of preschool children, by contrast, people are the prototypical animal, in which behaving being, rather than living being, is at the core.

To assess whether this reanalysis of people as one-animal-among-many has taken place, a second inductive inference task was given, exactly the same as the omentum task of the T1/T2-Neutral battery, except that participants were told that the newly taught organ is found inside dogs. Performance on this task was measured by the single response to people, yes or no.

Attribution to Tree

Embedded in the larger attribution task of the T1/T2-Neutral battery were questions about the properties of trees, including the four biological properties: breathes, has a heart, hears, and has babies. The central ontological kind of T2 is living thing, which includes both animals and plants. The formation of this concept involves reanalysis of the property breathing in terms of the role taking in air plays in supporting life, and reanalysis of the concept of baby as reproductive offspring. Though these reanalyses do not necessitate attribution of breathing and babies to trees, adults nonetheless often do so. Preschoolers in the grips of T1, on the other hand, rarely attribute these properties to trees, since trees are not seen as behaving beings. Performance on this task was measured with a difference score based on the relative attributions of bodily properties to trees versus the other inanimate objects in the attribution task.

Species Transformations

In order to assess the core of the concept of species kind identity, Keil (1989) studied the transformations participants judged would change the species of a given animal. Keil showed his participants a picture of a target animal (say, a raccoon), and told a story of how this animal was transformed into one that looked like a member of another species (say, a skunk). He found that the likelihood that a participant would judge that the raccoon had actually become a skunk depends upon the participant's age and the nature of the transformation, which ranged from costumes and temporary surface paint to permanent plastic surgery or an injection/pill given early in development.

In this sort of task, 3-year-olds judge that any transformation, including a costume change, yields an animal of the new species (DeVries, 1969); preschoolers judge that plastic surgery but not costume change yields a new species; fourth graders will accept injections but not plastic surgery or costumes, and adults judge that none of these transformations changes the animal's kind (Keil, 1989). In T1, physical characteristics are central to an animal's kind. Origins of the animal and its properties are peripheral, if acknowledged at all. For the 10-year-old's T2, origins of the animal and its properties are central to kind identity while its actual physical properties are peripheral.

Our tasks, taken directly from Keil (1989), included two stories of costume transformations (a goat being costumed to look like a sheep and a zebra being costumed to look like a horse) and two stories of surgery transformations (a raccoon turned into a skunk-look-alike and a tiger turned into a lion-look-alike). Performance was scored on the basis of how strongly the participant resisted a change in the animal's kind identity; the higher the score, the more resistant (and adultlike) the judgments.

9.3 An Important Caveat about the Two Batteries

None of the tasks employed here provide operational definitions of the concepts they are being used to diagnose. It is possible that some of the more "advanced" response patterns of the T2-Dependent battery could, however unlikely, be achieved without true understanding of the underlying concepts. For instance, a T2 judgment pattern on the animism task, in which only animals and plants are judged to be alive, could be achieved if a participant happens to have learned, as a piece of factual knowledge, that both plants and animals, and only plants and animals, are said to be alive, even though they have not yet constructed a biological concept of life that unites these two into a coherent, superordinate category. Similarly, participants could judge that plants have babies because they know that there are little ones, even though they have not yet constructed the concept of baby that is part of T2, involving a biological theory of reproduction.

One way to tell whether apparent T2 performance actually reflects T2 is to analyze consistency across tasks. For example, one participant with WS, who provided a T2 pattern of judgments on the Animism task (Level 6) had almost certainly simply learned that only plants and animals are called "alive." This is shown by the fact that 62% of her justifications were appeals to existence, utility, activities or irrelevant facts about the items (typical of preschoolers' justifications on this interview; see Carey, 1985) in contrast with 9% of the justifications of the matched controls who scored at Level 6. Similarly, if this participant had constructed the T2 concept of life, she should understand death as the cessation of life, due to breakdown of the bodily machine, but instead she achieved only Level 0 on the death task, indicating a concept of death close to that of preschoolers.

Therefore, in addition to measure-by-measure comparisons of the performance of the three groups on the tasks, consistency of performance across tasks was also analyzed.

9.4 Information Processing Demands of the Tasks of the Two Batteries

The participants with WS were predicted to perform at the same level as their matched controls on the T1/T2-Neutral battery, but much worse than their matched controls on the T2-Dependent battery. Conversely, they were predicted to perform much better than the younger controls on the T1/T2-Neutral battery, but at the same level or worse on the T2-Dependent battery. To ensure that this pattern of results, if obtained, reflects the predicted differences in concepts and conceptual structure between the populations, it is important that the task demands of the two batteries be equated. This was accomplished in several ways. First, identical tasks were included in both batteries, differing only in the knowledge structures they call upon. For example, the inductive projection of a novel property of dogs to people and other entities is part of the T2-Dependent battery because the projection to people is highly diagnostic of whether people are considered one animal among many with respect to bodily structure. On the other hand, the nearly identical task, inductive projection of a novel property of people to animals and other entities, was part of the T1/T2-Neutral battery, for this task reflects the animals-as-simple-variants-of-people prototype structure of T1, as well as the patterns of correlated properties that support similarity based inductive inferences (Osherson et al., 1990; Sloman, 1993). For similar reasons, the attribution of properties to animals is a T1/T2-Neutral task, but the same task construed over plants is a T2-Dependent task. Advanced performance with plants is facilitated by having constructed the ontological category of living things. And similarly, the costumes task places identical information-processing demands on the participant as does the operations task, yet young children always perform better on the costumes task than the operations task because the latter reflects the T2 concept of species kind. Secondly, wherever possible, the T2-Dependent tasks were scored on the bases of patterns of yes/no or forced-choice judgments (animism, projection from dog, attribution to plants, species transformations). Finally, when justifications and explanations were analyzed, the analysis did not depend upon the ability to provide explanations per se, but on the content of what was said (animism, death). On these tasks, young preschool children provide scorable data, so it was unlikely that the task demands would defeat the adolescents and adults with WS.

10. Results

The data were analyzed with respect to the predictions from the conceptual change position. Here we sketch the major results and overall patterns. Interested readers can find complete analyses and discussion of the results in Johnson & Carey (1998).

As can be seen in Table 1, both positions predicted that the older group of control participants (Matched Controls) would perform better than the younger group of control participants (Younger Controls) on both batteries. In addition, both hypotheses predicted that the participants with WS would perform at the level of the matched controls on the T1/T2-Neutral battery. The two positions differed only in their predictions for the T2-Dependent battery. The enrichment-only position predicted the same pattern of results for the T2-Dependent battery as for the T1/T2-Neutral battery, since conceptual change is not considered a prerequisite for the construction of the 10-year-old's biology. The conceptual change position, in contrast, predicted that the participants with WS would perform worse than their matched controls on this battery, at the level of the younger controls. Individual results from each task were aggregated and analyzed in three different ways.

Table 1: Predictions of Both Views for Each Battery

	WS vs. MC	WS vs. YC	MC vs. YC
T1/T2-Neutral Battery			
Accretionist View – enrichment only	=	>	>
Conceptual Change View – enrichment plus conceptual change	=	>	>
T2-Dependent Battery			
Accretionist View – enrichment only	=	>	>
Conceptual Change View – enrichment plus conceptual change	<	=	>
WS: Williams Syndrome; MC: Matched Controls; YC: Young controls; =: no significant difference; >: significantly better than; <: significantly worse than.

First, we tested the predictions of the conceptual change position using comparisons based on the relative performances of the participants with WS and Matched Control participants within each individually matched pair. The corresponding WS/Younger Control and Matched Control/Younger Control comparisons were based on overall group performances.

Summary results for each task and comparison are presented in Table 2. As predicted, participants with WS did not differ from their matched controls on any of the measures of T1/T2-Neutral knowledge of animals and bodily properties, except for one measure in which they marginally outperformed the controls. That is, their knowledge of bodily properties was sensibly organized and mental-age-appropriate with respect to the categories of animals and inanimate and animate objects. It also reflected use of the subtle distinction between universal and restricted bodily properties commonly used by lay adults, but not yet acquired by their normally developing matched controls. Furthermore, the lists of animal exemplars that they produced were qualitatively and quantitatively similar to those produced by their matched controls, as can be seen in the following examples:

WS(#10): lions, tigers, bears, raccoons, monkeys, apes, orangutans, Bengal tigers, elephants, walruses

MC(#10): Birds, cats, dogs, mice, tigers, cheetahs, lions, donkeys, zebras, giraffes, bears, rabbits, foxes, fish

YC(NP): Bears, camel, horse, cow, dog, cat, lamb, camel

Table 2: Summary Measures from All Tasks

	WS score (S.E.)	MC score (S.E.)	YC score (S.E.)	Value of statistical comparisons		
				WS vs. MC	WS vs. YC	MC vs. YC
T1/T2-Neutral Battery						
Animal Lexicon – net number of exemplars produced	14.4 (2.1)	14.8 (1.7)	8.0 (1.4)	=	>	>
Attribution of Properties to Animals – general percentages	95.0 (2.2)	97.0 (2.1)	80.0 (8.3)	=	>	>
Universal/Restricted Distinction – difference score of percentages	50.0 (11.2)	15.0 (15.0)	8.0 (10.7)	=	>	=
Projection of Novel Property from People – difference score of percentages	77.0 (8.0)	77.0 (8.0)	82.0 (8.0)	=	=	=
T2-Dependent Battery						
Animism – % correct on inanimates	53.0 (12.9)	86.0 (7.2)	83.0 (11.0)	<	=	=
Animism – level analysis	2.8 (0.6)	5.0 (0.4)	4.2 (0.8)	<	=	=
Death – level analysis	–0.7 (0.2)	1.1 (0.2)	-0.3 (0.3)	<	=	>
Attribution of Properties to Trees – difference score of percentages	20.0 (4.4)	32.5 (4.3)	8.3 (3.5)	<	=	>
Projection of Novel Property from Dog – yes/no projection to people	20.0 (13.0)	70.0 (15.0)	11.0 (11.0)	<	=	>
Species Costume Transformation – degree of resistance to change	1.8 (0.2)	2.9 (0.1)	2.2 (0.2)	<	=	>
Species Surgery Transformation – degree of resistance to change	1.4 (0.2)	2.2 (0.2)	1.2 (0.2)	<	=	>

WS: Williams Syndrome; MC: Matched Controls; YC: Young controls; S.E.: Standard Error; =: no significant difference; >: significantly better than; <: significantly worse than

In contrast, the list produced by this younger control participant was typical of that group's performance in general, in which they performed worse than the group with WS on three of the four tasks. The fourth task, the projection of a novel property from people, elicited a ceiling effect for all three participant groups. Though no developmental pattern was found with that measure, it nonetheless confirms that the knowledge that participants with WS have is not simply rote knowledge, but is embedded in productive conceptual structures which support novel inferences.

Overall, these results from the T1/T2-Neutral Animal Knowledge battery confirmed the first half of our hypothesis; that participants with WS are unimpaired on general knowledge of animals relative to their PPVT-R mental ages.

However, when probed for those concepts in the normal adult T2 biology that have been implicated in conceptual changes, the participants with WS performed markedly below their presumed mental ages. The participants performed with WS worse than their matched controls on every task in the T2-Dependent battery. In fact, their performance resembled that of young, normally developing preschoolers in every way, often falling below that of even the younger control group examined. They held no superordinate category of living thing which included both animals and plants, and could support the attribution of biological properties to trees. They refused to project a novel bodily property of dogs to people, thus revealing that they do not conceive of people as one-animal-among-many with respect to bodily structure. And they claimed that a raccoon, whether surgically altered to look like a skunk or simply dressed up in a skunk costume, was in fact a skunk, revealing no understanding of the role of reproduction and origins in determining biological kind identity. Participants with WS claimed that cars are alive because they move, are useful, or can be seen, and they conceived of death in terms of the departure or altered state of the dead person rather than in terms of the breakdown of a bodily machine. The animism and death interviews elicited particularly striking examples both of the immaturity of the responses of participants with MS relative to their matched controls, and also of the striking resemblance that they bear to those of the younger controls or even preschoolers reported in the literature. Take, for example, the following protocols taken from the animism interview.

WS(#5): Level 2; 43% over-attribution of life to non-living things; under-attribution of life to plants.

E: Is a car alive?
WS(#5): Yes, because it moves.

E: Is a cat alive?
WS(#5): Yes, cause they go, they move.

E: Is a cloud alive?
WS(#5): Yes, cause they move.

E: Is a tree alive?
WS(#5): No, cause it doesn't move.

Compare the following fragments of the interview from the Matched Control to the above participant with WS.

MC(#5): Level 6; no over-attributions of life to non-living things; no under-attributions of life to plants.

E: Is a car alive?
MC(#5): No, cause it doesn't move, it doesn't feel, it doesn't hear, it doesn't talk, it doesn't have feelings, it doesn't have a heart, it doesn't have a brain.

E: Is a cat alive?
MC(#5): Yes, because it has a heart, it has a brain, it can hear, it can move, it can feel, it has hearing.

E: Is a cloud alive?
MC(#5): Nope cause it can't think, hear, feel, speak. It doesn't have a brain, heart.

E: Is a tree alive?
MC(#5): Yes. (no explanation)

And, as can be seen from the following typical sample, the Younger Control participants (age 6) outperformed the adolescents and adults with WS on these interviews.

YC(LK): Level 5; no over-attributions of life to non-living things; under-attributions of life to plants.

E: Is a car alive?
YC(LK): No, it's still.

E: Is a cat alive?
YC(LK): Yes, it moves.

E: Is a cloud alive?
YC(LK): No, it doesn't have eyes.

E: Is a tree alive?
YC(LK): No, a tree doesn't have eyes.

The death interview revealed similar immature interpretations of death. Only 30% of the participants with MS defined death as the complement of life, whereas 70% of the Matched Control participants did this. The majority of participants with MS gave departure or altered state interpretations of death. "They slept," and "It means to not wake up, never come back," were both statements about death given by participants with WS. This sort of response was heard in the younger controls as well, in for example the child who defined death by saying "It means if you just fall to the ground and your eyes are shut and you're not moving at all, you're just standing there." The older Matched Controls, on the other hand, tended to point to the cessation of behavioral processes ("They can't think anymore. They can't feel anymore. They can't do any of the things they could do when they were alive.") and physical processes ("Your heart stops working, they stop breathing and they ... and everything stops inside you") when describing what happens to a person when they die.

All three groups elaborated their responses with emotional, religious, and procedural information about death, but participants with WS could be particularly eloquent in this respect: "They see God and God heals them from their wounds," and "They go to heaven, depending upon their quest in life, how they made their decisions, and how they felt about other people, and how much they have given."

In summary, the predictions made by the conceptual change position for WS performance on each batteries were strongly supported in this first analysis of the data. The participants with WS performed at or above the level of their PPVT-R mental age on tasks that tapped knowledge that is neutral with respect to the core domain of psychology and the constructed domain of vitalist biology (the concepts *animal, animal properties*, and *animal parts*). However, on tasks tapping the central concepts of the constructed domain of biology (*life, death, living thing, people-as-one-animal-among-many*, and *species kind*) participants with WS performed well below their mental age, often producing responses that resembled those of preschoolers.

We also examined the absolute achievement of each participant along the path from the core domain of psychology (T1) to the constructed domain of biology (T2) as diagnosed by the tasks in the T2-Dependent battery. It was predicted that if WS prevents conceptual change altogether, allowing only knowledge acquisition by enrichment, then the core concepts of the participants with WS as a group should never reflect T2. Similarly, on Carey's (1985) analysis, the Younger Control participants were at the beginning of the process of constructing T2, so they, too, should largely reveal T1 concepts of animals and plants. The Matched Control participants, on the other hand, were at the age at which a life-based, vitalist, intuitive biology (T2) has typically been constructed, and their performances as a group should reflect that.

In fact, this is what we found. The performance of each participant on each task was re-scored as a T1 (pre-conceptual change), a T2 (post-conceptual change), or an intermediary performance. Fifty-five percent of the WS performances overall remained grounded firmly in the T1 range, a figure comparable to that achieved by the Younger Controls (48%). Conversely, only 12% of the MC performances overall reflected T1 concepts.

The total number of T2 performances by each participant was also calculated. The histogram in Figure 1 shows the results of this analysis. No individual with WS scored a T2-level performance on more than 2 of the 7 measures. By contrast, 70% of the MC participants achieved a T2 performance on 3 or more of the 7 measures.

These analyses again illustrate the differential success of enrichment-based achievements and conceptual change-based achievements in participants with WS. For those concepts within the adult's constructed domain of biology that remain commensurable with the concepts of the core domain of psychology (i.e., for which conceptual change is not needed to support adultlike performance), people with WS perform well. However, when the adult's concepts are the result of conceptual change away from the core domain, the enrichment-alone processes available to people with WS fail to produce them and people with WS therefore perform poorly relative to their PPVT-R mental age.

One final measure was derived to compare achievement on the two batteries within individual participants. If the processes underlying enrichment of knowledge and conceptual change are truly distinct, then differential achievement on the two batteries should be detectable within individual subjects as well as within entire groups. Each participant with WS was therefore predicted to perform relatively better on the T1/T2-Neutral tasks than on the T2-Dependent tasks compared to the normally developing children. For the normally developing children in both groups, we expected that performance on the T1/T2-Neutral tasks would predict performance on the T2-Dependent tasks.

This is what we found. For each participant, we calculated a difference score between the degree of high-level performance on the T1/T2-Neutral battery and the degree of high-level performance on the T2-Dependent battery. A simple rank ordering of participants' difference scores revealed that the distribution of participants relative to this measure was not random across population groups. Nine of the 10 individuals with the highest difference scores had WS and 18 of the 19 remaining individuals were children developing normally, Mann-Whitney, $U = 20$, $p < .01$. The single participant with WS achieving a difference score in the normal range did so due to failure on both batteries rather than success on both. Thus we see that the differential impairment on the T2-Dependent tasks is restricted to the participants with WS.

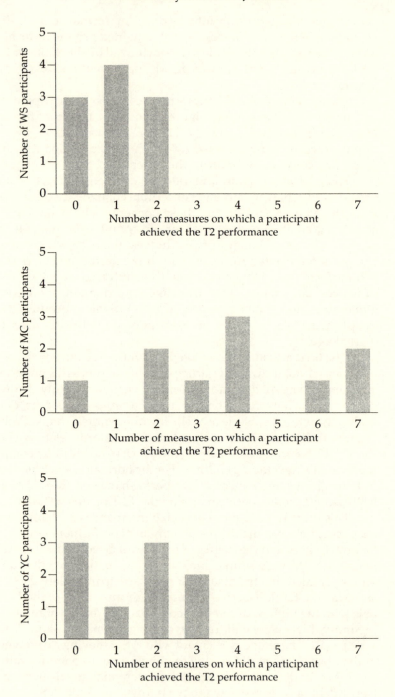

Figure 1.

11. Conclusions

11.1 Knowledge Enrichment and Conceptual Change

Adolescents and adults with WS were found to be differentially more impaired in the acquisition of concepts that were posited to require conceptual change than those that were not. When probed for concepts of life, death, living thing, species kind, and people-as-one-animal-among-many, highly articulate, seemingly well-informed individuals with WS were found to possess the conceptual understanding of normally developing 6-year-olds. Furthermore, these findings held despite matching task demands across the two batteries. Both the T1/T2-Neutral battery and the T2-Dependent battery were based largely on forced-choice judgment tasks, with only a small sampling of measures in each based on the production of more elaborate verbal responses. These results allow us to draw several conclusions.

First, in typical development there is a relationship between the amount of knowledge acquired through enrichment processes and the amount of knowledge acquired through conceptual change processes, such that one predicts the other. This is demonstrated most clearly in the correlation between performance on the two batteries within normally developing children ($r = .49$, $p < .05$, with age partialed out). However, contrary to the position of Churchland (1992) and enrichment-only theorists such as Spelke, Keil, Atran, and Springer, this correlation does not appear to derive from a single underlying learning process, as the dissociation in people with WS shows us. People with WS achieved L2-equivalent performances on the theory-Neutral battery while simultaneously performing at a 6-year-old or younger (T1) level on the theory-Dependent battery. This pattern of results held for every task and every participant with WS.

This pattern of results was predicted on the basis of our analysis of the relations between beginning and later knowledge in the two batteries. We argued that in the course of cognitive development, there are two different types of relations between successive conceptual states (CS1 and CS2). Sometimes CS2 is an enriched version of CS1, as is largely the case for the knowledge tapped by the T1/T2-Neutral battery; and sometimes CS2 is a new framework theory, the construction of which has required conceptual change away from CS1, as is largely the case for the knowledge tapped in the T2-Dependent battery. We predicted that participants with WS, on the basis of aspects of their mental retardation, would lack the ability to undergo conceptual change in the face of relatively preserved capacities for acquiring new enriched knowledge formulated over their current concepts.

Bellugi et al. (1993) report other data consistent with this prediction. In that work, adolescents with WS failed Piagetian tasks including conservation of number, weight, substance, and quantity. Although performance on conservation tasks is often taken as a reflection of reasoning ability (e.g., understanding that a greater extent in one dimension can be compensated for by a lesser extent in another), conservation of weight and matter also reflect important conceptual changes within the child's intuitive theory of matter (Carey, 1991; Piaget & Inhelder, 1941; Smith, Carey, & Wiser, 1985). Again, the concepts of the adolescents with WS appear to remain embedded in the T1 typical of preschool children.

Of course, participants with WS are not unimpaired on the T1/T2-Neutral battery. With one exception (the differentiation between universal and restricted bodily properties), they never perform at the level typical of their chronological age. Rather, the T1/T2-Neutral battery patterns with mental age as measured by the PPVT-R, on which participants with WS are also impaired relative to their chronological age. This result was predicted, and vindicates the choice of the PPVT-R as a matching instrument. However, it was by no means a foregone conclusion. The T1/T2-Neutral battery – that is, production of animals' names, inductive projection of a newly taught bodily property of people, and attribution of bodily properties to animals and inanimate objects – contained tasks very different from a receptive vocabulary task. Nonetheless, we expected that the PPVT-R would predict performance on this battery, for vocabulary acquisition of words such as those on the PPVT-R, like vocabulary acquisition of names of animal kinds, does not generally require conceptual change. Words on the PPVT-R name examples of kinds of which some exemplars are known to preschool children. What predicts difficulty on the T1/T2-Neutral battery, like the PPVT-R, is rarity of the knowledge, likelihood of having encountered it. We assume that people with mental retardation are less likely than normally developing people to encounter any given piece of information, and are generally slower to form associations, to enrich their existing knowledge base with new beliefs.

The data from the normally developing control participants also have implications in their own right for researchers debating the role of conceptual change in the domain of biology. This study was the first we know of in which a large collection of intuitive biological concepts was examined both within individuals and in a psychometric context. To our surprise, even the older controls had not completed the construction of T2, despite an average chronological age of nearly 10 and a mental age of nearly 11. Only two of the older participants (MA = 11;0 and 14;7) displayed T2 understanding across the board. This result is consistent with Carey's (1985) claim that the construction of the framework theory of living kinds is a long and slow process and is not completed until the end of the first decade of life. It is inconsistent with much of the recent work

pushing the acquisition of the living-kind ontology down into the preschool years, to ages more comparable with those at which the child's
theory of mind is clearly seen.

11.2 Theory of Mind and Core Knowledge

The characterization of biological knowledge of adolescents and adults
with WS supports the distinction between knowledge enrichment and
conceptual change, because individuals with WS are unable to achieve
the latter in the face of spared capacities in the former. This finding, in
turn, bears on controversies concerning the status of the 4-year-old's theory of mind as requiring conceptual change to achieve. The fact that individuals with WS acquire the preschooler's theory of mind early in
childhood, almost at the normal age, while never making the conceptual
changes that normal children make only a few years later, strongly suggests to us that the preschooler's theory of mind results from an unfold-
ing of core knowledge. At the very least, it does not require the learning
mechanisms that support later conceptual change.

In contrast to this conclusion, Gopnik & Meltzoff (1997) argue that
the construction of the 4-year-old's theory of mind requires the same
sorts of processes of conceptual change as does theory change in developed science, comparing the construction of the preschooler's theory of
mind to Darwin's construction of the theory of natural selection. They
argue as follows. First, the 4-year-old's understanding of mind deserves
the designation theory, as it determines a domain of unique phenomena,
a distinct ontology, and unique explanatory principles. Its concepts and
belief constitute a rich, interconnected, mutually defining whole. Second, studies of the components of the theory show them to develop together; the child who distinguishes appearance from reality also passes
the standard false-belief task, can evaluate sources of belief and pass
level-2 perspective-taking tasks. The child who fails on one of these is
likely to fail on others. This pattern of results supports the claim that this
is a coherent body of knowledge, that the concepts and beliefs are inter-
defined as in other theories. Third, they argue that training studies provide direct evidence that the processes supporting conceptual change
within this domain are similar to those that support conceptual change
in later developing theories. Slaughter & Gopnik (1996) showed, for example, that two experiences of feedback on a false-belief task, one week
apart, led to improvements on 3-year-olds' performance on a wide range
of theory of mind tasks, those implicated in the coherent developmental
patterns outlined above.

These results certainly support the interconnectedness and coherence
of the components of the 4-year-old's theory of mind. However, we draw
exactly the opposite conclusion from the training studies as do Gopnik
and Meltzoff. One hallmark of conceptual change is that it is difficult to

achieve. Widespread influence of two experiences ("No, Maxi says John thinks there are chocolates in the Smarties box, because Maxi knows that John didn't see the pencils"), each a week apart, is a fascinating finding, but hardly typical of the processes through which Darwin constructed the theory of natural selection. As Gruber (1974) documented through an analysis of Darwin's Transmutation Notebooks, this process took years to achieve, and even after Darwin worked out the theory, it failed to have widespread effect. He articulated it with great excitement, surrounded by exclamation points and stars, and then appeared to forget about it for 2 years, continuing to work within his original Monad theory of evolution, before finally returning to it.

More generally, the present case study offers the possibility of a test for whether any particular knowledge structure is part of core knowledge. Core knowledge is that which unfolds under the influence of substantial innate support during infancy and the preschool years and is achieved by individuals with mental retardation more or less on schedule. Constructed knowledge, including that involving conceptual change, is not achieved by such individuals, at least not by those without substantial, extraordinary, focused training (Campione et al., 1982). By this test, the 4-year-old theory of mind is part of core knowledge.

11.3. Metarepresentational Capacity and Conceptual Change

The third major conclusion from this case study is that the metarepresentational capacities that are part of the 4-year-old's theory of mind, substantial as they are, are not sufficient to ensure the first genuine conceptual changes in childhood. Contrary to Sperber's (1994) hypothesis, semantic evaluative abilities sufficient to support conceptual change are not part of the 4-year-old's metarepresentational repertoire. Children with WS, like children with Down Syndrome, develop the 4-year-old's metarepresentational capacities, around age 6 instead of around age 4, but in spite of the delay, apparently do so normally. Adolescents, even adults, with WS (and probably those with Down Syndrome) have not undergone the conceptual changes typical of middle childhood, in spite of being in possession of the metarepresentational capacities delivered by the theory-of-mind module at least since age 6. Therefore, these metarepresentational capacities not sufficient to support conceptual change in intuitive biological, physical and social theories.

The question then becomes, what is missing? Why do these individuals with mental retardation fail to undergo conceptual change in these domains? Normally developing children develop an intuitive vitalism by age 7 or 8 in the absence of explicit tuition in school, so it is unlikely that different educational experience account for the failure of adults with WS to construct this intuitive theory. One of our adults with WS had finished regular high school, including high-school biology, and had even completed two years of a normal junior college, yet was indistinguishable from the other WS participants on the T2-dependent battery.

One possibility is that later-developing metacognitive understanding and executive control processes are necessary for conceptual change. Not only do these develop in normal children later than age 4, they do not develop at all in children with mental retardation, in the absence of extended and explicit teaching (Bebko & Lahaorg, 1998; Campione et al., 1982; Montague, 1998). Examples include comprehension monitoring, the metaconcepts needed to explicitly evaluate an argument (e.g., the distinction between validity and truth), and the metaconcepts needed to evaluate explicitly the evidence for some belief (e.g., the distinction between evidence and theory). All these are developed later than the preschool theory of mind, sometimes much later, and are not spontaneously acquired by individuals with mental retardation. There is no direct evidence concerning late-developing metaconceptual knowledge of people with WS. However, since adults with WS resemble other populations with mental retardation with respect to metamemorial development (both metamemorial knowledge and strategic executive-control processes; Bertrand & Mervis, 1994), it is likely that they resemble other populations with mental retardation with respect to metaconceptual knowledge and control processes in general.

We do not doubt that later developing metaconceptual knowledge and executive control processes play a role in the processes that support theory development and conceptual change, even in the domain of intuitive biology, but there are two reasons to doubt that these fully explain the failure of adults with WS to achieve the vitalist T2. First, we need an explanation for why adolescents and adults with WS fail to acquire the relevant metaconceptual knowledge itself. Again, within the domain of metarepresentational capacity, children with WS exhibit core knowledge but fail to go significantly beyond it. One cannot appeal to the missing metaconceptual knowledge to explain this failure, for it is the missing metaconceptual knowledge we are trying to account for. Second, by age 10, normally developing children have constructed intuitive theories of biology, cosmology, matter, and social relations that go beyond core knowledge, requiring conceptual change. And in all of the cases looked at so far (biology, social relations, matter), adults with WS fail to make these conceptual changes, in spite of the fact that they are achieved by normally developing children between ages 6 and 10, ages at which explicit metaconceptual understanding of theory, evidence, contradiction, coherence is notably and spectacularly lacking (e.g., Kuhn et al., 1988; Carey, Evans, Honda, Unger, & Jay, 1989).

Much further research is needed to resolve these issues. In the absence of any specific evidence, we can offer our current speculations on why individuals with mental retardation like those with WS, who have good linguistic and metarepresentational abilities, fail to achieve the conceptual changes that allow normally developing children to go beyond core knowledge. First, we assume that mental retardation results from a general, low-level problem in computational power. Retarded individuals are slower encoders of perceptual information than are normal controls (e.g., Anderson, 1992). Second, we assume that the metarepresentational capacities that are part of the theory-of-mind module support noticing of contradictions, distinguishing appearance from reality, and so forth, for individuals with mental retardation as much as for normally developing ones. However, because of reduced computational capacity, they are simply less likely to do so on any given occasion.

In a case study of a bright, normally developing, preschooler achieving T2, Carey (1985) noted frequent comments that reflected exactly the semantic evaluation capacities on Sperber's list. For example, one day the child said:

> Child: That's funny, statues are not alive but we can still see them.

> Her mother replied: What's funny about that?

> Child: Well, Grampa's dead and that's sad because we can't see him anymore.

Here the child had noticed a contradiction within her undifferentiated concept of not alive (*dead/inanimate/absent/unreal/nonexistent/representation*). Statues are paradigm examples of inanimate objects, unreal representations, yet they are present, unlike her Grandpa who is also not alive, in the sense of dead. Further, she found this contradiction worthy of comment and puzzlement. Her mother tried to resolve the contradiction for her, distinguishing not alive in the sense of the end of animals' and peoples' life-cycles, from not alive in the sense in which tables and chairs are not alive, only succeeding in confusing the child further. The child's metarepresentational capacities allowed her to note the contradiction, but her lack of biological knowledge prevented her from understanding her mother's attempt to resolve it:

> Child: Yes, isn't that funny. Tables and chairs are not alive, but we can still see them.

Such exchanges are notably lacking between children with WS and their parents. Parents report to us that their children do not go through the maddening but charming "why" period of normally developing preschool children, except to ask why they are not allowed to do certain things. This observation bears careful documentation. The bootstrapping devices that underlie conceptual change (see Carey, 1999) require metarepresentational cognitive architecture, but they also require considerable computational capacity. The lack of the latter serves as a bottleneck, both in the construction of metaconceptual knowledge that goes beyond the core, and in the construction of the first theories that likewise transcend the core. These two consequences interact; the failure to develop metaconceptual knowledge and executive control makes the normal achievement of conceptual change all the more difficult for individuals with mental retardation relative to their normally developing age mates.

References

Anderson, M. (1992). *Intelligence and development: A cognitive theory.* Oxford: Basil Blackwell.

Atran, S. (1994). Core domains versus scientific theories: Evidence from systematics and Itza-Maya folkbiology. In L. A. Hirschfeld and S. A. Gelman (Eds.), *Mapping the mind: Domain specificity in cognition and culture.* New York: Cambridge University Press.

Au, T. K. (1994). Developing an intuitive understanding of substance kinds. *Cognitive Psychology 27* (1), 71–111.

Baron-Cohen, S. (1995). *Mindblindness: An essay on autism and theory of mind.* Cambridge, MA: MIT Press.

Baron-Cohen, S., Leslie, A. M., & Frith, U. (1985). Does the autistic child have a "theory of mind"? *Cognition 21,* 37–46.

Bebko, J.M., & Luhaorg, H. (1998). The development of strategy use and metacognitive processing in mental retardation: Some sources of difficulty. In J. A.Burack, R. M.Hodapp, & E. Zigler (Eds.), *Handbook of mental retardation and development.* New York: Cambridge University Press.

Bellugi, U., Birhle, A., Neville, H., Jernigan, T., & Doherty, S. (1993). Language, cognition, and brain organization in a neurodevelopmental disorder. In M. Gunnar and C. Nelson (Eds.), *Developmental behavioral neuroscience.* Minnesota Symposium. Hillsdale, NJ: Erlbaum.

Bertrand, J. & Mervis, C. (1994). Metamemory in people with Williams syndrome. Poster presented at the 1994 National Williams Syndrome Professional Conference, La Jolla, CA.

Bihrle, A., Bellugi, U., Delis, D., & Marks, S. (1989). Seeing either the forest or the trees: Dissociation in visuospatial processing. *Brain and Cognition, 11,* 37–49.

Campione, J., Brown, A., & Ferrara, R. (1982). Mental retardation and intelligence. In R. J. Sternberg (Ed.), *Handbook of human intelligence.* Cambridge: Cambridge University Press.

Carey, S. (1985). *Conceptual change in childhood.* Cambridge, MA: MIT Press.

Carey, S. (1988). Conceptual differences between children and adults. *Mind and language 3,* 167–181.

Carey, S. (1991). Knowledge acquisition: Enrichment or conceptual change? In S. Carey and R. Gelman (Eds.), *The epigenesis of mind: Essays on biology and cognition.* Hillsdale, NJ: Erlbaum.

Carey, S. (1995). On the origins of causal understanding. In D. Sperber, J. Premack, and A. Premack (Eds.), *Causal cognition: A multidisciplinary debate.* Oxford: Clarendon Press.

Carey, S. (1999). Sources of conceptual change. In E. K. Scholnick, K. Nelson, S.A. Gelman & P. Miller (Eds.), *Conceptual development: Piaget's legacy.* Hillsdale, NJ: Erlbaum.

Carey, S., Evans, R., Honda, M., Unger, C., & Jay, E. (1989). An experiment is when you try and see if it works: Middle school conception of science. *International Journal of Science Education 11,* 514–529.

Carey, S., & Gelman, R. (1991). *The epigenisis of mind: Essays on biology and cognition.* Hillsdale, NJ: Erlbaum.

Carey, S., & Spelke, E. S. (1994). Domain specific knowledge and conceptual change. In L. Hirschfeld & S. Gelman (Eds.), *Mapping the mind: Domain specificity in cognition and culture* (pp. 164–200). Cambridge: Cambridge University Press.

Carey, S., & Spelke, E. (1996). Science and core knowledge. *Journal of Philosophy of Science 63* (4), 515–533.

Chi, M. T. H. (1992). Conceptual change within and across ontological categories: Examples from learning and discovery in science. In R. Giere (Ed.), *Cognitive models of science: Minnesota studies in the philosophy of science.* Minneapolis, MN: University of Minnesota Press.

Churchland, P. M. (1992). A deeper unity: Some Feyerabendian themes in neurocomputational form. In R. Giere (Ed.), *Cognitive models of science: Minnesota studies in the philosophy of science.* Minneapolis, MN: University of Minnesota Press.

Coley, J. D. (1996). Emerging differentiation of folk biology and folk psychology: Attributions of biological and psychological properties to living things. *Child Development 66,* 1856–1874.

Crider, C. (1981). Children's conceptions of the body interior. In R. Bibace & M. E. Walsh (Eds.), *Children's conceptions of health, illness, and bodily functions.* San Francisco: Jossey-Bass.

DeVries, R. (1969). Constancy of genetic identity in the years three to six. *Monographs of the Society for Research in Child Development 34.*

Dunn, L. M. & Dunn, L. M. (1981). *Peabody picture vocabulary test* (Rev. ed.). Circle Pines, MN: American Guidance Service.

Feyerabend, P. (1962). Explanation, reduction, empiricism. In H. Feigl & G. Maxwell (Eds.), *Minnesota Studies in the Philosophy of Science 3* (pp. 41–87). Minneapolis, MN: University of Minnesota Press.

Flavell, J. H., Everett, B. A., Croft, K., & Flavell, E. R. (1981). Young children's knowledge about visual perception: Further evidence for the Level 1–Level 2 distinction. *Developmental Psychology 17,* 99–103.

Fodor, J. A., (1992). A theory of the child's theory of mind. *Cognition 44,* 283–296.

Frangiskakis, J. M., Ewart, A. K., Morris, C. A., Mervis, C. B., Bertrand, J., Robinson, B. F., Klein, B. P., Ensing, G. J., Everett, L. A., Green, E. D., Proschel, C., Gutowski, N. J., Noble, M., Atkinson, D. L., Odelberg, S. J., Keating, M. T. (1996). LIM-kinase1 hemizygosity implicated in impaired visuospatial constructive cognition. *Cell 86,* 59–69.

Frith, Uta (1989). *Autism: Explaining the enigma.* Cambridge, MA: Basil Blackwell.

Goldman, R., & Goldman, J. (1982). How children perceive the origin of babies and the roles of mothers and fathers in procreation: A cross-national study. *Child Development 53*, 491–504.

Goodale, M.A., & Milner, D.A. (1992). Separate visual pathways for perception and action. *Trends in Neuroscience 15*, 20–25.

Gopnik, A., & Meltzoff, A. (1997). *Words, thoughts, and theories.* Cambridge, MA: MIT Press.

Gopnik, A., & Wellman, H. M. (1994). The theory theory. In L. A. Hirschfeld and S. A. Gelman (Eds.), *Mapping the mind: Domain specificity in cognition and culture.* New York: Cambridge University Press.

Gruber, H. (1974). *Darwin on man: A psychological study of scientific creativity.* London: Wildwood House.

Hatano, G., & Inagaki, K. (1994). Young children's naïve theory of biology. *Cognition, 50*, 171–88.

Hacking, I. (1993). Working in a new world: The taxonomic solution. In P. Horwich (Ed.), *World changes: Thomas Kuhn and the nature of science.* Cambridge, MA: MIT Press.

Hirschfeld, L., & Gelman, S. (1994). *Mapping the mind: Domain specificity in cognition and culture.* New York: Cambridge University Press.

Inagaki, K., & Hatano, G. (1987). Young children's spontaneous personification as analogy. *Child Development 58*, 1013–1020.

Inagaki, K. & Hatano, G. (1993). Children's understanding of the mind-body distinction. *Child Development 64*, 5, 1534–1549.

Jernigan, T., & Bellugi, U. (1990). Anomalous brain morphology on magnetic resonance images in Williams syndrome and Down syndrome. *Archives of Neurology 47*, 529–533.

Johnson, S., & Carey, S. (1998). Knowledge enrichment and conceptual change in folk biology: Evidence from people with Williams syndrome. *Cognitive Psychology 37*, 156–200.

Johnson, S., Slaughter, V., & Carey, S. (1998). Whose gaze will infants follow? Features that elicit gaze-following in 12-month-olds. *Developmental Science 1* (2), 233–238.

Johnson, S., & Solomon, G. (1997). Why dogs have puppies and cats have kittens: Young children's understanding of biological origins. *Child Development 68* (3), 404–419.

Jones, K., & Smith, D. (1975). The Williams elfin facies syndrome: A new perspective. *Journal of Pediatrics 86*, 718–723.

Keil, F. C. (1989). *Concepts, kinds, and cognitive development.* Cambridge, MA: Bradford Books.

Keil, F. C. (1992). The origins of an autonomous biology. In M. R. Gunnar & M. Maratsos (Eds.), *Modularity and constraints in language and cognition: The Minnesota Symposia on Child Psychology 25*, Hillsdale, NJ: Erlbaum.

Keil, F. C. (1994). The birth and nurturance of concepts by domains: The origins of concepts of living things. In L. A. Hirschfeld and S. A. Gelman (Eds.), *Mapping the mind: Domain specificity in cognition and culture.* New York: Cambridge University Press.

Kitcher, P. (1988). The child as parent of the scientist. *Mind and Language 3*, 217–227.

Koocher, G. P. (1974). Talking with children about death. *American Journal of Orthopsychiatria 44*, 404–410.

Kuhn, D., Amsel, F., & O'Loughlin, M. (1988). *The development of scientific thinking skills*. San Diego, CA: Academic Press.

Kuhn, T. S. (1962). *The structure of scientific revolutions*. Chicago: University of Chicago Press.

Kuhn, T. S. (1977). *The essential tension: Selected studies in scientific tradition and change*. Chicago: University of Chicago Press.

Kuhn, T. S. (1982). Commensurability, comparability, communicability. *PSA 2*, 669–688. East Lansing: Philosophy of Science Association.

Landau, B., & Gleitman, L. (1985). *Language and experience: Evidence from the blind child*. Cambridge, MA: Harvard University Press.

Laurendeau, M., & Pinard, A. (1962). *Causal thinking in the child: A genetic and experimental approach*. New York: International Universities Press.

Leslie, A. M. (1994). ToMM, ToBy, and Agency: Core architecture and domain specificity. In L. A. Hirschfeld and S. A. Gelman (Eds.), *Mapping the mind: Domain specificity in cognition and culture*. New York: Cambridge University Press.

Levine, K. (1993). Cognitive profiles in Williams syndrome. Unpublished manuscript. Boston's Children's Hospital.

Mandler, J., Bauer, P., & McDonough, L. (1991). Separating the sheep from the goats: Differentiating global categories,. *Cognitive Psychology 23* (2), 263–298.

Markman, E. (1985). Comprehension monitoring: Developmental and educational issues. In S. F. Chipman, J. W. Segal, & R. Glaser (Eds.), *Thinking and learning skills: Vol. 2. Research and open questions*. Hillsdale, NJ: Erlbaum.

Meltzoff, A. N. (1995). Understanding the intention of others: Re-enactment of intended acts by 18-month-old children. *Developmental Psychology 31* (5), 838–850.

Milner, D. A., & Goodale, M. A., (1992). *The visual brain in action*. Oxford: Oxford University Press.

Montague, M. (1998). Research on metacognition in special education. In T. E. Scruggs & M. A. Mastropieri (Eds.), *Advances in learning and behavioral disabilities, Vol. 12*. London, UK: JAI Press.

Morris, C. (1994). The search for the Williams syndrome gene. Paper presented at the 1994 National Williams Syndrome Professional Conference, La Jolla, CA.

Nagy, M. H. (1948). The child's theories concerning death. *Journal of Genetic Psychology 73*, 3–27.

Nersessian, N. J. (1992). How do scientists think? Capturing the dynamics of conceptual change in science. In R. N. Giere (Ed.) *Cognitive models of science: Minnesota Studies in the Philosophy of Science 15*. Minneapolis: University of Minnesota Press.

Newport, E. L. (1990). Maturational constraints on language learning. *Cognitive Science 14*, 11–28.

Oakes, L., & Cohen, L. (1995). Infant causal perception. In C. Rovee-Collier, L. P. Lipsitt, (Eds.), *Advances in infancy research, Vol. 9*. Norwood, NJ: Ablex.

O'Neill, D., & Gopnik, A. (1991). Young children's ability to identify the sources of their beliefs. *Developmental Psychology 27*, 390–399.

Osherson, D., & Markman, E. (1975). Language and the ability to evaluate contradictions and tautologies. *Cognition 3*, 213–226.

Osherson, D., Smith, E., Wilkie, O., Lopez, A., & Shafir, E. (1990). Category-based induction. *Psychological Review 97* (2), 1985–2000.

Perner, J. (1991). *Understanding the representational mind*. Cambridge, MA: MIT Press.

Piaget, J. (1929). *The child's conception of the world*. London: Routledge and Kegan Paul.

Piaget, J., & Inhelder, B. (1941). *Le dévelopment des quantités chez l'enfant*. Neufchatel: Delchaux et Niestle.

Quine, W. V. O. (1960). *Word and object*. Cambridge, MA: MIT Press.

Reilly, J., Klima, E., & Bellugi, U. (1991). Once more with feeling: Affect and language in atypical populations. *Development and Psychopathology 2*, 367–391.

Scott, P., Mervis, C., Bertrand, J., Klein, S., Armstrong, S., & Ford, M. (1994). Lexical organization and categorization in people with Williams syndrome. Poster presented at the 1994 National Williams Syndrome Conference, La Jolla, CA.

Slaughter, V., & Gopnik, A. (1996). Conceptual coherence in the child's theory of mind: Training children to understand belief. *Child Development 67*, 2967–2988.

Sloman, S. A. (1993). Feature-based induction. *Cognitive Psychology 25*, 231–280.

Smith, C., Carey, S., & Wiser, M. (1985). On differentiation: A case study of the development of the concepts of size, weight, and density. *Cognition 21*, 177–237.

Smith, C., Snir, J., & Grosslight, L. (1992). Using conceptual models to facilitate conceptual change: The case of weight-density differentiation. *Cognition and Instruction 9* (3), 221–283.

Solomon, G. E. A., Johnson, S. C., Zaitchik, D., & Carey, S. (1996). Like father, like son: Young children's understanding of how and why offspring resemble their parents. *Child Development 67*, 151–171.

Spelke, E. (1991). Physical knowledge in infancy: Reflections on Piaget's theory. In S. Carey and R. Gelman (Eds.) *Epigenesis of mind: Essays on biology and cognition*. Hillsdale, NJ: Erlbaum.

Spelke, E. S., Breinlinger, K., Macomber, J., & Jacobson, K. (1992). Origins of knowledge. *Psychological Review 99*, 605–632.

Spelke, E., Phillips, A., & Woodward, A. (1995). Infants' knowledge of object motion and human action. In D. Sperber, J. Premack, and A. Premack (Eds.), *Causal cognition: A multidisciplinary debate*. Oxford: Clarendon Press.

Spelke, E. S., & Van de Walle, G. A. (1993). Perceiving and reasoning about objects: Insights from infants. In N. Eilan, W. Brewer, & R. McCarthy (Eds.), *Spatial representation* (pp. 132–161). Oxford: Basil Blackwell.

Sperber, D. (1994). The modularity of thought and the epidemiology of representations. In L. Hirschfeld & S. Gelman (Eds.), *Mapping the mind: Domain specificity in cognition and culture*. Cambridge: Cambridge University Press.

Springer, K. (1992). Children's beliefs about the biological implications of kinship. *Child Development 63*, 151–171.

Springer, K. (1995). How a naive theory is acquired through inference. *Child Development 66*, 547–58.

Springer, K., & Keil, F. (1989). On the development of biologically specific beliefs: The case of inheritance. *Child Development 60*, 637–648.

Springer, K., & Keil, F. (1991). Early differentiation of causal mechanisms appropriate to biological and nonbiological kinds. *Child Development 62*, 767–781.

Tager-Flusberg, H., Sullivan, K. & Zaitchik, D. (1994). Social cognitive abilities in young children with Williams syndrome. Paper presented at the 6th International Conference of the Williams Syndrome Association, San Diego.

Udwin, O., & Yule, W. (1990). Expressive language of children with Williams Syndrome. *American Journal of Medical Genetics Supplement 6*, 108–114.

Vosniadu, S., & Brewer, W. F. (1992). Mental models of the earth: A study of conceptual change in childhood. *Cognitive Psychology 24*, 535–585.

von Hofsten, C., Vishton, P., Spelke, E. S., Feng, Q, & Rosander, K. (1998), Predictive action in infancy: Tracking and reaching for moving objects. *Cognition 67*, 255–285.

Wellman, H. M. (1990). *The child's theory of mind.* Cambridge: MIT Press.

Wellman, H. M. (1993). Early understanding of mind: The normal case. In S. Baron-Cohen, H. Tager-Flusberg, & D. J. Cohen (Eds.), *Understanding other minds: Perspectives from autism.* Oxford, UK: Oxford University Press.

Wellman, H. M., & Gelman, S. A. (1992). Cognitive development: Foundational theories of core domains. *Annual Review of Psychology 43*, 337–375.

Williams, J. C. P., Barrett-Boyes, B. G., & Lowe, J. B. (1962). Supravalvular aortic stenosis. *Circulation 24*, 1311–1318.

Wiser, M. (1988). Can models foster conceptual change? The case of heat and temperature. *Educational Technology Center Technical Report*, Harvard University, Cambridge, MA.

Wiser, M., & Carey, S. (1983). When heat and temperature were one. In D. Gentner and A. Stevens (eds.), *Mental models* (267–297). Hillsdale, NH: Erlbaum.

Woodward, A. (1998). Infants selectively encode the goal object of an actor's reach. *Cognition 69*, 1–34.

Chapter 10

Consciousness and Metacognition

David Rosenthal

1. Metacognition and Conscious States

Metacognition has attracted considerable attention in recent psychological research. There has been extensive investigation, for example, of our metacognitive sense that information is present in memory even when that information is not consciously available, as well as investigation of the degrees of confidence people have about recall responses and about how well something has been learned. Moreover, the deficits that occur in such conditions as blindsight and visual agnosia and in certain forms of amnesia can usefully be seen as "[d]isruptions of metacognition" (Shimamura, 1994, p. 255). These and other investigations have highlighted the importance of studying the grasp we have of our own cognitive abilities and performance.[1]

Metacognitive functioning is plainly relevant to consciousness. Consider the so-called feeling-of-knowing (FOK) judgments that subjects make about what information is present in memory, even when that information is not currently accessible to consciousness, and also subjects' judgments of learning (JOLs) about how successfully something has been mastered. The metacognitive processes involved in both kinds of case result in subjects' conscious appraisals of their own cognitive condition. This has led one leading investigator to claim that metacognition can provide a useful model for studying the introspective access we have to our own mental states.[2]

Moreover, in blindsight, visual agnosia, and related disorders various indirect tests reveal that certain informational states occur of which subjects are wholly unaware, and which they routinely deny being in.[3] In the absence of the relevant neurological impairment, however, this visual and recognitional information would occur in the form of conscious mental states. So it is reasonable to hope that understanding these neural deficits will help us understand what it is that makes the difference between conscious and nonconscious mental states.[4]

Despite all this, current research into metacognition has not had all that much to say specifically about what it is in virtue of which conscious mental states are conscious. Consider, again, feeling-of-knowing judgments, which are representative of many of the phenomena on which investigation into metacognition has recently focused. A feeling-of-knowing judgment expresses a subject's sense "that a piece of information can be retrieved from memory even though that information currently cannot be recalled" (Miner & Reder, 1994, p. 47). In the terms used by Tulving & Pearlstone (1966, p. 115), the information is available to subjects but not accessible to them. Thus, in tip-of-the-tongue experiences,[5] conscious access to a word is blocked even though one consciously feels that the word is close to conscious recall. The relevant informational state in these cases is not conscious, but at best only potentially conscious. And in general, the mental states involved in feeling-of-knowing situations are not conscious mental states.[6]

How about research into blindsight and related neural deficits? Learning just what neurological processing is absent in these cases might well point to factors that, if present, would make those states conscious states.[7] But such research is still at a highly speculative stage.

Nonetheless, it is inviting to speculate that research into metacognitive functioning will be useful in understanding what it is for mental states to be conscious. What is the source of this theoretical intuition? At bottom, I think, it is due to the suggestion that for an informational or other mental state to be conscious is for one to be conscious *of* that state. More precisely, for a mental state to be conscious is for one to be conscious *that one is in that very state*.

It will be helpful, in this connection, to look again at the feeling-of-knowing situation. When one feels a word on the tip of one's tongue or has some other feeling-of-knowing experience, one has a conscious sense that the relevant informational state is there somehow, even though the state itself is not a conscious state. How can that be? As a first approximation, it is because one is conscious of being in some state or other that would fit the relevant informational bill, but one is not conscious of the particular informational state itself. So, despite one's conscious sense that the information is present, the particular informational state is not a conscious state. In feeling-of-knowing experiences one is conscious not of the state itself, but only that there is some relevant state. This lends provisional support to the idea that a mental state's being conscious consists in one's being conscious *of* that state.

As it stands, however, this is not quite right. On this account, the relevant informational states in feeling-of-knowing experiences fail to be conscious because one fails to be conscious *of* those states. But that is not what actually happens. Having a conscious sense that information is there somehow is one way of being conscious of the relevant informational state. One is conscious that one is in a state that bears the relevant information and, hence, conscious *of* that state as a state that bears that information. One is not, however, conscious of the state in respect of the information it bears.

We must therefore refine our first approximation. What matters is not just *that* one is conscious of the informational state, but *how* one is conscious of it. In feeling-of-knowing experiences, one is conscious of the target state as being a state that bears the relevant information, but not conscious of it in virtue of the actual information itself. Evidently what matters to a state's being conscious is not simply whether one is in some way conscious *of* the state, but whether one is conscious of the state in a way that gives one conscious access to its informational content. And for that to happen, one must be conscious that one is in a state *with that very information*. Informational states, after all, are individuated mainly in virtue of their content; so, if one is conscious of a state but not in respect of its content, one will have no subjective sense of that very state's being conscious. For a state to be conscious, one must be conscious of the state in virtue of its particular informational properties.

This fits well with the striking sense we have in feeling-of-knowing experiences that we are, somehow, both conscious and not conscious of the relevant informational state. As William James usefully notes, in tip-of-the-tongue experiences, the "gap" in our consciousness "is intensely active" (James, 1890/1950, p. 251). There is a vivid conscious difference between having one word on the tip of one's tongue and having another. We are conscious *of* the informational state somehow without being conscious of the information it bears.[8]

An analogy will help capture the oddness of such experiences. Somebody who knows that Mark Twain's real name is 'Samuel Clemens' could correctly be described as knowing *what* Twain's real name is; somebody who knows that Scott wrote *Waverly* could be truly said to know *who* wrote those novels. When we describe somebody's knowledge by way of a 'wh' complement – a clause governed by 'what', 'who', 'how', 'when', 'where', and the like – we abstract from the full content of that knowledge. We specify the knowledge only in terms of some question to which the knowledge would provide an answer.

In ordinary situations, we can truly describe somebody as knowing 'wh' – that is, as having knowledge specified with a 'wh' complement – only if the person has the relevant knowledge specified with a 'that' clause or its grammatical equivalent.[9] Feeling-of-knowing experiences occur precisely when the relevant knowing *that* isn't conscious. Suppose I have Twain's real name on the tip of my tongue; I have the feeling of knowing *what* that name is without, however, knowing consciously *that* his real name is 'Clemens'.

One sometimes has partial conscious access to the relevant information; one knows, say, that Twain's real name begins with 'c'.[10] One is conscious of the relevant informational state in respect of part of content, but not all. That suffices for the state to be conscious, though not conscious in respect of all its mental properties. And that corresponds to the way we experience such states. The way we are conscious of our conscious states in respect of of some, but not all, of their mental properties will be discussed at more length in section 5, below.

2. Metacognition and Higher-Order-Thoughts

We have seen that certain considerations pertaining to metacognitive phenomena make it inviting to hold that a mental state's being conscious is a matter of one's being conscious *of* that state. Close attention to feeling-of-knowing experiences, however, points to an even more fine-grained formulation. A mental state's being conscious consists not just in one's being conscious *of* that state, but in one's being conscious of it *under some relevant description*.

The requirement that one be conscious of the state under a relevant description has important consequences. There are two general ways in which we are conscious of things. One way is to see or hear the thing, or sense it in respect of some other sensory modality. Theorists who have recognized that a mental state's being conscious consists in one's being conscious of that state have almost invariably explained the particular way we are conscious of our conscious states in terms of our sensing or perceiving them.

There are several reasons why a perceptual model is attractive. Perhaps the most important has to do with the intuitive immediacy and spontaneity that characterizes the way we are conscious of our conscious mental states. When one has a conscious thought, perception, or feeling, one seems, from a first-person point of view, to be conscious of that state in a way that is entirely spontaneous and unmediated. There seems to be no reason for us to be conscious of the state, and no antecedent cause; it's simply the case that we are conscious of it. Moreover, nothing seems to mediate between those states and our awareness of them. So it may be tempting to hold that our awareness of our conscious states resembles in these respects the way we are aware of objects we perceive. From an pretheoretic, intuitive point of view, nothing seems to mediate between those objects and our perceptual awareness of them, and such awareness seems to arise spontaneously. Doubtless these analogies have done much to make an "inner sense" model of the way we are conscious of our conscious states seem inviting.

Sensing is not the only way of being conscious of things; we are also conscious of things when we think about them. Still, it may be tempting to think that sensing is the only way of being conscious of things that allows us to explain the intuitive spontaneity and immediacy characteristic of the way we are conscious of our conscious mental states.

Consider having a thought about some particular object, say, a particular house one saw yesterday. Having such a thought makes one conscious of that house. Suppose that the visually accessible properties of the house are insufficient to identify it uniquely; all that identifies it for one as a unique house is one's experience of seeing it. Perhaps, then, having thought about that very house requires that one have some relevant sensory image of it. One needn't, of course, actually sense the house to have a thought about it; but perhaps some relevant sensory content must figure in imagination for one's thought about that very house. And this may be the way it is with many cases of having thoughts about unique objects. If so, then at least in those cases, sensory content would always intervene between one's thoughts and the individual objects they are about. Since those thoughts would then be accompanied by suitable conscious sensory or imaginative states, they would presumably not seem to arise spontaneously.

This Aristotelian thesis about thinking and sensing[11] applies directly to the case at hand, since the conscious states we are conscious of are individuals. They are not individual objects, of course, but they are individual states. So if sensory content is often required for thoughts to be about unique individuals, we could not explain the intuitive immediacy and spontaneity of the way we are conscious of our conscious mental state by hypothesizing that we have thoughts about those states. We would instead need to adopt a sensory model of such consciousness.

But sensing is not in general necessary for thoughts to be about individuals. Individuation of the objects of thought takes place in many ways. In some cases we doubtless do pick out the objects of our thoughts by way of sensory content that pertains to those objects. But we also individuate objects of thought by describing them uniquely. Sometimes we describe them in terms of their unique relations to other individuals, and sometimes just as the unique individual satisfying some property at some particular time. Perhaps individuation of objects could not generally occur unless we individuated some objects by our sensing them. But even if that is so, it does not show that all individuals are picked out that way.

If objects of thought need not all be individuated by sensing them, it is hardly plausible that we need to individuate our own mental states that way. For one thing, it is natural to think of picking out mental states uniquely by reference to the individuating mental properties they instantiate during a particular time span. This type of procedure will work more successfully with one's own mental states than with physical objects, because restricting attention to one's own mental states cuts down the range of competing items with similar identifying properties. And that method of individuation aside, we may also be able sometimes to individuate mental states by reference to nonmental individuals. Even if I need to individuate a house by sensing it, once the house is picked out I can then individuate the thought I have at a particular time that that very house is large.

There are, in any case, other compelling reasons to doubt that we individuate, or are conscious of, our conscious states by sensing them. Sensing characteristically proceeds by way of a sensory modality dedicated to discerning the presence of a range of sensible properties, say, color and visible shape in the case of vision. But there is no sense organ dedicated to discerning our own mental states and no distinguishing range of sensible properties that those states exhibit.[12] Moreover, sense organs characteristically respond to whatever relevant properties fall within their sensory range. So, if the operation of some such organ were responsible for our being conscious of our conscious states, why would that organ respond only to some of those states and not to others? Why wouldn't all our mental states be conscious, instead of only some? Since we have no independent reason to think that any such sense organ actually exists, any answer to this question would very likely be unconvincing and ad hoc.

If the way we are conscious of our conscious states is not by sensing them, the only alternative is that we are conscious of those states by having thoughts about them. Can such a model square with our intuitive sense that the way we are conscious of our conscious states is immediate and spontaneous? Plainly it can. Recall that our consciousness of our conscious states need not actually be unmediated and spontaneous; it need only seem that way, from a first-person point of view. And thoughts do occur in ways that seem, from a first-person point of view, to be spontaneous and unmediated. All that's necessary for that is that we not be conscious of anything that causes those thoughts or otherwise mediates between them and the things they are about. So there must be no conscious inferences that lead to such thoughts, that is, no inferences of which we are conscious. And inference aside, we must also be unaware of anything else as mediating or causing those thoughts. For example, if sensory mediation of the sort discussed earlier did occur, we must not be conscious of it.

This model of the way we are conscious of our conscious mental states is the *higher-order-thought hypothesis* that I have defended elsewhere.[13] One is conscious of one's conscious states because every such state is accompanied by a higher-order-thought (HOT) to the effect that one is in that state.

Such HOTs cannot be dispositions to have the thought in question, since being disposed to have a thought about something doesn't make one conscious of that thing. And they must exhibit an assertoric mental attitude, since nonassertoric thoughts also don't make one conscious of things. These conditions rule out certain putative counterexamples, such as higher-order memories or the higher-order cognitive processing, which occur even when the lower-order mental states they are about aren't conscious states.[14] But memories are not stored as occurrent, assertoric intentional states, and higher-order processing will not exhibit an assertoric mental attitude.

HOTs need not themselves be conscious thoughts. Having a thought makes one conscious of the thing the thought is about even when we are not at all aware of having that thought – that is, even when the thought is not a conscious thought. This helps with our explanatory task. If we are conscious of a mental state by having a nonconscious thought about it, it's clear that our being conscious of that state will seem to be both unmediated and spontaneous. If we are unaware even of having the thought in question, how could it seem to us that anything causes it or mediates between it and the state it is about? More precisely, whenever one becomes conscious that one is conscious of a conscious state, the way one is conscious of that state will seem unmediated and spontaneous. Because one isn't ordinarily conscious of the HOTs in virtue of which one is conscious of those states, one won't normally think anything about how it is that one is conscious of them.

More important for present purposes, the HOT model helps with the explanatory task that arose in connection with certain metacognitive phenomena. In a feeling-of-knowing experience, one is conscious *of* a certain cognitive state even though that state is not a conscious state. The reason, I argued, is that one is conscious of the state in a way that fails to give one conscious access to its informational content. An informational state will not be a conscious state unless one is conscious of it in a way that gives one such access. And that means being conscious of the state under some relevant description.

But the mental state in virtue of which one is conscious of something under a description must have intentional content. One can be conscious of something under a description only if one is conscious of that thing in virtue of having a thought about it. So only the HOT model of the way we are conscious of our conscious states can do justice to the characteristic way in which we both are and are not conscious of informational states in feeling-of-knowing experiences. Consideration of these metacognitive phenomena helps us decide on the right model for explaining what it is for a mental state to be a conscious state.

3. The Transitivity Principle

I urged at the outset that metacognition is relevant to consciousness because what it is for a mental state to be conscious is at bottom a matter
of one's being conscious of that state. This account is not a definition, but
rather a hypothesis about what it is for mental states to be conscious. But
even so, one might object, as Alvin Goldman has, that this idea is circular.
We cannot explain a mental state's being conscious by reference to one's
being conscious of that state, since in effect that is appealing to consciousness to explain consciousness (Goldman, 1993, p. 366).

But no circularity occurs here. A mental state's being conscious –
what I have elsewhere called *state consciousness* – is distinct from the
manifestly relational property of a person's being conscious *of* something or other – what we can call *transitive consciousness*. We are transitively conscious of things when we sense them or have thoughts about
them. And we understand such transitive consciousness independently
of understanding state consciousness; otherwise we couldn't even entertain the possibility of conscious creatures' having thoughts and other
mental states that aren't conscious.

My claim, then, is that we can explain state consciousness in terms of
one's being transitively conscious of that state. I shall refer to this claim
as *the transitivity principle*. As intuitively obvious as this idea may seem,
there have been several objections lodged against it in the recent literature.

One of the more interesting of these objections derives from a second threat of circularity to which Goldman has usefully called attention.
Goldman considers the view that believing oneself to be in a particular
mental state is "criterial" (Goldman, 1996, p. 8) for that state's being conscious. This is a version of the transitivity principle; a state is conscious
if one is conscious of that state by believing that one is in that state. But,
as Goldman points out, a state is not conscious if one thinks one is in it
solely because one is taking somebody else's word for it. So we must distinguish cases in which the mental state one thinks one is in is conscious
from cases in which it is not.

We can rule out the counterexample by appeal to the requirement
that there be no conscious mediation between a conscious state and one's
thought about that state, that is, no mediation of which one is conscious.
If I believe that I am in some mental state only because you tell me that
and I take your word for it, I am conscious of your statement as mediating between my mental state and my thought that I am in that state.

Goldman regards this way of avoiding circularity as falling into circularity at yet another point. The requirement that one's HOT be noninferential and nonobservational, he urges, amounts to stipulating that
one's HOT be *introspective* (Goldman, 1996, p. 14). And introspective
HOTs are simply HOTs that are about conscious mental states.

But a HOT's being noninferential in the relevant way is a matter only of that HOT's not being based on any inference of which we are conscious. And that condition is not circular, since it mentions only the transitive consciousness of such inferences. Nor is a thought's being noninferential in this way the same as its being introspective. A thought need not be about mental states at all to arise independently of any inference or observation of which one is conscious. Not all spontaneous thoughts are introspective thoughts.

Indeed, Goldman's suggestion here seems to get things reversed. We are introspectively conscious of our mental states when we are conscious of those states, and conscious that we are. But when I am conscious of some mental state I am in solely because I take somebody else's word for it, my HOT that I am in that state will very likely be a conscious thought. By contrast, when my HOT is independent of others' remarks and similar considerations, that HOT typically fails, itself, to be conscious. The HOTs in virtue of which our mental states are sometimes conscious states are seldom introspective HOTs.

Fred Dretske has developed an ingenious argument against the transitivity principle. Consider a scene consisting of 10 trees, and another just like it but with one tree missing. And suppose that you consciously see first one scene and then the other, and that when you do, you consciously see all the trees in each scene. But suppose that despite all this you notice no difference between the two scenes. This sort of thing happens all the time, for example, when one scene is a slightly later version of the other but altered in some small, unnoticed way.

We may assume, with Dretske, that in such a case you will have conscious experiences of both scenes, including all the trees in each. Moreover, there will be some part of the conscious experience of 10 trees that is not part of the conscious experience of 9 trees. That part is itself a conscious experience – it is a conscious experience of a tree. But, because you notice no difference between the scenes, you are not transitively conscious of the difference between them. Dretske concludes from this that you will not be transitively conscious of the experience of the extra tree. And that would undermine the transitivity principle; the experience of the extra tree would be a conscious experience of which you are not transitively conscious.[15]

But Dretske's argument is not sound. As we saw with feeling-of-knowing experiences, one can be conscious of a mental state in one respect and yet not conscious of it in another. One may, for example, be conscious of a visual experience as an experience of a blurry patch, but not as an experience of a particular kind of object. Similarly, one could be conscious of the experience of the extra tree as an experience of a tree, or even just as part of one's overall experience, without thereby being in any way conscious of it as the thing that makes the difference between the experiences of the two scenes. This is presumably just what happens in the case Dretske constructs.[16] Dretske's case does not run counter to the transitivity principle.[17]

Ned Block has recently sought, in effect, to split the difference between the transitivity principle and its opponents. According to Block, the term 'conscious', as applied to mental states, is ambiguous as between two distinct properties. One is the property a mental state has when there is something it's like for one to be in that state; Block calls this property *phenomenal consciousness*. A state has the other property when, in Block's words, its content is "poised to be used as a premise in reasoning ... [and] for [the] *rational* control of action and .. . speech" (Block, 1995, p. 231, emphasis in the original).[18] This second property he calls *access consciousness*. And he maintains that the two properties are, conceptually at least, independent. If so, there would be no single property of state consciousness.

Block's distinction has considerable intuitive appeal. The concept of access consciousness is meant to capture the intuitive idea that a mental state's being conscious is a matter of having some conscious access to that state. A metacognitive model will very likely be helpful in understanding that sort of consciousness.

But there is also a resilient intuition that consciousness has something specifically to do with the qualitative character of bodily and perceptual sensations. It is that property which Block's concept of phenomenal consciousness is meant to capture. And, because qualitative character is presumably intrinsic to sensory states, Block urges that phenomenal consciousness is not a matter of our having access to those states. If he is right, a metacognitive model cannot help here. Moreover, if the property of phenomenal consciousness is intrinsic to sensory states, the transitivity principle will fail for that kind of consciousness.

Many theorists maintain that the qualitative character of sensory states cannot occur without our having conscious access to it. Elsewhere I have argued against that doctrine (Rosenthal, 1986a, sec. 3; 1991, sec 1; 1993b, pp. 357–358; 1997b, pp. 732–733). Sensory states occur in subliminal perception, peripheral vision, and blindsight, and those sensations are not conscious in any intuitive way whatever. Moreover, mundane aches and pains that last all day may be felt only intermittently, and an ache or pain that isn't felt does not count intuitively as being conscious.

Block's notion of phenomenal consciousness is meant to capture the idea of a state's having some intrinsic qualitative character. But unless one has conscious access to one's sensory states, none of the properties of these states has any connection with consciousness, intuitively understood.[19] It is precisely because such access is absent for the sensory states in blindsight and subliminal perception that we refuse to count those states as conscious.

Block seeks to avoid this conclusion by defining phenomenal consciousness in terms of there being something it's like to be in our sensory states. After all, whenever there is something it's like for one to be in a state, that state is plainly a conscious state. Moreover, since the various sensations in blindsight and subliminal perception differ in qualitative character, won't they differ also in respect of what it 's like to have them?

Not in any sense of the phrase 'what it's like' that has any bearing on consciousness. When one lacks conscious access to a state, there is literally nothing it's like for one to be in that state. Without access to a state one has no first-person perspective on it, and so there is nothing it 's like to be in it. As Thomas Nagel has insisted, what matters for consciousness is that there be something it's like *"for* the organism" (Nagel, 1979, p. 166). And there will be something it's like for the organism only if the organism has conscious access to the relevant state. Block's phenomenal consciousness is not a kind of consciousness at all unless it involves one's having access to the sensory states in question.[20]

Block distinguishes a third concept of consciousness, which he calls reflective consciousness (review of Dennett, p. 182) or monitoring consciousness ("On a Confusion," [1995], p. 235). A state is conscious in this way, according to Block, if one has a HOT about it. But the states he counts as being conscious in this reflective or monitoring way are states we are *introspectively* conscious of: states that we are conscious that we are conscious of. Block is right, therefore, to classify this as a distinct kind of consciousness. But he is mistaken to define it simply in terms of the having of HOTs. For a state to have monitoring consciousness, in his sense, it must be accompanied not just by a HOT, but by a *conscious* HOT.

Block, Dretske, and Goldman all seek to explain why they find the transitivity principle unconvincing by casting doubt on the power of higher-order states of whatever sort to make mental states they are about conscious. How could being conscious of a mental state make that state conscious when being conscious of a stone does not make the stone conscious?[21] In Block's version, why should being conscious of a mental state make it conscious when being conscious of a state of the liver does not (Block, 1994)?

This very question, however, embodies a question-begging assumption. Being conscious of a mental state results in no change in that state's intrinsic properties, any more than being conscious of a rock or a state of one's liver changes anything intrinsic to the rock or the state of the liver. But a state's being conscious, on the transitivity principle, is not an intrinsic property of that state, but a relational property. Perhaps Goldman is right that "[o]ur ordinary understanding of awareness or consciousness seems to reside in features that conscious states have in themselves, not in relations they bear to other states" (1993, p. 367). But it is well-known that common sense is often a highly unreliable guide about whether the properties of things are relational.[22] The rock objection is simply a vivid way of expressing the conviction shared by Dretske and Goldman that a mental state's being conscious is not relational.

Block's adaptation of the objection to states of the liver avoids the categorial disparity between states and objects. The question whether a rock is conscious is parallel not to whether a mental state is conscious, but to whether a person or other creature is conscious. It is plain that the property of a creature's being conscious – what I have elsewhere called *creature consciousness* (Rosenthal, 1993b, p. 355; 1997b, p. 729) – is distinct from the property of a mental state's being conscious, since a conscious creature can be in mental states that aren't conscious.[23] This is why the objection is more vivid when cast in terms of rocks. Whatever we say about state consciousness, creature consciousness is plainly not relational. It consists simply in a creature's being awake and responsive to sensory input.

Still, if state consciousness is relational, why wouldn't states of the liver be conscious if we were conscious of them in a way that seems unmediated? Since such seemingly unmediated access to states of our livers never occurs, it may not be entirely clear how our intuitions would go. But there is reason to think that we would not count such states as conscious. Suppose, only for the sake of illustration, that a particular mental-state token is identical with a particular brain-state token. And suppose that we follow the transitivity principle, and say that this mental state's being conscious consists in one's being conscious of it in a suitable way. Still, if one were conscious of that state solely by being conscious of being in a particular brain-state token, even in a seemingly unmediated way, we would not count that state as a conscious state. Conscious states are mental states we are conscious of *in respect of some mental properties*.[24]

4. Young Children and Metacognitive Development

The transitivity principle to one side, Dretske has appealed to certain metacognitive studies to argue specifically against the HOT model of state consciousness. Developmental work by John Flavell (1988), Alison Gopnik (1993), Josef Perner (1991), and Henry Wellman (1990) is sometimes taken to show that, before the age of about three years, children do not describe themselves as believing or experiencing things. Although they apply such words as 'think' and 'believe' to themselves and to others, there is reason to hold that these children do not mean what we mean by these words, since they tend not to distinguish what a person believes from what is actually the case.

In one well-known study (Perner, Leekam, & Wimmer, 1987), three-year-olds who saw a candy box opened to reveal pencils inside said that others who saw the box still closed would also believe it had pencils in it. These children apparently attribute beliefs when they take the beliefs to be true. Even more striking, this false-belief task yields the same sorts of result when the children apply it to themselves. Three-year-olds also say of themselves that, when they first saw the closed box, they believed that it contained pencils, although they had actually described themselves then as believing it contained candy (Gopnik & Astington, 1988; also Moore, Pure, & Furrow, 1990).

In many such studies, children three and younger elide the difference between what is actually the case and what they or others believe. So they ascribe to others and to their own past selves only beliefs whose content matches the way they currently take the world to be. They regard a person's believing something as always corresponding to that thing's actually being the case; saying how the world is believed to be does not, for them, differ significantly from just saying how the world is.[25] Since they ascribe no states whose content diverges from how they take things to be, the remarks these children make show little or no evidence of having the concept of a state that might so diverge.

Since content is all that matters to the way these children attribute beliefs to themselves and to others, it's tempting to conclude that they think of these states as involving only content; perhaps no mental attitude figures in their conception of these states. This divergence from the way adults and, indeed, slightly older children speak and think about these states encourages the idea that these children three and younger may simply not have the concepts of beliefs, thoughts, and experiences. Their use of such words as 'think', 'believe', and 'experience' does not express the ordinary folk-psychological concepts of these states.

Nonetheless, we can reasonably assume that these children are in many mental states that are conscious. And this, Dretske argues, causes difficulty for the HOT hypothesis, which holds that the mental states these children are in will be conscious only if they have HOTs about those states. And it is arguable that having such HOTs requires one to have concepts of the relevant types of state (Dretske, 1995, pp. 110–111).[26]

There is serious question about whether the data do show that these young children lack the relevant concepts, and question even about what concepts must figure in HOTs for these states to be conscious. But before getting to that, it's worth noting that children three and younger might in any case have HOTs about their mental states without ever expressing those HOTs in words. Even adults have thoughts they cannot express verbally, and doubtless children at various stages of cognitive development have many concepts that are not yet expressed in speech.

So these young children might have HOTs that draw the relevant distinctions even though their speech does not reveal any such HOTs.

One might simply reject the idea that these children have thoughts they never express in speech. The automatic, effortless way adults report their conscious states may make it seem that if one can speak at all, the only explanation for an inability to report one's conscious states must be that one lacks the requisite concepts. How could any language-using creature with the relevant concepts fail to be able to report its conscious states? [27]

We do readily express in words all the thoughts we are conscious of having, but not thoughts that are not conscious. And it is possible that some thoughts not only fail to be conscious but, given the psychological resources of these children, could not come to be conscious. These thoughts might well not be available for verbal expression. Indeed, this is the standard assumption for intentional states that are inaccessible to consciousness, for example, many states posited by cognitive and clinical psychologists. In any case, extrapolating from the adult situation is an unreliable way to determine what holds for young children. Much about early psychological development is still unclear, but it's plain that cognitive functioning in young children is in many ways strikingly different from that of adults. Since the inability of young children to talk about thoughts and experiences may well be due to some developmental factor that prevents them from expressing the relevant concepts in speech, we cannot conclude that concepts not expressed in the speech of these children also fail to figure in their mental lives.

These methodological caveats notwithstanding, the failure of children three and younger to use ordinary folk-psychological concepts of intentional states in speech does constitute some evidence that they may lack these concepts altogether. And that might create a problem for the HOT hypothesis. In feeling-of-knowing experiences, we saw, we are conscious *of* an informational state even though that state is not at that time conscious. The explanation was that we are conscious of these states in respect of the answers they would provide to specific questions, but not in respect of the specific informational content of the states. And that won't result in a state's being conscious. For a state to be conscious one must be conscious of it *as having* some particular informational content.

Content, however, is not the only mental property that characterizes intentional states; such states also exhibit some mental attitude that one has toward the content in question. So the question arises whether, in addition to having to be conscious of a state's specific intentional content for that state to be conscious, one must perhaps also be conscious of the state's mental attitude. If one did, a lack of any concepts for such attitudes would preclude one's forming HOTs of the requisite sort.

There is, moreover, good reason to think that this is so; a state will not be conscious unless one is conscious *of* that state in respect of its mental attitude as well as its content. If the way one is conscious of a state characterizes it only in terms of some content, that will not differ subjectively from one's being conscious of only of a particular state type, rather than any individual token. A state will not be conscious unless one is conscious of oneself as being in that state. When an intentional state is in question, one must be conscious of oneself as holding a particular mental attitude toward some intentional content.[28]

But one can be conscious of the mental attitude an intentional state exhibits without being conscious of that attitude in adult folk-psychological terms. And that would suffice for a state to be conscious, just so long as one is conscious of the intentional states as individual state tokens belonging to oneself. Even if three-year-olds have a concept of thoughts and beliefs on which the content of such states is always true, that weaker concept will suffice for their intentional states to be conscious. Even HOTs that represent target states as always having true content would enable these children to be conscious of themselves as being in the relevant state tokens. Their states would be conscious states.[29]

Indeed, there is compelling evidence that these children do conceive of the thoughts and beliefs they and others have as involving some mental attitude. They distinguish between one person's believing something and another person's believing the same thing. Beliefs are not for these children mere abstract contents; they are states of individual people. And that can be so only if they think of such states as involving some connection between an individual person and a content. Furthermore, even two-year-old children evidently distinguish believing from desiring, and understand that desires are not always fulfilled (Astington & Gopnik, 1991).[30] So even if the beliefs these children tend to attribute have contents they take to be true, they plainly conceive of believing as a type of mental attitude distinct from desiring.

I have assumed that the concepts children three and younger may have of intentional states may differ from the ordinary folk-psychological concepts of these states in order to show that even this would cause no difficulty for the HOT hypothesis. But the available evidence does not, in any case, establish that these children's concepts do differ from adult concepts. Even assuming that the children's speech accurately reflects the content of their thoughts, differences in how they attribute beliefs might be due not to their concepts of these states, but instead to the beliefs they have about these states. It might be that these children have just the concepts we do, but think different things about the intentional states they take themselves and others to be in.

Indeed, Jerry Fodor (1992) has developed a related hypothesis for explaining the relevant data, on which the children three and younger, though having the same concepts, differ in the way they attribute beliefs because their computational capacity is more limited than ours. In effect, it's more difficult for them to figure things out and work out the consequences of their thoughts. Though their concept of beliefs allow them to recognize and understand the occurrence of false as well as true beliefs, limitations in their computational resources lead them to take shortcuts in what behavior they predict and what beliefs they ascribe.

When unique predictions of behavior result from relying solely on desire and ignoring beliefs, these children operate in that way. Their thus disregarding beliefs would be indistinguishable from their simply assuming that beliefs match the way things actually are. On Fodor's hypothesis, moreover, these children assume that a person's beliefs are true when that assumption results in unique predictions about how things appear to the person. These practices impair predictive accuracy somewhat, but they represent an acceptable tradeoff given the children's limited computational abilities. The children end up believing that most or all of the beliefs that they and others have match what is true, but they do not believe this because they have a different concept of belief. On this account the enhanced computational resources of four-year-olds results in their increasingly taking into account the possibility of believing falsely.[31]

If Fodor's hypothesis is correct, the HOTs in virtue of which three-year-olds are conscious of their conscious states would involve the very same concepts as the HOTs of adults, whereas on the more standard hypothesis actual change in concepts occurs.[32] But it is unlikely that it matters which hypothesis is correct insofar as we are concerned with the way three-year-olds are conscious of their conscious states. How one is conscious of one's conscious states is a function not only of the concepts that figure in the relevant HOTs but of how, independently of these concepts, one thinks about states of the relevant type. On both hypotheses, three-year-olds will think of the beliefs they and others have as having content that largely or always matches what is actually true. This way of thinking about beliefs will in either case dominate what it's like for these children to have conscious beliefs.

Older children, of roughly four to five, also differ from adults in how they describe themselves cognitively. Unlike children of two or three, the beliefs these preschoolers ascribe to themselves and others do diverge in content from the way the preschoolers take things to be. In this respect, these children exhibit adult concepts of these states and think about those states the same way. But work by John Flavell, Frances Green, and Eleanor Flavell reveals dramatic differences between the metacognitive abilities of these children and those of adults (e.g., Flavell, Green & Flavell, 1993; 1995a; 1995b; & Flavell, 1993).

For one thing, these children seem to lack any notion of a continuous stream of consciousness. They think, for example, that people while awake may go for considerable stretches without thinking or feeling anything whatever. More striking, these children believe that people, while completely asleep, still think, hear, and feel things, and that they know at that time that they do. And they judge what a person is attending to and thinking about solely on the basis of immediate behavioral cues and environmental stimulation.

Because these preschoolers describe people while awake as going for periods of time without thinking or feeling anything at all, perhaps these children simply lack the ability to introspect their own ongoing stream of consciousness. If they could introspect, would they not know that thinking and feeling in the waking state is pretty much continuous?

But there is another explanation of these striking results. Children three and younger think about intentional states in somewhat different terms from adults, whether because they have different concepts of these states or different beliefs about them. Similarly, it may be that the way these older preschoolers describe thoughts and feelings reflects some different concepts they have of these states or at least a different rage of beliefs about them. The adult conceptions[33] of thoughts and feelings represent them as kinds of state that are often conscious, perhaps even, on some views, always conscious. Evidently these preschoolers do not think of thoughts and feelings in that way. Instead, their conception of these states is cast solely in terms of the states' content properties, the type of state in question, and the characteristic circumstances in which that state typically occurs.

Positing this difference in the conception these preschoolers have of thoughts and experiences helps explain the data. If these children do not think of thoughts and experiences as often or characteristically conscious states, it would be natural for them to regard people as being in such states even when they are asleep.[34] They would also see people as thinking or experiencing things only when some specific environmental or behavioral event points to the occurrence of a particular thought or experience. Presumably these children do think, feel, and experience things consciously; so there is something that it's like for them to think, feel, and experience. It is just that they do not yet think of themselves as being in conscious versions of these states, nor of the states themselves as possibly being conscious. They do not think of there being something it's like for them to be in conscious intentional states.[35]

Again, the HOT model fits well with this explanation. For a state to be conscious, one must be noninferentially conscious of being in that state. And one must be conscious of the state in respect of its content and mental attitude, though perhaps not in respect of a full conception of that content and attitude. But a state can be conscious without one's thinking of it as a conscious state, or even thinking of it as the type of state that could be conscious.

Indeed, one can readily see on the HOT model why one might not, at an early stage of development, think of one's conscious states as being conscious. In adults, HOTs are sometimes themselves conscious. When they are, one is conscious not only of one's thought or feeling, but also of having a HOT about that thought or feeling. Since a state's being conscious consists in having a HOT about it, when a HOT is conscious, one in effect is thinking about the mental state one's HOT is about *as a conscious state*. And, if one's HOTs are sometimes conscious, it will be evident to one that one's mental states are sometimes conscious. So one will conceive of mental states as being the sort of state that can, on occasion, be conscious.

By contrast, if one's HOTs are never themselves conscious thoughts, one will have no occasion to think of one's mental states, even those which are actually conscious, as being conscious states. One would think about and ascribe mental states, to oneself as well as to others, solely on the basis of behavioral cues and environmental stimulation. This suggests that the HOTs of four- and five-year-olds may well never be conscious, or hardly ever. If so, these children would have no basis on which to think of their thoughts and experiences as the sorts of state that might sometimes be conscious.[36]

Whenever we say anything, we express some intentional state that has the same content as what we say and a mental attitude that corresponds to our speech act's illocutionary force.[37] And almost without exception, whenever we say anything, the intentional state we express is conscious. Elsewhere I have argued that the HOT hypothesis can explain this striking regularity without following Descartes in invoking some unexplained connection between consciousness and speech (Rosenthal, 1990; 1998; see also Rosenthal, 1993a; 1986b).

Although $\ulcorner p \urcorner$ and $\ulcorner$I think that $p \urcorner$ have distinct truth conditions, adults recognize that the speech acts of saying these two things have the same performance conditions. Minor variation in conviction aside, whenever we say one we could equally well say the other. Moreover, this performance-conditional equivalence is, for adults, automatic and second nature. So whenever I say that $\ulcorner p \urcorner$, thereby expressing my thought that $\ulcorner p \urcorner$, I might equally well have said $\ulcorner$I think that $p \urcorner$. But saying that would have expressed my HOT to the effect $\ulcorner$I think that $p \urcorner$. Whenever I say anything, therefore, the automatic character of the performance-conditional equivalence between saying that thing and saying that I think it ensures that I will have a HOT to the effect that I do think that thing.

The developmental findings about children three and younger help us understand the performance-conditional equivalence invoked in this explanation. These children are already habituated to say $\ulcorner p \urcorner$ whenever they might say $\ulcorner$I think that $p \urcorner$ and conversely, though they would also say of others that they think that $\ulcorner p \urcorner$. So the automatic character of the adult performance-conditional equivalence between saying $\ulcorner p \urcorner$ and saying $\ulcorner$I think that $p \urcorner$ is a special case of the more general habit that children three and younger have of ascribing not only to themselves but to others as well only beliefs they take to be true. This habit is presumably central to young children's mastery of talking about believing and thinking. So the more general form of the performance-conditional equivalence will have become well-entrenched at a very early age.

The lack in four- and five-year-olds of HOTs that are conscious is presumably not due to any conceptual deficit, but to limits on the computational capacity needed to form the relevant HOTs. These third-order thoughts will, after all, be thoughts about thoughts about mental states. But even three-year-olds can say $\ulcorner$I think that $p \urcorner$, thereby verbally expressing a HOT to the effect that they think that $\ulcorner p \urcorner$. So why won't the HOTs of these children be conscious after all, given that verbally expressed thoughts are conscious?

Verbally expressed thoughts are conscious because of an automatic performance-conditional equivalence between saying $\ulcorner p \urcorner$ and saying $\ulcorner$I think that $p \urcorner$. But the embedding needed for the next level up arguably prevents that performance-conditional equivalence from being automatic and second nature. It is not at all natural, even for adults, to equate saying $\ulcorner$I think that $p \urcorner$ with saying $\ulcorner$I think that I think that $p \urcorner$ (see Rosenthal, 1990; 1998). So it is open for even the verbally expressed HOTs of four- and five-year-olds to be never or seldom conscious.

5. Nonveridical Metacognition and Consciousness

It is well-known that metacognitive judgments about subjects' cognitive states often fail to be fully accurate. Indeed, studies of feeling-of-knowing judgments, confidence judgments, and judgments of learning often, as noted earlier (p. 267; see esp. note 1), seek to assess their degree of accuracy, sometimes in comparison with one another or with other cognitive functions, such as ordinary recognition and recall.

It would not be surprising, therefore, if metacognition is never perfectly accurate, even in that form which pertains to our mental states' being conscious. Few today would endorse the traditional idea that our introspective grasp of what mental states we are in is invariably correct, to say nothing of the twin idea that introspection reveals all our mental states and does so in respect of all their mental features.[38]

As noted in connection with Block's concept of monitoring consciousness, introspective consciousness goes beyond the ordinary way in which mental states are conscious. When we introspect our mental states, we are conscious of them in a special way. We focus on them attentively and deliberately. And we are conscious of doing so. At the very least, therefore, the HOTs we have about our mental states when we introspect must be conscious HOTs.

But if our conscious HOTs can represent our mental states in ways that are less than fully accurate, presumably our nonconscious HOTs can do so as well. Indeed, inaccuracy among nonconscious HOTs, since it would seldom if ever be detected, may well occur far more often than we know it does with their conscious counterparts. HOTs result in our being conscious of ourselves *as* being in certain states, in particular, as being in states whose nature is *as* those HOTs represent them. And, if the HOTs in question aren't conscious thoughts, we won't be in a position to evaluate their accuracy.

It is to be expected, in any case, that HOTs would sometimes be inaccurate. In section 1, we considered the odd way in which we seem in feeling-of-knowing experiences both to be and not to be conscious of a cognitive state. I argued that we can understand such experiences in terms of our being conscious of the state as a state that holds the answer to a certain question but not in respect of that state's specific informational content. And I urged that we could best understand this difference, in turn, on the hypothesis that we are conscious of these states by having HOTs about them.

On this explanation, the HOTs in virtue of which mental states are conscious represent those states more or less fully. Moreover, the way our HOTs represent the states they are about actually influences what those states are like from a first-person point of view. What it's like for one to recall something consciously is strikingly different from what it's like simply to have that thing on the tip of one's tongue. And, because conscious recall and a tip-of-the-tongue experience may involve the very same informational content, the two will differ only in the way one is conscious of the target informational state. Whether one consciously recalls or has the information remain on the tip of one's tongue will depend on whether or not one's HOT represents the target in respect of its informational content.

Moreover, that target will be a conscious state only if the HOT does represent the state's informational content. So, if one had a HOT that represented the target as having, instead, some different content, it should seem to one as though one were actually in a conscious state that has that different content. What it's like for one depends on how one's HOTs represent the states they are about.

There are examples other than feeling-of-knowing experiences of the way differences in how our HOTs represent their targets affect what it's like for us to be in those target states. For example, what it's like for one to have a particular gustatory sensation of wine arguably depends on how much detail and differentiation goes into the HOT in virtue of which that sensation is conscious. Similarly for other sensory states; the degree of detail with which we are aware of a state makes a difference to what it's like for us to be in that state.[39] Indeed, if erroneous HOTs did not affect what it's like for us to be in target states, subjective errors could never occur, since what it's like to be in those target states would then always be accurate.

What HOT one has on any particular occasion, moreover, will depend not just on what target state one is in, but also on the size of one's repertoire of concepts, as well as on such transitory factors as one's current interests and how attentive one is. But if mental states do not by themselves determine what HOTs occur and how they represent their targets, there is no reason why those HOTs cannot sometimes misrepresent those targets. One would then be in a state of one type but have a HOT that represents one as being in a state of some different sort. And, since the content of one's HOT determines what it's like for one to be in a mental state, an erroneous HOT may well make it seem, from a first-person point of view, as though one were in a mental state that one is not in fact in.

There is reason to believe that this actually happens. Dental patients sometimes seem, from a first-person point of view, to experience pain even when nerve damage or local anesthetic makes it indisputable that no such pain can be occurring. The usual hypothesis is that the patient experiences fear along with vibration from the drill and consciously reacts as though in pain. Explaining this to the patient typically results in a corresponding change in what it's like for the patient when drilling resumes. But the patient's sense of what the earlier experience was like remains unaltered. The prior, nonveridical appearance of pain is indistinguishable, subjectively, from the real thing.

There is a also well-known tendency people have to confabulate being in various intentional states, often in ways that seem to make ex post facto sense of their behavior;[40] here it's plain that HOTs misrepresent the states that subjects are in. Similarly, it is reasonable to assume that repressed beliefs and desires often are actually conscious beliefs and desires whose content one radically misrepresents. Thus one might experience one's desire for some unacceptable thing as though it were a desire for something else, instead. The desire would not literally be unconscious; it would simply be a conscious desire whose character is distorted by inaccurate HOTs. And what it would be like to have that desire would fail accurately to reflect its actual content. Erroneous HOTs may well also figure in cases of so-called self-deception; there one's HOTs would misrepresent not what one desires but what one believes. These cases may even challenge our ability to distinguish in a nonarbitrary way between a HOT that misrepresents an actual target and a HOT whose target does not actually exist but is strictly speaking notional.

These two kinds of situation would presumably be indistinguishable from a first-person point of view.[41]

The variation in degree of detail with which consciousness represents our conscious states provides an important test for any explanatory model. Consider an ingenious proposal by Keith Lehrer (1991; 1997a, chap. 7; 1997b), which in a number of respects resembles the HOT hypothesis. A mental state is conscious, on Lehrer's model, in virtue of a mental process that leads from the state itself to a mental quotation of that state and then back to the state itself, this time considered as exemplifying the mental type to which it belongs. Lehrer argues that this process results in a metamental affirmation to the effect that the target state exemplifies the mental type in question. And, because the metamental affirmation that one is in a mental state of that type leads in turn to one's having easy, immediate knowledge about that target state, the affirmation makes the target a conscious state.

Lehrer recognizes that this metamental process is not immune from error (1997a, p. 170); it might go wrong, connecting a mental quotation of one token with some other token of a distinct type, treated as exemplar. As we have seen, such an occurrence would be undetectable from a first-person point of view. More important for present purposes, Lehrer notes that the metamental affirmation provides a thin characterization of the target, representing it only as being of that mental type which the target itself exemplifies. Lehrer urges that the information consciousness actually gives us about our conscious states is thin in this way, which doubtless is often so. But, as we see both from feeling-of-knowing experiences and from cases such as wine tasting, consciousness not only represents our conscious states more or less accurately, but also in strikingly greater and lesser detail. And it's unclear how such a model, on which our conscious states themselves determine how consciousness represents them, can make room for this variability in the way we are conscious of our conscious states.[42]

The foregoing considerations make it likely that inaccuracy affects not only our metacognitive judgments, but even the way our mental states are conscious. Moreover, there is considerable variation in the degree of detail that enters into both our metacognitive judgments and the way we are conscious of our conscious states. These parallels give us every reason to expect that research into metacognition and the errors that affect it will shed light on the nature of consciousness.

Acknowledgments

I am grateful to Alvin Goldman, Keith Lehrer, François Recanati, and Georges Rey for useful reactions to a slightly earlier version.

Notes

1 Excellent samples of such investigations can be found in Metcalfe & Shima-mura (1994); Nelson (1992); Weinert and Kluwe (1987); Forrest-Presley, Mackinnon, & Waller (1985). On dissociative neural deficits, see Milner & Rugg (1992), and many of the essays in Marcel & Bisiach (1988).

The term 'metacognition' seems to have been introduced into the psy-chological literature by John H. Flavell and coworkers (e.g., in Flavell & Wellman, 1977).

2 Nelson (1996). Cf. Nelson & Narens (1994).

3 On blindsight, see Weiskrantz (1986; 1990; 1991; 1997), and Marcel (1993). On visual agnosia, see Farah (1990; 1994).

4 Some studies suggest that frontal-lobe function subserves feeling-of-know-ing judgments, since deficits unique to the frontal lobe are correlated with impaired accuracy in such judgments, even when recall and recognition are normal. See Janowski, Shimamura, & Squire, 1989; Shimamura & Squire, 1986; and Nelson et al, 1990.

5 The tip-of-the-tongue (TOT) phenomenon that psychologists discuss in-volves having conscious access to partial information, perhaps the initial let-ters or phoneme of a name. In what follows I'll use the phrase 'tip of the tongue' in its commonsense usage to refer instead to cases in which we have a vivid sense, sometimes accurate, that the name or information could be ac-cessed though we cannot get conscious access even to partial information.

6 That is, the state that carries the information one feels one knows. As already noted, the *judgment* that one knows is of course conscious.

7 Larry Weiskrantz has reported research by colleagues aimed at such results (personal communication).

8 And, even when the states in question are all intentional states, there is typ-ically something it's like to have a tip-of-the-tongue or other feeling-of-knowing experience, as well as something different it's like when one re-trieves the actual information.

9 For a particularly useful discussion, see Vendler (1972, chap. 5).

10 See note 5 above.

11 Though Aristotle holds that images and thoughts are distinct (1907, Γ8, 432a14), he also insists that all thinking requires images (e.g., 1907 A1, 403a9–10, Γ7, 431a16, Γ8, 432a9, 14; 1972, 1, 449b31) and, indeed, that one "thinks in images" (1907, Γ7, 431b2; cf. Γ8, 432a5).

12 That is, characteristic properties susceptible of being sensed, as against, the distinguishing *sensory* properties of sensory states. On that distinction, see Rosenthal (1999).

13 For example, in Rosenthal (1986a); (1991); (1993b), all to appear with other papers in Rosenthal (in preparation), and in Rosenthal (1997b).

14 The objection from higher-order memories was raised by Alvin I. Goldman, in discussion; the objection from higher-order processing in the noncon-scious editing of speech and in the executing of certain motor intentions oc-curs in Marcel (1988, p. 140).

15 Dretske (1993), pp. 272–275; cf. Dretske (1995), pp. 112–113. Dretske holds that we are never transitively conscious of our conscious mental states, not

even in introspection. He argues that introspection resembles what he calls displaced perception. Just as we come to know how full the gas tank is by looking at the gauge, so we come to know what mental state we're in by noticing what physical object we're seeing. Although we come thereby to be conscious *that* we're in some particular mental state, we're not conscious *of* that state (Dretske, 1994/1995; 1995, chap. 2).

If Dretske is right about introspection, introspecting a mental state in effect means having a thought that one is that state. Dretske regards all thoughts as conscious; so this amounts to the claim that introspecting is having a *conscious* thought about one's mental states. This is exactly the account of introspection I have offered elsewhere (e.g., Rosenthal, 1986a, pp. 336–337; 1997, pp. 745–746). Dretske's view differs from mine only in his presupposition that all mental states are conscious states, and in denying that whenever one is conscious *that* something has a certain property one is thereby conscious *of* that thing.

16 Striking experimental results underscore how frequent cases occur in which one attentively sees two scenes that differ in a single respect, but without being conscious of the respect in which they differ. Grimes (1996) presented subjects with scenes that changed during saccades, as determined by eye trackers. Subjects were told to study the presentation material, and some were even told that a conspicuous change would occur. Most subjects fail on 7 of 10 trials to notice dramatic changes, such as a change in color of a large, salient object. Even people who informally view the presentation material without being fitted with eye trackers fail surprisingly often to notice such changes, presumably because of random saccades.

17 It is worth noting a complication in Dretske's discussion. Unlike being conscious of concrete objects and events, being conscious of a difference, according to Dretske, always amounts to being conscious "that such a difference exists" (Dretske, 1993, p. 275; cf. pp. 266–267). So he might insist that being conscious of a difference is always being conscious of it *as* a difference. But that cannot help. Even though the experience of the extra tree is that in virtue of which the two overall experiences differ, one can be conscious of the thing in virtue of which they happen to differ without being conscious that they do differ. As Dretske would put it, one can be conscious of that in virtue of which they differ but not of the difference between them. Indeed, he explicitly acknowledges that this very thing can happen: "[Those] who were only thing-aware of the difference between [the two arrays] were not fact-conscious of the difference between [them]" (Dretske, 1993, p. 275).

18 See also Block (1993, p. 184; 1992, pp. 205–206; 1990, pp. 596–598).

19 It won't help simply to assume that any state with sensory properties must be conscious in some way or other. If one has no conscious access to such a state, it won't be a conscious state in any intuitive sense.

20 Block's notion of access consciousness also has its troubles. That reconstruction trades on the idea that a state's playing various executive, inferential, and reporting roles involves one's having the kind of access to that state that is relevant to the state's being conscious. But that is often not the case. Many states play executive, inferential, and reporting roles without being conscious in any intuitive sense whatever. To reconstruct the kind of state consciousness that

involves having access to a mental state, we must provide that one actually be conscious of that state in an intuitively unmediated way. Given the argument in the text, we can conclude that, *pace* Block, phenomenal consciousness actually implies access consciousness. That fact is obscured by Block's reconstruction of access consciousness, since a state's playing various executive, inferential, and reporting roles does not intuitively seem to be what is needed for there to be something it's like to be in a sensory state. Being conscious of that state, by contrast, is exactly what is needed. See also Rosenthal (1997a).

Block's definition of access consciousness in terms of a state's being "poised" for various uses may be meant to capture the way conscious states seem more readily available for such use than nonconscious states. But even nonconscious states can be so poised. Defining access consciousness in such terms gives a dispositional mark of such consciousness. But that doesn't mean that access consciousness is a matter of one's simply being disposed to be conscious of one's mental states, as opposed to actually conscious of them. The states we are conscious of have many dispositional properties, among them being reportable and introspectible.

21 Goldman (1993, p. 366); see Dretske (1995, p. 109).

22 Dretske holds that a state's being conscious consists not in one's being conscious of the state, but in the circumstance that, in virtue of one's being in that state, one is conscious of something or conscious that something is the case. And that is an intrinsic property of every mental state. Because that property is intrinsic to all mental states, however, Dretske must hold that all mental states are conscious, which is highly implausible (1993, p. 271).

23 Cognitive and clinical theorists often posit nonconscious informational states specifically in connection with some mental subsystem. This encourages a tendency to describe all nonconscious mental states as states of subpersonal systems, in contrast with conscious states, conceived of as states of the whole creature. But there is good reason also to regard most nonconscious mental states as being states of the whole creature. Not only do nonconscious thoughts and desires, and the sensations that occur nonconsciously in peripheral vision and subliminal perception, have the very same distinguishing mental properties as conscious states; they sometimes come to be conscious. And it would be surprising if the shift from being nonconscious to being conscious involved a concomitant shift from being a state of a subpersonal system to being a state of the whole creature.

24 When I am conscious without apparent mediation of my veins' throbbing, I am conscious of two things: states of my veins, and a certain bodily sensation. Being conscious of the sensation in respect of its mental properties results in that sensation's being conscious. By contrast, being conscious of the veins, as such, may well result in no conscious state whatever.

Still, HOTs do not presuppose that one have a concept of mentality, since we can be conscious of a state in virtue of a mental property it has without being conscious that the property is a mental property.

25 In particular, the two are equivalent in truth conditions. The truth conditions for somebody's believing something of course also includes that person's existing and being in the relevant state, but the children presumably see these conditions as being obviously satisfied in both cases.

26 Dretske's argument affects the transitivity principle only indirectly, since it does, by itself, not preclude there being ways we might be conscious of our conscious states which do not require having any concepts at all of the relevant types of state. On the argument of section II, however, no other way will do, and elsewhere Dretske endorses those arguments (1993, p. 297).

27 This reasoning echoes Descartes's notoriously unconvincing argument that, if nonhuman animals had thoughts, they would surely express them in speech (letter to Newcastle, November 23, 1646, in Descartes 1984–1991, Vol. 3, p. 303), as though nothing more is needed for verbally expressing thoughts than having them.

28 This sort of consideration doubtless underlies the traditional view that consciousness attaches more directly to a state's mental attitude than to its content. Cf., e.g., Descartes's claim, in *Fourth Replies*, that it is with respect to "the operations of the mind," and not the contents of those operations, that "there can be nothing in our mind of which we are aware" (Descartes, 1984–1991, Vol. 2, p. 162).

29 Similar considerations apply to nonlinguistic animals, which presumably are also conscious of their conscious states in a way that fails to capture much about the specific attitudes those states exhibit. Indeed, nonlinguistic animals will also be conscious of the content of their conscious states in terms far simpler than those which figure in our HOTs, indeed, in terms that may be difficult to translate into our ways of describing things.

30 It's striking that some three-year-olds follow the candy-box pattern in judging others' likes and dislikes always to match their own (Flavell, Flavell, Green, & Moses, 1993).

31 Fodor (1992) also presents reasons for rejecting the standard hypothesis.

32 It is unclear that psychologists who take this second, more standard line have clearly distinguished between change in concept and change in the beliefs one has about the relevant things. If not, the difference between these hypotheses may be, at least in part, verbal rather than substantive.

33 I use 'conception' here as neutral between the concept one has of something and the central, characterizing beliefs one has about that thing.

34 An exception is seeing; these preschoolers report that people cannot see things when asleep. That fits well with this interpretation. Closed eyes constitute a behavioral cue that shows that a sleeping person is not seeing anything, but nothing parallel prevents one from regarding sleeping people as hearing and thinking.

    As noted, when Flavell and his associates asked these preschoolers whether people, while sleeping, know that they think, hear, and feel things, they give mostly affirmative answers. But knowing itself may be merely tacit and hence not conscious, and these replies may have referred only to such nonconscious, tacit knowing. Indeed, this is to be expected if these preschoolers do not think of mental states at all as being conscious states.

35 Flavell finds this interpretation congenial (personal communication).

36 It would then turn out that these children do not, after all, introspect, since introspection consists in having HOTs that are themselves conscious.

    The hypothesis that these children conceive of their mental states in terms of behavioral cues and environmental stimulation echoes, at the level of individual development, Wilfrid Sellars' idea that the characteristic way people have of reporting noninferentially about their own mental states might have been built on an earlier practice of reporting inferentially about their own mental states (Sellars, 1963, p. 189, §59).

37 An exception is insincere speech, but that is best understood as pretending to say things. See Rosenthal (1986b, sec. 4).

38 For a useful review, see Lyons (1986).

39 Compare Daniel Dennett's case of looking straight at a thimble but failing to see it as a thimble (1991, p. 336). One's sensation of a thimble is conscious, but conscious not *as* a sensation of a thimble but only, say, as a sensation of part of the clutter on a shelf. There are many cases in which the visual sensations one has of one's environment are conscious, but not conscious in respect of much of their significant detail. The best explanation of this is the coarse-grained character of the HOTs in virtue of which those sensations are conscious.

40 The classic study is Nisbett & Wilson (1977). That influential study focused both on cases in which subjects confabulate stories about the causes of their being in particular cognitive states and on cases in which they confabulate accounts about what states they are actually in.

41 Being inaccurately conscious of mental states is a possibility left open not only by the HOT model, but by any theory that upholds the transitivity principle. Some residual sense of the relative infallibility of consciousness may therefore underlie intuitive resistance to that principle. See, for example, Goldman (1996).

42 It is worth noting that the metamental affirmation posited by Lehrer's model cannot actually contain the target itself. Suppose the target is an intentional state. Its content can occur in the metamental affirmation, and that affirmation can represent the target's mental attitude. But the only mental attitude that can literally occur in the metamental affirmation itself is that which governs the entire content of the affirmation. This is evident from the fact that, whereas the metamental state must have an assertoric attitude, the target's mental attitude may be one of doubting, desiring, or denying. Since an intentional state can play the role of exemplar only if its mental attitude is suspended, the exemplar states in Lehrer's metamental affirmations cannot be the actual targets, but must be states derived from them. Similarly, targets cannot function as mental quotations of themselves, since mental quotations must also lack mental attitude.

This points to a difficulty. According to Lehrer, the metamental affirmation represents the target as being of the mental type exemplified by the target, and he explains our grasp of what that mental type is by appeal to our understanding of the mental token in question. But if the state that serves as exemplar is not the target state itself but some state derived from it, some additional account is needed of how we come to understand its content.

References

Aristotle (1907). *De anima*. Translation, introduction, and notes by R. D. Hicks. Cambridge: Cambridge University Press.

Aristotle (1972). *On memory*. Translated with commentary by Richard Sorabji. London: Duckworth.

Astington, Janet W., & Gopnik, Alison (1991). Developing understanding of desire and intention. In Andrew Whiten (Ed.), *Natural theories of mind: The evolution, development and simulation of second order representations* (pp. 39–50). Oxford and Cambridge, MA: Blackwell.

Block, Ned (1990). Consciousness and accessibility. *Behavioral and Brain Sciences 13* (4), 596–598.

Block, Ned (1992). Begging the question against phenomenal consciousness. *Behavioral and Brain Sciences 15* (2), 205–206.

Block, Ned (1993). Review of Daniel C. Dennett, *Consciousness explained*. *The Journal of Philosophy 90* (4), 181–193.

Block, Ned (1994). On a confusion about a function of consciousness. Unpublished manuscript version of Block (1995).

Block, Ned (1995). On a confusion about a function of consciousness. *Behavioral and Brain Sciences 18* (2), 227–247.

Davies, Martin, & Humphreys, Glyn W., Eds. (1993). *Consciousness: Psychological and philosophical essays*. Oxford: Basil Blackwell.

Dennett, Daniel C. (1991). *Consciousness explained*. Boston: Little, Brown.

Descartes, René (1984–1991). *The philosophical writings of Descartes (3 vols.)*. Eds. John Cottingham, Robert Stoothoff, and Dugald Murdoch. (Vol. 3 with Anthony Kenny.) Cambridge: Cambridge University Press.

Dretske, Fred (1993). Conscious experience. *Mind 102* (406): 263–283.

Dretske, Fred (1994–1995). Introspection. *Proceedings of the Aristotelian Society, 115*, 263–278.

Dretske, Fred (1995). *Naturalizing the mind*. Cambridge, MA: MIT Press/Bradford.

Farah, Martha J. (1990). *Visual agnosia: Disorders of object recognition and what they tell us about normal vision*. Cambridge, MA: MIT Press/Bradford.

Farah, Martha J. (1994). Visual perception and visual awareness after brain damage: A tutorial overview. In Carlo A. Umiltà & Morris Moscovitch (Eds.), *Attention and performance XV: Conscious and nonconscious information processing*. Cambridge, MA: MIT Press/ Bradford.

Flavell, John H. (1988). The development of children's knowledge about the mind: From cognitive connections to mental representations. In Janet W. Astington, Paul L. Harris, & David R. Olson (Eds.), *Developing theories of the mind*. Cambridge: Cambridge University Press.

Flavell, John H. (1993). Young children's understanding of thinking and consciousness. *Current Directions in Psychological Science 2* (2), 40–43.

Flavell, John H., & Wellman, Henry M. (1977). Metamemory. In Robert V. Kail, Jr. & John W. Hagen (Eds.), *Perspectives on the development of memory and cognition*. Hillsdale, N.J.: Erlbaum.

Flavell, John H., Flavell, Eleanor R., Green, Frances L., & Moses, Louis J. (1993). Young children's understanding of fact beliefs versus value beliefs. *Child Development 61* (4), 915–928.

Flavell, John H., Green, Frances L., & Flavell, Eleanor R. (1993). Children's understanding of the stream of consciousness. *Child Development 64*, 387–398.

Flavell, John H., Green, Frances L., & Flavell, Eleanor R. (1995a). Young children's knowledge about thinking. *Monographs of the Society for Research in Child Development 60* (1) (Serial No. 243), 1–95.

Flavell, John H., Green, Frances L., & Flavell, Eleanor R. (1995b). The development of children's knowledge about attentional focus. *Developmental Psychology 31* (4), 706–712.

Fodor, Jerry A. (1992). A theory of the child's theory of mind. *Cognition 44* (3), 283–296.

Forrest-Presley, D. L., Mackinnon, G. E., & Waller, T. Gary, Eds. (1985). *Metacognition, cognition, and human performance.* Orlando, FL: Academic Press.

Goldman, Alvin I. (1993). Consciousness, folk psychology, and cognitive science. *Consciousness and Cognition 2* (4), 364–382.

Goldman, Alvin I. (1996). The science of consciousness and the publicity of science. Unpublished paper, Department of Philosophy, University of Arizona.

Gopnik, Alison (1993). How do we know our minds: The illusion of first-person knowledge of intentionality. *Behavioral and Brain Sciences 16* (1), 1–14. With open peer commentary, 29–90, and author's response, Theories and illusion, 90–100.

Gopnik, Alison, & Astington, Janet W. (1988). Children's understanding of representational change and its relation to the understanding of false belief and the appearance-reality distinction. *Child Development 59* (1), 26–37.

Grimes, John (1996). On the failure to detect changes in scenes across saccades. In Kathleen Akins (Ed.), *Perception* (pp. 89–110). New York: Oxford University Press.

James, William (1950). *The Principles of Psychology.* (New York: Dover Publications. (Original work published 1890.)

Janowski, J., Shimamura, Arthur P., & Squire, Larry R. (1989). Memory and metamemory: Comparisons between patients with frontal lobe lesions and amnesic patients. *Psychobiology 17*, 3–11.

Lehrer, Keith (1991). Metamind, autonomy and materialism. *Grazer Philosophische Studien 40*, 1–11.

Lehrer, Keith (1997a). *Self-trust: A study of reason, knowledge, and autonomy* Oxford: Clarendon.

Lehrer, Keith (1997b). Meaning, exemplarization and metarepresentation. In Dan Sperber (Ed.), *Metarepresentations: A multidisciplinary perspective* (this volume).

Lyons, William (1986). *The disappearance of introspection.* Cambridge, MA: MIT Press/ Bradford.

Marcel, Anthony J. (1993). Slippage in the unity of consciousness. In *Experimental and theoretical studies of consciousness* (pp. 168–186). Ciba Foundation Symposium No. 174. Chichester: John Wiley & Sons.

Marcel, Anthony J. (1988). Phenomenal experience and functionalism. In Anthony J. Marcel & Edoardo Bisiach (Eds.), *Consciousness in contemporary science.* Oxford: Clarendon.

Marcel, Anthony J., and Bisiach, Edoardo, Eds. (1988). *Consciousness in contemporary science.* Oxford: Clarendon.

Metcalfe, Janet, & Shimamura, Arthur P., Eds. (1994). *Metacognition: Knowing about knowing*. Cambridge, MA: MIT Press/Bradford.

Milner, A. D., & Rugg, Michael D., Eds. (1992). *The neuropsychology of consciousness*. New York: Academic.

Miner, Ann C., & Reder, Lynne M. (1994). A new look at feeling of knowing: Its metacognitive role in regulating question answering. In Janet Metcalfe & Arthur P. Shimamura (Eds.), *Metacognition: Knowing about knowing* (pp. 47–70). Cambridge, MA: MIT Press/Bradford.

Moore, Chris, Pure, Kiran, & Furrow, David (1990). Children's understanding of the modal expression of speaker certainty and uncertainty and its relation to the development of a representational theory of mind. *Child Development*, 61 (3), 722–730.

Nagel, Thomas (1974). What is it like to be a bat? In Thomas Nagel, *Mortal questions* (pp. 165–179). Cambridge: Cambridge University Press. Originally published in *The Philosophical Review 83* (4), 435–450.

Nelson, Thomas O., Ed. (1992). *Metacognition: Core readings*. Boston: Allyn and Bacon.

Nelson, Thomas O. (1996). Consciousness and metacognition. *American Psychologist* 51 (2), 102–116.

Nelson, Thomas O., Dunlosky, John, White, David M., Steinberg, Jude, Townes, Brenda D., & Anderson, Dennis (1990). Cognition and metacognition at extreme altitude on Mount Everest. *Journal of Experimental Psychology: General* 119 (4) (December), 367–374.

Nelson, Thomas O., & Narens, Louis (1994). Why investigate metacognition? In Janet Metcalfe & Arthur P. Shimamura (Eds.), *Metacognition: Knowing about knowing* (pp. 1–25).

Nisbett, Richard E., & Wilson, Timothy DeCamp (1977). Telling more than we can know: Verbal reports on mental processes. *Psychological Review 84* (3), 231–259.

Perner, Josef (1991). *Understanding the representational mind*. Cambridge, MA: MIT Press/Bradford.

Perner, Josef, Leekam, Susan R., & Wimmer, Heinz (1987). Three-year-olds' difficulty with false belief: The case for a conceptual deficit. *British Journal of Developmental Psychology 5* (2), 125–137.

Rosenthal, David M. (1986a). Two concepts of consciousness. *Philosophical Studies* 49 (3), 329–359.

Rosenthal, David M. (1986b). Intentionality. *Midwest Studies in Philosophy 10*, 151–184.

Rosenthal, David M. (1990). Why are verbally expressed thoughts conscious? Report No. 32/1990, Center for Interdisciplinary Research (ZiF), University of Bielefeld, Germany. To appear in Rosenthal (in press).

Rosenthal, David M. (1991). The independence of consciousness and sensory quality. In Enrique Villanueva (Ed.), *Consciousness: Philosophical issues, 1, 1991* (pp. 15–36). Atascadero, CA: Ridgeview Publishing Company.

Rosenthal, David M. (1993a) Thinking that one thinks. In Martin Davies & Glyn W. Humphreys (Eds.), *Consciousness: Psychological and philosophical essays* (pp. 197–223). Oxford: Basil Blackwell.

Rosenthal, David M. (1993b). State consciousness and transitive consciousness. *Consciousness and Cognition 2* (4), 355–363.

Rosenthal, David M. (1997a). Phenomenal consciousness and what it's like. *Behavioral and Brain Sciences 20* (1), 64–65.

Rosenthal, David M. (1997b). A theory of consciousness. In Ned Block, Owen Flanagan, & Güven Güzeldere (Eds.), *The nature of consciousness: Philosophical debates* (pp. 729–753). Cambridge, MA: MIT Press.

Rosenthal, David M. (1998). Consciousness and its expression. *Midwest Studies in Philosophy 22*, 294–309.

Rosenthal, David M. (1999). *Consciousness and Mind.* Oxford: Clarendon.

Rosenthal, David M. (in preparation). The colors and shapes of visual experiences. In Denis Fisette, *Consciousness and intentionality: Models and modalities of attribution* (pp. 95–118). Dordrecht: Kluwer Academic Publishers.

Sellars, Wilfrid (1963). Empiricism and the philosophy of mind. In Wilfrid Sellars, *Science, perception and reality* (pp. 127–196). London: Routledge & Kegan Paul. Reprinted (1991) Atascadero, CA: Ridgeview Publishing Company. Republished (1997) as *Empiricism and the philosophy of mind.* Cambridge, MA: Harvard University Press.

Shimamura, Arthur P. (1994). The neuropsychology of metacognition. In Janet Metcalfe & Arthur P. Shimamura, (Eds.), *Metacognition: Knowing about knowing* (pp. 253–276). Cambridge, MA: MIT Press/Bradford.

Shimamura, Arthur P., & Squire, Larry R. (1986). Memory and metamemory: A study of the feeling-of-knowing phenomenon in amnesic patients. *Journal of Experimental Psychology: Learning, Memory, and Cognition 12*, 452–460.

Tulving, Endel, & Pearlstone, Z. (1966). Availability versus accessibility of information in memory for words. *Journal of Verbal Learning and Verbal Behavior 5*, 381–391.

Vendler, Zeno (1972). *Res cogitans.* Ithaca, NY: Cornell University Press.

Weinert, Franz E., & Kluwe, Rainer H., Eds. (1987). *Metacognition, motivation, and understanding.* Hillsdale, NJ: Erlbaum.

Weiskrantz, Lawrence (1986). *Blindsight: A case study and implications.* Oxford: Oxford University Press.

Weiskrantz, Lawrence (1990). Outlooks for blindsight: Explicit methodologies for implicit processes. The 1989 Ferrier Lecture. *Proceedings of the Royal Society B 239*, 247–278.

Weiskrantz, Lawrence (1991). Dissociations and associates in neuropsychology. In Richard G. Lister and Herbert J. Weingartner (Eds.), *Perspectives on cognitive neuroscience* (pp. 157–164). New York: Oxford University Press.

Weiskrantz, Lawrence (1997). *Consciousness lost and found: A neuropsychological exploration.* Oxford: Oxford University Press.

Wellman, Henry W. (1990). *The child's theory of the mind.* Cambridge, MA: MIT Press/Bradford.

Metarepresentations, Language and Meaning

Chapter 11

Meaning, Exemplarization and Metarepresentation

Keith Lehrer

The mind is essentially a metamind, or so I have argued (Lehrer, 1990a, 1990b). There are first-level states of representation and belief that are evaluated and either accepted or rejected at a metalevel through metamental ascent. They become the states of the metamind. The advantages of metamental ascent are those of representational transparency and mental plasticity. Without metarepresentation, we should be ignorant of what occurs at the first level, of our first-order representations and beliefs. Moreover, conflict at the first level is unavoidable for any complex representational system. Metamental ascent is required to represent that conflict and, therefore, to find a resolution of it.

In principle, it might be possible to achieve any first-level result without leaving the first level. The necessity for metamental ascent is psychological and pragmatic rather than logical or apodictic. We need metamental ascent to obtain knowledge of our first-order states, and to resolve our conflicts. The need is like the need for theoretical representation in science in order to resolve empirical conflict and obtain systematization at the empirical level. In principle, as Craig (1953) once showed us, we could obtain empirical systematization without theoretical representation, but, in fact, we cannot do it. Without theoretical representation, empirical systematization obtained in science is beyond our powers of ratiocination and extrapolation. The same thing is true of metamental ascent and the resolutions of first-level conflict. In principle, we can obtain the resolution of first-level conflict without metamental ascent, but, in fact, it is beyond our powers of ratiocination and extrapolation. In both cases, we need the understanding of the conflict that ascent to theory and the metamental provides.

Metarepresentation is, however, threatened by a regress. One problem was articulated by Sellars (1963) originally and later by Fodor (1979). Sellars formulated the argument as follows:

Thesis. Learning to use a language (*L*) is learning to obey the rules of *L*.

But, a rule which enjoins the doing of an action (*A*) is a sentence in a language which contains an expression for *A*.

Hence, a rule which enjoins the using of a linguistic expression (*E*) is a sentence in a language which contains an expression for *E* – in other words a sentence in a *meta*language.

Consequently, learning to obey the rules for *L* presupposes the ability to use the metalanguage (*ML*) in which the rules for *L* are formulated.

So that learning to use a language (*L*) presupposes having learned to use a metalanguage (*ML*). And by the same token, having learned to use *ML* presupposes having learned to use a *meta*-metalanguage (*MML*) and so on.

But this is impossible (a vicious regress).

Therefore, the thesis is absurd and must be rejected.
(Sellars, 1963, p. 321, italics in original)

Fodor's formulation is similar, though it refers to circularity rather than a regress:

> Learning a determination of the extension of the predicates involves learning that they fall under certain rules (i.e., truth rules). But one cannot learn that *P* falls under *R* unless one has a language in which *P* and *R* can be represented. So one cannot learn a first language unless one already has a system capable of representing the predicates in that language *and their extension.* And, on pain of circularity, that system cannot be the language that is being learned. But first languages *are* learned. Hence, at least some cognitive operations are carried out in languages other than natural languages. (Fodor, 1979, p. 64; italics in original)

The problem rests on an argument to the effect that metarepresentation and metamental ascent will lead to a regress or circularity when we attempt to explain how a language is acquired. The former used the argument to defend a holistic theory of representation, the latter to defend a nativist theory of representation. The argument is simple enough to formulate in the form of a regress. Suppose one is learning the meaning of representation r_0 at the language level 0. To understand the meaning of r_0 you must be able to formulate the meaning of r_0 as r_1 in a meaning rule at language level 1. However, to understand the meaning of r_1 you must be able to formulate the meaning of r_1 as r_2 in a meaning rule at language level 2. Thus, to understand something at language level 0 you will be led into a regress of metarepresentation which will never be complete. The circularity form of the argument says that you must formulate the rule of meaning for representation r_0 as r_1 in the same language, which is impossible if the language is the one being learned.

Moreover, the arguments have an importance beyond the issue of language acquisition. Metamental ascent to representation of our mental states to provide representational transparency and mental plasticity leads to a similar problem. Conflict resolution is either representationally opaque or representationally transparent. If it is representationally opaque, then we have no idea of the existence of the conflict or how it is resolved. Such ignorance deprives us of mental plasticity. Ignorant of the existence of the conflict and how it is resolved within us, we cannot use our knowledge of these matters to change the way in which we resolve conflict. Knowledge presupposes representation.

We might, of course, find some nonrepresentational method for changing how we function. We might, for example, discover chemical means to change the way in which we function, but such changes are no more an expression of mental plasticity than is the retraining of the eye to eliminate double vision. I assume, however, that mental plasticity is representational plasticity. I have argued that conflict resolution requires representational transparency and mental plasticity (Lehrer, 1990a, 1997) . I assume the results here. The problem is that the requirement of representational transparency appears to lead to the regress that Sellars articulated as a problem for an account of language acquisition.

Suppose there is a conflict between states r_0 and s_0 at the first-level L_0. If the conflict is representationally transparent, then I must have a representation of those two states, r_1 and s_1, at a metalevel L_1, the result of metamental ascent. Does that suffice for transparency and plasticity? It might seem to do so, for r_0 and s_0 are represented by r_1 and s_1 respectively and, therefore, the two former states are representationally transparent. The conflict between those two states is resolved at the metalevel in terms of the states r_1 and s_1. Suppose that the latter two states are not represented. In that case, the resolution of the conflict at the metalevel will be opaque again, and the person will have no idea how the conflict is resolved unless the two metalevel states in L_1 are represented at the next level L_2 by two states r_2 and s_2. Thus, the argument for metalevel representation leads to a regress. Whatever the level at which resolution of conflict occurs, it must be represented to obtain representational transparency and mental plasticity. Mental plasticity requires representational transparency, and a regress threatens.

Sellars' Theory of Meaning

How are we to avoid the regress? Fodor's (1979) way is to suppose that there is an innately understood language of thought which we understand without needing to formulate the meaning of items contained therein. If one asks, however, how the language of thought is understood, the problem iterates. Sellars' way out was to argue that we understand the meanings of words because of the language system we acquire without knowing the meaning of any items in the system prior to acquiring the system. If one asks how we learn the system, the problem iterates. Both Fodor and Sellars have had interesting and valuable things to say about the iteration problem. I wish to argue that the major insight about how to avoid the regress is contained in the work of Sellars (1963), in his theory of meaning, which I wish to articulate and defend. Roughly, the point is that meaning sentences, though metalinguistic sentences, do not express a relationship between a word and something else. They have a different function which ends the regress in a representational and metarepresentational loop.

Sellars' point is best illustrated by the simple example he often used. Consider the following meaning sentence:

MF   "Rouge" in French means red

which, unlike the sentence

M   "Red" in English means red,

is informative to a speaker of English. This sentence MF might be reformulated in various ways as follows:

MFQ   "Rouge" in French means the quality red

DFU   "Rouge" in French designates redness.

Compare the reformulations of these sentences concerning "red" as follows:

MQ   "Red" in English means the quality red

DU   "Red" in English designates redness.

The first thesis is that MF and M contain the basic semantic information contained in the other sentences. The other information, in effect, tells us what kind of word "Red" in English is, a quality word, for example. Moreover, the theses concerning "rouge" tell us about a word in a different language, French, and thereby tell us of the relationship between two languages, at least indirectly, by referring to one and using the other. Nevertheless, if any information is conveyed by any of these sentences about the relationship between a word and the world, that information is conveyed by M as well as by all the rest. So, we may concentrate on M for an account of the simplest if least informative formulation of what a word means. If we can formulate the meaning of every word of the language in this manner and understand the formulation without winding up in a regress, what remains is theoretical development and extrapolation from M.

So, let us consider that sentence as a minimal formulation of meaning:

M "Red" in English means red.

How should we analyze that sentence? Does it tell us about the relationship of a word to something extralinguistic? Sellars argued that it does not. We should not understand the use of the word "red" at the end of the sentence as a use of the word intended to refer to anything. It is, instead, a use of the word intended to make an exhibit, or, as I will say, *exemplar*, of the word, to use it as an exemplar to stand for a class of words having a role in language.

There is, of course, a similarity between M and the equivalence sentence

EM "Red" in English has the same meaning as "Red" in English

just as there is a similarity between the meaning of

MF "Rouge" in French means red

and

EMF "Rouge" in French has the same meaning as "red" in English.

But similarity is not identity. EM and EMF contain no use of the word "red," only a mention of it. Someone might understand the meaning of both sentences who did not understand the meaning of either "rouge" or "red" as a monolingual English speaker, if such can be imagined, might understand the meaning of

$EMFG$ "Rouge" in French has the same meaning as "rot" in German

without understanding the meaning of "rouge" or "rot." Such a speaker understands that the two words have the same meaning but does not understand the meaning of either word. By contrast, the English speaker who understands MF understands the meaning of "red" and, for that matter, the person who understands M understands the meaning of "red". Nevertheless, part of the role, though not all of it, of the end use of "red" in both MF and M is to call attention to the role of the word "red" in discourse within the language used, in this case, English.

Sellars went on to suggest that M and MF might be analyzed by treating the end use of the word "red" as a special kind of mentioning by introducing his dot-quotes and converting "means red" into a predicate containing the dot-quoted "red" (Sellars, 1963). The result would be as follows:

$M\bullet$ "Red" in English is a $\bullet$red$\bullet$

and

$MF\bullet$ "Rouge" in French is a $\bullet$red$\bullet$.

The dot-quoted version makes the point that the sentence affirms that the original quoted word is a member of class of words of which "red" is an exemplar and has the linguistic role of the word dot-quoted. If you do not understand the word dot-quoted, then you do not understand what role is being indicated, and the sentence fails to accomplish its purpose. The contrast between the quoted and dot-quoted mention and use of "red" is that you do not have to understand the quoted use to understand what is said about the word, but you do have to understand the dot-quoted word to understand what is said about the quoted word.

Content

The foregoing account was from the meaning of words to the content of sentences. Thus, if we start with the sentence

SC "That is red" in English has the content that is red,

we may treat the use of the unquoted sentence "that is red" at the end of SC as an exemplar of a sentence having a certain linguistic role, and we may consider SC as affirming that "That is red" plays that role. This gives us an analysis of SC which can be expressed with dot-quotes as

$SC\bullet$ "That is red" in English is a $\bullet$That is red$\bullet$.

Moreover, if we suppose that there is a language of thought more or less isomorphic to conventional languages, we can use the same method to give an account of the meaning of expressions in the language of thought. Thus,

SCT "That is red" in thought has the content that is red

gets expressed with dot-quotes as

$SCT\bullet$ "That is red" in thought is a $\bullet$That is red$\bullet$.

Finally, the use of the dot-quoted exemplar involved in these sentences helps to explain why it so easy for us to report on the content of our thoughts. We do it by dot-quoting the sentence or thought, converting it to an exemplar. A process of quotation and disquotation yields a report of content. The report extends only as far as our understanding of the thought or sentence, just as a report of meaning resulting from dot-quotation extends only as far as our understanding of the word dot-quoted. The use of dot-quotes explains the ease of minimal reports of meaning and content. Quotation and disquotation is all there is to it.

Exemplarization

Now, all of these reflections put a great burden on the expressions "understanding of the word," and I will explain this understanding below. But we should not, for that reason, fail to grasp the importance of the proposal. It is that words can be used in a language to represent a role that they, and other words that are members of a specific class of words, play in various languages. Included therein is the role of an exemplar which is used, rather than mentioned, but used to represent a class of words of which it itself is a member. A word used in this way becomes an *exemplaric representation* of a class of words including itself playing a linguistic role. The crux of the proposal is that exemplaric representation avoids the regress with a loop. How this is so requires explanation that goes beyond what Sellars has written and requires the assumption of a process of making a word into a representational or metarepresentational exemplar. I will call this process *exemplarization* and explain how it resolves the regress.

What does it mean to exemplarize something? S exemplarizes X if and only if S uses X as an exemplar of a class of symbols having some role of which X itself is a member. X is an exemplar if and only if X stands for a class of objects of which X is a member. Does using X as an exemplar bring back all the problems of intentionality? I wish to argue that it need not. Consider quotation and disquotation of a word. I make remarks about the word as a word. That is like making remarks about anything else. Now suppose I want to make remarks concerning what the word is about. I just disquote the word and use it to say what I want concerning the things that the word is about. The basis of it is quotation and disquotation. That is the solution to the problem of intentionality. Moreover, thought about something is a matter of quotation and disquotation of some mental state in a similar loop of exemplarization.

Nelson Goodman (196 8) provided us with many examples of exemplarization in conventional symbolic systems. If, for example, you ask me what the dance of the *pas de deux* in *Don Quixote* is, and I dance it with Sylvie Guillem to show you what it is, our dancing would be an exemplar of the *pas de deux* from *Don Quixote* representing the other dances of the *pas de deux* by other dancers or, if you prefer, representing a certain kind of dance with the role of a *pas de deux* in the ballet. If you understand our dancing in this way, you are treating our dancing as an exemplaric representation of the *pas de deux*. Exemplarization is, in fact, a standard form of representation of dance, as Goodman indicates, because of the limitations of other symbolic systems for representing dance. It should not escape notice, however, that exemplarization reveals a special mental or metamental capacity whereby something becomes a metarepresentation by looping referentially back upon itself to represent other things of the same kind or sort.

Meaning, Belief and Opacity

Exemplarization explains why there is more to the representation of meaning than the representation of extension. The proof that there is more is the usual one: you cannot substitute one representation for another with the same extension, whenever it is used, and preserve truth value. Assuming "witch" and "wizard" have the same extension, namely, the null extension, you cannot substitute one for the other in all contexts of use and preserve truth value. Intentional contexts, belief contexts, for example, exhibit this most clearly. "Jean believes that all wizards are male" does not have the same truth value as "Jean believes that all witches are male," as Jean would surely inform us. The reason is that "witch" and "wizard" have a different meaning even if they both denote the same thing, namely, nothing at all.

This is the problem of referential opacity. Exemplarization provides an explanation and a solution. The usual solution is that there is a different mode of representation of what Jean believes in one sentence and in the other. Now, suppose that we regard Jean as someone who exemplarizes or might exemplarize the mental tokens in a sentence that Jean uses to represent the content of what he believes. Jean might then exemplarize "witch," and the class of words "witch" exemplarizes for Jean would not include "wizard." The exemplaric representations of "witch" and "wizard" are different, and that accounts for the difference in mode of representation. The difference in mode of representation is a difference in exemplarization of representations. Exemplarization explains opacity.

Does this mean every difference in a sentence Jean might use to represent the content of what Jean believes introduces opacity? Every difference introduces potential opacity but not actual opacity. It depends on how Jean exemplarizes the word X to represent a class of words playing a role in the language. If Y is included in the same exemplarization class as X, then "Jean believes that a is X," and "Jean believes a is Y" have the same truth value. This condition, though sufficient, may not be necessary. Jean may regard some complex expression C as playing the same descriptive role as X, though not the same syntactical role, and, as a result, not include C in the exemplarization class of X, though he or she accepts C as a definition of X. Should we then say that "Jean believes that a is X" has the same truth value as "Jean believes that a is C"? Jean might or might not agree that he believed that a is C when he believed that a is X, for he might say that it had not occurred to him that X is defined as C though he recognizes that it is so defined. The case seems to me to be borderline and shows that truth, like other notions, has borderline cases.

Now this reflection may raise a doubt about the substitution of Y for X even when Y is in the exemplarization class of X for Jean. For, again, it might not occur to Jean that Y is in the exemplarization class of X for Jean, though, when asked, he recognizes that it is so included. Here I would say that we should disagree with Jean and affirm that he did believe that a is Y though it did not occur to him that he did, but I would not be dogmatic about this. Again, truth becomes vague in belief contexts and, though we may decide to eliminate the vagueness one way or another for the purposes of philosophical reconstruction, the justification for our decision to do so must be in terms of those purposes rather than a simple appeal to antecedent intuition. However we decide problematic cases, exemplarization will provide the basic account of opacity.

The capacity for exemplarization was assumed by Sellars, of course, because he assumed that we understand sentences like M as well as the variations of it by treating "red" as an exemplar. Sellars, like Goodman, favored a kind of psychological nominalism, however, and the introduction of an operation of exemplarization threatens to bring in the bugbear of kinds or sorts as the exemplar is exemplarized to represent things of the same kind or sort as itself. Put another way, exemplarization seems to assume an understanding of what it is for something to be of the same sort or kind as other things.

I will not spend a great deal of time over this matter except to mention the solution that Thomas Reid proposed, namely, that generalizing from an individual yields a conception of a general quality or sort (Reid, 1785/ 1895, pp. 295–405). Such an account assumes a capacity to generalize, to parcel things into sorts, but it does not presuppose the existence of universals. We must presuppose the capacity to generalize, but all animals generalize. Moreover, connectionist models of generalization offer an account of how a system might generalize without any antecedent representations of universals, not even resemblance. We have, I propose, the capacity to generalize, which we share with many other animals, and a capacity to exemplarize built upon that capacity, which we may share with some other animals. Finally, as Reid suggested, the way in which we parcel things into sorts is driven by utility, with the result that different animals may generalize in different ways and have different general conceptions. How much of the way we generalize is innate and how much is driven by tutelage and circumstance is not germane to my concerns here, though it seems to me that the general capacity to generalize is innate.

Having progressed to this point, we can see how to avoid Fodor's solution to the problem. Fodor assumed that we need a language of thought, complete with innately understood meaning of words therein, to learn a conventional language. We need, he argued, the innately understood language in order to learn to understand the conventional one by mapping it into the innately understood language of thought. I am suggesting that what is required innately is only a capacity to generalize and exemplarize. Rather than needing to map the words of a conventional language into an innately understood language of thought to understand what they mean, what is needed is an innate capacity to generalize and exemplarize. Generalization is needed for exemplarization, and exemplarization is needed to avoid the regress with a loop. We do not need to have an innate understanding of the dancing of the *pas de deux* from *Don Quixote* in order to understand the dancing representationally or metarepresentationally. We only need to exemplarize the dance in terms of a performance of it and treat the performance as exemplaric representation. Assuming the innate capacities of generalization and exemplarization, the regress of representation and metarepresentation ends before it begins in the loop of exemplaric representation. This is, no doubt, a form of circularity as Fodor suggests, but one that is rendered harmless by the psychological reality of exemplarization.

What I am suggesting is that one may understand a word before one can understand a representation of what it means. Consider again sentence M which is the simplest sentence formulating the meaning of a word:

   M "Red" in English means red.

The sentence exemplarizes the second use of "red" as the dot-quoted version of the sentence:

   $M\bullet$ "Red" in English is a •red•

makes clear. However, to understand either M or $M\bullet$, one must understand "red," for without such understanding, one will not understand what sort or kind of word is exemplarically represented by the end or dot-quoted use of "red" in these sentences. It is as a result of understanding "red" that one understands a representation of what it means, and not the other way around. Understanding a representation of the meaning is a simple consequence of exemplarizing over the understood word.

But what is it to understand the word? Without offering a detailed account, the understanding of the word requires generalization and inferential patterning in a semantic field guided by conditions of relevance expressed by Dan Sperber and Deirdre Wilson (1986) yielding dispositions to apply the word and draw conclusions involving it. I have, with Adrienne Lehrer, (1995), attempted to articulate a theory of understanding a word in terms of functions of application of the word and network relations within a semantic field. This story is complicated in empirical development and theoretical articulation, but the idea is familiar and simple enough. The understanding of a word arises as one acquires dispositions to apply the word and to draw inferences involving it. These dispositions constitute vectors of understanding in the idiolect of the individual. The vectors of individuals may be aggregated within the individual and within society in terms of the relative weights assigned to the vectors. The public language is an aggregation of vectors within individuals, and may be realized within the idiolect of some individual or constitute a fiction of the average speaker of the language. The presence of these dispositions involving the word, combined with grammatical and pragmatic factors, yield an understanding of it.

Such understanding of a word may fall short of our representing the meaning of the word in even the minimal way involved in sentence *M* above. Nevertheless, an understanding of the word is essential to an understanding of the minimal representation of the meaning of the word in a sentence such as *M*. What is needed to get from the understanding of the word to a minimal representation of the meaning of the word is simply the exemplarization of it. The understanding of a word is not the result of understanding a minimal representation of the meaning of the word. On the contrary, understanding a minimal representation of the meaning of the word in a sentence like *M* presupposes the understanding of the word.

It is, moreover, important to realize that not all generalizing and patterning are limited to words of a conventional language. As the example of the dance illustrates, various activities, experiences and objects can be exemplarized. I have argued (1996, 1997) that the exemplarization of our inner states, especially conscious ones, converts them into exemplaric representations essential to our immediate knowledge of them. We exemplarize conscious states so that they become representational exemplars of states including themselves and, thus, the source of immediate representation of themselves. There is no more to the immediacy of consciousness than the loop of quotation and disquotation. Exemplarization extends, moreover, beyond conscious states to others. There is good empirical support for the thesis of the exemplaric representational character of experience in the work of Larry Barsalou (1990) and others (Barsalou & Olseth, 1995).

Thus, our understanding of the word "red" rests on the exemplarization of experience of red objects and, perhaps, red sensations, as we generalize and convert states and sensations into exemplaric representations. There is an understanding of representation prior to an understanding of the words in a conventional language. I do not object to calling an understanding of such representations a *language of thought*, as Daniel Andler suggested (in conversation, March, 1994), for I think that generalization and exemplarization are based on things other than words before we learn a conventional language. I deny that such representations provide us with a complete language that is presupposed for learning the meaning of words in the conventional language. On the contrary, understanding the words is presupposed for understanding what they mean by exemplarization of them. Exemplarization creates representation in a metamental loop of quotation and disquotation. We revolve out of the regress of metarepresentation in a loop of level-ambiguous exemplarization.

References

Barsalou, L. W. (1990). On the indistinguishability of exemplar memory and abstraction in category representation. In T. K. Srull & R. S. Wyer (Eds.), *Advances in social cognition: Volume 3. Content and process specificity in the effects of prior experiences* (pp. 61–88). Hillsdale, NJ: Erlbaum.

Barsalou, L. W. and Olseth, K. L. (1995). The spontaneous use of perceptual representations during conceptual processing. In *Proceedings of the seventeenth annual meeting of the Cognitive Science Society* (pp. 310–315). Hillsdale, NJ: Erlbaum.

Craig, William (1953). Replacement of auxiliary expressions. *Philosophical Review 65*, 38–55.

Fodor, Jerry (1979). *The language of thought.* Cambridge, MA: Harvard University Press.

Goodman, Nelson (1968). Languages of Art. Indianapolis and New York: Bobbs-Merrill.

Lehrer, Adrienne, & Lehrer, Keith (1995). Fields, networks and vectors. In F. Palmer (Ed.), *Grammar and meaning* (pp. 26–47). New York: Cambridge University Press.

Lehrer, Keith (1990a). *Metamind.* Oxford: Oxford University Press.

Lehrer, Keith (1990b). Metamental ascent: Beyond belief and desire. (Presidential Address). In *Proceedings and Addresses of the American Philosophical Association 63*, 3: 19–36.

Lehrer, Keith (1996). Consciousness. In A. Schramm, (Ed.) *Philosophie in Österreich* (pp. 20–32). Vienna: Hölder-Pichler-Tempsky.

Lehrer, Keith (1997). *Self-trust: A study of reason, knowledge and autonomy.* Oxford: Oxford University Press.

Reid, Thomas (1785/1895). In Sir William Hamilton (Ed.), *The Works of Thomas Reid, D. D.: Vol.1* (8th ed., pp. 395–405). Edinburgh: James Thin.

Rosenthal, David (1986). Two concepts of consciousness. *Philosophical Studies 49*, 329–359.

Sellars, Wilfrid (1963). *Science, Perception and Reality.* New York: Humanities Press.

Sperber, Dan, and Wilson, Deirdre, (1986). *Relevance.* Cambridge, MA: Harvard University Press.

Chapter 12

The Iconicity of Metarepresentations

François Recanati

1. Preliminaries

1.1 Extensionality

In contemporary philosophy there is a huge body of literature devoted to the analysis of metarepresentations, especially belief reports like

(1)   John believes that kangaroos have tails.

On the face of it, such metarepresentations seem to contain a primary representation, namely, 'Kangaroos have tails', and something like an operator 'John believes (that)', which makes a sentence out of a sentence. In this respect, 'John believes that S' appears to be very much like 'It is not the case that S'.

A major difference between 'John believes that' and the sentence-forming operator 'it is not the case that' is that the latter is *extensional*: the truth-value of the complex representation is a function of the truth-value of the primary representation. In this instance, the Principle of Extensionality is respected:

> *Principle of Extensionality*
>
> Given any sentence that contains as a part a sentence S, its truth-value is unchanged if we substitute for S any other sentence S' having the same truth-value as S.[1]

In contrast, 'John believes that' is not extensional: the truth-value of the complex statement does not depend merely on the truth-value of the embedded sentence. John may believe that grass is green without believing that snow is white, even though 'Grass is green' and 'Snow is white' have the same truth-value. Consequently, the Principle of Extensionality is violated.

The Principle of Extensionality is a consequence of a more general principle:

Generalized Principle of Extensionality (GPE)

The truth-value of a sentence is unchanged if we replace a constituent of that sentence by another one with the same extension.

The extension of a singular term (be it a 'genuine singular term', i.e., a name or an indexical, or a definite description) is an object; the extension of a predicate is a class of objects; and the extension of a sentence is a truth-value (i.e., 'true' or 'false', as the case may be). The GPE therefore entails various *replacement principles*, one of which is the Principle of Extensionality:

Extensional replacement principles:

• Substitutivity of Co-Denoting Prima Facie Singular Terms:

A prima facie singular term *t* (i.e. a name, an indexical, or a description) can be replaced *salva veritate* by some other term *t'*, provided *t* and *t'* have the same extension.

• Substitutivity of Co-Extensive Predicates:

A predicative expression *F* can be replaced *salva veritate* by another predicative expression *G* if the class of objects that satisfy *F* is identical to the class of objects that satisfy *G*.

• Principle of Extensionality (Substitutivity of Equivalent Sentences):

A sentence *S* can be replaced by a sentence *S'* in any complex sentence in which *S* occurs if *S* and *S'* have the same truth-value.

The first of these replacement principles should not be confused with another principle, the Principle of Substitutivity of Singular Terms, which concerns only genuine singular terms (names and indexicals), but not descriptions. Someone who rejects the GPE (and hence rejects the first extensional replacement principle) will want to retain the Principle of Substitutivity, which holds in many non-extensional contexts (such as the modal context 'It is necessary that . . .'). I will return to this distinction between the two principles later (§2.4).

The GPE is more general than the simple Principle of Extensionality, but it can still be generalized much further. First, it is not only the truth-value of a sentence, but *the extension of any sort of expression whatsoever*, which is unchanged if, in that expression, a constituent is replaced by another one with the same extension. Second, it is not only the extension of an expression, but its semantic value *at all levels* which arguably is a function of the semantic values of its parts. This last principle, which entails the GPE, I call the Generalized Principle of Compositionality (GPC).

Different types (or levels) of semantic value can be ascribed to expressions; the unitary notion of 'meaning' is therefore rather misleading. As against that unitary notion Frege insisted on distinguishing the *Sinn* ('sense' or 'content') of an expression and its *Bedeutung* ('reference' or 'extension'). He argued for a twofold Principle of Compositionality:

> The extension of an expression is a function of the extensions of its parts, and the content of an expression is a function of the contents of its parts.

Kaplan added a further distinction between 'character' (linguistic meaning) and 'content', in order to account for those cases in which the content of an expression partly depends upon the context in which the expression is tokened (Kaplan, 1989). In Kaplan's framework, which I will adopt in what follows, there are three distinct aspects of 'meaning'. Depending on the level of analysis, the semantic value of an expression can be either its *character*, or its *content* (Frege's 'sense') or its *extension* (Frege's 'reference').[2]

The Generalized Principle of Compositionality can now be stated as consisting of three sub-principles, the third of which is identical to the GPE:

Generalized Principle of Compositionality (GPC)

The semantic value of an expression at all levels is a function of the semantic values of its parts; that is:

(a) the character of an expression is a function of the characters of its parts

(b) the content of an expression is a function of the contents of its parts

(c) the extension of an expression is a function of the extensions of its parts (= GPE)

Given that the GPC entails the GPE which entails the Principle of Extensionality, belief reports, which violate the Principle of Extensionality, raise an obvious problem for those who defend the GPE or the GPC. Now the attachment of philosophers and logicians to this group of principles is so great that, more often than not, they have attempted to save the Principle of Extensionality by showing that its violations are 'only apparent', given a particular analysis of belief reports. In building theories to that effect, however, they have been led to sacrifice what, following Davidson, Barwise and Perry have called 'semantic innocence' (Barwise & Perry, 1981).

1.2 Innocence

Most philosophers analyze 'John believes that S' as consisting of a two-place predicate 'believes' and two singular terms, namely, 'John' and 'that S'. The standard argument in favor of that analysis is the validity of certain inferences involving belief sentences, for example, the following:

> John believes that grass is green
>
> Everything John believes is true
>
> Therefore, it is true that grass is green

If we rephrase 'It is true that grass is green', in which there is a dummy subject, into 'That grass is green is true', then the argument can easily be accounted for on the assumption that 'that grass is green' is a term (possibly a definite description, as several authors suggest). The inference pattern is:

> a is F (That grass is green is believed by John)
>
> Every F is G (Everything believed by John is true)
>
> Therefore, a is G (That grass is green is true)

In this framework, the GPE seems to apply, for the truth-value of the belief report is unchanged if we replace either of the singular terms flanking the two-place predicate 'believes' by a codenoting expression. The following inferences are both licensed by one of the replacement principles which the GPE entails, namely, the principle of Substitutivity of Co-Denoting Prima Facie Singular Terms:

> John believes that S
>
> John is the landlord
>
> Therefore, the landlord believes that S

> John believes that S
>
> That S is the most crazy thing I ever heard
>
> Therefore, John believes the most crazy thing I ever heard

However, we still have the problem of analyzing the complex singular term 'that S'. It contains the sentence S, but the reference of the 'that'-clause is *not* a function solely of the extension of the embedded sentence. If we replace the sentence by another one with the same truth-value but a different content, the truth-value of the complex sentence will shift. Again, John may believe that grass is green without *eo ipso* believing that snow is white. This is a violation of the GPE.

Many philosophers have dealt with this problem by appealing to the thesis of Semantic Deviance, according to which the extension of an expression is affected when it is embedded within a 'that'-clause. For Frege, who put forward a radical version of the thesis, the extension of a sentence systematically shifts in such circumstances. Once embedded, 'Grass is green' no longer denotes its truth-value (viz., True) but it comes to denote its truth-*condition* (viz., the proposition that grass is green). In other words, the extension of a sentence is not its normal extension, namely its truth-value, when the sentence is embedded in a belief context; an embedded sentence refers to its (normal) *content*. So if we replace 'Grass is green' by 'Snow is white' in a 'that'-clause, we do *not* replace an expression with another one with the same extension. *In the context of the belief sentence*, 'Grass is green' and 'Snow is white' do not have the same extension. The Principle of Extensionality is therefore respected, appearances notwithstanding.

Some philosophers, like Quine, do not like the idea that the embedded sentence refers to a 'proposition' or 'content', because they are suspicious of such entities. But they stick to the thesis of Semantic Deviance: they maintain that when a sentence is embedded in a belief report, its semantic value is affected.[3] 'That'-clauses, in this respect, are similar to quotation contexts: when we put a sentence in quotation marks, it no longer represents what it ordinarily represents. The sentence is mentioned rather than used. The same thing holds, Quine says, for non-extensional contexts in general. Non-extensional contexts in general are assimilated to quotation contexts, in which words stop behaving in the normal way. Thus

It is contingent that grass is green

is read as

That grass is green is contingent

and this is construed as similar to

"Grass is green" is contingent

where the sentence occurs within quotation marks. Because the representation is mentioned rather than used, we cannot expect the GPC to apply in those contexts. As Quine says,

> From the standpoint of logical analysis each whole quotation must be regarded as a single word or sign, whose parts count no more than serifs or syllables. A quotation is not a *description*, but a *hieroglyph*; it designates its object not by describing it in terms of other objects, but by picturing it. The meaning of the whole does not depend upon the meanings of the constituent words. The personal name buried within the first word of the statement

(1) 'Cicero' has six letters

e.g., is logically no more germane to the statement than is the verb 'let' which is buried within the last word. Otherwise, indeed, the identity of Tully with Cicero would allow us to interchange these personal names, in the context of quotation marks as in any other context; we could thus argue from the truth (1) to the falsehood

'Tully' has six letters (Quine 1951, p. 26)

By parity of reasoning, 'that S' in 'John believes that S' counts as logically a single word, whose semantic value does not depend upon the semantic values of its parts. (If the words in the embedded sentence did their normal compositional job, in accordance with the GPC, the Principle of Extensionality *would* apply.)

In the case of quotation, the thesis of Semantic Deviance is extremely plausible. Does the first word of (2) and (3) below have, for example, the same extension? No, the first one refers to cats, the second one refers to the word 'cats'.

(2)   Cats are nice

(3)   'Cats' is a four-letter word

(Note the difference in number between the two words: one is singular, the other plural.) But what about belief sentences and 'that'-clauses in general? Consider (4)

(4)   John believes that grass is green

Is it credible to say that the words 'Grass is green' do not represent what they normally represent? In what sense? Does 'grass' in the embedded sentence refer to anything else than grass? As Davidson emphasized,

> If we could recover our pre-Fregean semantic innocence, I think it would seem to us plainly incredible that the words 'The earth moves', uttered after the words 'Galileo said that', mean anything different, or refer to anything else, than is their wont when they come in different environments. (Davidson, 1984, p. 108)

I fully agree with Davidson that we should at least try to "recover our pre-Fregean innocence," that is, to do without the thesis of Semantic Deviance. In an 'innocent' framework, the semantic value of an expression in the embedded part of a belief report is construed as its *normal* semantic value (whatever that may be).

Ironically, many of those who explicitly defend semantic innocence in the analysis of belief reports (e.g., Crimmins & Perry, 1989) do so within the standard framework. They hold that 'that'-clauses refer to the proposition which the embedded sentence would express, were it uttered in isolation. But, I will argue (§2.1), that is not 'innocent' in the strong sense in which Davidson and Barwise and Perry talk about pre-Fregean innocence. One way of achieving innocence in that strong sense is to capture a central, though neglected, feature possessed by belief reports and other metarepresentations: the feature of 'iconicity', to which I now turn.

1.3 Iconicity

Belief sentences belong to a class of sentences which have, or seem to have, the (syntactic) property that they contain other sentences. For example, the sentences

> If Peter comes, John will be happy

> Peter comes and John will be happy

both contain the sentence 'Peter comes' and the sentence 'John will be happy'. Similarly,

> It is true that John will be happy

> Peter believes that John will be happy

> Later today, John will be happy

all seem to contain the sentence 'John will be happy'. Whenever we have a complex sentence dS which contains a sentence S in this manner, the following schema yields true instances:

> *Schema (I)*

> One cannot entertain the proposition that dS without entertaining the proposition that S.

For example:

> One cannot entertain the proposition that John believes that grass is green without entertaining the proposition that grass is green.

> One cannot entertain the proposition that it is not the case that Peter is smart without entertaining the proposition that Peter is smart.

> One cannot entertain the proposition that if it rains the road will be wet without entertaining the proposition that the road will be wet.

Here, like Frege in "The Thought" (1956), I rely on an intuitive understanding of what it is to 'entertain' (or 'grasp' or 'apprehend') a proposition, as opposed to asserting it or judging it to be true.

The property I have just mentioned holds for all sentences that contain a sentence as part, with the exception of sentences that contain another sentence in quotation marks.[4] Sentences with 'that'-clauses, in particular, satisfy schema (I): one cannot entertain the proposition such a sentence expresses without entertaining the proposition expressed by the embedded sentence. This is true of a belief report such as 'John believes that S' as much as of an extensional sentence such as 'It is true that S'.

If we want to make sense of this intuitive observation, we will be inclined to take the containment relation seriously. The following principle suggests itself:

Principle of Iconicity

Attitude reports and other metarepresentations contain the object-representation not only syntactically (in the sense that dS contains S), but also semantically: the proposition Q expressed by dS 'contains' as a part the proposition P expressed by S – and that's why one cannot entertain Q without entertaining P.

This principle itself makes sense only in the context of a certain type of semantic theory – a theory which construes propositions (the contents of utterances) as structured entities; that is indeed the sort of theory I have in mind. I leave it to proponents of the other sorts of semantic theory to decide whether and how they would be willing to account for the intuitive observation noted above.

A theory that conforms to the Principle of Iconicity can only be 'innocent'. The proposition that is the content of S, is also what S contributes to the content of the complex sentence dS. Thus the content expressed by S (hence its extension) is the same, whether S occurs in isolation or is embedded within a belief report.

The Principle of Iconicity is so named because, if it is true, metarepresentations essentially *resemble* the representations they are about – they share a lot of content with them. Indeed that is the intuition I am trying to convey. Consider example (5):

(5)   Tom: The moon is made of green cheese

Bob: According to Tom, the moon is made of green cheese

Tom's utterance represents the moon as being made of green cheese. Bob's utterance, which is a metarepresentation, has a different subject-matter: it is about Tom's utterance (or the belief it expresses), as the prefix 'According to Tom' makes clear. Yet, via the contained sentence, Bob's metarepresentational utterance displays the content of Tom's utterance and therefore replicates it to some extent. *Both Tom's utterance and Bob's include a representation of the moon as being made of green cheese.* That representation is offered by Tom as a representation of the way the world actually is – and by Bob as a representation of the way the world is according to Tom.

The Principle of Iconicity goes against the received wisdom concerning metarepresentations. As undergraduates, we learn that if a metarepresentation *m* represents an object-representation *r* and *r* is about *x*, then *m* is about *r* and *not* about *x*. If the Principle of Iconicity is correct, just the opposite is true: Whenever a metarepresentation *m* represents an object-representation *r* and *r* is about *x*, then *m* is bound to be about *x* (as well as about *r*). In other words, metarepresentations are fundamentally *transparent*.

Before proceeding, let me point out that not all metarepresentations in the general sense of 'representations of representations' fall into the same basket here. There is a difference between, for example, (6) and (7)

(6)   Tom stated Leibniz's Law

(7)   Tom stated that identical objects have all their properties in common.

Both statements are about a statement, namely, Tom's statement of Leibniz's Law. However, the content of Tom's statement (viz., Leibniz's Law) is displayed only in (7). It follows that only (7) is an iconic metarepresentation, that is, a metarepresentation which displays the content of the object-representation and thereby replicates it. Proposition (6) is not iconic – it does not satisfy schema (I): One *can* entertain the proposition that Tom stated Leibniz's Law without entertaining the proposition that identical objects have all their properties in common (= Leibniz's Law); but one *cannot* entertain the proposition that Tom stated that identical objects have all their properties in common without entertaining the proposition that identical objects have all their properties in common. So it makes a big difference whether we use a standard singular term (or description) or a 'that'-clause. This difference is ignored in standard accounts. From now on, I will reserve the term 'metarepresentation' for those representations of representations which *do* satisfy schema (I) and which, I claim, have the semantic property of iconicity. For example:

According to John, grass is green

John believes that grass is green

John says that grass is green

In John's mind, grass is green

In the picture, grass is green

In the film, grass is green

Etc.

I take those metarepresentations to constitute a natural class, and it is that class which I am trying to characterize via the Principle of Iconicity.

2. Metarepresentational Operators

2.1 Trouble with the Standard Analysis

According to the standard analysis, the sentential complement in a metarepresentation such as 'John believes that Peter likes grass' *names* a proposition. But that is not what the complement sentence does when it is not embedded. Unembedded, the sentence *expresses* the proposition which, once embedded, it names. Hence, by construing 'that'-clauses as names, it seems that the standard account violates semantic innocence.

To be sure, many philosophers (including myself) have attempted to provide innocent versions of the standard account. The usual strategy consists in drawing a distinction between the embedded sentence ('Peter likes grass') and the complete 'that'-clause ('that Peter likes grass'). The embedded sentence, it is said, expresses a proposition, and it is that proposition which is named by the 'that'-clause (consisting of the embedded sentence plus the complementizer 'that'). In this way, innocence is allegedly saved: the sentence does the same thing – it expresses a certain proposition – whether it is embedded or not; it never names a proposition, since that is a job for the complete 'that'-clause.

I do not think this strategy works, however. First, the distinction between the embedded sentence and the complete 'that'-clause has no obvious equivalent when we turn to metarepresentations like 'In the film, Peter likes grass' or 'According to John, Peter likes grass'. There is no 'that'-clause in such examples – only the sentence 'Peter likes grass'. Second, even when the distinction makes syntactic sense, it is unclear that it enables us to preserve semantic innocence. I will show that by considering an analogous case, that of quotation.

Faced with an instance of quotation, for example, " 'Cat' is a three-letter word," we have two options. We can say that the word 'cat' in this context does something different from what it normally does: it is used 'autonymously' (self-referentially). Or we can say that it is the complex expression " 'cat' " (consisting of the word 'cat' *and the quotation marks*), which denotes the word 'cat'. If, by taking the second option, we refrain from ascribing to the word 'cat' a deviant function in quotation contexts, we will be led to deny that the word 'cat' really occurs; rather, with Tarski and Quine, we will say that it occurs there only as a 'fragment' of the longer expression, much as 'cat' occurs in 'cattle'. From the semantic point of view, the relevant unit is indeed the complete quotation; the word 'cat' itself thus disappears from the picture. *In this way, innocence is lost as surely as it is when we take the first option.* A truly innocent account is one that would *both* acknowledge the occurrence of the expression at issue in the special context under consideration *and* ascribe it, in that context, its normal semantic function. (Of course, there is no reason to expect an account of quotation to be semantically innocent in that sense.)

Similarly, we have two options with regard to attitude reports, in the standard framework. If we say that the complement sentence, once embedded, names the proposition which it would normally express, we accept that the embedded sentence does not do what it normally does. On the other hand, if, in order to protect innocence, we draw a sharp distinction between the embedded sentence (which expresses a proposition) and the 'that'-clause (which names it), *we run the risk of making the former disappear from the logical scene.* For the relevant semantic unit is the complete 'that'-clause. At the level of logical form, the sentence 'John believes that S' has the form aRb – it consists of a two-place predicate and two singular terms. The embedded sentence plays a role only via the 'that'-clause in which it occurs. Which role? Arguably a *presemantic* role analogous to that of the demonstration which accompanies a demonstrative.[5] If that is right, then semantically the complexity of the 'that'-clause matters no more than the pragmatic complexity of a demonstrative-*cum*-demonstration or the pictorial complexity of a quotation.

The difficulty we are facing is this. We want to say that (i) 'believes' in 'John believes that Peter likes grass' expresses a relation between John and what he believes; and that (ii) what John believes is actually expressed (displayed) by the embedded sentence 'Peter likes grass'. Because of (i), we think that 'believes' is a two-place predicate, that is, an expression which makes a sentence out of two terms. On this construal, what follows 'believes' must be a term, not a sentence; hence we view 'that' as converting the embedded sentence into a term. Because of (ii), however, we think the embedded sentence must remain a sentence; it must *not* be converted into a term.[6]

The difficulty stems from the fact that a predicate, in the logical sense, demands terms to fill its argument places. Since a sentence is not a term, there are two options for the analysis of belief reports. Proponents of the standard analysis say that the embedded sentence is converted into a term which fills the second argument place of the first-order predicate 'believes'. As we have seen, this threatens innocence. But there is another option: we can say that the embedded sentence is (and remains) a bona fide sentence, and deny that the verb really corresponds to a first-order predicate with two argument places. The latter option, suggested by Quine, has been pursued by Arthur Prior.

2.2 Prior's adverbial analysis

To make sense of the Quine-Prior suggestion, we must introduce the notion of a functor.[7] A functor makes a sentence out of one or several expressions which can be either terms or sentences. In '*Rab*', '*R*' makes a sentence out of two terms, '*a*' and '*b*'; in '*&pq*' (a Polish-like notation for '*p&q*'), '*&*' makes a sentence out of two sentences '*p*' and '*q*'. Both the predicate '*R*' and the connective '*&*' are functors. There is no reason why there should not exist functors of a mixed variety ('connecticates'), that is, functors making a sentence out of a term and a sentence. 'Believes that' is such a functor, according to Prior: it makes a sentence out of a term (e.g., 'Paul') and a sentence (e.g., 'Grass is green'). When a term is provided, the connecticate becomes a monadic propositional operator 'Paul believes that . . .', which makes a sentence out of a sentence. 'Paul believes that' thus belongs to the same logical category as other sentence-forming operators like 'it is not the case that' or 'it is necessary that'.

In this framework, we can maintain that the verb is a 'two-place predicate' in the *grammatical* sense, that is, a verb which comes with two 'argument roles' (one of the roles being filled by a sentential argument). Yet it does not function as a predicate in the logical sense, but as a connecticate, when the verb takes a sentence as second argument.[8] In such contexts, the verb in combination with the first argument contributes an operator, much as a sentential adverb would. Thus 'John believes that grass is green' is more or less equivalent to 'According to John, grass is green'.

In the case of 'believe', the second argument place can be filled either by a noun-phrase, as in (8), or by a sentence, as in (9). This is supposed to show that in (9) the embedded sentence itself has the status of a noun-phrase. Indeed (9) is only a stylistic variant of (10), which contains a 'that'-clause; and there is but a short step from (10) to (11), in which it can hardly be doubted that the 'that'-clause has the status of a noun-phrase. Note that the relation of (9) to (11) is the same as the relation of (8) to (12):

(8)   John believes that story

(9)   John believes Peter will come

(10)   John believes that Peter will come

(11)   That Peter will come is something which John believes

(12)   That story is something which John believes

All this is supposed to show that the standard, relational analysis is correct, and that Prior's proposal is hopeless. But this conclusion is too hasty. To see why, let us consider attitude verbs other than 'believe'.

There are cases in which the second argument place can be filled *only* by a sentence. In such cases, we are intuitively much less tempted to treat the sentence as a noun-phrase, and the verb as expressing a relation. Consider 'complain,' for example. As Rundle points out: "You can complain about something or object to something, but you can neither complain nor object something. So, although you can complain or object that *P*, it would seem wrong to regard 'that *P*' as filling the role of object" (Rundle, 1979, p. 283). Thus (14) is fine, but neither (13) nor (15) is acceptable:

(13)   *John complains that story

(14)   John complains that Peter will come

(15)   *That Peter will come is something which John complains

Even when the verb at issue *can* take a straightforward term as direct object, Rundle points out, there often is no temptation to treat the 'that'-clause as actually filling the object role. Thus, in (16)

(16)   John explained that he had been delayed

the proposition that John had been delayed, allegedly denoted by the 'that'-clause, is not *what* John explained. 'That he had been delayed' is not the thing which John explained; rather, it is the explanation itself. (What John explained was the fact that he was late.) The relation, in (16), between the verb and the statement that John had been delayed is similar to what we find either in direct speech or in 'free indirect speech':

(17)   John explained: 'I have been delayed'

(18)   John explained: he had been delayed.

In neither case should we say that the quoted words provide the direct object of the verb. Contrast (17) with (19):

(19)   John explained 'I have been delayed' by providing a synonym.

In (17) and (18), the verb (together with its first argument) has a prefatory character, similar to that of a parenthetical clause. Likewise, 'John explained that the train had been delayed' is more or less equivalent to 'The train had been delayed, John explained', or to 'According to John's explanation, the train had been delayed'. It is *not* equivalent to 'John explained the proposition that the train had been delayed'.

Similar observations are made by Friederike Moltmann in a couple of recent papers. As she points out,

> Many attitude verbs do take referential NPs of the sort *the proposition that S*, but then obtain a different reading, the reading they have when taking ordinary referential NPs:
>
> (a) John imagined that he will win.
>
> (b) John imagined the proposition that he will win.
>
> (c) John imagined Mary

(a) John expects that he will win.

(b) John expects the proposition that he will win.

(c) John expects Mary.

(a) John heard that Mary closed the door.

(b) John heard the fact/the proposition that Mary closed the door.

(c) John heard Mary.

An attitude verb taking a referential complement, as in the (b)- or (c)-examples above, systematically displays a different reading from the one it has when it takes a clausal complement. (Moltmann, 1998, §1)

Moltmann concludes that there is "a fundamental distinction between the semantic value of *that*-clauses and *the proposition that S*: The semantic value of a *that*-clause does not act as an object recognized as such by an agent standing in an attitudinal relation to it; rather it acts only as an 'un-reflected' content . . . It is a semantic value merely expressed, not referred to by the *that*-clause" (Moltmann, 1997, §2.1).

The upshot of these considerations is that a case can be made for a non-relational analysis of attitude sentences and other metarepresentations. We are not forced to parse the complex sentence 'John believes that grass is green' as

John BELIEVES that-grass-is-green

Instead of construing 'believes' as a two-place predicate expressing a relation between John and the proposition that grass is green, we can construe it as the connecticate 'believes-that':

John BELIEVES THAT grass is green

On this view, urged by Arthur Prior, 'John believes that' is a unary sentential operator, on a par with the operators used in modal logic: 'it is possible that', 'it is necessary that', and so forth (see Hintikka, 1962, for a similar treatment).

2.3 Higher-Order Predication

The adverbial analysis raises an obvious objection. It does not account for the intuition that 'believes' in 'John believes that grass is green' expresses a relation between John and what he believes. That intuition is supported by the validity of inferences like (20).

(20)   John says that grass is green

Everything John says is true

Therefore, it is true that grass is green

As we have seen, such inferences (and the 'relational' intuition which they support) can easily be accounted for on the assumption that 'that'-clauses are terms (§1.2). How will they be accounted for if we give up that assumption?

To account for (20), we may follow Ramsey and analyze the major premiss as 'For all p, if John says that p, then it is true that p' (Ramsey, 1990, p. 39). That is what Prior does. In support of that move, let us consider another type of case in which we have a valid inference very much like (20):

(21)   Australian deconstructionists are rare

Everything rare is precious

Therefore, Australian deconstructionists are precious

There are reasons to believe that 'rare' is not a first-order predicate. If it were, we could reason as follows:

Australian deconstructionists are rare

John is an Australian deconstructionist

Therefore, John is rare

But this is as nonsensical as

Australian deconstructionists are less than 50

John is an Australian deconstructionist

Therefore, John is less than 50

Following Frege, let us construe '... are rare' and '... are less than 50' as *second-order* predicates. It is, as Frege puts it, the 'concept' of an Australian deconstructionist that is said to be rarely instantiated, or instantiated by less than 50 persons. On this view 'Everything rare is precious' is an instance of second-order quantification. A more obvious example of second-order quantification is

(22)   John is something that I am not, namely Australian

which should be analyzed as 'For some F, John is F and I am not F'.

If we make room for such higher-order quantification and predication, then (20) raises no problem for the view that 'John says that' is a sentential operator. If we can quantify predicates, then surely we can quantify sentences. Proposition (20) will thus be construed as instantiating the following pattern of inference

$\delta\sigma$

For every p, if δp then $\delta' p$

Therefore, $\delta'\sigma$

where 'δ' and 'δ'' respectively stand for two sentential operators (e.g., 'John says that' and 'It is true that') and 'σ' for a sentence (e.g., 'grass is green'), while 'p' is a sentential variable. This entails, of course, that we reject Quine's claim that quantification is fundamentally 'objectual' and involves existential commitments. When we quantify predicates or sentences, we do not quantify objectually: higher-order quantification is non-objectual, as Prior stressed in many places. A quantified sentence like (22) commits us to no more and no less that the corresponding substitution instance: 'John is Australian but I am not'. If the latter does not existentially commit us to properties, neither does the former.

To say that the quantification (or predication) is second-order is to say (*inter alia*) that the predicate or proposition talked about are not objectified (i.e., transformed into things). The gist of the higher-order approach advocated by Frege is this:

> There are two different ways in which we can talk about concepts. We can reify the concept, construe it as an object and engage in first-order talk about it. That, according to Frege, is what we do when we say things like 'the concept of horse is multiply instantiated', since 'the concept of horse' is (for Frege) a singular term. But we can also engage in second-order talk about concepts, in which case the concept talked about is 'expressed' rather than 'referred to'. In 'Australian deconstructionists are less than 50' the concept of an Australian deconstructionist is expressed, it is not referred to (as it is in 'the concept of an Australian deconstructionist is instantiated by less than 50 persons').

If we accept Frege's distinction between the two ways of talking about concepts, we can extend it and account for the iconicity of *oratio obliqua* by construing it as higher-level talk about propositions. On this view, propositions are not reified when we use the 'x Vs that p' construction. Thus we capture the distinction between 'John stated Leibniz's Law' and 'John stated that identical objects have all their properties in common'.

Note that, if we take this line, *there no longer is a tension between the adverbial analysis and the relational analysis*. 'Believes' *can* be construed as a two-place predicate in the logical sense, if it is a higher-level predicate. Since the second argument place of the 'believes' predicate is filled by a sentence, the predicate taken together with its first argument has the status of an adverb operating on the sentence.[9]

2.4 Substitutivity

From now on I will assume the operator analysis, according to which metarepresentations, whether explicitly adverbial ('According to John, Peter likes grass') or not ('John believes that Peter likes grass'), consist of two components: a sentential operator ('according to John', 'John believes that') and a sentence ('Peter likes grass').

The first thing to note, in connection with that analysis, is that the operators at issue – metarepresentational operators, such as 'John believes that' – are not extensional. The Principle of Extensionality is violated: even though the sentence 'John believes that S' (under the analysis in question) contains the sentence S as constituent, it is not possible to replace S by an equivalent sentence without possibly affecting the truth-value of the complex sentence. This is acceptable for, as Prior says,

> there is no more reason for accepting [the Principle of Extensionality] as true than there is for believing that the earth is flat, and it is in one way a rather similar belief. What we say by our sentences (or better, how we say things are) may vary in innumerable other 'dimensions' than that of truth-value; for any given p, it may not only be or not be the case that p, but may also be believed by Paul or by Elmer or by everybody or by nobody that p, it may be possible or impossible or necessary that p, it may be desirable or undesirable or a matter of indifference whether p, and so on, and for a given f, whether it is or is not the case that $f(p)$ may depend solely on whether it is or is not the case that p, but it may on the contrary depend on a variety of these other factors in the situation . . . The so-called law of extensionality was an interesting early effort at generalization in a scientific logic, and no doubt does hold within the first area to be thoroughly examined – the functions required in the foundations of mathematics – but in no other science that I've heard of do the practitioners cling to the first guesses of their teachers, in the face of the most obvious counter-examples, with the fervour of religious devotees. (Prior, 1976, pp. 150–151)

According to Tom Baldwin, Prior's rejection of the Principle of Extensionality merely shows that the significance of that principle was not apparent to him (Baldwin, 1982, pp. 256–257). The only thing I can say is that it is not apparent to me either. Like Prior, I think the Principle of Extensionality is false. Hence I reject the GPC:

Generalized Principle of Compositionality (GPC)

The semantic value of an expression at all levels is a function of the semantic value of its part; that is:

(a) the character of an expression is a function of the characters of its parts

(b) the content of an expression is a function of the contents of its parts

(c) the extension of an expression is a function of the extensions of its parts (= GPE)

What I reject is the third part of the GPC, namely, the GPE (Generalized Principle of Extensionality). The extension of an expression is not in general a function of the extensions of its parts. The reason that is so is that the extension of an expression primarily depends on its *content* (and the way the world is); now the content of an expression depends on more than merely the extensions of its parts: it depends on their contents. Thus if, in a complex expression, you replace a constituent by another one with the same extension but a different content, you change the content of the complex expression, hence (possibly) its extension.[10]

Rejecting the GPE leaves us with a more restricted principle of compositionality:

> *Restricted Principle of Compositionality (RPC)*
>
> (a) the character of an expression is a function of the characters of its parts;
>
> (b) the content of an expression is a function of the contents of its parts;
>
> (c) the extension of an expression is *not* a function of the extensions of its parts.

Contrary to the GPC, the RPC does not entail that expressions with the same extension can be substituted *salva veritate*. But it suggests that expressions with the same *content* can be substituted *salva veritate*. This entails various intensional replacement principles, including the Principle of Substitutivity of Singular Terms: that two directly referential terms with the same extension can be substituted *salva veritate* (since two directly referential terms with the same extension have the same content).

> *Intensional Replacement Principles:*
>
> • A genuine singular term t (e.g., a name or an indexical) can be replaced *salva veritate* by some other term t' provided t and t' have the same extension (hence the same content).
>
> • A predicative expression F can be replaced *salva veritate* by another predicative expression G if F and G express the same concept.
>
> • A sentence S can be replaced *salva veritate* by a sentence S' in any complex sentence in which S occurs if S and S' express the same proposition.

The problem is that those replacement principles do not seem to be unrestrictedly valid. Like the extensional replacement principles, they have numerous counter-examples. Intensional replacement principles work well for modal sentences such as 'It is necessary that S', but apparently they do not work for belief sentences. For even *synonymous* expressions – expressions that certainly have the same content – cannot be substituted *salva veritate* in belief sentences. John can believe that Paul is an ophthalmologist without believing that Paul is an eye-doctor. If that is right, then metarepresentational operators like 'John believes that' are not merely 'intensional' (i.e., non-extensional); they are *hyperintensional* in that replacing an expression by another one with the same content may change the truth-value of the sentence in which the change occurs.[11]

Failures of extensionality led us to give up the GPC in favour of the RPC. Should failures of intensional replacement lead us to give up the RPC as well? Are there hyperintensional operators, which violate the RPC, much as there are intensional operators which violate the GPC? I do not think so. If two sentences S and S' have the same content, they express the same proposition. Now if the propositions they respectively express are the same, whatever is true of one proposition must be true of the other. Hence if John believes that S, and the proposition that S is the same as the proposition that S', it must be true that John believes that S'. This seems to show that, if two sentences have the same content, they *must* be substitutable even under the 'John believes that' operator.[12]

Now consider the alleged counter-example to the RPC:

(a) John believes that Paul is an ophthalmologist

(b) 'Ophthalmologist' has the same content as 'eye-doctor'

(c) John believes that Paul is an eye-doctor

By virtue of (b), 'Paul is an ophthalmologist' (= S) and 'Paul is an eye-doctor' (= S') have the same content and express the same proposition σ. Both (a) and (c) apparently consist of that proposition in the scope of the operator δ corresponding to the phrase 'John believes that'; hence it seems that (a) and (c) must express the same proposition $\delta\sigma$. How then could (a) and (c) differ in truth-value? How, without giving up the RPC, can we account for our clear intuitions that (a) can be true and (c) false?

One way of accounting for our intuitions consists in acknowledging the *context-sensitivity* of the phrase 'John believes that'. By substituting 'Paul is an eye-doctor' for 'Paul is an ophthalmologist', you change the context in which the phrase 'John believes that' is tokened, and that can affect the semantic value of that phrase, if it is context-sensitive. Thus we can imagine that the same phrase 'John believes that' corresponds to distinct (though related) operators depending on the context. Thus in (a) 'John believes that' corresponds to some operator δ. The inference goes through if we *fix* that operator: if δp, and Ipq (the proposition that p is identical to the proposition that q), then δq. But what we have in (c) is not quite the operator δ, but the *phrase* 'John believes that'. That phrase, in (a), corresponds to the operator δ, but if it is context-sensitive it may well change its content in (c) and correspond in that context to a distinct operator δ', in such a way that the inference no longer goes through: from the fact that δp, and the fact that the proposition that p is identical to the proposition that q, it does not follow that $\delta' q$. All that follows is the proposition that δq (but that proposition is arguably *not* what [c] expresses).

On this analysis, when a sentence S cannot be replaced *salva veritate* by a sentence S' with the same content within the complex sentence dS, the culprit is the prefix d whose content changes from context to context. The substitution itself changes the context and causes the shift in semantic value of the prefix. Because of the possible context-sensitivity of the prefix d, all the intensional replacement principles, including the Principle of Substitutivity, are false, strictly speaking. But the RPC (and, of course, the laws of identity) remain true. On this account, the intensional replacement principles come out true *only if* the semantic values (contents) of all expressions in the sentence are 'fixed' and prevented from shifting as a result of the replacement itself. Under such artificial conditions, the counter-examples vanish.

To illustrate that point, consider Quine's well-known counter-example to the Principle of Substitutivity of Singular Terms (Quine 1943):

> Giorgione was so-called because of his size

'Giorgione' and 'Barbarelli', being co-extensive proper names, presumably have the same content; yet they cannot be substituted *salva veritate*. This is because the replacement would change the context for the adverb 'so', whose semantic value is context-sensitive. But if we fix the reference (hence the content) of the adverb 'so', then, evidently, the Principle of Substitutivity unproblematically applies. If Giorgione was so-called, that is, called 'Giorgione', because of his size, and Giorgione = Barbarelli, then, of course, Barbarelli was 'so' called (in the now *fixed* sense: 'called "Giorgione"') because of his size. Similarly, there is no reason to assume that the function expressed by 'John believes that' will be the same irrespective of the sentence which fills the blank after 'that'; but if we artificially fix the function expressed by the prefix, then, evidently, it will be possible to replace the embedded sentence by any other sentence expressing the same proposition, without affecting the truth-value of the complex sentence dS. If we fix the value of d, the complex sentence will express the same proposition δp before and after the replacement, instead of expressing δp before and $\delta' p$ after the replacement.

My aim in this section was not to urge a particular explanation of failures of substitutivity in belief contexts. I merely wanted to show that, unless it is properly qualified,[13] the Principle of Substitutivity is false, so that its failures should cause us no more worry than the failures of the Principle of Extensionality. I now turn to the central task of clarifying the contribution which the metarepresentational prefix d ('In the film', 'According to John', 'John believes that', etc.) makes to the meaning of the complex metarepresentation.

3. Simulation and Beyond

3.1 Metarepresentation and Simulation

Iconicity is the property in virtue of which metarepresentations contain the representation they are about (the 'object-representation'), both syntactically and semantically. Among the theories which capture that property of metarepresentations, we can distinguish two groups. Theories of the first group maintain that there is a difference between the content of the metarepresentation and the content of the object-representation; the latter is a proper part of the former. According to theories of the second group, there is no such difference: the metarepresentation has the same content as the object-representation and differs from it only in some other dimension.

Modal theories of metarepresentations belong in the first group. A modal theory analyzes a metarepresentation dS as consisting of the object-representation S and a circumstance-shifting prefix d. While S is true in a circumstance c iff a certain condition p obtains, dS is true in a circumstance c iff condition p obtains in a different circumstance c', where c' bears a certain relation R to c. An example of modal representation is: 'It will be the case that grass is green'. It consists of 'grass is green' and a circumstance-shifting prefix 'it will be the case that'. While 'grass is green' is true in a circumstance c iff grass is green in c, 'It will be the case that grass is green' is true in c iff grass is green in a distinct circumstance c' such that c' is later than c. (There are complications regarding the indexicality of tense which I pass over.) Similarly, the metarepresentation 'John believes that grass is green' is true in c iff grass is green in all possible circumstances c' compatible with what John believes in c. In that framework there is a clear difference between the truth-conditional content of S and that of dS.

Because of that difference between the content of S and the content of dS, it is in general possible to assert the complex proposition that dS (e.g., the proposition that John believes that grass is green) without asserting the component proposition that S (e.g., the proposition that grass is green). In general, the content of a sentence is not asserted unless that sentence occurs in isolation. When it occurs only as a component of a longer sentence, the proposition expressed by the complex sentence, not that expressed by the component sentence, is asserted.

I think the modal approach to metarepresentations is essentially correct. Before actually putting forward a theory along these lines, however, we must consider a theory belonging to the second group: the simulation theory. The basic notion it uses, that of simulation, will turn out to be an essential ingredient of the account to be put forward later.

For theories of the second group, the reason that the proposition that S is not asserted when a metarepresentation dS is issued (i.e., uttered or entertained) is not that S is embedded instead of occurring in isolation. There are well-known cases in which a proposition is not asserted even though the sentence which expresses it is uttered in isolation: that happens whenever the speaker is not seriously attempting to characterize the actual world, but merely evoking some imaginary world. For example, suppose that, misled by unreliable weather reports, we are caught in the middle of a storm and I say, 'The weather is indeed lovely'. My utterance is clearly ironic: I do not *assert* that the weather is lovely – I am not characterizing the world as it is but, rather, the world as the weather reports misleadingly depicted it. Irony, here as elsewhere, involves a form of pretense or mimicry.[14] Now the sentence in this example is uttered in isolation, but we can imagine that a certain prefix serves to indicate that the sentence which follows is not really asserted. A good example of that sort of thing is provided by children's games of make-believe. In such a game, my son says to my daughter:

> On serait un roi et une reine

This utterance expresses the proposition that my children are King and Queen respectively. That proposition is not asserted because the world of reference is not the actual world, but some imaginary world evoked by the game. The function of the conditional mood in French is precisely to shift the world from the actual world to some imaginary world.[15] Besides the conditional mood (or the 'imparfait', a tense which serves the same function in children's games) there are specific adverbials, such as 'pour de faux', which signal that the utterance is not a serious assertion purporting to characterize the actual world, but a pretend assertion (or question, or request) purporting to characterize the imaginary world of the game. In this type of case – when an adverbial such as 'pour de faux' is used – the proposition expressed by the utterance dS is arguably the very proposition expressed by S; the only function of the prefix is to indicate that the proposition in question is not asserted – that the speaker is merely pretending. So we have a complex sentence dS, but it is not because S is not 'uttered in isolation' that it is not asserted; rather, it is because the sentence is not (seriously) asserted that it has been prefixed with 'pour de faux', to make clear what the speaker is doing.

The simulation theory is the view according to which metarepresentational prefixes such as 'John believes that' have such a pragmatic function: they indicate that the speaker is not characterizing the actual world, but, say, John's belief-world, much as the ironist, in our earlier example, playfully (simulatively) describes the world as it would have been, had the meteorological predictions been correct. The point of the ironist is to show how much the 'world' thus described differs from the actual world. The point of the belief ascriber is, simply, to show how the world is according to the ascribee. In both cases, according to the theory, the utterance is not a genuine assertion but an instance of pretend assertion. Such a theory clearly belongs to the second group: for the only contribution of the prefix is pragmatic; there is no difference between the content of S and the content of dS – dS expresses the proposition that S while signalling that that proposition is not seriously asserted.

The notion of a prefix 'indicating' or 'signalling' the force of an utterance makes sense only with respect to language or communication. But it is an important fact about *thoughts* that we can entertain thoughts either assertively or not. Assertive thoughts are thoughts which we entertain concerning the actual world. But we can also entertain thoughts concerning imaginary worlds. In such a case, the representation of a state of affairs is 'de-coupled' from the actual world.[16] This de-coupling is effected through mental simulation.

Mental simulation is the activity we engage in when we imagine some world distinct from the actual world – when we pretend that the world is different from what it actually is (Kahneman & Tversky, 1982). In the example of pretend play I gave above (my son saying to my daughter, 'On serait un roi et une reine'), the representation that my children are King and Queen respectively is non-assertively entertained, in the sense that the world of reference is not the actual world, but the imaginary world of the game. There is no essential difference between children's pretend play, thus described, and the fictional activity of adults. When an author (or storyteller) says 'Once upon a time, there was a King and a Queen', she deploys an imaginary world, in exactly the same way as my children in their game of make-believe. The pretense in those examples is communicational, but it need not be. What is involved is an act of *mental* simulation: we pretend that the world is different from what it actually is, as we do when we imagine a counterfactual possibility.

According to the simulation theory, when we say or think that John believes that S (or that, according to John, S), we simulate John's mental state and assert that S within the simulation. As Quine says, "we project ourselves into what ... we imagine the [ascribee]'s state of mind to [be], and then we say what, in our language, is natural and relevant for us in the state thus feigned" (Quine, 1960, p. 218). Thus the operator in 'John believes that S' really is a 'pretense' operator.

In support of the simulation theory, consider propositions (23) and (24):[17]

(23)   Peter believes that John's phone number is 325-248

(24)   Peter believes that John has the same phone number as Mary

From (23) and (24) we have no difficulty inferring (25).

(25)   Peter believes that Mary's phone number is 325-248

How does the inference proceed? The simulation theory offers a straightforward answer to that question. If to think that John believes that S is to think that S within a certain pretense, then the subject who is given (23) and (24) as premises holds the following under the pretense in question:

(23*)   John's phone number is 325-248

(24*)   John has the same phone number as Mary

The subject is therefore in a position to infer that

(25*)   Mary's phone number is 325-248

To be sure, this is inferred 'under the pretense', hence the subject holds (25*) only under the pretense also. But to hold (25*) under the pretense in question *is* to hold (25), according to the simulation theory. The transition from (23) and (24) to (25) is therefore explained.

The simulation theory as I have described it is fairly close to (radical versions of) what is described under that name in the literature of philosophy of mind. Thus Gordon says that "to attribute a belief to another person is to make an assertion, to state something as a fact, *within the context of practical simulation*" (Gordon, 1986, p. 168).[18] A merit of that theory is that it is as 'innocent' as a theory of metarepresentations can be. Iconicity is a built-in feature of the simulation theory: if to metarepresent is to simulate the object-representation, then the metarepresentation can only resemble the object-representation.

I think that iconicity can indeed be accounted for by linking metarepresentation to simulation. But the link forged by the simulation theory is too simple and too direct. The simulation theory, I will argue, conflates two different things: the exercise of simulation and its exploitation.

3.2 Conditionals and simulation

In the early 1970s, two authors – the Oxford philosopher John Mackie and the French linguist Oswald Ducrot – put forward a pragmatic analysis of conditionals that is exactly like the 'simulation theory', and which has the same merits and the same defects as the simulation theory. We may call it the 'simulation theory of conditionals'. The distinction I want to make between actual simulation and something which presupposes simulation but differs from it ('post-simulation') is best introduced by first considering the case of conditionals.

According to Ducrot and Mackie, a conditional utterance serves to perform two distinct illocutionary acts: (i) the antecedent introduces a *supposition:* it invites the hearer to consider a certain possibility; (ii) the consequent is asserted or put forward *within* that supposition.[19] The two illocutionary acts, therefore, are the act of 'supposing' and the act of 'asserting under a supposition'. The former is typically performed by means of the phrase 'Suppose that ...' or 'Imagine that ...'. Insofar as "the primary function of 'if' is to introduce a supposition, to invite us to consider a possibility," it "can be expanded into 'suppose that', and the consequent can be regarded as being put forward within the scope of that supposition" (Mackie, 1973, p. 98). The conditional 'If Peter comes, he will be tired' is therefore equivalent to a pair of utterances:

(26)   Imagine/suppose that Peter comes.

(27)   He will be tired.

Proposition (27) is asserted only 'within the supposition' introduced by (26). We are to imagine a situation in which Peter comes; it is the imaginary situation thus introduced – not the actual world – which we characterize in (27). Proposition (27) therefore is not an assertion *tout court*, but a pretended assertion concerning the imaginary situation that (26) invites us to consider. Such a simulative assertion is similar to the 'On serait un roi et une reine' previously mentioned: for the latter also characterizes some imaginary situation previously evoked.

Even though this is a speech act analysis that "explains conditionals in terms of what would probably be classified [and is indeed classified by Ducrot] as a complex illocutionary speech act, the framing of a supposition and putting something forward within its scope" (Mackie, 1973, p. 100), Mackie insists that the act of supposition in question is not essentially or primarily linguistic:

> Supposing some possibility to be realized and associating some further how-things-would-be with it is something that can be done merely by *envisaging* the possibilities and consequences in question. Among the reasons why this is important is that it makes comprehensible the otherwise puzzling fact that animals which seem not to use language – at any rate, not a language with any such grammatical structure as ours – seem capable of reasoning conditionally. (Mackie, 1973, p. 100)

One consequence of the Ducrot-Mackie account is that conditionals are not, strictly speaking, true or false. The act of supposing is certainly not evaluable in that dimension; and the statement which is made 'under the supposition' is only a prete⋯⋯   ⋯rtion, an assertion which can be evaluated only within the preten⋯⋯ ⋯nat the imaginary situation depicted by the antecedent actually obtains. The theory therefore "abandons the claim that conditionals are in a strict sense statements, that they are in general any sort of descriptions that must either be fulfilled or be not fulfilled by the way things are, and hence that they are in general simply true or false" (Mackie, 1973, p. 93).[20]

The problem is that conditionals often seem to be true or false in a fairly straightforward sense. For example, we can say: 'It is true that if Peter comes, he will be tired' (Mackie, 1973, p. 102). What does that mean, if the conditional 'If Peter comes, he will be tired' is not, strictly speaking, true or false? To be sure, one can invoke the redundancy theory to dispose of this difficulty – by arguing that 'It is true that if *P, Q*' says no more and no less than 'If *P, Q*'. But that misses the point. The point is that a conditional such as 'If Peter comes, he will be tired' may legitimately be construed as stating a fact concerning the actual world. Even a counterfactual conditional such as 'If Peter came, he would be tired' can be so construed. As Stalnaker says,

> Counterfactuals are often contingent, and contingent statements must be supported by evidence. But evidence can be gathered, by us at least, only in this universe . . . It is because counterfactuals are generally about possible worlds which are very much like the actual one, and defined in terms of it, that evidence is so often relevant to their truth . . . The conditional provides a set of conventions for selecting possible situations which have a specified relation to what actually happens. This makes it possible for statements about unrealized possibilities to tell us, not just about the speaker's imagination, but about the world. (Stalnaker, 1991, pp. 44–45)

And David Lewis:

> It is . . . the character of our world that makes counterfactuals true . . . The other worlds provide a frame of reference whereby we can characterize our world. By placing our world within this frame, we can say just as much about its character as is relevant to the truth of a counterfactual: our world is such as to make an (A-and-C)-world closer to it than any (A-and-not-C)-world [where A and C correspond to the antecedent and the consequent of the counterfactual]. (Lewis, 1986, p. 22)

What Stalnaker and Lewis say of counterfactuals holds even more clearly for indicative conditionals. If I say:

If John opens the fridge, he will be scared to death

my reason for saying that is that I know John, and I know what is in the fridge. It is John's *actual* character which supports the fact that if he opens the fridge (the actual fridge, with its actual contents) he will be scared to death. Had John's character, or the contents of the fridge, been different, the conditional would not hold. In that sense, the conditional is about the actual world.

The simulation theorist might reply as follows:

Let us replace the conditional by the corresponding Ducrot-Mackie pair:

> Suppose John opens the fridge.

> He will be scared to death.

There is no doubt that the simulation theory applies here: a supposition is made, and something is put forward in the scope of that supposition. The 'assertion' that John will be scared to death can be disputed or accepted only by someone who engages in the simulation and imagines John's opening of the fridge. Now, if the pretend assertion is accepted (if the hearer agrees with the speaker), that means that the speaker and the hearer view the imaginary situation in the same way; and they do so presumably because they have the same information concerning John and the fridge in the actual world. So the connection with the actual world exists, yet the utterance does not *say* something about the actual world. The utterance says something only about an *imaginary* situation, but the suppositional procedure through which that situation is constructed in imagination takes the actual world as its starting point, so that the utterance provides some evidence concerning the actual world, or the way the speaker takes it to be. The same thing holds, arguably, for the conditional: it does not *say* something about the actual world, even though what it says concerning the imaginary situation depicted by the antecedent is grounded in the speaker's information concerning the actual world. To say that the conditional makes an assertion concerning the actual world simply because it is connected to the actual world in that way would be to fall prey to what Barwise and Perry call the 'fallacy of misplaced information' (Barwise & Perry, 1983, p. 38).

Well, perhaps; but there is, I will argue, a significant difference between the conditional 'If John opens the fridge, he will be scared to death' and the corresponding Ducrot-Mackie pair. The Ducrot-Mackie pair states something only within the supposition that John will open the fridge; not so with the conditional.

3.3 Conditionals versus Conditional Assertions

Note, first, that conditionals can be embedded, for example, within belief sentences: 'Paul believes that if John opens the fridge, he will be scared to death'.[21] Following Peter Long (1971, pp. 142–143), Mackie himself ultimately accepts that conditionals are, or function as, genuine 'statements' (i.e., they express true or false propositions) in such contexts. Peter Long distinguishes between two uses of conditionals: the 'propositional employment' and the 'non-propositional employment'. In the propositional employment, 'If P then Q' means that Q is inferable from P. In its non-propositional employment, the sentence asserts that Q within the supposition that P. Long, followed by Mackie, holds that the non-propositional (simulative) use is primary: the propositional use presupposes the non-propositional use. As Mackie admits, this theory is much weaker than the full-blown simulation theory; it is also, I think, much closer to truth. Be that as it may, what matters for my purposes is the distinction between two things: asserting a proposition within the scope of a supposition; and asserting that a proposition follows (is inferable) from a supposition. I take it that conditionals are typically used to do the latter. If I am right, the simulation theory conflates the two things.

To bring that point home, let us consider natural deduction systems of logic, in which we find both conditionals and assertions-within-the-scope-of-a-supposition. Mackie acknowledges that the 'suppositional procedure' is at work in such systems, where we introduce temporary assumptions and reason in terms of them (Mackie, 1973, p. 99). To assume something, in natural deduction, *is* to make a supposition in the Ducrot-Mackie sense: we assume the truth of an auxiliary premiss P, and infer from it (and other premisses) a certain proposition Q. Q is not asserted, as it is inferred only 'under the assumption'. We only pretend to assert Q, or assert it 'within the scope' of the assumption that P. If Q is self-contradictory, we can discharge the assumption and assert the negation of the auxiliary premiss (reductio ad absurdum). If Q is not self-contradictory, we can discharge the assumption and assert the conditional $P \rightarrow Q$ (conditional proof).

For example, suppose that we want to prove '$\neg p$' from '$p \rightarrow \neg p$'. We can do it as set out in Table 1.

	Assertion	**Assumption**	
(1)	$p \rightarrow \neg p$		(Premiss)
(2)		p	(Auxiliary premiss)
(3)		$\neg p$	([1], [2], *Modus Ponens*)
(4)		$p \,\&\, \neg p$	([2], [3], *&-Introduction*)
(5)	$\neg p$		([2], [4], *Reductio ad absurdum*)

We start by assuming the negation of the proposition we want to prove (step 2 above); within that assumption, we derive a contradiction (steps 3 and 4); we then discharge the assumption and infer the negation of the auxiliary premiss (step 5).

Of interest here is the clear distinction (marked through placement in the appropriate column) between the propositions that are asserted and those that are merely 'assumed', that is, simulatively asserted. The propositions we find at steps (1) and (5) are asserted; the intermediate propositions, (2), (3), and (4), are all assumed.

Now let us consider an instance of Conditional proof. Suppose that we want to prove '$\neg q \to \neg p$' from '$p \to q$'. We can do it as in Table 2.

	Assertion	**Assumption**	
(1)	$p \to q$		(Premiss)
(2)		$\neg q$	(auxiliary premiss)
(3)		$\neg p$	([1], [2], *Modus Tollens*)
(4)	$\neg q \to \neg p$		([2], [3], *Conditional proof*)

We assume the antecedent of the conditional we want to prove (step 2); from that proposition and the initial premiss we infer the consequent (step 3). Because the antecedent, $\neg q$, was not really asserted, but merely assumed, the consequent, $\neg p$, is not asserted either. But the inference rule of Conditional proof enables us to infer the conditional $\neg q \to \neg p$ from the fact that, under the assumption that $\neg q$, the proposition that $\neg p$ can be derived.

When we look at the above representation of the proof, we see very clearly that there is a difference between line 3 and line 4. At line 3, we find the simulative assertion of the consequent in the scope of the assumption corresponding to the antecedent. That this assertion is fictitious is shown, again, by placement in the appropriate column. At line 4, however, we find the conditional, which *is* asserted. The conditional is not in the scope of the supposition; but it holds because, and to the extent that, the consequent is assertible within the scope of the supposition.

Line 4 corresponds to what I call the 'post-simulative mode': we exploit the simulation effected at the previous level (lines 2 and 3) to say something about the imaginary situation envisaged in (2). During the simulation, we (non-assertively) say things within the scope of the supposition; after the simulation, we are in a position to assert *that* the supposition in question supports the consequent. What we say at the post-simulative level we do not say from within the simulation, but from the outside, as it were. The post-simulative mode implies taking a reflective stance toward the simulation which it presupposes.

3.4 The Post-Simulative Mode

The distinction between the exercise of simulation and its post-simulative exploitation goes some way toward explaining the otherwise puzzling fact that conditionals emerge late in children's development (in the second half of the third year), later than morphosyntactically similar sentences. Presumably, the reason for that is semantic: conditionals are distinguished from 'when'-sentences, for example, by the fact that they talk about *imaginary* situations; hence they are cognitively more complex than formally similar types of sentence used to talk about the actual world. However, Bowerman has argued against that explanation, citing evidence to the effect that "well before children produce conditionals they appear to be not only capable of entertaining situations contrary to reality but also in some cases of marking them as counterfactual" (Bowerman, 1986, pp. 290–291). Hence the puzzle and Bowerman's aporetic conclusion: "These negative outcomes suggest that further work is needed on our theoretical assumptions about what determines timing of acquisition" (Bowerman, 1986, p. 304).

Bowerman is certainly right, but I think the cognitive complexity hypothesis should not be given up too hastily. As I suggested above, it is one thing to be able to imagine counterfactual situations and to engage into overt pretense; it is quite another to be able to state, from the outside, objective facts concerning the imaginary situations thus evoked. If I am right, there are two types of fact regarding imaginary situations: (i) facts that hold *within* the situations in question, and that can only be simulatively asserted; and (ii) objective facts *about* those situations, to the effect that they support such and such facts of the first type. Those objective facts can be asserted *tout court*, and they are typically expressed by means of conditionals. Conditionals, therefore, are not equivalent to Ducrot-Mackie pairs.

To illustrate the distinction between the two sorts of fact, let us consider a much simpler type of case, involving only real situations. As John Perry (1992) pointed out, if I say or think 'It is raining', my utterance or thought concerns the place where I am, but the place in question is not represented explicitly (reflectively) in the utterance or thought. The representation that it is raining concerns that particular place because it is the place in which the representation is tokened. In contrast, if I say 'It is raining here' or 'It's raining in Paris', the place where it is raining is articulated *in* the representation. The difference is not merely a difference in wording. The simple assertion that it is raining states a simpler fact (a fact with fewer constituents); that fact, however, is 'relativized' to a particular context, namely to the place where the speaker is located. (On relativization, see Barwise, 1989, pp. 253–254; Recanati, 1999, pp. 127–129). In the other case, when I say 'It is raining here' or 'It's raining in Paris', the place is an explicit constituent of the fact which is stated, but that fact is no longer relativized to the context in question. In other words, what changes from one utterance or thought to the next is both the fact that is explicitly stated and the context relative to which the utterance or thought is interpreted. In Recanati (1997), I analyzed the latter difference as follows:

> When I say 'In Paris, it is raining', this makes sense only insofar as the location Paris is virtually contrasted with some other location, such as London or the country. This is a point which European 'structuralism' has much insisted on: whatever is singled out in speech is extracted from a 'paradigm' or contrastive set. If no other location was implicitly considered, the specification of the location would play no role and could be omitted. The fact that the location is singled out shows that the situation with respect to which the locationally specific representation is interpreted includes the mentioned location *and others from the same paradigm*. The situation might be, for example, the Continent of Europe (which contains Paris, Rome, Vienna, etc.). But the locationally non-specific 'It is raining' can be interpreted with respect to a smaller situation, viz. Paris itself (to the *exclusion* of any other location). (Recanati, 1997, pp. 54–55)

In that sort of example, we can say that the simple representation 'It is raining' is asserted *within* a particular context or situation, namely, the situation which it concerns; while the more complex representation 'It is raining here' or 'It is raining in Paris' is *about* that situation but is not asserted *within* it. In the more complex utterance or thought, the place where it is raining is considered from the outside and explicitly represented. I think we find the same contrast between Ducrot-Mackie pairs and the corresponding conditionals, except that the situation at issue is imaginary rather than real. In a Ducrot-Mackie pair, the 'consequent' (the second member of the pair) is asserted *within* the supposition made by the 'antecedent' (the first member); but a conditional asserts *that* the imaginary situation corresponding to the antecedent supports the consequent.

Similarly, there is a striking contrast between, for example, the pretended assertions made by the story-teller, *concerning* some imaginary situation, and (serious) metarepresentational assertions *about* the story and the imaginary situation it depicts. The former do not talk about the actual world but are asserted within a context of mental simulation; the latter do talk about the actual world, by explicitly characterizing the imaginary situation depicted by the story. Thus when I say 'In the film,

Robin Hood meets Sherlock Holmes', I talk about the actual world and an aspect of it: the film that I saw yesterday. It is an objective fact concerning the actual world that, in the film I saw yesterday, Robin Hood meets (met) Sherlock Holmes. To be sure, the fact that Robin Hood met Sherlock Holmes is only a fact in a certain fictional world, but that is not the fact which the metarepresentation states: what the metarepresentation says is that *that fact holds in the world pictured by the film* – and that is a different fact from the fictitious fact in question.

Using that distinction we can reanalyze the simulative solution to the 'phone number problem' (§3.1). We must not conflate the metarepresentations (1 and 2 below) and the associated assumptions (3 and 4). In solving the phone number problem by the simulation method, we start from the metarepresentations (1) and (2), which are our premises; by simulatively projecting ourselves into Peter's shoes, we assume the ascribed beliefs (auxiliary premises 3 and 4); having done so, we can reason within that assumption and derive (5); then we discharge the assumption and assert the metarepresentation (6), which results from re-embedding (or, as I once put it, 'retrojecting') (5) into the original matrix.

	Assertion	Assumption	
(1)	Peter believes that John's number = 325-248		(Premiss)
(2)	Peter believes that John's number = Mary's number		(Premiss)
(3)		John's number = 325-248	([1], Projection)
(4)		John's number = Mary's number	([2], Projection)
(5)		Mary's number = 325-248.	([3], [4], Symmetry and Transitivity of =)
(6)	Peter believes that Mary's number = 325-248		([5], Retrojection)

There is a clear difference between the pretend assertion (5) and the metarepresentation (6), much as there was a difference between the pretend assertion of the consequent and the assertion of the conditional in the instance of Conditional proof discussed above (§3.3). The difference between (5) and (6) is the same as the difference between (1) and (3) and between (2) and (4): it is a difference between a metarepresentation *about* a 'belief world' and a simulated assertion made 'from within' a belief world which we assume.

That is not to deny that there is a close connection between simulation and metarepresentation; there is indeed, but the simulation theory much overstates it. Simulative assertions such as 'On serait un roi et une reine' *are not metarepresentations at all* – they are primary representations, much like a film or a novel consists of primary representations of (non-actual) facts. Similarly for irony, free indirect speech, and so forth. In such cases, the speaker (thinker) is not making a serious assertion, but only pretending. In metarepresentations something quite different happens: we seriously characterize the actual world by mentioning facts which hold in imaginary situations. Here is the reason that our representations concern the actual world: The imaginary situations we are talking about are related to things in the actual world (and represented as such), so that to say something about the imaginary situations in question is to say something about the actual world. Thus to say something about what happens to Holmes (in such and such an imaginary situation) is to say something about a real-world object, namely, the novel in which that situation is described. It is that fundamental insight which modal theories capture when they make the truth-value of the metarepresentation at a given circumstance c depend upon the truth-value of the object-representation at a distinct circumstance c' appropriately related to c.

4. Representing Metarepresentations

4.1 Facts Concerning Situations

If what I have said so far is correct, there are two main distinctions which a proper theory of metarepresentations must draw. First, there is a distinction between saying something about a situation and saying something within (or better, with respect to) a situation. That distinction is illustrated by the contrast between 'It's raining' (said at location l) and 'It's raining at l'. Second, there is a distinction between two sorts of situation: real situations (such as the place l in the above example), and imaginary situations, such as those described by novels, or those which correspond to the antecedent of conditionals. Conditionals and metarepresentations are statements *about* imaginary situations; while simulative assertions are statements made *with respect to* some imaginary situation.

In standard semantic theories, the first distinction cannot be represented. 'It's raining' and 'It's raining at l' are taken to express the same proposition, consisting of a two-place relation *Rain* (t, p) and a sequence of two arguments: a time and a place. The place is not articulated at all in the sentence, while the time is (via the present tense); despite this differ-ence, the content of the utterance is said to be the same in both cases – only the wording is supposed to change.

Dissatisfied with this approach, we can give up standard semantics and opt for the non-standard variety that Barwise and Etchemendy call 'Austinian semantics' (Austin, 1971; Barwise & Etchemendy, 1987; Re-canati, 1996; 1997; 1999). The basic idea is that each statement is inter-preted with respect to a particular situation which it 'concerns'. The complete content of an utterance, therefore, is an 'Austinian proposition' consisting of two components: the fact which the utterance explicitly states, and the situation which that fact concerns.

Facts, or states of affairs, are structured entities (consisting of an n-place relation, a sequence of appropriate arguments, and a polarity) very much like propositions in the Russell-Kaplan sense; in what follows they will be represented by standard predicate-calculus formulas, or by nat-ural language sentences. In general at least, the situation which the ut-terance concerns is not a constituent of the fact which it states; but it is a constituent of the global, Austinian proposition. At the Austinian prop-osition level, the fact which the utterance states is presented as 'holding in' the situation which it concerns. In this framework 'It's raining' is rep-resented as follows:

(28)   [Paris] $\models$ << It's raining >>

On the left-hand-side, in square brackets, we find the situation (here a location, namely, Paris) that the utterance concerns. On the right-hand-side, within double angle brackets, we find the fact that the utterance explicitly states, which does not contain that situation as constituent. That fact can be analyzed as involving a 1-place relation (*Rain*, con-strued as a property of times) and an appropriate argument (the present time).

In Austinian semantics, a representation is true if and only if the fact it states holds in the situation the representation concerns. Consider the canonical example (from Barwise & Etchemendy, 1987, pp. 121–122). Looking at a poker game, I say 'Claire has the ace of hearts'. My utterance expresses the fact that Claire has the ace of hearts, and the situation it concerns is the poker game I am watching. For the utterance to be true, it is not sufficient if the fact it expresses obtains; that fact must hold *in the situation the utterance concerns*, that is, in the poker game in question. As Barwise and Etchemendy point out, if I am mistaken and Claire is not among the players of the game, my utterance is not true – even if Claire is playing poker in some other part of the city and has the ace of hearts there. It is true only if Claire has the ace of hearts *in that poker game*. Similarly, the utterance 'It is raining', uttered with respect to a certain location, is true if and only if it is raining *at that location*.

Two cognitive mechanisms at work in discourse can be defined in this framework: *Reflection* and *Projection* (Recanati, 1997). If the subject comes to *reflect on* the situation which the representation concerns and makes it explicit, the representation, hence the fact which it expresses or articulates, becomes more complex. The simple representation 'It's raining' is replaced by 'It is raining here' or 'It is raining in Paris', which expresses a fact involving the *two-place* relation $Rain\ (t,\ p)$ between times and places. As I said above, when the situation is made explicit in this way, generally by contrast with other possible situations, the situation which the utterance concerns (i.e., that which figures in the left-hand side of the Austinian proposition) is correspondingly enlarged. Thus the subject who says 'Its raining in Paris' or 'It's raining here' normally has in mind other locations (e.g., other capitals of Europe), and is attempting to state a fact concerning not just Paris, but, more globally, the meteorological situation in, for example, continental Europe. The new utterance can be represented as

(29)   [Europe] $\vDash$ << It's raining in Paris >>

That is a *minimal* reflection of (28): the only difference between (28) and (29) is that the situation which the representation in (28) concerns is a constituent of the fact stated by the representation in (29), which representation therefore concerns a larger situation. But reflections need not be minimal. Reflection operates whenever we start with a representation 'concerning' a certain situation, for example, a situation given in the context, and make that situation explicit in a second representation which is 'about' it but 'concerns' a larger situation. An example of (non-minimal) reflection is provided in the following discourse:

(30)   Look, it's raining! It's always like that in this city ...

The first utterance of (30) states a fact concerning the location where the utterance is situated (viz., Paris); the second utterance is explicitly about that location, and concerns a larger situation (one that includes Paris and the other locations with which it is implicitly contrasted).

Instead of representing minimal reflections by increasing the arity of the relation, we can leave the relation as it was prior to Reflection and simply copy the pre-reflective Austinian proposition into the right-hand-side of the post-reflective Austinian proposition:

(29*)   [Europe] $\vDash$ << Paris $\vDash$ << It's raining >> >>

I find that notation more perspicuous and I will use it in what follows.

Projection is very similar to Reflection, except that it operates in the other direction. A situation is first mentioned (i.e., it is a constituent of some fact which is stated); the speaker then 'projects herself into that situation' or assumes it, and states something with respect to that situation, as if it were given in the external context (while it is only given 'in the discourse'). This phenomenon is illustrated by the following example:

(31)   Berkeley is a nice place. There are bookstores and
         coffee shops everywhere.

In the second utterance ('There are bookstores and coffee shops everywhere') the quantifier 'everywhere' ranges over locations in Berkeley; yet Berkeley is not represented in the utterance – it is not a constituent of the fact which the utterance states. Nor is Berkeley 'contextually given' in the sense in which Paris was in the previous example: I assume that the above discourse does not take place *in* Berkeley but, say, in London. Berkeley is represented in the *previous* utterance, however, and this enables it to be used as the situation 'with respect to which' the second utterance is interpreted. In Recanati (1997), I analyzed the example as follows:

> The first sentence of (31) talks directly about Berkeley considered as an object: it states a fact of which Berkeley is a constituent. But the second sentence of (31) does not talk about Berkeley in this manner. The second sentence of (31) expresses a fact internal to Berkeley rather than a fact 'about' Berkeley in the sense of including Berkeley as a constituent. The second sentence of (31) is interpreted with respect to the Berkeley situation without mentioning that situation. That is possible because the Berkeley situation has already been mentioned – in the first sentence. This is a standard instance of projection. (Recanati, 1997, p. 61)

Because Projection operates, the two sentences of (31) do not concern the same situation. The first sentence, which expresses a fact containing Berkeley as a constituent, concerns a situation 'larger than' the Berkeley situation itself; it may concern, for example, the United States (in which there are many cities, not all of which are nice by European standards), or California, or perhaps the set of cities with big universities ... What matters is the contrast with the second utterance, which concerns a much smaller situation: Berkeley itself. It is that smaller situation which provides the domain for the quantifier 'Everywhere'. Proposition (31) can therefore be represented thus:

(31a)   [USA] ⊨ << Berkeley is a nice place >>

(31b)   [Berkeley] ⊨ << There are coffee shops everywhere >>

4.2 Imaginary Situations

Insofar as they 'contain' facts (the facts which hold in them), situations can be, and often are, represented as sets of facts. There is a problem with that representation, however. If situations are represented as sets of facts, the support relation between situations and facts will be represented in terms of set membership; but a set has its members essentially, and this will prevent us from representing the contingency of the support relation.[22]

It is presumably a contingent fact that it is raining in Chicago. That contingency will not be captured if the set of facts associated with a situation (e.g., the Chicago situation) is considered as definitive of that situation. If a situation *is* the set of facts it supports, then it cannot be a contingent fact that a situation supports (contains) such and such a fact. That is why we must distinguish situations from the sets of facts they determine. Situations determine sets of facts *only relative to a world*. Thus, in the actual world, it is raining in Chicago. But the Chicago situation might have been different – it might have contained different facts.

On the present view, a world w consists of a domain of entities, Dom (w); and a function W from entities in that domain to sets of facts concerning those entities. The set of facts associated with a situation $s \in$ Dom (w) is the set $W(s)$. Different worlds can associate different sets of facts with the same situations if the situations in question are in the domains of those worlds. A situation s supports an atomic fact σ with respect to a world w if and only if that fact belongs to $W(s)$. Since the support relation turns out to be relative to a world, instead of '$s \models \sigma$' we must write:

$$s \models_w \sigma$$

By default – in the absence of an explicit subscript – the support relation will be interpreted as relative to @, the actual world.

As I suggested above, for a representation to be de-coupled is for it to be relative to an imaginary situation. But what is an imaginary situation? Is it a situation that is not in the domain of @? Certainly not. Hypothetical situations are typical cases of imaginary situation, yet they may well belong to Dom (@). Suppose I utter (32):

(32)　　If John went to Lyons, he took the 1:30 train

I am considering a hypothetical situation, namely, a situation in which John went to Lyons. Suppose that John indeed went to Lyons. Then the hypothetical situation turns out to be in the domain of @ (in the sense that @ associates a set of facts with that situation). Yet it still is an hypothetical (hence an imaginary) situation. So we cannot define an imaginary situation as a situation that does not belong to the domain of @.

Situations can be in the domain of several worlds; a situation does not essentially belong to the domain of this or that world. When we mention a situation as supporting a certain fact, however, the support relation *is* relative to a world. I therefore suggest the following definition: An imaginary situation is a situation that is presented as supporting a certain fact *with respect to a world w different from* @.

The definition I have just given raises a problem. What is the possible world at issue in conditionals? According to Stalnaker, it is "that world in which the antecedent is true which is most similar, in relevant respects, to the actual world" (Stalnaker, 1999, p. 68). But we run into a difficulty if we so characterize the world w with respect to which the imaginary situation denoted by the antecedent of a conditional is presented as supporting the fact expressed by the consequent. Whenever the antecedent of an indicative conditional turns out to be true, the world w in question turns out to be identical to @: for example, if John actually went to Lyons, then the actual world *is* that world in which the antecedent of (32) is true which is most similar to the actual world. But if that is so, then we cannot appeal to the difference between @ and w to capture the intuitive distinction between real situations and hypothetical situations. In the described circumstances, the hypothetical situation in which John went to Lyons would turn out to be a real situation by the above definition.

The above definition of imaginary situations could perhaps be defended by pointing out that it brings 'modes of presentation' into the picture. Even if the antecedent of an indicative conditional turns out to be true, still the hypothetical situation denoted by that antecedent is not 'presented as' supporting the consequent *with respect to* @, but with respect to a world w, *which may, but need not, be identical to* @. The hypothetical situation is hypothetical precisely because one does not know whether or not it is actual. So one appeals to a world w possibly distinct from @, and one says that, with respect to that world, the situation denoted by the antecedent supports the consequent. That world may turn out to be the actual world, but it is not presented as such.

Introducing modes of presentation for worlds would hopelessly complicate an already complicated picture, however. A much simpler solution consists in acknowledging that w need be not a unique world but may be a set of worlds. On this view, the hypothetical situation corresponding to the antecedent is said, by the conditional, to support the consequent with respect to a class of worlds,[23] namely, those worlds in which the antecedent is true which are relevantly similar to the actual world. The set of worlds in question may turn out to contain the actual world (if the antecedent turns out to be true simpliciter), but it contains other worlds as well. Thus we can stick to our definition of an imaginary situation, reformulated as follows: An imaginary situation is a situation that is presented as supporting a certain fact with respect to a world w different from @, or with respect to a class of worlds containing a world w different from @.

We are now in a position to analyze mental simulation. There is mental simulation whenever a representation *concerns* an imaginary situation, as in (33):

(33) $[s] \vDash_w \sigma$

In (33), the subject imagines some aspect or portion of a world w distinct from the actual world. She characterizes the imaginary situation s, thus envisaged, as supporting the fact that σ. This representation fits all the instances of mental simulation we have mentioned: children's games of make-believe, fiction, irony, supposition, and so forth.

In discussing the simulation theory of conditionals, I mentioned that an act of mental simulation can set up a context for other acts of mental simulation within its scope. That is what happens in Ducrot-Mackie pairs:

Suppose he comes back tonight

He will be tired

We won't worry him by mentioning the fire

'He will be tired' and 'We won't worry him by mentioning the fire' characterize the hypothetical (imaginary) situation in which he comes back tonight. In the initial act of 'supposing', the subject pretends that the world is as supposed; it is the imaginary world w thus deployed through the pretense that indexes the support relations in the subsequent Austinian propositions.

$$[s] \models_w << \text{He will be tired} >>$$

$$[s] \models_w << \text{We won't worry him by mentioning the fire} >>$$

Note that the first utterance, 'Suppose he comes back tonight,' is a metarepresentation (with directive illocutionary force); hence the act of mental simulation it initiates may be construed as achieved through some form of Projection. However, the example is too complex and I will not analyze it here. Instead, I will consider a simpler example of Projection involving imaginary situations.

In Recanati (1997), I gave the following examples of Projection involving imaginary situations:

(34)   John is totally paranoid. Everybody spies on him or wants to kill him, including his own mother.

(35)   I did not know you were so much interested in knights. You should read *A Connecticut Yankee in King Arthur's Court*, by Mark Twain. There are a lot of knights.

In (34), the first utterance ('John is totally paranoid') concerns a real situation s'. That situation s' is presented as supporting << John is paranoid >>. Now a paranoid is someone who believes himself to be in a certain type of situation. Let us call the situation John believes himself to be in s. That situation is an aspect of his 'belief world', bw. It supports certain 'facts' in John's belief world, but those need not be facts in the actual world. Now the second sentence of (34) concerns that imaginary situation *s*. The speaker does not seriously assert that everybody spies John or wants to kill him: she expects the hearer to understand that fact as holding in John's belief world, more specifically in the imaginary situation *s* John believes himself to be in. Such a shift in point of view is constitutive of 'free indirect speech', of which (34) is a typical instance. Free indirect speech generally involves an operation of Projection: an imaginary situation is first mentioned, then assumed.

(34a) $[s']$ $\models_@$ << John is paranoid >>

(34b) $[s]$ $\models_{bw}$ << Everybody spies on him, etc. >>

The other example is similar. In the second sentence of (35), Twain's fiction (a portion of the actual world) is mentioned. Now Twain's fiction has a certain content, that is, it describes a certain situation as supporting certain facts. The situation in question is imaginary in the sense that the facts it is presented as supporting only hold in the 'world' of the fiction. Now the third sentence of (35) is directly interpreted with respect to that imaginary situation. It is in that situation that there are a lot of knights. This is similar to the Berkeley example (4.1), except that the situation which is assumed is an imaginary situation instead of a real one.

§4.3 The Proper Treatment of Metarepresentations

The representations from which Projection operates in the last two examples are not 'metarepresentations' in the sense in which I have been using this term in this paper (§1.3). They are about 'representations', namely, John's belief system or Twain's book, both of which have a certain content; but they are not metarepresentations because the content of the representations they are about is not actually displayed. We can, however, replace the representations from which Projection operates, in those examples, by genuine metarepresentations:

(36)   *John believes that he is being persecuted.* Everybody spies on him and even his mother wants to kill him.

(37)   *In Twain's book, a nineteenth-century man finds himself in King Arthur's England.* There are a lot of knights and funny medieval things.

In those examples, the first sentence (italicized) is a metarepresentation. Now most philosophers and linguists would analyze the second sentence in (37) as an *elliptical* metarepresentation. Once the allegedly elided material has been restored, (37) becomes:

(37*)   In Twain's book, a nineteenth-century man finds himself in King Arthur's England. *In that book* there are a lot of knights and funny medieval things.

It is clear, however, that the second sentence of (36) is an instance of 'free' indirect speech; now free indirect speech is not 'elliptical' indirect speech, and it would be a mistake to construe (36) as merely an elliptical version of

(36*)   John believes that he is being persecuted. *He believes that* every-
              body spies on him and *that* even his mother wants to kill him.

Similarly, (37) is not merely an elliptical version of (37*). There is a se-mantic difference between the initial metarepresentation in both exam-ples and the pretend assertion that follows. The pretend assertion is no more an elliptical metarepresentation than the metarepresentation is a pretend assertion. The metarepresentation mentions some imaginary situation (viz., that described in Twain's book, or that John believes him-self to be in); that situation is simulatively assumed in the pretend as-sertion that follows.

To account for the difference between the metarepresentation and the pretend assertion that follows, we must apply the distinction be-tween 'concerning' and 'being about' to the special case of imaginary sit-uations. Like all representations, a metarepresentation states a fact con-cerning a situation. The situation the metarepresentation concerns is a real situation involving, for example, a certain book or the mental states of a certain person; and the fact it states is about an imaginary situation, namely, that which the book or the beliefs describe. The metarepresen-tation 'John believes that he is being persecuted' therefore expresses the Austinian proposition:

$$[s'] \vDash_@ << s \vDash_{bw} \text{John is being persecuted} >>$$

where s' is the real situation which the metarepresentation concerns (a situation involving John and his beliefs); and s is the imaginary situation John believes himself to be in. On this analysis, a metarepresentation is not an instance of mental simulation, for the situation that it concerns (in this example at least) is a real-world situation, not an imaginary sit-uation. The imaginary situation s is mentioned *in* the metarepresenta-tion, but it is not that situation which the metarepresentation concerns. That is why the metarepresentation gives rise to a serious assertion, rather than a pretend assertion. In (36), however, the metarepresentation is followed by a pretend assertion concerning the imaginary situation which the metarepresentation mentions. Proposition (36) can therefore be represented as:

(36a) $[s'] \vDash_@ << s \vDash_{bw} \text{John is being persecuted} >>$

(36b) $[s] \vDash_{bw} << \text{Everybody spies on him, etc.} >>$

The same sort of analysis can be offered for (37). The initial metarepre-sentation 'In Twain's book, a nineteen-century man finds himself in King

Arthur's England' mentions the situation described in Twain's book as supporting the fact that a nineteen-century man finds himself in King Arthur's England. It is that imaginary situation, assumed through Projection, which the second utterance of (37) concerns.

On this analysis, a metarepresentation states a fact *about* the imaginary situation described by some representation r (a film, a book, a belief, a belief system, a picture, or whatnot); namely the fact that that situation supports a further fact σ. Hence there are three levels of semantic analysis for metarepresentations. First there is a distinction between (i) the fact σ which the imaginary situation is said to support, and (ii) the fact *that* the imaginary situation supports σ. The fact (ii) is the fact which the metarepresentation states, while (i) is a fact internal to the situation which the object-representation represents. Next there is the distinction between (ii), the fact which the metarepresentation states, and (iii), the complete Austinian proposition which the metarepresentation expresses, to the effect that the real situation that the metarepresentation concerns supports the fact (ii).

The general structure of a metarepresentation dS is given in the formula:

$$[s'] \vDash_{@} << F(r) \vDash_{w} \sigma >>$$

The material within angle brackets corresponds to the fact which the metarepresentation states, that is, to its propositional content in the traditional sense. '$F(r) \vDash_{w} \ldots$' is the operator corresponding to the metarepresentational prefix d ('in the film', 'John believes that', etc.), and σ is the content of the sentence S. In this formula 'F' is a function from representations to the situations they describe; '$F(r)$' thus denotes the situation which the object-representation r describes.

In this framework, many pressing questions arise. In particular, we must say what is it for a situation s' to support *the fact that another situation s supports* σ. Without going into the details, my answer to that question is the following. For s' to support the fact that $s \vDash \sigma$, two conditions must be satisfied: (i) s must be accessible from s', and (ii) s must support σ. The accessibility condition has already been illustrated in connection with the poker game example (§4.1). Even if it is a fact that Claire has a good hand (assuming that she is presently playing cards somewhere), still that fact does not hold in the poker game we are watching, for Claire is nowhere to be found in that situation. (We suppose that she is playing somewhere else.) We can construe Claire herself as a situation supporting the 0-adic fact of having a good hand: Claire $\vDash$ << has-a-good-hand >>. It is not the case that the poker game situation we are watching supports the complex fact << Claire $\vDash$ << has-a-good-hand >> >> because the "situation Claire" is not accessible from that poker game situation.

When, as in the poker-game example, a situation is, or corresponds to, a spatio-temporal region in which there are objects having properties and standing in relations to other objects, both the locations included in the region and the objects it contains are accessible – indeed, whatever is 'in' a situation is accessible from it. But that is not the only form of accessibility we must consider. In the sort of case we are most concerned with, a situation s is accessible from a situation s' even though s is not literally 'in' s'. Indeed, *s and s' do not even belong to the same world.*

In the actual world there are entities (e.g., books, utterances, pictures, or mental states) that have content. Their having the content which they have is a contingent property of these entities. Through their contents, the entities in question give us access to imaginary situations (i.e., they project possible worlds with respect to which the situations which they depict support certain facts). Thus the Sherlock Holmes stories depict certain situations which support certain facts in the 'fictional world' imagined by Conan Doyle. In this type of case a real-world situation s' (involving a certain book) gives us access to an imaginary situation s (that which is depicted in the book) – a situation which belongs to a possible world (or a set of possible worlds) distinct from the actual world. Since, in the possible worlds in question, s supports the fact that σ, and s is accessible from s', the real-world situation s' actually supports the fact that (in those possible worlds) s supports σ.

Another pressing question regards conditionals. I have emphasized the similarity between conditionals and metarepresentations. Conditionals, too, mention imaginary situations while concerning real situations. The difference seems to be that a conditional locates the imaginary situation it talks about via the condition that it supports such and such a fact (corresponding to the antecedent), while a metarepresentation presents the situation it talks about as the situation described by some representation r. How much of a difference is that? Perhaps a conditional is a sort of self-referential metarepresentation, in which the representation r is the act of mental simulation which the antecedent invites the interpreter to perform. Even if we take this approach, however, we will have to account for the following datum: the representation r is explicitly mentioned in the metarepresentation – it is a constituent of the fact which the metarepresentation states – while the act of simulation to which the antecedent of the conditional invites the interpreter is not explicitly mentioned; it may be involved, but only at the character level – not at the level of content. That observation may lead us to modify the above formula to make clear that r is a genuine constituent of the fact stated by the metarepresentation. For the time being, however, I will be content with the tentative analysis encapsulated in the formula.

To conclude, let us return to the issue of iconicity. A metarepresentation mentions a representation *r*, and asserts something about it: that it has such and such a content (i.e., that the situation it represents supports such and such facts). Now that content is *displayed*, it is not named or otherwise designated. That feature of iconicity which metarepresentations exhibit must be accounted for, and I think it can be accounted for in terms of a corresponding feature of representations.

Representations are real world items which 'represent' the world as being thus and so. (Remember Pascal's famous dictum: "L'univers me comprend, mais je le comprends.") Now to understand a representation, that is, to access its content, there is no other way than simulation: we understand a representation *r* as meaning that *p* if and only if we are able to think: '*p*. That is how the world is according to *r*'. That is, we must be able to *entertain* the content of *r*, and that means viewing (or pretending to view) things in the way *r* states them to be. An organism that is capable of understanding representations is therefore an organism that is capable of simulation. That is true for all representations, be they books, paintings, photographs, utterances, or beliefs and other mental states: to ascribe a content to such items is to simulatively entertain a certain representation and to assertively hold: that is how *r* represents things.[24] There simply is no other way of understanding a representation. The capacity of understanding representations, therefore, is a capacity for 're-constructive simulation' (Ryle, 1933, pp. 73–74).

The iconicity of metarepresentations is a feature that they possess because the content of a representation can only be accessed via simulation. Since a metarepresentation says what the content of a representation *r* is, it can only display that content, that is, simulate *r*, by actually representing the world as *r* itself represents it to be. But it does so within the scope of an assertion about *r*. Hence a metarepresentation is not an assertion in the scope of an act of simulation, as the simulation theory claims; rather, it is an act of simulation in the scope of a serious assertion.

Notes

1 This formulation is adapted from Russell (1940), p. 260.
2 Actually we need even more levels than that. Frege's senses can be interpreted in two different ways: as unstructured 'intensions', in the sense of contemporary model-theoretic semantics, or in the sense of 'structured contents'. As Cresswell (1985) has shown, structured contents themselves can be analyzed as structures made up of intensions. In what follows I will use 'content' in the sense of 'structured content'.
3 In "Opacity," Kaplan stresses the similarities between Frege's and Quine's respective strategies (Kaplan, 1986).

4 This gives some support to Arthur Prior's claim that "nothing could be more misleading and erroneous than to treat sentences containing … other sentences in quotations-marks as a paradigm case to which the things that we are really interested in (thinking that, fearing that, bringing it about that) should be assimilated" (Prior, 1971, p. 61).

5 That, of course, is controversial. On the standard construal, 'that'-clauses are semantically complex: 'that' has a semantic value, the embedded sentence has a semantic value, and the semantic value of the complex (the 'that'-clause) is determined by the semantic values of its constituents. On this view, the embedded sentence plays a fully semantic role. But this view comports badly with the claim that 'that'-clauses are *names* (genuine singular terms). For genuine singular terms are semantically simple: they have their referent directly assigned by a semantic rule such as '*Nixon* refers to Nixon' or '*I* refers to the speaker' or '*that* refers to whatever the speaker is demonstrating'. If an expression is semantically complex, then arguably it is not a name but a quantifier (Neale, 1993; see also Lepore & Ludwig, forthcoming, where it is shown that complex demonstratives are best treated as restricted existential quantifiers in which a demonstrative appears in the nominal restriction). If we really want to treat 'that'-clauses as names, we have to deny their semantic complexity and ascribe them a purely syntactical complexity. That is the view to which I alluded in the text: 'that'-clauses consist of the word 'that' and a sentence, but the sentence plays only a presemantic role, like the demonstration which accompanies a demonstrative.

6 The two requirements are reconciled if, following Davidson (1984), we consider that there are two sentences instead of one: the first sentence ('John believes that') expresses the relation and consists of a two-place predicate flanked by two terms; the second sentence ('Peter likes grass') expresses a proposition, namely, a proposition to which the first sentence refers. But I take it as obvious that there is a *single* sentence — that is precisely where the difficulty comes from. Evans once criticized Russell for his 'butchering' of surface syntax; I find that Davidson fares no better than Russell on this score.

7 In this paragraph I rely on Orenstein (forthcoming).

8 This will be qualified below, after the distinction between first-order and higher-order predicates has been introduced.

9 On this analysis 'believes' is a two-place predicate with heterogeneous arguments. A similar analysis could be provided for predicates like 'find' in constructions such as 'I found him great'. The verb in this construction expresses a three-place predicate with two individuals and a predicate as arguments.

10 When we say that two expressions (e.g., 'Tegucigalpa' and 'the Capital of Honduras') 'have the same extension', what we mean is that they have the same extension *in the current circumstance*, that is, at the present time and in the actual world. Now the prefix in a metarepresentation arguably indicates that the internal sentence — the sentence which follows the prefix — must be evaluated with respect to a circumstance c' (e.g., John's 'belief world') distinct from the current circumstance c in which the metarepresentation itself is being evaluated. Hence it is only normal that we cannot always substitute an expression for another one in the internal sentence, even though they have

the same extension *in the current circumstance*; for the current circumstance is irrelevant when we evaluate the internal sentence and the expressions it contains. Such failures are to be expected whenever a circumstantial shift occurs. For example, I cannot substitute 'Clinton' for 'the President of the United States' in a sentence like 'Some years ago the President of the United States was an actor', simply because the prefix 'Some years ago' relevantly shifts the circumstance, in such a way that the so-called identity 'Clinton = the President of the United States', which holds in the current circumstance, becomes irrelevant. On the other hand, if two expressions have the same content, they will have the same extension in *every* possible circumstance of evaluation and substitutability will thereby be guaranteed.

11 See Davies (1981), pp. 47–48; Neale (1990), pp. 125–128. Neale credits Cresswell (1975) for coining the label 'hyperintensional'. Note that I am using 'intensional' in the sense of 'non-extensional', while the authors I have just mentioned follow Carnap (1947) and use 'intensional' in a more restrictive manner: an intensional operator for them licenses intensional substitutions, hence a hyperintensional operator is, by definition, not intensional.

12 One possible reaction to this argument consists in rejecting it as flawed. Propositions (the contents of sentences in context) are not 'objects' — at least not on the operator analysis. To say that John believes that S is not to say that a certain 'object' (the proposition that S) has a certain 'property' (the property of being believed by John). Hence we cannot use the law that identical objects have all their properties in common to conclude, from the fact that the proposition that S is the same as the proposition that S', that John must believe that S' if he believes that S. Indeed we *know* that S and S' cannot be freely substituted under 'John believes that' even though they express the same proposition.

   That reaction rests on a serious mistake. As Prior pointed out, even if we do not reify propositions — even if we do not treat them as genuine objects — we can talk of propositional identity (Prior, 1971, pp. 53 ff.). Propositional identity may be construed as an operator rather than as a predicate in the logical sense. Thus we can use the dyadic operator I = 'the proposition that ... is identical to the proposition that ...'. That connective makes a sentence out of two sentences, and the resulting sentence is true whenever the constituent sentences have the same content. In terms of this operator, it will be possible to formulate laws of propositional identity similar to the ordinary laws of identity: *Every proposition is identical to itself* (that is, 'For every p, the proposition that p is identical to the proposition that p'), and *Identical propositions have all their properties in common* (that is, 'If the proposition that p is identical to the proposition that q, then δp if and only if δq'). The above argument against hyperintensionality will therefore be statable without begging the question against the operator analysis.

13 A suitably qualified version of the Principle of Substitutivity can be found in Marcus (1993), 108.

14 See, for example, Sperber & Wilson (1981, pp. 306–311); Ducrot (1984, pp. 210–213); Clark & Gerrig (1984); Walton (1990, pp. 222–224); Perrin (1996, chap. 5); Clark (1996, pp. 371 ff.).

15 Bally describes the conditional in French as the 'mood of potentiality', as opposed to the indicative, which is the mood of actuality (Bally, 1965, p. 49).
16 That phrase comes from Leslie (1987), but I use it freely here.
17 This example comes from Dinsmore (1991, p. 84 ff.). Dinsmore stresses the analogy between the simulative approach, inspired by Fauconnier's work on 'mental spaces' (Fauconnier 1985), and the use of assumptions in natural deduction.
18 See also Pratt, who describes the above type of reasoning as 'reasoning within the scope of an imagined cognitive predicament' (Pratt, 1990, p. 369).
19 Mackie (1973, p. 93); Ducrot (1972, p. 167–168). Similar theories of 'conditional assertion' can be found in Quine (1962, p. 12); von Wright (1963); and Belnap (1970). See also the 1971 symposium on Conditional assertion (with articles by D. Holdcroft and P. Long) in the *Proceedings of the Aristotelian Society*, Suppl. vol. 45, pp. 123–147.
20 Quine's position concerning indicative conditionals in natural language is different. The statement which is made 'under the supposition' is a genuine assertion, for Quine, just in case the antecedent is true. When the antecedent is false, "our conditional affirmation is as if it had never been made" (Quine, 1962, p. 12). Thus indicative conditionals with true antecedents are true or false, while indicative conditionals with false antecedents are neither true nor false.
21 Ducrot (1972, p. 180) mentions one such example, but he does not seem to realize that it raises a problem for the simulation theory strictly understood.
22 I owe this observation to R. Stalnaker.
23 The same move must be made with respect to metarepresentations. 'Belief worlds', 'fictional worlds', and so forth, cannot really be worlds because they are not sufficiently determinate: they too must ultimately be thought of as *sets* of worlds (see, e.g., Hintikka, 1973, p. 199; Ross, 1997, pp. 49–54).
24 Thus the possession of content may be considered as a 'secondary quality' of objects: for a real world object such as a film or a book to possess a 'content' is for it to possess the power to prompt us to (simulatively) entertain that content.

References

Austin, John (1971). Truth. In his *Philosophical papers* (2nd ed., pp. 117–133). Oxford: Clarendon Press. (Essay originally published 1950.)

Baldwin, Tom (1982). Prior and Davidson on indirect speech. *Philosophical Studies* 42, 255–282.

Bally, Charles (1965). *Linguistique générale et linguistique française* (4th ed.). Bern: Francke.

Barwise, Jon (1989). *The Situation in logic*. Stanford, CA: Center for the Study of Language and Information.

Barwise, Jon, & Etchemendy, John (1987). *The liar*. New York: Oxford University Press.

Barwise, Jon, & Perry, John (1981). Semantic innocence and uncompromising situations. *Midwest Studies in Philosophy 6*, 387–403.

Barwise, Jon, & Perry, John (1983). *Situations and attitudes*. Cambridge, MA: MIT Press.

Belnap, Nuel (1970). Conditional assertion and restricted quantification. *Noûs 4*, 1–12.

Bowerman, Melissa (1986). First steps in acquiring conditionals. In E. Traugott, A. Ter Meulen, J. Reilly, & C. Ferguson (Eds.), *On conditionals* (pp. 285–307). Cambridge: Cambridge University Press.

Carnap, Rudolf (1947). *Meaning and necessity.* Chicago: University of Chicago Press.

Clark, Herb (1996). *Using language*. Cambridge: Cambridge University Press.

Clark, Herb, & Gerrig, Richard (1984). On the pretense theory of irony. *Journal of Experimental Psychology: General 113*, 121–126.

Cresswell, Max (1975). Identity and intensional objects. *Philosophia 5*, 47–68.

Cresswell, Max (1985). *Structured meanings*. Cambridge, MA: MIT Press.

Crimmins, Mark, & Perry, John (1989). The prince and the phone booth. *Journal of Philosophy 86*, 685–711.

Davidson, Donald (1984). On saying that. In his *Inquiries into truth and interpretation* (pp. 93–108). Oxford: Clarendon Press. (Essay originally published 1968).

Davies, Martin (1981). *Meaning, quantification, necessity.* London: Routledge.

Dinsmore, John (1991). *Partitioned representations*. Dordrecht: Kluwer.

Ducrot, Oswald (1972). *Dire et ne pas dire*. Paris: Hermann.

Ducrot, Oswald (1984). *Le dire et le dit*. Paris: Minuit.

Fauconnier, Gilles (1985). *Mental spaces*. Cambridge, MA: MIT Press.

Frege, Gottlob (1956). The thought: A logical enquiry. (Trans. by A. and M. Quinton.) *Mind 65*, 289–311.

Gordon, Robert (1986). Folk psychology as simulation. *Mind and Language 1*, 158–171.

Hintikka, Jaakko (1962). *Knowledge and belief*. Ithaca: Cornell University Press.

Hintikka, Jaakko (1973). Grammar and logic: some borderline problems. In J. Hintikka, J. Moravcsik, & P. Suppes (Eds.), *Approaches to natural language* (pp. 197–214). Dordrecht: Kluwer.

Holdcroft, David (1971). Conditional assertion. *Aristotelian Society Proceedings, Supplementary Volume 45*, 123–139.

Kahneman, Daniel & Tversky, Amos (1982). The simulation heuristic. In D. Kahneman, P. Slovic, & A. Tversky (Eds.), *Judgment under uncertainty: Heuristics and biases* (pp. 201–207). Cambridge: Cambridge University Press.

Kaplan, David (1986). Opacity. In L. Hahn & P. A. Schilpp (Eds.), *The philosophy of W. V. Quine* (pp. 229–289). La Salle, IL: Open Court.

Kaplan, David (1989). Demonstratives. In J. Almog, H. Wettstein & J. Perry (Eds.), *Themes from Kaplan* (pp. 481–563). New York: Oxford University Press.

Lepore, Ernest & Ludwig, Kirk (forthcoming). Complex demonstratives.

Leslie, Alan (1987). Pretense and representation: The origins of "theory of mind." *Psychological Review 94*, 412–426.

Lewis, David (1986). *On the plurality of worlds*. Oxford: Blackwell.

Long, Peter (1971). Conditional assertion. *Aristotelian Society Proceedings, Supplementary Volume 45*, 141–147.

Mackie, John (1973). *Truth, probability, and paradox*. Oxford: Clarendon Press.

Marcus, Ruth (1993). *Modalities*. New York: Oxford University Press.

Moltmann, F. (1997). On the semantics of clausal complements. Unpublished manuscript.

Moltmann, F. (1998). Nonreferential complements and secondary objects. Unpublished manuscript.

Neale, Stephen (1990). *Descriptions*. Cambridge, MA: MIT Press.

Neale, Stephen (1993). Term limits. *Philosophical Perspectives 7*, 89–123.

Orenstein, Alex (forthcoming). Propositional attitudes without propositions. In P. Kotatko and A. Grayling (Eds.), *Meaning*. Oxford: Clarendon Press.

Perner, Josef (1991). *Understanding the representational mind*. Cambridge, MA: MIT Press.

Perrin, Laurent (1996). *L'ironie mise en trope*. Paris: Kimé.

Perry, John (1992). Thought without representation. In his *The problem of the essential indexical and other essays* (pp. 205–225). New York: Oxford University Press. (Essay originally published 1986.)

Pratt, Ian (1990). Psychological inference, rationality, closure. In P. Hanson (Ed.), *Information, language and cognition* (pp. 366–389). New York: Oxford University Press.

Prior, Arthur (1971). *Objects of thought*. Oxford: Clarendon Press.

Prior, Arthur (1976). Oratio Obliqua. In his *Papers in Logic and Ethics* (pp. 147–158). London: Duckworth. (Essay originally published 1963.)

Quine, Willard Van Orman (1951). *Mathematical logic* (2nd ed.). Cambridge, MA: Harvard University Press.

Quine, Willard Van Orman (1943). Notes on existence and necessity. *Journal of Philosophy 40*, 113–127.

Quine, Willard Van Orman (1960). *Word and object*. Cambridge, MA: MIT Press.

Quine, Willard Van Orman (1962). *Methods of logic* (2nd ed.). London: Routledge & Kegan Paul.

Ramsey, Frank (1990). *Philosophical papers*. Cambridge: Cambridge University Press.

Recanati, François (1996). Domains of discourse. *Linguistics and Philosophy 19*, 445–475.

Recanati, François (1997). The dynamics of situations. *European Review of Philosophy 2*, 41–75.

Recanati, François (1999). Situations and the structure of content. In K. Murasugi & R. Stainton (Eds.), *Philosophy and linguistics* (pp. 113–165). Boulder, CO: Westview.

Ross, Jeff (1997). *The semantics of media*. Dordrecht: Kluwer.

Rundle, Bede (1979). *Grammar in philosophy*. Oxford: Clarendon Press.

Russell, Bertrand (1905). On denoting. *Mind 14*, 479–493.

Russell, Bertrand (1918). Knowledge by acquaintance and knowledge by description. In his *Mysticism and logic and other essays* (pp. 209–232). London: Longmans, Green.

Russell, Bertrand (1940). *An inquiry into meaning and truth*. London: George Allen and Unwin.

Ryle, Gilbert (1971). Imaginary objects. In his *Collected Papers*: vol. 2, *Collected essays*,

1929–1968 (pp. 63–81). London: Hutchinson. (Essay originally published 1933.)

Sperber, Dan, & Wilson, Deirdre (1981). Irony and the use-mention distinction. In P. Cole (Ed.), *Radical pragmatics* (pp. 295–318). New York: Academic Press.

Stalnaker, Robert (1991). A theory of conditionals. In F. Jackson (Ed.), *Conditionals* (pp. 28–45). New York: Oxford University Press. (Essay originally published 1968.)

Stalnaker, Robert (1999). Indicative conditionals. In his *Context and Content* (pp. 63–77). Oxford: Oxford University Press. (Essay originally published 1975.)

Strawson, Peter (1977). *Logico-linguistic papers*. London: Methuen.

Walton, Kenneth (1990). *Mimesis as make-believe*. Cambridge, MA: Harvard University Press.

von Wright, Georg Henrik (1963). On conditionals. In his *Logical Studies* (pp. 127–165). London: Routledge & Kegan Paul.

Chapter 13

Social Externalism and Deference

Steven Davis

Consider the *de dicto* intentional states[1] of Ruth's believing arthritis is a painful disease and her believing that psoriasis is a painful disease.[2] Whatever we take these intentional states to be they are distinct. One way of marking the difference is to take them to have different intentional contents and the contents to have different constituents. The former has as its content that arthritis is a painful disease, while the latter has as its content that psoriasis is a painful disease. Furthermore, the content that arthritis is a painful disease contains the concepts *arthritis*, *being painful* and *disease*, while the content that psoriasis is a painful disease contains the same concepts, except that the concept *arthritis* is replaced with the concept *psoriasis*. We can regard the concepts that a content contains as playing a role in individuating that content. Hence, what marks the difference between the two contents and the intentional states that have them is that the former has the concept *arthritis*, while the latter has the concept *psoriasis*.

For an individual to have a concept F, is for him to have a *de dicto* intentional state that has a content that has the concept F as one of its constituents or to have the standing disposition to have such an intentional state. Hence, Ruth has the concept *arthritis*, since she believes that arthritis is a painful disease. An individual's *conception* of Fs is to be distinguished from the concept F that he possesses (Burge, 1993a, p. 316). An individual's conception of Fs is a weighted subset of the individual's set of beliefs about what he takes Fs to be.[3] There can be a gap between an individual's conception of Fs and his concept F, a gap that can arise in two ways. He might have a mistaken conception of what Fs are, and thus, a mistaken grasp of the concept F, or have an incomplete conception of Fs and thus, not have a complete understanding of the concept F. Ruth might believe that arthritis is a disease of the joints and that it can occur in the thighs, and thus, have a mistaken conception of the concept *arthritis* that she possesses. Or she might not believe that arthritis is a disease of the joints and thus, have an incomplete grasp of her concept *arthritis*.

Concepts are representational. The concept *F* cannot be this concept, if it is not of **Fs**. If there were a concept that did not apply to **Fs**, it could not be the concept *F*. Thus, it is necessary that the concept *F* apply to **Fs** (Burge, 1993a, p. 310). For example, the concept *arthritis* is not the concept *arthritis*, if it is not of arthritis. This principle about concepts also applies to vacuous concepts. The concept *unicorn* is not this concept if it does not apply to unicorns. Hence, a concept *F*'s applying to **Fs** does not imply that there are **Fs** (1993a, p. 310). It follows on this account of concepts that a sufficient condition for distinguishing between concepts is possible non-coextensiveness of the terms that express them. The concept *F* is identical to the concept *G* if it is possible that there are **Fs** that are not **Gs** or **Gs** that are not **Fs**. Since concepts are representational, so too are contents. The content that arthritis is a painful disease represents that arthritis is a painful disease and the content is true just in case it is true that arthritis is a painful disease. So in general we can say that the intentional state that *p* contains the representational content that *p* and the content that *p* is true just in case it is true that *p*. Just as possible non-co-extensiveness distinguishes concepts, possible non-equivalence is sufficient for distinguishing contents. The content that *p* is identical to the content that *q*, if it is possible that *p* and *q* have different truth values. Possible difference of truth value is not the only sufficient condition for distinguishing between intentional contents. Having different concepts as constituents is also sufficient for distinguishing them. The content that *p* is identical to the content that *q*, if the content that *p* contains a concept that the content that *q* does not contain, or the content that *q* contains a concept that the content that *p* does not contain. In turn, this gives us a sufficient condition for distinguishing intentional states. *A's Ø-ing that p* is identical to *A's Ø-ing that q*, if the content that *p* is identical to the content that *q*.[4]

The term 'representation', like 'statement' or 'belief', is ambiguous; it can be applied to a state, that is, to a representing, and to the content of the state. Thus, Ruth's believing that arthritis is a painful disease is a representing and thus, a representation; the content that arthritis is a painful disease is also a representation. In what follows I shall use 'representation' to apply to the content of a representing and use 'representing' to apply to intentional states that contain contents that are representations. Representings come in levels. Let us call Ruth's belief that arthritis is a painful disease, '*a first-level representing*' and the content that is a constituent of it, '*a first-level representation*'. A first-level representation is a content that does not represent a representing, and a first-level representing is a representing that has as a content a first-level representation. For there to be an intentional state that is a first-level representing, the intentional state need not have a content that represents that a subject has that intentional state. Thus, in believing that arthritis is a painful disease, Ruth need not believe that she has this belief. Ruth can, however, reflect on her belief. She can think to herself that she believes that arthritis is a painful disease. In so thinking, the content of Ruth's thought is that she believes that arthritis is a painful disease – that is, its content is a representation of another of her intentional states. Let us call the content of an intentional state that is a representation of another intentional state a *metarepresentation* and the intentional state that has as its content a metarepresentation a *metarepresenting*.[5]

What intentional states we have and what their nature is might seem to be a personal matter that is up to us. Our intentional states, one might think, are determined solely by our own internal physical states, including our dispositions to behave, the effect that stimuli have on us, our skills, capacities and abilities, all non-intentionally described. Contrary to this internalist view is the view that what is external to our inner states determines our intentional states and the concepts that constitute them. Burge's arguments for externalism come in two forms, one in which an account of a subject's intentional states is given by his physical environment and the other by the kinds of objects to which he is related and the social practices in which he participates, including the linguistic practices, of the members of his linguistic community. I shall call the former 'kind externalism' and the latter 'social externalism', and shall concentrate my attention on the second sort of externalism.[6] My main focus is to examine what role deference plays in Burge's argument for social externalism. The thesis that I shall defend is that a certain type of deference, what I shall call '*conditional deference*', is a necessary condition for concept possession, and thus plays an essential role in Burge's argument for social externalism.

I shall begin by considering and then rejecting one form of social externalism, linguistic externalism that appeals to linguistic meaning, in which deference plays a role. The thought is that the semantic norms articulated in the linguistic meanings attributed to terms of a language individuate the concepts expressed by the terms.[7] Consequently, it is to these norms that speakers must defer in their use of the terms to have the concepts expressed by the terms.[8] Against this view, Burge has convincingly argued that semantic norms given in meaning characterizations do not fix cognitive value, and thus cannot individuate concepts and the contents that are constituted by them (Burge, 1986b, pp. 707–713). Burge presents two arguments that show that the conditions for individuating conventional linguistic meaning are distinct from those that individuate cognitive value. The first is Fregean and rests on the dubitability of meaning characterizations; the second rests on the sorts of belief attributions that we make across changes in "meaning" (Burge, 1986b, p. 714).

The semantic norms of a linguistic community that specify the conventional linguistic meanings of terms for ordinary perceptual objects[9] are the characterizations that the most competent speakers of the language settle on, characterizations that competent speakers usually reach by reflecting in part on what are regarded as normal examples of the objects to which the term is applied (Burge, 1986b, pp. 704–705). Typically, the aim is to characterize the kind of objects to which the term is standardly applied by giving characteristics of the kind that are essential or central to an object's being of that kind (Burge 1986b, p. 703). These characterizations are, however, dubitable and defeasible. Consider the meaning characterization of 'swan' before English speakers set eyes on the black swans of Australia, a characterization that we can say gives the 'theory' accepted among those taken to be knowledgeable about what swans are. 'Swans are large white birds with graceful necks and black markings around the eyes'.[10] This characterization was a norm for how 'swan' was to be used by English speakers before the discovery of the black swans of Australia; an English speaker who used it otherwise would have been open to criticisms from his linguistic community. Despite this characterization's having been accepted by those in the know as giving the conventional meaning of 'swan', there would have been nothing amiss in someone doubting it, even before the black swans of Australia were discovered. That it can be doubted shows that 'swan' and 'large white bird with graceful neck and black markings around the eye' do not have the same cognitive value, although they would have been regarded to be synonymous. Hence, Burge's Fregean point is that the conditions for individuating the conventional meaning of an expression are distinct from the conditions for individuating the cognitive value of an expression.[11]

Burge's second argument is that the most competent among us, even if his characterization accords with the normal examples to which the term applies, and he has satisfied others that his characterization has met whatever criticisms are on offer, can still be mistaken; he can be wrong about what characterizes a class of entities (Burge, 1986b, p. 706). Obviously, the meaning characterization given to 'swan' before the black swans of Australia were discovered was defeasible, since it turned out to be false. That the characterization was defeasible shows that it cannot individuate the concept *swan*. If we were to suppose that it individuates this concept, then it would have been impossible for an English speaker to come to believe that there were black swans in Australia, something clearly that English speakers came to believe. The assumption of our practice of belief attribution is that there is no change in the concept *swan* across the changes in belief and in the conventional linguistic meaning characterization for 'swan'. Hence, the meaning characterization that was accepted before the news about Australian black swans affected this characterization did not individuate the concept *swan*.[12] The characterization I have chosen to illustrate Burge's arguments about the difference between the conditions for the individuation of cognitive value and conventional linguistic meaning turned out to be false. But a characterization's being false is not essential to the arguments. Any characterization of the conventional linguistic meaning of an expression, even if it is a true characterization, is open to doubt and can be false. The reason that it can be mistaken rests on Quine's point that there is no principled difference between matters of fact and truths of 'meaning'. Hence, to give the meaning of an expression is to state a fact of the matter that is no different in kind from ordinary matters of fact that even if true, could be false.

The underlying reason for the difference between the conditions for the individuation of conventional linguistic meaning and cognitive value expressed by a term for an ordinary perceptual object is the way in which the conditions for individuation are fixed. The conventional linguistic meaning of a term is fixed by "[o]rdinary, thorough, unimpeded, rational reflection by members of a community on the totality of their actual communal practices – all patterns of assertion, deference, teaching, persuasion ... (Burge, 1986b, p. 719). These do not, Burge argues, fix the cognitive value of the term. He claims that "[r]eflection on and analysis of linguistic use at any given time need not suffice to explicate cognitive value correctly" (1986b, p. 719). Since conventional linguistic meaning does not fix cognitive value, thought is not determined by meaning. Consequently, Burge's arguments show that conventional linguistic meaning and the uses of expressions, in one sense of 'use', are not individuators of intentional states, at least for those intentional states that contain concepts for perceptual objects.[13]

An argument similar to Burge's second argument can be mounted to cut against taking the best available theory about Xs accepted by the most knowledgeable in a community to be an individuator of the concept X and the intentional states that contain the concept. Take what I have given above as the meaning characterization of 'swan' and reconstrue it as a theory accepted by those who were regarded by others in the English-speaking community to have been the most knowledgeable about swans. If it does not have enough content to be a 'theory', it can be filled out with additional information. Let us call the theory so filled out T, and suppose further that it was accepted among English speakers before any of them had seen the black swans of Australia. T cannot individuate the concept *swan*, since if it did, those English speakers who landed on Australia could not have come to believe that swans were black, something that they surely came to believe. Hence, theories about Xs, or more simply the set of beliefs about Xs, that are accepted by those regarded to be the most knowledgeable in a community cannot individuate concepts for ordinary perceptual objects. The point again is Quinean. Since there is no principled difference between truths of fact and truths of 'meaning', any argument that has as its conclusion that the latter do not individuate concepts and the intentional states that contain them can be reformulated as an argument that shows that the former cannot serve as concept and content individuators.

In light of Burge's arguments against taking conventional linguistic meaning to individuate cognitive value, what then of social externalism? The two arguments that show that linguistic meaning does not fix cognitive value set a necessary condition for the adequacy for any argument for social externalism. In determining what individuates a concept X, no appeal can be made to the linguistic meaning of 'X' or to a set of beliefs about what Xs are, whether these are held by some identifiable set of individuals in the community, the 'experts' say, or are somehow spread out across members of the community. Let us call this condition for the adequacy of an argument for social externalism, the *Burge Test*. The main argument for social externalism has been Burge's *arthritis* thought experiment. I shall first consider a variant of his argument. Second, I shall show how it passes the Burge test. Third, I shall take up the role that deference plays in social externalism and the place that metarepresentation has within an account of deference. I shall argue that deference does not play a role in the determination of concepts, but is a condition for individuals to possess certain concepts. Lastly, I shall argue that there is a normative element involved in an account of deference and thus in the possession conditions for certain intentional states.

Let us turn to a variant of Burge's *arthritis* thought experiment (Burge, 1979, p. 80).[14] Let us imagine that in the actual world, A, Oscar is able to use the term 'ottoman' in enough different contexts that we are warranted in attributing to him *de dicto* beliefs using 'ottoman' in the content clauses of a variety of belief attributions and thereby, attributing to him the concept *ottoman*. He believes that his mother and his uncle Harry have ottomans, that ottomans are smaller than double beds, that they were introduced into the West from the Ottoman empire, and so on. Further, let us suppose that Oscar acquires 'ottoman' in his idiolect from his mother who teaches him the term by uttering it while pointing to her ottoman that is her most prized possession. In addition, let us assume that Oscar comes to think falsely that all and only pieces of furniture without backs or arms, including benches and wooden stools, are ottomans. Oscar's problem is that he has a mistaken conception of his concept *ottoman*, but this is not sufficient to bar our correctly attributing to him *ottoman* contents. Oscar persists in his use of 'ottoman' until he visits his furniture maker and, pointing to the wooden stool he has brought to be repaired says, 'I'd like my ottoman fixed'. The furniture maker corrects Oscar and tells him what an ottoman is. Oscar stands corrected and henceforth uses 'ottoman' in the way that others use it in his speech community (Burge, 1979, p. 77). We can view the furniture maker as the expert and Oscar's standing corrected as his deferring to the expert.

Let us now consider a counterfactual situation, α, in which there is no change in Oscar's physical history, including his behaviour, his stimulus patterns, and so forth, non-intentionally described, including how Oscar is introduced to the term 'ottoman'. His mother teaches him the term by pointing to her most prized possession, while saying 'ottoman'. Thus, in A and α, Oscar acquires 'ottoman' by being in causal contact with exactly the same object. In α, however, 'ottoman' is used as a term for pieces of furniture without backs or arms, including benches and stools. That is to say, in α speakers use the term in the way that Oscar mistakenly uses it in A. As Burge puts it, "['ottoman'], in the counterfactual situation, differs both in dictionary definition and extension from ['ottoman'] as we use it" (Burge, 1979, p. 79). Moreover, let us suppose that people in α do not think of ottomans as separate kinds of furniture; they have no term for cushioned seats without backs or for upholstered footstools. In both A and α, Oscar is related to the same physical objects by the same causal relations, he has the same stimulus patterns and he behaves in the same way, including uttering the same sentences in the same situations, all non-intentionally described. When Oscar goes to his furniture maker and pointing to his wooden stool says, 'I'd like my ottoman fixed', the furniture maker does not correct what he says, since 'ottoman' is used by the furniture maker and others in Oscar's community in the way that Oscar uses it mistakenly in A. In α, neither Oscar nor anyone else has the concept *ottoman*. Because of this, we cannot correctly attribute to Oscar in the counterfactual situation the sorts of intentional states that we can attribute to him in A using 'ottoman' in the content clauses of intentional state attributions (Burge, 1979, p. 78). Burge concludes that, "[t]he difference in [Oscar's] mental contents is attributable to differences in his social environment" (Burge 1979, p. 79). What exactly are the 'differences in [Oscar's] social environment' that individuate his intentional states? What seems to individuate Oscar's intentional states in both A and α are the linguistic practices of Oscar's linguistic communities, since by hypothesis everything else is kept constant from A to α. In particular, the individuating difference between A and α is a difference in the way that 'ottoman' "was conventionally applied and defined to apply" (Burge, 1979, p. 78). There are then two features of the difference: in A and α 'ottoman' is used to apply to different sets of object, and it is so defined by a "standard, non-technical dictionary definition" (Burge, 1979, p. 78). We might say that there is a difference between A and α in the 'use' of 'ottoman', in its semantic referent and in its conventional linguistic meaning. It is these, then, that in A and α seem to individuate Oscar's intentional states.

It would appear on the face of it that the *ottoman* thought experiment runs afoul of the Burge Test, since the thought experiment appeals to 'a standard, non-technical dictionary definition' and the use of 'ottoman' in *A* and *α*, both of which the Burge Test appears to rule out as possible individuators of cognitive value. Let us begin with Burge's appeal in the thought experiment to a standard dictionary definition, an appeal that I take to be an appeal to conventional linguistic meaning. Although conventional linguistic meaning and cognitive value do not have the same conditions for individuation, understanding the former is quite often a guide to understanding the latter (Burge, 1986b, p. 718). Hence, even though the conventional linguistic meaning of a term does not individuate the concept expressed by the term, it is the best guide that we have about what the concept is. The relation between conventional linguistic meaning and concept determination is similar to the relation between the best available theory about some natural kind, *X*, and what *X*s are. The best available theory is the best way we have for understanding what *X*s are, but the theory itself does not individuate the kind. If it did, with change in theory we would have change in kind, but our practice of kind attribution holds kinds constant across theory change (Burge, 1986b, p. 716)

What about the different uses of 'ottoman' in *A* and *α*? Burge is quite explicit that although use determines conventional linguistic meaning, on a certain sense of 'use' it does not fix cognitive value: "In certain senses, 'use', socially conceived, necessarily 'fixes' conventional linguistic meaning; but 'use' (individualistically or socially conceived) does not necessarily 'fix' cognitive value" (Burge, 1986b, p. 710).

There are different ways in which 'use' can be understood. On one construal, the use of an expression is determined by the different kinds of sentences in which it can occur and the different sorts of linguistic acts these sentences can be used to perform, acts, for example, of asserting, expressing beliefs, expressing desires, and so forth. In turn these acts determine the conventional linguistic meaning of the expression. On this view, we might take it that some linguistic acts in which the term, '*X*', occurs are more privileged than others for determining its conventional linguistic meaning, namely those speech acts which express intentional contents to which speakers are ostensibly committed and in which the term is used so that some property is attributed to *X*s. On the assumption that the speakers say what they believe what we have is the speakers' theory about *X*s.[15] Although this might determine the conventional meaning of '*X*', it cannot individuate the concept *X*, since it runs afoul of the Burge Test. The speakers' theory about *X*s can change, but across the change, the concept *X* remains the same.

There is however another way in which 'use' can be understood which meets the Burge Test.[16] The use to which the *ottoman* thought experiment appeals is not the use of sentences to perform various speech acts. The thought experiments that establish social externalism turn on the same term's being used by members of a speech community to apply to different kinds across A and α, while everything else is kept constant across the worlds (Burge, 1979, pp. 78–79). In the *ottoman* thought experiment what varies across A and α, then, is that Oscar and members of his speech community use 'ottoman' with different extensions. In A, for Oscar and other members of his speech community the semantic referent of 'ottoman' is ottomans, while in α, for Oscar and other members of his speech community it is any piece of furniture without a back on which one can sit or rest one's feet. As we have seen, for two terms to express different concepts, it is sufficient that they have different extensions.[17] It is, then, this social fact, the use of a term with a certain semantic referent in a linguistic community, on which the arguments for social externalism depend.

What makes it the case that a term has the particular semantic referent that it does? Does it depend on the beliefs of Oscar or other members of his linguistic community? Does it rest in A, for example, on their believing that 'ottoman' refers to pieces of upholstered furniture without backs or arms that can be used as a foot rest or for sitting on? Let us assume that it does. What they believe would not give the conventional linguistic meaning of 'ottoman', but would determine the semantic referent of their term and give a set of properties necessary for things falling under the concept *ottoman*. It would follow from what they believe about the referent of 'ottoman' that they believe that ottomans are upholstered pieces of furniture, and so forth. We could view this as their 'theory' about ottomans. The problem with this way of accounting for the semantic referent of 'ottoman' and the concept *ottoman* is that it does not pass the Burge Test. Oscar and the other members of his linguistic community could be mistaken about what ottomans are. Suppose that they were mistaken, discovered that they were so mistaken and revised their views about ottomans accordingly. There would have been, then, a change in their 'theory' about what ottomans were. But before and after the theory change, they would have the same concept *ottoman*, and their uses of 'ottoman' would have as their semantic referent ottomans. What would have changed is their conception of ottoman. Hence, what they believe about ottomans cannot individuate the concept *ottoman* or determine the semantic referent of 'ottoman'.

This is a problem, however, for Burge's arguments for social externalism only if what the members of Oscar's linguistic community believe is necessary for determining the semantic referent of 'ottoman'. But, for familiar Kripkean reasons, what they believe about ottomans is not necessary for determining the semantic referent of 'ottoman', since it is possible that in Oscar's linguistic community 'ottoman' would have ottomans as its semantic referent without anyone knowing enough about ottomans that would pick out all and only ottomans (Kripke, 1980, p. 81). What determines the semantic referent of the term is the well-known story about a historical chain stretching from speakers' current dispositions to use 'ottoman' to the introduction of the term, where, in A, ottomans were fixed as the semantic referent of the term and, in α, pieces of furniture without a back on which one can sit or rest one's feet. What about the reference fixing? Does it pass the Burge Test? We can also imagine that the reference fixing, itself, does not involve essentially any *de dicto* intentional state that would open the reference fixing to the possibility that it did not pass the test. Rather, we can take it that the semantic referent of 'ottoman' is fixed by someone introducing the term by pointing in A to ottomans and in α to pieces of furniture without a back on which one can sit or rest one's feet and saying in the respective worlds, "I shall call those things and anything like them 'an ottoman'." What distinguishes the reference fixings in α and in A is that the reference classes for the reference fixings do not have the same extensions. Hence, Burge's arguments for social externalism pass the Burge test.[18]

I would now like to turn to the roles that deference plays in the argument for social externalism and that metarepresentation plays in an account of deference. Let us reconsider Oscar and his ottoman. First, I shall show that deference to the furniture maker or even a disposition to defer to any expert is not essential to Burge's argument for social externalism. Second, I shall argue that a conditional disposition to defer about ottomans is necessary for the argument. Lastly, I shall try to lay out what this sort of deference is and how it involves metarepresentation. In the story above, we have Oscar going to his furniture maker, pointing to his wooden footstool and telling him that he would like his ottoman repaired. The furniture maker corrects him and Oscar accepts his correction. Oscar's reason for giving up what he believed about his footstool and accepting what the furniture maker tells him is that Oscar believes that the furniture maker knows more about ottomans than he does. For Oscar to change his belief about his footstool because he believes that the furniture maker knows more about ottomans than he does is for Oscar to defer to the furniture maker. Actual deference, however, is not essential to Burge's argument. As Burge points out, Oscar's dropping dead just after he voices his desire to have his ottoman repaired and before he has deferred to his furniture maker would not affect the argument for social externalism (Burge, 1979, p. 79). Oscar would have had *de dicto ottoman* intentional states, even if he had not deferred to his furniture maker. Hence, Oscar's actually deferring to the furniture maker is not essential to the argument. What is essential, perhaps, is that Oscar have the disposition to defer to the furniture maker about ottomans. This too is not necessary for the argument. Oscar might think, mistakenly, that he knows more about ottomans than the furniture maker, and thus not have a disposition to defer to him. Hence, Oscar need neither actually defer to the furniture maker nor have a disposition to defer to him.

It might be thought that the problem above can be avoided by not restricting the range of Oscar's deference to the furniture maker. What might be necessary for the argument for social externalism is that Oscar have the disposition to defer to experts about ottomans, whoever they are. There are two ways in which such a disposition to defer can be understood. The first presupposes that Oscar believes that there are others who know more about ottomans than he does.[19] Let us call them 'experts'. Since Oscar is rational, he wishes to have only true beliefs, including his beliefs about ottomans. Because of this, he is disposed to change his *ottoman* beliefs in light of being corrected by someone he regards to be an expert. The disposition that Oscar has with respect to his beliefs about ottomans is the sort of disposition that most of us have with respect to a great many of our concepts, since we believe that there are experts that are more knowledgeable than we are about these concepts, experts to whom we are disposed to defer. The second way in which the disposition to defer can be understood does not presuppose the belief that there are experts about ottomans. Rather, it is a conditional disposition. Oscar is disposed to defer to anyone, if such a person exists, who offers him considerations[20] that Oscar regards to have a bearing on the truth or falsity of his *ottoman* beliefs.[21] It is the second sort of disposition that I shall argue is necessary for someone to have the concept *ottoman*.

I would now like to turn to arguments that show that the first way of understanding deference that presupposes believing that there are experts is not essential to the argument for social externalism. There are two roles that deference might play in the argument: firstly, it could be taken to be a condition on the individuation of the concept *ottoman*, or secondly, a condition on the possession of the concept. I shall show that it plays neither role. Let us suppose that Oscar becomes more sophisticated about ottomans. He learns what the 'experts' take ottomans to be and because of this, drops his belief that wooden footstools are ottomans. He becomes as adept as the 'experts' in picking out ottomans. He then begins to reflect on the nature of ottomans and to develop his own theory about what they are that leads him to doubt the received opinion about them, and comes to believe that ottomans are religious objects that are not, despite appearances, used for sitting on or for a footrest. He thinks that everyone else is deluded about ottomans and what they think they remember about their use. Because of this, he is not disposed to defer to others about ottomans.[22] Despite Oscar's non-standard views about what ottomans are, we are warranted in attributing to him before, during and after his change of view *de dicto ottoman* intentional states. It is correct to say about him that

> Before he began to study ottomans, Oscar believed that wooden footstools were ottomans. He then became more sophisticated and came to believe

what the experts believed about them, namely, that ottomans are upholstered pieces of furniture without backs and arms that are used for sitting
on and for resting one's feet. On further thought he developed his own
views about ottomans, and came to believe that they are religious objects
that are not used for sitting on or for a footrest.

In so attributing to him these *de dicto* beliefs, we are attributing to him
the same concept *ottoman* across his change of beliefs. Hence, Oscar's increasing knowledge about what is the standard view about ottomans,
and his developing a non-standard theory about them does not change
the individuating conditions for the concept *ottoman* that he has through
these changes of belief about ottomans. Consequently, if deference plays
a role in individuating the concept *ottoman*, it should play this role across
Oscar's change of beliefs. After he develops his non-standard theory, Oscar thinks that everyone else is deluded about what ottomans are. Because of this, he no longer seems to be disposed to defer to others about
what ottomans are. Since he maintains the same concept *ottoman* across
his changes in belief, deference does not appear to play a role at any time
in individuating his concept *ottoman*.

We can arrive at the same conclusion by considering sameness of
concept across individuals, rather than sameness of concept with respect
to one individual across changes in his beliefs. Both Oscar and his furniture maker have the same concept *ottoman*.[23] Since they have the same
concept, it is obvious that whatever plays a role in individuating Oscar's
concept *ottoman* must play the same role in individuating the furniture
maker's concept *ottoman*. In the description of the argument for social externalism above, Oscar is disposed to defer to his furniture maker, but the
converse is not the case. Suppose that the furniture maker is convinced
that he is the world's authority on ottomans. Given his views about his
ottoman expertise, he would not be disposed to defer to others about ottomans. Since he does not seem to have the disposition to defer to others
and has the concept *ottoman*, a disposition to defer about ottomans does
not play a role in individuating his concept *ottoman*. Since Oscar has the
same concept *ottoman* as the furniture maker, his disposition to defer to
the furniture maker cannot play a role in individuating his concept *ottoman*.[24] It appears then that deference that presupposes the belief in the
existence of experts does not play a role in individuating concepts or the
de dicto intentional states that contain them.[25]

Perhaps a disposition to defer to experts is a necessary condition not
for concept individuation, but concept possession. A moment's reflection shows that this is not the case. Take the furniture maker who is an
expert and regards himself to be the world's authority on ottomans. Because of this, he has no disposition to defer to experts about ottomans,
although he has the concept *ottoman*. Oscar, however, is not an expert.

He has a mistaken conception of his concept *ottoman*. Perhaps, a disposition to defer to experts is a necessary condition for someone who has a partial or mistaken conception of a concept to possess a concept.[26] The problem is that presumptuousness is an all too familiar human failing. Despite Oscar's mistaken beliefs about ottomans, that is, his mistaken conception of the concept *ottoman*, there is nothing that rules out the possibility that he thinks that he knows more about ottomans than anyone else. In fact, he might even believe that only he is an expert about ottomans. Hence, he does not believe that there are experts about ottomans to whom he is disposed to defer.[27] That Oscar does not have a disposition to defer that presupposes the belief in experts does not mean that he is using 'ottoman' idiosyncratically nor does it rule out attributing to him *de dicto ottoman* intentional states. He might have learned 'ottoman' in the standard way, by being exposed to ottomans and using the term in various situations that warrant attributing to him a variety of beliefs about ottomans, and thus attributing to him the concept *ottoman*.

Deference about what ottomans are, however, is not yet out of the picture. There is still the conditional deference that does not presuppose that Oscar believes that there are experts to whom he is disposed to defer, but only that Oscar is disposed to defer to anyone who knows more about ottomans than he does, if there is such a person. To have such a conditional disposition is for Oscar to be willing to change any of his beliefs about ottomans in light of considerations that he recognizes show that they are mistaken. The question is whether such a disposition is necessary for Oscar to have *ottoman* beliefs and thus, the concept *ottoman*. It might seem that it is not, since the possibility is open that he might be disposed to hold onto his ottoman beliefs "come what may" (Quine, 1953, p. 41). Hence, if he had such a Quinean disposition, he would not have the disposition to be open to any corrections of these beliefs, and thus, would not have the conditional disposition to defer. It would follow then that conditional deference is not necessary for concept possession and hence, for the argument for social externalism, since if the Quinean consideration is correct, Oscar could have *ottoman* beliefs and the concept *ottoman* without having any disposition to defer, including the conditional disposition to defer.[28]

I believe that this is mistaken. Before turning to my criticism of the Quinean argument above, it must be redescribed so that it does not presuppose that Oscar has the concept *ottoman* and thus, beg the question. The issue is whether without having a disposition to defer, Oscar can have *ottoman* beliefs, and thus have the concept *ottoman*. The Quinean argument is supposed to show this, but the argument framed in terms of 'holding onto *ottoman* beliefs, come what may' presupposes that Oscar has the concept *ottoman*, since for Oscar to have such *de dicto* beliefs is for him to have the concept *ottoman*, since on my construal of *de dicto ottoman* beliefs, the concept *ottoman* is a constituent of such beliefs. For the Quinean argument not to presuppose that Oscar has the concept *ottoman*, I shall rephrase it in terms of 'holding onto sentences come what may'. Furthermore, I shall take it that for someone to hold onto a sentence come what may is for him to have the standing disposition to assent to queried tokenings of the sentence without being open to changing his assent to dissent in light of whatever considerations are presented to him, either through his own experience or the testimony of others. For a subject to have the disposition to defer[29] to others regarding a set of sentences to which he assents is for him to be open to change his assent to dissent in light of what others make manifest[30] to him about these sentences. So if someone holds onto a set of sentences come what may, it follows that he does not have a disposition to defer with respect to these sentences. Recasting the Quinean argument in terms of dispositions to assent to sentences we can say that Oscar has the disposition to assent to a set of sentences containing 'ottoman', but he is not open to changing this assent to dissent in light of whatever is presented to him. Hence, with respect to these sentences, Oscar does not have the disposition to defer.

Not having a disposition to defer with respect to a given set of sentences that Oscar holds onto come what may does not show that he does not have a disposition to defer about his use of 'ottoman' that is necessary for him to have the concept *ottoman*. A disposition to defer is not just a disposition to defer about the 'ottoman' sentences with respect to which Oscar has a current disposition to assent, come what may. It is a projectable disposition to defer about any of the possible 'ottoman' sentences for which Oscar could come to have a standing disposition to assent, come what may. For the Quinean argument above to show that it is not necessary for his having the concept *ottoman* that he has a conditional disposition to defer, it must show that it is possible that firstly, Oscar has the disposition to hold onto, not only his current 'ottoman' sentences to queried tokenings of which he has a current disposition to assent, come what may, but also to hold onto any 'ottoman' sentences about which he could come to have a disposition to assent, come what may and secondly, Oscar has *ottoman* beliefs and thus, the concept *ottoman*.

Let us suppose that the initial set of 'ottoman' sentences that Oscar holds onto, come what may, does not contain indexical sentences of the form, 'That is an ottoman'. There is, however, nothing that excludes such sentences from being added to the set. If Oscar is capable of using 'ottoman', then he could come to have dispositions to assent to various queried tokenings of this sentence. The dispositions are, however, not dispositions to assent to queried tokenings of the sentence, simpliciter, but to assent to them with particular assignments of semantic referents to instances of 'that'. Let us imagine that Oscar comes to develop a disposition to assent to queried tokenings of 'That is an ottoman', come what may, where the semantic referents of the different tokens of 'that' are various wooden footstools. That is, Oscar is not open to changing his disposition to assent to a disposition to dissent to tokenings of the sentence in which the tokens of 'that' has as its semantic value various wooden footstools, despite its being made manifest to him that wooden footstools are not ottomans. In effect, with respect to any of his 'ottoman' sentences, including tokenings of, 'That is an ottoman', Oscar is not open to changing his disposition to assent to a disposition to dissent in light of evidence to the contrary which has as its source his own experience or the testimony of others. Hence, he does not have a disposition to defer with respect to these sentences. The question is whether Oscar's having the disposition to assent to this set of sentences and his not having the disposition to defer is compatible with his having *ottoman* beliefs, and thus, the concept *ottoman*. If it is, then we have an argument that shows that a disposition to defer is not necessary for having the concept *ottoman*.

One way to argue for the compatibility is to take Oscar's pattern of assent and dissent with respect to his 'ottoman' sentences and his lack of a disposition to defer as showing that he is using 'ottoman' idiosyncratically. As Peacocke puts the point, deference in cases of this sort "is what distinguishes ... partial understanding (and partial misunderstanding) of a word in a communal language, from the quite different case of an individual's taking over a word from his community and using it in his own individual, different sense" (Peacocke, 1992, p. 29).[31] The thought is, then, that Oscar is using 'ottoman' idiosyncratically, to express a "different sense," or as I have put it, a different concept from the one that is standardly associated with the term. In Oscar's linguistic community 'ottoman' expresses the concept *ottoman*, but Oscar uses 'ottoman' to express "his own individual" concept. Let us suppose that Oscar uses 'ottoman' to express the concept *wooden footstool* and that he does not defer in his use of the term to the communal linguistic norms that apply to its use. Let us grant Peacocke that this is sufficient for its being a case of an idiosyncratic use of the term. So in Oscar's idiosyncratic use of 'ottoman', perhaps we have a case which supports the Quinean argument above in which a speaker does not have a disposition to defer about his use of a term, or about the sentences containing the term to which he assents, but yet where we are warranted in attributing to him a concept and beliefs that contain the concept.

The situation that we are imagining is one in which Oscar uses 'ottoman' idiosyncratically to express the concept *wooden footstool*, and he is not open to the norms governing the use of 'ottoman' in his linguistic community. We can imagine that Oscar believes that the members of his linguistic community are in error about what ottomans are, and thus, about how 'ottoman' should be used. Let us grant that Oscar does not defer about the communal use of 'ottoman', but this is not enough for the

Quinean argument. What is required is that Oscar would not defer to corrections of his own idiosyncratic use of the term. Using a term idiosyncratically does not bar a speaker from making mistakes in using it, nor from others being warranted in correcting his mistakes. Suppose that Oscar spies across the room something he takes to be a wooden footstool, but that in fact is a broken chair without a back. He says, 'That's an ottoman'. [32] We have learned the way he uses the term and accepted that he uses the term idiosyncratically. Correcting him, we say, 'That's not true. That's just a broken chair without a back'. Now for him not to have a disposition to defer about his use of 'ottoman', he would have to reject our correction of what he said. That is, he would have to refuse to change his assent to dissent, although our correction was manifest to him.

For Oscar not to have the disposition to defer, not only would he have to refuse to change his assent to dissent with respect to the sentences he utters, but with respect to any sentence containing 'ottoman' to which he would assent and to any corrections of his assent that were made manifest to him. However, were he to do this, it is not clear that Oscar's utterances of 'ottoman' would express any concept. What concept would it be? We have supposed that his utterances of 'ottoman' are idiosyncratic uses of the term that express the concept *wooden footstool*. But he now assents to, 'That is an ottoman', where the semantic referent of 'that' is a broken chair without a back. A case of this sort does not bar Oscar from having the concept *ottoman*. Using a term to express a concept is compatible with error. Let us imagine, however, that Oscar were to assent to various queried tokenings of 'That is an ottoman', in which the semantic referent of 'that' changes from occasion to occasion. On some occasions it is a broken chair without a back, on others it is a teddy bear and on others, a cow. Moreover, he is unwilling to change his assent to dissent in light of corrections. Were this to be the case, in Oscar's idiolect, 'ottoman' would have to include within its extension chairs without backs, teddy bears and cows. But then it is difficult to see why we should take 'ottoman' in Oscar's idiolect to express the concept *wooden footstool* or any other concept. What would it be? Perhaps we can say it is the disjunctive concept *wooden footstool or teddy bear or cow*. But even this move is not available, since the above point can be generalized. It is possible for Oscar to come to have the disposition to assent to queried tokenings of 'That is an ottoman' where the semantic value of 'that' is anything that we can imagine, and also to dissent to such tokenings with similar variation in the semantic value of 'that' without on any occasion being willing to defer to the corrections of others. In such a case, it is difficult to see what concept Oscar's use of 'ottoman' could express. Notice that matters change if Oscar is willing to accept corrections to his use of 'ottoman'. The upshot is that it is a necessary condition for a subject to have a term in his idiolect which he can use to express a concept that he have a conditional disposition to defer to others about the use of 'otto-man'. Hence, the Quinean argument does not show that a speaker can hold onto any of the sentences to which he assents, come what may. Correspondingly, the argument does not provide grounds for supposing that he could hold onto any of his beliefs, come what may. Thus, it gives us no reason for thinking that he could have a concept without having a conditional disposition to defer.

I would like to consider another objection to my claim that it is a necessary condition for concept possession that a subject has a conditional disposition to defer. We attribute intentional states to animals, even animals quite low down on the evolutionary scale, for example, bees. Imagine the following case. There are flowers that are on a boat that is some meters off shore. A bee, let us call it 'Beescar', finds its way to the boat, returns to its hive and indicates to other bees that there is nectar on the boat. It is quite natural to say that Beescar believes that there is nectar on the boat. Thus, it would appear to follow that on the view being presented here of concept possession, Beescar has the concepts *nectar* and *boat*. Since it is implausible to suppose that Beescar has a conditional disposition to defer, it seems that we have a case in which having such a disposition is not a necessary condition for concept possession.[33]

The argument that I have given for a conditional disposition to defer being a necessary condition for concept possession applies only to *de dicto* intentional states. So if the Beescar case is to be a counterexample to this argument, it must show that Beescar's believing that there is nectar on the boat is a *de dicto* intentional state. A necessary condition for an intentional state, $A \, \emptyset\text{-}ing$ that p, to be *de dicto* is that 'p' contains terms for which substitution of co-referential terms fails to preserve the truth value of '$A \, \emptyset s$ that p'. An intentional state can be partially or fully *de dicto* depending on whether all or some of the terms in 'p' are open to substitution. If all the terms in 'p' are open to substitution, then $A's \, \emptyset\text{-}ing \, that$ p is not partially a *de dicto* intentional state. So the question is whether Beescar's believing that there is nectar on the boat is a *de dicto* intentional state. It is evident that in 'Beescar believes that there is nectar on the boat', 'nectar' and 'the boat' are open to substitution of co-referential terms. If Beescar believes that there is nectar on the boat and the boat is my mother's favorite sloop, then it believes that there is nectar on my mother's favorite sloop. Or, at least its believing the latter is as plausible as its believing that there is nectar on the boat. Clearly, if 'the boat' can be exchanged for 'my mother's favorite sloop' *salva veritate*, then it can be exchanged for any co-referential expression *salva veritate*. A similar argument can be mounted that would show that 'nectar' is also open to substitutivity *salva veritate*. Hence, if Beescar believes that there is nectar on the boat, its believing this is not a *de dicto* intentional state. The argument can be generalized to show that Beescar does not have any *de dicto* intentional states. This, of course, is not a conclusive argument against those who claim that animals, other than humans, can have *de dicto* intentional states, but not have a conditional disposition to defer. But I shall leave a discussion of this for another time.[34]

Let us return to conditional deference. It is a species of the status deference that has been widely studied by linguists, anthropologists and conversational analysts. The status deference on which they have concentrated their attention occurs where there is a difference in power, position and authority between participants in a conversation in which one of the participants is of a lower or higher status, a ranking that is recognized by the participants in the conversation. The difference in status can arise because of a difference in location in a social hierarchy, where this difference can be attributed to a wide range of properties, including differences in age, sex, wealth, family, race, religion, occupation, caste, and so forth. Such differences are marked in some languages by lexical items, for example, *tu/vous*,[35] in French or by a wider range of lexical items and even word endings, for example, in Japanese and Javanese. Status deference can also be indicated by conversational styles, by voice timber, and by the kinds of speech acts which can be performed in a conversation.

Let us return to the *ottoman* thought experiment, and imagine that Oscar persists in his errant uses of 'ottoman' until he takes his wooden footstool to be repaired, when pointing to it, he says to his furniture maker, 'I would like my ottoman repaired'. The furniture maker informs him that what he is pointing to is not an ottoman, but a wooden footstool and tells him what an ottoman is. Oscar, chagrined, accepts the criticism and changes his beliefs accordingly. Oscar's deference to the furniture maker is not marked linguistically, but it still is an instance of status deference where the difference in status between Oscar and the furniture maker is a difference in the position that they have in a hierarchy, in this case in an epistemological hierarchy. Where there is epistemological deference, one of the participants in a conversation is taken to know more than the others; Oscar takes the furniture maker to know more than he does about ottomans.[36]

We can have a clearer understanding of the disposition to defer and the role that metarepresentation plays in it by looking in detail at an actual case and then asking what sorts of capacities must one have that make it possible to defer, when it is appropriate. Let us begin with an agent who we shall assume to be fully reflective about his beliefs and his reasons for holding and changing them. Such an over intellectualized account cannot provide a completely accurate picture of deference, since it cannot be applied to young children who clearly have beliefs and thus, concepts.[37] But it is a way to begin. Once the fully reflective story is before us, we can then propose ways in which the account can be trimmed to apply to the not fully reflective.

Let us take Oscar and assume that he is fully reflective about his beliefs. He has a wide range of beliefs that we are warranted in attributing to him using 'ottoman' in the content clause of *de dicto* belief attributions, including the mistaken belief that ottomans are wooden footstools. He, then, goes to his furniture maker with his grandfather's wooden footstool and has the following conversation with him:

> *Oscar* (pointing to his grandfather's footstool): I would like my ottoman that I inherited from my grandfather to be repaired.

> *Furniture maker*: That's not an ottoman; it is just a footstool. It can't be an ottoman, since it is not upholstered.

Considering what the furniture maker says, Oscar gives up his belief and comes to believe that unupholstered footstools are not ottomans. That is to say, he defers to the furniture maker (Burge, 1979, p. 77).

Let us look more closely at the conversation and the beliefs surrounding it. Let us assume that there is no irony, metaphor, and so on involved in the conversation and that both Oscar and the furniture maker understand what the other says and implies. There are two contributions to the conversation and an upshot. Superficially the conversation consists in Oscar's and the furniture maker's saying what they do and expressing the corresponding beliefs. Thus, they both express what I have called a first level representation. But there is a more structure to the conversation than that. What Oscar says is addressed to the furniture maker, and the furniture maker's remark is a denial of what Oscar says. The upshot of the conversation that is of interest here is that Oscar changes his belief. His change of belief consists in his giving up his belief that what he has is an ottoman and his coming to believe that what he has is not an ottoman, but a footstool. The question is: What reason does Oscar have for changing his belief? We might take Oscar to reason in the following way:

> I have said to the furniture maker that I have an ottoman, but he denies that this is the case. He is an authority about furniture, and thus about ottomans. So I should accept what he says, since he knows more about ottomans than I do. But to accept what he says I can no longer believe that what I have is an ottoman, since to believe this and accept what the furniture maker says would be to have contradictory beliefs. Since I ought not to have contradictory beliefs, I shall give up my former belief. And since I accept the furniture maker's claim for authority, I shall accept what he says.[38]

Oscar's change of belief, then, consists in his accepting the furniture maker's claim for authority about ottomans and his applying the epistemic norm that one should not have contradictory beliefs. So in changing his belief, Oscar defers to the furniture maker. To defer, we might say, is to accept a claim for authority. As we can see, Oscar's changing his belief is shot through with metarepresentations. Oscar represents to himself what the furniture maker has said and what he denies. In addition he represents to himself his own first-level representations, for example, what he believes about ottomans.

What, then, is one's reason to accept a claim for authority? As Alan Gibbard puts it, it is to have as one's reason for believing something that someone else believes it (Gibbard, 1990, p. 174). Gibbard takes this kind of appeal to authority to be what he calls *contextual authority*: "Authority is contextual ... if it stems from a presupposition that the speaker is guided by norms the audience shares, so that the audience can use the speaker's reasoning as proxy for his own" (Gibbard, 1990, p. 174). I take it that Gibbard's view is that if Oscar accepts on authority from the furniture maker what the furniture maker says about what he inherited from his grandfather, then Oscar presupposes that he and the furniture maker share the same epistemic norms and that what he, Oscar, lacks, and knows he lacks, is the particular experiences that the furniture maker has about ottomans. So Oscar regards the furniture maker as serving as a stand-in for him. Oscar thinks: Had I the same experiences as the furniture maker, I would come to have the same beliefs as he has about ottomans. To accept something on authority is always to accept it on authority from someone. This presupposes that the person from whom one accepts something on authority is, himself, an authority about what one accepts on authority. To take someone to be an authority is to take that person to have a particular epistemic status with respect to what one accepts on authority from him, namely, that he is knowledgeable about what one accepts on authority from him.

Authority is chainable. Suppose that I tell Oscar that he is mistaken about ottomans; they are not footstools. And I cite as my authority what I read in a dictionary. Oscar might well take what I tell him on authority, even though I am not an authority about ottomans. But for Oscar to accept what I tell him on authority is for him to accept on authority what I read in the dictionary. This rests on there being someone who is an authority, namely, the person who is the source of the dictionary entry. So Oscar's accepting something on authority from me rests epistemically on the authority from whom I accept on authority what I tell Oscar. Accepting something on authority should be distinguished from accepting something from an authority. Suppose that I am the bugler in the army and my commanding officer tells me that reveille will be at 5:00 a.m. tomorrow instead of 6:00 a.m. I believe what he tells me not because he is an authority about reveille, but because it is in his power to determine at what time reveille will be called. But this is not the kind of authority that is involved when one accepts something on authority. When one accepts something on authority, the sort of authority that is involved is an authority by virtue of having what is taken to be knowledge about a certain domain, not by virtue of having certain institutional powers.

Gibbard's account of what it is to accept something on authority seems to be too demanding an account. It is possible that Oscar can accept something on authority without his presupposing that he and the furniture maker share all the same epistemic norms or that they have the same capacities to reason given their shared norms. All that he need presuppose is that, were he in the same epistemic position and had he the same intellectual capacities as the furniture maker, he would come to accept the same norms as the furniture maker and in light of the same experiences that the furniture maker had, would reason to the same conclusion as the furniture maker about whether what he has is an ottoman. Although Oscar need not presuppose that he and the furniture maker share exactly the same norms, he must presuppose that they share the same set of higher order epistemic norms so that if he were in the same position as the furniture maker, he would reason in such a way that he would come to have the same norms as the furniture maker. So Oscar presupposes at least that some of the norms he has are the same as the furniture maker's, namely the higher order norms that lead to the acceptance of norms that might cover some particular domain, for example, the particular norms adopted by furniture makers: regard something to have been heavily repaired if it has a great deal of furniture wax on it.

The account above of deference that involves Oscar in a set of metarepresentations might seem to be an overly stringent account of deference. One might argue that in ordinary conversations people are entitled to accept what is said to them without making any presuppositions about the reasoning and norms of their interlocutors. Tyler Burge claims that: "A person is entitled to accept as true something that is presented as true and that is intelligible to him, unless there are stronger reasons not to do so" (Burge, 1993b, p. 467). Burge calls this the *Acceptance Principle*, a principle that he claims is itself not used to justify what people are entitled to accept in accordance with the principle. Burge takes the *Acceptance Principle* as the epistemic default. In various sorts of contexts, in philosophical or political discussion, for instance, we do not accept what we are told, rather we take a critical stance towards it and seek reasons for accepting it (Burge, 1993b, p. 468). These are, however, not the ordinary sorts of situations that make up most conversations. Let us consider a simple example. If someone tells me that it is raining, I am entitled to accept what he says as true, just because he is a rational source of information, I understand what he says and have no reason not to accept what he says. The speaker is making no claim to authority and I do not believe what he says because I accept him as an authority about whether it is raining. So it would appear that Gibbard's account of why we accept what we are told does not apply to quite ordinary situations. Why should it apply to Oscar and the furniture maker? The reason is that Oscar has prima facie grounds for not accepting what the furniture maker tells him, namely, that he believes that what he inherited from his grandfather is an ottoman, a belief that the furniture maker denies. Hence, the claim for authority is necessary for Oscar's acceptance, because what the furniture maker says is an explicit denial of what he believes, a belief that he must have a reason for overriding. Consequently, Oscar must have a reason for accepting what the furniture maker tells him over and above its being from a rational source, being intelligible to him and being presented as being true. This reason is the furniture maker's claim for authority. Hence, Oscar must metarepresent what the furniture maker says to him and consider this a reason for overriding his belief that what he inherited from his grandfather is an ottoman.

Let us try to locate where norms play a role in Oscar's changing his belief in light of what the furniture maker tells him. First, as we have seen, one of the reasons for Oscar's giving up his former belief in accepting what the furniture maker tells him is the norm that one should not hold contradictory beliefs. This norm does not, however, encompass the full range of epistemic disharmony that can occur between what one believes and what one comes to believe because of accepting an other's claim to authority. But I shall not take up this issue here. Second, there is Gibbard's account of what is involved in accepting a claim for authority. On Gibbard's view, leaving aside the complexities raised above, Oscar's reason for giving up what he believes and accepting what the furniture maker tells him is that he takes the furniture maker to be an authority and trusts the furniture maker to reason in the same way he would, using the same set of shared norms, had he experienced what the furniture maker had. So Oscar trusts the furniture maker because he trusts that he would reason from norms that both he and the furniture maker share to the same conclusion as the furniture maker, had he the same experiences as the furniture maker. As Gibbard puts it, accepting something on authority rests on self-trust (Gibbard, 1990, p. 178). But this presupposes that there is a set of norms that Oscar accepts. Hence, for Oscar to accept on authority what the furniture maker claims he cannot be normless. Since accepting something on authority is to defer, it follows that to defer, one must have a certain set of norms that one accepts.

Let us return to Oscar's willingness to change his beliefs, a willingness that is constituted in part by his disposition to defer. For him to have the disposition to defer is not for him to accept something on authority, but for him to have the disposition to accept something on authority. To have this disposition, Gibbard argues, is for Oscar to trust someone else to reason as he would from the same norms to the same conclusion, had he the same experiences as the person in question. Consequently, the disposition to accept something on authority, and thus, the disposition to defer, rests on Oscar's disposition to reason from certain norms. The norms in question are not norms that Oscar would have, were he to defer, but norms that he actually has. Thus, certain epistemic norms are part of the structure of the disposition to defer.

The account I have given of the disposition to defer is overintellectualized. It is psychologically implausible to attribute to children such conscious self-reflective metarepresentational capacities. Yet, they have intentional states that have concepts as constituents. It might even be thought that young children do not have the capacity to defer. This, I think, is mistaken. At a very early age children take correction of what they say and do and recognize that they are being corrected. More importantly, they recognize that certain persons serve as an authority about what they say and do. For example, a very common occurrence is for infants to point to an object and to try out a word, and then look for a parent or other care-giver for approval. The structure of the disposition to defer in infants might be somewhat different from the fully conscious self-reflective disposition to defer described above, but my conjecture is that it will contain important similarities. An important question that I cannot discuss here is to what extent the disposition to defer and its attendant epistemic norms are innate.

Let us leave aside the nature of the disposition to defer in infants and return to the disposition to defer that I described above. I would like to summarize the points I have made about representation and metarepresentation. I take intentional states to be representations and an intentional state that has as its content a representation of another intentional state, a metarepresentation. So Oscar's believing that his inheritance from his grandfather is an ottoman is a representation and his believing about this belief that he must give it up, because he accepts on authority what the furniture maker tells him, is a metarepresentation. Hence, the disposition to change one's beliefs and to defer is an ability that involves the ability to have metarepresentations; in fact it is shot through with this ability. This does not tell us what representations or metarepresentations are. I leave this to others. But it does tell us that the capacity to have metarepresentations are as plentiful as our *de dicto* intentional states, the possession of which involves a disposition to defer, and this is more than enough.

Acknowledgments

I would like to thank Jonathan Berg, Christopher Gauker, Georges Rey and Dan Sperber for their help with the paper.

Notes

1 For a complete account of intentionality, intentional events, as well as states, should be included in the account. For the sake of simplicity, however, I shall talk only of intentional states.

2 The view of *de dicto* intentional states that I shall adopt here is due in part to Tyler Burge who in a series of papers (1979, 1982, and 1993) has sketched a rather comprehensive theory of the structure of *de dicto* intentional states, their contents, the concepts that constitute the contents and the relationship between these and meaning. See also Rey (1983, and 1985) for similar distinctions.

3 The members of the subset might be determined by those beliefs that the individual thinks most centrally characterize Fs.

4 We can say something stronger about the identity conditions for intentional states. A's $\emptyset$-ing that p = B's Ψ-ing that q if and only if $A = B$, $\emptyset$-ing = Ψ-ing and the content that p = the content that q.

5 The underlying justification for the apparatus in the preceding four paragraphs is that it is implicit in the interpersonal and intrapersonal comparisons we make of intentional states and in our psychological theories of abilities, dispositions, behaviour, etc., that appeal to intentional states.

6 Burge's arguments for social externalism are to found in (Burge, 1979, 1982, and 1986b). Burge (1979) emphasizes the role that kinds play in determining what intentional state a subject has, while Burge (1982) emphasizes the role that social practices play in accounting for the intentional states of a subject. Burge (1986a) contains his argument for kind externalism.

7 A stronger version of this view would identify linguistic meanings with concepts.

8 The view represented here is externalist in the sense that the meanings of a speaker's terms are determined by how the terms are used by members of his linguistic community.

9 As Burge points out, a similar case can be made for theoretical terms, but including them in the discussion would greatly and unnecessarily complicate the account that is being given here of social externalism (Burge, 1986, p. 716 and n. 16). For this reason I shall leave them out of the discussion.

10 I gloss over the distinction between an object level characterization, "A sofa is . . ." and a term level characterization, " 'Sofa' means . . .," characterizations that Burge is careful to distinguish (Burge, 1986, pp. 703–704). The distinction is not important for the argument considered here.

11 The most general form of this argument is found in Burge (1978), where Burge shows that despite the synonymy of, for example, 'fortnight' and 'fourteen days', they do not express the same concepts. See also Burge (1986, p. 715).

12 It is important to notice that the Burgean view about concepts that I have adopted here accords with our practices of belief attribution that we make in ordinary cases like the one here involving the black swans of Australia. The Burgean view about concepts does not propose how we ought to attribute beliefs, contrary to other views about belief and concept attribution, but follows the lead of our actual practices, practices that are presupposed by psycholog-

ical theorizing and should not be abandoned in doing psychology, unless there are good reasons within psychological theory itself for replacing them.

13 In what follows I shall introduce a sense of 'use' that plays a role in concept individuation.

14 My appeal is actually to a variant of a variant of the *arthritis* argument. The variant of Burge's *arthritis* argument is his *sofa* argument. This should not be taken to suggest that the *arthritis* argument cannot be deployed as an argument for social externalism (Burge, 1979). It can, but I find that it muddies the waters to use 'arthritis', since it is a natural kind term. The reason that I use a variant of the *sofa* argument is that most people know what a sofa is and thus might find attributing to Oscar a mistaken conception of the concept *sofa* not very plausible.

15 I have greatly simplified matters here about how to arrive at what a community of speakers' theory about *X*s are. We might not want to include all the intentional contents attributing some property to *X*s to which every member of the speech community is committed. We might take some of the intentional states or some of the speakers to be more privileged than others in determining the community's theory about *X*s. But on whatever way we weigh the intentional states or the contribution of individual speakers in determining the community wide theory about *X*s, we end up with a theory.

16 The Frege test drops out of consideration here, since it is a test for showing that two terms, '*X*' and '*Y*' that occur as substitution instances in, '*X* is *Y*', express different concepts. As we shall see, the intentional content at issue is not of this form.

17 Of course, for two terms to express different concepts, it is not a necessary condition that they have different extensions. Since a difference of extension is not a necessary and sufficient condition for a difference of concepts, we cannot say that it fixes cognitive value.

18 It might be thought that in this and the preceding paragraph I am giving necessary and sufficient conditions for concept individuation. I am not. What I am appealing to here are conditions for fixing semantic reference. The structure of my argument is the following: If in *L* '*a*' and '*b*' have different semantic referents, then they express different concepts. '*a*' and '*b*' have different semantic referents in *L* if and only if speakers of *L* are such that with respect to '*a*' and '*b*' they have distinct dispositions to use the terms each of which have an appropriate historical connection with different kinds of things, *a*'s and *b*'s, to which the semantic referents of, respectively, '*a*' and '*b*' are fixed. It follows from this that if speakers' current disposition to use '*a*' and '*b*' have appropriate historical connections with different kinds of things and with reference fixings, then the two terms express different concepts. But what does not follow is that a difference in historical chains terminating in referent fixings is necessary for concept individuation. Hence, historical chains do not individuate concepts.

19 It is a disposition of this sort that is at play, I believe, in Putnam's division of linguistic labour (Putnam, 1975, p. 228).

20 I say 'considerations', rather than 'evidence', since it is anything that has a bearing on the correctness or incorrectness of Oscar's *ottoman* intentional states.

21 To be more precise about the two dispositions, the first can be understood as the following: Oscar believes that there are experts about ottomans and he is disposed to defer to them. The second can be understood as the following: Oscar is disposed to defer to anyone who knows more than he does about ottomans, if there be such a person.

22 This example is taken from Burge (1986, p. 707). But Burge uses it as part of an argument to cast doubt on conventional linguistic meaning and cognitive value having the same individuation conditions. My purpose here is to raise questions about the place that deference plays in the individuation of cognitive value.

23 It might be thought that there is a distinction to be made here between type and token. It could be argued that although Oscar and the furniture maker are related to the same concept type, they have different tokens of the type. Oscar's disposition to defer is what distinguishes his token from the furniture maker's. I think that this is mistaken on two counts. First, if the notion of token of a concept makes sense, it would not be Oscar's deferring that distinguishes his token from the furniture repairman, but rather the spatio-temporal location of the tokens. Second, what is of interest here is not distinguishing tokens, but distinguishing types, and Oscar and the furniture repairman are related to the same concept type.

24 The same sort of argument can be used to show that neither partial understanding nor mistaken understanding of a concept plays a role in individuating a concept.

25 In the arguments above, I have assumed that with respect to a single individual there is sameness of concept and content across change of beliefs and that there is sameness of concept and content between two individuals with different sets of beliefs. Contrary to this, holists about intentional individuation opt for similarity where I have claimed there is identity. I take it that the arguments that constitute what I have called the Burge Test can be used against intentional state holism, but I shall not take up this issue here.

26 See Peacocke (1992, p. 29). I shall take up Peacocke's views more fully below.

27 If the ottoman example is implausible, imagine that it is not Oscar, but Einstein and it is the concept *mass* that is in question. This example was suggested to me by Georges Rey.

28 The point draws on Quine's views on theory revision, but it is not Quine's, since he eschews intentionality and with it any talk of concepts.

29 The deference here and in what follows is conditional deference, since I have shown that the deference that presupposes the existence of experts is not necessary for having a concept.

30 For something to be manifest to a subject he must understand its relevance to the matter at hand.

31 Peacocke takes deference to be one of the conditions on the attribution of intentional states and not a condition on their possession.

32 Let us suppose that if Oscar had been queried with the sentence, he would have assented to it.

33 This objection was suggested to me by Alvin Goldman and Daniel Dennett.

34 See Davidson (1982) for a further discussion of this issue.

35 *Tu/vous* is also used to indicate a different sort of non-deferential relation that turns on the perceived level of intimacy of participants in a conversation.

36 A person can have epistemic authority, not only because he is knowledgeable about a particular domain, but also because he is better placed perceptually than someone else. Suppose that Oscar and the furniture maker are equally knowledgeable about ottomans, but in a given situation the furniture maker has a better perceptual take on a piece of furniture, because his view, but not Oscar's, is unobstructed. In this case about this particular piece of furniture, he is in a better position than Oscar to determine whether it is an ottoman. For this reason, Oscar ought to defer to the furniture maker about whether the piece of furniture is an ottoman. I shall not consider these sorts of cases of authority and deference.

37 Since I am taking having a disposition to defer as a necessary condition for someone's having concepts that are constituents of *de dicto* intentional states, anyone, including children, who has such intentional states must have a disposition to defer. See more on this below.

38 This is not to suppose that Oscar consciously goes through the steps of reasoning in this way. Rather, all that need be supposed is that if Oscar were queried for his reasons for changing his beliefs, he would be able to give his reasons for doing so.

References

Burge, Tyler (1978). Belief and synonymy. *The Journal of Philosophy 75* (3), 119–138.

Burge, Tyler (1979). Individualism and the mental. *Midwest Studies in Philosophy 4*, 73–121.

Burge, Tyler (1982). Other bodies. In A. Woodfield (Ed.), *Thought and object* (pp. 97–120). New York: Oxford University Press.

Burge, Tyler (1986a). Individualism and psychology. *The Philosophical Review 45*, 3–45.

Burge, Tyler (1986b). Intellectual norms and foundations of mind. *The Journal of Philosophy 83* (12), 697–720.

Burge, Tyler (1993a). Concepts, definitions and meaning. *Metaphilosophy 24*, 309–325.

Burge, Tyler (1993b). Content preservation. *The Philosophical Review 100* (4), 457–488.

Davidson, Donald (1982). Rational animals. In E. Lepore & B. McLaughlin (Eds.), *Actions and events: perspectives on the philosophy of Donald Davidson* (pp. 473–481). Oxford: Basil Blackwell.

Donnellan, Keith (1993). There is a word for that kind of thing: An investigation of two thought experiments. *Philosophical Perspectives, Language and Logic 7*, 155–171.

Gibbard, Allan (1990). *Wise choices, apt feelings.* Oxford: Clarendon Press.

Kripke, S. (1980). *Naming and necessity.* Cambridge, MA: Harvard University Press.

Loar, Brian, (1986). Social content and psychological content. In H. Grimm and
    D. D. Merrill (Eds.), *Contents of thought* (pp. 99–110). Tucson, AZ: University
    of Arizona Press.
Peacocke, Christopher, (1992). *A study of concepts*. Cambridge, MA: MIT Press.
Putnam, Hilary (1975). The meaning of meaning, *Philosophical papers*: Vol. 2.
    Mind, language and reality (pp. 215–271). Cambridge: Cambridge University
    Press.
Quine, W. V. O. (1953). Two dogmas of empiricism. In *From a logical point view*
    pp. 20–46). Cambridge, MA: Harvard University Press.
Rey, Georges (1983). Concepts and stereotypes. *Cognition 15*, 237–262.
Rey, Georges (1985). Concepts and conceptions: A reply to Smith, Medin and
    Rips. *Cognition 19*, 297–303.

Chapter 14

Metarepresentations in Staged Communicative Acts

Raymond W. Gibbs, Jr.

Introduction

Speakers often say things to others that appear, on one level anyway, not to be serious. Consider the following conversation between two parents (Bill and Pat) and their teenage son (Grant) from the documentary film series *The American Family*. The conversation takes place in the family's backyard by the swimming pool. Grant knew earlier that his parents wanted to talk about his apparent disinterest in summer work. In the preceding scene, Grant complained to his sister, Delilah, about his parents' request to have this chat, so it is clear that Grant, and his parents to some extent, were not looking forward to this confrontation. The conversation starts with Bill summoning Grant over to where Bill and Pat are sitting by the pool.

(1)   *Bill*: Come over here a little closer . . . I think

(2)   *Grant*: Well, I'd rather stay out of this

(3)   *Bill*: You . . . want to stay out of swinging distance

(4)   *Grant*: Yeah, I don't want to hurt you.

Right away, at the opening moments of the conversation, we see how the participants, via their use of teasing and irony, attempt to express a variety of communicative intentions. When Grant says in (2) that he would rather stay out of the conversation, which is likely a serious comment reflecting his unhappiness about having this chat, his father, Bill, in (3), provides in a nonserious manner a reason why Grant might not wish to come closer to sit down and talk. In making his assertion, Bill is only pretending that he and Grant may get into a physical fight, which Grant would, in this hypothetical scene, wish to avoid. In (4) Grant continues the pretense by saying that he does not wish to hurt his father, assuming, of course, that this would happen if a physical fight did break out. Grant's comment in (4) might be intended literally or seriously on one level, but his action here is to join the pretend scenario by remarking in a jocular manner how he might possibly hurt his father if a fight did occur. All of this teasing and irony fulfills the need for father and son to defuse what must be mutually recognized as a potentially uncomfortable situation of the parents criticizing Grant for his unwilliness to work.

The remarkable feature of about even this brief bit of conversation is that the participants (and we as audience) do not appear to experience any difficulty interpreting what was meant by any of these nonserious utterances. In no sense were these expressions conscious, calculated risks, because they seemed to easily fit in the natural flow of the conversation. Nonserious language, like that seen in this brief exchange between Grant and his father, seems especially useful in informing others about one's own attitudes and beliefs in indirect ways. Speakers do not always want to make explicit what they think, and so say things in such a way that listeners must infer their true beliefs (Brown & Levinson, 1987; Sperber & Wilson, 1995).

My aim in this chapter is to show the serious side of nonserious communication and to demonstrate how speaker's or listener's recognition of specific *metarepresentations* affects their joint production and understanding of nonserious speech. In the same way that metalanguage is language about language, and metacognition is knowledge about knowledge, metarepresentation involves representations of representations. Inferring metarepresentations is a critical part of how speakers and listeners coordinate their mutual beliefs in successful communication. This is especially true in cases where a speaker is alluding to some attributed thought or utterance of another individual (a second-order belief). I shall illustrate the ubiquity of metarepresentations in different kinds of nonserious speech, called *staged communicative acts* (Clark, 1996), and discuss the role of metarepresentational reasoning in the on-line processing of nonserious, staged utterances in conversation.

Nonserious Speech and Staged Communicative Acts

Little attention has been given to nonserious language use in philosophy, linguistics, and psychology (see Clark, 1996). As Austin once pointed out: "Language in such circumstances (e.g., play acting, pretense) is in special ways – intelligibly – used not seriously, but in ways parasitic upon it in normal ways . . . All this we are excluding from consideration" (Austin, 1961, p. 22). Most language scholars, following Austin, have indeed just assumed, to the extent that they have considered it at all, that nonserious, pretend language is deviant and not especially worthy of serious theoretical consideration. Yet explaining how people produce and interpret nonserious speech is essential for any psychological theory of language use, and, I would argue, is critical for contemporary theories of linguistic meaning in philosophy and linguistics. People frequently tease one another, speak ironically, sarcastically, use understatement, and hyperbole in ways that are not meant to be understood literally. Speaking nonseriously not only expresses propositional information, but also allows people to manage and manipulate social relations in some very subtle, interesting ways, as well as to indirectly communicate their attitudes and beliefs.

Clark (1996) dubs nonserious language *staged communicative acts*. The key ingredient in these acts is pretense. For example, in Grant and Bill's brief exchange, Bill pretends as if a physical fight is likely to break out and Grant immediately extends the pretense by claiming that he would hurt his father if such a fight were to occur. This scenario is staged in the sense that the speaker, Bill, creates for his audience, Grant and Pat, a brief, improvised scene in which an implied Bill (the actor in the scene who might start the fight) makes an assertion to an implied Grant (the actor in the scene who would be the recipient of implied Bill's punches). When Grant continues the pretense, he assumes the role of co-author of the hypothetical scenario by making an assertion in which an implied Grant (the recipient of Bill's opening punch in the fight) performs a sincere utterance within the play, as it were, for an implied Bill (the one who would get hurt in the play, should Grant fight back). As co-authors of this hypothetical scenario, both Bill and Grant wish for each other, and perhaps for Pat as side-participant, to imagine the scene and to appreciate their pretense in staging it, It appears, then, that pretense it fundamental to the teasing, and jocular irony that Bill and Grant communicate. By engaging in pretense, Bill and Grant enable themselves to conceptualize of the upcoming conversation, which has a serious side, in a nonserious manner, one which should, even if momentarily, help defuse the potentially emotional confrontation between Grant and his parents.

Layers of Meaning as Metarepresentational Reasoning

One of the important ways to understand how pretense involves metarepresentational reasoning is to acknowledge how staged communicative acts reflect different layers of meaning (see Clark, 1996 for a discussion of layering in both oral and written language). Consider, again, Grant's utterance in (4) where he says *I don't want to hurt you*. When Grant makes this assertion, he is taking action at two layers. He is first making an assertion (layer 1). Yet on a different level, Grant is joining in on his father's pretense that he could hurt his father should a physical fight break out between them, something that Grant wishes not to do (layer 2). By joining the pretense, Grant builds upon the hypothetical situation (in layer 2), which bluntly contrasts with the actual situation (in layer 1). Grant intends his father, Bill, to appreciate why he is highlighting the contrasts, in order to mock his father and the topic of the upcoming conversation.

Layering reflects metarepresentational reasoning because a speaker is alluding to, or echoing, some attributed utterance or thought of another person, thus creating a representation of a representation (i.e., a second-order belief). When Bill and Grant say what they do, each of them is alluding, at one layer, to their implied roles in the hypothetical, pretend scenario they jointly construct. By alluding to these implied speakers' beliefs, Bill and Grant, and other listeners, must recognize the second-order nature of the beliefs if they are to understand what Bill and Grant intend to communicate. Metarepresentational reasoning of this sort is a special characteristic of staged communicative acts.

Why might listeners ordinarily infer complex metarepresentations? What drives listeners to draw certain conclusions about what speaker's mean is the *principle of relevance* (Sperber & Wilson, 1995). Staged communicative acts are just one way of striving for relevance in one's communication. Staged communicative acts, like that seen in Bill and Grant's brief exchange, are interpreted by ordinary listeners as expressions of and clues to the speaker's thoughts. Every utterance is more or less a truthful interpretation of a thought that a speaker wants to communicate. An utterance is *descriptively* used when the thought interpreted is itself entertained as a true description of a state of affairs; it is *interpretively* used when the thought interpreted is entertained as an interpretation of some further thought, say, an attributed thought or utterance, or it can be an interpretation of some thought that might be desirable to entertain in some context (Wilson & Sperber, 1992). Bill and Grant's exchange involves staged communicative acts that must be understood interpretively, rather than descriptively, precisely because these utterances are complex metarepresentations in the sense of being representations of pretend thoughts.

I want to flesh out these ideas in what follows and eventually suggest some of the ways in which metarepresentations are critical to understanding of staged communicative acts, but not necessarily all aspects of figurative speech.

Pretense and Metarepresentations

The idea that pretense involves metarepresentations, in that the pretender must represent his own or another's representation of a counterfactual state of affairs, was first proposed by Leslie (1987). Leslie claimed that an important connection exists between pretense in children's play and their metarepresentational abilities. In developmental research, pretend play is seen as a significant landmark in the child's acquisition of a "theory of mind," that is, the child's ability to make inferences about another's beliefs, or to mentally represent another's mental representations. Even young children know the difference between pretending and real acting. These children, do not, for example, really eat the mud pies that they are pretending to have made, and if they know that they are pretending, then they must surely represent themselves as engaging in pretense, which is a metarepresentation.

Children who pretend are generally ascribed a "double knowledge" about an object, situation, or event. For instance, children can pretend that a banana is a telephone, but at the same time they know that is really a banana (something to eat) and not a telephone. Leslie argued that during an act of pretense, the primary representation, for instance *is a banana*, is copied onto another context, "*this is a banana.*" The secondary representation is "decoupled" from reality, and its reference, truth, and existence relationships are momentarily suspended. This decoupled expression will be a second-order, metarepresentation in that it will be a representation of the primary representation. Of course, simply copying a primary representation does not constitute a metarepresentation. A person must be able to compute a relation between the agent, and the primary and secondary representations, as in Agent – PRETENDS – "this is a banana." This relational structure is referred to as a *M-representation* (Leslie & Roth, 1993).

Following Leslie's idea, we can say that our understanding of Bill and Grant's exchange requires that we compute some relation between the agents, and their respective primary and secondary representations. Unlike the case of a child pretending while playing alone, ordinary conversation where staged acts are communicated requires people to establish joint pretense.

Let us go back and consider an even more complex way that metarepresentational reasoning works in staged communicative acts. The next segment of the *American Family* conversation continues with Bill elaborating on the reason for the conversation right after Grant says in (4) "I don't want to hurt you."

(5)   *Bill*: Well . . . I mean . . . I was talking with your mother, ya know, and I told her that you weren't interested in doing any more work, ya see . . . and I don't blame you . . . I think that's a very honest reaction, there's nothing wrong with feeling, umm . . . its a natural thing to do not wanting to work . . .

(6)   *Grant*: No, ah . . . it's not that I don't want to work, it's just ah . . .

(7)   *Pat*: What kind of work did you have in mind, Grant? Watching
          the television, and listening to records . . .

(8)   *Grant*: I don't need your help, Mom.

(9)   *Pat*: Playing the guitar, driving the car . . .

(10)   *Grant*: Ah . . .

(11)   *Pat*: Eating, sleeping . . .

Pat's performance is complex, for she stages it with an extended rhetorical question to express her main point. Rhetorical questions are one
type of staged communicative acts. When Pat says "What kind of work
do you have in mind, Grant?" she is only pretending to ask a question;
she really does not expect an answer. In (7), (9), and (11), Pat sarcastically echoes, via her rhetorical question, Grant's putative belief that
watching television, listening to records, playing the guitar, and so on,
constitute meaningful work activities. Pat's sarcasm reflects her ironic
understanding of Grant's claim that he wants to work while at the same
time doing little other than watching TV, listening to records, playing
the guitar, and so on.

     In saying what she does, Pat stages a brief scene in two layers. In
layer 2, implied Pat asks Grant if he believes that playing the guitar, listening to music, driving the car, eating, and sleeping really constitute his
idea of work. In layer 1, Pat and Grant (and Bill as side-participant)
jointly pretend that the event in layer 2 is taking place. Pat wishes for
Grant (in layer 1) to imagine a particular scene in which Grant believes
that playing the guitar, listening to music, eating, sleeping, and so on
constitute work. In the actual world, both Pat and Grant know that real
work involves something quite different from these activities. So in creating layer 2, Pat has highlighted several contrasts between the two
scenes. Pat might actually take pleasure in mocking Grant in this way,
or at least, take some pleasure in expressing her apparent anger toward
Grant for his not working in the way that his parents wished for him to
do that summer.

     This analysis of Pat's utterance reinforces the importance of
metarepresentational inferences in understanding different staged communicative acts. By alluding to Grant's putative belief that sleeping, eating, playing the guitar, and so on constitute work, Pat's utterance must
be understood interpretively as expressing a complex metarepresentation (a representation of Grant's putative belief).

     Consider one last set of two exchanges between Bill, Grant, and Pat
to illustrate further how metarepresentational reasoning is central to
staged communicative acts. Following Pat's rhetorical question, Bill says
after a rather pregnant moment of silence:

(12)   *Bill*: No, ah, listen Grant, you are a very good boy, we're very proud of you.

(13)   *Grant*: Yeah, I know you are.

(14)   *Bill*: No, we are ... you don't give us any trouble ya know ...

(15)   *Grant*: Well, you sure are giving me a hell of a lot.

(16)   *Bill*: Well that's my job, I think ... if, ah, I don't, why nobody else will and that's what I'm here for you ... is to kind of see that you get off to a good start ... lucky you may be with the deal, that's my job, is to see that you get to see how life's going to be ...

(17)   *Grant*: Yeah ...

(18)   *Bill*: ... and, ah, if I don't then nobody else will ... a lot of kids go around don't even have that privilege of having a mean old man ...

(19)   *Grant*: Yeah, sure is a privilege too.

Later on in the conversation, Pat goes off on Grant for other alleged "crimes" he has committed during his summer of non-work:

(20)   *Pat*: Okay, I'll tell you what, you are totally revolting around the house, you never do anything you're supposed to do ...

(21)   *Grant*: Now, let's get into the heavy stuff, Mom, really start going now.

(22)   *Pat*: You are, you don't clean up after yourself ...

(23)   *Grant*: That's not true, you know that's not true ... that's not true.

(24)   *Bill*: Well ...

(25)   *Pat*: Alright, you see it ... let me say this: you see it one way and I see it another ... now if you'll ask Delilah ...

(26)   *Grant*: And you're older than me and you know more than me so that's, you know, you're right so that you see it is right ...

Consider Grant's two statements in (19) and (26). Both of these are classic instances of irony based on *echoic mention* (Sperber & Wilson, 1981; 1995; Wilson & Sperber, 1992). In (19), Grant echoes his father's previous statement that "most kids don't have the privilege of having a mean old man" by saying "Yeah, sure is a privilege too" and, by doing so, constructs a pretended scenario with two layers: layer 1 makes a serious assertion about Grant's belief as to the way he should feel about having Bill as his father, while in layer 2 Grant only pretends to feel privileged in having a mean old man as his father. The contrast between these two layers produces the irony and communicates Grant's mockery of his father's beliefs about what kind of father he is to Grant. In (26), Grant does not explicitly echo any of the his mother's statements in the present conversation, but is very likely echoing aspects of her earlier stated beliefs about her being older and wiser than Grant. Again, by echoing this belief, Grant constructs a pretend situation in which his mother adopts the belief attributed to her, which contrasts directly with the present situation of Grant's arguing for a different view, this producing an ironic effect. Both these utterances require sophisticated metarepresentational reasoning to be understood, because the thoughts interpreted are interpretations of some further thought or utterance, attributed to someone other than the speaker (i.e., Pat).

Ironic / sarcastic performances call attention to an unexpected incongruity between what might have been (layer 2) and what is (layer 1). Metarepresentational reasoning is clearly entailed in irony as conversational participants infer second-order beliefs that they jointly construct in pretend scenarios. But the metarepresentational reasoning in irony, and other staged communicative acts, appears to be more complex than that required by young children who successfully solve theory of mind tasks. In irony, the metarepresentations inferred must be transcended, viewed critically, and indeed mocked. The greater complexity in understanding how the representations alluded to by an ironic utterance must be transcended suggests one reason why children who exhibit some metarepresentational skills are still unable to understand many ironic situations and utterances (Lucariello & Mindolovich, 1995).

I have only scratched the surface in talking about some of the ways in which metarepresentational thinking functions in the use and understanding of staged communicative acts. It is clear that any attempt to explain how the participants in the *American Family* discussion and how we, as overhearers, jointly create meaning demands an explicit recognition of the importance of pretense in nonserious speech and show how the ability to think metarepresentationally motivates how such talk occurs.

Besides irony, teasings, and rhetorical questions, there are several other kinds of staged communicative acts. For instance, hyperbole and understatement are closely related to irony, in that each misrepresents the truth to a certain degree (Gibbs, 1994). Hyperbole distorts the truth in that speakers assert more than is objectively warranted, as when Professor Smith says to Professor Jones "I have ten thousand papers to grade before noon." Understatement also distorts the truth because speakers say less than is objectively warranted, as when someone comments about a very drunk person that "He seems to have had a bit too much to drink." Similar to irony, when people use hyperbole and understatement, they pretend as if some state of affairs holds in the world in order to communicate ideas or attitudes regarding their stated propositions. When Professor Smith says "I've got ten thousand papers to grade before noon," he is adopting the pretense of actually having ten thousand papers to grade in order to express the idea that he has a great deal of work to do in a short period of time. Hyperbole and understatement may require complex metarepresentations in the sense that each of these nonserious utterances alludes to hypothetical thoughts of the speaker, one that the speaker does not fully endorse, given his likely true understanding of the real situation (e.g., Professor Smith knows that he only has some small number of papers to grade, even if this is still a lot).

Another type of staged communicative act is indirect speech acts. For instance, when someone makes an indirect request such as "Can you pass the salt?" the speaker is only pretending that some obstacle prevents the addressee from complying with the request (Gibbs, 1986a). Similarly, when someone says "It sure is hot in here," the speaker only pretends to comment on the room temperature because he or she really wants some listener to open a window (Kreuz & Glucksberg, 1989). In addition, consider the case of *lateral indirect speech acts* (Clark & Carlson, 1982), as when Mary says to Beth with Steve present "Don't you think that Steve should take out the garbage?" Here Mary only pretends to be asking Mary her opinion when in fact she is laterally making a request for Steve to actually take out the garbage. Understanding any of these utterances requires metarepresentational reasoning whereby the listener recognizes the contrast between different layers of meaning, especially in the sense of alluding to a hypothetical thought that the speaker only momentarily pretends to adopt.

Finally, staged communicative acts can be expressed nonverbally. For instance, imagine that the two of us are seated across from one another at a boring lecture. Suppose that at one point I yawn. Now in some circumstances, such as when I catch your eye before yawning, this gesture (or facial expression) might be intended to communicate to you that I believe the lecture to be boring, whereas in other circumstances you will simply understand my gesture as being a natural act without any specific communicative purpose (even if you understand from this nonverbal behavior that I am tired). When I pretend to yawn and know that you are watching, my intention is to stage an action with two layers: my serious yawning action (layer 1) and my obvious adopting the pretense of yawning (layer 2). Recognizing how layer 2 is a metarepresentation is a critical part of how people interpret many nonlinguistic actions, especially those that are part of ostensive-inferential communication.

Processing Staged Communicative Acts

How do ordinary listeners comprehend staged communicative acts in conversation? Irony, sarcasm, teasing, hyperbole, understatement, and indirect speech acts are all types of nonliteral language and are traditionally viewed, along with metaphor, as classic tropes. I will argue, and present some experimental evidence supporting the idea, that not all aspects of figurative language are staged communicative acts. Following the claims of Sperber and Wilson's relevance theory (1995; see also Happe, 1993; Sperber, 1994a), I shall suggest that staged communicative acts are different from metaphor precisely because of the use of metarepresentational reasoning in the production and interpretation of staged acts – something that is not required for understanding metaphor.

Traditional theories of figurative language do not see irony as differing from metaphor in that each violates various communicative norms (Foeglin, 1991; Grice, 1989; Searle, 1979). According to this traditional view, which I have dubbed the *standard pragmatic model* (Gibbs, 1994), understanding what any nonliteral utterance mean requires that listeners analyze a sentence's literal meaning before other figurative meanings can be derived. Another implication of this model is that understanding tropes requires that a defective literal meaning be found before the search for a nonliteral meaning can begin. Figurative meaning can be ignored if the literal meaning of an utterance makes sense in context. Finally, additional inferential work must be done to derive figurative meanings that are contextually appropriate.

The results of many psycholinguistic experiments have shown these claims to be false (see Gibbs, 1994, for a review). Listeners and readers can often understand the figurative interpretations of metaphor (e.g., billboards are warts on the landscape); metonymy (e.g., The ham sandwich left without paying); sarcasm (e.g., You are a fine friend); idioms (e.g., John popped the question to Mary); proverbs (e.g., The early bird catches the worm); and indirect speech acts (e.g., Would you mind lending me five dollars?) without having to first analyze and reject their literal meanings when these tropes are seen in realistic social contexts. These studies specifically demonstrate that people can read figurative utterances as quickly as – sometimes more quickly than – they can read literal uses of the same expressions in different contexts or equivalent non-figurative expressions. Research also shows that people quickly apprehend the nonliteral meaning of simple comparison statements (e.g., surgeons are butchers) even when the literal meanings of these statements fit perfectly with context (Glucksberg, Gildea, & Bookin, 1982; Shinjo & Myers, 1989). Even without a defective literal meaning to trigger a search for an alternative figurative meaning, metaphor, to take one example, can be automatically interpreted. Moreover, experimental studies demonstrate that understanding metaphor, metonymy, irony, and indirect speech acts requires the same kind of contextual information as do comparable literal expressions (Gibbs, 1986b; 1986c; Gildea & Glucksberg, 1983; Keysar, 1989). These observations and experimental findings demonstrate that the standard pragmatic view of nonliteral language use has little psychological validity, at least insofar as very *early* cognitive processes are concerned (see also Recanati, 1995).

In recent years, several other proposals have been made that better capture what goes on psychologically in the understanding of such staged communicative acts as irony. According to *echoic mention theory* (Jorgensen, Miller, & Sperber, 1984; Sperber & Wilson, 1981; Wilson & Sperber, 1992), there is no nonliteral proposition that listeners must substitute for the literal proposition. Rather, listeners are *reminded* echoically of some familiar proposition (whose truth value is irrelevant), and of the speaker's attitude toward it. For instance, when Grant says to his father "Sure is a privilege, too," his ironic or sarcastic intention is clear from the fact that Grant has echoed his father's previous assertion that many kids do not have the privilege of having a mean old man to help show them the way in life.

Empirical research demonstrates that people judge ironic utterances such as "Sure is a privilege too, which have explicit echoic mentions, as being more ironic than statements that do not have such mentions (Gibbs, 1986b; Jorgensen et al., 1984). People also process sarcasm based on an explicit echo faster than they do sarcastic expressions based on less explicit or nonexistent echoes (Gibbs, 1986b). These findings imply that listeners would quickly comprehend Grant's sarcastic utterance in (19) because it directly echoes his father's statement that not many kids have the privilege of having a mean old man like him. Although ironic utterances mostly accomplish their communicative intent by reminding listeners of some antecedent event, not all such reminders are echoic, nor do they all refer to actual or implied utterances (Kreuz & Glucksberg, 1989). Many ironic remarks merely remind listeners of the attitudes and expectations that they might share with speakers. For example, Pat's rhetorical question about what kind of work Grant had in mind does not echo any previous statement or thought. It simply alludes to what Pat is pretending must be Grant's beliefs, given that all he has done that summer is play the guitar, listen to the stereo, and so forth. When listeners recognize this pretense, they should understand that the speaker is expressing a derogatory attitude toward the idea expressed, the imaginary speaker, and the imaginary listener.

The fact that verbal irony involves pretense, and not just echoic mention or reminding (Clark & Gerrig, 1984) suggests to some scholars that pretense provides the main umbrella under which to best explain irony and other staged communicative acts (Clark, 1996). My own view is that pretense theory and reminder theory have much in common because both theories note how the communicative purpose of irony is to call attention to some idea or attitude that both speaker and listener can derogate (Kreuz & Glucksberg, 1989; Williams, 1984). In this sense, I think of echoic-mention theory as a subpart of pretense theory. But the important point is that both theories acknowledge the importance of metarepresentations in how people use and understand irony. Moreover, both views suggests that irony is different from metaphor in requiring the recognition of a thought about an attributed thought (second-order metarepresentation), in order to understand a speaker's intentions (and the "weak" implicatures that become manifest from this).

One testable hypothesis that follows from this idea about the metarepresentational character of irony is that irony should be more difficult to comprehend than metaphor because irony requires the ability to recognize a second-order belief. Both metaphor and irony require some understanding of a speaker's or writer's intentions. Because the propositional form of a metaphor only loosely corresponds to the speaker's actual thought, understanding metaphor clearly requires a first-order theory of mind. Looking at what a metaphor literally means is clearly not sufficient for understanding what people mean by their use of these expressions. Few scholars would disagree with this conclusion. .

On the other hand, irony is more difficult to understand than metaphor, and possibly literal expressions, because listeners or readers must compute second-order metarepresentations (a thought about an attributed thought). This view of irony, as requiring complex metarepresentational reasoning in order to be understood (i.e., the Irony as Metarepresentational Thought or IMT view), differs considerably from the traditional, standard pragmatic model, which assumes that understanding irony should not necessitate any ability that interpreting metaphor does not also demand (Happe, 1993).

Several studies in developmental psychology support the idea that interpreting irony and metaphor might be different. For instance, Happe (1993) confirmed with autistic and normal subjects that second-order metarepresentation ability is necessary to comprehend irony as an expression of a speaker's attitude to an attributed thought. However, normal subjects who failed second-order theory-of-mind tasks are as successful in understanding metaphors as are people who exhibit second-order metarepresentational ability. The inability to report thoughts about thoughts is, therefore, seen as a major reason why autistic individuals exhibit communicative problems (Happe, 1994).

These conclusions from the developmental work (also see Luciarello & Mindolovich, 1995) generally support the idea from relevance theory that irony use requires metarepresentational thought (the IMT hypothesis).

Further Experimental Tests of the Hypothesis, Irony as Metarepresentational Thought (IMT)

Differences in learning the meanings of individual metaphors and ironies does not necessarily imply that the cognitive processes involved in comprehending ironic and metaphoric statements are different. But what is the best way of experimentally testing the idea that irony processing differs from metaphor comprehension? Making a comparison between irony and metaphor processing requires that certain assumptions be made about what constitutes cognitive effort in linguistic processing. The main assumption that must be adopted is that language processing occurs in real time, beginning with the earliest moments in which low-level linguistic processes operate (e.g., phonological, orthographic, syntactic, and semantic) and extending in time up to where listeners or readers arrive at an interpretation that best fits their beliefs about the speaker's or writer's communicative intentions. One way of describing this process is to follow the *principle of relevance*, and assume that during linguistic interpretation people attempt to maximize contextual effects while minimizing processing effort (Sperber & Wilson, 1995).

To discover what actually occurs during real-time linguistic processing, psycholinguists often measure the amount of time it takes individuals to read different linguistic expressions, such as metaphors and ironies, in different discourse contexts. Participants in these computerized, reaction-time experiments are often asked to push a button as soon as they comprehend what they have just read. The decision made is subjective and is thought to represent something about the "click of comprehension" phenomenally suggested by people's experience of understand language. Reaction-time experiments generally show that people take between 1 and 4 sec to read and understand different nonliteral utterances such as metaphors and ironies. These studies often compare the time needed to read figurative utterances versus the time needed to process literal expressions. Average differences of 200 to 300 msec in the comprehension times of figurative versus literal sentences may appear to be negligible in terms of everyday communication, but such differences can mark important variations in the sequence of mental processes used in understanding figurative utterances and staged communicative acts (Gibbs, 1994).

Of course, it does not make much sense to simply measure the time it takes people to read various ironies in context and compare these latencies with the times to read metaphors in different contexts. After all, ironies and metaphors can vary tremendously in their syntactic, semantic, and stylistic complexity. Simply comparing the processing times for random groups of ironies and metaphors does not provide the kind of control needed to establish the psychological validity of the

IMT hypothesis. We need, instead, to find a way of either comparing reading times for roughly equivalent ironies and metaphors in identical contexts or of comparing reading times for the same sentences, expressing either ironic or metaphoric meanings, in slightly different contexts. Only under either of these experimental conditions can any legitimate decision be made about the claim that irony requires additional processing over metaphor because irony demands more complex metarepresentational reasoning to be understood.

I want now to present the findings of several psycholinguistic experiments that examined the irony-metaphor hypothesis. This work is very much in its infancy, yet the data obtained thus far is interesting and worthy of immediate consideration.

In the first set of studies, earlier published as Gibbs, O'Brien, & Doolittle (1995), I looked at people's processing of irony, which, I believe in retrospect, bears on the claim that understanding irony requires special metarepresentational reasoning. Consider the following two situations:

John and Bill were taking a statistics class together.
Before the final exam, they decided to cooperate during the test.
So they worked out a system so they could secretly share answers.
After the exam John and Bill were really pleased with themselves.
They thought they were pretty clever for beating the system.
Later that night, a friend happened to ask them if they ever tried to cheat.
John and Bill looked at each other and laughed, then John said,
"I would never be involved in any cheating."

John and Bill were taking a statistics class together.
They studied hard together, but John was clearly better prepared than Bill.
During the exam, Bill panicked and started to copy answers from John.
John didn't see Bill do this and so didn't know he was actually helping Bill.
John took the school's honor code very seriously.
Later than night, a friend happened to ask them if they ever tried to cheat.
John and Bill looked at each other, then John said,
"I would never be involved in any cheating."

Both of these situations end with the identical statement that in each case is understood as verbal irony. The speaker in the first story specifically intends for his audience to understand what is said as ironic, but the speaker in the second situation does *not* intend for his utterance to be understood ironically. In the second story, only the addressees and overhearers see the irony in what the speaker actually said. It is quite possible for people to understand a speaker's utterance as irony even though the speaker did not intend the utterance to be understood as irony. Several experimental studies showed that people understand utterances in stories like the second one above as having ironic meaning even if the speaker did not intend for the utterance to be understood in this way (Gibbs et al., 1995). In fact, readers see the final statements in the unintentional stories as being more ironic than was the case for intentionally ironic statements. Thus, although irony often reflects speakers' communicative goals to identify aspects of ironic situations, speakers may unintentionally create irony by what they say.

Another way of distinguishing between these two types of irony is to suggest that understanding intentional irony requires more complex metarepresentational reasoning to understand what the speaker pretended to communicate by what he said. That is, when a speaker says, "I would never be involved in any cheating," he intentionally desires for his addressee to recognize the sarcasm in his statement. Listeners must recognize the attributed belief (perhaps shared by the speaker and listener) that a person should not, and would not, cheat (a second-order belief). Understanding unintentional irony, on the other hand, does not require listeners to draw these same types of complex metarepresentational inferences (i.e., about what the speaker said nonseriously or staged). Thus, listeners need not construct a hypothetical scenario to which the speaker's utterance, on one level, refers.

If people engage, on more complex metarepresentational reasoning, to comprehend intentional irony more readily than unintentional irony, then reading intentional ironies should take more time than processing unintentional ironies. We measured the amount of time it took experimental participants to read each line of 24 stories, like the pair presented above, on a computer screen in a self-paced reading task. The results of a reading-time study in Gibbs, O'Brien, & Doolittle (1995) showed that people took much *less* time to read unintentionally ironic statements than to process intentionally ironic statements. It appears that people find that it is easier to comprehend verbal ironies that spontaneously *create* ironic situations than it is to make sense of ironies that *remind* listeners of speakers' attitudes or beliefs. Of course, one could argue that participants in this study may not have understood the unintentionally ironic statements as being all that ironic. Yet, again, these same participants rated the unintentionally ironic statements as being *more* ironic than were the intentionally ironic statements. So it appears that people did, in fact, see the final statements in the unintentional stories as being ironic even more so than was the case for the intentionally ironic statements.

The traditional view of irony cannot account for these empirical findings. However, the data are consistent with the IMT hypothesis in that ironic statements incorporating more complex metarepresentations (i.e., the intentional ironies) take more time to process than ironic remarks that do not reflect second-order beliefs (i.e., the unintentional ironies).

Let us now consider a study that looks directly at irony processing versus metaphor processing. Consider the following two stories, each of which end with the expression, "This one's really sharp."

You are a teacher at an elementary school.
You are discussing a new student with your assistant teacher.
The student did extremely well on her entrance examinations.
You say to your assistant,
"This one's really sharp."

You are a teacher at an elementary school.
You are gathering teaching supplies with your assistant teacher.
Some of the scissors you have are in really bad shape.
You find one pair that won't cut anything.
You say to your assistant,
"This one's really sharp."

The expression, "This one's really sharp," has a metaphorical meaning in the first context as the teacher refers to the student's intellectual abilities using a familiar metaphorical comparison according to which the mind is conceived of as a cutting instrument (the sharper the cutting instrument, the greater a person's intellectual abilities). The same expression in the second context has an ironic meaning. Even though the teacher is literally referring to a cutting instrument (i.e., the scissors), she refers to it ironically as possessing a desired property (e.g., sharpness) that, in reality, is does not possess. This comparison provides the ideal situation for assessing the irony-metaphor hypothesis, because the same sentence is read in slightly different contexts (i.e., where the teacher makes an evaluative statement about some person or thing).

Under the IMT hypothesis, people reading these stories should take longer to read the ironic use of "This one's really sharp" than to process the metaphoric use of this expression. In a self-paced reading-time study recently conducted with Herb Colston, we tested this prediction by having 24 undergraduate students read stories like the ones shown above, half of which ended with ironic expressions and half with metaphoric expressions. After reading the last line of each story, participants were shown a possible paraphrase of the last line and had to judge whether it was similar in meaning to the last expression. This was included to ensure that people correctly understood the critical last lines as having appropriate ironic or metaphoric meaning. We found that people indeed take longer to read the ironic statements (2,013 msec) than the metaphoric ones (1,791 msec). This result supports the hypothesis that irony requires extra processing over metaphor because of the extra metarepresentational reasoning needed to understand the pretense behind what speakers say.

Finding that, at least in some cases, irony takes longer to process than metaphor provides one kind of support for the IMT. But did people actually engage in more complex metarepresentational reasoning when reading ironic remarks than they did when reading metaphoric statements? The reading-time data reported above do not directly reveal what kinds of inferences people make when reading ironic and metaphoric comments. In a follow-up study, Herb Colston and I presented a different group of undergraduate students with the same stories and final (ironic or metaphoric) remarks used in the first experiment. After reading the last line of each story, the participants rated their agreement with a set of statements that probed for the different inferences people might have drawn when reading the ironic and metaphoric comments. Participants gave their ratings on a 7-point scale, where higher ratings reflect higher levels of agreement with the different statements.

The first statement examined people's assessments of the speaker's beliefs in understanding the ironies and metaphors. For instance, when participants read the stories described above ending with either ironic or metaphoric uses of "This one's really sharp," they rated the following statements.

Irony: The teacher's remark reflects her current belief that the scissors are not sharp.

Metaphor: The teacher's remark reflects her current belief that the student is smart.

The data revealed no difference in people's ratings for the metaphor (6.54) and irony (6.59) questions. Thus, in both cases, listeners recognize that the speaker's statement reflect something about her beliefs.

The second statement looked at the importance of pretense in understanding the speaker's meaning in the final utterance. Pretense is an important part of ironic communication and we expected readers to infer that a speaker was adopting pretense when using irony but not metaphor. Participants rated their agreement with the following statements.

Irony: The teacher's remark reflects the fact that she is only pretending that the scissors are sharp.

Metaphor: The teacher's remark reflects the fact that she is only pretending that the student is a cutting instrument.

The data showed that people gave higher ratings to the ironic comments (4.81) than to the metaphoric ones (3.00), a statistically significant difference: people thought that the ironic statements involved pretense to a greater degree than the metaphoric comments did.

The third statement looked at people's recognition of the allusion to prior beliefs in the speaker's final utterance in each story. Once again, irony reflects via pretense, or echoic mention, a speaker's prior belief or verbally expressed opinion that no longer holds, given a new context. Listeners will not be able to understand most instances of irony unless they correctly infer how the speaker's utterance alludes to some previous belief or opinion. Participants rated their agreement with the following statements

Irony: The teacher's remark refers to her prior belief (meaning her belief about the scissors before the conversation) that the scissors should be sharp.

Metaphor: The teacher's remark refers to her prior belief (meaning her belief about the student before the conversation) that the student should be sharp is only pretending that the student is a cutting instrument.

Not surprisingly, people gave much higher ratings of agreement to these statements having read the ironic (5.66) comments, than they did to the metaphoric ones (1.94), a highly significant difference: people thought that ironies allude to prior beliefs to a greater degree than metaphoric remarks do.

The next statement looked at people's possible recognition of the speaker's multiple beliefs in understanding ironies and metaphors. If irony depends on listeners' recognition of the speaker's complex meta-representational beliefs, we expected that participants would give higher ratings of agreement to the ironic remarks than they would to the metaphoric ones.

Irony: The teacher's remark reflects her multiple beliefs in that she is both referring to her present belief that the scissors are not sharp and to her prior belief that the scissors should be sharp.

Metaphor: The teacher's remark reflects her multiple beliefs in that she is both referring to her present belief that the student is a cutting instrument and her prior belief that the student should be smart.

People gave much higher agreement ratings to the ironic statements (5.87) than to the metaphoric ones (2.01), a reliable statistical difference. This finding shows that understanding irony reflects more complex recognition of the speaker's multiple beliefs than does understanding metaphor. Listeners clearly viewed ironic statements as reflecting a speaker's second-order attributions in a way that they did not do for metaphors.

The final statement examined people's recognition that ironic statements mock prior beliefs more so than does metaphor. Again, understanding that a speaker mocks someone else, or some social norm, is essential to understanding irony, but not metaphor. Participants rated their agreement with the following statements.

Irony: The reason that the teacher possibly refers to her prior belief that the scissors should be sharp is to mock this expectation, given that the scissors are not sharp.

Metaphor: The reason that the teacher possibly refers to her prior belief that the student should be sharp is to mock this expectation, given that the student is smart."

The agreement ratings were, again, significantly higher for the ironic statements (6.15) than for the metaphoric ones (2.89). This result is consistent with the claim that irony mocks speakers' or listeners' prior beliefs more so than does metaphor.

In summary, the results from this follow-up experiment suggest that people are clearly conscious of how irony differs in critical ways from metaphors, especially with regard to how irony involves pretense and uses complex metarepresentational reasoning to mock an individual's prior beliefs. Together with the reading-time results, the two experiments provide strong, if preliminary, support of the IMT hypothesis.

It is important to acknowledge some other empirical findings that are relevant to my assessment of the irony-metaphor hypothesis. As mentioned earlier, several psycholinguistic studies indicate that people do not necessarily analyze the literal meanings of ironic remarks before determining what these statements mean figuratively (Gibbs, 1986b; 1986c). The particular findings in support of this conclusion are that people take no more time, and often less time, to read a statement like, "You're a fine friend," in a context where this expression has a ironic meaning than they do to read this same statement in a context where it has a literal meaning. But if people understand irony, as one type of staged communicative acts, via making a second-order attribution about another person's beliefs (i.e., the irony-metaphor hypothesis) – that is, they understand irony interpretively rather than descriptively – then one would expect irony to be more difficult to process than roughly equivalent literal statements. This clearly is not always true.

The solution to this problem might be found by considering how context influences linguistic interpretation. Consider one short-story context from the Gibbs (1986b) studies:

Gus just graduated from high school and he didn't know what to do with his life. One day he saw an ad about the Navy. It said that the Navy was not just a job, but an adventure. So Gus joined. Soon he was aboard a ship doing all sorts of boring things. One day as he was peeling potatoes, he said to his buddy, "This sure is an exciting life."

The reason why people might find the ironic remark, "This sure is an exciting life," as easy to process as when this same sentence was seen in a literal context (e.g., where the speaker said something truthful about the exciting life he was leading) is that the context itself sets up an ironic situation through the contrast between what Gus expected when he joined the Navy and the reality of its being rather boring. Because people conceptualize of many situations ironically (Gibbs, 1994; Lucariello, 1994), and thus already infer the irony of a metarepresentation, they can subsequently understand someone's ironic or sarcastic comment without having to engage in the additional computation often required when irony is encountered in conversation.

The main "take-home" message of all this is that there are various contextual factors that influence linguistic processing and so it might not be the case that irony always take longer to process than literal or metaphoric language because of its special metarepresentational character. In fact, people still need to draw metarepresentational inferences when understanding most ironies, but part of these inferences can occur before one actually encounters an ironic utterance.

Conclusions

People's ability to make complex metarepresentational inferences are a critical part of how they produce and interpret nonserious utterances, called staged communicative acts, in conversation. These staged acts are ubiquitous in everyday speech, and people appear to employ their metarepresentational reasoning skills with little conscious effort in ordinary conversation (similar skills must underlie people's abilities to makes sense of plays and extended written narratives in which the levels of metarepresentations can be even more complex). Many aspects of figurative language, especially those requiring pretense, demand metarepresentational inferences to be successfully understood.

There is, at least, some experimental evidence to support the idea that certain staged communicative acts, especially irony, may indeed require more processing effort to understand than tropes like metaphor precisely because of irony's complex metarepresentational character. At the same time, it may very well be the case that people can in some situations quickly understand complex cases of irony (i.e., those involving at least second-order belief inferences) because listeners or readers already draw metarepresentational inferences as part of their understanding of the context in which some ironic utterances are produced. Consequently, the existing psycholinguistic evidence supports some aspects of relevance theory's claims about irony and metarepresentation (Happe, 1993; Sperber, 1994b; Sperber & Wilson, 1995).

My claim that metarepresentational reasoning is an essential ingredient in a psycholinguistic theory of staged communicative acts raises several important challenges for future theoretical and empirical work. First, linguists and psycholinguistics must continue to explore the degree to which different aspects of metarepresentational reasoning underlies ordinary language use and understanding (see Wilson, this volume). Second, language scholars must give greater recognition to the differences in using utterances descriptively as opposed to interpretively, especially with regard to the role that complex metarepresentations play in understanding interpretively stated utterances. Third, psycholinguists must find additional ways of experimentally testing both the *processes* by which complex metarepresentational utterances are understood and the different *products* that become manifest when listeners understand speakers' intentions in verbal communication. A special challenge here is to find ways of falsifying hypotheses that emerge from different linguistic analyses of metarepresentations in discourse. Finally, the most general challenge that studying metarepresentations in language poses for language scholars in all academic disciplines is to recognize how the coordination of mutual beliefs in ordinary speech reflects essential connections between the ways people think and the ways they produce and understand language.

References

The American Family (1973). Television series, Public Broadcasting System, United States.

Austin, J. (1961). *How to do things with words*. Oxford: Clarendon Press.

Brown, P., & Levinson, S. (1987). *Politeness*. Cambridge: Cambridge University Press.

Clark, H. (1996). *Using language*. New York: Cambridge University Press.

Clark, H., & Carlson, T. (1982). Hearers and speech acts. *Language 58*, 332–373.

Clark, H., & Gerrig, R. (1984). On the pretense theory of irony. *Journal of Experimental Psychology: General 113*, 121–126.

Foeglin, R. (1991). *Figuratively speaking*. New Haven: Yale University Press.

Fowler, H. (1965). *A dictionary of modern English usage* (2nd ed., revised by E. Gowers). Oxford: Oxford University Press.

Gibbs, R. (1986a). What makes some indirect speech acts conventional. *Journal of Memory and Language 25*, 181–196.

Gibbs, R. (1986b). On the psycholinguistics of sarcasm. *Journal of Experimental Psychology: General 115*, 3–15.

Gibbs, R. (1986c). Comprehension and memory for nonliteral utterances: The problem of sarcastic indirect requests. *Acta Psychologica 62*, 41–57.

Gibbs, R. (1994). *The poetics of mind: Figurative thought, language, and understanding*. New York: Cambridge University Press.

Gibbs, R., O'Brien, J., & Doolittle, S. (1995). Inferring meanings that are not intended: Speaker's intentions and irony comprehension. *Discourse Processes 20*, 187–203.

Gildea, P., & Glucksberg, S. (1983). On understanding metaphor: The role of context. *Journal of Verbal Learning and Verbal Behavior 22*, 577–590.

Glucksberg, S., Gildea, P., & Bookin, H. (1982). On understanding nonliteral speech: Can people ignore metaphors? *Journal of Verbal Learning and Verbal Behavior 21*, 85–98.

Grice, H. (1989). *Studies in the way of words.* Cambridge: Harvard University Press.

Happe, F. (1993). Communicative competence and theory of mind in autism: A test of relevance theory. *Cognition 48*, 101–119.

Happe, F. (1994). Understanding minds and metaphors: Insights from the study of figurative language in autism. *Metaphor and Symbolic Activity 10*, 275–295.

Jorgensen, J., Miller, G., & Sperber, D. (1984). Test of the mention theory of irony. *Journal of Experimental Psychology: General 113*, 112–120.

Keysar, B. (1989). On the functional equivalence of literal and metaphorical interpretation in discourse. *Journal of Memory and Language 28*, 375–385.

Kreuz, R., & Glucksberg, S. (1989). How to be sarcastic: The echoic reminder theory of verbal irony. *Journal of Experimental Psychology: General 118*, 374–386.

Leslie, A. (1987). Pretense and representation: The origins of theory of mind. *Psychological Review 94*, 412-426.

Leslie, A., & Roth, D. (1993). What autism teaches us about metarepresentation. In S. Baron-Cohen, H. Tager-Flusberg, & D. Cohen (Eds.), *Understanding other minds: Perspectives from autism.* Oxford: Oxford University Press.

Lucariello, J. (1994). Situational irony: A concept of events gone awry. *Journal of Experimental Psychology: General 123*, 129–145.

Lucariello, J., & Mindolovich, C. (1995). The development of complex metarepresentational reasoning: The case of situational irony. *Cognitive Development 10*, 551–576.

Recanati, F. (1995). The alleged priority of literal interpretation. *Cognitive Science 19*, 207–232.

Searle, J. (1979). Metaphor. In Andrew Ortony (Ed.), *Metaphor and thought* (pp. 92–123). New York: Cambridge University Press.

Shinjo, M., & Myers, J. (1987). The role of context in metaphor comprehension. *Journal of Memory and Language 26*, 226–241.

Sperber, D. (1994a). Understanding verbal understanding. In J. Khalfa (Ed.), *What is intelligence?* (pp. 179–198). New York: Cambridge University Press.

Sperber, D. (1994b). The modularity of thought and the epidemiology of representations. In L. Hirschfeld & S. Gelman (Eds.), *Mapping the mind: Domain specificity in cognition and culture* (pp. 39–67). New York: Cambridge University Press.

Sperber, D., & Wilson, D. (1981). Irony and the use-mention distinction. In P. Cole (Ed.), *Radical pragmatics* (pp. 295–318). New York: Academic Press.

Sperber, D., & Wilson, D. (1995). *Relevance: Communication and cognition* (2nd ed.). Cambridge, MA: Blackwell.

Williams, J. (1984). Does mention (in pretense) exhaust the concept of irony? *Journal of Experimental Psychology: General 113*, 127–129.

Wilson, D., & Sperber, D. (1992). On verbal irony. *Lingua 87*, 53–76.

Wilson, D. (2000). Metarepresentation in Linguistic Communication. This volume.

Chapter 15

Metarepresentation in Linguistic Communication

Deirdre Wilson

1. Introduction

Several strands of research on metarepresentation have a bearing on the study of linguistic communication. On the whole, there has been little interaction among them, and the possibility of integrating them with an empirically plausible pragmatic theory has not been much explored. This chapter has two main aims: to illustrate the depth and variety of metarepresentational abilities deployed in linguistic communication, and to argue that a pragmatic account of these abilities can both benefit from, and provide useful evidence for, the study of more general metarepresentational abilities.

A metarepresentation is a representation of a representation: a higher-order representation with a lower-order representation en ed-ded within it. The different strands of research on metarepresentation that have a bearing on the study of linguistic communication vary in the type of metarepresentations involved and the use to which they are put. First, there is the philosophical and psychological literature on mind-reading (or "theory of mind"), which deals with the ability to form *thoughts* about *attributed thoughts* (Carruthers & Smith, 1996; Davies and Stone 1995a, 1995b; Whiten 1991). Suppose a child sees a ball being put into a box. Having formed the thought in (1), he may go on, by observing his companions, to form thoughts of the type in (2):

(1)   The ball is in the box.

(2) (a) John thinks the ball is in the box.

    (b) John thinks the ball is not in the box.

    (c) John thinks Sue thinks the ball is in the box.

    (d) John thinks Sue thinks the ball is not in the box.

There is a now a substantial body of work on how this metapsychological ability develops and how it may break down. It may be present to
varying degrees. People may differ, for example, in their ability to attribute to others beliefs incompatible with their own. A child who believes (1) and lacks this ability would be limited to the metarepresentations in (2a) and (2c). A child with first-order "theory of mind" could
attribute to others beliefs that differ from his own, as in (2b); a child with
second-order "theory of mind" could attribute to others beliefs about the
beliefs of others that differ from his own, as in (2d) (Astington, Harris,
& Olson, 1988; Fodor, 1992; Frye & Moore, 1991; Gopnik & Wellman,
1992; Leslie, 1987; Lewis & Mitchell, 1994; Scholl & Leslie, 1999; Smith
& Tsimpli, 1995). Autistic people are typically said to be lacking in first-
order or second-order metapsychological abilities of this type (Baron-
Cohen, 1995; Baron-Cohen, Leslie, & Frith, 1985; Baron-Cohen, Tager-
Flusberg, & Cohen, 1993; Happé, 1993; 1994; Leslie, 1991).

Second, there is the Gricean pragmatic literature on the attribution
of speaker meanings. Grice shifted attention away from a code model
of communication and towards an inferential account in which the formation and recognition of communicators' intentions was central.
Thanks to his work, the idea that verbal comprehension is a form of
mind-reading has been relatively uncontroversial in pragmatics for
more than thirty years (Bach & Harnish, 1979; Davis, 1991; Kasher, 1998;
Grice, 1989; Levinson, 1983; Neale, 1992; Sperber & Wilson, 1986/1995).
Grice treats the comprehension process as starting from a metarepresentation of an *attributed utterance* and ending with a metarepresentation of
an *attributed thought*. Suppose Mary says (3) to Peter:

(3) You are neglecting your job.

In understanding her utterance, Peter might entertain a series of
metarepresentations of the type in (4):

(4) (a) Mary said, "You are neglecting your job."

     (b) Mary said that I am neglecting my job.

     (c) Mary believes that I am neglecting my job.

     (d) Mary intends me to believe that I am neglecting my job.

     (e) Mary intends me to believe that she intends me to believe that
          I am neglecting my job.

Unlike the literature on mind-reading, the Gricean pragmatic literature
deals with the specific metacommunicative ability to attribute speaker
meanings on the basis of utterances. It might thus be seen as forming a
bridge between the literature on mind-reading and the philosophical, lit-

erary, and linguistic literature on quotation, which is the third strand of research on metarepresentation that I will look at here.

The literature on quotation is mainly concerned with *utterances* about *attributed utterances*. Unlike the Gricean pragmatic literature, it deals with a type of metarepresentation used not in *identifying* the speaker's meaning but as *part of* the speaker's meaning. For example, Peter might report Mary's utterance in (3) in one of the following ways:

(5) (a) Mary said to me, "You are neglecting your job."

  (b) Mary told me I was not working hard enough.

  (c) According to Mary, I am "neglecting" my work.

  (d) Mary was pretty rude to me. I am neglecting my job!

This illustrates the four main types of quotation discussed in the literature: direct quotation, as in (5a), indirect quotation, as in (5b), mixed direct and indirect quotation, as in (5c), and free indirect quotation, as in (5d). Here, both the higher-order representation and the lower-order representations are utterances and both are components of the speaker's meaning: they are part of what Peter intends to communicate by uttering (5a) through (5d) (Cappelen & Lepore, 1997a; Coulmas, 1986; Davidson, 1968/1984; 1979/1984; McHale, 1978; Noh, 1998a; Partee, 1973; Saka, 1998).

So far, all the lower-order representations I have looked at have been attributed utterances or thoughts. There is a further, more disparate literature on non-attributive representations of a more abstract nature, linguistic, logical, or conceptual. Consider the examples in (6):

(6) (a) 'Dragonflies are beautiful' is a sentence of English.

  (b) 'Shut up' is rude.

  (c) It's true that tulips are flowers.

  (d) *Roses and daisies are flowers* entails that roses are flowers.

  (e) I like the name 'Petronella'.

  (f) 'Abeille' is not a word of English.

  (g) *Tulip* implies *flower*.

Here the higher-order representation is an *utterance* or *thought* and the lower-order representation is an *abstract representation*: for example, a sentence type, as in (6a), an utterance type, as in (6b), a proposition, as in (6c) and (6d), a name, as in (6e), a word, as in (6f), or a concept, as in (6g). Such cases have been approached from a variety of perspectives: for example, the philosophical literature on quotation includes some discussion of non-attributive *mentions* of words or concepts (see also Garver, 1965); and the ability to make judgements about grammaticality, to think about sentence or utterance types, or to consider evidential or entailment relations among propositions or thought-types, has given rise to a substantial experimental and developmental literature (Gombert, 1990; Morris and Sloutsky, 1998; Overton 1990).

Metarepresentation, then, involves a higher-order representation with a lower-order representation embedded inside it. The higher-order representation is generally an utterance or a thought. Three main types of lower-order representation have been investigated: *public representations* (e.g., utterances); *mental representations* (e.g., thoughts); and *abstract representations* (e.g., sentences, propositions). How do these metarepresentational abilities fit together, with each other and with the architecture of the mind? I will argue that it is worth considering them together and attempting to integrate them with an empirically plausible pragmatic theory. In the section 2, I will consider how the Gricean metacommunicative ability used in attributing speaker meanings might fit with the more general metapsychological abilities studied in the literature on mind-reading, and argue that some of Grice's assumptions about pragmatics must be modified if a serious attempt at integration is to be made. In section 3, I will sketch a pragmatic theory that might fit better with existing research on mind-reading. In section 4, I will show how this theory might help with the analysis of quotation and other types of linguistic metarepresentation.

2. Gricean Pragmatics and Mind-Reading

Grice sees both communicator and audience as deeply involved in metarepresentation: the communicator in metarepresenting the thoughts she wants to convey, the audience in metarepresenting the communicator's intentions. Clearly, this metacommunicative ability has a lot in common with the more general mind-reading ability illustrated in (2). It is conceivable that there is no difference between them, and that the ability to identify speaker meanings is nothing but the general mind-reading ability applied to a specific, communicative domain. Arguably, this is the approach that Grice himself would have favored (see Sperber, this volume). An alternative hypothesis is that the metacommunicative ability is a specialization of the more general mind-reading ability, developed for use in the communicative domain. This possibility is currently being explored in work on relevance theory, and is the one I will develop here (Sperber 1996; this volume; Origgi & Sperber, in press).

If either of these possibilities is to be seriously investigated, however, some of Grice's pragmatic assumptions will have to be dropped. His framework does not fit straightforwardly with existing research on mind-reading, for several reasons. In the first place, his conception of communication involves, if anything, not too little metarepresentation but too much. For a Gricean speaker's meaning to be conveyed, the speaker's intentions must be not merely recognized but transparent, in a sense that seems to be definable only in terms of an infinite series of metarepresentations. The speaker must not only (1) intend to inform the hearer of something, and (2) intend the hearer to recognize this informative intention, but (3) intend the hearer to recognize the higher-order intention in (2), and so on *ad infinitum*. In other words, for a speaker's meaning to be conveyed, the speaker's informative intention – and every contextual assumption needed to identify it – must become *mutually known* (Recanati, 1986; Schiffer, 1972; Searle, 1969; Smith, 1982; Sperber & Wilson, 1986/1995). However theoretically justified this conclusion, it creates a practical problem: it is hard to see how an infinite series of metarepresentations could ever be mentally represented . The search for a definition of speaker meaning that would simultaneously satisfy the theoretical requirement of transparency and the practical requirement of psychological plausibility was a major preoccupation of early inferential accounts (Clark & Carlson, 1981; Clark & Marshall, 1981; Garnham & Perner, 1990; Gibbs, 1987; Sperber & Wilson, 1986/1995; 1987; 1990a).

A second problem is that Grice seems to have thought of the attribution of meaning as involving a form of conscious, discursive reasoning quite unlike the spontaneous inferences deployed in mind-reading. Here is his "working-out schema" for the identification of conversational implicatures:

(a)   He has said that *p*.

(b)   There is no reason to suppose that he is not observing the maxims, or at least the CP [= Co-operative Principle].

(c)   He could not be doing this unless he thought that *q*.

(d)   He knows (and knows that I know that he knows) that I can see that the supposition that he thinks that *q* is required.

(e)   He has done nothing to stop me thinking that *q*.

(f)   He intends me to think, or is at least willing to allow me to think, that *q*.

(g)   And so he has implicated that *q*. (Grice, 1975/1989, p. 50)

It is hard to imagine even adults going through such lengthy chains of inference in the attribution of speaker meanings. Yet preverbal infants seem to be heavily involved in inferential communication, as the following example (from a 14-month-old infant) shows:

> Mother enters the room holding a cup of tea. Paul turns from his playpen in her direction and obviously sees it. (i) He cries vestigially and so attracts his mother's attention; immediately he points toward her and smacks his lips concurrently. [Paul's way of asking for food or drink.]
>
> *Mother*: No, you can't have this one, it's Andy's.
>
> Mother gives me [i.e. Andy Lock, the observer of the incident] the cup of tea, and I put it on the mantelpiece to cool. Paul crawls across to me and grasps my knees. (ii) I turn to look at him; he looks toward the mantelpiece and points, turns back to me, continues to point, and smacks his lips. (Lock,1980, pp. 95–96).

Surveying a range of examples of this type, and noting the presence of such typical features of inferential communication as attracting the audience's attention, pointing, gaze alternation, and ritualized gestures such as lip-smacking and vestigial crying, Bretherton (1991) concludes: "I suggest that the most parsimonious explanation of these phenomena is that, by the end of the first year, infants have acquired a rudimentary ability to impute mental states to self and other ... and, further, that they have begun to understand that one mind can be interfaced with another through conventional or mutually comprehensible signals" (Bretherton, 1991, p. 57). While it is easy to accept that preverbal infants engage in inferential communication, it is hard to imagine them going through the sort of conscious, discursive reasoning illustrated in Grice's "working-out schema."

In fact, the problem is more serious. Gricean pragmatics substantially underestimates the amount of inference involved in linguistic communication. As the "working-out schema" shows, Grice saw the starting point for inferential comprehension as the recovery of a literal meaning (or "what is said"), which was determined independently of speakers' intentions. Yet there is good evidence that speakers' intentions help to determine not only what is implicated but also "what is said." This is most obvious in disambiguation and reference resolution, but (as I will show in later sections) there is a very wide range of further cases in which sentence meaning substantially under-determines "what is said" (Carston, 1988; 1998; Recanati 1989; 1999; Sperber & Wilson 1986/1995; 1998b; Wilson & Sperber, in preparation). To accommodate these, Grice's "working-out schema" for implicatures would have to be supplemented with further schemas designed to deal with disambiguation, reference assignment, and other linguistically under-specified aspects of "what is said": for example, resolution of lexically vague expressions, and interpretation of semantically incomplete expressions like 'too big'. While reflective inferences of this type do occur (for example in repairing misunderstandings or reading the later work of Henry James), disambiguation and reference assignment are, in general, intuitive processes that take place below the level of consciousness, and an adequate pragmatic theory should recognize this.

The ability to engage in inferential comprehension plays a role in language acquisition, where there is experimental evidence that young children attribute speaker intentions in acquiring lexical meanings. In one study (Tomasello & Kruger, 1992), the experimenter used a novel verb in telling a child what she was about to do. She then performed an apparently accidental action (marked by saying "Whoops"), and an apparently intended action (marked by saying "There!" and looking pleased). The child assumed that the verb described the apparently satisfactory action rather than the apparently accidental one. Paul Bloom, who surveys a variety of examples of this type, concludes that "even very young children infer the referential intention of the speaker (through attention to cues that include line-of-regard and emotional indications of satisfaction) when determining the meaning of a new word" (Bloom, 1997, p. 10). As with inferential communication in preverbal infants, it is easier to think of this as an intuitive rather than a reflective process.

If lexical comprehension involves an element of mind-reading, the ability of autistic people to grasp an intended lexical meaning should also be impaired. Here is an illustration from the autobiography of someone with Asperger's syndrome:

> [During my first year at school], we were required to take naps each day. I vividly remember my teacher announcing, "Children, find your mats and take your nap." I refused. Again the teacher called my parents. Again my parents made their way to the school.
>
> "Liane, why won't you take your nap?" my parents wondered of me.
>
> "Because I can't."
>
> "You see!" the teacher said smugly.
>
> "Why can't you take your nap?" my parents continued.
>
> "Because I don't have a mat."
>
> "You most certainly do have a mat. There it is in your cubby," the teacher replied.

"I do not have a mat."

"You see what I mean?" the teacher asked my parents. "She is an obstinate child."

"Why do you say you don't have a mat?" the folks asked, not giving up on me.

"That is not a mat. That is a rug," I honestly and accurately replied.

"So it is," said my father. "Will you take a nap on your rug?"

"If she asks me to," I said matter-of-factly . . .

I wasn't trying to be difficult, I was trying to do the right thing. The trouble was, the teacher assumed I understood language like other children. I did not. (Willey, 1999, pp. 19–20).

But the impairment in Asperger's syndrome seems to lie at the intuitive rather than the reflective level. If anything, failures at the intuitive level are compensated by an increase in the sort of reflective reasoning envisaged in Grice's "working-out schema," as the following comment (from the same writer) suggests:

If [my husband] were to tell me he was disappointed he had missed me at lunch, I would wonder if he meant to say he was sad – which is simply regretfully sorry; unhappy – which is somewhere between mad and sad; disheartened – which is a lonely sad; mad – which makes you want to argue with someone over what they had done; angry – which makes you want to ignore the person you are feeling this way towards; furious – which makes you want to spit; or none of the above. In order for me really to understand what people are saying I need much more than a few words mechanically placed together. (Willey, 1999, p. 63)

Here the author describes a conscious attempt to resolve a lexical vagueness that most people would deal with spontaneously and unreflectively. This again suggests that the basic metacommunicative capacity is an intuitive rather than a reflective one.

Grice himself might not have been opposed to the idea of an intuitive metacommunicative capacity. What mattered to him was that this capacity – whether intuitive or reflective – was not code-based but inferential: "The presence of a conversational implicature must be capable of being worked out; for even if it can in fact be intuitively grasped, unless the intuition is replaceable by an argument, the implicature (if present at all) will not count as a CONVERSATIONAL implicature; it will be a CONVENTIONAL implicature" (Grice, 1975, p. 50). Grice's fundamental contribution to pragmatics was to show that much of verbal comprehension is inferential; but an empirically plausible pragmatic theory should also be concerned with how the inferential processes go. Here, it is not the intuitions but the "working-out schema" that ought to be replaced.

A third problem is that, despite the elaborate-looking "working-out schema," Grice's framework suggests no explicit procedure for identifying the content of a particular speaker meanings. Grice showed that hearers have certain very general expectations – which he analyzed in terms of a Co-operative Principle and maxims of truthfulness, informativeness, relevance, and clarity – and look for meanings that satisfy those expectations. But how exactly is this done? How does the hearer decide, for instance, that someone who uses the word 'mat' intends to refer to a rug, or that someone who says "I was disappointed not to see you" is angry and expects an apology? If we look for guidance to the "working-out schema" for implicatures, we find that the content of the implicature is introduced at step (c), but no explanation is given of how it is derived. In fact, the function of the "working-out schema" is not to help the hearer construct a hypothesis about the content of the implicature but merely to show how, once constructed, it might be confirmed as part of the speaker's meaning. But until we have some idea of how hypotheses about the speaker's meaning are constructed, we will be unable to see how the metacommunicative and metapsychological abilities might fit together.

In this chapter, my main concern is with empirical questions about the role of metarepresentation in identifying the content of speakers' meanings. In section 3, I will outline a pragmatic theory – relevance theory – which suggests a comprehension procedure that might replace Grice's "working-out schema" and form the basis of a metacommunicative module. As to the theoretical problem of how to define speaker's meaning without getting into an infinite regress, Grice himself proposed a possible way out. He suggested that although full transparency in communication is not in practice achievable (because of the infinity of metarepresentations required), communicators might simply *deem* it to be achieved (Grice, 1982). This has the unfortunate consequence of making speaker's meaning an idealization that is never achieved in real life. At the end of section 3, I will suggest an alternative solution that avoids this unfortunate consequence and shows how the theoretical goal of transparency and the practical goal of psychological plausibility might be reconciled.

3. Relevance Theory and Communication

Relevance theory (Sperber & Wilson 1986/1995, 1987) is based on a definition of relevance and two general principles: the *Cognitive Principle* that human cognition tends to be geared to the maximization of relevance; and the *Communicative Principle* that utterances create expectations of relevance:

Cognitive Principle of Relevance:

Human cognition tends to be geared to the maximization of relevance.

Communicative Principle of Relevance:

Every utterance (or other act of inferential communication) communicates a presumption of its own optimal relevance. (Sperber & Wilson, 1986/1995, p. 260)

Relevance is treated as a property of inputs to cognitive processes and analyzed in terms of the notions of cognitive effect and processing effort. When an input (for example, an utterance) is processed in a context of available assumptions, it may yield some cognitive effect (for example, by modifying or reorganizing these assumptions). Other things being equal, the greater the cognitive effects, the greater the relevance of the input. However, the processing of the input, and the derivation of these effects, involves some mental effort. Other things being equal, the smaller the processing effort, the greater the relevance of the input.

It follows from the Cognitive Principle of Relevance that human attention and processing resources are allocated to information that seems relevant. It follows from the Communicative Principle of Relevance (and the definition of optimal relevance [Sperber & Wilson, 1986/ 1995, pp. 266–278]) that the speaker, by the very act of addressing someone, communicates that her utterance is the most relevant one compatible with her abilities and preferences, and is at least relevant enough to be worth his processing effort. This, in turn, suggests a comprehension procedure that might form the basis for a modularized metacommunicative ability.

Inferential comprehension starts from the recovery of a linguistically encoded sentence meaning, which is typically quite fragmentary and incomplete. The goal of pragmatic theory is to explain how the hearer, using available contextual information, develops this into a full-fledged speaker's meaning. The Communicative Principle of Relevance motivates the following comprehension procedure, which, according to relevance theory, is automatically applied to the on-line processing of attended verbal inputs. The hearer takes the linguistically decoded sentence meaning; following a path of least effort in the accessing of contextual information, he enriches it at the explicit level and complements it at the implicit level until the resulting interpretation meets his expectation of relevance; at which point, he stops.

Relevance-theoretic comprehension procedure: follow a path of least effort in computing cognitive effects.

(a) Consider interpretations in order of accessibility.

(b) Stop when your expectation of relevance is satisfied.

The mutual adjustment of explicit content and implicatures, constrained by expectations of relevance, is the central feature of relevance-theoretic pragmatics (Carston, 1998; Sperber & Wilson, 1998b; Wilson & Sperber, in preparation).

The expectations of relevance created (and adjusted) in the course of the comprehension process may be more or less sophisticated. Sperber (1994) discusses three increasingly sophisticated strategies, each requiring an extra layer of metarepresentation, which might correspond to stages in pragmatic development. The simplest strategy is one of *Naïve Optimism*. A Naïvely Optimistic hearer looks for an interpretation that seems relevant enough: if he finds one, he assumes that it was the intended one and attributes it as the speaker's meaning; if he does not, he has no further resources and communication will fail. In Sperber's terms, a Naïvely Optimistic hearer assumes that the speaker is both competent and benevolent – competent enough to avoid misunderstanding and benevolent enough not to lead him astray. Suppose a mother tells her child:

(7)   I'll write you a letter.

'Write you a letter' may mean *write a letter of the alphabet for you, write a message for you*, or *write a message to you*. The mother has spoken competently if the first interpretation that her child finds relevant enough is the intended one; she has spoken benevolently if this interpretation not only seems relevant but is genuinely so. A Naïvely Optimistic hearer has no need to think about the speaker's thoughts in identifying the speaker's meaning; the only time he needs to metarepresent the speaker's thoughts is when, having found an acceptable interpretation, he concludes that it is the intended one.

A more complex strategy, which requires an extra degree of metarepresentation, is one of *Cautious Optimism*. A Cautiously Optimistic hearer assumes that the speaker is benevolent but not necessarily competent. Instead of taking the first interpretation he finds relevant enough and attributing it as the speaker's meaning, he can ask himself on what interpretation the speaker *might have thought* her utterance would be relevant enough. This extra layer of metarepresentation allows him to avoid misunderstanding in two types of case where a Naïvely Optimistic hearer would fail.

The first is the case of *accidental relevance*. An utterance is accidentally relevant when the first interpretation that seems relevant enough to the hearer is not the intended one. Suppose that – for reasons his mother could not plausibly have foreseen – the first interpretation of example (7) that the child finds relevant enough is one on which his mother is offering to help him practise his handwriting. A Naively Optimistic hearer would accept this as the intended interpretation. A Cautiously Optimistic hearer would be able to consider whether his mother could have expected her utterance, on this interpretation, to be relevant enough to him.

An utterance may also be *accidentally irrelevant*. An obvious example is when someone mistakenly tells you something you already know. Another arises with slips of the tongue. Suppose Mary tells Peter:

(8)   I've been feeding the penguins in Trafalgar Square.

A Naively Optimistic hearer would restrict himself to the linguistically encoded meaning, would be unable to find an acceptable interpretation, and communication would fail. By adopting a strategy of Cautious Optimism, and asking himself on what interpretation Mary *might have thought* her utterance would be relevant enough to him, Peter may conclude that she meant to say 'pigeon' instead of 'penguin'. Clearly, most ordinary hearers are capable of this.

While a cautiously optimistic hearer can deal with speaker incompetence, his assumption of speaker benevolence may still lead him astray. The strategy of *Sophisticated Understanding* allows hearers to cope with the fact that speakers are not always benevolent: they may intend an interpretation to *seem* relevant enough without in fact being so. For example, in saying (8), Mary may be lying about where she has been. A Cautiously Optimistic hearer might be able to cope with her slip of the tongue, but only if he does not realize she is lying: a benevolent communicator could not intend to inform him of something she knows to be false. Using the strategy of Sophisticated Understanding, Peter may be able to identify Mary's meaning even if he knows she is lying, by asking himself under what interpretation she *might have thought he would think* her utterance was relevant enough. In identifying the intended interpretation, he therefore has to metarepresent Mary's thoughts about his thoughts. Most adult speakers are capable of this.

To sum up. A Naïvely Optimistic hearer need not metarepresent the speaker's thoughts at all in identifying the speaker's meaning; he simply takes the first interpretation that seems relevant enough and treats it as the intended one. A Cautiously Optimistic hearer considers what interpretation the speaker *might have thought* would be relevant enough; at the cost of an extra layer of metarepresentation, he can cope with cases where the speaker tries to be relevant enough but fails. Finally, a hearer using the strategy of Sophisticated Understanding considers what interpretation the *speaker might have thought he would think* was relevant enough; at the cost of a further layer of metarepresentation, he can cope with deceptive cases in which nothing more than the appearance of relevance is attempted or achieved (see Sperber, this volume, for discussion).

These strategies have implications for the development of the meta-communicative ability. A child starting out as a Naïve Optimist should make characteristic mistakes in comprehension (in disambiguation and reference assignment, for example) and there is some experimental evidence for this (Bezuidenhout & Sroda, 1996; 1998). Roughly speaking, the move from Naïve Optimism to Cautious Optimism coincides with the acquisition of first-order "theory of mind," and there should also be implications for verbal comprehension in people with autism and Asperger's syndrome (Leslie & Happé, 1989; Happé, 1993; for general discussion of the relation between relevance theory and mind-reading, see Nuti, in preparation).

At the end of section 2, I pointed out an undesirable consequence of Grice's solution to the infinite-regress problem. On his account, transparency in communication, although *deemed* to be achieved, is never in fact achievable, so that full-fledged communication never occurs. Relevance theory suggests an alternative definition of communication that avoids this unfortunate consequence. The first step is to replace the notion of mutual knowledge (or mutual belief) with a notion of *mutual manifestness* (Sperber & Wilson, 1986/1995, chap. 1, § 8). Manifestness is a dispositional notion, which is weaker than knowledge (or belief) in just the required way:

Manifestness

An assumption is manifest to an individual at a given time iff he is capable at that time of mentally representing it and accepting its representation as true or probably true.

An assumption cannot be known or believed without being explicitly represented;[1] but it can be manifest to an individual if it is merely capable of being non-demonstratively inferred. By defining communication in terms of a notion of mutual manifestness, the theoretical requirement of transparency and the practical requirement of psychological plausibility can be reconciled. (For discussion of mutual knowledge versus mutual manifestness, see Garnham & Perner, 1990; Sperber & Wilson, 1990a.)

Relevance theory analyzes inferential communication in terms of two layers of intention: (1) the *informative intention* to make a certain set of assumptions manifest (or more manifest) to the audience, and (2) the *communicative intention* to make the informative intention mutually manifest (Sperber & Wilson, 1986/1995, chap. 1, §§ 9–12):

Ostensive-inferential communication

The communicator produces a stimulus which makes it mutually manifest to communicator and audience that the communicator intends, by means of this stimulus, to make manifest or more manifest to the audience a set of assumptions *I*.

When the stimulus is an utterance, the content of the speaker's meaning is the set of assumptions *I* embedded under the informative intention. As long as the informative intention is made mutually manifest, transparency is achieved. An infinite series of metarepresentations is available in principle; however, it does not follow that each assumption in the series must be mentally represented. Which metarepresentations are actually constructed and processed in the course of interpreting a given utterance is an empirical question. On this account, the attribution of a full-fledged speaker's meaning involves a fourth-order metarepresentation of the type shown in (4e) above: "She intends me to believe that she intends me to believe ...". This is complex enough to suggest a modularized meta-communicative ability, but finite enough to be implemented.

In this section, I have outlined a comprehension procedure that might form the basis for a modularized metacommunicative ability, itself a sub-part of the more general metapsychological ability or "theory of mind." The procedure is governed by an expectation of relevance created and adjusted in the course of the comprehension process, which may be more or less sophisticated, with implications for development and breakdown. In section 4, I will turn to the content of the speaker's meaning (that is, the set of assumptions *I* embedded under the informative intention) and show that this may also contain a metarepresentational element that is very rich and varied.

4. Relevance Theory and Linguistic Metarepresentation

4.1 Resemblance in Linguistic Metarepresentation

As noted above, the literature on quotation is mainly concerned with utterances about attributed utterances, such as those in (5), repeated below.

(5) (a) Mary said to me, "You are neglecting your job."

(b) Mary told me I was not working hard enough.

(c) According to Mary, I am "neglecting" my work.

(d) Mary was pretty rude to me. I am neglecting my job!

Direct quotation, as in (5a), has been linked by different analysts to a variety of related phenomena: demonstrations, pretences, play-acting, mimesis, and non-serious actions (Clark & Gerrig, 1990; Recanati, 1999; Sternberg, 1982a; Walton, 1990). When a literary example such as example (9) is read out on the radio, it is easy to see why direct quotation has been treated as belonging to "a family of non-serious actions that includes practising, playing, acting and pretending" (Clark & Gerrig, 1990, p. 766):

(9)   "Out of the question," says the coroner. "You have heard the
           boy. 'Can't exactly say' won't do, you know. We can't take that
           in a court of justice, gentlemen. It's terrible depravity. Put the
           boy aside." (Dickens, 1996, p. 177)

Similar claims have been made for free indirect quotation, as in (5d).

     However, if we are interested in a notion of metarepresentation that
extends to the full range of cases, public, mental and abstract, these
analyses will not do. It is hard to see how notions such as pretence, mimesis, and play-acting, which apply to public representations, can help
with cases where the lower-order representation is chosen for its content or abstract properties: for example, the indirect speech report in
(5b), the non-attributive mentions in (6), or indirect reports of thought
such as (10):

(10)   What, reduced to their simplest reciprocal form, were Bloom's
           thoughts about Stephen's thoughts about Bloom and Bloom's
           thoughts about Stephen's thoughts about Bloom's thoughts
           about Stephen? He thought that he thought that he was a jew
           whereas he knew that he knew that he knew that he was not.
           (Joyce, 1960, p. 797)

Nor do they help with cases where the higher-order representation is
mental rather than public, as in the mental attributions of utterances or
thoughts that underlie the metapsychological and metacommunicative
abilities (cf. (2) and (4) above). What is worth retaining from these analyses is the idea that quotation involves the exploitation of resemblances.
I will argue that all varieties of metarepresentation, public, mental and
abstract, can be analyzed in terms of a notion of *representation by resemblance*, leaving the way open to a unified account.

     In some of the literature on quotation, it has been assumed that
identity rather than resemblance is the normal or typical case. Direct
quotations are treated as verbatim reproductions of the original utterance, and indirect quotations as reproductions of its content (for discussion, see Cappelen & Lepore, 1997a; 1997b; Davidson, 1968/1984; 1979/
1984; Noh, 1998a; Saka, 1998). This assumption is too strong. In many
cases, indirect quotation involves paraphrase, elaboration, or exaggera-
tion rather than strict identity of content. For example, (5b) is a paraphrase of the original in (3), and it might be used to report a more re-
motely related utterance such as (11), which merely contextually implies
or implicates that Peter is neglecting his job:

(11)   You spend too much time at the theatre.

Particularly in academic circles, where even typographical errors are
often reproduced verbatim, the idea that direct quotation is based on

resemblance rather than identity may be harder to accept. But the degree of accuracy required in verbatim reporting depends on culture and circumstance – reproduction of phonetic features, hesitations, mispronunciations, and repairs may or may not be relevant. Moreover, not all direct quotation is verbatim, as the following examples show:

(12) (a)   Descartes said, "I think, therefore I am."

    (b)   I looked at John and he's like, "What are you saying?"

    (c)   And so the kid would say, "Blah blah blah?" [tentative voice with rising intonation] and his father would say "Blah blah blah" [in a strong blustery voice], and they would go on like that. (Clark & Gerrig, 1990, p. 780)

    (d)   And I said, "Well, it seemed to me to be an example of this this this this this this and this and this," which it was you know. (Clark & Gerrig, 1990, p. 780)

Example (12a) is a translation; the expression 'he's like' in (12b) indicates that what follows should not be taken as a verbatim reproduction; and in (12c) and (12d) the expressions "blah blah blah" and "this this this" indicate very loose approximations indeed (for discussion, see Clark & Gerrig 1990; Coulmas, 1986; Gutt, 1991; Wade & Clark, 1993.)

A quotation, then, must merely resemble the original to some degree. Resemblance involves shared properties. As the above examples suggest, the resemblances may be of just any type: perceptual, linguistic, logical, mathematical, conceptual, sociolinguistic, stylistic, typographic. Typically, direct quotation, as in (5a), increases the salience of formal or linguistic properties, and indirect quotation, as in (5b), increases the salience of semantic or logical properties. We might call these resemblances *metalinguistic*, on the one hand, and *interpretive*, on the other (Sperber & Wilson, 1986/1995, chap. 4, §§ 7–9; Noh, 1998a; Wilson & Sperber, 1988b). Mixed quotation, as in (5c), exploits both metalinguistic and interpretive resemblances, while reports of thought, and metarepresentations of thought in general, are typically interpretive.

Interpretive resemblance is resemblance in content: that is, sharing of implications. Two representations resemble each other (in a context) to the extent that they share logical and contextual implications. The more implications they have in common, the more they resemble each other. Identity is a special case of resemblance, in which two representations share all their implications in every context. In interpreting a quotation or, more generally, a linguistic metarepresentation, the hearer must make some assumption about the type and degree of resemblance involved. According to the relevance-theoretic comprehension procedure, he should not expect strict identity between representation and original: following a path of least effort, he should start with the most salient hypothesis about the intended resemblances, compute enough implications to satisfy his expectation of relevance, then stop. Resemblance, rather than identity, is the normal or typical case (Gibbs, 1994; Sperber & Wilson, 1990b; 1998b; Wilson & Sperber, in preparation).

Developmental studies of quotation have provided useful data on the production side, tracing the development of propositional-attitude verbs such as 'think', 'want', 'hope', 'fear', for example (Bartsch & Wellman, 1995; Bretherton & Beeghly, 1982; Wellman, 1990). Here I will look mainly at the comprehension side and argue that language contains a huge variety of metarepresentational devices whose comprehension might interact in interesting ways with the metapsychological and metacommunicative abilities. I will also try to show that the recognition and interpretation of linguistic metarepresentations involves a substantial amount of pragmatic inference, bearing out my claim in the section 2 that Gricean pragmatics has considerably under-estimated the inferential element in comprehension.

4.2 Decoding and Inference in Linguistic Metarepresentation

The semantic and philosophical literature has been mainly concerned with overtly marked quotations such as (5a) through (5c), whose presence is linguistically indicated by use of higher-order conceptual representations such as *Mary said*, or *Peter thought*. Literary and stylistic research has been more concerned with free indirect cases such as (5d), where the presence, source, and type of the metarepresentation is left to the reader to infer. Consider (13):

(13)   Frederick reproached Elizabeth. She had behaved inconsiderately.

The second part of (13) has three possible interpretations: it may be an assertion by the narrator that Elizabeth had behaved inconsiderately, a free indirect report of what Frederick said, or a free indirect report of what he thought. The literature on "point of view" in fiction provides a wealth of clues to the presence of free indirect reporting, and critical procedures by which indeterminacies as to source and type of metarepresentation might be resolved (Banfield, 1982; Cohn, 1978; Fludernik, 1993; Sternberg, 1982b; Walton, 1976).

To take just one example, consider (14), a passage from *Persuasion* that describes the reactions of the hero, Wentworth, on seeing the heroine, Anne Elliot, after a gap of many years. Anne's sister has just told her that Wentworth has informed a friend that Anne was "so altered he would not have known her." Anne is shocked and upset. Jane Austen continues:

(14)   Frederick Wentworth had used such words, or something like
            them, but without an idea that they would be carried round to
            her. He had thought her wretchedly altered, and, in the first
            moment of appeal, had spoken as he felt. *He had not forgiven
            Anne Elliot. She had used him ill; deserted and disappointed him; and
            worse, she had shewn a feebleness of character in doing so, which his
            own decided, confident temper could not endure. She had given him
            up to oblige others. It had been the effect of over-persuasion. It had
            been weakness and timidity.*

            *He had been most warmly attached to her, and had never seen a
            woman since whom he thought her equal; but, except from some nat-
            ural sensation of curiosity, he had no desire of meeting her again. Her
            power with him was gone for ever.* (Austen, 1990, pp. 61–62. Italics
            added.)

As noted by Leech & Short (1981, p. 339), three interpretations have been
proposed for different parts of the italicized passage in example (14).
Mary Lascelles (1939/1965, p. 204) treats the first part as a straightforward authorial description and the last part as a free indirect report of
what Wentworth said. Wayne Booth (1961, p. 252) reads the whole passage as a free indirect report of Wentworth's thoughts. This disagreement has critical consequences. For Lascelles, the passage amounts to an
"oversight" on Austen's part, since it fails to present events from the
point of view of Anne Elliot, which is consistently maintained in the rest
of the novel. For Booth, it is not an oversight at all. By showing us Wentworth's thoughts at this one decisive point in the story, Austen creates
a genuine doubt in our minds about what the outcome will be. "It is deliberate manipulation of inside views in order to destroy our conventional security. We are thus made to go along with Anne in her long and
painful road to the discovery that Frederick loves her" (Booth, 1961,
p. 252). Later critics have tended to prefer Booth's interpretation as
yielding a more "coherent" reading.

    In literary examples of this type, the interpretation process may be
deliberate and time-consuming, calling on evidence from sources beyond the immediate context. In other cases, the presence of a quotation
may be straightforwardly detected even though it is not overtly marked.
Here are some examples from the "Question and Answer" column in a
newspaper:

(15) (a) Why is it that we curry favour?

     (b) Why is it that someone who tries to convert others prosely-
          tizes?

     (c) Why is it that we trip the light fantastic if we go out for a good
          evening?

(d) Why is it that we have to take off our shoes before entering a mosque?

(e) Why is it that gorillas beat their chests?

(f) Why is it that we get butterflies in our stomachs when we are nervous?

Although none of these questions contained quotation marks, some of them were clearly metalinguistic ("Why is it that we *say* we "curry favour"), while others were straightforwardly descriptive. In the published responses, questions (15a) through (15c) were treated as metalinguistic, (15d) and (15e) were treated as descriptive, and (15f) was treated as both. Intuitively, considerations of relevance help the reader decide how these utterances were intended: it is easier to see how (15a) through (15c) would be relevant as metalinguistic rather than descriptive questions, while the reverse is true for (15d) and (15e). The relevance-theoretic comprehension procedure should shed light on how these utterances are understood.

A hearer following the relevance-theoretic comprehension procedure should consider interpretive hypotheses in order of accessibility. Having found an interpretation that satisfies his expectation of relevance, he should stop. The task of the speaker is to make the intended interpretation accessible enough to be picked out. Notice that the best way of doing this is not always to spell it out in full. In appropriate circumstances, the hearer may be able to infer some aspect of the intended interpretation with less effort than would be needed to decode it from a fully explicit prompt. Returning to (10), for instance, it is relatively easy for the reader to infer that the pronouns in the final sentence must be understood as follows:

(10')   Bloom thought that Stephen thought that Bloom was a jew, whereas Bloom knew that Stephen knew that Bloom knew that Stephen was not.

This interpretation is justified in terms of both effort and effect. It is the most accessible one, since it is exactly patterned on the immediately preceding utterance, in which the intended referents are overtly marked. It is acceptable on the effect side, since it answers a question raised by the immediately preceding utterance and achieves relevance thereby. The less explicit formulation in (10) is thus stylistically preferable to the one in (10'), which would cost the hearer some unnecessary linguistic effort.

Linguistic metarepresentations vary from the fully explicit and conceptual, as in (5a) and (5b), to the fully inferred, as in (13). Most languages also have a range of quotative devices that indicate an attributive intention without foregrounding it to the degree shown in (5a) or (5b).

English has hearsay adverbs ('allegedly', 'reportedly'), adjectives ('self-confessed', 'so-called'), particles ('quote-unquote'), parentheticals ('as Chomsky says', 'according to Bill'), and noun-phrases ('Derrida's claim that', 'the suspect's allegation that'). French also has hearsay prepositions ('selon'), connectives ('puisque') and morphology (the "reportative conditional"); German has hearsay modals ('will'). Japanese has a hearsay particle ('tte') which, if added to the second part of (13), would mark it unambiguously as an attributed utterance; Sissala has an interpretive particle ('re') which does not distinguish between attributed utterances and thoughts. Quotation marks, "finger dancing," and intonation provide further orthographic and paralinguistic resources for indicating attributive use. These devices work in very varied ways, and their semantic properties and pragmatic effects deserve more attention than I can give them here (for discussion, see Blass, 1989; 1990; Ducrot, 1983; Ifantidou-Trouki, 1993; Ifantidou, 1994; Itani, 1996; Noh, 1998a; Wilson & Sperber, 1993).

Most languages also have a range of what might be thought of as self-quotative or self-attributive expressions, which add a further layer of metarepresentation to the communicated content. Parallel to 'he thinks' and 'he says' are 'I think' and 'I say'; and most of the hearsay expressions mentioned above have epistemic or illocutionary counterparts. Consider (16) and (17):

(16) (a)   Allegedly, the Health Service is on its last legs.

(b)   Confidentially, the Health Service is on its last legs.

(c)   Unfortunately, the Health Service is on its last legs.

(17) (a)   There will be riots, the security forces warn us.

(b)   There will be riots, I warn you.

(c)   There will be riots, I fear.

In (16a) and (17a), the parenthetical comment is used to attribute an utterance to someone other than the speaker; in (16b), (16c), (17b), and (17c), it carries speech-act or propositional-attitude information about the speaker's own utterance (Blakemore, 1991; Recanati, 1987; Urmson, 1963). Into this category of epistemic or illocutionary expressions fall mood indicators (declarative, imperative), evidentials ('doubtless'), attitudinal particles ('alas'), and indicators of illocutionary force ('please'), which, by adding a higher-order metarepresentation to the basic layer of communicated content, might be seen as bridging the gap between the metacommunicative ability studied in Gricean pragmatics and the literature on quotation proper (Chafe & Nichols, 1986; Clark, 1991; Fillmore, 1990; Ifantidou, 1994; Papafragou, 1998a; 1998b; 1998c; Recanati, 1987; Wilson & Sperber, 1988a; 1993).

As with freer forms of quotation, these higher-order metarepresentations need not be linguistically marked. Compare (18a) and (18b):

(18) (a) The grass is wet, because it's raining.

    (b) It's raining, because the grass is wet.

Although syntactically similar, these utterances would normally be understood in different ways. Example (18a) would be understood as making the purely descriptive claim that the rain has caused the grass to get wet. The speaker of (18b) would normally be understood as communicating that the fact that the grass is wet has caused her to *say*, or *believe*, that it's raining. In (18a), the causal relation is between two states of affairs; in (18b), it is between a state of affairs and an utterance or thought. In interpreting (18b), the hearer must construct a higher-order representation of the type 'she says', or 'she thinks', and attribute it as part of the speaker's meaning (for further discussion of epistemic or illocutionary interpretations, see Blakemore, 1997; Noh, 1998b; Papafragou, 1998a; 1998b; Sweetser, 1990.

In example (18b), the inferred higher-order representation may be either epistemic or illocutionary. In other cases, this indeterminacy may be pragmatically resolved. Suppose someone comes up to me in the street and says:

(19)   Your name is Deirdre Wilson.

The information that my name is Deirdre Wilson is patently irrelevant to me. What the speaker intends to communicate must be that she *knows*, or *believes*, that my name is Deirdre Wilson; only on this interpretation will (19) be relevant enough.

In still further cases, what has to be pragmatically resolved is whether some higher-order information made manifest by the utterance is part of the speaker's meaning or merely accidentally transmitted. Consider (20):

(20) (a) *Mary* (whispering): I'm about to resign.

    (b) *Mary* (frowning): You're late.

    (c) *Mary* (puzzled): The radio's not working.

Here, paralinguistic features such as facial expression, gestures, and intonation provide a clue to Mary's attitude to the proposition she is expressing, which may or may not be salient enough, and relevant enough, to be picked out by the relevance-theoretic comprehension procedure.[2] In section 4.3, I will look at a range of cases in which the speaker's attitude to an attributed utterance or thought makes a major contribution to relevance, and must be treated as part of the communicated content.

4.3 Reporting and Echoing

The literature on quotation has been much concerned with reports of speech and thought, which achieve relevance mainly by informing the hearer about the content of the original. There is a wide range of further, *echoic*, cases, which achieve relevance mainly by conveying the speaker's attitude to an attributed utterance or thought. Echoic utterances add an extra layer of metarepresentation to the communicated content, since not only the attribution but also the speaker's attitude must be represented.

The attitudes conveyed by echoic utterances are very rich and varied: the speaker may indicate that she agrees or disagrees with the original, is puzzled, angry, amused, intrigued, sceptical, and so on – or any combination of these. Here I will limit myself to three broad types of attitude: endorsing, questioning, and dissociative. Suppose Peter and Mary have been to see a film. As they come out, one of the following exchanges occurs:

(21)   *Peter*: That was a fantastic film.

(22)   *Mary*: (a) (happily) Fantastic.

               (b) (puzzled) Fantastic?

               (c) (scornfully) Fantastic!

In (22) Mary echoes Peter's utterance while indicating that she agrees with it; in (22) she indicates that she is wondering about it; and in (22) she indicates that she disagrees with it. The resulting interpretations might be as in (23):

(23) (a)   She believes I was right to say/think *P*.

     (b)   She is wondering whether I was right to say/think *P*.

     (c)   She believes I was wrong to say/think *P*.

Like regular quotations, echoic utterances may be metalinguistic or interpretive: the attitude expressed may be to the form of the original (e.g., a word, an accent, a pronunciation) or to its content. In (22b), for example, Mary may be wondering whether Peter meant to say the word 'fantastic', or to pronounce it as he did; or she may be wondering whether he really believes the film was fantastic, and why.

As with regular quotations, the speaker's attitude may be more or less overtly marked ('I agree that', 'I doubt that', 'I wonder whether'), or left to the hearer to infer, as in (22). Apart from intonation, facial expressions, and other paralinguistic features, most languages also have various attitudinal devices, parallel to the hearsay devices above, which may increase the salience of the intended interpretation. Credal attitudes to attributed contents are conveyed by factive verbs ('he knows', 'he admits', 'they point out') and parentheticals ('as Chomsky says', 'as these arguments have shown') (on factives and credal attitudes, see Kiparsky & Kiparsky, 1971; Sperber, 1997). Questioning attitudes are conveyed by expressions such as 'eh?', 'right?', 'aren't you?', as in (24):

(24) (a)   You're leaving, eh?

(b)   You don't want that piece of cake, right?

(c)   You're thinking of resigning, aren't you?

There is also a range of more or less colloquial dissociative expressions. Suppose Peter tells Mary that he is planning to enter the New York marathon, and she replies as in (25):

(25) (a)   You're bound to win, *I don't think.*

(b)   You're sure to win. *Not.*

(c)   You're going to run the marathon, *huh*!

Here, the addition of the italicized expressions makes it clear that the main clause is attributive, and that Mary's attitude is a sceptical or dissociative one.

A central claim of relevance theory has been that verbal irony is tacitly dissociative: the speaker expresses a wry, or sceptical, or mocking attitude to an attributed utterance or thought (Sperber & Wilson, 1981; 1986/1995, 1990b, 1998a; Wilson & Sperber, 1992). Consider Mary's utterance in (22c) above. This is clearly both ironical and echoic. Relevance theory claims that it is ironical *because* it is echoic: irony consists in echoing a tacitly attributed thought or utterance with a tacitly dissociative attitude. This analysis has been experimentally tested, and the theoretical claims behind it have been much discussed (Clark & Gerrig, 1984; Curcó, 1998; Gibbs, 1994; Jorgensen, Miller, & Sperber, 1984; Kreuz & Glucksberg, 1989; Kumon-Nakamura, Glucksberg, & Brown, 1995; Martin, 1992; Sperber, 1984; Sperber & Wilson, 1998a). There is good evidence that irony involves attributive metarepresentation, and that this extra layer of metarepresentation makes irony harder than metaphor to understand for people with autism who have not attained a second-order "theory of mind" (Happé 1993; on the development of metaphor and irony, see Winner 1988).

Verbal irony is interpretive: the speaker conveys a dissociative attitude to an attributed content. Parody might be thought of as its metalinguistic counterpart: the speaker conveys a dissociative attitude not (only) to an attributed content but to the style or form of the original. Typically, the resemblance is quite loose. Consider (26a), a mocking inversion of the saying in (26b):

(26) (a) Our friends are always there when they need us.

    (b) Our friends are always there when we need them.

This is a case of echoic allusion, which allows the speaker to make a serious assertion with (26a) while simultaneously making fun of the related utterance in (26b).[3] A further type of case, which is not normally treated as echoic, is (27b):

(27) (a) *Prince Charles:* Hello, I'm Prince Charles.

    (b) *Telephone operator:* And I'm the Queen of Sheba.

It has been suggested (I think by Dan Sperber) that the response in (27b) might be treated as an echoic allusion. The speaker aims to make salient a rather abstract property that her utterance shares with (27a): obvious falsehood or absurdity (see Noh 1998a for discussion). In all these cases, the claim that attribution is based on resemblance rather than identity plays an important role.

Consider now the contrast between denial and negation. Negation is properly semantic; denial (typically conveyed by use of negative sentences) is a speech act, whose function is to reject some aspect of an attributed utterance or thought. In other words, denial is echoic. Here are some examples:

(28) (a) *Peter:* Oh, you're in a miserable foul mood tonight.

    (b) *Mary:* I'm not in a miserable foul mood; I'm a little tired and would like to be left alone. (Carston, 1996, p. 322)

(29)   Around here we don't eat tom[eiDouz] and we don't get stressed out. We eat tom[a:touz] and we get a little tense now and then. (Carston, 1996, p. 320)

(30)   Mozart's sonatas weren't for violin and piano, they were for piano and violin. (Horn, 1989, p. 373]

(31)   I didn't manage to trap two mongeese; I managed to trap two mongooses. (Horn, 1989, p. 373)

In (28b), Mary echoes and rejects Peter's description of her; in (29), the speaker objects to the American pronunciation of 'tomatoes' and the expression 'stressed out'; in (30), she rejects the description of Mozart's sonatas as 'for violin and piano'; and in (31), she rejects the claim that she managed to trap two 'mongeese' rather than two 'mongooses'. Such denials fit straightforwardly into the pattern of previous sections. Like regular quotations, they may be interpretive, as in (28), or metalinguistic, as in (29) through (31). As with irony and free indirect quotations, the presence of the attributive element is not overtly marked.

In fact, the picture of denial just given is not the standard one. Linguists generally define denial as involving the rejection of an attributed *utterance*, treating rejections of attributed thoughts as cases of regular negation. For example, van der Sandt claims that the "essential function" of echoic denials is "to object to a previous utterance" (van der Sandt, 1991, p. 331). His category of denials would include (28) through (31), which all metarepresent attributed utterances, but would exclude rejections of attributed thoughts. Horn (1989, §§ 3.2; 6) takes an even more restrictive view. He points out (correctly) that an utterance such as (28) may be used to reject not only previous utterances but also attributed thoughts or assumptions that are "in the discourse model"; however, instead of concluding that all these cases are echoic denials, he decides to exclude all of them from his category of echoic use. For him, the only genuine cases of echoic denial are metalinguistic, based on resemblances in form. Carston (1996) offers what seems to me a more satisfactory account. She includes in the category of echoic denials the full set of cases involving both attributed utterances and attributed thoughts. On her account, examples (28) through (31) would all be treated as echoic, as would any utterance used to metarepresent and reject an attributed utterance or thought (for discussion, see Burton-Roberts, 1989; Carston, 1996; Horn, 1985; 1989; Iwata, 1998; McCawley, 1991; Noh, 1998a; van der Sandt, 1991).

"Echo questions" are formally distinguishable from regular interrogatives by their declarative syntax and rising intonation. Their treatment has generally run parallel to the treatment of metalinguistic negation. Consider (22b) above, or (32b) through (34b):

(32) (a) *Peter*: You finally managed to solve the problems.

   (b) *Mary*: Managed? I solved them in two minutes.
        (Noh, 1998a, p, 218)

(33) (a) *Peter*: I need a holiday.

   (b) *Mary*: You need a holiday? What about me?

(34) (a) *Tourist*: Where can I find some tom[eiDouz]?

   (b) *Londoner*: You want tom[eiDouz]? Try New York.

All four questions are clearly echoic in the sense defined above: the speaker echoes and questions some aspect of the form or content of an attributed utterance. However, as with echoic denials, linguistic analyses of echoic questions have generally been over-restrictive. "Echo questions" are generally defined as echoing prior utterances, not thoughts.

> Echo questions are distinguished from other questions by their restricted
> context. An echo occurs in dialogue as a reaction to a prior utterance and is

interpretable only with respect to it, while other questions may be the first or the only utterance in a discourse. (Banfield, 1982, p. 124).

Echo questions generally require a linguistic context in which the original utterance ... has been previously uttered within the discourse. (Horn, 1989, p. 381)

Yet there seem to be clear cases of echoic questions used to metarepresent attributed thoughts. Compare examples (35a) through (35c):

(35) (a) *Mary* (seeing Peter walk towards the door): Just a minute. You're going shopping?

(b) ? *Mary* (seeing Peter walk towards the door): Just a minute. Henry VIII had six wives?

(c) *Mary* (seeing Peter walk towards the door): Just a minute. Did Henry VIII have six wives?

Here, the echoic question in (35a) and the regular interrogative in (35c) are pragmatically appropriate, but the echoic question in (35b) is not. The obvious way of explaining this would be to treat the utterances in (35a) and (35b) as echoing and questioning thoughts that Mary attributes to Peter. In (35a), his behavior gives her ground for inferring his thoughts even though he has not spoken; in (35b), it does not. This would enable us to maintain the parallel between verbal irony, denials, and echoic questions: all are tacitly attributive and all may be used for the attribution both of utterances and of thoughts (Blakemore, 1994; Escandell-Vidal, 1998; Noh, 1998a; 1998c).

4.4 Non-Attributive Cases

So far, the only lower-order representations I have looked at have been attributive. As noted in section 1, there are also non-attributive cases: mentions of sentence types, utterance types, or proposition types, as in (6), repeated below.

(6) (a) 'Dragonflies are beautiful' is a sentence of English.

(b) 'Shut up' is rude.

(c) It's true that tulips are flowers.

(d) *Roses and daisies are flowers* entails that roses are flowers.

(e) I like the name 'Petronella'.

(f) 'Abeille' is not a word of English.

(g) *Tulip* implies *flower*.

These are worth considering because they are not obviously linked to the metapsychological or metacommunicative abilities, and might contrast in interesting ways with attributions of utterances and thoughts.

To understand the cases of mention in (6), the hearer must be able to recognize linguistic, logical, or conceptual resemblances between representations considered in the abstract rather than tied to a particular individual, place, or time. Because no attribution is involved, this ability might be present even if the intuitive metapsychological or metacommunicative capacity is impaired. Indeed, there is evidence from the autobiographical writings of people with autism (several of whom have been students of linguistics) of a serious interest in linguistic form (Frith & Happé, 1999; Willey, 1999; Williams, 1992). Here is how one of them describes her fascination with language:

> Linguistics and the act of speaking itself have always been among my keenest interests . . . Words, and everything about them, hold my concentration like nothing else. On my overstuffed bookshelf sit several thesauruses, a half dozen dictionaries, famous quotations books, and a handful of personal reflection journals. Language appeals to me because it lends itself to rules and precision even more often than it does to subjectivity . . . Some words can please my eyes, given that they have the symmetry of line and shape I favor. Other words can fascinate me by the melodies they sing when they are spoken. Properly handled . . . words can work miracles on my sensibilities and my understanding of the world, because each one has its own personality and nuance and its own lesson to teach. (Willey, 1999, p. 30)

This is in marked contrast to the comments of the same writer on her inability to discern the intentions behind other people's use of words.

Relevance theorists have argued that there are several further types of non-attributive metarepresentation which have been less widely recognized, and which clearly contrast with the attributive cases discussed above. For example, regular (non-attributive) interrogatives and exclamatives have been treated in relevance theory as representations of *desirable thoughts* (or desirable information); and regular (non-attributive) negations and disjunctions have been treated as representations of *possible thoughts* (possible information). Parallel to these, we might expect to find (non-attributive) representations of possible and desirable utterances. I will end this survey with a few illustrations of each.

In relevance theory, regular (non-echoic) interrogatives such as those in (36) have been treated as the metarepresentational counterparts of imperatives:

(36) (a) Is today Tuesday?

   (b) What day is it today?

   (c) When are we leaving?

Imperatives represent *desirable states of affairs*; interrogatives represent *desirable thoughts*. Someone who utters an imperative is thinking about a state of affairs, which she regards as desirable from someone's point of view. Someone who utters an interrogative is thinking about a thought (or item of information), which she regards as desirable from someone's point of view. Since information can be desirable only because it is relevant, this amounts to claiming that interrogatives represent relevant answers (Clark, 1991; Sperber & Wilson, 1986/1995, chap. 4, § 10; Wilson & Sperber, 1988a).

   This account of interrogatives has some advantages over alternative analyses. For example, in speech-act theory, interrogatives are generally treated as encoding requests for information (Bach & Harnish, 1979; Harnish, 1994; Searle, 1969). One problem with the speech-act approach is that not all interrogative utterances are requests for information; they may be offers of information, rhetorical questions, examination questions, idle speculations, and so on. The relevance-theoretic account solves this problem in the following way. An interrogative utterance merely indicates that the speaker regards the answer as relevant to *someone*. It will only be understood as a request for information if two further contextual conditions are fulfilled: (1) the speaker regards the answer as relevant to herself; and (2) the hearer is in a position to provide it. In other conditions, it will be differently understood. For example, it will be understood as an offer of information if (1) the speaker regards the answer as relevant to the hearer, and (2) the speaker herself is in a position to provide it. Other types of interrogative speech act also fall out naturally from this account (Clark, 1991; Sperber & Wilson, 1986/1995, chap. 4, § 10; Wilson & Sperber, 1988a; 1988b).

   The analysis of interrogatives as inherently metarepresentational brings them into interesting contact with the literature on mind-reading. On the relevance-theoretic account, the production and interpretation of interrogatives necessarily involves a higher order of metarepresentational ability than standard declaratives, but differs in two respects from examples that have been central in the "theory-of-mind" literature: first, the metarepresented proposition is not attributive, and second, it is not treated as either false (as in the false-belief task) or true (as in pretence). The fact that it is not attributive means that we might expect someone who fails second-order "theory of mind" tasks to pass tasks involving regular interrogatives, but fail on echo questions, for example.

If interrogatives metarepresent desirable thoughts, we might expect to find utterances used to metarepresent desirable utterances. There is no shortage of candidates. Here are some possible examples:

(37) (a)   *Vicar to bride*: I, Amanda, take you, Bertrand, to be my lawful wedded husband.

  (b)   *Bride*: I, Amanda, take you, Bertrand, to be my lawful, wedded husband.

(38)   *Mary to Peter* (as doorbell rings): If that's John, I'm not here. (Noh, 1998b)

(39) (a)   *Quiz-show host*: The first man to walk on the moon was?

  (b)   *Contestant*: Neil Diamond.

In (37a), the vicar metarepresents an utterance that he wants the bride to produce. In the "speech-act conditional" in (38), the consequent is used to metarepresent an utterance that Mary wants Peter to produce; (38) expresses something equivalent to 'If that's John, *say* I'm not here' (Sweetser, 1990; Noh, 1998b; van der Auwera, 1986). The quiz-show question in (39) might be analyzed on similar lines: the host is not producing a regular interrogative but metarepresenting an utterance he wants the contestant to produce. Further illustrations include the utterances of prompters in a theatre and solicitors whispering answers to their clients in court.

The literature on standard mentions contains many examples of utterances used to represent possible thoughts and utterances. For instance, mentions of propositions, as in (6c) and (6d) above, amount to metarepresentations of possible thought types; and mentions of utterances, as in (6b) above, amount to metarepresentations of possible utterance types. But there may be a much wider range of candidates. Consider (40a) through (40c).

(40) (a)   Ducks don't bite.

  (b)   Maybe I'll leave.

  (c)   Either William will become a soldier or Harry will.

Regular (non-attributive) uses of negation, modals, and disjunctions, as in (40a) through (40c), seem to presuppose the ability to think about possible thoughts and evaluate their truth or falsity, which would make all these examples metarepresentational. The development of attributive and non-attributive negatives, modals, and interrogatives contrast in interesting ways, shedding light on the interaction between metalogical, metacommunicative, and metapsychological abilities

(Bloom, 1991; Gombert, 1990; Morris & Sloutsky, 1998; Noveck, Ho, & Sera, 1996; Overton, 1990; Papafragou, 1998c).

Apart from standard mentions of utterance types, as in (6b) above, metarepresentations of possible utterances might include the following advertisements from a recent Glenfiddich whisky campaign in England:

(41)   *Picture of a newspaper with the headline*: French admit Britain is best.

        Caption: Till then, there's Glenfiddich to enjoy.

(42)   *Picture of a newspaper with the headline*: World's funniest man is a Belgian.

        Caption: Till then, there's Glenfiddich to enjoy.

Drafts, essay plans, and rehearsals of future conversations might provide further examples. There is evidence, then, that all four categories of non-attributive representation are filled.

5. Conclusion

This survey was designed to show something of the depth and variety of the metarepresentational abilities used in verbal comprehension. Language is full of metarepresentational devices, which are often quite fragmentary or incomplete: I have argued that they provide no more than triggers for spontaneous metacommunicative processes by which speakers' meanings are inferred. I have outlined a pragmatic comprehension procedure which might help to resolve indeterminacies in meaning and form the basis for a modularized metacommunicative ability, itself a sub-part of a more general metapsychological ability or "theory of mind."

The processing of linguistic metarepresentations also interacts in more specific ways with the metapsychological ability. As I have shown, linguistic metarepresentations vary both in degree of explicitness and in the type of original they are used to represent: utterances, thoughts, or abstract representations. By comparing comprehension in these different types of case, it might be possible to gain new insight into the metapsychological and metacommunicative abilities. To take just one example, there are cases, such as (20) above, in which the mind-reading ability directly feeds the comprehension process, by interpreting para-linguistic information – gestures, facial expressions, intonation, and so on – to provide information about the speaker's mood or epistemic state, which may, in turn, be picked out by the pragmatic comprehension procedure and attributed as part of a speaker's meaning. Inferring these aspects of speaker's meaning is likely to prove particularly difficult for people whose general mind-reading ability is weak. It would be interesting to check whether the use of overt linguistic devices would facilitate comprehension and, if so, in what way.[4] For example, is it easier to attribute a false belief when expressed or implied by an utterance ("The ball is in the cupboard") than by inferring it on the basis of non-communicative behavior?

From the linguist's point of view, there are also benefits to be gained by considering metarepresentational devices in the context of the more general metapsychological and metacommunicative abilities. As I have shown, in studying linguistic metarepresentations, linguists have tended to concentrate on cases involving the attribution of utterances, and many echoic utterances and "hearsay" devices may have broader uses than existing research suggests. Studies of lexical acquisition are already being conducted within a broader metacommunicative and metapsychological framework; the acquisition of specifically metarepresentational devices within this framework should also yield interesting results.

Acknowledgments

I would like to thank Richard Breheny, Robyn Carston, Herb Clark, Steven Davis, Corinne Iten, Eun-Ju Noh, Milena Nuti, Anna Papafragou, François Recanati, Neil Smith, Dan Sperber, Tim Wharton and the members of CREA for interesting discussions on the topic of this paper. I would also like to thank CREA for its generous hospitality while the paper was being written.

Notes

1 Or at least deducible from assumptions explicitly represented. Since the full set of metarepresentations in a Gricean definition of speaker's meaning are not deducible from any finite subset, I will ignore this complication here. (See Sperber & Wilson, 1990a, for discussion.)
2 These are perhaps the clearest cases in which the mind-reading ability makes a direct contribution to communicated content, by providing access to information about the speaker's mental states, which may then be picked out by the relevance-theoretic comprehension procedure for attribution as a speaker's meaning.
3 See Martin (1992) and Sperber & Wilson (1998a) for discussion of such cases, which, like many of my previous examples, present serious problems for traditional (non-attributive) analyses of verbal irony.
4 Even overtly metarepresentational devices may leave a lot to be inferred, as the example with "disappointed" (above, p. 419) shows.

References

Austen, Jane (1990). *Persuasion* (World's Classics). Oxford: Oxford University Press.

Astington, Janet, Harris, Paul, & Olson, David, Eds. (1988). *Developing theories of mind.* Cambridge: Cambridge University Press.

Bach, Kent, & Harnish, Robert M. (1979). *Linguistic communication and speech acts.* Cambridge, MA: MIT Press.

Banfield, Anne (1982). *Unspeakable sentences: Narration and representation in the language of fiction.* Boston: Routledge & Kegan Paul.

Baron-Cohen, Simon (1995). *Mindblindness: An essay on autism and theory of mind.* Cambridge, MA: MIT Press.

Baron-Cohen, Simon, Leslie, Alan, & Frith, Uta (1985). Does the autistic child have a "theory of mind"? *Cognition 21,* 37–46.

Baron-Cohen, Simon, Tager-Flusberg, Helen, & Cohen, Donald, Eds. (1993). *Understanding other minds: Perspectives from autism.* Oxford: Oxford University Press.

Bartsch, Karen, & Wellman, Henry (1995). *Children talk about the mind.* Oxford: Oxford University Press.

Bezuidenhout, Anne, & Sroda, Mary Sue (1996). Disambiguation of reference by young children: An application of relevance theory. Paper presented at the Relevance Theory Workshop, Tokyo, March 1996.

Bezuidenhout, Anne, & Sroda, Mary Sue (1998). Children's use of contextual cues to resolve referential ambiguity: An application of relevance theory. *Pragmatics and Cognition 6,* 265–299.

Blakemore, Diane (1991). Performatives and parentheticals. *Proceedings of the Aristotelian Society 91,* 197–214.

Blakemore, Diane (1994). Echo questions: A pragmatic account. *Lingua 4,* 197–211.

Blakemore, Diane (1997). Restatement and exemplification: A relevance-theoretic reassessment of elaboration. *Pragmatics and Cognition 5,* 1–19.

Blass, Regina (1989). Grammaticalisation of interpretive use: The case of *re* in Sissala. *Lingua 79,* 229–326.

Blass, Regina (1990). *Relevance relations in discourse: A study with special reference to Sissala.* Cambridge: Cambridge University Press.

Bloom, Lois (1991). *Language development from two to three.* Cambridge: Cambridge University Press.

Bloom, Paul (1997). Intentionality and word learning. *Trends in Cognitive Sciences 1,* 9–12.

Booth, Wayne (1961). *The rhetoric of fiction.* Chicago: Chicago University Press.

Bretherton, Inge (1991). Intentional communication and the development of an understanding of mind. In Douglas Frye & Chris Moore (Eds.), *Children's theories of mind: Mental states and social understanding* (pp. 49–75). Hillsdale, NJ: Lawrence Erlbaum.

Bretherton, Inge, & Beeghly, Marjorie (1982). Talking about internal states: The acquisition of an explicit theory of mind. *Developmental Psychology 18,* 906–921.

Burton-Roberts, Noel (1989). *The limits to debate: A revised theory of semantic presupposition.* Cambridge: Cambridge University Press.

Cappelen, Herman, & Lepore, Ernie (1997a). Varieties of quotation. *Mind 106*, 429–450.

Cappelen, Herman, & Lepore, Ernie (1997b). On an alleged connection between indirect speech and theory of meaning. *Mind and Language 12*, 278–296.

Carruthers, Peter, & Smith, Peter (1996). *Theories of theories of mind*. Cambridge: Cambridge University Press.

Carston, Robyn (1988). Implicature, explicature and truth-theoretic semantics. In Ruth Kempson (Ed.), *Mental representations: The interface between language and reality* (pp. 155–181). Cambridge: Cambridge University Press. Reprinted in Steven Davis (Ed.), *Pragmatics: A reader* (pp. 33–51). Oxford: Oxford University Press.

Carston, Robyn (1996). Metalinguistic negation and echoic use. *Journal of Pragmatics 25*, 309–330.

Carston, Robyn (1998). *Pragmatics and the explicit-implicit distinction*. Doctoral dissertation, University College London. To be published by Blackwell, Oxford.

Chafe, Wallace, & Nichols, Johanna, Eds. (1986). *Evidentiality: The linguistic coding of epistemology*. Norwood, NJ: Ablex.

Clark, Billy (1991). *Relevance theory and the semantics of non-declaratives*. Doctoral dissertation, University of London.

Clark, Herbert, & Carlson, Thomas (1981). Context for comprehension. In J. Lang & Alan Baddeley (Eds.), *Attention and performance, Vol. 9* (pp. 313–30). Hillsdale, NJ: Lawrence Erlbaum.

Clark, Herbert, & Gerrig, Richard (1984). On the pretense theory of irony. *Journal of Experimental Psychology: General 113*, 121–126.

Clark, Herbert, & Gerrig, Richard (1990). Quotations as demonstrations. *Language 66*, 764–805.

Clark, Herbert, & Marshall, Catherine (1981). Definite reference and mutual knowledge. In Aravind Joshi, Bonnie Webber, & Ivan Sag (Eds.), *Elements of discourse understanding* (pp. 10–63). Cambridge: Cambridge University Press.

Cohn, Dorrit (1978). *Transparent minds: Narrative modes for presenting consciousness in fiction*. Princeton: Princeton University Press.

Coulmas, Florian, Ed. (1986). *Direct and indirect speech*. Berlin: Mouton de Gruyter.

Curco, Carmen (1998). indirect echoes and verbal humour. In Villy Rouchota & Andreas Jucker (Eds.), *Current issues in relevance theory* (pp. 305–325). Amsterdam: John Benjamins.

Davidson, Donald (1968/1984). On saying that. In his *Inquiries into truth and interpretation* (pp. 93–108). Oxford: Oxford University Press.

Davidson, Donald (1979/1984). Quotation. In his *Inquiries into truth and interpretation* (pp. 79–92). Oxford: Oxford University Press.

Davies, Martin, & Stone, Tony, Eds. (1995a). *Mental simulation: Philosophical and psychological essays*. Oxford: Blackwell.

Davies, Martin, & Stone, Tony, Eds. (1995b). *Folk Psychology*. Oxford: Blackwell.Davis, Steven, Ed. (1991). *Pragmatics: A reader*. Oxford: Oxford University Press.

Dickens, Charles (1996). *Bleak house*. Penguin Classic Edition. Harmondsworth: Penguin.

Ducrot, Oswald (1983). Puisque: Essai de description polyphonique. In M. Herslund et al. (Eds.), *Analyse grammaticale du français*. Special issue, *Revue romane 24*, 166–185.

Escandell-Vidal, Victoria (1998). Metapropositions as metarepresentations. Paper delivered to the Relevance Theory Workshop, Luton, September 1998.

Fillmore, Charles (1990). Epistemic stance and grammatical form in English conditional sentences. *Chicago Linguistic Society 26*, 137–162.

Fodor, Jerry (1992). A theory of the child's theory of mind. *Cognition, 44*, 283–296.

Fludernik, Monika (1993). *The fictions of language and the languages of fiction: The linguistic representation of speech and consciousness*. London: Routledge.

Frith, Uta, & Happé, Francesca (1999). Theory of mind and self-consciousness: What is it like to be autistic? *Mind and Language 14*, 1–22.

Frye, Douglas, & Moore, Chris, Eds. (1991). *Children's theories of mind: Mental states and social understanding*. Hillsdale, NJ: Lawrence Erlbaum.

Garnham, Alan, & Perner, Josef (1990). Does manifestness solve problems of mutuality? *Behavioral and Brain Sciences 13*, 178–179.

Garver, Newton (1965). Varieties of use and mention. *Philosophy and Phenomenological Research 26*, 230–238.

Gibbs, Ray. (1987). Mutual knowledge and the psychology of conversational inference. *Journal of Pragmatics 11*, 561–588.

Gibbs, Ray (1994). *The poetics of mind: Figurative thought, language and understanding*. New York: Cambridge University Press.

Gombert, Jean (1990). *Metalinguistic development*. Hassocks, Sussex: Harvester.

Gopnik, Alison, & Wellman, Henry (1992). Why the child's theory of mind really is a theory. *Mind and Language 7*, 145–171.

Grice, H. Paul (1975). Logic and conversation. In Peter Cole & Jerry Morgan (Eds.), *Syntax and semantics 3: Speech acts* (pp. 41–58). Reprinted in his *Studies in the way of words* (pp. 22–40). Cambridge, MA: Harvard University Press.

Grice, H. Paul (1982). Meaning revisited. In Neil Smith (Ed.), *Mutual knowledge* (pp. 223–243). London: Academic Press.

Grice, H. Paul (1989). *Studies in the way of words*. Cambridge, MA: Harvard University Press.

Gutt, Ernst-August (1991). *Translation and relevance: Cognition and context*. Oxford: Blackwell.

Happé, Francesca (1993). Communicative competence and theory of mind in autism: A test of relevance theory. *Cognition 48*, 101–119.

Happé, Francesca (1994). *Autism: An introduction to psychological theory*. Cambridge MA: Harvard University Press.

Harnish, Robert M. (1994). Mood, meaning and speech acts. In Savas Tsohatzidis (Ed.), *Foundations of speech-act theory*. London: Routledge.

Horn, Laurence (1985). Metalinguistic negation and pragmatic ambiguity. *Language 61*, 121–174.

Horn, Laurence (1989). *A natural history of negation*. Chicago, IL: Chicago University Press.

Ifantidou-Trouki, Elly (1993). Sentence adverbials and relevance. *Lingua 90*, 69–90.

Ifantidou, Elly (1994). *Evidentials and relevance*. Doctoral dissertation, University College London.

Itani, Reiko (1996). *Semantics and pragmatics of hedges in English and Japanese.* Tokyo: Hituzi Syobo.

Iwata, Seizi (1998). Some extensions of the echoic analysis of metalinguistic negation. *Lingua 105,* 49–65.

Jorgensen, Julia, Miller, George, & Sperber, Dan (1984). Test of the mention theory of irony. *Journal of Experimental Psychology: General 113,* 112–120.

Joyce, James (1960). *Ulysses.* London: The Bodley Head.

Kasher, Asa, Ed. (1998) *Pragmatics: Critical concepts. Vols. 1–6.* London: Routledge.

Kiparsky, Carol, & Kiparsky, Paul (1971). Fact. In Danny Steinberg & Leon Jakobovits (Eds.), *Semantics: An interdisciplinary reader* (pp. 345–369). Cambridge: Cambridge University Press.

Kreuz, Roger, & Glucksberg, Sam (1989). How to be sarcastic: The echoic reminder theory of irony. *Journal of Experimental Psychology: General 118,* 374–386.

Kumon-Nakamura, Sachi, Glucksberg, Sam, & Brown, Mary (1995). How about another piece of pie: the allusional pretense theory of discourse irony. *Journal of Experimental Psychology: General 124,* 3–21.

Lascelles, Mary (1939/1965). *Jane Austen and her art.* Oxford: Oxford University Press.

Leech, Geoffrey & Short, Michael (1981). *Style in fiction: An introduction to English fictional prose.* London: Longman.

Leslie, Alan (1987). Pretense and representation: The origins of "theory of mind." *Psychological Review 94,* 412–426.

Leslie, Alan (1991). The theory of mind impairment in autism: Evidence for a modular mechanism of development? In Andrew Whiten (Ed.), *Natural theories of mind: Evolution, development and simulation of everyday mindreading* (pp. 63–78). Oxford: Blackwell.

Leslie, Alan, & Happé, Francesca (1989). Autism and ostensive communication: The relevance of metarepresentation. *Development and Psychopathology 1,* 205–212.

Levinson, Stephen (1983). *Pragmatics.* Cambridge: Cambridge University Press.

Lewis, Charlie, & Mitchell, Peter, Eds. (1994) *Children's early understanding of mind: Origins and development.* Hillsdale, NJ: Lawrence Erlbaum.

Lock, Andrew (1980). *The guided reinvention of language.* New York: Academic Press.

Martin, Robert (1992). Irony and universe of belief. *Lingua 87,* 77–90.

McCawley, James (1991). Contrastive negation and metalinguistic negation. *Chicago Linguistic Society 27: Parasession on Negation,* 189–206.

McHale, Brian (1978). Free indirect discourse: A survey of recent accounts. *PTL: Journal for Descriptive Poetics and Theory of Literature 3,* 235–287.

Morris, Anne, & Sloutsky, Vladimir (1998). Understanding of logical necessity: Developmental antecedents and cognitive consequences. *Child Development 69,* 721–741.

Neale, Stephen (1992). Paul Grice and the philosophy of language. *Linguistics and Philosophy 15,* 509–59.

Noh, Eun-Ju (1998a). *The semantics and pragmatics of metarepresentations in English: A relevance-theoretic approach.* Doctoral dissertation, University College London. To be published by John Benjamins, Amsterdam.

Noh, Eun-Ju (1998b). A relevance-theoretic account of metarepresentative uses in conditionals. In Villy Rouchota & Andreas Jucker (Eds.), *Current issues in relevance theory* (pp. 271–304). Amsterdam: John Benjamins.

Noh, Eun-Ju (1998c). Echo questions: Metarepresentation and pragmatic enrichment. *Linguistics and Philosophy 21*, 603–628.

Noveck, Ira, Ho, Simon, & Sera, Maria (1996). Children's understanding of epistemic modals. *Journal of Child Language 23*, 621–643.

Nuti, Milena (in preparation). *Pragmatics and mindreading.* Doctoral dissertation, University College London.

Origgi, Gloria, & Sperber, Dan (in press). Issues in the evolution of human language and communication. To appear in Peter Carruthers & Andrew Chamberlain (Eds.), *Evolution and the human mind: Language, modularity and social cognition.* Cambridge: Cambridge University Press.

Overton, Willis, Ed. (1990). *Reasoning, necessity and logic: Developmental perspectives.* Hillsdale, NJ: Lawrence Erlbaum.

Papafragou, Anna (1998a). *Modality and the semantics-pragmatics interface.* Doctoral dissertation, University College London. To be published by Elsevier, Amsterdam.

Papafragou, Anna (1998b). Inference and word meaning: The case of modal auxiliaries. *Lingua 105*, 1–47.

Papafragou, Anna (1998c). The acquisition of modality: Implications for theories of semantic representation. *Mind and Language 13*, 370–399.

Partee, Barbara (1973). The syntax and semantics of quotations. In Stephen Anderson & Paul Kiparsky (Eds.), *A Festschrift for Morris Halle* (pp. 410–418). New York: Holt, Rinehart & Winston.

Recanati, François (1986). On defining communicative intentions. *Mind and Language 1*, 213–242.

Recanati, François (1987). *Meaning and force.* Cambridge: Cambridge University Press.

Recanati, François. (1989). The pragmatics of what is said. *Mind and Language, 4*, 295–329. Reprinted in Steven Davis (Ed.), *Pragmatics: A reader* (pp. 97–120). Oxford: Oxford University Press.

Recanati, François (1991). *Oratio obliqua, oratio recta: The semantics of metarepresentations.* Paris: Bibliothèque du CREA. To be published by MIT Press, Cambridge, MA.

Rouchota, Villy, & Jucker, Andreas, Eds. (1998). *Current issues in relevance theory.* Amsterdam: John Benjamins.

Saka, Paul (1998). Quotation and the use-mention distinction. *Mind 107*, 113–135.

Schiffer, Stephen (1972). *Meaning.* Oxford: Clarendon Press.

Scholl, Brian, & Leslie, Alan (1999). Modularity, development and "theory of mind." *Mind and Language 14*, 131–153.

Searle, John (1969). *Speech acts.* Cambridge: Cambridge University Press.

Smith, Neil, Ed. (1982). *Mutual knowledge.* London: Academic Press.

Smith, Neil, & Tsimpli, Iauthi-Maria (1995). *The mind of a savant: Language learning and modularity.* Oxford: Blackwell.

Sperber, Dan (1984). Verbal irony: Pretense or echoic mention? *Journal of Experimental Psychology: General 113*, 130–136.

Sperber, Dan (1994). Understanding verbal understanding. In J. Khalfa (Ed.), *What is intelligence?* (pp. 179–198). Cambridge: Cambridge University Press.

Sperber, Dan (1996). *Explaining culture: A naturalistic approach.* Oxford: Blackwell.

Sperber, Dan (1997). Intuitive and reflective beliefs. *Mind and Language 12*, 67–83.

Sperber, Dan, & Wilson, Deirdre (1981). Irony and the use-mention distinction. In Peter Cole (Ed.), *Radical pragmatics* (pp. 295–318). New York: Academic Press.

Sperber, Dan, & Wilson, Deirdre (1986/1995). *Relevance: Communication and cognition.* Oxford: Blackwell.

Sperber, Dan, & Wilson, Deirdre (1987). Précis of *Relevance: Communication and cognition. Behavioral and Brain Sciences, 10*, 697–754. Reprinted in Asa Kasher (Ed.), *Pragmatics: Critical concepts. Vol. 5* (pp. 82–115). London: Routledge.

Sperber, Dan, & Wilson, Deirdre (1990a). Spontaneous deduction and mutual knowledge. *Behavioral and Brain Sciences 13*, 179–184.

Sperber, Dan, & Wilson, Deirdre (1990b). Rhetoric and relevance. In John Bender & David Wellbery (Eds.), *The ends of rhetoric: History, theory, practice* (pp. 140–156). Stanford, CA: Stanford University Press.

Sperber, Dan, & Wilson, Deirdre (1998a). Irony and relevance: A reply to Seto, Hamamoto & Yamanashi. In Robyn Carston & Seiji Uchida (Eds.), *Relevance theory: Applications and implications* (pp. 283–293). Amsterdam: John Benjamins.

Sperber, Dan, & Wilson, Deirdre (1998b). The mapping between the mental and the public lexicon. In Peter Carruthers & Jill Boucher (Eds.), *Language and thought: Interdisciplinary themes* (pp. 184–200). Cambridge: Cambridge University Press.

Sternberg, Meir (1982a). Proteus in quotation-land: Mimesis and the forms of reported discourse. *Poetics Today 3*, 107–156.

Sternberg, Meir (1982b). Point of view and the indirections of direct speech. *Language and Style 15*, 67–117.

Sweetser, Eve (1990). *From etymology to pragmatics: Metaphorical and cultural aspects of semantic structure.* Cambridge: Cambridge University Press.

Tomasello, Michael, & Kruger, Ann Cale (1992). Joint attention on action: Acquiring verbs in ostensive and non-ostensive contexts. *Journal of Child Language, 19*, 311–333.

Urmson, Jim (1963). Parenthetical verbs. In Charles Caton (Ed.), *Philosophy and ordinary language* (pp. 220–240). Urbana: University of Illinois Press.

van der Auwera, Johan (1986). Conditionals and speech acts. In Elizabeth Traugott, Alice ter Meulen, Judy Reilly, & Charles Ferguson (Eds.), *On conditionals* (pp. 197–214). Cambridge: Cambridge University Press.

van der Sandt, Robert (1991). Denial. *Chicago Linguistic Society 27: Parasession on Negation*, 331–344.

Wade, Elizabeth, & Clark, Herbert (1993). Reproduction and demonstration in quotations. *Journal of Memory and Language 32*, 805–819.

Walton, Kendall (1976). Points of view in narrative and depictive representation. *Nous 10*, 49–61.

Walton, Kendall (1990). *Mimesis as make-believe: On the foundations of the representational arts.* Cambridge, MA: Harvard University Press.

Wellman, Henry (1990). *The child's theory of mind.* Cambridge MA: MIT Press.

Whiten, Andrew, Ed. (1991). *Natural theories of mind: Evolution, development and simulation of everyday mindreading.* Oxford: Blackwell.

Willey, Liane Holliday (1999). *Pretending to be normal: Living with Asperger's syndrome.* London: Jessica Kingsley.

Williams, Donna (1992). *Nobody nowhere*. New York: Avon Books.

Wilson, Deirdre, & Sperber, Dan (1988a). Mood and the analysis of non-declarative sentences. In Jonathan Dancy, Julius Moravcsik, & Charles Taylor (Eds.), *Human agency: Language, duty and value* (pp. 77–101). Stanford, CA: Stanford University Press. Reprinted in Asa Kasher (Ed.), *Pragmatics: Critical concepts. Vol. 2* (pp. 262–289). London: Routledge.

Wilson, Deirdre, & Sperber, Dan (1988b). Representation and relevance. In Ruth Kempson (Ed.), *Mental representation: The interface between language and reality* (pp. 133–153). Cambridge: Cambridge University Press.

Wilson, Deirdre, & Sperber, Dan (1992). On verbal irony. *Lingua 87*, 53–76.

Wilson, Deirdre, & Sperber, Dan (1993). Linguistic form and relevance. *Lingua 90*, 1–25.

Wilson, Deirdre, & Sperber, Dan (in preparation). Truthfulness and relevance. Paper delivered to the San Marino conference on Grice's Heritage, May 1998.

Winner, Ellen (1988). *The point of words: Children's understanding of metaphor and irony*. Cambridge MA: Harvard University Press.

Vancouver Studies in Cognitive Science

List of volumes published

List of volumes in progress